PRAXISEUROPARECHT

Edited by
Prof. Karel Van Hulle
Head of Unit, European Commission, Brussels
Dr. Harald Gesell
Rechtsanwalt, Linklaters Oppenhoff & Rädler, Cologne

European Corporate Law

Nomos

Proposal for quotations: *Author,* in: Van Hulle/Gesell, European Corporate Law, Part 1, II, Mn. 33

Die Deutsche Bibliothek – CIP-Einheitsaufnahme

Die Deutsche Bibliothek verzeichnet diese Publikation in der Deutschen Nationalbibliografie; detaillierte bibliografische Daten sind im Internet über http://dnb.ddb.de abrufbar.

Die Deutsche Bibliothek – CIP Cataloguing-in-Publication-Data

Die Deutsche Bibliothek lists this publication in the Deutsche Nationalbibliografie; detailed bibliographic data is available in the Internet at http://dnb.ddb.de.

ISBN 3-8329-1811-6

1. Auflage 2006

List of Authors

Dr. Csaba Berecz (LL.M.), Budapest, Part 2, XI
Jorge M Bleck, Lisbon, Part 2, XX
Akvilė Bosaitė, Vilnius, Part 2, XV
Elijus Burgis (LL.M.), Vilnius, Part 2, XV
Virginie Buseine, Paris, Part 2, VIII
James Coleman, London, Part 2, XXV
Peteris Dalderis, Riga, Part 2, XIV
Sofia Egídio, Lisbon, Part 2, XX
Dr. Eszter Fedák, Budapest, Part 2, XI
Carsten Flaßhoff (LL.M.), Cologne, Part 1, II, Part 2, IX
Alain Garnier, Paris, Part 2, VIII
Nicolas Gauzès, Luxembourg, Part 2, XVI
Dr. Harald Gesell, Cologne, Part 1, II
Gianluca Ghersini, Milan, Part 2, XIII
Heili Haabu, Tallinn, Part 2, VI
Sakari Helminen (LL.Lic.), Turku/Helsinki, Part 2, VII
Prof. Karel Van Hulle, Brussels, Introduction
Svante Johansson, Stockholm, Part 2, XXIV
Dr. Florian Kirchhof, Ljubljana, Part 2, XXII
Dr. Michael Krömker, Cologne, Part 1, II, Part 2, IX
Dr. Florian Kusznier (LL.M.), Vienna, Part 2, I
Maura McLaughlin, Dublin, Part 2, XII
Michał Mieciński, Warsaw, Part 2, XIX
Hanns-William Mülsch, Berlin, Part 2, XXVI
Andrew Muscat, Valetta, Part 2, XVII
Elena Papandreou (LL.B.), Nicosia, Part 2, III
Katia Papantonopoulou, Athens, Part 2, X
Raino Paron (LL.M.), Tallinn, Part 2, VI
Dr. Sven Piegsa (LL.M.), Berlin, Part 2, XXVI
Eric Pottier (LL.M.), Brussels, Part 2, II
Giovanna Puppo, Milan, Part 2, XIII
César Ramírez (LL.M.), Madrid, Part 2, XXIII
Pieter Riemer, Amsterdam, Part 2, XVIII
Prof. Álvaro Sáinz, Madrid, Part 2, XXIII
Dr. Alexander Schall (MJur), Hamburg, Part 1, I
Jean-Michel Schmit (LL.M.), Luxembourg, Part 2, XVI
Lukas Sevcik, Prague, Part 2, IV
Henk Arnold Sijnja, Amsterdam, Part 2, XVIII
Niels Bang Sørensen, Copenhagen, Part 2, V
Jani Soršak, Ljubljana, Part 2, XXII
Daniel Torsher, Bratislava, Part 2, XXI
Miroslav Trencan, Bratislava, Part 2, XXI
Stelios Triantafyllides (M.A., LL.M.), Nicosia, Part 2, III
Steven Turnbull, London, Part 2, XXV
Dr. Cezary Wiśniewski, Warsaw, Part 2, XIX
Christina Zakopoulou (M.Sc.equiv.), Athens, Part 2, X
Lauris Zubulis, Riga, Part 2, XIV

Summary of Contents

Table of Contents

Cross-References

Within a chapter

Cross-references within a chapter refer to marginal numbers.
Example:
Mn. 3 = marginal number 3 in the respective chapter.

To a chapter of Part 1 – Legal Framework and Comparison

Cross-references to the chapters of the first part of the book have been made in accordance with the following example:
Part 1, II, Mn. 33 = Part 1, chapter II, marginal number 33.

To a Chapter of Part 2 – National Law

Cross-references to the chapters of the second part of the book have been made in accordance with the following abbreviations:

Austria	A	France	F	Lithuania	LT	Slovenia	SLO
Belgium	B	Germany	D	Luxembourg	L	Spain	E
Cyprus	CY	Greece	GR	Malta	M	Sweden	S
Czech Republic	CZ	Hungary	H	Netherlands	NL	United Kingdom	UK
Denmark	DK	Ireland	IRL	Poland	PL	Excursus: Societas Europaea	S.E.
Estonia	EST	Italy	I	Portugal	P		
Finland	FIN	Latvia	LV	Slovakia	SK		

Examples:
Part 2, CZ, Mn. 4 = Part 2, Chapter IV (Czech Republic), marginal number 4.
Part 2, S.E., Mn. 17 = Part 2, Chapter XXVI (Societas Europea), marginal number 17.

Glossary/Abbreviations

AB	Akcinė bendrovė (Lithuanian Stock Corporation)
ABĮ	Akcinių bendrovių įstatymas (Lithuanian Law on Companies)
AC	Appeal cases – Law Reports
A.E.	Anonymi Etairia (Greek Stock Corporation)
AG	Aktiengesellschaft (Austrian/German Stock Corporation, depending on the respective chapter)
AGM	Annual general meeting
AJPES	Slovenian Agency for Public Evidence
AktG	Aktiengesetz (Austrian/German Stock Corporation Act, depending on the respective chapter)
All ER	All England Report
App.	Appeal
ApS	Anpartsselskab (Denmark: Limiteld Liability Company)
ApSL	Danish Limited Liabilities Companies Act
ArbVG	Arbeitsverfassungsgesetz (Austria: Labour Constitution Act)
Art.	Article
a.s.	Akciová společnost (Czesk Stock Corporation) or akciová spoločnost (Slovak Stock Corporation); depending on the respective chapter
A/S	Aktieselskab (Dansk Stock Corporation)
AS	Aktsiaselts (Estonian Stock Corporation) or akciju sabiedrība (Latvian Stock Corporation); depending on the respective chapter
ÄS	Estonian Commercial Code
ASL	Danish Stock Corporations Act
BB	Betriebs-Berater (a German legal journal)
BCLC	Butterworth's Company Law Cases (British law report)
BGH	Bundesgerichtshof (German Federal Supreme Court)
BGHZ	Collection of judgements of the German Federal Supreme Court
B.V.	Besloten vennootschap (Dutch Stock Corporation)
BVBA	Besloten vennootschap met beperkte aansprakelijheid (See SPRL)
CA	British Companies Act 1985, Irish Companies Act, Maltese Companies Act 1995; depending on the respective chapter
Cas.	Case
CC	Companies Code, Código das Sociedades Comerciais (Portuguese Companies Code) or Slovak Commercial Code; depending on the respective chapter
C.Com	Code de Commerce (French Commercial Code)
CFR	US-Code of Federal Regulations
CGI	Code Général des Impôts (French General Code on Taxation)
CK	Civilinis kodeksas (Lithuanian Civil Code)
CMF	Code Monétaire et Financier (French Monetary and Financial Code)
CMVM	Comissão de Mercado de Valores Mobiliáros (Portuguese Securities Market Commission)
CRC	Código do Registo Comercial (Portuguese Commercial Registry Code)
CRO	Irish Companies Registration Office
Ctv.	Hungarian Company Registration Act

DCC	Burgerlijk Wetboek (Dutch Civil Code)
D&O insurance	Directors' & Officers' liability insurance
d.o.o.	Družba z omejeno odgovornostjo (Slovenian Limited Liability Company)
DStR	Deutsches Steuerrecht (a German legal journal)
E.B.L.R.	European Business Law Review
EBOR	European Business Organization Law Review
EC	European Community
ECFR	European Company and Financial Law Review
ECJ	European Court of Justice
ECRS	Väärtpaberite Keskregister (Estonian Central Register of Securities)
ECT	Treaty establishing the European Community
Ed	Editor
EEA	European Economic Area (i.e. the EU plus Iceland, Liechtenstein and Norway)
EGM	Extraordinary General Meeting
EKEG	Eigenkapitalersatzgesetz (Austrian Equity Capital Subrogation Act)
EKL	Latvian European Stock Corporation Act
EPE	Eteria Periorismenis Efthinis (Greek Limited Liability Company)
Et seq.	And following
EU	European Union
FĮĮ	Finansų įstaigų įstatymas (Lithuanian Law on Financial Institutions)
Fn.	Footnote
FS	Festschrift
GAAP	Generally Accepted Accounting Principles (as applied in the respective country))
GM	General meeting
GmbH	Gesellschaft mit beschränkter Haftung (Austrian/German Limited Liability Company)
GmbHG	Gesetz betreffend die Gesellschaften mit beschränkter Haftung (Austrian/German Limited Liability Companies Act)
Gt.	Hungarian Companies Act
HGB	Handelsgesetzbuch (Austrian/German Commercial Code)
IA 1986	Insolvency Act 1986 (UK Insolvency Code)
IAS	Intarnational Accounting Standards
IC	Código da Insolvência e da Recuperação de Empresas (Portuguese Insolvency Code)
ICC	Italian Commercial Code
i.e.	id est (that is)
ĮFAĮ	Įmonių finansinės atskaitomybės įstatymas (Lithuanian Law on Financial Statements)
IFRS	International Financial Reporting Standards
InsO	Insolvenzordnung (German Insolvency Code)
KCL	Komerclikums (Latvian Commercial Law Act)
Kft.	Korltolt felelősségű társaság (Hungarian Limited Liability Company)
KG	Kommanditgesellschaft (German Limited Partnership)
KO	Konkursordnung (Austrian Insolvency Act)

KSH	Ustawa – kodeks spólek handlowych (Polish Act on Commercial Partnerships and Companies Code)
LAS	Lithuanian Accounting Standards
Lda	Sociedade por Quotas (Portuguese limited liability company)
Limited Liability Company	The term "Limited Liability Company" and the term "Private Company Limited by Shares" should be understood as synonyms in this publication; both are intended to refer to the respective national corporate form with limited liability that usually has a smaller number of shareholders (or quotaholders or members) and cannot be listed at a stock exchange
LLC	Luxembourgian Law of Commercial Companies
LNN	Latvian Law on Taxes and Duties
Ltd.	See Private Company Limited by Shares
LUGP	Latvian Law on Annual Accounts of Companies
LUUM	Latvian Law on the Insolvency of Companies
M&A	Mergers and Acquisitions
Mn.	Marginal number
NBPR	National Board of Patents and Registration (Finland)
NJ	Nerderlandse Jurisprudentie (Dutch journal)
N.V.	Naamloze vennootschap (Belgian/Dutch Stock Corporation)
ObchZ	Obchodní zákoník (Czech Commercial Code)
OGM	Ordinary General Meeting
OHG	Offene Handelsgesellschaft (German Partnership)
OÜ	Asaühing (Estonian Limited Liability Company)
Oy	Osakeyhtiö (Finnish Limited Liability Company)
Oyj	Julkinen osakeyhtiö (Finnish Stock Corporation)
OYL	Osakeyhtiölaki (Finnish Companies Act)
PankrS	Pankrotiseadus (Estonian Bankruptcy Act)
PCL	Irish Private Company Limited by Shares (see Limited Liability Company)
PCLS	Irish Public Company Limited by Shares (see Stock Corporation)
Plc.	Public Company Limited by Shares
Private Company Limited by Shares	See Limited Liability Company
Procurist/Prokurist	Holder of a special statutory authority under the respective laws of a Member State to represent a company
Public Company Limited by Shares	See Stock Corporation
RPS	Raamatupidamise seadus (Estonian Accounting Act)
Rt.	Részvéntytársaság (Hungarian Stock Corporation)
RvdW	Rechtspraak van de Week (Dutch Journal)
S.A.	Société anonyme (Belgian/French/Luxembourg Stock Corporation), spólka akcyjna (Polish Stock Corporation), Sociedade Anónima (Portuguese Stock Corporation) or Sociedad Anónima (Spanish Stock Corporation)
SARL/S.à.r.l.	Société à responsibilité limitée (French/Luxembourg Limited Liability Company)
SAS	Société par actions simplifiée (French Simplified Stock Corporation)
SC	Código dos Valores Mobiliários (Portuguese Securities Code)

S.E.	Societas Europaea (European Stock Corporation; European (Public) Company)
S.p.A.	Società per Azioni (Italian Stock Corporation)
Sec.	Section
SIA	Sabiedrība ar ierobežotu atbildību (Latvian Limited Liability Company)
SL	Sociedad de responsabilidad Limitada (Spanish Limited Liabibility Company)
S.r.l.	Società a responsabilità limitata (Italian Limited Liability Company)
Sp.z o.o.	Spólka z ograniczoną odpowiedzialnoįcią (Polish Limited Liability Company)
SPRL	Société à responsabilité limitée (Belgian Limited Liability Company)
s.r.o.	Společnosts ručením omezenym (Czech Limited Liability Company) or společnost' s ručením obmezenym (Slovak Limited Liability Company); depending on the respective chapter
Stock Corporation	The term "Stock Corporation" and the term "Public Company Limited by Shares" should be understood as synonyms in this publication; both are intended to refer to the respective national corporate form with limited liability which usually has a larger number of shareholders and can be listed at a stock exchange (but is also often used without a listing)
Subs.	Subsection / paragraph
UAB	Uždaroji akcinė bendrovė (Lithuanian Limited Liability Company)
UfR	Ugeskrift for Retsvæsen (a Danish legal journal)
UK	United Kingdom
URG	Unternehmensreorganisationsgesetz (Austrian Companies Reorganisation Act)
UZ	Zákon o účetnictví (Czech Act on Accounting)
VAT	Value Added Tax
VPRĮ	Vertybinių popierių rinkos įstatymas (Lithuavian Law on Securities Market)
WGE	Wet giraal effectenverkeer (Dutch Securities Giro Transfer Act)
ZCP	Zákon o cenneyh papírech (Czech Securities Act)
ZDDV	Slovenian Value Added Tax Act
ZDP	Zákon o daní z příjmů (Czech Income Taxes Act)
ZFPPod	Zakon o finančnem psolovanju podjetij (Slovenian Financial Operations of Companies Act)
ZGD	Zakon o gospodarskih družbah (Slovenian Companies Act)
ZGR	Zeitschrift für Unternehmens- und Gesellschaftsrecht (a German Legal Journal)
ZIP	Zeitschrift für Wirtschaftsrecht (a German Legal Journal)
ZKP	Zákon o podnikáni na kapitalovém trhu (Czech Act on Capital Markets)
ZNVP	Zakon o nematerialziranih vednostnih papirjih (Slovenian Book Entry Securities Act)
ZSR	Zakon o sodnem registru (Slovenian Court Register Act)
ZTVP	Zakon o trgu vrednostnih papirjev (Slovenian Securities Market Act)

Introduction

European Corporate Law: United in Diversity

*Prof. Karel Van Hulle**

The official motto of the European Union is truly reflected in the present status of company law in the various Member States of the EU. While one can find much similarity, particularly in those areas where harmonisation efforts have taken place, there are still many divergencies, which result from different legal traditions but also from different socio-economic developments. In this respect, the internal market is far from complete. There are a number of areas where the lack of harmonisation has been the cause of practical difficulties, leading to a number of important rulings by the European Court of Justice. The Court's rulings in cases such as *Centros, Überseering* and *Inspire Art* have given raise to an abundant legal literature and have clearly provoked a renewed interest in European corporate law. This interest had already been awakened by the work of the Group of High Level Experts, under the chairmanship of Prof. Jaap Winter, which was appointed by the European Commission in 2001 in order to provide the Commission with an expert opinion on those issues where further EU action in the area of company law might be useful or indeed necessary. The extensive mandate provided for by the Commission was subsequently broadened when as a result of corporate scandals, particularly in the US, certain aspects of company law, such as the role of non-executive directors and of supervisory boards, management remuneration and the responsibility of management for the preparation of financial information received more public attention.

The Winter Group submitted its Report on a Modern Regulatory Framework for Company Law in Europe in November 2002. The Group identified a number of issues where action from the EU was urgently needed, i.e. corporate governance, capital maintenance and cross-border restructuring and mobility of companies. These matters should be dealt with by the EU in the short term. A number of other issues were tabled for action in the medium or long term. Important were also the comments in the Group's Report on the legal instrument to be used. Action at EU level does not necessarily mean the adoption of a Directive or a Regulation. It can sometimes be more efficient and effective to proceed by way of Recommendation or by setting up a mechanism whereby interested parties can meet and discuss best practice.

In May 2003, the European Commission came forward with its response. Two Communications were issued, one dealing with company law in general and another one dealing with issues relating to the statutory audit. In the company law area, 23 actions (from short to long term) were proposed. In the area of statutory audit, 10 actions (short and medium term) were listed. There is no doubt that both documents constitute the most comprehensive policy documents that were ever issued by the Commission in the area of company law.

Most of the short term actions announced in the Commission's Communication on company law have meanwhile been implemented:

- adoption on 14 December 2004 of a Commission Recommendation fostering an appropriate regime for the remuneration of directors of listed companies;
- adoption on 15 February 2005 of a Commission Recommendation on the role of non-executive or supervisory directors of listed companies and on the committees of the (supervisory) board;
- adoption by the European Parliament and the Council (20 September 2005) of a Directive on cross-border mergers in the EU; creation of a European Forum to promote convergence in Europe in the area of corporate governance;
- adoption by the Commission of a proposal to amend the Second Company Law Directive (implementation of the proposals to simplify the provisions on capital maintenance);
- adoption of a proposal to amend the Fourth and Seventh Company Law Directives (collective responsibility of board members for the financial statements, improved transparency about

* Head of Unit at the *European Commission*. The views expressed in this contribution are entirely personal.

related party transactions and about off-balance sheet transactions, introduction of a corporate governance statement).

Meanwhile, preparatory work has started on what could become a proposal for a Directive on cross-border voting and on the cross-border transfer of a company's registered office (Fourteenth Directive). The launch of a feasibility study is also being prepared on an alternative to the present capital maintenance regime and its relation to profit distribution. Finally, the Commission recently announced that it will launch a study on the difficult issue of "one share, one vote", a subject which already caused a lot of controversy in the context of the Thirteenth Directive on take over bids.

As far as the Communication on statutory audit is concerned, the most important action, i.e. the replacement of the present Eighth Directive by a new Directive introducing a comprehensive regulation of the audit function, has been virtually completed after the adoption by the Council in October 2005 of the amendments introduced by the European Parliament. Work is also under way on the preparation of a study that will be launched in the near future on the economic impact of auditors' liability regimes, a study which has been specifically requested by the European Parliament during the debate on the Eighth Directive.

Although the initiatives mentioned before were taken after appropriate consultation of Member States, the European Parliament and all interested parties, the present Commission attaches more than ever importance to better regulation. All future Commission initiatives will have to be accompanied by an impact assessment which examines the practical impact of what is being proposed. Proposed and adopted measures will be constantly reviewed and evaluated and where necessary withdrawn. As a consequence of this approach of better law making, the Commission recently decided to withdraw a number of initiatives, such as the proposed Statute for a a European Mutual Society and even adopted measures such as the Twelfth Company Law Directive on the single member company. Attention will also be paid to further simplification of the existing set of regulations and to a codification of the adopted Directives.

Company law is only one element in the regulatory environment of business undertakings. Nevertheless, the impact of company law rules on the business community cannot be underestimated. It is therefore important to proceed with caution. The internal market clearly does not call for uniform company law. There must be proper competition between legal systems so as to allow for creativity. On the other hand, the ever changing business environment calls for a close monitoring of the market so as to be able to identify those areas where action is needed in order to remove obstacles which stand in the way of progress towards a better functioning internal market, which should ultimately be to the benefit of all parties concerned.

To enable and enhance the afore-mentioned competition between the company law systems of the Member States, a high level of transparency is needed as a catalyst. Only if investors and potential founders know and understand the variety of corporate forms available in the EU and the opportunities specific types of corporations in the individual Member States offer, they will make a selection on an informed basis; this selection, in turn, will increase competition. Whereas first steps have been taken in the past to increase transparency by comparing certain types of companies, this was restricted to corporate forms of a limited number of selected Member States so far; a comprehensive comparison and analysis of corporate forms from all EU Member States, however, was missing – and overdue.

This textbook provides an overview of all forms of public limited liability companies (in this book referred to as "stock corporations") and private limited liability companies (in this book referred to as "limited liability companies") that are available in any Member State and of the European Company (SE). That forms the basis of a thorough analysis of this set of corporate forms from a number of different angles that may be crucial in the decision-making process of an investor.

Part 1 – Legal Framework and Comparison

I. European Framework for the Mobility of Companies

by Dr. Alexander Schall (MJur)[*]

1 Introduction

1 Numerous forms of companies from all the Member States are trading in the EU. All these companies are subject to different requirements for their birth, life and death. They vary with respect to issues like corporate governance, creditor protection or co-determination. These differences complicate trading in the EU and are thus obstacles for the realisation of the Common Market.

2 There are three ways in which European law tries to counter these adverse effects. First, it provides for the mutual recognition of the companies from Member States in Art. 43, 48 ECT. These provisions grant the freedom of establishment, in particular the opening of branches in other Member States. However, the scope of this right has for decades been restricted under Continental jurisdictions with a view to pseudo-foreign companies. The ECJ-jurisdiction in *Centros*, *Übeseering* and *Inspire Art* did away with these restrictions.[1] This opened the door for UK limited companies to the Continent. The most important market appears to be Germany where there are by now more than 20,000 pseudo-foreign UK limited companies in operation.[2]

3 Secondly, European law tries to overcome the national differences by harmonisation. The creation of a common set of company law rules facilitates trading and establishing branches within the Common Market. For this purpose, several directives have been adopted, e.g., with respect to the capital structure of stock corporations, the powers of companies organs or disclosure principles.[3] In addition, the European Insolvency Regulation, although it does not (yet) provide for a uniform corporate insolvency law (as exists in the US), establishes uniform principles determining the applicable law in a winding up.

4 Thirdly, European law has long since been willing to offer a pan-European corporate form free from national requirements, namely the European stock corporation (*Societas Europaea*). However, necessary compromises on the political level have left us with not one, but 25 different forms of the S.E., thus counteracting the original aim of supra-nationality.[4] Bearing that in mind, it remains doubtful whether there will be a need and a political will to go on and create a European Private Company.

2 The Freedom of Establishment, the Rules on Conflict of Laws and Pseudo-foreign Companies

5 Companies are creatures of the law. Each jurisdiction forms its own companies. Any capacity of companies to act in another jurisdiction is dependent on their recognition by that state. Within the EU, recognition of companies from one Member State by all the others is granted in Art. 43, 48 ECT. As a result, enterprises are not forced to establish local subsidiaries to trade in other Member States.

6 However, the guaranteed recognition under Art. 43, 48 ECT has always had a weak flank with respect to so-called pseudo-foreign companies, i.e. companies which are incorporated in a Member

* Assistant-professor in law, *Institute for Law and Economics, University of Hamburg*.

1 See Mn. 12 et seq.

2 This number can be derived from the sudden but constant rise of new UK limited incorporations since the *Überseering* judgment set in relation to those European economies where the migration phenomenon is perceived. It is confirmed by the recently reported number of 17,400 German directors registered in UK limited companies in 2004, see Wirtschaftswoche, 7.4.2005, 26. The number of pseudo-foreign companies is, however, not reflected in the commercial register, as the obligation to register as a branch is often avoided for various reasons.

3 See Mn. 38 et seq.

4 See Mn. 75.

State different from where they actually trade to avoid stricter domestic requirements (e.g. minimum capital). This was due to the rules on conflict of company laws which were a domain of national legislation. While it was clear that companies from other Member States could invoke the freedom of establishment, the conflict rules did not provide a clear definition of what actually constituted a "foreign company". Several approaches were posited and led to a very different picture,[5] before the jurisdiction of the ECJ stepped in and clarified the situation.

2.1 The Incorporation Theory

7 According to the incorporation theory, the rules applicable to a company are determined by the state in which the company has been incorporated and remains registered.[6] This is a straightforward formal definition of a company's "nationality". It is followed for example in the UK, the Netherlands and most Nordic countries. The incorporation theory avoids difficult material criteria such as where the main business is done or where the administrative decisions are taken.

8 As a consequence, this formal approach enables founders to choose their company law by registering in a country different from where the business is actually done. As a result, it allows de facto "contracting out" of local company law and thus undermines the mandatory requirements which should be complied with to gain the privilege of limited liability in the host state. An even more liberal approach is offered by the registration theory which further allows changing the company law of origin by re-registering in another country.

2.2 The Real Seat Theory

9 The opposing "real seat theory" was developed to avoid this factual choice of company law and evasion of domestic rules.[7] Under this approach, the "nationality" of the company is determined by the real seat of its administration, i.e. where the main decisions are taken. A company is only deemed foreign by the host state if it is governed from abroad, not from within the host state. For example, if the actual administration of a Liberian limited company were located in Germany, this company would be denied separate legal personality and limited liability granted by the laws of Liberia. Instead, it would be treated as a German business. To gain legal personality and limited liability in Germany, the business would have to be incorporated anew under German law. Conversely, if a German GmbH moved its real seat abroad, it would be dissolved by operation of law. The same applied, for example, to an Italian company relocating its registered office to Luxemburg.[8] As a result, under company laws which follow the real seat theory, there may be no divergence between the registered office and the actual centre of administration. This hinders both the moving in of foreign companies and the moving out of domestic companies. The material criterion of the real seat raised considerable problems, for example, in cases where the company does not have a discernible "real seat".[9] But it proved an efficient way to prevent evasion of domestic company law, and thus became widespread on the Continent.

5 For historic details see (in German) the – partly outdated – account by Kindler, Münchener Kommentar zum BGB, Band 10, 3rd edition 1999, Internationales Handels und Gesellschaftsrecht, 258 et seq.

6 See e.g. (for the UK) Davies, Gower and Davies' Principles of Modern Company Law, 7th edition 2003, 103 et seq.

7 See Klinke, ECFR 2005, 270, 283 et seq.; in German: Behrens, in: Ulmer/Habersack/Winter (eds), Großkommentar zum GmbHG, Bd. 1 (2005), Allg. Einl. Mn. B 1 et seq. (to be published 2006).

8 The B&C Case of the Cassazione, Corte di Cassazione Civile, Sezioni Unite, 23.1.2004, n. 1244, Rivista italiana di diritto privato e processuale, 2005, 1381, noted Mucciarelli (2005) ECFR 512 (while Italy follows the incorporation theory, Luxembourg adheres to the real set theory).

9 See e.g. *Multinational Gas and Petrochemical Co v Multinational Gas and Petrochemical Services Ltd* (1983) Ch 258 (Court of Appeal) = (1983) 2 All ER 563 where the vehicle was designed without any real seat to avoid fiscal implications.

2.3 Hybrid Concepts

Between these two poles, several hybrid concepts have emerged. Their common feature is the splitting of the applicable company law, for example, with respect to internal (corporate governance, shareholders) and external (creditor protection) issues.[10] This caused practical inconvenience. It was refuted by proponents of both the incorporation and the real seat approaches who insisted on a uniform regime for the applicable company law. 10

2.4 The Conflict of Laws Doctrines in Light of European Law

In the European Union (or Community, as it then was), incorporation theory and real seat theory co-existed from the beginning – a reality which the European legislator accepted in the drafting of many rules.[11] Notwithstanding that, it has been argued for a long time that the real seat theory was in conflict with European law. The *Sedes materiae* was Art. 48 ECT which grants *freedom of establishment to any company validly established* under the laws of a Member State. This freedom is restricted if, under the real seat approach, the relocation of the real seat leads to non-recognition of the incorporated company requiring re-incorporation under the laws of the recipient state. Thus, it appears that any company validly incorporated in a Member State should be able to invoke freedom of establishment against such restrictions. Nevertheless, it was a long and winding road before the freedom of establishment finally prevailed over the conflict principles of the real seat approach. 11

2.5 The Jurisdiction of the ECJ

2.5.1 Daily Mail

In 1988, the first case on the interdependence of the freedom of establishment and national company law was decided by the ECJ.[12] *Daily Mail* has been understood as a fierce defence of the real seat approach and a refutation of the critique uttered by the incorporationists. This is interesting as the case did not refer to conflict rules directly. Rather, it concerned an unmeritorious tax case. To avoid the taxation of its hidden reserves accumulated in the UK, Daily Mail resolved to move the real seat of its business to the Netherlands. To prevent this form of "tax evasion", UK law contained a provision under which the relocation of the real seat required the approval of the government. Not surprisingly, the British government abstained from authorising the relocation of Daily Mail. The appeal against this decision led the parties before the ECJ. 12

The ECJ held that Daily Mail could not invoke Art. 48 ECT on two grounds. The first was that the freedom of establishment could not be invoked directly but was subject to – still outstanding – implementation by secondary law. This ground no longer holds today. It has been expressly revoked by the ECJ in *Centros*.[13] The crucial reason is therefore the second one. The Court explained that a company only exists within the legal framework of its "home state". This legal framework therefore enjoys priority over the freedom of establishment. If the home law provides, for example, that a company ceases to exist if it leaves the country without authorisation, that company loses its legal personality and can thus no longer invoke freedom of establishment. The state which has spent its life may take it away again before Europe can interfere. 13

It should be noted that this interpretation is at odds with the wording of Art. 48 ECT which grants freedom of establishment to companies validly incorporated (and not: existing) under the law of a Member State. Nevertheless, contrary to the priority-of-harmonisation argument, it has not been given up by the ECJ in the subsequent cases. Rather, the ECJ distinguished them on the ground that 14

10 For a German post-*Inspire Art* take, see Altmeppen, FS Röhricht (2005), 3, 11 et seq.; contra: Sandrock, BB 2004, 987.

11 e.g. Art. 48 ECT, Art. 7 European Company Statute.

12 Case C-81/87 *Daily Mail* (1988) ECR I-5483; noted Cerioni, JBL 1999, 59; Behrens, IPRax 1989, 354.

13 See Mn. 15 et seq.

Daily Mail concerned restrictions imposed by the home country, whereas *Centros*, *Überseering* and *Inspire Art* dealt with restrictions imposed by the host.[14]

2.5.2 Centros

15 Ten years later, in 1998, the *Centros* case was heard before the Court.[15] A UK limited company had been denied registration of its branch in Denmark on grounds that it was not doing actual business in the UK ("pseudo-foreign company"). The complaint by the Danish incorporators was allowed by the ECJ. Denmark had argued that Art. 48 could not be invoked because of abuse. The UK limited company was only a vehicle to circumvent the Danish minimum capital requirement. But the Court answered that establishing a pseudo-foreign company meant not abusing but using the freedom of establishment.[16] The Court then went on to put the Danish restriction to the test of Art. 48 ECT. The Court adopted the same broad view of the scope of Art. 48 ECT that it had developed with respect to other basic freedoms. These freedoms are not restricted to discriminations. Rather, they are restricted to any measures which make trading for foreigners more onerous. The denial of registration thus restricted the freedom of establishment. This restriction could not be justified. The specific provision in Art. 46 ECT does not cover creditor protection. A general justification on grounds of public interest can not be invoked either. The Court applied a scheme well known from other cases. A restriction of basic freedoms is justified if it is applied in a non-discriminatory manner, if it is justified for compelling reasons of public interest, if it is apt to achieve this objective and if it is not more onerous than necessary (= proportionate).[17] Denmark had argued that the denial of registration should ensure compliance with the minimum capital requirement which was necessary for creditor protection. But the Court had no difficulty answering that the creditors would not have been protected if the company had also been doing business in the UK. Therefore, the restriction could not be "necessary".

16 It is obvious that the Court in *Centros* disapproved of the underlying reasoning of the real seat theory. Instead, it *de facto* pleaded for competition of company laws and protection of creditors via disclosure.[18] However, the case was not the demise of the real seat theory yet as both Denmark and the UK followed the incorporation theory. Thus many legal writers argued that the *Daily Mail* prerogative of national company law and conflict rules still was valid.[19]

2.5.3 Überseering

17 Four years later, another case went up to the ECJ.[20] The Dutch company *Überseering* B.V. did building business in the border regions of Germany and the Netherlands. Its shares were sold to owners living (and possibly managing the company's business) in Germany. When it tried to sue a debtor under a contract, the Geman court held that the transfer of the shares had led to a relocation of the real seat to Germany. This had the effect, according to the then prevailing principles of the real seat theory, that the company was a *nullum* and had no legal standing to sue. The case made its way to the *Bundesgerichtshof* (BGH), the German Federal Supreme Court. The judges decided to ask the ECJ directly whether the consequences of the real seat theory, as it then stood, were in line with European law.

18 The ECJ clarified that any company established under the laws of a Member State must be accepted by any other Member State *as such*, irrespective of its real seat.[21] As a result, it was now

14 See Mn. 15 et seq.

15 Case C-212/97 *Centros* (1999) ECR I-1459, noted Merkt, (2001) 3 Int.Comp.Corp.L.J. 119.

16 Ibid, para. 18 et seq.; *Segers* (1986) ECR I-2375, para. 16; confirmed in C-167/01 *Inspire Art* para. 95 et seq.

17 Ibid, para. 34; C-19/92 *Kraus* (1993) ECR I-1663; C-55/94 *Gebhard* (1995) ECR I-4165, para 37; confirmed in C-196/01 *Inspire Art*, para. 133.

18 See Merkt, ECFR 2004, 3, 16 et seq.

19 E.g. Kindler (Fn. 5), 358 et seq.

20 Case C-208/00 *Überseering* (2002) ECR I-09919.

21 It is interesting to note that the chamber of the BGH which decided to pose the question was not the one in charge of company law. So, parallel to the pending *Überseering* case, the company law chamber modified the real seat theory.

clear that a UK limited or a Dutch B.V. could neither be denied legal capacity nor be regarded as a German partnership. Thus, the central position of the real seat theory on incoming companies could no longer be upheld. However, the Court refrained from declaring itself directly on the theories. This may be understood from judicial self-restraint. Unfortunately, it left room for interpretations on how far the foreign companies might still be subjected to domestic requirements, for example by "defence legislation".

2.5.4 Inspire Art

The last case in the line, *Inspire Art*,[22] dealt with the scope which remained for the application of domestic company law on pseudo-foreign companies. It concerned Dutch defence legislation. The Netherlands did not follow the real seat doctrine and accepted legal personality of pseudo-foreign companies under their law of origin. Instead, to defend the domestic requirements (in particular legal capital), they had enacted defence legislation requiring disclosure of the pseudo-foreign character of the company and *de facto* compliance with the domestic minimum capital.[23] The ECJ disallowed the Dutch Act. First, it held that the Eleventh Directive on disclosure requirements for branches did not permit further disclosure duties.[24] Secondly, it found that the indirect implementation of the legal capital via directors' duties impeded trading and thus restricted the freedom of establishment. It reconfirmed that the running of a pseudo-foreign company was no abuse of Art. 48 ECT. Finally, it found no justification for the restriction of Art. 48 ECT imposed by the Act. The ECJ left open whether minimum capital requirements are necessary for efficient protection at all.[25] The lack of necessity was, like in *Centros*, already shown by the fact that local legal capital could not protect creditors against "real" foreign companies. If disclosure suffices here, it must suffice there as well. **19**

2.6 The Legal Treatment of Corporate Relocations post *Inspire Art*

2.6.1 Restrictions by Host States on Moving In

The survival of *Daily Mail* makes it necessary to distinguish between restrictions imposed by the host state on moving in and by the home state on moving out. With respect to the former, the ECJ decisions have not gone so far as to approve or disapprove one of the opposing conflict of laws concepts. However, it can be drawn from them that they favour the incorporation theory.[26] The ECJ has made it very clear that legal personality and limited liability of companies incorporated in one Member State must be accepted as such in all other Member States, irrespective of the "real seat" of the company. Therefore, the principles of the real seat theory as to "pseudo-foreign" companies[27] cannot be upheld with respect to "incoming" companies. Furthermore, the ECJ ruled that any restrictions on the trading of foreign companies need to be justified in light of Art. 43, 48 ECT. In this regard, the comparison to the rules for "real" foreign companies plays an essential role. For example, as local creditor protection rules (for example, capital maintenance) could not be **20**

Instead of denying any legal standing, it now preferred to treat the "pseudo-foreign company" as a partnership under German law. This would have at least enabled *Überseering* B.V. to sue before a German court, albeit with the flip side of being treated as a mere partnership with unlimited shareholder liability (which could, of course, again have been seen as a violation of the freedom of establishment). Under the new approach, the question posed by the other chamber of the BGH to the ECJ would have been obsolete. But it was too late, and the ECJ seized the opportunity to clarify the matter.

22 Case C-167/01 Inspire Art *(2003) noted de Kluiver, ECFR 2004, 121.*

23 This was enforced by a management liability. The managers of the pseudo-foreign company were personally liable for the company's debts as long as the company traded without having raised capital amounting to the Dutch requirement.

24 Ibid, para. 66 et seq.

25 This had been bluntly denied by Alber AG, opinion of 30 January.

26 See Klinke, ECFR 2005, 270, 289 et seq., 294 et seq.; Sester/Cardenas, ECFR 2005, 398, 401.

27 See Mn. 9.

applied to real foreign companies, they cannot be applied to pseudo-foreign companies either. The law of origin principle is in line with the general ECJ jurisdiction on the fundamental freedoms.[28]

21 It results that EU companies generally need to be treated under the **law of origin**, as posited by the **incorporation theory**. However, many uncertainties remain with respect to the scope left for domestic requirements. This has sparked considerable debate in the countries which found themselves as favoured host states after *Inspire Art*, in first place Germany, where the legal writing[29] can be summarised as follows:

22 The law of origin certainly covers the formation of the company, the company structure, the powers of the board, shareholders' remedies and directors' duties[30] (but see below for insolvency-related misfeasance). Form requirements on share transfers in the host state do not apply.[31] According to prevailing opinion, the same is true for statutory co-determination at board level.[32] The company's name must comply both with the laws of origin and with German law and is protected by German legal tools.[33] It is not clear yet whether a pseudo foreign company can invoke the statutory provisions of the German *Umwandlungsgesetz* (Transformation Act) for restructuring (mergers, split-offs).[34] The company can be sued in the state of origin as well as in Germany. The same is true for directors or shareholders.[35] Conversely, the company's access to court is no longer restricted. The disclosure duties follow from the Eleventh Directive.[36] The company has to register its branch in Germany. Accounts under the law of origin suffice.[37] However, as the pseudo-foreign companies are generally taxed by the host state, they will have to deliver German accounts as well. Moreover, as the British Companies House is reported to accept these German accounts for companies not trading in the UK, the legal rule is de facto turned upside down.

23 However, according to Art. 3, 4 European Insolvency Regulation, insolvency proceedings are conducted under the law where the centre of main interest ("CoMI") usually is. This rule is not restricted to mere procedural law but also includes substantial insolvency law, for example the provisions on avoidance[38] (transactions at an undervalue, preferences) which define the assets available

28 Klinke, ibid, 295.

29 See e.g. Hirte/Bücker (eds.) Grenzüberschreitende Gesellschaften (2005); Lutter (ed), Europäische Auslandsgesellschaften in Deutschland (2005), Eidenmüller, Ausländische Kapitalgesellschaften (2004). The current focus is mainly on creditor protection regimes, see Mn. 24 et seq.

30 Riegger, ZGR 2004, 510, 517 et seq.

31 Art. 11 para. 1 EGBGB (Introductory Act to the German Civil Code): *lex causae* for the share transfer is the *lex societatis*, i.e. UK law; *lex loci* is German law containing a form requirement in Sec. 15 Subs. 4 GmbHG (German Private Limited Companies Act). See in detail Kalss, ECFR 2004, 340, 360 et seq.

32 Müller-Bonani in Hirte/Bücker (Fn. 29) § 13 (17) et seq.; Zimmer in Lutter (Fn. 29), 369 et seq.; Riegger, ZGR 2004, 510, 518 et seq.; contra: Grundmann/Möslein, ZGR 2003, 317, 350 et seq. For an overview on co-determination in Europe see Part 1, II, Mn. 161 et seq.

33 Mankowski in Hirte/Bücker (Fn. 29), § 12 (48) et seq.; Karsten Schmidt in Lutter (Fn. 29), 15 et seq.

34 As to the possibility of a merger, the ECJ in the SEVIC case (case C-411/03, judgment of 13 December 2005) has meanwhile held that the general refusal under German law to register a merger between a German and a foreign company (having its seat in another Member State) is contrary to European law. The decision was passed in response to a question posed by the regional court (Landgericht) Koblenz, LG Koblenz, 16.9.2003 – 4 HKT 1/0, ZIP 2003, 2210 = EWiR 2004, 139 (noted Mankowski). See further below, Mn. 46, and Hirte in Hirte/Bücker (Fn. 29) § 1 (78).

35 This can be derived from Council Regulation (EC) No. 44/2001 of 22 December 2000 on jurisdiction and enforcement in civil and commercial matters, see in particular Arts. 2 para. 1, 60 para. 1, 5 No 5 and 22 No 2 as to companies. Shareholders and officers may either be sued in Germany (where they live) or in the UK (Art. 5 No 1, company law as *lex causae*). See in detail Leible in Hirte/Bücker (Fn. 29) § 11; Wagner in Lutter (Fn. 29), 223 et seq.

36 See Mankowski in Hirte/Bücker (Fn. 29) § 12 (10) et seq.; Westhoff in Hirte/Bücker (Fn. 29) § 17 (43) et seq. In light of the ECJ jurisdiction, it is no longer possible to object to the application of the regulation on branches on the basis of the overcome argument that the branch of a pseudo-foreign company is not really a branch, but the (real) seat.

37 Riegger, ZGR 2004, 510, 515 et seq.

38 But see Art. 13 restricting the applicability of avoidance provisions of the host state to transactions which would also be challengeable under the laws of the state of origin. As a result, e.g., the German § 135 InsO under which the payback of capital replacement can be challenged could not be applied to such transactions with an English or French company wound up in Germany, Forsthoff/Schultz in Hirte/Bücker (Fn. 29) § 15 (38); contra: Huber in Lutter (Fn. 29), 191 et seq.

for distribution. Thus, the presumed overcome distinction between real foreign and pseudo-foreign companies is preserved. The former are wound up under the laws of the home state, the latter under the laws of the host state.

This division between company law of origin and insolvency law of domicile has sparked a vigorous debate in Germany about the applicable **creditor protection regime**, in particular the potential liabilities of directors and shareholders for the debts of the company (e.g. piercing the veil, equitable subordination, wrongful trading).[39] As a general rule, the law of origin prevails here as well. *Inspire Art* has clarified that no legal capital requirement can be superimposed on foreign companies. However, the European Insolvency Regulation opens the back door for the law of the host state. This undermines *Inspire Art* in several ways. First, the ECJ jurisdiction is based on the assumption that, within the EU, the laws of origin will provide sufficient and comparable creditor protection. But in so far as this protection is achieved via insolvency law, it will not catch the trading of pseudo-foreign companies. For example, the creditors of a pseudo-foreign UK limited can (arguably) not rely on the fraudulent or wrongful trading remedies under Secs. 213, 214 IA 1986.[40] The same is true for the handy British petition right under Sec. 123 Subs. 1 (a) IA 1986 under which default suffices to prove insolvency.[41] Thus, the CoMI approach may pierce the coherent creditor protection system of the Member States. 24

Moreover, the approach to creditor protection differs considerably within Europe. This is not only true for legal capital, but also for insolvency law. Many Member States like Germany, France or Austria establish a directors' duty to file for insolvency in order to put insolvent companies off the market while others adhere to a more flexible approach, for example by requirements for directors to take into account the interests of the creditors (UK).[42] As will be shown below, this may cause material conflicts of duties under the laws of host and home state. 25

Even worse, the distinction between "insolvency law" and "company law" leads to major legal uncertainty. For example, if the German insolvency–related management or shareholder liabilities (duties to file for insolvency, equitable subordination, piercing the veil) are classified as "insolvency law" rather than as "company law" they can be applied to pseudo-foreign companies notwithstanding *Inspire Art*. This facilitates "tendency interpretation" with the aim of applying as much domestic creditor protection law as possible to foreign companies. 26

These legal uncertainties caused by the CoMI approach may well prevent healthy competition of company laws on the Single Market (as wished by the ECJ) and rather attract businessmen of dubious virtue seeking shelter from clear cut laws and registration requirements.[43] This development is deplorable for both home and host state. With respect, the ECJ may have underestimated the consequences of its jurisdiction. Companies are legal *persons* and deserve different treatment from mere products like beer, wine and widgets. It may be that Europe was not yet sufficiently mature for the free movement of companies. 27

In light of these uncertainties, profound analysis of the applicable rules is required for each cross border constellation within the EU. As a general rule, it may be stated: If the law of origin provides sufficient creditor protection, liabilities under the law of the host state cannot be applied as they would impose the burden of a double regime on the company. This cannot be justified under Art. 43, 48 ECT. This holds true even if the respective liability is rooted in the insolvency law of the host 28

39 See only the most recent articles by Schall, EBLR 2005, 1577 et seq.; in German: Goette, DStR 2005, 197; Röhricht, ZIP 2005, 505; Hirte/Mock, ZIP 2005, 474; Schall, ZIP 2005, 965; further in detail Forsthoff/Schultz in Hirte/Bücker (Fn. 29) § 15; Fleischer in Lutter (Fn. 29), 79 et seq.; Huber in Lutter (Fn. 29) 131 et seq., 307 et seq.; Eidenmüller (Fn. 29), § 3, § 4 and § 9 (41) et seq.

40 Cf. Schall, EBLR 2005, 1577 et seq. and ZIP 2005, 965, 972; Röhricht, ZIP 2005, 505, 506; contra: Mock/Schildt in Hirte/Bücker (Fn. 29) § 16 (46). Another example: in the case of a pseudo-foreign French S.A.R.L., there may be no *action en comblement du passif* as it was classified as "insolvency law" in an old decision of the ECJ, 22.2.1979, Case C-133/78 (1979) 733.

41 Under German insolvency law, a failed attempt to execute is required, i.e. normally the creditor will have to sue the doomed company for an award.

42 There is no harmonisation with respect to duties to file for insolvency, neither for private nor for public companies, see Mn. 29.

43 Cf. Tröger, EBOR 2005, 119; Kirchner/Painter/Kaal, ECFR 2005, 159 et seq.: Schall, EBLR 2005, 1577 et seq.; less sceptic Sester/Cardenas, ECFR 2005, 398, 402.

state. Therefore, the applicability under Art. 3, 4 European Insolvency Regulation is not as such sufficient to justify the restrictions of Art. 43, 48 ECT. This argument is further supported by Art. 13 of the Regulation. When it comes to challenging transactions, the insolvency law of the host states only applies under the proviso that it accords with the law of origin. This shows that if a material liability differs from the law of origin, the insolvency law of the host state cannot be applied. This rationale should be extended to *all* material liabilities rooted in local insolvency laws. Exceptions would only be possible if the law of origin left material lacunas in the creditor protection regime.

29 In the important case of UK limited companies trading in Germany, this leads to the following result:[44] UK law provides sufficient creditor protection. This leaves no space for additional German liabilities. Note that problems with limited liability arise once the equity is lost. According to the balance sheet, the remaining assets belong to the creditors. However, particularly in small companies, the manager-shareholders will be induced to carry on trading on the back of their creditors, to use the remaining assets for risky attempts to survive or at least to siphon them away into their own pockets. UK law does not allow this kind of conduct. The statutory prohibition can be found in Sec. 213, 214 IA 1986 (fraudulent and wrongful trading). These statutory duties, however, merely reflect the Common law rule that if the equity is lost, the best interest of the company is not defined by the interests of the shareholders as a whole, but of the creditors as a whole.[45] The directors are subject to this interest as fiduciaries. If they breach their duties, they are liable towards the company.[46] Unlike wrongful trading, this is a company law liability which applies abroad.[47] The same is true for piercing the veil under the fraud exception.[48] These causes of action cover corporate misfeasance near insolvency in an encompassing way and leave no space for domestic German rules. This is in particularly true for the duty to file for insolvency (Sec. 64 Subs. 1 GmbHG, "*Insolvenzantragspflicht*"). This may well conflict with the UK directors' duty to continue trading if it is in the best interest of the creditors, for example if the survival prognosis of the currently over-indebted business is positive. For the same reason, the German duty to cohere the assets (Sec. 64 Subs. 2 GmbHG) and the law of capital replacement (e.g. Secs. 32 a, 32b GmbHG) are not applicable. Neither is the German veil-piercing claim ("*existenzvernichtender Eingriff*"). It is superfluous next to the duty for the benefit of the creditors and the fraud exception of UK law which sufficiently cover insolvency-related misfeasance. At the end of the day, the German claims are not applicable because they serve the same purpose (avoiding trading at the expense of the creditors) in a different way that may be apt for the GmbH but not for UK companies.[49] Conversely, the UK may just as well be prevented from applying its domestic law to foreign companies under Sec. 426 Subs. 5 IA.[50]

2.6.2 Restrictions by Home States on Moving Out

30 While incoming companies need to be treated under the principles of the incorporation theory, a different picture emerges as to outgoing companies. The ECJ has not overruled but only distinguished its *Daily Mail* decision. This cannot be explained by a tax-based interpretation of *Daily Mail*. The ECJ has closed this door in *Hughes de Lasteyrie du Saillant*[51]. In this case, the ECJ subjected an onerous French fiscal provision impeding the moving out of individuals (taxation of unrealised gains) to Art. 43 ECT without even mentioning *Daily Mail*. This indicates that *Daily*

44 In detail Schall, EBLR 2005, 1577 et seq. and (in German) ZIP 2005, 965, 972 et seq.

45 *West Mercia Safetywear v Dodd* (1988) 4 BCC 30, 33; *Kinsela v Russel Kinsela Pty Ltd* (1986) 10 ACLR 395.

46 This liability will normally be enforced by the liquidator. But it is, unlike wrongful trading, not restricted to insolvency proceedings and might therefore also be attached by a creditor.

47 It is rooted in the fiduciary position of the directors. Cf. also the statutory fair dealing provisions in Part X CA 1985 and their internationality under s.347 CA.

48 Cf. *Trustor AB v Smallbone (No 3)* (2001) 3 All ER 987. While hardly applied in the UK, piercing the veil might play a bigger role abroad, see Schall EBLR 2005, 1577 et seq.

49 Schall, EBLR 2005, 1577 et seq. and ZIP 2005, 965, 974.

50 That happened in the BCCI case, see *Re Bank of Credit and Commerce International S.A.* (1993) BCC 787; Goode Principles of Corporate Insolvency (1997) 502 et seq.

51 Case C-9/02 *Hughes de Lasteyrie du Saillant v Ministère de l'Economie, des Finances et de l'Industrie* (2004) noted Parleani, ECFR 2004, 379.

Mail was indeed based on the peculiarities of company law and not – not even between the lines – on preserving the Member States' prerogative in the field of tax law.

The survival of *Daily Mail*, even if it may be explained by rather psychological factors,[52] allows the upholding of the restrictions imposed by home states under the real seat theory. If the law of origin so provides, the company may not relocate its actual place of business abroad. This may provide, for example, a convenient option to avoid the loss of taxation. However, given the wording of Art. 48 ECT,[53] it is not clear whether *Daily Mail* can really live on to save relocation restrictions by the home state.[54] 31

2.7 Further Impact of the Basic Freedoms on European Company Law

Another important development in Europe was the challenge of several provisions in Member States rendering the takeover of public companies impossible ("**Golden Shares**").[55] These provisions aimed to make sure that important public utility companies of strategic interest (for example, energy suppliers, airports) could not escape domestic state control and come into foreign hands. However, in most cases, these provisions were disapproved for infringement of the free movement of capital as the restrictions went too far and exceptions granted were too complicated and uncertain.[56] As a consequence of this development, the German "VW-Act" (protecting Volkswagen from hostile takeovers) has been widely deemed contrary to European law and is probably soon up for repeal. Therefore, Porsche and DaimlerChryssler now plan to acquire major shareholdings as an anticipated defence measure against prospective foreign bidders. Moreover, freedom of establishment and free movement of capital have become a viable remedy against cumbersome **tax provisions**.[57] 32

3 Harmonisation of European Company Laws

3.1 Overview and Current Trends

The national company laws within the EU are overarched in manifold ways by European law. Harmonisation led to a high level of convergence in particular with respect to public companies, while the rules on private companies still differ considerably. There is for example, no European legal capital requirement for private companies, a fact that may well be viewed as the root cause for the *Centros* development. 33

National provisions implementing Directives must be interpreted in accordance with European law.[58] The literal meaning is of high importance in this context – maybe higher than in the national laws of the different Member States. For example, under German private law, the literal meaning of a provision can be overcome to reach either an unwritten restriction or extension of a provision arguing from the underlying objectives and policies (*teleologische Reduktion / Extension*), while this would seem odd to a Common lawyer feeling strongly bound to the wording of Acts ("Golden 34

52 *Daily Mail* was decided in 1988. At that time, the UK was governed by the Euro-sceptic Margaret Thatcher. A decision against the UK might have caused a severe backlash to the European project. By the time of *Centros*, the Court had become far more powerful. Political resistance had decreased. Moreover, this time the decision "favoured" the UK. Thus the Court could feel strong enough to revoke its priority of harmonisation argument. However, the priority of the home law argument could not be revoked without admitting that the ECJ had erred in Daily Mail. Thus the Court may have been relieved to find a way to distinguish *Centros* from *Daily Mail*.

53 See Mn. 14.

54 In the same sense Klinke, ECFR 2005, 270, 296 with no. 124.

55 See e.g. C-483/99 (2002) ECR I-4781 *Commission v France* (Elf Aquitaine), obs. Storck, ECFR 2004, 36, 56 et seq.; C 98/01 *Commission v United Kingdom* (Heathrow Airport). See in more detail the report by Klinke, ECFR 2005, 270, 304 et seq.

56 Different only in C-503/99 *Commission v Belgium* where the requirement of legal certainty was complied with.

57 In detail Klinke, ECFR 2005, 270, 296 et seq.; C-9/02 *Hughes de Lasteyrie du Saillant* noted Parleani, ECFR 2004, 379; C-463/00 *X and Y*, noted Krebs/Bödefeld BB 2004, 407; C-319/02 *Manninnen*; C-324/00 *Lankhorst-Hohorst*; C-168/01 *Bosal*;

58 Art. 249 para. 3 ECT; cf. ECJ C-106/89 *Marleasing*, para. 8 *et seq*. In German: Canaris, "Die richtlinienkonforme Auslegung und Rechtsfortbildung im System der juristischen Methodenlehre" in FS Bydlinski (2002), 47 et seq.

rule").[59] The literal meaning may, however, be difficult to gauge with a view to the many different versions of equal validity.[60] European law further accepts (unlike English law) arguments from the history of the enactment as it forms part of the Directive (in its recitals).[61] National courts concerned with the interpretation of provisions based on Directives may, and last-instance-courts[62] must, find their way to the ECJ to solve legal questions arising in this context.[63]

35 Further issues arise if a national provision simultaneously implements European law and regulates further cases not covered by any Directive. This has, for example, happened in the German *Umwandlungsgesetz* Transformation Act which caters not only for mergers and divisions of stock corporations (Third and Sixth Directives) but also for transformations of other enterprises such as private limited companies (GmbH), partnerships and limited partnerships. That raises the question about the European impact on interpretation (if any). According to orthodoxy national law not directly derived from Directives does not need to be interpreted in accordance with European law (unless the **national** law requires uniform interpretation). Nor may the national courts address the ECJ.[64]

36 Looking at European legislative efforts, it is interesting to note that the spin has shifted in recent years. In the beginning, Europe often adopted Continental, in particular German, rules, for example, corporate bodies with unlimited powers to bind the company or legal capital for stock corporations. A turning point in the Continental predominance could be seen in the failure of the Fifth Directive to harmonise the company structure and of the Ninth Directive to impose the overcomplicated German group law definitions on European level. Instead, European legislation went to define groups from case to case on a "control" approach.[65] As to the company structure, one might however observe a kind of "indirect implementation". The Thirteenth Directive requires disclosure of all obstacles to one – share, one vote (for example, shareholder agreements for acting in concert, double voting rights) and requires the Member States to impose sanctions for non-compliance – a strong incentive to adopt the simple and straightforward structure apparently favoured by European company law.[66]

37 Today, European legislation is strongly influenced by American and British concepts of company law.[67] There is a widespread impression that they offer a more modern, flexible and liberal approach to issues like corporate governance, fair value accounting or creditor protection. Theories of Law and Economics play an increasingly important role in this development. For example, the Takeover Directive is strongly influenced by the Anglo-Saxon belief in efficient market control where bad management will be punished by successful takeover bids. As a consequence, Europe is increasingly under pressure to reconsider its legislation with a view to these new concepts. This is in particular true for the areas of accounting and capital maintenance.[68] Last but not least, it should be noted that the focus of European harmonisation has shifted from company law to capital market law in recent years (see e.g. the Thirteenth Directive and the IAS-Regulation). The predominant driver for harmonsiation today appears to be the free movement of capital, whereas with regard to classical company law, regulatory competition may prevail.

59 For a recent example see *Ricketts v Ad Valorem Factors* (2003) EWCA Civ 1706 = (2004) 1 All ER 894 = EWiR 2005, 517 (noted Schall).

60 See e.g. ECJ C-135/83 (1985) ECR 469, para. 9 et seq.

61 Art. 253 ECT.

62 It is not entirely clear whether last instance court is to be understood as (only) the Supreme Court (eg House of Lords, Cour de Cassation, BGH, Cassazione) or whether it can be any court being the ultimate instance of the respective case.

63 Art. 234 ECT.

64 Habersack, para. 39a.

65 The rise of the control approach diminished the role of the traditional German group law definitions in Secs. 15 et seq. AktG, see Schall in Spindler/Stiltz, Kommentar zum Aktiengesetz, (to be published 2006), Pre Sec. 15 (1) et seq.

66 Hirte, ECFR 2005, 1, 10 et seq.

67 Cf. Fleischer, ECFR 2005, 378 et seq.; Conac, ECFR 2005, 487 et seq. (with a view to French law).

68 See in particular the critical report on legal capital by Jonathan Rickford, Member of the High Level Group of European Company Law Experts, in (2004) 15 EBLR 919; contrast Schön, EBOR 2004, 429. Pleading for a compromise Miola, ECFR 2005, 413 et seq.

3.2 Overview of the Current European Company Law Directives

3.2.1 The First Directive on Company Data

The **First Directive**[69] is concerned with disclosure of the "personal data" of the company and the persons beyond the corporate veil. It requires the publishing of the articles, the board members, their powers to bind the company, and the annual accounts (Art. 2). This includes information on whether each director can bind the company individually (*Einzelvertretungsbefugnis*) or whether this power is only vested with the board (majority vote) or all its members (*Gesamtvertretungsbefugnis*). In Germany, the BGH has added a supplementary duty to register whether or not the directors are subject to the rule against self-dealing. By contrast, Companies House in the UK does not inform users that the power to bind the company is only vested with the board as a whole[70] – arguably a violation of European law. Nor is there any information on the no-conflict rule (and its eventual disposition by the articles) although this equitable principle clearly restricts the unlimited powers of the board.[71] Art. 3 introduced a duty to register companies and keep their files in central or local registers and to publish and avail this information to the public. As a new alternative, e-registration has now been introduced. Art. 7 to 9 deal with the validity of the company's acts. The most prominent provision is Art. 9 which provides that the organs of the company have unlimited powers of attorney which may not be restricted via the objects or the articles. This principle of German origin[72] aims to facilitate the course of business and led to the abolition of the *ultra-vires* doctrine with respect to third parties.[73] Nevertheless, the unlimited powers of the corporate bodies are subject to restrictions by general concepts of abuse of authority in many Member States.[74] Art. 8 provides that irregularities in nominating the board members do not affect the validity of acts vis-à-vis third parties unless they have knowledge thereof. Art. 7 establishes a personal liability for persons acting in the name of a company before it has acquired legal personality.[75] The final part (Art. 10 to 12) restricts the nullity of companies which is *inter alia* dependent on an antecedent court order. 38

3.2.2 The Second Directive on Capital Maintenance

The **Second Directive**[76] implemented strict capital raising and maintenance provisions for European stock corporations for the sake of creditor protection. It is centred on the continental view that legal capital (and not disclosure) is the consideration for limited liability.[77] All public companies have to raise at least minimum capital of EUR 50,000 (Art. 6)[78] which is by the way a negligible amount for a plc.[79] Member Sates are free to set higher thresholds.[80] The shares must be half paid up (plus the full premium). Contributions in kind must be made fully available to the management 39

69 First Council Directive 68/151/EEC of 9 March 1968 on coordination of safeguards which, for the protection of the interests of members and others, are required by Member States of companies within the meaning of the second paragraph of Article 58 of the Treaty, with a view to making such safeguards equivalent throughout the Community Official Journal L 065, 14/03/1968 P. 0008 – 0012.

70 Individual managers will have to show actual authority. If they are held out as managers, ostensible authority may apply.

71 *Movytex Ltd v Bulfield* (1988) BCLC 104 (ChD) per Vinelott J.

72 Edwards, p 35; Habersack, para. 100.

73 Sec. 35 CA.

74 See Payne, ECFR 2004, 235, 243 et seq., in particular at p. 244 Fn 40.

75 Sec. 41 AktG; Sec.11 CA.

76 Second Council Directive 77/91/EEC of 13 December 1976 on co-ordination of safeguards which, for the protection of the interests of members and others, are required by Member States of companies within the meaning of the second paragraph of Article 58 of the Treaty, in respect of the formation of public limited liability companies and the maintenance and alteration of their capital, with a view to making such safeguards equivalent, *Official Journal L 026 , 31/01/1977 P. 0001 – 0013.*

77 Schall, EBLR 2005, 1577 et seq.

78 The official text speaks of 25,000 European units of account.

79 E.g., in a recent German case before the BGH on equitable subordination in an AG, the debt financing by shareholders was ten times as high as that minimum capital.

80 For an overview see Antunes, ECFR 2005, 323, 337 with no. 64.

from the beginning and are subject to a mandatory audit. The directive does, however, not provide for any safeguards against the circumvention of these restrictions on contributions in kind. The Member States are free to adopt any if they think fit. This has been done in Germany under the doctrine of "real capitalisation" (*Grundsatz der realen Kapitalaufbringung*). This doctrine prohibits disguised contributions in kind, like setting off the payment against the purchase price of an asset. In such cases, the contribution in cash is not discharged and must be paid in again. The shareholder is left with a personal claim in restitution for the asset which he cannot set off and which will be valueless in the company's insolvency – a common and efficient means for German liquidators to replenish the assets. In Germany, Aaron Salomon would thus have had to pay the EUR 20,000 once more despite having already lost his business.[81] In Member States that do not prohibit disguised contributions however, the restrictions of the Second Directive are of course perceived as meaningless.[82] This would become even more obvious if, deviating from Art. 7, services were accepted as contributions in kind because salaries of manager-shareholders could then be construed as disguised contributions.

40 The Directive provides for strict capital maintenance. Contributions must not be returned to the shareholders. Distributions may only be made from profits and free reserves (Art. 15). The company may not subscribe for own shares (Art. 18). Buy back of shares, redeemable shares and reductions of capital are severely restricted (Art. 19 to 22 and Art. 30 to 39). Financial assistance is prohibited (Art. 23, 24). The underlying doctrine of capital maintenance is rooted in all European legal systems including the UK. The Common Law has followed (and will follow)[83] the principle "no payment out of capital"[84] – of course, however, without requiring minimum capitalisation. This sharply contrasts with the US where the permissibility of distributions (including repurchase of shares) depends mainly on the equitable solvency test and where "disguised" returns of capital, for example by way of undervalue transactions are subject to the insolvency law ("fraudulent conveyance").

41 Although legal capital is the consideration for limited liability, the Directive does *not* provide for a duty of the directors to stop trading and file for insolvency if all capital is lost and the company is overindebted. The directors merely have to call a general meeting to decide on appropriate measures in the case of loss of half the company's capital (Art. 17), and in some Member States, the company has to be liquidated afterwards if the capital is not replenished again.[85] But this is not a mandatory consequence under Art. 17 which only requires the GM to *consider* whether the company be wound up or other measures be taken.[86] Thus, the establishment of any duty to file for insolvency lies within the discretion of the Member States. As has been shown above,[87] this leads to grave differences of the creditor protection regimes of the Member States and serious conflicts in cross-border situations. The situation is worsened by the fact that the Directive does not provide for any other additional creditor protection safeguards (for example, equitable subordination).

42 The Directive regulates the increase of capital (Art. 25 *et seq.*). In particular, it provides for a subscription right of shareholders if the capital is raised. This shows that the Directive aims to protect both (minority) shareholders and creditors.[88] Indeed, the safeguards for contributions in kind and the requirement to pay and maintain the full premium can be traced back under German law to fraud on investors in the second half of the 19th century.[89] However, it has been criticised that the Directive complicates trading in shares. For example, it causes the common split of nominal

81 The leading English case on the principle of limited liability, *Salomon v Salomon & Co Ltd* (1897) AC 22 included inter alia a disguised contribution in kind.

82 See Rickford, EBLR 2004, 921, 935.

83 DTI *Company Law Reform* Whitepaper (2005) 40 et seq.

84 See only Secs. 263, 277 CA; *Re Halt Garage (1964) Ltd* (1982) 3 All ER 1016 (ChD); *Aveling Barford Ltd v Perion Ltd* (1989) BCLC 626 (ChD); Davies (Fn. 3) 281 et seq.

85 Miola, ECFR 2005, 413 et seq.

86 Miola, ibid.

87 See Mn. 20 et seq.

88 In fact, the first capital rules were designed with a view to investor protection, Miola, ECFR 2005, 413 et seq.

89 See the legislative materials on the reform of German stock coporation law in 1884.

and real share value and petrifies the inconvenient prohibition of no par value shares (Art. 8).[90] It is therefore under attack with regard to the alternative US system where efficient investor and creditor protection may arguably be achieved in a less burdensome way.[91]

The Second Directive further supplemented the disclosure requirements of the First Directive by demanding information, *inter alia*, on the company's name and type, its objects and its capital structure (Art. 2, 3). 43

Last but not least, it should be noted that shareholders may be barred from invoking rights granted under European Directives by national law for "abuse of rights". However, such doctrines may not amount to a partial derogation of European law.[92] 44

3.2.3 The Third Directive on Mergers and the Sixth Directive on Divisions of Public Companies

(i) The **Third Directive** regulates[93] mergers of public companies. Public companies may be merged by the acquisition of one company by another (Art. 5 to 22) or by formation of a new company (Art. 23). The Directive requires a merger draft by the management boards (Art. 5). This draft must, *inter alia*, contain the share exchange ratio and the amount of any cash payment, the terms of the allotment and the beginning of profit participation, information on the evaluation of the assets and liabilities, the articles of the transferee company and rights conferred in exchange for previous special rights of members (if any). The draft is to be disclosed (Art. 6) and approved by both shareholder meetings with a qualified majority (Art. 7 – for exceptions in the acquiring company, see Art. 8). The management must further prepare a detailed report explaining the terms and the legal and economic background of the merger (in particular the exchange ratio) and describing any valuation problems (Merger Report, Art. 9).[94] Moreover, the draft terms are subject to examination by independent experts who also draw a written report for the shareholders (Expert Report, Art. 10). The legal completion of the merger leads simultaneously to (a) the complete transfer of the assets and liabilities of the acquired company to the acquiring company,[95] (b) the shareholders of the acquired company becoming shareholders of the acquiring company and (c) the dissolution of the acquired company without liquidation (Art. 19). Creditors with debts not yet due need to be protected adequately, for example by a right to claim security (Art. 13). Once the merger is accomplished, it is practically impossible to be undone again. That is why Art. 22 prevents *restitutio in integrum* for irregularities once the transaction is registered. 45

The Third Directive is restricted to transactions within a Member State, just as the Sixth Directive is to the division of public companies. Cross-border transactions are now regulated by the Tenth Directive.[96] Nevertheless the German Law on Transformation of Companies[97] had become subject to challenge before the ECJ in the aftermath of Inspire Art. The challenge was directed against the restriction of the Umwandlungsgesetz on companies with their seat[98] in Germany. This restriction was introduced with a view to the planned EU regulation. However, earlier ECJ judgments had already made it clear that the freedom of establishment applies irre- 46

90 E.g. Sec. 97-98 CA 1985 (UK); Sec. 9 AktG (Germany); Art. L 225-128 Ccomm (France). In the UK, that has been the law since *Oregum Gold Mining Co of India Ltd v Roper* (1892) AC 125 (House of Lords). On the inconvenience for troubled companies cf. Sealy, Cases and Materials in Company Law, 7th edition 2001, 371.

91 Cf. Rickford, (2004) 15 EBLR 919. But see the forthcoming report of the Arbeitskreis Kapitalreform.

92 ECJ C-367/96 *Kefalas*; C-42/95 *Siemens-Nold*; C-441/93 *Parfitis*.

93 Third Council Directive 78/855/EEC of 9 October 1978 based on Article 54 para. 3 (g) of the Treaty concerning mergers of public limited liability companies, *Official Journal L 295 , 20/10/1978 P. 0036 – 0043*.

94 It is debated whether Member States may allow the unanimous waiver of this right by the shareholders e.g. Secs. 8 Subs. 3, 9 Subs. 3 UmwG). This should be so, bearing in mind that Art. 9 is explicitly designed to protect shareholders, Habersack, para. 230.

95 This is not subject to any consent of third parties, e.g. creditors, as they are protected via the right to claim security.

96 See Mn. 55 et seq.

97 I.e. mergers, split-offs, re-registrations (even from companies to partnerships).

98 Both "real" and officially registered.

spective of any process in harmonisation matters. That is why the restriction was consequently disallowed by the ECJ.[99]

47 (ii) The **Sixth Directive**[100] on division of public companies is a mirror image of the Third Directive on mergers. A company may be divided in several ways. It may be split up on two other (existing or new) companies and cease to exist while the shareholders receive shares in the acquiring companies. Or it may transfer a part of its assets (spin-off) to another (new or existing) company in exchange for shares in the company which will be received either by itself or directly by its shareholders. The main difference to the merger is that the assets and liabilities are not concentrated in one legal entity, but split up on at least two smaller companies (partial succession). Therefore, creditor protection is achieved via the joint and several liability of all involved companies (Art. 12 No 3) for the debts of the divided company which may or may not cease to exist.

3.2.4 The Fourth Directive on Company Accounts, the Seventh Directive on Group Accounts, the Eight Directive on Auditors and their Supplements

48 (i) The **Fourth Directive**[101] introduced common rules for the annual accounts of companies. However, the harmonisation of accounting rules only referred to the form, not to the substance. The basic difference between the English "true and fair view concept" and the German "prudence principle" could only partially be overcome. For the Common lawyer, the balance sheet must inform the shareholder/investor as accurately as possible about the true value of the enterprise and the fair amount of distributions. By contrast, in Germany, the overriding principle of the balance sheet is creditor protection. German law prefers the undervaluation and hidden gains to overvaluation and hidden losses which may result in dangerous distributions. That is why it favours historical cost accounting and depreciation of assets to volatile assessment of the current value. The Fourth Directive acknowledges the true and fair view principle (Art. 2 (3) to (5)). However, the Directive remains neutral in substance, for example by demanding prudent valuation (Art. 31 (1) (c) and by granting manifold options to the Member States, including the option to revalue certain fixed assets (Art. 33). Therefore most harmonisation is achieved on a formal basis. The Directive prescribed, *inter alia*, the layout of the balance sheet (Art. 9, 10) and of the profit and loss account (Arts 23 to 26), certain valuation rules (Art. 31 *et seq.*) and mandatory audit requirements. It has been supplemented by Directives on banking and insurance enterprises.[102]

49 The Directive introduced the annual report on the development of the company's business and its position (Art. 46). Although information on the company's likely future development shall be included, the report has been constructed primarily retrospectively. This changed in the aftermath of the accounting scandals at the beginning of the Millennium (Enron, Worldcom, Parmalat etc). The Modernisation Directive requires a lot more detailed information particularly from listed companies on the risks and chances of the future development plus specific disclosure on the risk management and hedging of the company. This Directive was implemented in different ways by the Member States. For example, the UK introduced the OFR (Operating and Financial Review) for listed companies. It requires detailed information on the company's future strategies and policies, too. In addition, there is the (less far reaching) enhanced annual report for other companies. By contrast, Germany enhanced the annual report along the lines

99 ECJ judgment dated 13 December 2005 (case C-411/03, SEVIC).

100 Sixth Council Directive 82/891/EEC of 17 December 1982 based on Article 54 para. 3 (g) of the Treaty, concerning the division of public limited liability companies, *Official Journal L 378 , 31/12/1982 P. 0047 – 0054.*

101 Fourth Council Directive 78/660/EEC of 25 July 1978 based on Article 54 para. 3 (g) of the Treaty on the annual accounts of certain types of companies, *Official Journal L 222 , 14/08/1978 P. 0011 – 0031.*

102 Council Directive 86/635/EEC of 8 Dec 1986 on the consolidated accounts of banks and other financial institutions, OJ L 372, 31/12/1986, p 0001 – 0017; Council Directive 91/674/EEC of 19 Dec 1991 on the annual accounts and consolidated accounts of insurance undertakings.

of the OFR for all companies, but without requiring disclosure of sensitive policies and strategies.[103]

A specific "contra-German" modification of the Directive was enacted in 1990.[104] It extended the disclosure requirements for annual accounts from "real" limited liability companies (ltd, plc) to certain partnerships which were similar to companies. That was in particular the case of the German GmbH & Co KG. This is a limited partnership where only limited companies are unlimited partner(s). This amendment hit hard on the German economy. It consists mostly of small and medium enterprises which fear the disclosure of their figures. Take a highly specialised supplier. If the margins are disclosed, he is open to attack from cost cutters and competitors. To further avoid disclosure, German enterprises must now resort to unlimited "dummy partners" (for example, family members). **50**

(ii) The **Seventh Directive**[105] elaborated common rules on consolidated group accounts. The crucial question of when is a company only a company and when are companies a group is determined by the "control principle". Consolidated group accounts merely require the capability to control a subsidiary via a majority of votes. It is not necessary to show a common group strategy or a single economic unit.[106] Moreover, there are some specific provisions on the accounting for major (but not majority) holdings. **51**

(iii) The **Eighth Directive**[107] introduced requirements for the qualification (Art. 3 to 19) and liability of auditors (Art. 26). Eligible are only persons of good repute (Art. 3) with university entrance level, a theoretical instruction course, practical training and an examination of professional competence of university (Art. 4 et seq.). **52**

It should be noted that securing the quality and independence of the audit (for example, via audit committees) and of the auditors has become a major issue in the aftermath of the burst of the Internet bubble and the accounting scandals. Appropriate measures need to be taken to re-gain the trust of the investors, albeit this may not be so vital in bank-financed Europe as it was in the equity-financed US (Sarbanes-Oxley). Furthermore, it has transpired by now that quality management is preferable to ever extending auditor liability. This is because the potential liability risks are enormous and, in the end, no longer insurable. That is why liability towards investors should remain restricted to fraudulent conduct or special contractual relationships[108] whereas professional self-control and market control (Arthur Andersen) should generally suffice. **53**

(iv) **Recent Modifications**: The Fourth and Seventh Directives were modified in 2001 in order to allow Member States to permit or to require the fair valuation of certain financial instruments, particularly in consolidated accounts. [109] The objective was to establish conformity with International Accounting Standard 39 (Recognition and measurement of financial instruments) which required certain financial instruments, including derivatives, to be carried in the balance sheet at their fair value. This means an important departure from the historical cost concept, which was the approach underlying of the Fourth Directive. In order to ensure conformity between the Accounting Directives and the International Accounting Standards which had been amended in the meantime and in order to make it possible for Member States to amend their **54**

103 Winnefeld, Münchener Handbuch des Bilanzrechts, 4th edition (to be published 2006), sub K 2. On the situation in France under the NRE Law see Storck, ECFR 2004, 36, 52 et seq.

104 Council Directive 90/604/EEC of 8 November 1990 amending Directive 78/660/EEC on the annual accounts and Directive 83/349/EEC on the consolidated accounts concerning the exception for small and medium enterprises and the disclosure of annual accounts in Ecu, OJ L 317/57 of 16 November 1990.

105 Seventh Council Directive 83/349/EEC of 13 June 1983 based on the Article 54 para. 3 (g) of the Treaty on consolidated accounts, *Official Journal L 193 , 18/07/1983 P. 0001 – 0017.*

106 Contrast German law where a group requires "uniform governance" (*einheitliche Leitung*, Sec. 18 AktG).

107 Eighth Council Directive 84/253/EEC of 10 April 1984 based on Article 54 para. 3 (g) of the Treaty on the approval of persons responsible for carrying out the statutory audits of accounting documents, *Official Journal L 126, 12/05/1984 P. 0020 – 0026.*

108 See Sec. 826 BGB or Sec. 311 Subs. 2 and 3 BGB (in Gemany); *Caparo Industries v Dickman* (1990) 2 AC 605; *Galoo Ltd v Bright Grahame Murray* (1995) 1 All ER 16 (CA); *Al Saudi Banque v Clark Pixley* (1990) Ch 313.

109 Directive 2001/65/EC of the European Parliament and Council of 27 Dec 2001 amending Directives 78/660/EEC, 83/349/EEC and 86/635/EEC as regards the valuation rules for the annual and consolidated accounts of certain types of companies as well as of banks and other financial institutions, OJ L 283, 27/10/2001, p. 0028 – 0032.

national accounting legislation so as to bring it closer to IAS, the Accounting Directives were again amended and modernised in 2003 ("Modernisation Directive").[110] At that time, the existing conflicts with IAS were removed and accounting options which were available under IAS but were not allowed under the Accounting Directives were introduced. The Commission also issued a Recommendation and an Interpretative Communication concerning the Fourth and Seventh Directives.[111] In 2004, the Commission introduced a new proposal to amend the Accounting Directives, in the aftermath of the accounting scandals of Enron, Worldcom and particularly Parmalat (see below). This shows the EU's growing emphasis on regulating capital markets which has started with the 2001 Directive on securities traded on stock exchanges.[112] This Directive has been supplemented in 2004 by way of a further Directive[113] which provides for enhanced annual and periodical reporting and requires disclosure of material blockholdings in listed companies, starting from 5 per cent (Art 9). A further cornerstone in the harmonisation of European capital markets is the Directive on takeover bids.[114]

55 (v) The **IAS-Regulation** was introduced in 2002.[115] It provides that all listed EU companies must prepare their consolidated accounts in accordance with adopted International Accounting Standards (IAS/IFRS) from 2005 onwards. Companies which only have debt securities listed on a regulated stock exchange may continue to apply national accounting rules until 2007, if so allowed by their Member State (for instance Belgium or France). The same transitional rule applies to those companies which apply US GAAP for the purpose of a listing in the US. They may continue to apply US GAAP until 2007, if their Member State specifically allows this (for instance, Belgium or Germany). For those listed EU companies that apply IAS, the Seventh Directive no longer applies unless the matter is not specifically dealt with under IAS (such as certain disclosures, the consolidated annual report, the audit requirement). The International Accounting Standards (IAS/IFRS) are set by the International Accounting Standards Board (IASB), a private organisation which is based in London. Only those International Accountings Standards which have been endorsed by the European Commission must be complied with. As a result of the endorsement, the IAS become part of European law. The Commission Regulations adopting the standards are published in the Official Journal. The standards are attached to each Regulation in all official languages of the EU. Listed EU companies may continue to apply national accounting rules in their annual accounts. Member States may however allow or require them to also apply IAS in their annual accounts. They may also allow or require other companies (not listed) to apply IAS in their annual and/ or consolidated accounts.

If all companies with limited liability (public and private) in the EU were to apply IAS in their annual and consolidated accounts, comparability of financial information would increase tremendously. However, it is very unlikely that this will happen in the near future. Reasons for this are: the close linkage which exists in many Members States between accounting and taxation, which makes it difficult to apply IAS in annual accounts, as this would inevitably

110 Directive 2003/51/EC of the European Parliament and of the Council of 18 June 2003 amending Directives 78/660/EEC, 83/349/EEC , 86/635/EEC and 91/674/EEC on the annual and consolidated accounts of certain types of companies, banks and other financial institutions and insurance undertakings, OJ L 178, 17 June 2003.

111 On 30 May 2001 the Commission adopted a Recommendation on the recognition, measurement and disclosure of environmental issues in the annual accounts of companies (C(2001)453/EC – Official Journal L 156 of 13.06.2001). On 7 January 1998 the Commission adopted an interpretative communication concerning certain articles of the fourth and seventh Council Directives on accounting (Official Journal C 16 of 20.01.1998). On 13 September 1995 the Commission adopted a recommendation on the use of the statistical classification of economic activities in the European Communities for breaking down net turnover by type of activity (Official Journal L 225 of 22.09.1995).

112 Directive 2001/34/EC of the European Parliament and of the Council of 28 May 2001 on the admission of securities to official stock exchange listing and on information to be published on those securities, Official Journal L 184, 06/07/2001 P. 0001 – 0066. Cf. further K. J. Hopt/E. Wymeersch (eds.), Capital Markets and Company Law, 2003.

113 Directive 2004/109/EC of the European Parliament and of the Council of 15 December 2004 on the harmonisation of transparency requirements in relation to information about issuers whose securities are admitted to trading on a regulated market and amending Directive 2001/34/EC; Official Journal L 390, 31/12/2004 P. 0038 – 0057.

114 See Mn 62.

115 EC-Regulation 1606/2002 of Parliament and Council on the application of international accounting standards (IAS) of 19 July 2002, OJ L 243/1 of 11 September 2002.

lead to adverse tax consequences; the linkage between financial reporting and profit distribution which means that the profit following from the annual accounts defines the amount which is available for distribution (a problem under IAS because of the extensive use of fair value accounting); the lack of adaptation of IAS to the specific needs of small and medium-sized companies (IAS have been conceived for large listed companies and not for the majority of small and medium-sized companies for which the standards are far too complicated).

3.2.5 The Tenth Directive on Cross-Border Mergers

The **Tenth Directive** on cross-border mergers of companies with limited liability[116] is now enacted. It enables cross-border mergers of companies domiciled in different Member States. Deviating from the Third and Sixth Directives, it encompasses both private and public companies.[117] It however excludes all kinds of partnerships,[118] even if similar to limited liability companies.[119] **56**

The merger procedures are of course similar to the Third Directive. Companies with limited liability may merge by acquisition or by formation of a new company. Each company is on principle subject to its national provisions which – at least with respect to public companies – are already largely harmonised. The Tenth Directive merely confirms and complements certain aspects while extending them to other company forms. For example, the core element in Art. 5, the Merger Plan, must additionally announce the legal form of the future entity. **57**

The supervision of the cross-border merger is subject to a two stage process (Art. 10). First, the legality of the procedure is scrutinised and certified by the authority competent for the transferor company (or companies). The decision is binding on the authority competent for the transferee company which then examines the legality on the other side, including compliance with the cross-border requirements and with requirements for the foundations of a new company, as the case may be. **58**

The most important point of the Directive is the compromise on co-determination in Art. 16. This has been subject to hefty debate and for a long time prevented any consent at all. The compromise developed in the Tenth Directive is similar to the solution of the S.E.-Statute.[120] In principle, the S.E.-rules apply if one company is subject to co-determination under national law and employs more than 500 employees. This means that employer and employee representatives have to negotiate the future co-determination regime, and that there is a default rule in case the negotiations fail (most prominently, the furthest reaching national model might apply). However, there are modifications. Different from the S.E.-statute, the furthest reaching national model is only applicable if aggregately more than one third (not: one quarter) of the employees were subject to co-determination. Moreover, the maximum number of employee representatives under a monistic board structure may be confined to one third by the Member States. This opens a major route out of German at par co-determination. **59**

3.2.6 The Eleventh Directive on Foreign Branches

The **Eleventh Directive**[121] set up common disclosure requirements for foreign branches of companies in Member States. The first part (Art. 1 to 6) introduces common rules for branches of companies from other Member States. Companies from other Member States have to register their **60**

116 Directive of the European Parliament and of the Council on cross-border mergers of limited liability companies, 19 Sept 2005 based on the proposal of 18 Nov 2003, COM (2003) 703(01). The original proposal had been withdrawn in 2001.

117 E.g., the Plc, the Ltd and the LLP in the UK, the SA and the SARL in France, the GmbH, the AG and the KGaA in Germany.

118 E.g. partnerships and limited partnerships in the UK, oHG and KG in Germany.

119 Like in particular the German GmbH & Co KG, see Mn. 49 and Council Directive 90/604/EEC of 8 November 1990 with regard to disclosure.

120 See Mn. 75 and Part 2, S.E.

121 Eleventh Council Directive 89/666/EEC of 21 December 1989 concerning disclosure requirements in respect of branches opened in a Member State by certain types of company governed by the law of another State, *Official Journal L 395 , 30/12/1989 P. 0036 – 0039.*

branches in the host state. According to the ECJ's jurisdiction in *Centros* and *Inspire Art*[122], this also applies if the company has no business activity in the state of origin, ie the "branch" is the "real seat" of the company. The company's name, legal form, organs with power of attorney and the place where it is registered have to be disclosed. Moreover, the local agents[123] have to be named. The accounts need to filed in the language of the host state, but under the rules of the law of origin. This is a privilege which was supposed to prevent the onus of a double accounting regime which was deemed an infringement of the freedom of establishment.[124] However, this does not assist 'pseudo-foreign' companies as they are subject to the host state's taxation and therefore have to provide apt local accounting anyways. As a consequence, the theoretical approach of the Eleventh Directive is turned upside down in practice. Many pseudo-foreign limited companies try to get away with handing in German accounts in the UK. This seems to be accepted for the time being.[125]

61 The second part (Art. 7 to 10) contains rules on branches of companies from non-Member States. These provide only for a minimum level of harmonisation whereas the rules of the first part are conclusive and may neither be tightened nor relaxed by Member States.[126]

3.2.7 The Twelfth Directive on Single-Member Companies

62 The **Twelfth Directive**[127] required all Member States to recognise single-member companies, whether they were formed as such or emerged later on by the acquisition of all shares by one member. Before, the existence of one-person-companies was not generally accepted in Europe. This was partly due to the (failed) attempts to limit abuse of limited companies (as opposed to personally liable sole traders) via minimum member requirements. But these requirements have always attracted circumvention and could not be upheld.[128] Furthermore, it provided specific disclosure requirements.[129] Non-compliance with these requirements usually triggers a fine,[130] but does not render the disposition void.

3.2.8 The Thirteenth Directive on Takeover Bids

63 The **Thirteenth Directive**,[131] which had failed in an earlier attempt,[132] now regulates takeover bids in the Common Market. It aims to facilitate takeovers by creating a level playing field in Europe.[133] The underlying idea is to increase corporate governance by allowing efficient market control. The model type is seen in one share, one vote.[134] Deviations are not forbidden, but have to be disclosed. The Member States should (but need not) provide for management neutrality (Art. 9).[135] The protection of minority shareholders is mainly granted by a mandatory takeover bid (Art. 5) which however suffers from a wide discretion of the Member States to set the trigger

122 See Mn. 17 et seq.

123 Even those with only limited powers to bind the company, Habersack, para. 130 (contentious).

124 See preamble (first recital).

125 There are also illegal tricks like declaring the company dormant in the UK despite its vivid business activity in Germany.

126 Cf. ECJ C-167/01 *Inspire Art* noted de Kluiver, ECFR 2004, 121. No special disclosure requirements for "pseudo-foreign" companies.

127 Twelfth Council Company Law Directive 89/667/EEC of 21 December 1989 on single-member private limited-liability companies, OJ L 395 , 30/12/1989 P. 0040 – 0042.

128 See only *Salomon v A Salomon Co Ltd* (1897) AC 22 (HL) where the wife and the five children were nominee shareholders to meet the requirement of seven incorporators. One might wonder, however, if in these childless times the usefulness of those restrictions could revive.

129 Sec. 382B CA; Sec. 35 Subs. 2 GmbHG.

130 Sec. 382B Subs. 2 CA.

131 Directive 2004/25/EC of the European Parliament and of the Council of 21 April 2004 on takeover bids, Official Journal L 142, 30/04/2004 P. 0012 – 0023. Note that it is not officially called the Thirteenth Directive, albeit it is generally perceived as such.

132 On the long history of its adoption see Edwards, ECFR 2004, 416, 417 et seq.

133 Enriques, ECFR 2004, 440, 447 et seq.

134 Hirte, ECFR 2005, 1.

135 On this last minute compromise Edwards, ECFR 2004, 416, 435 et seq.

threshold.[136] Art. 14 introduces the squeeze out of minority shareholders which is counterbalanced by a right to sell out in Art 15. The applicable law is determined in Art. 4.[137] The competent authority sits usually where the target is listed.

3.2.9 The European Insolvency Regulation

Last but not least, as shown above,[138] the **European Insolvency Regulation** plays an important role within the post *Inspire Art* world, in particular with respect to private companies. It provided for common rules on the insolvency of companies dealing in other Member States. It is an open question to what extent and under what conditions material manager or shareholder liabilities for insolvency-related misfeasance are caught by Art. 3 and 4. The answer should be in the affirmative for if they are construed as contributions in the winding up, for example the British provisions on fraudulent or wrongful trading (Secs. 213, 214 IA 1986). The same holds for duties to file for insolvency as they are closely connected to insolvency proceedings.[139] **64**

3.3 Overview of Future Harmonisation Measures

3.3.1 Proposals

There are several European harmonisation proposals on the horizon. **65**

(i) The **Fourth, Seventh** and **Eighth Directives** will be tightened by two further amending Directives following recent accouting scandals (Enron, Worldcom and particularly Parmalat).[140] **66**
The proposal amending the **Fourth and Seventh Directives** will establish collective responsibility of the members of the administrative, management and supervisory bodies of companies towards the company for ensuring that the annual and consolidated accounts are drawn up and published in accordance with the requirements of the Directives, enhance transparency about related parties' transactions and about off-balance sheet transactions and introduce a corporate governance statement.
The proposal amending the **Eighth Directive** (which has already been approved by Council and European Parliament) will introduce a comprehensive framework for the regulation of the audit function, including a strengthening of the education requirements for auditors, introduction of a requirement for all auditors to be registered, introduction of a requirement for all auditors to be subject to a quality assurance regime, introduction of public oversight, introduction of a requirement for all statutory audits to be carried out on the basis of International Standards on Auditing adopted by the European Commission, introduction of a system of cooperation between oversight bodies of Member States and of cooperation between oversight bodies of Member States with similar bodies in third countries (such as the PCAOB in the US). During the discussions in the European Parliament it was also agreed that the Commission would carry out a study concerning the liability of auditors in order to find a solution for the problem that auditors are often used as a "deep pocket" after a corporate scandal.

(ii) Moreover, the Commission proposes to **relax** the **Second Directive** to facilitate capital-related measures taken in public limited companies by enabling Member States to eliminate specific **67**

136 Enriques, ECFR 2004, 440, 447 et seq.

137 See in detail Siems, ECFR 2004, 458.

138 See Mn. 20 et seq.

139 But note that in the case of a conflict of these duties with the company law of origin, the latter will prevail on grounds of freedom of establishment, notwithstanding the classification as insolvency law under Arts 3, 4 European Insolvency Regulation (see Mn. 28).

140 Proposal for a Directive of the European Parliament and of the Council amending Council Directives 78/660/EEC and 83/349/EEC concerning the annual accounts of certain types of companies and consolidated accounts (COM(2004) 725 final – Not yet published in the Official Journal). Proposal for a Directive of the European Parliament and of the Council of 16 March 2004 on statutory audit of annual accounts and consolidated accounts and amending Council Directives 78/660/EEC and 83/49/EEC (COM(2004) 177 final – Not yet published in the Official Journal).

reporting requirements.[141] Companies will be enabled to react more promptly and in a less costly and protracted manner to developments in the markets.

68 (iii) The transfer of company seats within the EU will be regulated in a planned **Fourteenth Directive**.[142] Apparently, this regulation will be restricted to the transfer of registered seats. As a consequence, the *Daily Mail* issue of whether companies can be hindered by the home state to relocate their real seat will remain unclear.[143]

69 (iv) Also, there is a planned proposal for a **Directive on shareholders' rights**, focused on harmonising the law around the general meeting of public companies (voting, notice, information).[144] It is not clear yet whether the Directive will include unlisted companies.

3.3.2 Remaining Gaps

70 Some **lacunas** in the line of European company law directives will however remain. There are no plans to revive the Fifth Directive on the company structure. Nor will the Ninth Directive come in its original, German-dominated form. This is due to major differences on the theory of companies. The most prominent point is the role of workers' participation. The German model of co-determination grants employee representatives seats in the supervisory board, next to shareholder representatives. In certain cases, they occupy 50 per cent of the seats. This model is sharply rejected by other Member States like the UK. The debate about employee representation has for a long time been in the way of harmonisation measures like the S.E. or the Directive on cross-border mergers.

71 This difference can however only partly be understood from the different role trade unions play in Europe. Of course, in Germany their influence is guaranteed by the constitution. The establishment of non-governmental powers was one way to create safeguards against another centralised dictatorship in post-war Germany. By contrast, in the UK, trade unions were marginalised in the Eighties under the reign of Thatcherism.

72 However, the debate on co-determination also symbolises a deeper diversion of views about in whose interest a large public company shall be governed – a divergence which has been a major obstacle to further harmonisation in Europe. Two models oppose. The pluralist model can, for example, be found in Germany. German lawyers have always viewed shareholders as mere investors, not as owners of the AG. Rather, a public company conducting huge business concerns the interest of several important stakeholders, in particular the employees, the shareholders, the creditors and the general public. That being so, the AG shall be governed in balanced accordance of all these interests. The shareholders' interests are not paramount. This amounts to a kind of expropriation of the shareholders which is particularly expressed in the dual structure of the AG. The management board governs the AG within its free discretion. It is appointed and controlled by the supervisory board, not by the shareholders directly. The shareholders do not have any right to interfere with the running of the company. While the shareholder is downgraded to a mere investor, the employees are upgraded to "owners" who sit on the supervisory board and control the management.[145] All this shall facilitate a fair balance of equal ranking interests.

73 The setting back of the shareholders renders it difficult to govern a public company subsidiary. That is why the complicated German group law provisions (contractual groups, dominion agreements etc) are necessary to facilitate groups at all. It also impedes (hostile) takeovers of companies. That is why there are (faint) considerations as to whether the German co-determination and the dual

141 Proposal for a Directive of the European Parliament and of the Council amending Council Directive 77/91/EEC as regards the formation of public limited liability companies and the maintenance and alteration of their capital (COM(2004) 730 – Official Journal C 24 of 29.01.2005).

142 Planned proposal for a Fourteenth Company Law Directive on the cross-border transfer of the registered office of limited companies.

143 Leible, ZGR 2004, 531 et seq.

144 For an overview see the six country comparison (US, UK, Germany, France, Canade, Switzerland) by Zetsche, ECFR 2005, 107 et seq.

145 The upgrading of non-owners to owners is a typical German feature which can also be observed in the landlord – tenant relationship.

board system might infringe the free movement of capital.[146] One certainly cannot argue that both institutions have been recognised by several Directives.[147] The same could be said about the real seat theory which strongly influenced the drafting of European law[148] – but it did not save this theory in the end. However, it should be borne in mind that the "Golden Share" jurisdiction of the ECJ[149] merely concerned limitations for the benefit of public bodies.

The opposite side is the "monist approach". For example, in the UK, the shareholders are viewed as the owners of the company. The management is under a fiduciary duty to act in their best interest. The shareholders can dismiss directors any time[150] and even interfere with the management of the company if they so wish. From this monist (and capitalist) perspective, it is well understood that creditors only come into play once the equity is lost while employees are hardly taken into account at all. The governance of subsidiaries does not pose major problems nor require specific contracts. This fundamental difference in the interest approach illuminates why there is much more divergence than convergence in European company models and why both the Fifth and Ninth Directives were bound to fail up to now. The mere difference between a single board with NED and a dual board with a formal split of management and supervision would not be so important as such.[151] 74

Recently, the two poles seem to move closer towards a compromise. In the new UK company law, the "enlightened shareholder" will be introduced. He is not interested in reaping short term benefits (for example, by shedding workforce) and plundering the company but in sustainable earnings and growth of the company over a longer period. Meanwhile German lawyers have come to accept similar notions as guidelines for governing the AG.[152] However, these developments are still young and need to be perceived and analysed more deeply. Whether they will facilitate more harmonisation of European company law in future, for example the introduction of a European Private Company, remains to be seen. 75

4 European Companies

4.1 The European Company (Societas Europaea)

After 30 years of negotiations, the EU has finally created its own public company: the Societas Europaea (S.E.). The European Company Statute has been enacted in October 2004 and has since then been implemented in most jurisdictions. The S.E. is a special stock corporation aimed at big multinational players.[153] The original idea was to provide one set of rules all over the Common market. This aim has however not been achieved. The main obstacle was of course employee participation, a conflict which, as just set out, merely reflects the different notions on in whose interest companies shall be governed.[154] When negotiating the S.E., these structural differences could not be overcome. That is why the European legislator had to settle for a compromise to make the S.E. finally fly. Therefore, the S.E. follows the law of the equivalent national stock corporation. There are only two major qualifications. The first is the option for Member States to offer for the S.E. another optional company structure (one-tier or two-tier, as the case may be) even if such structure has previously not been available in the respective jurisdiction.[155] The second is the possibility to opt out, after a complicated bargaining procedure, of mandatory domestic co-determination rules at board level as exist, for example, in Germany.[156] The S.E.-Statute is based on the real seat principle and forbids any division between the registered and the real seat (Art. 7). That 76

146 Cf. Hirte, ECFR 2005, 1, 12.
147 E.g. Art. 14 of the Takeover Directive, Art. 16 of the Tenth Directive.
148 See only Art. 48 ECT or Art. 7 S.E.-Statute.
149 See Mn. 32.
150 Sec. 303 CA.
151 Cf. Hopt/Leyens, ECFR 2004, 135, 160 et seq.
152 Hefermehl/Spindler in Münchener Kommentar zum Aktiengesetz, 2nd edition 2002, § 76 Mn. 52 et seq.
153 The creation of a S.E. requires the merger of companies from *different* Member States.
154 See Mn. 69 et seq.
155 For Germany cf. Teichmann, BB 2004, 53 et seq. On board structures in Europe in general Hopt/Leyens, ECFR 2004, 135; Antunes, ECFR 2005, 323, 359 et seq.
156 The compromise formula on this most controversial issue was essential to bring the S.E. to life.

raises the question of a conflict with the freedom of establishment.[157] At present, academic interest for the S.E.[158] seems to exceed its practical importance, probably due to the complicated rules and the failure of one single regime. This should however not prejudice the need for a European Private Company.

4.2 The European Private Company

77 After the difficult birth of the S.E., the European legislator does not seem inclined to press for the creation of a European Private Company.[159] Indeed, it should be noted that in a big GmbH, co-determination is mandatory, too. This shows that co-determination debate could not be avoided with a European Private Company. However, bearing in mind the post *Inspire Art* difficulties, the case for a European Private Company seems stronger.[160] The crucial difference within European private companies does not lie in the interests of the company. Even in Germany it is (maybe too)[161] well understood that the shareholders govern the GmbH.[162] The main difference is rooted in the legal capital. For many continental jurists, this is the *quid pro quo* of limited liability whereas, for the English lawyer, it is just a nuisance. In his view, the consideration for limited liability is strict disclosure.[163] The gist of the debate on legal capital seems to indicate that at least a mandatory minimum capital requirement may be difficult to defend. So it may well be that the European Private Company will be available as a kind of European limited liability company following the deregulated British model, e.g. no legal capital and no form requirements. The liability might be construed via the "best interest" approach, in particular with the shift to the interests of the creditors near insolvency. Also, an easy petition right for creditors should be provided. A deregulated company like that could be of particular interest for start ups or transaction vehicles.

157 See e.g. Schindler, RdW 2003, 122 et seq.

158 See e.g. (in German) Habersack, ZGR 2003, 724; Maul, ZGR 2003, 743.

159 The Action Plan of the Commission, COM(2003) 284 final proposes a study of demand, see van Hulle/Maul, ZGR 2004, 484, 501does not see any priority for the issue.

160 Pleading in this sense Hommelhoff, Vorschläge für eine europäische Privatgesellschaft, 1999; id., ECFR 2006 (to be published).

161 For example, the priority of the shareholders is not directly limited via the interests of the shareholders near insolvency. This has led to a highly complicated creditor protection regime, see Schall, EBLR 2005, 1577 et seq.

162 Secs. 45 et seq. GmbHG.

163 Rickford, ECFR 2004, 391, 408.

II. National Differences within the EU Framework

*by Dr. Harald Gesell, Carsten Flaßhoff (LL.M.) and Dr. Michael Krömker**

1 Analysis

1.1 Export of Company

1 The "export" of companies, i.e. the relocation of a company that was incorporated in one Member State into another Member State, is an issue which for decades has only been the subject of theoretical discussions between legal scholars, but in recent years has gained in relevance and become a practical issue. At the theoretical level, there are essentially two ways for effecting such a relocation. On the one hand, a company could move its registered office/corporate seat to another Member State, being struck from its home register and subsequently registered in another Member State. On the other hand, a company could simply move its head office and business activities to another Member State whilst keeping the registration in the country of incorporation.

1.1.1 Corporate Seat/Registered Office

2 The relocation of the corporate seat/registered office from one Member State to another would require specific EU legislation on the corporate formalities required, especially the de-registration in the country of incorporation and the registration in the host country and an answer to the question whether the legal entity should remain governed by the corporate law of its country of incorporation or should acquire the corporate form of a legal entity of its host country. Currently, however, there is no such EU legislation in force, though a consultation process is being undertaken on a Fourteenth Directive on the cross-border transfer of the registered office of limited companies.[1] Consequently, the relocation of the corporate seat/registered office from one Member State to another Member State is either not addressed in the company acts of the vast majority of Member States or, as in the Czech Republic, Italy, Slovakia and Spain[2] is only allowed subject to an international agreement providing for such relocation. Other than by using an S.E.,[3] the relocation of the corporate seat/registered office from one Member State to another must therefore currently be considered impossible throughout the EU.

1.1.2 *De Facto* Seat

3 The relocation of the *de facto* seat (i.e. moving the head office and/or the entire business activity to another Member State whilst keeping the registration in the country of incorporation) has to be seen from two perspectives: the corporate law of the company's home country (where it was originally incorporated and registered) and that of the host country (where it shall be moved to).

(i) Host Country

4 With regard to the host country's perspective, one used to have to distinguish between countries applying the real seat theory (not allowing a relocation into their country), countries applying the incorporation theory (allowing a relocation into their jurisdiction) and hybrid forms of those theories.[4] In the cases "Überseering" and "Inspire Art",[5] the ECJ ruled that – irrespective of this theoretical discussion – Member States must not hinder corporate entities registered in another Member State

* *Linklaters Oppenhoff & Rädler*, Cologne. The authors wish to thank James Coleman, *Linklaters*, London, for his contributions to this chapter.

1 See Part 1, I, Mn. 68.

2 See Part 2, CZ, Mn. 2/50; I, Mn. 2/40; SK, Mn. 2/40; E, Mn. 2/28.

3 See Part 2, S.E., Mn. 4 et seq.

4 For details on this theoretical approach see Part 1, I, Mn. 7 et seq.

5 See Part 1, I, Mn. 17 et seq.

from carrying out their business activities in their territory. Any national contravention has to be seen as a violation of the Freedom of Establishment of an investor granted by the EC Treaty and therefore as unlawful. Consequently, all Member States as host countries have to accept the relocation of the head office and/or entire business activity of a company registered in another Member State into their own territory and may generally not impose any restrictions on those companies.

(ii) Country of Incorporation

5 When coming to the perspective of the country of incorporation, however, the situation is not as clear, because the afore-mentioned case law of the ECJ did not (at least not expressly) cover the question whether the Freedom of Establishment requires the Member States also to allow their own corporate entities to relocate their *de facto* seat to another Member State whilst at the same time keeping their registration in the country of incorporation. For the time being, the attitude of the various Member States to such an 'export' of their corporate entities can be categorized as follows:

Member States who do allow such 'export', are Cyprus, the Czech Republic, Denmark, Estonia, Finland, the United Kingdom, Italy, Latvia, Lithuania, Malta, the Netherlands, Poland and Sweden;[6] also French law is likely to be interpreted in the same way.[7]

In addition, there are a number of other jurisdictions which only allow the relocation into another country if the host country accepts it; amongst these are Belgium, Luxembourg, Portugal, Slovenia and Slovakia.[8] In light of the afore-mentioned case law of the ECJ, under which all host countries will have to accept such relocation, all those five Member States now should allow the relocation of the *de facto* seat of their own companies to another Member State; this, however, is not yet finally clarified in those jurisdictions. Regardless thereof, in Luxembourg and Slovenia the relocation of the *de facto* seat would result in the loss of their status as a Luxembourg or Slovenian company, as the case may be (which is usually not what an investor intends).

A level of uncertainty remains in Austria where there has not yet been any local case law after the latest ECJ judgments.[9]

The only Member States who clearly do not allow such an 'export' of their corporate entities are Greece, Germany, Hungary, Ireland and Spain.[10]

The situation is summarised in the following schedule:

6 See Part 2, CY, Mn. 6/38; CZ, Mn. 3/51; DK, Mn. 2/37; EST, Mn. 2/41; FIN, Mn. 3/49; LV, Mn. 2/37; LT, Mn. 2 et seq./52; UK, Mn. 2/42; I, Mn. 2/25; M, Mn. 2/36; NL, Mn. 4/52; PL, Mn. 2/38; S, Mn. 3/57.

7 See Part 2, F, Mn. 5.

8 See Part 2, B, Mn. 2/33; L, Mn. 2/37; P, Mn. 3/45; SLO, Mn. 2/32; SK, Mn. 2/40; it is not yet clarified in practice whether those countries now have to allow the relocation of the *de facto* seat of their own companies to another Member State in light of the latest ECJ rulings, under which all host countries will have to accept such relocation.

9 See Part 2, A, Mn. 2/36.

10 See Part 2, D, Mn. 3/45; GR, Mn. 2/31; H, Mn. 2/42; IRL, Mn. 2/32: E, Mn. 2/28.

'Export' of corporate entities is			
allowed	**allowed, if host country accepts***	**unclear**	**not allowed**
Cyprus Czech Republic Denmark Estonia France (likely) Finland Italy Latvia Lithuania Malta the Netherlands Poland Sweden United Kingdom	Belgium Portugal Slovakia ——— Luxembourg Slovenia	Austria	Germany Greece Hungary Ireland Spain
* which it has to, according to ECJ case law			

6 In light of the ECJ judgments "Überseering" and "Inspire Art",[11] legal scholars are in dispute whether a Member State may still restrict a corporate entity incorporated under its own laws from moving its *de facto* seat abroad in the future, although in general Member States are allowed to impose certain restrictions on the corporate entities registered in their own territory and do not have to assure equal treatment of those "own entities" with corporate entities registered in other Member States ("Principle of Discrimination of Nationals"). Therefore, the above mentioned national restrictions remain applicable for the time being as long as no different legislation has been introduced or the ECJ has ruled otherwise.

1.2 Transformation into a Foreign Entity

7 Transformations of corporate entities can be effected in several ways, the two main of which are the change of the corporate form on the one hand and a "true" merger of one or more companies on the other into a foreign entity (with all transferring companies ceasing to exist and all their assets and liabilities being transferred to the surviving entity by operation of law).

8 Most European jurisdictions, such as Belgium, Cyprus, the Czech Republic, Denmark, Estonia, Finland, France, Hungary, Ireland, Lithuania, Poland, Portugal, Slovakia, Sweden, Spain and the United Kingdom do not allow the transformation of their domestic corporate entities into foreign corporate entities by way of a true merger or by a change of the corporate form into that of a foreign corporate entity.[12] After the ECJ judgment of 13 December 2005 in the case SEVIC (case C-411/03) – which might be interpreted as a complete abolishment of general restrictions on cross-border mergers by national laws of EU Member States – it is questionable whether this position can be upheld in future. An exception to this general rule – for certain corporate forms – offers a merger with an S.E.[13] Most alternative structures, which usually involve the transfer of a business, often result in adverse tax effects as it generally leads to an exposure of hidden reserves to taxation

11 See Part 1, I, Mn. 17 et seq.

12 See Part 2, B, Mn. 3/34; CY, Mn. 7/39; CZ, Mn. 4/52; DK, Mn. 3/38; EST, Mn. 3/42; FIN, Mn. 4/50; F, Mn. 7/57; UK, Mn. 3/43; H, Mn. 3/43; IRL, Mn. 3/33; LT, Mn. 5/53; PL, Mn. 3/39; P, Mn. 4/46; SK, Mn. 3/41; S, Mn. 4/61; E, Mn. 3/29.

13 For details see Part 2, S.E., Mn. 6 et seq.

in the country of the transferring entity. An exception to this rule is Spain which provides for a tax neutral way for the transfer of assets in certain cases.[14]

9 Under certain circumstances, a cross border merger is allowed in Austria, Germany, France, Italy, Luxembourg, Malta and Slovenia.[15] In some of these countries, such as Austria, France and Germany, this possibility, however, is not based on express provisions of the domestic Companies Act but on solutions invented in legal practice (e.g. the setting up of a complicated legal structure involving the incorporation and collapse of several companies and partnerships in the involved jurisdictions). It goes without saying that the possibility of a cross border merger will also depend on whether the other country involved also accepts the planned form of transformation. However, the ECJ has clarified that a Member State may not categorically hinder foreign corporate entities from merging with its local companies.[16]

10 National rules will be harmonised and cross border mergers thus be allowed as soon as the Tenth Directive on Cross Border Mergers[17] has been implemented into the national laws of the Member States.

1.3 Incorporation

11 In all 25 EU jurisdictions the incorporation of a corporate entity requires at least the signing of one or more constitutional documents (be they called deed of incorporation, memorandum of association and/or articles of association), their submission to a public register and the registration of the company with such register. The status as an independent legal entity is usually acquired at the moment of registration with the register. In other respects, the incorporation procedures differ in the various EU jurisdictions, especially as regards the minimum number of founders, as well as the formalities, duration and costs of the incorporation procedure.

1.3.1 Minimum Number of Founders

12 A time consuming formality with regard to the incorporation of a corporate entity in some EU jurisdictions can be the statutory requirement to have a minimum number of incorporators. This either results in the need to transfer the shares of the other incorporator(s) to the investor immediately after the incorporation or even makes the long-term involvement of minority shareholders necessary. Such restrictions may make it more difficult to establish complex holding structures in an international group of companies.

13 Belgium,[18] e.g., requires stock corporations to have a minimum of two shareholders. In practice this also applies to Belgian limited liability companies, where sole incorporatorship/shareholdership is legally allowed but will trigger unlimited shareholder liability. The Czech Republic (as far as the limited liability company is concerned) and Slovakia[19] do not allow a single shareholdership if the shareholder itself has in turn a single shareholder. The same restriction applies in Poland, however, only in the foundation phase. After registration of a Polish limited liability company, the shares can be held by one shareholder which itself has in turn a single shareholder.[20]

14 Portugal[21] requires a minimum number of two (limited liability company) or five shareholders (stock corporation), respectively, but provides for exceptions in certain cases, e.g., if a stock corporation is incorporated by the State or another company. More than one founder of a stock cor-

14 See Part 2, E, Mn. 3/29.

15 See Part 2, A, Mn. 3/37; D, Mn. 4/46; GR, Mn. 3/32; F, Mn. 7/57/84; I, Mn. 3/41; L, Mn. 3/38; M, Mn. 3/37; SLO, Mn. 3/33.

16 ECJ judgment dated 13 December 2005 (case C-411/03, SEVIC)

17 See Part 1, I, Mn. 56 et seq.

18 See Part 2, B, Mn. 4/35.

19 See Part 2, CZ, Mn. 6; SK, Mn. 4/43.

20 See Part 2, PL, Mn. 4/40.

21 See Part 2, P, Mn. 5/47.

poration is also required in Cyprus (seven), the United Kingdom (two), France (seven),[22] Ireland (seven), Luxembourg (two), Malta (two) and Slovakia (two, unless the founder is another company).[23]

1.3.2 Formal Requirements

From a formal point of view, a distinction must be made between those jurisdictions where the involvement of a notary is required and those where the public register is the only public authority verifying the compliance of the incorporation documents with statutory requirements. **15**

In most jurisdictions, the incorporation documents are set up by way of a notarial deed. Notarial involvement is also required in Latvia and Lithuania,[24] where the documents are set up privately but a certification from a notary public has to be obtained confirming that all legal stipulations have been adhered to. **16**

No involvement of a notary is required in the common law jurisdictions (the United Kingdom, Ireland, Malta, Cyprus), France and some Scandinavian Member States (Denmark, Finland and Sweden),[25] where only the incorporation document(s) have to be filed with the competent register. The same applies to the incorporation of Slovenian limited liability company if it is incorporated by a sole founder.[26] **17**

Finland additionally has a legislative bill underway, changing the Companies Act as of 1 September 2006 in a way that an Oy – the Finnish equivalent to a limited liability company – could be incorporated with extremely short articles of association only containing the company name, the corporate seat and the object of the company. The new act will contain default provisions on the topics which usually need to be addressed in articles of association. While it is unlikely that the majority of incorporators will make use of this possibility, it will be helpful for those investors who need to establish a legal entity under significant time pressure. **18**

1.3.3 Duration

The duration of an incorporation procedure very much depends on its complexity. Complicated and lengthy constitutional documents, the appointment of foreign directors, the obtaining of publicly certified signatures from foreign countries etc. can be very time consuming and make it difficult to give an exact estimate on how long it takes to incorporate a company in a particular EU jurisdiction. Assuming, however, the existence of standard constitutional documents and no issues being raised during any review by the public registers, the incorporation of a limited liability company will on average take between one and three weeks, whilst the incorporation of a stock corporation usually takes at least two weeks. **19**

The incorporation procedure in Spain and Sweden may be exceptionally long. In Spain the incorporation of either an S.L. (limited liability company) or an S.A. (stock corporation) will require a minimum of six weeks and, if directors from other jurisdictions are to be appointed, even longer.[27] In Sweden an investor has to expect an incorporation procedure lasting about five to six weeks.[28] **20**

Same-day registrations are possible in Denmark, Finland, the United Kingdom, Malta and – under certain circumstances – Portugal.[29] Denmark even provides for an online registration procedure taking 15 to 20 minutes. **21**

22 Note, however, that France has introduced a simplified stock corporation (SAS), which can be incorporated by one founder; see Part 2, F, Mn. 58.

23 See Part 2, CY, Mn. 8/40; UK, Mn. 4/45; F, Mn. 8; IRL, Mn. 34; L, Mn. 39; SK, Mn. 43; M, Mn. 4/38.

24 See Part 2, LV, Mn. 5/39; LT, Mn. 6/54.

25 See Part 2, F, Mn. 8/59/86; UK, Mn. 4/45; IRL, Mn. 4/34; M, Mn. 4/39; CY, Mn. 8/40; FIN, Mn. 5/51; DK, Mn. 4/39; S, Mn. 5/62.

26 See Part 2, SLO, Mn. 4/34.

27 See Part 2, E, Mn. 4/30.

28 See Part 2, S, Mn. 5/62.

29 See Part 2, DK, Mn. 4/39; FIN, Mn. 5/51; UK, Mn. 4/45; M, Mn. 4/39; P, Mn. 5/48.

1.3.4 Minimum Costs

22 The minimum statutory costs of incorporation (notary, registration and publication fees) in most Member States will on average not exceed an aggregate amount of EUR 300 to 800 for a limited liability company and EUR 600 to 1,000 for a stock corporation.

23 Higher minimum fees will, however, be charged in Italy (approximately EUR 3,000) and in the Netherlands (approximately EUR 2,700) for the incorporation of limited liability companies.[30] The minimum costs of incorporation are also relatively high for the incorporation of a stock corporation in Belgium (approximately EUR 1,860), Italy (approximately EUR 5,000), the Netherlands (approximately EUR 2,700), Poland (approximately EUR 1,740) and Spain (approximately EUR 1,225).[31]

24 An incorporation is cheapest in Denmark, where no fees are charged, the United Kingdom (approximately EUR 30) and Ireland, where the incorporation costs of a limited liability company are approximately EUR 50 to 100.

1.4 Recurrent Costs and Efforts

25 The annual costs and efforts incurred by companies in the EU post-incorporation vary according to the jurisdiction of incorporation and range from insignificant to fairly substantial figures. The main causes for such a broad range of costs are primarily the different requirements relating to the payment of annual registration fees, the auditing of annual accounts, as well as the respective filing and publication obligations in each Member State. The size and turnover of a company are inevitably of relevance, with recurrent costs and efforts generally increasing with those factors.

1.4.1 Limited Liability Companies

26 There is, however, a marked similarity in the treatment of limited liability companies throughout the EU where recurrent costs will usually be low and efforts expended minimal. In most Member States a limited liability company will not face filing and publication costs and/or annual registration fees in total exceeding EUR 100. In Denmark, Finland, Hungary and Lithuania these costs in fact are practically non-existent.[32] Annual costs for these formalities exceeding EUR 500 can only be found in Belgium, Greece, Italy and Poland.

27 In the United Kingdom, Ireland and Malta it will also be necessary to appoint a company secretary and maintain a formal "registered office".[33] There will only be a cost of complying with such obligations if the company requires a professional company secretary to fulfil certain corporate housekeeping duties such as maintenance of statutory books and to ensure compliance with corporate filing requirements, in which case – taking the United Kingdom as an example – these will be approximately GBP 500 (approximately EUR 750) per annum inclusive of the maintenance of the registered office. Where such professional assistance is not required it is usual that an employee or director of the company will act as the company secretary with the company's headquarters as the registered office resulting in no additional expense to the company. A similar peculiarity can be found in Luxembourg, where it is usual to register the company with a domiciliary agent who will provide filing and registration services at a cost between EUR 2,000 and EUR 3,000 per annum for its services.[34]

28 Limited liability companies in France, the United Kingdom, Italy and Poland[35] are obliged to hold a physical annual shareholders' meeting. Once again, the costs and efforts vary depending on the size.

30 See Part 2, I, Mn. 5; NL, Mn. 9.
31 See Part 2, B, Mn. 37; I, Mn. 43; NL, Mn. 54; E, Mn. 30; PL, Mn. 4/41.
32 See Part 2, DK, Mn. 6; FIN, Mn. 7; H, Mn. 6; LT, Mn. 8..
33 See Part 2, M, Mn. 6/40; UK, Mn. 7/47.
34 See Part 2, L, Mn. 6.
35 See Part 2, F, Mn. 11/60; UK, Mn. 7/47 (although in the United Kingdom private companies could elect to dispense with holding AGMs, thereby reducing recurring costs and efforts); PL, Mn. 6/42.

A further trigger for annual costs is the need for the company's annual accounts to be audited by an independent auditor as prescribed by the Fourth Directive. Only some jurisdictions have made use of the possibility to give relief from the auditing requirement for small and medium-sized enterprises which do not meet defined financial thresholds. Among these are Belgium, the Czech Republic, Estonia, Germany, the United Kingdom, Latvia, Lithuania, Luxembourg and Slovakia. [36] **29**

1.4.2 Stock Corporations

It should be noted that in all countries, recurrent costs and efforts for a small stock corporation are likely to be similar to those incurred by limited liability companies. **30**

Recurrent costs and efforts, however, are greater where large stock corporations are concerned due to the more onerous obligations and restrictions imposed on such companies in order to protect both creditors and shareholders, the latter because they will tend to be less involved in the running of the business. The main differences result from the obligatory requirements to hold AGMs, which in some countries may cost from EUR 100,000 for those listed stock corporations with a significant shareholder base.[37] **31**

If the stock corporation is listed, it must comply with the regulatory requirements of the relevant stock exchange, which generally aim at greater transparency enabling investor and creditor protection and are achieved by the imposition of various disclosure and filing obligations, which may be costly as well as time consuming. **32**

1.5 Shares and Share Transfers

1.5.1 Share Characteristics

Participation interests in companies located in the EU, be they called shares, quotas, parts, participations or interests (in this section referred to as "shares"), can vary in form and be either certificated or dematerialised, registered or bearer shares (or a combination thereof). **33**

In the majority of jurisdictions,[38] shares in a limited liability company will be uncertificated, with the managing directors/board of directors generally assuming responsibility for maintaining a share (or shareholders') register. In Finland, Germany, Lithuania and Sweden it is possible for limited liability company shares to be certificated (though in practice this is rarely done)[39] whilst certification in the form of registered shares is the norm in the United Kingdom and those Member States whose corporate legal systems have Anglo-Saxon roots.[40] Bearer shares issued by limited liability companies in the EU are uncommon and are possible only in a small number of jurisdictions.[41] **34**

The majority of jurisdictions in the EU allow domestic stock corporations to issue registered or bearer shares.[42] However, they vary as to the certification requirement. While there are countries providing for obligatory certification (at least in the form of one "global share certificate" representing all shares) other Member States, such as France or – in case of a listed company – the United Kingdom and Sweden, oblige stock corporations to have dematerialised shares.[43] **35**

36 See Part 2, B, Mn. 29/59; EST, Mn. 38/66; CZ, Mn. 47/88; D, Mn. 41/77; L, Mn. 6/41; LT, Mn. 49; LV, Mn. 34/57; SK, Mn. 37/70; UK, Mn. 39.

37 See e.g. Part 2, D, Mn. 49.

38 See e.g. Part 2, A, Mn. 7 and Mn. 8; DK, Mn.8; EST, Mn. 8; D, Mn. 9; GR, Mn. 7; H, Mn.8; I, Mn. 8; LV, Mn. 7; L, Mn.8; PL, Mn. 7; P, Mn.9; SK, Mn. 8; SLO, Mn. 6; E, Mn. 8.

39 In Sweden, e.g., this will result in the shares becoming bearer instruments (see Part 2, S, Mn. 9), as opposed to Germany where the certificate only works as a (disprovable) means of evidence. I.e. the share will not be transferred by endorsing the certificate, but in the same way as a non-certificated share, (see Part 2, D, Mn. 10).

40 See Part 2, CYP, Mn. 12; IRL, Mn. 8 and M, Mn. 7.

41 See e.g. Part 2, UK, Mn. 8; S, Mn. 9.

42 See Part 2, A, Mn. 42; B, Mn. 38; CZ, Mn. 56; DK, Mn. 43; D, Mn. 50; GR, Mn. 36; H, Mn. 48; LV, Mn. 41; L, Mn. 42; PL, Mn. 43; P, Mn. 50; SK, Mn. 45 and SLO, Mn. 37.

43 See Part 2, F, Mn.13; UK, Mn. 48; S, Mn. 64.

1.5.2 Transfer Requirements[44]

(i) Limited Liability Companies

36 A large number of Member States permit shares in a limited liability company to be transferred only by way of notarial deed,[45] or in written form with signatures certified by a notary public,[46] whilst the remainder do not generally require such a level of formality and allow shares to be transferred pursuant to simple (e.g. oral) agreements[47] or written declarations.[48] It is often the case that the company must, as a minimum, be notified so that the relevant share (or shareholders') register can be updated (e.g., in France, Germany, Lithuania, Luxembourg, Poland, Slovenia and Slovakia).[49] Many jurisdictions allow the articles to set out the exact mechanisms of transfer and, in some cases, to adopt either a more relaxed (e.g., the Czech Republic) or stricter (e.g., Austria, Belgium, Greece, Hungary and Italy) approach than that provided by statute.[50]

(ii) Stock Corporations

37 The transfer requirements regarding shares in stock corporations are more varied and can differ substantially from Member State to Member State. Probably the greatest similarity in approach lies with bearer shares where physical delivery of the certificate will generally be sufficient to transfer title. In Germany, where certification is obligatory, the individual unregistered shares will normally be represented by a global share certificate which is held by a depository and in which case the individual share will be transferred by way of the assignment of a delivery claim against the depository.[51]

38 The transfer of registered shares which are certificated can be effected in most jurisdictions through endorsing the certificate (e.g., Austria, Czech Republic, Denmark, Germany, Poland, Slovakia, Slovenia) whilst other jurisdictions allow transfers to be effected by way of a simple transfer document which, in contrast to the general position for limited liability companies, does not need to be notarised.[52]

39 Dematerialised shares may be transferred by written agreement and, in almost all jurisdictions, the transferor or transferee must ensure that the share register is updated. A number of Member States require the register to be updated (i) before a transferee may exercise his rights as a shareholder (e.g., in Germany and Sweden) or (ii) to give effect to the transfer (e.g., in Lithuania and Luxembourg).[53]

40 Certain Member States, such as France, the United Kingdom, Ireland and Greece, require furthermore the payment of transfer or stamp taxes.[54]

44 For the avoidance of doubt, this section covers the contractual transfer of shares, by way of singular succession, only – disregarding share transfers by way of global succession, e.g. under the rules of inheritance or a merger or spin-off.

45 See Part 2, A, Mn.7; EST, Mn. 7 (unless the shares are registered with the Estonian Central Register of Shares); D, Mn. 9; GR, Mn. 7; L, Mn. 8; P, Mn. 8; SLO, Mn. 6; E, Mn. 9.

46 See Part 2, CZ, Mn. 11; PL, Mn. 7; I, Mn. 7 (please note, however, that in Italy the notarised agreement is only required for enforcement vis-à-vis third parties and the company, while the mere transfer inter partes only requires a simple agreement); SK, Mn. 9.

47 See Part 2, B, Mn. 11; DK, Mn. 8; FIN, Mn. 9; F, Mn. 15; H, Mn. 7; LV, Mn. 8; LT, Mn. 11; S, Mn. 9.

48 See e.g. Part 2, in the UK and Ireland, where title can be transferred by way of a stock transfer form. See Part 2, IRL, Mn. 8; UK, Mn. 9.

49 See Part 2, F, Mn. 13; D, Mn. 9; LT, Mn. 11; L, Mn. 8; PL, Mn. 7; SK, Mn. 8.

50 See e.g. Part 2, CZ, Mn. 10.

51 See Part 2, D, Mn. 50.

52 Notarisation is optional in Greece, see Part 2, GR, Mn. 36.

53 See Part 2, L, Mn. 43; LT, Mn. 57; S, Mn. 64.

54 See Part 2, F, Mn. 15; GR, Mn. 36; IRL, Mn. 9/37; UK, Mn. 48.

1.5.3 Restrictions on Transfer

Many Member States appear to base transfer restrictions on the understanding that limited liability companies will often be formed by a small group of individuals who wish to jointly pursue a business aim and that the ability of a shareholder to transfer his interest to an outside third party could be prejudicial to the joint corporate success. In a number of jurisdictions, therefore, transfers of shares in a limited liability company may require board approval[55] or even shareholder approval[56] (though the discretion may be limited to some extent by law), whilst other Member States provide for statutory pre-emption rights , particularly in favour of other shareholders, which may affect a transfer (e.g., Estonia, Hungary and Lithuania).[57] **41**

Transfers of shares in stock corporations are, however, substantially less restricted, undoubtedly reflecting the fact that stock corporations are vehicles in which shareholders often participate purely as investors and where a stock exchange listing is often desired. To the extent there are restrictions, these will generally have to be set out in the articles of association.[58] **42**

Note that, apart from the above-mentioned corporate law restrictions, share transfers may also be restricted under national public law in certain sensitive industry sectors, such as the telecommunications or defence industry. **43**

1.5.4 Offers of Shares to the Public

Throughout the EU, limited liability companies are generally not able to issue shares to the public, either because this is expressly prohibited by law (e.g., the United Kingdom, Ireland, Italy, Malta, Poland, and Sweden)[59] or because it is impracticable to do so given, e.g., the existence of notarisation obligations, pre-emption rights which cannot be disapplied, or because the private form cannot be listed on an exchange. Thus offers of shares to the public are very much the preserve of the stock corporations which, without exception, are able to make such offers subject to compliance with statutory and regulatory obligations. **44**

1.6 Corporate Bodies

At their core, corporate structures used throughout the EU are, almost without exception,[60] firmly based on the legal concept of a division between those owning or investing in a particular enterprise (the shareholders, quota-holders, members etc.) and those responsible for the management and internal control of the company (the board, managing directors etc.). However, Member States have taken very differing approaches regarding the level of shareholder involvement in corporate affairs and in particular board structure and composition. **45**

As regards board structure, one will find two main approaches: the UK-style one-tier system, namely the directors of the company, and the two-tier system, which, e.g., can be found in the German stock corporation where the management is divided into a management body (board of directors) in charge of the day-to-day management of the company and a controlling body (supervisory board) which oversees the legality and feasibility of the actions of the board of directors. The one-tier system can be subdivided further into board structures where all directors have executive functions and other board structures where some directors have executive functions and the others are acting on a non-executive basis, thereby having a position with a stronger supervisory function. **46**

55 E.g., Cyprus, United Kingdom and Ireland, see Part 2, CY, Mn.12; UK, Mn. 9; IRL, Mn. 8.

56 E.g., Belgium (if not made to certain connected persons), Luxembourg (if to a non-shareholder), Poland (if stipulated in the articles) and Germany (if stipulated in the articles), see Part 2, B, Mn. 7; CZ,11; , L, Mn. 8; PL, Mn. 7, D, Mn. 9.

57 See Part 2, EST, Mn. 7; H, Mn. 7; LT, Mn. 10.

58 See e.g. Part 2, B, Mn. 38; EST, Mn. 46; F, Mn.14; PL, Mn. 44; E, Mn. 35 and S, Mn. 65.

59 See Part 2, IRL, Mn. 10; I, Mn. 8; M, Mn. 8; PL, Mn. 7; S, Mn. 10; UK, Mn. 9.

60 Note, e.g., Greece, where the limited liability company only requires one corporate body, namely a partners' meeting; see Part 2, GR, Mn. 9.

1.6.1 Limited Liability Companies

47 The majority of limited liability companies in the EU follow the UK style one-tier board system where the directors or managers are responsible for day-to-day management and where the shareholders in shareholders' meetings have certain matters reserved to them and will be ultimately responsible for controlling the management.[61] The one-tier board system is, however, not always obligatory and Austria, the Czech Republic, Finland,[62] Germany, Latvia, Lithuania, Poland,[63] Slovakia and Slovenia allow limited liability companies to form a supervisory board if so decided. The main purpose behind the formation of a supervisory board is to control the management and, in most jurisdictions, certain business transactions will be stipulated for which supervisory board approval is required.

48 In relation to larger limited liability companies, certain European jurisdictions have considered it appropriate to have a compulsory system in place either to ensure a strict or partial separation of supervisory and executive functions, or in order to provide opportunities for employees to participate in the management process.[64] In Austria, Estonia, Germany, Hungary, Italy[65] and Poland e.g., a two-tier structure and the establishment of a supervisory board becomes mandatory in the event certain thresholds regarding, *inter alia*, number of employees, share capital or number of shareholders (depending on the jurisdiction concerned) are exceeded.

1.6.2 Stock Corporation

49 Many Member States consider the additional supervision institutionally assured by a two-tier board system necessary in relation to a stock corporation and such a system is therefore obligatory in the majority of jurisdictions,[66] with the principal exceptions being Belgium, Cyprus, the United Kingdom, Greece, Ireland, Luxembourg, Malta and Spain, which continue to adhere to a strict one-tier system.[67] The establishment of a supervisory board is discretionary in Finland, France, Lithuania and Portugal.[68]

50 Of interest is the position in Italy where it is believed necessary that there is some form of review and control of management actions and where shareholders are able to decide between one of three different models in the bylaws of the stock corporation.[69] The traditional method is to have a management board and a board of statutory auditors (which has a similar role to a supervisory board in other European jurisdictions) both of which are appointed by the shareholders. Alternatively, the shareholders can adopt either a German style two-tier system, where they appoint a supervisory board which in turn appoints the board of directors, or an Anglo-Saxon style single board structure which appoints a supervisory committee of non-executive directors.

1.6.3 Appointment

51 The members of a one-tier board are appointed exclusively by the shareholders' meeting. With a two-tier system, some countries such as Germany and Austria[70] provide that the shareholders appoint the supervisory board which (in most cases, only as far as the limited liability company is concerned) in turn appoints the management board. In this structure, the shareholders therefore only

61 See Part 2, A, Mn. 10; B, Mn. 9; CY, Mn. 14; CZ, Mn. 13; DK, Mn. 10; EST, Mn. 9; UK, Mn. 10; H, Mn. 9; IRL, Mn. 11; LV, Mn. 9; LT, Mn. 14; L, Mn. 9; M, Mn. 9; PL, Mn. 8; P, Mn. 10; SK, Mn. 10; SLO, Mn. 7; E, Mn. 10.

62 Provided the company has a share capital in excess of EUR 80,000; see Part 2, FIN, Mn. 12.

63 Unless certain thresholds are met, in which case a supervisory board becomes obligatory; see Part 2, PL, Mn. 8.

64 For details as to employee representation please refer to Mn. 155 et seq.

65 In Italy a board of statutory auditors is obligatory for a limited liability company once certain financial thresholds are met but the responsibilities are very similar to those typically allocated to a supervisory board in other European jurisdictions; see Part 2, I, Mn. 8 and 15.

66 Including in Slovenia, if certain financial thresholds are met; see Part 2, SLO, Mn. 38.

67 See Part 2, B, Mn. 39; CY, Mn. 46; UK, Mn. 49; GR, Mn. 38; IRL, Mn. 38; L, Mn. 44; M, Mn. 42; E, Mn. 36.

68 See Part 2, FIN, Mn. 59; F, Mn. 67; LT, Mn. 65; P, Mn. 53.

69 See Part 2, I, Mn. 49.

70 See Part 2, A, Mn. 49; D, Mn. 55.

have an indirect influence on the composition of the management board. Other countries applying the two-tier system, such as the Czech Republic and Slovakia, provide that the shareholders' meeting has the exclusive authority to appoint both the management board and the supervisory board (unless the articles of association stipulate otherwise or employee election requirements exist).[71] In Finland and Germany, where the general rule is that the supervisory board is appointed by the shareholders' meeting, a minority of the supervisory board members may also be appointed in another manner, e.g. directly by a certain shareholder.[72]

1.7 Duties and Liabilities of Directors

There is a wide range of duties with which the management (managing directors, board of directors, officers, members of the supervisory board) has to comply in all Member States. As a common basis, however, the directors have to act with the diligence of a prudent businessman and in the best interests of the company. Their duties will usually also include the obligation to make all relevant filings to the competent registers and authorities and not to make any payments out of the company's assets in violation of local capital maintenance rules. Should the directors act in breach of their duties, this will usually result in a personal liability of those directors towards the company. 52

Whereas the primary duties on an abstract level are all very similar throughout the EU, there are significant national differences when considering the specific duties, the applicable standards for measuring compliance, as well as the scope of liability. 53

1.7.1 Joint and Several Liability

As regards personal liability, in most of the Member States the directors are jointly and severally liable for any breach of an individual director's obligations resulting in damage to the company, irrespective of the identity of the director who caused the damage. The rationale behind this concept is the joint responsibility of all directors in a sense that those directors not directly having breached their duties at least did not correctly supervise their co-directors. 54

However, one may argue that if a director was not involved in an action causing a damage and also otherwise acted with due managerial care, there is no legal ground for his personal liability. Following this argumentation, some of those countries which provide for a joint and several liability under certain circumstances allow a release from the joint and several liability of the director not having acted. The release is usually granted to a director if there was a prior allocation of duties between several directors, the director did not take part in the relevant action or omission and he can prove that he supervised his colleagues with due managerial care.[73] However, others of the Member States providing for a joint and several liability of the directors pursue the concept of joint liabilities strictly and thus do not allow a defence in the abovementioned manner.[74] 55

Other countries, such as Denmark, Finland, France, Greece (as far as the limited liability company is concerned), Poland, Slovakia, Sweden and the United Kingdom only stipulate the requirement of a joint and several liability in the case of a joint breach of a duty.[75] In other words: a director not having taken part in a breach is not liable. 56

1.7.2 Effect of Prior Instructions by the Shareholders

Many Member States release directors from their liability if they acted in accordance with a lawful instruction by the shareholders' meeting. Amongst these are Austria and Germany (both only as regards the limited liability company), the Czech Republic, Denmark, Estonia, Greece (as far 57

71 See Part 2, CZ, Mn. 64; SK, Mn. 50 and 53.

72 See Part 2, FIN, Mn. 19; D, Mn. 55.

73 See Part 2, A, Mn. 17; D, Mn. 19/58; GR, Mn. 42 (as regards the A.E.); I, Mn. 65 (as regards the S.A. in case the board member formally objected to the breach); M, Mn. 15/49; NL, Mn. 30; S, Mn. 28.

74 See Part 2, EST, Mn. 18; LT, Mn. 25; P, Mn. 17.

75 See Part 2, DK, Mn. 17/52; FIN, Mn. 21; F, Mn. 27; GR, Mn. 14; PL, Mn. 16/54; SK, Mn. 15/54; S, Mn. 28/68; UK, Mn. 16.

as the stock corporation is concerned), Hungary, Latvia, Portugal and Slovakia.[76] No release from liability is granted where the directors acted in accordance with unlawful instructions.

Other countries, such as Poland and Spain,[77] expressly do not provide for the possibility of such release, irrespective of whether the instruction by the shareholders was lawful or not.

1.7.3 Effect of Subsequent Discharge in Shareholders' Meeting

58 Likewise, the Member States are divided into countries providing for a discharge of the directors in the annual shareholders' meeting, after which the company is excluded from ascertaining claims against directors, and other countries not providing for this possibility of discharge. Among the countries providing for a release from the director's liability by way of discharge are Austria, Denmark, Estonia, Finland, Germany (as far as the limited liability company is concerned), Greece, Luxemburg, the Netherlands, Poland, Portugal and Sweden.[78] Of course, the approval in the shareholders' meeting is not obligatory in these countries and only relates to breaches which were apparent to the shareholders at the time of the annual meeting. Other countries such as France, Italy, Latvia, Lithuania, Malta, Slovakia, Slovenia, Spain and the United Kingdom do not provide for the possibility to grant the managers a general discharge in the annual meeting.[79] This, however, does not mean that the company may not waive a particular claim against a director.

1.7.4 D&O Insurance

59 A possible means of protecting a company from damages incurred from managerial misconduct is liability insurance for directors (so-called D&O insurance). This is widely known – and allowed – in all Member States. Related premiums may usually be directly paid or reimbursed to the directors by the company.[80] Note, however, that the latter is disputed in the Netherlands.[81] Although allowed, D&O insurance is uncommon in Greece and Lithuania.[82]

60 A unique concept is followed by Portugal, which even obliges the board members of Portuguese stock corporations to provide either a guarantee assuring the settlement of potential claims brought forward against them and exceeding an amount of EUR 5,000 or to provide a respective insurance.[83]

1.7.5 Statute of Limitations

61 In most Member States, claims against directors become time-barred after five years, starting in the majority of jurisdictions from the point in time when the breach is committed. Latvia and Lithuania provide for a 10-year statute of limitations.[84] Others, such as France, Ireland (both three years) and Malta (two years) provide for considerably shorter periods.[85] Finland takes a different approach and provides for a three-year statute of limitations as regards claims by the company and a 10-year statute of limitations as regards claims by the shareholders or third parties. This, however, will change to a uniform period of five years when the new Finnish Companies Act enters into force on 1 September 2006.[86]

76 See Part 2, A, Mn. 17; CZ, Mn. 19; DK, Mn. 17/52; EST, Mn. 17; D, Mn. 17; GR, Mn. 43; H, Mn. 19; LV, Mn. 16; P, Mn. 17; SK, Mn. 15/56.

77 See Part 2, PL, Mn. 15; E, Mn. 13.

78 See Part 2, A, Mn. 17; DK, Mn. 17/52; EST, Mn. 19; FIN, Mn. 22; D, Mn. 19; GR, Mn. 14/43; L, Mn. 16/53; NL, Mn. 31; PL, Mn. 15; P, Mn. 17; S, Mn. 29.

79 See Part 2, F, Mn. 30; I, Mn. 19; LV, Mn. 17; LT, Mn. 25; M, Mn. 15/49; SK, Mn. 17/56; SLO, Mn. 12/46; E, Mn. 13.

80 Although the premiums reimbursed by the company in that way may be considered as taxable income of the insured director under local tax laws.

81 See Part 2, NL, Mn. 30.

82 See Part 2, GR, Mn. 14/42; LT, Mn. 27.

83 See Part 2, P, Mn. 61.

84 See Part 2, LV, Mn. 15/47; LT, Mn. 26.

85 See Part 2, F, Mn. 31; IRL, Mn. 16; M, Mn. 15.

86 See Part 2, FIN, Mn. 23.

1.7.6 Liability *vis-à-vis* Third Parties

It goes without saying that the directors are liable *vis-à-vis* the company if they breach their duties. As regards liability *vis-à-vis* the company's creditors, the Member States can be divided into three groups. First, there are those which do not provide for a liability *vis-à-vis* the company's creditors (except for a liability based on tort). Amongst these are France, Germany, Latvia and Luxembourg (the latter only as regards misconduct which does not constitute a violation of legal or statutory provisions).[87] A second group of countries, such as Belgium, Estonia, Finland, Portugal, Spain and Sweden, stipulate a director's liability both *vis-à-vis* the company and *vis-à-vis* the company's creditors.[88] A third group of Member States – in between the two afore-mentioned groups – only holds directors liable *vis-à-vis* third parties in the event of financial difficulties of the company. Amongst these are Ireland, Malta, Poland and Slovenia.[89] **62**

There are no special provisions for the director's liability towards the shareholders. If a shareholder has a claim against the company on the basis of a transaction that was concluded at arm's length terms, the directors of the company are liable towards such shareholder in the same way as described in the paragraph above. **63**

1.7.7 Wrongful Trading/Fraudulent Trading

The common law jurisdictions Ireland, Malta and the United Kingdom traditionally provide for rules regarding wrongful trading. Denmark has similar provisions.[90] Wrongful trading regulations create a duty of care on the part of the directors towards the company's creditors which will be triggered at the point at which the directors knew or ought to have known that there was no reasonable prospect that the company would avoid going into insolvent liquidation. If the company then indeed goes into insolvent liquidation, the liquidator is entitled to sue the directors. The only defence the directors have is to show that they took every step with a view to minimising the potential loss to the company's creditors as they ought to have taken. Directors who fail in this defence have to contribute to the assets of the company such an amount as the court thinks proper.[91] **64**

In the case of fraudulent misconduct, directors are furthermore subject to both civil and criminal liability under so-called fraudulent trading rules. These, however, are not a peculiarity of the common law jurisdictions but in general apply equally in all EU jurisdictions, although there is not always a term such as "fraudulent trading" under which this concept is summarised. **65**

1.7.8 Duty to Apply for Insolvency Proceedings

A statutory duty of the directors to file for insolvency proceedings applies in continental European jurisdictions, e.g. in Austria, Estonia, France, Germany, Latvia, Lithuania, Luxemburg, Slovakia and Slovenia.[92] This duty is triggered, if the company is unable to pay its debts or is over-indebted from a balance sheet perspective (i.e. the assets do not cover the liabilities of the company anymore). The common law jurisdictions do not provide for such a duty, but apply the regulations on wrongful trading[93] and directors' disqualifications[94] instead. **66**

1.7.9 Directors' Disqualifications

A further common law instrument enforcing the director's duty of care which is stricter than in continental Europe is the possibility of a director's disqualification. It enables the court to prohibit a **67**

87 See Part 2, F, Mn. 29; D, Mn. 20/59; LV, Mn. 15/47; L, Mn. 16/53.
88 See Part 2, B, Mn. 14/45; EST, Mn. 19; FIN, Mn. 21; P, Mn. 17; E, Mn. 13; S, Mn. 30.
89 See Part 2, IRL, Mn. 16; M, Mn. 15; PL, Mn. 16; SLO, Mn. 12/46.
90 See Part 2, DK, Mn. 16/51.
91 See Part 2, UK, Mn. 17.
92 See Part 2, A, Mn. 16/51; EST, Mn. 22/54; F, Mn. 33/71; D, Mn. 18/58; LV, Mn. 17/47; LT, Mn. 24/66; SK, Mn. 19/54; SLO, Mn. 12/46.
93 See Mn. 64 et seq.
94 See Mn. 67.

person from being involved in the future in the management of companies, whether as a director or otherwise, if he has shown him- or herself to be unfit for such a position. The disqualification rules allow the court to review the director's entire conduct regarding the management of a company if that company has fallen into insolvent liquidation or into administration or where an administrative receiver has been appointed for the company.[95]

68 The courts in continental Europe usually have less discretion. A disqualification in those countries is mostly the direct consequence of certain criminal convictions (such as fraud).[96] The mere involvement in an insolvency of a company *per se* is not a sufficient basis to disqualify a director.

1.8 Shareholders' Liability

69 In all of the EU jurisdictions, the limited liability company and stock corporation are legal entities separate from their shareholders and responsible for their own actions, with the shareholders being liable only to the extent of their unpaid contributions. This principle of limited shareholder liability has been of fundamental importance in the development of the present market by inviting investors to participate in the financing of companies and at the same time limit their exposure to financial risks.

70 Given the commercial importance of maintaining limited shareholder liability, the courts throughout the EU have been reluctant to pierce this corporate veil. As an exception to this rule, the courts do pierce this veil in order to counter specific fraudulent or otherwise abusive actions of shareholders either to protect creditors (e.g., where payments are made to shareholders in breach of capital maintenance provisions or – though rarely – where there is a qualified under-funding or thin capitalisation of the company)[97] or where the corporate form is being used as a means to circumvent certain statutory obligations. As regards the latter, the courts in Cyprus,[98] e.g., look to protect the interests of the tax authorities by piercing the corporate veil to counter tax fraud or tax evasion.

71 National courts are otherwise most likely to pierce the corporate veil in those situations in which a parent company as majority shareholder[99] exercises its influence to the detriment of a group company.[100] The courts in Hungary, e.g., hold a majority shareholder liable who constantly exercises its influence in such way.[101] German courts do not grant the privilege of limited liability to shareholders of a limited liability company (and most likely also of a stock corporation) who withdraws assets from the company which are required for the settlement of obligations of the company to third parties.[102] A similar principle is applied in Lithuania.[103] Apart from the shareholder's liability *vis-à-vis* the company to compensate illegal repayments of share capital (and a withdrawal of assets may be interpreted as such), a shareholder committing such a tort is also likely to be directly liable to third party creditors of the company for damages incurred by this action.

1.9 Capitalisation and Financing

1.9.1 Basic Concepts

72 It is a commonplace that any company needs to have an equity that is in sound proportion to the level of business this company is doing. The equity works as a buffer against the debts of the company and, in principle, enables the company to obtain sufficient liquidity to meet its debts when

95 See Part 2, UK, Mn. 17.
96 See e.g. Part 2, D, Mn. 18; B, Mn. 16/47.
97 E.g. Austria and Spain: see Part 2, A, Mn. 19 et seq./52; E, Mn. 14/39. In Belgium, founding shareholders can be held liable for under-capitalization, if the company enters into insolvency within a period of three years after its incorporation, see Part 2, B, Mn. 21.
98 See Part 2, CY, Mn. 24.
99 Usually holding an interest of 50 per cent and above or otherwise having a controlling influence on the company.
100 See e.g. Part 2, I, Mn. 24; NL, Mn. 33/66; E, Mn. 14/39.
101 See Part 2, H, Mn. 20 et seq./58.
102 See Part 2, D, Mn. 21 et seq./61 et seq.
103 See Part 2, LT, Mn. 30/67.

due. If the equity is too low, this increases the risk that the company may become over-indebted and/or technically insolvent, if for some time more of the business hazards materialize then of the business opportunities.

This puts not only the shareholders at risk to lose their investment, but also the creditors of the company. As the later, contrary to the shareholders, have no means to influence the financial situation of the company, they need to be protected by the law. Conceptually, this creditor protection can be addressed by a legislator from an *ex ante* and an *ex post* perspective. 73

Ex post mechanisms can mainly be found (i) in wrongful and fraudulent trading rules,[104] in regulations on (ii) the disqualification[105] and (iii) personal liability of directors in cases of violations of the respective company and insolvency laws and (iv) in the possibility granted to insolvency administrators to nullify and set aside certain transactions which have occurred in a period prior to insolvency proceedings. Whereas the first two measures are mainly applied in common law jurisdictions, all EU jurisdictions – without exception – have adopted rules regarding the two last-mentioned measures, which only vary in their details. 74

From an *ex ante* perspective the requirement of a fixed share capital can further strengthen the protection of creditors. It defines a minimum amount of the equity buffer mentioned above, thus providing a sort of solid basis for the company to commence and conduct business.[106] This concept is completed by the rules on capital maintenance which shall assure that this equity buffer will be preserved within the company. At the same time, a minimum capital as the price for the limited liability of a company assures a certain level of seriousness on the shareholder's side. The EU jurisdictions are in agreement that stock corporations require this *ex ante* protection and thus, based on the Second Directive,[107] have each adopted minimum capital requirements and further rules on maintenance of the share capital. 75

On the basis of these arguments most EU jurisdictions, other than Cyprus, the United Kingdom and Ireland,[108] require limited liability companies to have a minimum share capital. Generally, it can be said that the jurisdictions which do not require the founding shareholders of a limited liability company to make a minimum contribution to the company believe that the *ex post* mechanisms together with the *ex ante* self-help possibilities of creditors (gathering information, implementation of floating charges, request for personal guarantees from shareholders or directors) are sufficient to provide creditor protection. On the other hand, these jurisdictions at the same time do provide for capital maintenance rules in a way very similar to the continental European approach where the founding shareholders have decided to contribute share capital to the respective company. 76

It is interesting to see that the above concepts of capitalisation, financing and creditor protection do not lead to dramatic differences in the practical day-to-day business. Irrespective of the share capital of a company, banks will usually not grant long-term loans without security from the directors or shareholders (mortgages, personal guarantees etc.), suppliers will insist on a retention of title for goods delivered and employees will look to ensure they are paid at the end of each month of employment. Consequently, most of the following topics will be addressed similarly in most jurisdictions and the remaining differences do not necessarily depend on the general approach of creditor protection to which a certain country adheres. 77

1.9.2 Minimum Share Capital

Whereas the share capital of a company forms the theoretical minimum amount available to the company's creditors[109] it also may be an obstacle for investors when considering a business activity 78

104 See Mn. 64 et seq.
105 See Mn. 67 et seq.
106 However, it remains questionable whether a fixed minimum share capital irrespective of the actual business of the company indeed can serve this purpose.
107 See Part 1, I, Mn. 39 et seq.
108 See Part 2, CY, Mn. 26; UK, Mn. 21; IRL, Mn. 19.
109 It goes without saying that the minimum share capital of course can be used by the company and cannot be understood as a "reserve of assets".

in a certain jurisdiction. Thus, the Member States are torn between efficient creditor protection and attracting investors with low minimum capital requirements, thereby stimulating economic growth.

(i) Stock Corporations

79 To avoid a "Delaware effect"[110] through a gradual relaxation of the national minimum capital requirements and to ensure a minimum equivalent protection for shareholders and creditors of stock corporations, the EU has introduced the Second Directive[111] which stipulates that Member States must provide for a minimum share capital of stock corporations at least meeting an amount of EUR 25,000.[112]

80 Cyprus, Estonia, Slovakia and Slovenia[113] have implemented this requirement without significant change and provide for an attractive minimum share capital between approximately EUR 25,000 and EUR 28,000, (considerably below the average EU-wide amount of around EUR 55,000).

Relatively high minimum capital requirements can be found in Austria, Finland, the United Kingdom and Hungary[114] which oblige shareholders to contribute into a stock corporation an amount of at least EUR 70,000 to EUR 80,000. The minimum capital requirements in Italy and Poland[115] are higher still and amount to approximately EUR 120,000. This is also the minimum share capital required for the establishment of an S.E., irrespective of the Member State where it is incorporated.

(ii) Limited Liability Companies

81 As regards limited liability companies, the EU has not harmonised national minimum capital requirements and therefore has left room for competition between countries intending to attract investors.

82 While some countries such as Austria (EUR 35,000), Germany (EUR 25,000), Greece (EUR 18,000) and the Netherlands (EUR 18,000)[116] impose on investors relatively high initial capital payments, other Member States provide for virtually no minimum capital (Cyprus, the United Kingdom and Ireland)[117] or only a relatively low minimum capital. E.g., Finland, Portugal, Spain and most countries having joined the EU on 1 May 2004[118](except for Hungary and Poland)[119] rank below the EU-wide average amount of approximately EUR 9,000 for limited liability companies.

(iii) Contribution Methods (cash/in-kind)

83 Contributions to capital to be made by the shareholders can usually be rendered both in cash and in kind. The latter, however, in most cases is only permitted if expressly allowed in the respective articles of association. Furthermore, most Member States require the contributions in kind to be valued by an independent auditor who, in some jurisdictions such as France, Greece and Italy –

110 "Delaware effect" describes a race to the bottom between jurisdictions as regards the legal requirements stipulated for companies. Historically the concept is derived from the struggle between Federal States in the United States – where no national corporate law exists – to attract founders with the laxest requirements on the incorporation of a company. Delaware had won this struggle, now being the State where over half of the U.S. corporations are registered. It should be mentioned, though, that this race to the bottom not only had downsides. Due to the fact that under U.S. law the courts at the corporate seat of a company have jurisdiction over corporate law issues, Delaware meanwhile has courts renowned for their corporate expertise, thus assuring very sophisticated corporate law judgments.

111 See Part 1, I, Mn. 39 et seq.

112 Article 6 Subs. 1.

113 See Part 2, CY, Mn. 50; EST, Mn. 54; SK, Mn. 61; SLO, Mn. 49.

114 See Part 2, A, Mn. 54; FIN, Mn. 63; UK, Mn. 57; H, Mn. 60.

115 See Part 2, I, Mn. 69; PL, Mn. 58.

116 See Part 2, A, Mn. 23; D, Mn. 25; GR, Mn. 18; NL, Mn. 35.

117 See Part 2, CY, Mn. 26; UK, Mn. 21; IRL, Mn. 19.

118 See Part 2, CZ, Mn. 28; EST, Mn. 25; FIN, Mn. 30; LV, Mn. 21; LT, Mn. 33; M, Mn. 20; P, Mn. 24; SK, Mn. 23; SLO, Mn. 17; E, Mn. 16.

119 See Part 2, H, Mn. 23; PL, Mn. 19.

as far as the stock corporation is concerned –[120] must be appointed by a public authority, such as a court or state ministry. Other jurisdictions, such as Germany and Italy – as far as the limited liability company is concerned –[121] only require contributions in kind to be valued in a private valuation report by the shareholders. In practice, however, even in Germany and Italy, the contribution report is usually audited as the contributor may want to ensure he is not liable to the company in the event the actual value of the in-kind contribution falls short of the value he has undertaken to contribute – a liability known in all EU jurisdictions. Some jurisdictions, such as Poland and Luxembourg, even apply a more relaxed method and make a distinction between limited liability companies where no valuation of contributions in kind is required (the value is estimated by the shareholders and the management board, but there is no requirement to back it up by private valuations), and stock corporations where the contributions in kind must be valued by an independent auditor appointed by the registration court.

(iv) Time of Contribution

Finally, most jurisdictions do not oblige shareholders to make their full contribution upon incorporation. Usually, an amount between a quarter and half of the share capital needs to be contributed at the date of incorporation and/or application for registration in the competent public register. The remaining amount is usually to be contributed to the company within a certain period of time or upon express request by the company. Only some jurisdictions, such as Denmark, Estonia, Finland, Greece, Lithuania, Luxembourg, Poland, Portugal and Sweden stipulate the requirement to contribute the entire share capital to a limited liability company upon its incorporation (if such company is only incorporated with the statutory minimum capital).[122] **84**

1.9.3 Maintenance of Capital and Liquidity

(i) System

It is believed that where shareholders have decided to provide their company with a certain share capital – irrespective of whether the respective jurisdiction obliges the shareholders to do so – it needs to be assured that the agreed contributions are indeed made to the company and that the amount remains within the company, to assure a solid financing of the company and improve protection against insolvency. While certain practical problems are handled differently in the Member States, the principles of "real capital contribution and maintenance" have generally been accepted by all EU jurisdictions. **85**

As regards stock corporations, national rules have been harmonised on the basis of the Second Directive.[123] The Member States have also implemented systems of capital contribution and maintenance for limited liability companies. These, however, are not necessarily based on the requirements of the Second Directive – which they need not be – but often apply similar (or identical) principles. **86**

(a) Stock Corporations

Rules regarding the contribution, maintenance, increase and reduction of share capital have been harmonised to a large extent by way of the Second Directive which stipulates, *inter alia*, the following:[124] **87**

- The subscribed capital must be formed of assets capable of economic assessment. Undertakings to perform work or supply services may not form part of these assets (Article 7). **88**

120 See Part 2, F, Mn. 38; GR, Mn. 18/47; I, Mn. 26.
121 See Part 2, D, Mn. 20; I, Mn. 26.
122 See Part 2, DK, Mn. 22; EST, Mn. 24; FIN, Mn. 30; GR, Mn. 18; L, Mn. 20; LT, Mn. 33; PL, Mn. 18; P, Mn. 24; S, Mn. 35.
123 See Part 1, I, Mn. 39 et seq.
124 Note that Member States may provide for stricter rules.

89 ■ Shares must not be issued at a price lower than their nominal value (Article 8).

90 ■ At the time of incorporation, at least 25 per cent of the nominal value of the shares must be paid-up. In-kind contributions must be transferred to the company within a period of five years after incorporation (Article 9).

91 ■ In-kind contributions require a valuation by independent auditors (Article 10).

92 ■ Acquisitions of assets from a founding shareholder within a period of two years after the date of incorporation for a consideration that exceeds 10 per cent of the amount of subscribed capital require the approval of the shareholders' meeting (Article 11).

93 ■ Shareholders may not be released from their obligation to pay up their contributions (Article 12).

94 ■ Distributions to shareholders need to be made out of profits or freely available reserves less any losses brought forward (Article 15). Distributions made contrary to this stipulation must be returned by the shareholders if they knew or should have known about the irregularity (Article 16).

95 ■ A loss of half of the subscribed share capital obliges the management to call a shareholders' meeting which has to decide on the measures to be taken (Article 17).

96 ■ The company may not subscribe for its own shares (Article 18).

97 ■ The company generally is not allowed to acquire its own shares. The main exception to this rule is an authorisation by the shareholders' meeting given for a period not exceeding 18 months, entitling the company to acquire own shares not exceeding 10 per cent of the subscribed share capital if the acquired shares are fully paid-up and the acquisition does not result in the balance sheet equity falling below the subscribed capital plus other reserves which may not be distributed under the relevant company law (Article 19).

98 ■ Rights attached to shares are suspended as long as the shares are held by the company; a reserve unavailable for distribution needs to be created on the liabilities side of the balance sheet as long as the company holds own shares (Article 22).

99 ■ A company may not finance the acquisition of own shares by a third party (Article 23) and generally should not accept own shares as security (Article 24).

100 ■ In the case of a capital increase, the old shareholders generally need to be granted a pre-emptive right for the new shares (Article 29).

101 ■ In the case of a reduction of share capital, the creditors may claim security for claims which have not fallen due by the date of the publication of the reduction (Article 32).

102 ■ A reduction of the subscribed capital may not lead to the subscribed share capital falling below the minimum amount of share capital (Article 34).

(b) Limited Liability Companies

103 As indicated, the EU jurisdictions also provide for a sophisticated system ensuring both the actual initial contribution of the share capital to the company and its later maintenance where limited liability companies are concerned. Some countries apply concepts similar to those known for stock corporations, others have adopted regulations which are only applicable in their respective jurisdictions. In the following we highlight some national regulations of particular interest, thereby trying to illustrate – without being exhaustive – where common standards are applicable and in which ways capital maintenance can be addressed differently.[125]

Legal Reserve

104 The requirement to create a legal reserve in addition to the subscribed share capital – known in all European stock corporations – is also applicable for Belgian, Czech, Estonian, French and Luxembourg limited liability companies, where profits have to be put into such legal reserve until

125 Distributions, shareholder loans and the acquisition of own shares and related financing are addressed below; see Mn. 108 et seq./131 et seq./116 et seq.

it has reached an amount of 10 per cent of the share capital.[126] This reserve is only available for the compensation of losses and cannot be distributed.

Hidden contributions in kind

Some countries also require the approval of the shareholders in shareholders' meeting for transactions of the company with (founding) shareholders when these transactions exceed a specific amount within a certain period of time; a principle also known in all EU stock corporations. The relevant legal provisions intend to avoid circumvention of strict regulations on in-kind contributions by contributing cash at a first stage and, at a later stage, selling an asset to the company without having audited the value of the respective asset (so-called hidden contributions in kind). Countries applying this principle are the Czech Republic, Denmark, Luxembourg, Poland, Slovakia and Sweden.[127] The Czech Republic and Slovakia oblige the management to seek shareholders' approval if the transaction with the shareholder exceeds 10 per cent of the share capital and takes place within three and two years, respectively, after the date of incorporation and also requires the consideration to be valued by an independent auditor. Denmark requires approval if (i) the transaction exceeds 10 per cent of the share capital, and an amount of approximately EUR 6,715, (ii) is not an ordinary business transaction, and (iii) takes place within a period of 24 months. The same period applies for Poland where the transaction has to exceed 25 per cent of the share capital and an amount of approximately EUR 12,000. Luxembourg and Sweden also apply the 24-months period but have a 10 per cent threshold as regards the value of the transaction. Germany is aware of the same problem and has taken a more rigid approach. So-called hidden contributions in kind are treated as completely invalid – irrespective of their value in relation to the total share capital – and the shareholder concerned remains obliged to render (again) his cash contribution in total.[128] **105**

Loss of share capital

Most EU jurisdictions stipulate the requirement that the shareholders' meeting has to be called by the management if a certain portion of the registered share capital – usually 50 per cent – is lost. The shareholders' meeting will have to decide on the appropriate measures to be taken. In Italy, the management will already have to call the shareholders' meeting after a loss of one third of the share capital.[129] In this regard it is interesting to note that under current Finnish law the shareholders are obliged to put the company into liquidation in a second shareholders' meeting if it had been resolved in a prior meeting to continue business and in a period of 12 months at least half of the share capital has not been restored.[130] **106**

Capital reductions

Common law jurisdictions and continental European countries treat reductions of registered share capital in a slightly differing manner. Most continental European countries, such as Germany, generally provide for a procedure under which the plan to reduce the share capital must be published, claims of creditors must be settled or secured, a shareholders' resolution must be adopted and finally the reduction must be registered. Simplified procedures are allowed in certain cases if no actual distributions will be made but losses are to be settled on the balance sheet only. The Anglo-Saxon system,[131] on the other hand, requires an express court approval as well as an authorisation in the articles of association, a "special resolution" by the shareholders, and ultimately the registration/publication of the reduction. The court will take into account whether interests of creditors are sufficiently protected and shareholders are treated equally. Upon the court's approval the registrar will be allowed to register the reduction. Malta[132] has in principle adapted the continental European system but provides that no prior information of creditors is necessary. In turn, however, the **107**

126 See Part 2, B, Mn. 22; CZ, Mn. 33; EST, Mn. 29; F, Mn. 102; L, Mn.25.
127 See Part 2, CZ, Mn. 33; DK, Mn. 24; L, Mn. 22; PL, Mn. 21; S, Mn. 42; SK, Mn. 24.
128 See Part 2, D, Mn. 27/65.
129 See Part 2, I, Mn. 28 et seq.
130 See Part 2, FIN, Mn. 34 (about to be changed under the new Finnish legislation entering into force on 1 September 2006).
131 Applied by Cyprus, United Kingdom and Ireland; see Part 2, CY, Mn. 27/51;IRL, Mn. 20; UK, Mn. 31.
132 See Part 2, M, Mn. 24.

reduction does not become valid unless no creditor objections have arisen within three months after registration.

(ii) Distributions

108 As a general rule, distributions to shareholders may only be made in the form of dividends, proceeds resulting from a formal reduction of the registered share capital and liquidation proceeds.

109 Distributions in the form of dividends are in general only allowed out of the net profits of the company or reserves available for the purpose of distribution after deduction of losses carried forward and amounts to be put into a legal reserve (if applicable in the respective jurisdiction).

(a) Minimum Dividend

110 Some EU jurisdictions provide for a minimum dividend. In Greece[133] the shareholders of a stock corporation are entitled to a so-called first dividend in the amount of 6 per cent of the paid up share capital, provided the company has generated sufficient profit. The shareholders of Portuguese limited liability companies and stock corporations[134] can demand that 50 per cent of the distributable profits are paid to the shareholders unless the articles of association provide otherwise or the shareholders have resolved otherwise with a three-quarter majority. Swedish law[135] provides that a minority of at least 10 per cent of the shareholders can request that, after certain deductions, 50 per cent of the net profit of a business year is distributed as dividends. The same applies to Finnish companies where, however, the minority may not demand a distribution exceeding 8 per cent of the company's equity.[136]

111 German law applies a different concept for its limited liability companies on the basis of the rulings of its Federal Supreme Court ensuring an equitable dividend for minority shareholders.[137] The basic idea of these regulations is to avoid majority shareholders exploiting minority shareholders by retaining the entire profits in the company.

(b) Interim Dividends

112 Interim dividends, i.e. advance dividends not based on approved annual accounts for the past business year, are allowed in most EU jurisdictions. An interim dividend can be distributed if the management of a company, acting as a prudent businessman, on the basis of an interim balance sheet is of the opinion that the annual accounts at the end of a business year will show a distributable profit justifying the advance payment to the shareholders. It goes without saying that interim dividends are only possible where the restricted share capital of the company is not infringed.

113 Whilst most countries allowing interim dividends leave this decision to the management,[138] other countries, such as Germany (if a limited liability company is concerned) and Hungary require a shareholders' resolution to authorise an advance payment to the shareholders.[139]

114 Czech, Estonian, Latvian, Finnish and Slovak laws do not allow interim dividends.[140] The same applies to Austria and Belgium as far as the limited liability company is concerned.[141] Slovakia does not allow interim dividends as regards its stock corporations.[142] In Germany, interim dividends by stock corporations are not allowed before the end of a business year and may only be granted under

133 See Part 2, GR, Mn. 51.
134 See Part 2, P, Mn. 31/68.
135 See Part 2, S, Mn. 41/74.
136 See Part 2, FIN, Mn. 35/65.
137 See Part 2, D, Mn.30.
138 See e.g. Part 2, B, Mn. 52 (as relates to the stock corporation); CY, Mn. 28/52; F, Mn. 41/78/103; IRL, Mn. 22/43; M, Mn. 25/55; NL, Mn. 40/71; PL, Mn. 26/60; UK, Mn. 27/61.
139 See Part 2, D, Mn. 31; H, Mn. 28/67.
140 See Part 2, CZ, Mn. 36; EST, Mn. 30; FIN, Mn. 36 et seq./65 (likely to be changed under new Finnish Companies Act); LV, Mn. 25; SK, Mn. 27/64; S, Mn. 43/74.
141 See Part 2, A, Mn. 27; B, Mn. 23.
142 See Part 2, SK, Mn. 64.

certain circumstances on the basis of annual accounts (already drawn-up but not yet approved by the shareholders), if so allowed in the articles of association and sanctioned by a resolution of the board of directors.[143] This is, however, a rare occurrence in practice. A similar principle is applied in Luxembourg.[144] Under a different concept for the limited liability company, German law allows for a quasi-interim dividend: On the basis of a shareholders' resolution the capital reserve of the company can be dissolved and the reserved amount be paid out anytime during the fiscal year of the company.[145]

In Sweden, likewise, interim dividends are not allowed in either type of companies. Interestingly, however, a company can declare dividends at extraordinary shareholders' meetings, based on a balance sheet adopted at an earlier shareholders' meeting, adjusted for previously declared and distributed dividends. Such dividends can be declared until the next annual shareholders' meeting where the new annual accounts are adopted.[146] **115**

(iii) Acquisition of Own Shares and Related Financing

A company may be interested in acquiring its own shares for a number of purposes, the main reasons being the use of its shares for employee participation programmes, their use as an acquisition currency in M&A transactions or – as far as listed companies are concerned – in order to achieve an improvement in the stock market price. On the other hand, the acquisition of own shares by a company bears the risk of endangering the company's solvency and infringing the restricted share capital (as the shares are not assets which can be used for the settlement of third party claims in insolvency or liquidation proceedings). The same applies if a company accepts its own shares as a security. Similar problems can occur if a company grants loans or other forms of financial assistance to facilitate the acquisition of its shares by a third party. **116**

In light of this concern, Member States have implemented rules ensuring that the share capital is actually contributed to the company and that the capital maintenance rules are not circumvented by the acquisition of own shares. **117**

(a) Acquisition of Own Shares by Stock Corporations

As regards stock corporations, regulations on the acquisition of own shares have been harmonised on the basis of the Second Directive.[147] Article 18 of the Second Directive stipulates that stock corporations may not subscribe for their own shares. Acquisitions of own shares at a later stage are only allowed if such an acquisition is authorised by the shareholders in a shareholders' meeting. Article 19 of the Second Directive states that the authorisation may only be granted for a period of up to 18 months and the nominal value of the acquired shares may not exceed 10 per cent of the subscribed share capital. The proposed acquisition may not result in the net assets of the company falling below the total amount of the subscribed share capital and the undistributable reserves, and only fully paid-up shares can be acquired. **118**

The Second Directive does stipulate some exemptions from these restrictions, above all where the acquisition is necessary to prevent a serious and imminent harm to the company or where the shares are used for distribution to the company's employees or employees of an associated company, provided the distribution of such shares occurs within 12 months after the acquisition. **119**

The Member States are allowed to provide for further exemptions in very limited cases such as the acquisition of shares in the course of a reduction of the share capital, the acquisition of shares as a result of a universal transfer of assets, the acquisition of fully paid-up shares free of charge or the acquisition of shares by virtue of a legal obligation or resulting from a court ruling. Most Member States have made use of these further exemptions. Where they have done so, the shares acquired **120**

143 See Part 2, D, Mn. 66.
144 See Part 2, L, Mn. 65.
145 See Part 2, D, Mn. 31.
146 See Part 2, S, Mn. 43/74.
147 See Part 1, I, Mn. 39 et seq.

by way of one of these further exemptions must be disposed of within not more than three years after the acquisition, unless the aggregate nominal value of these shares does not exceed 10 per cent of the subscribed capital. Otherwise, these shares must be cancelled (Article 20 of the Second Directive).

121 Rights attached to shares held by the company itself, including, *inter alia*, the voting right, are suspended for the period in which the company holds the shares. Furthermore, Article 22 of the Second Directive states that if the shares are included among the assets shown in the balance sheet, a reserve of the same amount must be created on the equity and liabilities side of the balance sheet and must be unavailable for distribution.

122 The above rules apply equally to the company accepting its own shares as security.

(b) Acquisition of Own Shares by Limited Liability Companies

123 Equal to stock corporations, the Member States entirely prohibit a limited liability company from subscribing for its own shares. This is due to the concept that the share capital – irrespective of how low it may be in each jurisdiction – must actually be contributed to the company.

124 Most EU jurisdictions also prohibit the acquisition of own shares by the company at a later point in time.[148] Where a company in these jurisdictions receives own shares by means other than an acquisition (e.g. due to the enforcement of a court ruling against one of its shareholders, or by way of global succession under a merger or spin-off) it is obliged to dispose of these shares within a short period of time, e.g., in Austria without undue delay[149] and in Latvia within one year.[150]

125 Estonia, Finland, Germany, the United Kingdom, Hungary, Ireland, Lithuania, Malta, Poland, Portugal and Slovenia allow the acquisition of own shares by a limited liability company, at least under certain conditions.[151] All these jurisdictions, other than Germany and Slovenia, at least require the authorisation by the shareholders' meeting. Some of these countries provide for further restrictions. Ireland and Lithuania, e.g., limit the maximum interest to be held by the company itself to 10 per cent of the share capital; Hungary applies a one-third threshold. Estonia, Hungary and Poland oblige the company to dispose of all of the acquired shares within one year after the acquisition while Finland requires the companies to do so in three years.

126 In this regard Germany is the most liberal jurisdiction as it allows the acquisition of own shares by a limited liability company without any special statutory restrictions. It goes without saying, however, that in all jurisdictions where such acquisitions are allowed, they are only permitted for fully paid-up shares. Furthermore, the acquisition may not result in an infringement of the restricted share capital and may not leave the company with no shareholders.

(c) Financial Assistance

127 A stock corporation is not allowed to advance funds, make loans, grant security or any other form of financial assistance related to the acquisition of its own shares by a third party (Article 23 of the Second Directive). The only two exceptions allowed in this regard are transactions by banks and other financial institutions in their normal course of business and transactions relating to the acquisition of shares by the company's employees or employees of an associated company.

128 In jurisdictions where the acquisition of own shares by a limited liability company is not allowed those companies are also not allowed to grant any financial assistance in connection with the acquisition of their own shares, above all by way of granting loans to a potential third party buyer. The same applies to Estonian, Finnish and Portuguese limited liabilities companies, although they are allowed to acquire their own shares.[152]

148 See e.g. Part 2, A, Mn. 29; CY, Mn. 29; CZ, Mn. 37; DK, Mn. 27; GR, Mn. 24; I, Mn. 33; LV, Mn. 27; PL, Mn. 27; SK, Mn. 28; E, Mn. 19.

149 See Part 2, A, Mn. 29.

150 See Part 2, LV, Mn. 27.

151 See Part 2, EST, Mn. 31; FIN, Mn. 38; D, Mn. 32; H, Mn. 29; IRL, Mn. 23 et seq.; LT, Mn. 39; M, Mn. 26 et seq.; P, Mn. 32 et seq.; SLO, Mn. 23.

152 See Part 2, EST, Mn. 33; FIN, Mn. 40; P, Mn. 34.

The "white-wash" procedure regarding financial assistance is peculiar to the United Kingdom and Ireland. Although *prima facie* prohibited, a limited liability company may provide financial assistance provided the directors make a statutory declaration of solvency and the financial assistance is approved by a special resolution of the shareholders.[153] This resolution can be contested before court by minority shareholders holding at least 10 per cent of the subscribed share capital. This Anglo-Saxon approach regarding financial assistance, contrary to the continental European approach, is not focused on the strict maintenance of a certain balance sheet number (i.e. the share capital) but purely on the solvency of the company for which the directors become liable by way of the declaration of solvency. **129**

Interesting in this regard is Italy, where loans in the context of certain M&A transactions used to be seen as a violation of rules on financial assistance. In January 2004 the Italian legislator introduced a kind of "safe harbour", which now allows – under certain circumstance – the financing of an acquisition vehicle by way of shareholder loans and the subsequent merger of the indebted acquisition vehicle with the target of the M&A transaction.[154] **130**

(iv) Company as Lender or Guarantor

The lending of money by a company to a third party or a shareholder bears three main practical risks. First, the company may be using its funds for a purpose other than its object of business as set forth in its articles of association. Second, interest to be paid by a shareholder as borrower may be below market terms and thus circumvent specific rules regarding distributions to shareholders. Third, liquidity may be transferred to a shareholder while the balance sheet is not affected. The granting of a security by a company provides further problems to the extent that the company does not receive any consideration or benefit for the security but solely enters into a risk which may be unpredictable. **131**

While some EU jurisdictions deal with these problems on the basis of general rules (directors' duties etc.), they are addressed specifically by the majority.[155] **132**

Most Member States have taken a liberal stance as regards the lending of funds by a company to third party borrowers or shareholders or the securing of third party or shareholder loans by the company through guarantees, mortgages or other means of security. To avoid hidden distributions circumventing national regulations on distributions to shareholders, some of those countries, however, require the loans to be made at arm's length terms.[156] **133**

Germany at first sight could be considered the most liberal jurisdiction regarding loans to shareholders, at least when considering the limited liability company. However, this first impression in reality turns out to be theoretical. Although the loan does not even have to reflect market conditions as long as the registered share capital is maintained,[157] rules become stricter where the registered share capital is partially lost. Under those circumstances a loan is only considered legal if it is made at arm's length terms, is in the best interests of the company and is fully secured and consequently there is no reasonable doubt that the repayment claim of the company will be honoured. Earlier liberal approaches had in practice enabled abusive actions by shareholders and thus led to severe rulings by the German Federal Supreme Court holding shareholders liable for "actions endangering the existence of a company",[158] a concept the scope of which is difficult to determine and which leaves a high level of uncertainty as to the legality of group financing by way of up-stream loans/guarantees, cash-pools etc. **134**

Other jurisdictions are likewise reluctant in allowing loans or securities by the company and make use of the concept of "commercial justification" or "corporate benefit". This concept means that **135**

153 See Part 2, UK, Mn. 33; IRL, Mn. 25. In the UK the white-wash procedure additionally requires an assessment of the company's solvency by the auditors of the company.

154 See Part 2, I, Mn. 33.

155 Although problems regarding financial assistance in the acquisition of own shares do fall within the scope of company lending, they are not addressed in this Section but can be found under Mn. 133.

156 See Part 2, D, Mn. 35/69; IRL, Mn. 26/46; M, Mn. 30/58; SLO, Mn. 25/53.

157 Note, however, that an interest below market conditions may be taxable income.

158 See Part 2, D, Mn. 23 and Mn. 62.

any loan or security granted by the company needs to be within the company's object of business as stipulated in its constitutional documents and has to lead to a benefit for the company. Austria, Belgium and Cyprus apply this principle to the granting of security by the company.[159] The United Kingdom, Italy, Latvia and Luxembourg require a corporate benefit for both the granting of a loan (irrespective if to a third party or a shareholder) and the granting of security.[160]

136 The Baltic and Scandinavian Member States provide for different rules in this regard. Denmark, Estonia and Sweden generally prohibit loans to shareholders (but allow loans to third parties if in the best interests of the company). However, they do allow the granting of loans to parent companies (in Denmark only to parent companies incorporated in the EU/EEC) or other group companies.[161] Finland only allows a loan to be granted to a shareholder out of freely distributable assets and against the granting of a security, although there is a bill underway relaxing these restrictions and which, once in force, will only apply general principles on the equal treatment of shareholders and on respecting the object of the company.[162] Latvia and Lithuania generally allow the granting of loans and securities in favour of third parties and shareholders. Latvia, however, applies a rule under which the transaction may be void if it triggers the insolvency of the company and the parties were aware of the circumstances.[163] Lithuania allows the granting of loans to third parties and shareholders under the condition that interests out of these loans may not form a significant part of the income of the company and further provided that the funds granted under the loans do not exceed the amount of the company's equity capital.[164]

(v) Company as Borrower

137 In principle, shareholders are free in the financing of their company, i.e. they can freely decide whether and to what extent they want to contribute new equity to the company or to provide it with shareholder loans.[165]

138 The freedom to finance the company as the shareholders wish becomes problematic as soon as the company comes close to insolvency. The majority of creditors do not notice such financial difficulties until the company has applied for insolvency proceedings. Shareholders of closely held companies with more detailed insight into the financials of their companies often have such knowledge at an earlier point in time. As prudent business people they would decide at this stage to supply the company with more equity capital or to put it into liquidation or insolvency proceedings. Very often, however, faced with such a situation, shareholders tend to finance a company with a loan or to suspend a repayment claim regarding a shareholder loan which has fallen due. In light of creditor protection this is problematic behaviour as a shareholder would thereby obtain a preferred ranking for his claims by devious means. This is because in insolvency proceedings such a loan repayment claim generally would be considered as ranking equal with usual third party claims, which are to be satisfied before the capital contributions of the shareholders[166] can be repaid.

139 Nevertheless, most EU Member States believe that such problems are sufficiently addressed by the rules of insolvency law, which usually allow the insolvency administrator to nullify certain transactions which have occurred within a specific time period before the company has entered into insolvency. Additionally, insolvency laws severely punish actions of deliberate creditor discrimination by way of criminal law. Therefore, Belgium, the Czech Republic, Denmark, Estonia, Finland, France, the United Kingdom, Greece (as far as the limited liability company is concerned),

159 See Part 2, A, Mn. 31/61; B, Mn. 26/56; CY, Mn. 30/54.
160 See Part 2, UK, Mn. 34/67; I, Mn. 34/74; LV, Mn. 29/54; L, Mn. 30/70.
161 See Part 2, DK, Mn. 29/61; EST, Mn. 34/63; S, Mn. 46 et seq./78.
162 See Part 2, FIN, Mn. 41/68.
163 See Part 2, LV, Mn. 29/54.
164 See Part 2, LT, Mn. 42/73.
165 Note, however, that a certain equity/debt ratio may be required under national thin capitalisation rules. Thin capitalisation rules intend to hinder foreign shareholders to disguise actual profits of a company as interests under the loan and thus to move profits from a country with high tax rates to a country with lower tax rates. Tax law, however, is not addressed in more detail in this publication.
166 Capital contributions are subordinated to all other claims of the company's creditors.

Hungary, Ireland, Luxembourg, Malta, Slovakia, Spain and Sweden do not have specific rules on shareholder loans given to the company and shareholder security granted in favour of the company in the case of a financial crisis of the company.[167]

Austria, Germany, Greece (as far as the stock corporation is concerned), Italy, Poland, Portugal **140**
and Slovenia provide for rules avoiding the above-mentioned preferred ranking of the shareholder loans in case of insolvency proceedings. Under Portuguese law, shareholder loans in general are to be considered as subordinated debt in the case of an insolvency of the company, irrespective of whether they were granted during a crisis of the company or not.[168] Austria considers shareholder loans granted by a controlling shareholder (holding more than 25 per cent or otherwise having a controlling influence on the company) as equity – and thus last ranking in insolvency proceedings – if those loans were granted during a crisis of the company.[169] The same rule applies to stock corporations in Germany and Slovenia and – irrespective of the percentage of interest held by the shareholder – to German and Slovenian limited liability companies.[170] Greece applies this rule to stock corporations where the shareholder has a "dominant influence".[171] Poland makes use of this rule in relation to loans granted by shareholders of limited liability companies or stock corporations if the loan agreement was concluded within two years of the beginning of the company's insolvency proceedings.[172]

Note, however, that in practice loans by shareholders in the other jurisdictions – like the UK – **141**
are often subordinated at the request of lending banks or other third party creditors.[173]

1.10 Publication and Filing Requirements

It is recognised throughout the EU that maintaining commercial registers and making certain in- **142**
formation with regard to both limited liability companies and stock corporations publicly available is important to ensure that shareholders, creditors and other third parties have a degree of transparency regarding the legal nature, financial strength and operations of the corporate entity they are either participating in or contracting with.

Each Member State differs in the exact nature and scope of the information to be made public **143**
but, as a minimum, complies with the provisions of the First Directive and Fourth Directive.[174] Consequently, the constitutional documents, the appointment and termination of directors and officers, the amount of share capital subscribed, a balance sheet and profit and loss account,[175] the registered office and details of any winding-up or the appointment of any liquidators are all documents or information which have to be provided and kept updated (e.g., through the submission of annual returns).[176] This information often has to be supplemented by further disclosures, such as shareholder lists or registers, director and shareholder resolutions, the disapplication of pre-emption rights and authorities to allot shares. Certain jurisdictions (e.g. Spain)[177] may impose additional publicity obligations in the event there are foreign shareholders or investors. Stock corporations will generally have greater publication obligations which increase further if listed.

The information to be made public must be filed at the relevant commercial register usually **144**
within certain deadlines and, in relation to particular corporate acts, these may only have effect

167 See Part 2, B, Mn. 27/57; CZ, Mn. 427/85, DK; Mn: 30/62; EST, Mn. 36/64; FIN, Mn. 42/69; F, Mn. 47/78/107; GR, Mn. 26; H, Mn. 32/75; IRL, Mn. 27/47; L, Mn. 31/71; M, Mn. 31/59; SK, Mn. 32/68; E, Mn. 22/47; S, Mn. 52/79; UK, Mn. 36/68.

168 See Part 2, P, Mn. 39/74.

169 See Part 2, A, Mn. 32/62.

170 See Part 2, D, Mn. 70; SLO, Mn. 54.

171 See Part 2, GR, Mn. 55.

172 See Part 2, PL, Mn. 32/64.

173 See Part 2, UK, Mn. 36/68.

174 See Part 1, I, Mn. 38 and 48 et seq.

175 Though there are specific exclusions for some corporate forms.

176 Required, e.g., in Cyprus, the United Kingdom and Ireland; see Part 2, CY, Mn. 32/56; IRL, Mn. 28/48; UK, Mn. 37 et seq./69.

177 See Part 2, E, Mn 23.

once actually placed on the register. Alongside a duty to make information public at the commercial register, there may be an obligation to publish it in a specific newspaper or official gazette.

145 The commercial registers themselves are organised on an either central[178] or local basis (either maintained at the local registry or court).[179] Almost all may be inspected by any member of the general public[180] with a number also providing online access (e.g. the Czech Republic, Denmark, Estonia, Finland, Germany (in part), Slovakia, Sweden and the United Kingdom).[181] The extent, however, to which an individual may rely upon the information contained in the commercial register varies from Member State to Member State, with Germany and France,[182] e.g., allowing the general public a high degree of reliance on accuracy of the information published, and Member States such as the United Kingdom preferring the registers to act as, in effect, simple depositories for corporate documents.

146 A failure to file may result in fines being levied on either the management or the company. National differences, however, exist as regards the enforcement of such fines in practice. Whilst German commercial registers are usually very reluctant to fine a company unless a third party applies for the fine to be levied, others, such as Ireland and the United Kingdom enforce them on a strict basis and, in the event of persistent violations, may cause the company to be removed from the companies' register.[183]

1.11 Financial Reporting

147 Accounting standards have been much in focus since the Enron and WorldCom scandals and significant attempts have been made to improve and harmonise financial reporting on a global basis.

1.11.1 Accounting Standards

148 In Europe a significant step towards uniform financial reporting and transparency was taken when the Council of Ministers approved Regulation 1606/2002 pursuant to which all EU companies listed on a regulated exchange are under an obligation as of 1 January 2005 to prepare their consolidated financial statements in accordance with IAS/IFRS. Whereas individual Member States could have extended such obligations to other corporate entities (including non-listed companies) and to annual accounts, this has, almost without exception, not been the preferred approach, with a significant number looking to retain local GAAP and ensure a controlled convergence with international standards over time, using the Modernisation Directive[184] as a tool to achieve that goal.

149 In the majority of the European jurisdictions, therefore, local GAAP continue to form the basis for the preparation of annual financial statements of listed companies. Cyprus[185] and Malta[186] are the sole jurisdictions in which IAS/IFRS are applied instead of local GAAP (both for listed and non-listed companies), whilst in other countries, as for example Denmark, Germany (for information purposes only), Luxembourg, the Netherlands, and the UK[187], IAS/IFRS may be used by listed companies also in annual financial statements. Other member states such as Estonia, Italy, Lithuaniaand Slovenia even require this[188]. Although local GAAP are prevalent, many jurisdictions allow the use of IAS/IFRS where local GAAP are silent. This is particularly the case in the new Member States.[189]

178 See e.g. Part 2,, B, Mn. 28; CY, Mn. 23 et seq.; CZ, Mn. 44 et seq.; DK, Mn. 31; EST, Mn. 37; FIN, Mn. 43; UK, Mn. 376; IRL, Mn. 28; LT, Mn. 46; L, Mn. 33; M, Mn. 32; S, Mn. 53.
179 See e.g. Part 2, F, Mn. 50; D, Mn. 39; GR, Mn. 27; H, Mn. 33; I, Mn. 36; SLO, Mn. 27; E, Mn. 23.
180 In Greece it is necessary to show a legitimate interest: see Part 2, GR, Mn. 27.
181 See Part 2, CZ, Mn. 44; D, Mn. 40; DK, Mn. 31; FIN, Mn. 45; EST, Mn. 37; UK, Mn. 37; SK, Mn. 34; S, Mn. 53.
182 See Part 2, D, Mn. 39; F, Mn. 49.
183 See Part 2, IRL, Mn. 28; UK, Mn. 37; SLO, Mn. 28.
184 See Part 1, I, Mn. 54.
185 See Part 2, CY, Mn. 35.
186 See Part 2, M, Mn. 33
187 See Part 2. DK, Mn. 64; L. Mn. 34/74; D Mn. 41/72; UK, Mn. 70.
188 See Part 2, EST, Mn. 66; I, Mn. 77; LT, Mn. 76 and SLO, Mn. 29/58.
189 See e.g. Part 2, PL, Mn. 35/66

With respect to non-listed companies, the situation is again rather complex. As far as the use of IAS/IFRS in the consolidated financial statements is concerned, this is allowed inter alia in Belgium, the Czech Republic,Denmark, Estonia, Finland, France, Germany, Greece, Hungary, Ireland, Spain, Slovakia and the UK[190]. Sometimes special conditions must be satisfied. 150

As far as the use of IAS/IFRS in the annual financial statements is concerned, this is allowed for example in Estonia, Finland, Germany (for information purposes only), Greece, Italy, Ireland and Luxembourg.[191] Here again, special conditions may have to be satisfied. No Member States apart from Cyprus and Malta[192] require the use of IAS/IFRS in the annual financial statements, except, in some cases, for banks and/or insurance undertakings.[193]

1.11.2 Formal Requirements

Irrespective of the reporting standards used, there has been a considerable extent of EU-wide harmonisation as to the form of the financial statements and in related auditing and filing obligations. The Fourth Directive[194] introduced common rules for the annual accounts of companies. It prescribed, *inter alia*, the layout of the balance sheet and the profit and loss accounts, the annual report, certain valuation rules and mandatory audit requirements. The rules on consolidated group accounts were further elaborated in the Seventh Directive.[195] The said harmonisation efforts offer shareholders and other third parties greater transparency by ensuring in the entire EU comparability and equivalence in the format of financial information of companies which have to be made available to the public. 151

Annual financial statements (i.e. annual accounts) must therefore comprise a balance sheet, a profit and loss account and notes to the accounts. They will often be accompanied by an annual report , although small companies may be relieved from this requirement in some jurisdictions. 152

The financial statements for both limited liability companies and stock corporations in the EU are normally required to be drawn up on an annual basis[196] and must be approved by the shareholders' meeting and filed with the relevant commercial register. Timings vary significantly, with the majority of Member States requiring the financial statements to be prepared and presented to the annual shareholders' meeting within a three to six-months period, though Cyprus and the United Kingdom have longer periods. 153

Member States have, however, taken different approaches with regard to auditing requirements. While the general rule prescribed by the Fourth Directive is that both limited liability companies and stock corporations must have their financial statements audited, only some jurisdictions have made use of the possibility to give relief from the auditing requirement for small companies which do not exceed the thresholds defined in the Fourth Directive. Among these are Belgium, the Czech Republic, Estonia, Germany, the United Kingdom, Latvia, Lithuania, Luxembourg and Slovakia.[197] 154

1.12 Employee Participation in Corporate Bodies

The participation of employees in an enterprise has to be considered from two different angles. On the one hand, employees may take part in taking certain operational decisions – e.g., by consultation requirements in case of dismissals and restructurings – through unions, works councils, etc. 155

190 See Part 2, B, Mn. 29; CZ, Mn. 47; DK, Mn. 32; EST, Mn. 38; F, Mn. 52; FIN, Mn. 52; D. Mn. 46; GR, Mn. 28; H Mn. 39; IRL, Mn. 30; E, Mn. 25; SK, Mn. 25; UK, Mn. 39.

191 See Part 2, EST, Mn. 37; FIN, Mn. 46; D, Mn. 41; GR, Mn. 28; IRL, Mn. 29; L, Mn. 34.

192 See Part 2, Mn. 152.

193 See e.g. Part 2, EST, Mn. 26; I, Mn. 77.

194 See Part 1, I, Mn. 48 et seq.

195 See Part 1, I, Mn. 51.

196 Listed stock corporations may be obliged to additionally draw up and disclose quarterly statements under security exchange laws.

197 See Part 2, B, Mn. 29/59; EST, Mn. 38/66; CZ, Mn. 47/87; D, Mn. 42/72; UK, Mn. 38/71; L, Mn. 13/50; LT, Mn. 49/76; LV, Mn. 34/57; SK, Mn. 37/70.

These aspects traditionally form part of the labour law and have no direct influence on the corporate structure.

156 On the other hand, a considerable number of European countries also provide for employee participation at the level of the corporate bodies of companies. In these countries a number of employee representatives are granted membership at (management or supervisory) board level with all duties and liabilities of an ordinary board member, thereby giving the employees a considerable degree of influence in the corporate decision making process.

157 Employee representation in corporate bodies of private companies is alien to Belgium, Cyprus, Estonia, the United Kingdom, France, Greece, Ireland, Italy, Latvia, Lithuania, Malta, Poland, Portugal and Spain.[198]

158 The countries which provide for employee representation in corporate bodies are Austria, the Czech Republic, Denmark, Finland, Germany, Hungary, Luxembourg, the Netherlands, Slovakia (with regard to stock corporations only), Slovenia and Sweden. The board members representing the employees are usually either directly appointed by the employees or nominated by them and formally appointed by the shareholders. Whilst the mentioned countries all have in common[199] the aspect of employee representation in both the limited liability companies and stock corporations, they differ considerably as to the applicable thresholds triggering the requirement and as to the level of influence given to the employee representative.

159 Employee representation in the Czech Republic,[200] Denmark,[201] Slovakia[202] and Sweden[203] is required where the workforce in the corporate entity is at a level far below 100 employees. Other countries, such as Germany[204] (although having a reputation for a high level of employee participation) and Luxembourg,[205] require a minimum work force of 500 or more employees to trigger such a requirement.

160 The level of influence granted to employees differs in both the number of employees to be placed in a corporate body and in the (merely supervisory or more significant managerial) function of this corporate body. Since Denmark, Luxembourg and Sweden provide for a one-tier board system,[206] employee representatives are automatically involved in certain managerial decisions to be taken.[207] This aspect is not common to most countries having a two-tier board system, although Slovenian companies with more than 500 employees and German companies having more than 2,000 employees or, if they belong to the coal and steel industry, having more than 1,000 employees need to provide for a so-called "labour director" at the managerial board level. This labour director has the same duties and liabilities as all other executive directors, but internally will be primarily responsible for labour and social matters.

161 The countries applying a two-tier board system usually require that one-third of the total number of members of the supervisory board should consist of employee representatives. Germany provides an exception to this as far as companies with a workforce exceeding 2,000 employees are concerned, where half of the members of the supervisory board must be employee representatives. In all jurisdictions, however, the employee representatives can always be overruled, e.g. by a casting vote of the chairman who is always appointed by the shareholders' side.

198 See Part 2, B, Mn. 31; CY, Mn. 36; EST, Mn. 39; F, Mn. 53; GR, Mn. 29; IRL, Mn. 30; I, Mn. 38; LV, Mn. 35; LT, Mn. 50; M, Mn. 34; PL, Mn. 36; P, Mn. 43; E, Mn. 26; UK, Mn. 40; note that in some of these countries employee participation is known in state-owned businesses (see e.g. Greece, Part 2, GR, Mn. 29) or former state-owned businesses (the latter as regards Poland, PL, Mn. 36/67). France in certain cases also allows employee representatives to attend board meetings. They, however, do not have voting rights, F, Mn. 53.

199 In Luxembourg only with respect to the S.A..

200 See Part 2, CZ, Mn. 48/89.

201 See Part 2, DK, Mn. 34/65 et seq.

202 See Part 2, SK, Mn. 71.

203 See Part 2, S, Mn. 57/82.

204 See Part 2, D, Mn. 42/73.

205 See Part 2, L, Mn. 35/75.

206 See Part 2, DK, Mn. 10/50; L, Mn. 75; S, Mn. 13/67.

207 Not necessarily relating to the day-to-day business.

Interestingly, in Finland the company may freely choose whether the employees should be represented on the supervisory board, the board of directors or in the management.[208] 162

2 Conclusion

With its judgments on the free movement of the *de facto* seat of companies the ECJ has created new opportunities for investors in Europe. Entrepreneurs can now chose between a variety of stock corporations and limited liability companies from various EU jurisdictions irrespective in which Member State they actually intend to carry out their business. 163

Those jurisdictions whose types of corporations are available (i.e. who allow their corporations to be 'exported' to another Member State) comprise at present:

- Cyprus
- Czech Republic
- Denmark
- Estonia
- France (likely)
- Finland
- Italy
- Latvia
- Lithuania
- Malta
- the Netherlands
- Poland
- Sweden
- United Kingdom

as well as, in our view (although not yet confirmed by local case law):

- Belgium
- Portugal
- Slovakia

and (although of less practical use):

- Luxembourg
- Slovenia

Before making such a choice the investor, however, will have to review in detail to what extent corporate forms from other jurisdictions actually do offer a more preferential framework.

Irrespective thereof, any investor doing a location check to find the best place within the EU to set up a subsidiary (e.g., as a sub-holding of its European activities) has to take into account, *inter alia*, also the types of corporations available within the respective EU Member State. Thus, also those jurisdictions come into play which do not allow their corporate entities to be 'exported' to other Member State, i.e. 164

- Greece
- Germany
- Hungary
- Ireland
- Spain

as well as

- Austria,

where the question of 'exportability' is unclear at present.

The above analysis shows that company laws throughout the EU have already been harmonised to a considerable extent, above all as regards publication and financial reporting requirements and the capital maintenance rules in stock corporations. On the other hand, there are still a number of significant differences, partially in relation to entire concepts, partially only regarding minor details. Nevertheless, it is remarkable that despite these differences, it seems that all Member States have considered and addressed – one way or the other – the same issues. 165

Capital maintenance in limited liability companies and the liability of directors are issues, where the national differences of corporate law within the EU become particularly apparent. While – in simplified terms – continental European jurisdictions tend to stress the requirements for a strict maintenance of the registered share capital, common law jurisdiction focus stronger on a maintenance of the company's liquidity by imposing on the directors a direct liability towards the company's creditors in case the solvency of the company is endangered (wrongful trading rules, solvency test in case of capital reductions etc.). But even under these difference concepts, the practical results in a significant number of cases are quite similar. 166

In addition to different solutions for similar issues, there are of course also a number of unique concepts to be found in individual Member States, e.g. the German co-determination rule according 167

208 See Part 2, FIN, Mn. 47/72.

to which the employees are entitled to elect half of the members of the supervisory board of a German company with more than 2,000 employees.

168 In light of the above, there are in essence two conclusions to be drawn: On the one hand, there are quite a number of issues in relation to which investors and entrepreneurs within Europe can chose the preferential corporate form. On the other hand, there is no single "best" corporate form combining all advantages. Instead, investors and entrepreneurs will have to analyse the particular situation to find the corporate form which suits their purposes by offering the particular advantages they need most.

Part 2 – National Law

I. Austria

*by Dr. Florian Kusznier (LL.M.)**

1 The Limited Liability Company ("GmbH")

Literature: Koppensteiner, GmbH-Gesetz (2nd Edition 1999); Reich-Rohrwig, Das österreichische GmbH-Recht in systematischer Darstellung, Band I (2nd Edition 1997).

The limited liability company (*Gesellschaft mit beschränkter Haftung*, "GmbH") is by far the most widely used and most popular type of company in Austria. As of 1 October 2003, over 90,000 GmbHs were registered in the Austrian companies register (*Firmenbuch*). This contrasts with around 2,000 stock corporations (*Aktiengesellschaften*, "AG"). 1

1.1 Export of Company

While neither statutory provisions nor case law exist which explicitly deal with the cross-border relocation of a company seat, an article published in 2004 has pointed to persuasive arguments in favour of the possibility of the factual seat of an Austrian company being transferred to another EU Member State.[1] Given the lack of case law on this issue, the impact of the ECJ-judgments Überseering and Inspire Art[2] cannot be estimated at this point and thus a cautious approach needs to be taken in practice. 2

1.2 Transformation into a Foreign Entity

There are no statutory provisions which deal explicitly with the transformation of an Austrian GmbH into a foreign entity. However, in a small number of cases, such transactions have been successfully implemented.[3] Austrian legal scholars advocate the admissibility of cross-border mergers and transformations, even though criticism has been voiced with respect to certain aspects of those cases where such a transformation has taken place.[4] The Austrian statute implementing Council Regulation (EC) No. 2157/2001 does not allow for a merger of an Austrian GmbH with an S.E. 3

1.3 Incorporation

The articles of association (or, where there is only one founder, the declaration on the establishment of the company) of a GmbH need to be drawn up in the form of an Austrian notarial deed (Sec. 4 Subs. 3 Limited Liability Companies Act, "GmbHG") and registration of the company in the companies register is required.[5] The costs of incorporation amount to approximately EUR 1,500- 4

* *Schönherr Rechtsanwälte*, Vienna.

1 Adensamer/Eckert, Umzug von Gesellschaften in Europa, insbesondere Wegzug österreichischer Gesellschaften ins Ausland, GeS 2004, p. 52 et seq.

2 See Part 1, I, Mn. 17 et seq and 19.

3 OGH 20 March 2003, 6 Ob 283/02 i; Eckert, Die Überwindung der Palström-Doktrin, ecolex 2002, p. 97; Wenglorz, Die grenzüberschreitende "Heraus"-Verschmelzung einer deutschen Kapitalgesellschaft: Und es geht doch!, Betriebs-Berater 2004, p. 1061. Whether such a transaction can be successfully implemented will, to a large degree, depend on the court having jurisdiction or even the judge handling the matter.

4 Pro: Kalss, Verschmelzung – Spaltung – Umwandlung (1997) Sec. 219 AktG Mn. 5, Vorb UmwG Mn. 13; M. Doralt, OGH zur verschmelzenden Umwandlung über die Grenze – ein Meilenstein im internationalen Gesellschaftsrecht?, GesRZ 2004, p. 26; More cautious: Rüffler, Die Umwandlung auf den deutschen Alleingesellschafter – eine Kritik an der Entscheidung des OGH 6 Ob 283/02 i, GesRZ 2004, p. 3; Nowotny, Unternehmenszusammenschlüsse über die Grenze – Traditionelle Wege auch weiterhin gefragt, ÖStZB 2004, p. 384.

5 Excerpts from the companies register can be obtained electronically. The actual physical files are kept at the Regional Court (*Landesgericht*) located at the company's registered seat, or the Vienna Commercial Court (*Handelsgericht Wien*) for companies with their registered seat in Vienna.

1,800 (notary fees are in the range of EUR 1,000 but may be higher if the company has a high share capital; court fees amount to approximately EUR 300 for a GmbH with two managing directors and minimum share capital; company tax of 1 per cent of the share capital will be levied and needs to be paid before registration).

5 Upon registration, a copy of the articles, a list of the shareholders, a list of the managing directors and sample signatures of all managing directors need to be filed in the companies register. The filing must be signed by all managing directors. Furthermore, a confirmation by an Austrian credit institution must be furnished, evidencing payment of the share capital of an amount totalling at least EUR 17,500 into the company's bank account.[6]

1.4 Recurrent Costs and Efforts

6 Corporate housekeeping with respect to a GmbH is straightforward and does not incur any significant expenditure. Costs and expenses are generally incurred only to the extent that filings need to be made in the companies register (e.g. filing of the annual accounts) but are insignificant and should not exceed EUR 400 annually. There is no annual registration fee.

1.5 Shares and Share Transfers

7 The shares of a GmbH may not be divided into different classes. Pursuant to Sec. 39 Subs. 2 GmbHG, the voting power of a shareholder is proportionate to his share: EUR 10 awards one vote, unless the articles provide for a different voting power. If they do, each shareholder must, nevertheless, have at least one vote. Shares in a GmbH are freely transferable and inheritable (Sec. 76 GmbHG) but share transfer agreements (except in the course of wills) must be drawn up in the form of an Austrian[7] notarial deed (Sec. 76 Subs. 2 GmbHG). The articles of association may impose additional restrictions on the transfer of shares, such as, for example, requiring the company's prior consent to a transfer (Sec. 76 Subs. 2 GmbHG).[8] Shares in an Austrian GmbH must not be issued in the form of share certificates (Sec. 75 Subs. 3 GmbHG). Consequently, title to a share in an Austrian GmbH can only be evidenced by way of an uninterrupted chain of notarial transfer deeds. No taxes are levied on the transfer of shares in a GmbH as such but capital gains and real estate transfer taxes may arise in individual cases.

8 Pursuant to Sec. 78 Subs. 1 GmbH, only those persons who or entities which are registered as such in the companies register are recognised as shareholders of a GmbH. Correspondingly, Sec. 26 Subs. 1 GmbHG provides that the managing directors must file any change of shareholders of a GmbH with the companies register without undue delay. Thus, a share transfer needs to be notified to the management immediately after it has taken place.

9 The listing of shares in an Austrian company on the stock exchange requires share certificates to be issued (Sec. 1 Subs. 2 Stock Exchange Act) by the company. A GmbH is thus precluded from a stock exchange listing.[9]

1.6 Corporate Bodies

10 Generally, there are only two mandatory corporate bodies in an Austrian GmbH: (i) the managing directors; and (ii) the shareholders' meeting. Only in a limited number of circumstances must a

6 The minimum share capital of an Austrian GmbH is EUR 35,000, of which EUR 17,500 must be paid up in cash upon formation (Sec. 6 Subs. 1 and Sec. 6a Subs. 1 GmbHG). The requirement of a cash payment does not apply in the case of in-kind contributions accompanied by a valuation report in line with the Second Directive, Art. 10.

7 Or German, see Koppensteiner, GmbHG^2, Sec. 76 Mn. 24; Trenkwalder in: Kalss (Ed.), Die Übertragung von GmbH-Geschäftsanteilen in 14 europäischen Rechtsordnungen (2003), Austria, p. 30.

8 Unless the articles expressly state otherwise, consent of "the company" is to be interpreted to mean consent by shareholders' resolution.

9 Mn. 7; see also Kalss, Anlegerinteressen, Der Anleger im Handlungsdreieck von Vertrag, Verband und Markt (2001), p. 46 et seq.

supervisory board be set up (Sec. 29 GmbHG),[10] but it may nevertheless be established by the shareholders if they so wish.

1.6.1 Managing Directors

Only individuals may be appointed as managing directors of a GmbH but (apart from very limited exceptions, e.g. under professional conduct rules) no other restrictions apply. The managing directors represent the company in and out of court when dealing with third parties (Sec. 18 Subs. 1 GmbHG). If more than one managing director has been appointed, the managing directors represent the company jointly, unless one or more of them has/have been granted individual power of representation.[11] **11**

In addition to the managing directors, holders of special commercial power of attorney (*Prokuristen*) are frequently appointed to run the day-to-day business of the company, especially where the company has non-resident managing directors. Appointment of these special representatives needs to be filed in the companies register. **12**

1.6.2 Shareholders' Meeting

Sec. 35 Subs. 1 GmbHG stipulates a range of measures which fall into the exclusive competence of the shareholders' meeting, e.g. approval of the annual accounts, distribution of profits and the appointment and withdrawal of managing directors. Other core competences include dissolution of the company, mergers and amendments of the articles. The shareholders may issue instructions to the managing directors (Sec. 20 Subs. 1 GmbHG). **13**

Most shareholder resolutions require a simple majority to be adopted, unless the articles set out a higher threshold. Certain measures, including, for example, amendments to the articles (Sec. 50 Subs. 1 GmbH) and mergers (Sec. 98 GmbHG), do, however, require a three-quarters majority of the votes cast. **14**

1.6.3 Supervisory Board

The supervisory board's core competence is to monitor the managing directors (Sec. 30 j Subs. 1 GmbHG). The managing directors need to report to the supervisory board at least once a year with a forecast on the overall development, assets and liabilities, financial condition and results of operation of the company. In addition, they have to prepare, at the very least, quarterly reports detailing the actual development of the company compared to the annual forecast (Sec. 28a Subs. 1 GmbHG). **15**

1.7 Duties and Liabilities of Directors

The managing directors of a GmbH owe a duty of care and diligence expected of a prudent businessman towards the company (Sec. 25 Subs. 1 GmbHG). This includes the actual conduct of business of the company as well as compliance with reporting and filing requirements (e.g. preparation and filing of the annual accounts, notification of changes of shareholders,[12] appointment or withdrawal of managing directors and institution of insolvency proceedings). **16**

The managing directors are jointly liable to the company for any damage caused as a result of a breach of their duties (Sec. 25 Subs. 2 GmbHG). This joint liability generally cannot be restricted by an allocation of responsibilities. However, in such a case, a managing director who is not directly responsible may claim that he exercised a sufficient level of care and diligence if he supervised **17**

10 If the share capital exceeds EUR 70,000 *and* the number of shareholders exceeds 50, *or* where the company has more than 300 employees on an annual average basis.

11 To achieve this, the articles must provide for the general possibility of granting individual power of representation to a managing director. The actual decision which managing director(s) is to be given this power has to be included in the shareholders' resolution on his/their appointment.

12 See Mn. 8.

the other managing director(s) to an appropriate extent. A direct instruction by the shareholders releases the managing directors from their liability, unless the instruction is null and void, i.e. if implementing it would contravene statutory law.[13] Equally, discharge releases the managing directors from their liability provided the shareholders were aware of all underlying circumstances. Additionally, managing directors may seek protection under D&O insurance. Claims pursuant to Sec. 25 GmbHG become statute-barred after five years.

18 Examples of breaches of directors' duties include instances of repayment of share capital[14] or failure to request commencement of insolvency proceedings upon either inability to pay or over-indebtedness of the company (Secs. 66 and 67 Insolvency Act, *Konkursordnung*, "KO"). Moreover, managing directors may become personally liable pursuant to the Companies Reorganisation Act (*Unternehmensreorganisationsgesetz*, "URG") if they fail to institute reorganisation proceedings even though the financial standing of the company would require such proceedings to be instituted.

1.8 Shareholders' Liability

19 The principle of the separation of assets is an overriding principle under Austrian corporate law (Sec. 61 Subs. 2 GmbHG). Piercing of the corporate veil, resulting in a direct shareholder liability for liabilities of the company, can thus only be contemplated in extraordinary circumstances, e.g. in the event of qualified under-funding of the company or upon irreversible mixing of the shareholders' and the company's funds.[15]

20 Qualified under-funding is seen to exist in cases where it is evident that the contributed equity capital is entirely out of proportion to the company's purpose of business and thus the business is more likely than not to be developed in a way that would be detrimental to the company's creditors.[16]

21 Mixing of the shareholders' funds with the company's funds may justify piercing the corporate veil if it has occurred to the extent that it can no longer be established whether the shareholders have used the company to enrich themselves to the detriment of the creditors of the company.[17]

1.9 Capitalisation and Financing

1.9.1 Basic Concepts

22 The core concepts of the capitalisation provisions of Austrian corporate law are the principles of (i) capital contributions, (ii) capital maintenance and (iii) separation of assets: in return for the contribution of assets of "actual value" to the company and maintenance of these assets in the company, the shareholders benefit from the separation of assets between the company's funds and the shareholders' funds.[18]

1.9.2 Minimum Share Capital

23 The minimum share capital of an Austrian GmbH is EUR 35,000. At least EUR 17,500 must be paid up in cash upon formation of the company (Sec. 6 Subs. 1 and Sec. 6 a Subs. 1 GmbHG). Alternatively, assets can be transferred to the company by way of an in-kind contribution (upon formation or at a later stage, e.g. in the course of a capital increase). In this scenario, a valuation report by an independent expert needs to be commissioned, verifying that the value of the assets corresponds, at the very least, to the issuance value of the shares issued in exchange (Sec. 6a Subs. 4 GmbHG).[19]

13 Koppensteiner, GmbHG^2, Sec. 25 Mn. 17 et seq.
14 See also Mn. 24.
15 Koppensteiner, GmbHG^2, Sec. 61 Mn. 34 et seq.
16 Saurer in: Doralt/Nowotny/Kalss, AktG, Sec. 48 Mn. 9 et seq.
17 Saurer in: Doralt/Nowotny/Kalss, AktG, Sec. 48 Mn. 17.
18 With limited exceptions in extraordinary circumstances, see Mn. 19 et seq.
19 See also Mn 5.

1.9.3 Maintenance of Capital and Liquidity

(i) System

The shareholders of a GmbH are only entitled to dividends, distributions as a result of a decrease of the share capital or liquidation proceeds, but must not otherwise receive any payments from the company (Sec. 82 Subs. 1 GmbHG). The company is entitled to reclaim any payments made in breach of these restrictions (Sec. 83 Subs. 1 GmbHG) and the managing directors are personally held liable if they have distributed the company's funds and have not observed the statutory restrictions (Sec. 15 Subs. 3 No. 1 GmbHG). **24**

In the event that repayment cannot be obtained from either the recipient or the managing directors, all shareholders of the company become liable for the distributed amount pro rata of their participation in the company (Sec. 83 Subs. 2 GmbHG). **25**

(ii) Distributions

As outlined above,[20] the only distributions that shareholders are entitled to receive are (i) dividends, (ii) distributions as a result of a decrease of the share capital and (iii) liquidation proceeds. **26**

Dividends can only be distributed on the basis of the adopted annual accounts and thus may be distributed only once a year. The distribution of advance or interim dividends is not possible in an Austrian GmbH.[21] **27**

To protect the creditors of a GmbH, special procedures need to be observed in the event of a reduction of the share capital or liquidation of the company. These include a public announcement and direct notification to the creditors of these measures and the provision of security or the settlement of their claims, respectively (Sec. 55 Subs. 2 and Sec. 91 Subs. 1 GmbHG). Only thereafter distributions to the shareholders may be made (Sec. 57 Subs. 1 and Sec. 91 Subs. 3 GmbHG). **28**

(iii) Acquisition of Own Shares and Related Financing

An Austrian GmbH may not acquire its own shares (Sec. 81 GmbHG). The only exception to this set forth in the GmbHG is where own shares are purchased during the course of execution proceedings to achieve fulfilment of a claim which the company has against a shareholder. In this scenario, the company is under an obligation to sell the shares again without undue delay.[22] Another generally accepted exception is an acquisition without any consideration being paid since this does not result in a reduction in company funds.[23] **29**

(iv) Company as Lender or Guarantor

A GmbH is generally not restricted under Austrian company law from pursuing lending activities. However, in the case of loans to the company's shareholders – and thus where a group of companies in particular is concerned – the provisions on capital maintenance impose certain limitations. In order that such lending is not seen as "disguised dividends" and thus distributions, which would be a breach of Sec. 82 GmbHG,[24] loans must be concluded at arm's length. The same applies to the provision of security by the company for the loans of a shareholder.[25] **30**

In the context of group-wide financing facilities, the provision of security by an Austrian GmbH may fall foul of the regulations on capital maintenance if security is provided without any visible **31**

20 See Mn. 24.
21 But see Mn. 58 for the AG.
22 Koppensteiner, GmbHG^2, Sec. 81 Mn. 12.
23 This, however, only applies insofar as the share capital of the company is fully paid up. Otherwise the company itself might become pro rata liable for payment of the outstanding portion of the share capital (Sec. 70 Subs. 1 GmbHG).
24 See Mn. 24.
25 Koppensteiner, GmbHG^2, Sec. 82 Mn. 17.

"commercial justification".[26] Whether provision of security is commercially justified will in particular depend on which benefits accrue to the company in the context of the particular transaction.

(v) Company as Borrower

32 A GmbH may borrow both from third parties and its shareholders. With respect to loans from shareholders, the provisions of the Equity Capital Surrogate Act (*Eigenkapitalersatzgesetz*, "EKEG") are particularly important. The EKEG provides that a loan granted by shareholders during a period of financial crisis is treated as a contribution of equity capital and must not be repaid until the crisis is over (Sec. 1 and Sec. 14 Subs. 1 EKEG). The EKEG applies to loans made by shareholders who exercise a controlling influence on the company or who hold a participation interest of 25 per cent or more in the share capital (Sec. 5 EKEG). The EKEG also applies to security provided by shareholders in return for a loan given to them by the company (Sec. 15 EKEG).[27]

1.10 Publication and Filing Requirements

33 Generally, the filing requirements set out in the GmbHG are addressed to the managing directors of a GmbH. They require filing the appointment and recall of managing directors, the annual accounts, changes in the shareholding structure, corporate reorganisations (e.g. mergers) and amendments to the articles. In line with the requirements of the First Directive,[28] the Austrian companies register is publicly accessible. The documents filed in the companies register can thus be inspected and copies obtained. Excerpts from the companies register can be obtained electronically via a centralised web-based service to which the courts, notaries and attorneys have access.[29] Third parties may rely on the content of the register.

1.11 Financial Reporting

34 The drawing-up of the annual accounts of an Austrian GmbH is the responsibility of the managing directors. The accounts must be drawn up in accordance with the provisions of the Austrian Commercial Code (*Handelsgesetzbuch*, "HGB") within the first five months of the following business year (Sec. 222 Subs. 1 HGB), and must be filed with the companies register nine months after the balance sheet date at the latest. The annual accounts generally consist of the balance sheet, the profit and loss account, the management report and explanatory notes (Sec. 193 Subs. 4 in connection with Sec. 222 Subs. 1 HGB).

Certain forms of relief in line with the Fourth Directive[30] are, however, also available for small and medium-sized companies under the HGB. In Austria small companies are those not exceeding two of the three following criteria: a balance sheet total of EUR 3.65 million, a turnover of EUR 7.3 million and a workforce of 50 employees (on an annual average basis). Medium sized companies are those exceeding at least two of the afore-mentioned criteria but not exceeding two of the three following criteria: a balance sheet total of EUR 14.6 million, a turnover of EUR 29.2 million and a workforce of more than 250 employees (on an annual average basis). Small companies are inter alia released from the requirement to draw up a management report (*Lagebericht*), may draw up considerably less-detailed annual accounts and do not need to file their profit and loss accounts with the commercial register (i.e. are required to file only the – simplified – balance sheet). Small GmbH do not need to have their annual accounts audited by an independent auditor (unless they are required to have a supervisory board by law, Sec 268 Commercial Code). Medium sized companies may draw up (and file with the register) shorter annual accounts. Both small and medium-sized companies only need to publish in the Federal Gazette the fact that they have filed their annual

26 Saurer in: Doralt/Nowotny/Kalss, AktG, Sec. 52 Mn. 67.
27 See in detail Dellinger/Mohr, EKEG (2004), Sec. 15 Mn. 1 et seq.
28 See Part 1, I, Mn. 38.
29 See also Fn. 5. A fee is charged for access to this service.
30 See Part 1, I, Mn. 48 et seq.

accounts – but not the actual annual accounts (which large stock corporations are required to publish).

1.12 Employee Participation in Corporate Bodies

The employees of a GmbH are entitled to seats on the supervisory board of a GmbH, provided the company has more than 300 employees on an annual average basis (Sec. 29 Subs. 1 No. 2 GmbHG). The number of employee representatives depends on the number of shareholder representatives on the supervisory board. The employees are entitled to nominate one representative for every two shareholder representatives and an additional member in the event that there is an uneven number of shareholder representatives (Sec. 110 Subs. 1 and Subs. 5 Labour Constitution Act, *Arbeitsverfassungsgesetz*, "ArbVG"). The minimum number of shareholder representatives is three (Sec. 30 GmbHG). The minimum number of employee representatives is thus two. **35**

2 The Stock Corporation ("AG")

Literature: Doralt/Nowotny/Kalss, Kommentar zum Aktiengesetz (2003); Jabornegg/Strasser, Kommentar zum Aktiengesetz, (4th Edition 2002).

2.1 Export of Company

What has already been said with respect to the GmbH at Mn. 2 above applies equally to the question of the transfer of the seat of an AG. **36**

2.2 Transformation into a Foreign Entity

The question of transforming an Austrian AG into a foreign entity must be seen in the light of the comments made with respect to the GmbH at Mn. 3 above. The case underlying an article by Eckert concerned the merger of an Italian stock corporation with an Austrian AG.[31] The Austrian statute implementing Council Regulation (EC) No. 2157/2001 allows for a merger of an Austrian AG with an S.E. **37**

2.3 Incorporation

Until an amendment of the Stock Corporation Act (*Aktiengesetz*, "AktG") which entered into force on 8 October 2004, formation of a stock corporation required the participation of at least two founders. Sec. 35 AktG now provides for the possibility of forming an AG with only one founder.[32] The costs of incorporation will usually amount to several thousand Euros. **38**

The articles of association of an AG need to be drawn up in the form of an Austrian notarial deed (Sec. 16 Subs. 1 AktG) and registration of the company in the companies register is required. The founders, the management board and the supervisory board have to draw up formation reports (Sec. 24 Subs. 1 and Sec. 25 Subs. 1 AktG). **39**

Upon registration, a copy of the articles along with the formation reports of the founders, the members of the management board and the members of the supervisory board, as well as a list of the members of the supervisory board, a list of the managing directors and sample signatures of all managing directors, need to be filed in the companies register. The filing must be signed by all founders, all members of the supervisory board and all members of the management board (Sec. 28 Subs. 1 AktG). Furthermore, a confirmation by an Austrian credit institution must be furnished, evidencing payment of the share capital of an amount totalling at least EUR 17,500 into the company's bank account. **40**

31 Eckert, ecolex 2002, p. 97 (full quote at Fn. 3).

32 The details of the sole shareholder need to be filed in the companies register (Sec. 35 Subs. 1 AktG).

2.4 Recurrent Costs and Efforts

41 The costs arising from the carrying out of the corporate housekeeping of an AG will depend to a considerable extent on the actual company. While a closely-held AG will not incur major costs, the expenses will rise significantly for larger (or even listed) AGs. Compared with a GmbH, the costs will, however, invariably be higher; for example, while written resolutions can be passed in a GmbH on most matters, formal shareholders' meetings need to be held in an AG – and the minutes need to be notarised and filed in the companies register.

2.5 Shares and Share Transfers

42 An Austrian AG can either have shares with a par value[33] or non-par value shares and can issue either bearer or registered shares (Sec. 8 Subs. 1 and Sec. 10 Subs. 1 AktG). Additionally, there may be different classes of shares, in particular preference shares and regular shares. Preference shares may only be issued up to a maximum of one third of the AG's share capital (Sec. 115 Subs. 2 AktG). Provided these preference shares are entitled to a special dividend, the voting right of the holders of such preference shares may be excluded. Furthermore, an Austrian AG may introduce a maximum voting right threshold but not a system where particular shares carry more than one vote. In most cases, the company will not print actual share certificates but will issue interim certificates instead. While bearer shares are transferred by physical handover, both interim certificates and registered shares are transferred by endorsement (Sec. 61 AktG). In the event that no interim certificates are issued but the shares are only electronically recorded, transfer will take place by way of book-entry transactions.[34]

43 As a consequence of the latest amendment to the AktG, a shareholder acquiring all the shares in an AG must notify the management board of this. The management board in turn must file the details of the sole shareholder in the companies register (Sec. 35 Subs. 2 AktG).[35]

2.6 Corporate Bodies

44 In contrast to the GmbH, there are three mandatory corporate bodies in an AG: (i) the management board; (ii) the supervisory board; and (iii) the shareholders' meeting.

2.6.1 Management Board

45 The members of the management board of an AG are appointed by the supervisory board for a maximum fixed period of five years (Sec. 75 Subs. 1 AktG). During their period of appointment, they can only be recalled for cause (Sec. 75 Subs. 4 AktG). If the management board consists of more than one member, the members represent the company jointly, unless one or more of them has/have been granted individual power of representation (Sec. 71 Subs. 2 AktG).

46 In contrast to the GmbH, the management board of an AG acts independently and neither the supervisory board nor the shareholders' meeting can issue instructions to the management board (Sec. 70 Subs. 1 AktG).[36] A range of measures does, however, require the supervisory board's prior consent (Sec. 95 Subs. 5 AktG).

2.6.2 Shareholders' Meeting

47 The shareholders' meeting of an AG, when compared to a GmbH, has significantly fewer options at its disposal to influence the business of the company. In particular, it cannot issue instructions to the management board. The shareholders do, however, have exclusive competence to appoint the

33 Of at least EUR 1 or multiples thereof.

34 See in detail Micheler, Wertpapierrecht zwischen Schuld- und Sachenrecht (2004).

35 See also Mn. 33.

36 Nowotny in: Doralt/Nowotny/Kalss, AktG, Sec. 70 Mn. 6.

members of the supervisory board (Sec. 87 Subs. 2 AktG) and to decide on the distribution of profits (Sec. 126 Subs. 1 AktG).

In extraordinary circumstances, the management board is under a fiduciary duty to obtain the approval of the shareholders prior to the implementation of a measure, in particular in circumstances having far-reaching implications on the future substance or business of the company.[37] Furthermore, pursuant to Sec. 237 Subs. 1 AktG, the transfer of the "entire" business of an AG requires consent of the shareholders. This shareholders' resolution requires a majority of three-quarters of the share capital.[38] **48**

2.6.3 Supervisory Board

The members of the supervisory board are elected by the shareholders' meeting for a maximum fixed period of five years (Sec. 87 Subs. 2 AktG). During their period of appointment, they can be recalled at any time by shareholders' resolution. This resolution requires a majority of three-quarters of the votes cast (Sec. 87 Subs. 3 AktG) unless the articles provide for a different majority.[39] **49**

The supervisory board of an Austrian AG consists of three members unless the articles set forth a higher number (maximum of 20) (Sec. 86 Subs. 1 AktG). Its core duties are: (i) monitoring the management board; (ii) approval of the annual accounts;[40] and (iii) the appointment and recall of the members of the management board. **50**

2.7 Duties and Liabilities of Directors

The managing directors and the members of the supervisory board of an AG owe a duty of care and diligence expected of a prudent businessman towards the company (Sec. 84 Subs. 1 and Sec. 99 AktG). The scope of their duties is generally comparable to those of the managing directors of a GmbH.[41] Also, as is the case for managing directors of a GmbH, the members of a management board of an AG may become personally liable for any damage caused as a result of a breach of their duties (Sec. 84 Subs. 2 AktG). What has been said in respect of the managing directors of a GmbH[42] equally applies to the AG provided, however, that shareholders of an AG may not issue direct instruction to the managing directors. **51**

2.8 Shareholders' Liability

What has been said with respect to the GmbH[43] applies equally to the AG. **52**

2.9 Capitalisation and Financing

2.9.1 Basic Concepts

The core concepts outlined for the GmbH[44] also apply to the AG. **53**

37 Bachner in: Doralt/Nowotny/Kalss, AktG, Sec. 103 Mn. 28 et seq., analysing the German "Holzmueller" doctrine.

38 The "entire" business is generally interpreted as also encompassing transfers of *material assets* of an AG – see Bachner in: Doralt/Nowotny/Kalss, AktG, Sec. 237 Mn. 4. Below this threshold, the management board may still be under an obligation to obtain the shareholders' consent along the lines of the "Holzmueller/Gelatine" doctrine – see the Chapter on Germany, Part 2, XVI, Mn. 53 for more details.

39 Which may also be a lower majority requirement; Kalss in: Doralt/Nowotny/Kalss, AktG, Sec. 87 Mn. 35.

40 Unless the management board and supervisory board opt for an approval by the shareholders' meeting (Sec. 125 Subs. 2 AktG).

41 See Mn. 16 et seq.

42 See Mn 16 et seq.

43 See Mn. 19 et seq.

44 See Mn. 22 et seq.

2.9.2 Minimum Share Capital

54 The minimum share capital of an Austrian AG is EUR 70,000. At least EUR 17,500 must be paid up in cash upon formation (Sec. 7 and Sec. 28a Subs. 1 AktG). The provisions on in-kind contributions to a GmbH[45] apply equally to the AG (Sec. 20 and Sec. 25 Subs. 2 and 4 AktG).

2.9.3 Maintenance of Capital and Liquidity

(i) System

55 The principle that shareholders are entitled to dividend payments only by the company is set out in Sec. 52 AktG. In addition, the shareholders of an AG may also receive distributions both as a result of a decrease in the share capital and as liquidation proceeds in accordance with the special provisions set out for these measures. No other payment may be made by the company to its shareholders.

56 As is the case with the GmbH, the shareholders of an AG must repay all payments received in breach of the capital maintenance rules (Sec. 56 AktG). In contrast to the GmbH,[46] there is, however, no subsidiary liability of the other shareholders of an AG if repayment cannot be obtained from the recipient.[47]

57 Furthermore, the approval of the shareholders' meeting is required for contracts between the company and a founding shareholder if such a contract is concluded during the first two years after registration of the company and the consideration paid by the company amounts to 10 per cent or more of the share capital (Sec. 45 Subs. 1 AktG).

(ii) Distributions

58 What has been said with respect to the GmbH also applies to the AG. However, pursuant to Sec. 54 a AktG, the management board may under certain circumstances authorise the payment of an advance dividend after the first half of a business year of an AG.

(iii) Acquisition of Own Shares and Related Financing

59 An AG may under limited circumstances acquire own shares up to a maximum of 10 per cent of the share capital (Sec. 65 Subs. 2 AktG). For listed companies, no special justification needs to be demonstrated if the acquisition has been authorised by a resolution of the shareholders' meeting (Sec. 65 Subs. 1 No. 8 AktG). This authorisation may be given for a maximum period of 18 months.

60 Pursuant to Sec. 66a AktG, an AG is precluded from providing financial assistance (in particular loans, the provision of security and advances) for the acquisition of (i) own shares of the company or (ii) shares in its parent company.[48]

(iv) Company as Lender or Guarantor

61 The comments made in respect of the GmbH[49] apply equally to the AG.

(v) Company as Borrower

62 The comments made in respect of the GmbH[50] apply equally to the AG.

45 See. Mn. 23.
46 See Mn. 25.
47 Csoklich in: Doralt/Nowotny/Kalss, Sec. 59 Mn. 3.
48 For details see Kalss in: Doralt/Nowotny/Kalss, AktG, Sec. 66 a Mn. 4 et seq.
49 See Mn. 30 et seq.
50 See Mn. 32.

2.10 Publication and Filing Requirements

What has been said with respect to the GmbH[51] applies equally to the AG. Additional disclosure and reporting requirements pursuant to, for example, the Takeover Act, the Stock Exchange Act and the Austrian Corporate Governance Code apply to listed companies.[52] **63**

2.11 Financial Reporting

The accounting regulations applicable to an AG correspond to those that apply to a GmbH.[53] **64**

2.12 Employee Participation in Corporate Bodies

In an AG, the establishment of a supervisory board is mandatory, irrespective of the number of employees. The method of calculating the number of employee representatives required has already been outlined above.[54] **65**

51 See Mn. 33.
52 For an excellent overview see Gruber in: Doralt/Nowotny/Kalss, AktG, Sec. 18 Mn. 31 et seq.
53 See Mn. 34.
54 See Mn. 35.

II. Belgium

*by Eric Pottier (LL.M.)**

1 The Limited Liability Company ("SPRL/BVBA")

Literature: Business Law Guide to Belgium, Chapter 2, IV, A (Kluwer Law International, 2003)

The SPRL/BVBA (*société privée à responsabilité limitée/besloten vennootschap met beperkte aansprakelijkheid*) is the company structure most commonly used for small businesses (family-owned) in Belgium. Most legal provisions governing the SPRL/BVBA are contained in the Companies Code (the "CC"). In contrast to the stock corporation ("SA/NV"),[1] the shareholders of the SPRL/BVBA have considerable influence over the company. At the end of 2003 there were approximately 178.600 SPRLs/BVBAs registered in Belgium in contrast to 82.700 SAs/NVs 1

1.1 Export of Company

An SPRL/BVBA will only be considered to be a Belgian company if it is managed from Belgium (theory of effective management as opposed to incorporation theory). An SPRL/BVBA can emigrate and become a foreign company, with continuity of legal personality, by moving its seat of effective management abroad if the host country accepts this immigration of the company with continuity of legal personality. Merely moving the registered office abroad will not suffice.[2] If the seat of effective management is moved to a country which uses the incorporation theory, the company will still remain Belgian as a result of the theory of *renvoi*. 2

1.2 Transformation into a Foreign Entity

Belgian law does not expressly provide for the transformation of a domestic company into a foreign entity. This can be achieved only indirectly by transferring the business of the SPRL/BVBA business to a foreign company. 3

According to Sec. 2 Subs. 2 of the Council Regulation of 8 October 2001 on the Status of a European Company ("the Regulation"), an SPRL/BVBA can be part of an S.E. by means of incorporation of a holding S.E., which is allowed when at least two of the companies creating the holding are governed by the law of different EU Member States or when these companies have a subsidiary which has been governed by the law of another EU Member State for at least two years. An SPRL/BVBA can also be part of an S.E. by means of incorporation of a subsidiary S.E. (Sec. 2 Subs. 3 of the Regulation) under the same conditions. An SPRL/BVBA cannot be merged into an S.E. Such merger into an S.E. is, according to Sec. 2 Subs. 1 of the Regulation, only permitted for an SA/NV. The same applies for the transformation into an S.E. (Sec. 2 Subs. 4 of the Regulation).

The Belgian SPRL/BVBA taking part in the formation is governed by Belgian law.

A minimum capital of EUR 120,000 is required to create a new S.E. and a minimum amount of EUR 61,500 has to be paid up.[3]

1.3 Incorporation

An SPRL/BVBA is incorporated by way of a notarial deed of incorporation executed by at least two shareholders, unless the sole shareholder is a physical person[4] (Sec. 211 CC). If an 4

* *Linklaters De Bandt*, Brussels. Written with the assistance of Catherine Hatert (LL.M.) and Priscilla Maters (LL.M.).

1 See Mn. 32 et seq.

2 Conseil d'Etat, 29 June 1987, No. 28.267 (1989).

3 P. Nicaise in: La société européenne: une société de type européen, JT, 2002, p. 481.

4 If an individual is already the sole shareholder of another SPRL/BVBA, he/she will be jointly liable as a guarantor for the liabilities of any SPRL/BVBA of which he/she subsequently becomes the sole shareholder, except as a result of a transfer upon death (Sec. 212 CC).

SPRL/BVBA is incorporated by one legal entity acting alone, such legal entity will be jointly liable for all liabilities of the SPRL/BVBA as long as this legal entity remains sole shareholder of the SPRL/BVBA (Sec. 213 Subs. 2, al. 1 CC).

If a shareholder – which is a legal entity – acquires all shares in an existing SPRL/BVBA, this does not trigger the dissolution of the SPRL/BVBA. The sole shareholder will, however, be required to have a new shareholder join the company within one year or to wind up the company within one year. If the sole shareholder fails to do so, it can be held jointly liable as a guarantor for all liabilities incurred by the SPRL/BVBA from the date on which the sole shareholder acquired all the shares until the date a new shareholder joins the company or the date of publication of the company's dissolution (Sec. 213 Subs. 2 al. 2 CC).

The SPRL/BVBA acquires legal personality and becomes a corporate entity upon filing of the deed of incorporation with the clerk's office of the commercial court (Sec. 2 Subs. 4 CC).[5] In principle, an SPRL/BVBA may not enter into any transaction (e.g. lease of premises or purchase of assets) until it has acquired legal personality. It is, however, possible for one or more persons to carry out a transaction on behalf of a company prior to the moment it acquires legal personality.

5 The incorporation process takes about one to three weeks. Incorporation costs (notary fees and costs, publication costs and the 0.5 per cent registration tax on capital, excluding legal fees) for a company incorporated with a minimum capital of EUR 18,550 amount to approximately EUR 900.

1.4 Recurrent Costs and Efforts

6 Recurrent costs and efforts relating to a Belgian SPRL/BVBA are minimal and relate only to the publication of annual accounts and their filing with the National Bank of Belgium at an annual cost of approximately EUR 400. Other costs and efforts materialise only in the event that certain corporate steps are taken which require notarisation, filing with the Crossroads Bank of Enterprises (*Banque-carrefour des entreprises/Kruispuntbank van Ondernemingen*)[6] or publication.

1.5 Shares and Share Transfers

7 The capital of an SPRL/BVBA is divided into equal shares. The shares issued by an SPRL/BVBA are in registered form and can only be capital shares (Sec. 232 CC). Shares can be issued with or without par value, and can be voting as well as non-voting shares, in which case the non-voting shares cannot represent more than one-third of the capital (Sec. 240 CC). Except for transfers to other shareholders, to certain close relatives or to other persons designated in the articles of association, share transfers require (upon penalty of nullity) the consent of at least half of the shareholders owning at least three-quarters of the capital (after deduction of the shares to be transferred);[7] the articles of association or other documents can further restrict the transferability of the shares (Sec. 249 CC). To be effective *vis-à-vis* third parties, the share transfer must be registered in the share register (Sec. 250 CC).

8 An SPRL/BVBA may not solicit funds from the public nor can it obtain a listing on a stock exchange market.[8]

1.6 Corporate Bodies

9 The SPRL/BVBA provides for two compulsory corporate bodies, one or more managers (acting alone or as a board) and the shareholders' meeting.

5 See Mn. 28.

6 The Crossroads Bank of Enterprises is a Belgian institution existing since July 2003 which operates a centralised computer database charged with the registering, preserving, managing and making available of all basic information on enterprises. The files of Belgian companies are no longer held in the "commercial register", which was cancelled with the introduction of the Crossroads Bank of Enterprises, but by the Register of Legal Entities, which is part of the Crossroads Bank of Enterprises.

7 Business Law Guide to Belgium, No. 348, p. 73.

8 Business Law Guide to Belgium, No. 335, p. 71.

1.6.1 Managers

An SPRL/BVBA is managed by one or more managers (*gérants/zaakvoerders*), physical persons or legal entities, who may but need not be shareholders; where a legal entity is appointed as manager, it must appoint a permanent representative (physical person) to act on its behalf and who will be subject to the same civil and criminal liability as the legal entity (Sec. 61 CC). Each manager acting alone can represent the company but the articles of association may provide differently (e.g. a majority of the board of managers or two managers acting jointly). In addition, the manager(s) can delegate specific powers to person(s) of his/her/their choice. **10**

Managers have the power to do all things which are not expressly reserved by law or in the articles of association to the shareholders' meeting (Sec. 257 CC). Restrictions on the management or powers of representation are not enforceable. No daily management body is provided for in the CC: all managers have powers of daily management.[9] **11**

1.6.2 Shareholders' Meeting

The shareholders' meeting is vested with specific powers reserved for the shareholders by the CC, such as any amendment to the company's articles of association (Sec. 286 CC), the approval of annual accounts (Sec. 284 CC) or the appointment of the manager(s) and the auditor (Sec. 256 CC). In the absence of any more restrictive provision in the company's articles of association, the resolutions of the shareholders' meeting usually require the approval of a simple majority of the votes cast, regardless of the number of shares present or represented at the meeting.[10] The shareholders cannot give any instruction to the manager to carry out a particular action. Shareholders representing one-fifth of the capital can, however, request the management to convene a shareholders' meeting (Sec. 268 CC) and put particular topics on the agenda of the meeting (Sec. 268 CC implicitly). During shareholders' meetings, the managers have to answer the questions raised by the shareholders with respect to their report or items on the agenda. **12**

Extraordinary shareholders' meetings decide on modifications to the articles of association in the presence of a Belgian notary[11] (Sec. 286 CC). Special shareholders' meetings concern a residual category of topics (e.g. replacement of managers).[12] **13**

1.7 Duties and Liabilities of Directors

Managers are not personally liable for the company's liabilities or obligations but the managers will, in specific cases, be held personally liable for shortcomings in the exercise of their mandate and for non-compliance with (i) the CC or (ii) the articles of association (Sec. 262 CC). The general rules of tort liability are also applicable. **14**

Managers are jointly and severally liable *vis-à-vis* the company or any third parties for all damages caused by any violation of the CC or the articles of association (Sec. 263 CC). A manager will be discharged from any liability if he/she (i) did not personally participate in the violation of law, (ii) did not otherwise make any mistake and (iii) denounced the violation at the first shareholders' meeting following the date on which he/she obtained knowledge of the violation. In addition to the general liability of managers, the managers can be held liable for any breach of the rules relating to the protection of the company's share capital listed in Sec. 314 CC.

According to Sec. 265 CC, any manager, former manager or person who, without having been formally appointed as a manager of an SPRL/BVBA, nevertheless acted in fact as a manager and performs the duties of a manager may be held personally liable for all or part of the company's

9 Business Law Guide to Belgium, No. 353, p. 74.

10 Unanimous written shareholders' resolutions are possible for all shareholders' decisions not requiring a notarial deed.

11 The majority requirement is for three-quarters of the votes cast, in some cases higher (e.g. four-fifths for modification of corporate purpose), exceptionally lower (one-quarter for dissolution where the net assets have decreased below one-quarter of the registered capital).

12 There is no quorum requirement but a simple majority unless the articles of association provide otherwise.

debts (up to the amount of the net liabilities) in the event of the company's bankruptcy when the liabilities surpass the assets, if such manager has committed an act of manifest gross negligence that contributed to the company's bankruptcy.[13]

Under Belgian law, if, as a result of incurred losses, the net assets of an SPRL/BVBA are lower than half of the corporate capital, the managers must convene a shareholders' meeting, which must take place within two months after such loss was discovered or should have been discovered. The shareholders have to decide either to dissolve (with a special quorum and majority) the company or to continue its activities. Identical rules exist if the net assets are lower than one-quarter of the corporate capital. In such case, one-quarter of the votes of the shareholders' meeting is sufficient for a resolution to dissolve the company (Sec. 332 CC).[14]

Claims against managers in respect of activities in connection with their duties become time-barred after five years from the date such activities were performed or, if wilfully concealed, as from the date of their discovery (Sec. 198 Subs. 1 CC). The five year term applies to any kind of liability, including tort liability.

15 Managers may incur criminal liability for offences committed while carrying out their duties; in some cases, managers can be held criminally liable for an offence committed by the company itself.

16 At the annual shareholders' meeting, release of liability can be granted to the managers with regard to liability *vis-à-vis* the company.

According to the Royal Decree of 24 October 1934, a judge may prohibit a person from acting as manager if such person has been convicted by a criminal court for criminal actions defined in Article 1 of the Royal Decree. When convicted for criminal actions in the context of an insolvency of a company, a person may be prohibited from carrying out any commercial activity (Art. 1 *bis*). The judge has a wide discretion but the interdiction may not be shorter than three years or longer than ten years.

1.8 Shareholders' Liability

17 As a general rule, the shareholders may not be held liable for the debts incurred or transactions carried out by the company. Their maximum exposure is in principle limited to the amount of their contribution to the company's capital (Secs. 61 and 210 CC).

18 In exceptional cases, shareholders can be held personally liable in the event of "piercing of the corporate veil".

Founding shareholders are jointly liable for (i) that part of the capital that was not validly subscribed for at the time of incorporation and for the shortfall between the minimum capital required and the capital actually subscribed; (ii) non-compliance with rules relating to the paying up of capital and shares at the time of incorporation; (iii) damages resulting from the company's dissolution, omission of certain items in the deed of incorporation or over-evaluation of the contribution in kind at incorporation; (iv) under-capitalisation if the company goes bankrupt within a period of three years of incorporation; and (v) the paying up of shares in the case of non-compliance with the prohibition on companies subscribing for their own shares or certificates (Sec. 229 CC).

1.9 Capitalisation and Financing

1.9.1 Basic Concepts

19 The SPRL/BVBA financing regulations are based on the concept of a restricted share capital counterbalancing the notion of limited shareholder liability. The share capital of the company is therefore intended to form a capital fund which represents the minimum amount available to the company's creditors.[15]

13 Business Law Guide to Belgium, No. 224, p. 52.
14 Business Law Guide to Belgium, No. 309-310, p. 67.
15 Business Law Guide to Belgium, No. 332, p. 70.

1.9.2 Minimum Share Capital

The capital of an SPRL/BVBA must amount to at least EUR 18,550 (Sec. 214 CC). At the date of incorporation, a minimum of EUR 6,200 must be paid up.[16] In addition, each share must be paid up to at least 20 per cent. Shares representing a contribution in kind must be fully paid up at the time of incorporation (Sec. 223 CC). **20**

1.9.3 Maintenance of Capital and Liquidity

(i) System

The SPRL/BVBA benefits from an effective capital protection system which compensates for the absence of personal liability on the part of shareholders. All founding shareholders can be held liable for under-capitalisation; such liability applies if the company goes bankrupt within a period of three years from incorporation. **21**

Capital is protected by the allocation of net profits to a legal reserve until such reserve amounts to 10 per cent of the capital (Sec. 319 CC). Managers also have the obligation to convene a shareholders' meeting when losses cause the net assets to fall below half of the registered capital. The shareholders' meeting will decide upon the dissolution or continuation of the company (Sec. 332 CC). **22**

(ii) Distributions

The annual shareholders' meeting decides on the distribution of profits. The articles of association may stipulate certain rules as to profit distribution. There are restrictions on the payment of dividends so as to prohibit net assets from falling below the level of paid-up or, if superior, called-up capital plus the amount of the reserves not available for distribution (Sec. 320 CC). **23**

Distribution of interim dividends is not possible.

(iii) Acquisition of Own Shares and Related Financing

Subject to strict conditions and majority and quorum requirements, it is possible for the SPRL/BVBA to acquire its own shares. The acquisition by the company of its own shares will require the creation of a statutory reserve for own shares in the balance sheet (Sec. 325 CC). The SPRL/BVBA may repurchase a maximum of 10 per cent of shares representing the subscribed capital (Sec. 322 CC). An SPRL/BVBA is prohibited (with certain exceptions) from providing financial assistance or granting loans or security with a view to the acquisition by third parties of the company's shares (Sec. 329 CC). **24**

As long as the SPRL/BVBA holds title to the redeemed shares, it cannot exercise most of the shareholders' rights attaching to such shares (e.g. voting rights, right to dividends, etc.) (Sec. 325 CC). **25**

(iv) Company as Lender or Guarantor

A grant of a security or guarantee (regardless of the beneficiary) by an SPRL/BVBA must be in the corporate interest of the company (direct or indirect economic or commercial benefit) and must fall within the scope of its corporate purpose. **26**

(v) Company as Borrower

There are no specific restrictions applying to shareholders financing the company. In the event of insolvency shareholder loans rank pari passu with non-shareholder loans. **27**

16 Contributions in kind need to be certified by an auditor; contributions in cash are evidenced by a bank certificate.

1.10 Publication and Filing Requirements

28 The company may not start its business activities prior to registration with the Crossroads Bank of Enterprises (Sec. 67 CC). A copy of the deed of incorporation must be filed with the clerk's office of the commercial court (Sec. 67 CC). The Crossroads Bank of Enterprises is centralised.[17] The files of Belgian companies registered with the Crossroads Bank of Enterprises cannot be accessed online. There are no additional filing obligations with respect to foreign shareholders.

A wide range of documentation must be published in the Annexes to the Belgian State Gazette (e.g. excerpts of the deed of incorporation and changes thereto[18] and of other corporate resolutions).[19] In addition, other information (e.g. exploitation seat, additional offices, receipt of certain permits and authorisations, etc.) has to be disclosed in the company's file with the Crossroads Bank of Enterprises. The annual accounts need to be filed with the Central Balance Sheet Office of the National Bank of Belgium.

Several penalties apply in the case of non-filing or late filing of the annual accounts. In addition, administrative penalties may be imposed by the Minister of Economic Affairs. These penalties may amount to a total of EUR 200 per month of delay, part of a month being counted as a full month, subject to a maximum of EUR 1,200. If the annual accounts are not filed on time, any damage suffered by third parties will be deemed to be the consequence of this non-compliance (Sec. 92 Subs. 1 al. 3 and Sec. 98 CC). A company can be dissolved and removed from the register at the request of any interested party or the Public Prosecutor, if it has failed to file its accounts for three consecutive years (Sec. 182 CC). The Central Balance Sheet Office of the National Bank of Belgium may not investigate offences or impose penalties but the judicial and fiscal authorities have the ability to enforce the penalties.

1.11 Financial Reporting

29 In some circumstances, the supervision of the company's activities and financial statements must be exercised by an auditor (*commissaire/commissaris*), appointed by the shareholders' meeting and chosen from among the members of the Institute of Certified Auditors (*Institut des Réviseurs d'Entreprises/Instituut der Bedrijfsrevisoren*) (Sec. 130 CC).[20] In companies where no auditor is required to be appointed, each shareholder has an individual right to audit the corporate books and accounts (Sec. 166 CC).

30 Annual accounts must be approved by the shareholders' meeting within six months of the closing of the financial year (Sec. 92 Subs. 1 CC) and must be filed with the National Bank of Belgium 30 days thereafter (Sec. 98 CC). The annual accounts must be drawn up in accordance with Belgian GAAP. The drawing up of annual accounts in accordance with other accounting principles such as US GAAP or IAS/IFRS is not permitted unless an authorisation thereto has been obtained from the Ministry of Economic Affairs (Sec. 125 CC).

1.12 Employee Participation in Corporate Bodies

31 Employees do not have the right to appoint members of an SPRL/BVBA's corporate bodies.

17 See Mn. 6.

18 For example, registered office, capital, legal form, corporate purpose, financial year, scope of powers and manner in which powers are exercised by persons authorised to manage and represent the company.

19 For example, appointment and dismissal of managers, auditors or liquidators.

20 Pursuant to Sec. 15 CC, this obligation is imposed on all companies:
– either exceeding at least two of the following criteria:
(i) annual average of 50 employees;
(ii) annual turnover: EUR 6,250,000.00 (not including VAT);
(iii) balance sheet total: EUR 3,125,000.00;
– or employing on average 100 persons or more per year.
If the company is part of a group that is required to draw up and file consolidated accounts, the above-mentioned criteria should be calculated on a consolidated basis, i.e. taking into account the company's affiliated companies.

2 The Stock Corporation ("SA/NV")

Literature: Van Lancker, Listed in Belgium: A legal guide for Euronext and Nasdaq Europe Companies (Intersentia, 2003); Business Law Guide to Belgium, Chapter 3 (Kluwer Law International, 2003)

The SA/NV (*société anonyme/naamloze vennootschap*) is the other important corporate entity offering limited shareholder liability in Belgium.[21] Its advantage is that it has easy access to capital markets and therefore greater scope for raising funds to finance its business activities. However, as this will usually result in a large number of shareholders, its governance structure and rules on capital protection are particularly strict. **32**

2.1 Export of Company

The possibility of relocating a Belgian domestic company to a foreign country will apply to an SA/NV in the same manner as for an SPRL/BVBA.[22] An SA/NV can emigrate from Belgium and become a foreign company, with continuity of legal personality, by moving its seat of effective management abroad if the host country accepts this immigration of the company with continuity of legal personality. **33**

2.2 Transformation into a Foreign Entity

Belgian law does not expressly provide for the transformation of a domestic company into a foreign entity. **34**

An SA/NV can be merged into an S.E. The merger is only possible for an SA/NV (Sec. 2 Subs. 1 of the Regulation). The same applies for the transformation into an S.E. (Sec. 2 Subs. 4 of the Regulation). According to Sec. 2 Subs. 2 of the Regulation, an SA/NV can also be part of an S.E. by means of incorporation of a holding S.E., which is allowed when at least two of the companies creating the holding are governed by the law of different EU Member States or when these companies have a subsidiary governed by the law of another EU Member State for at least two years.

An SA/NV can also be part of an S.E. by means of incorporation of a subsidiary S.E. (Sec. 2 Subs. 3 of the Regulation) under the same conditions. The Belgian SA/NV taking part in the formation is governed by Belgian law.

A minimum capital of EUR 120,000 is required to create a new S.E. and a minimum amount of EUR 61,500 has to be paid up.[23]

2.3 Incorporation

An SA/NV is incorporated by at least two shareholders, who may be physical persons or legal entities, by way of a deed of incorporation prepared and executed by a notary public. The SA/NV acquires legal personality and becomes a corporate entity upon filing of the deed of incorporation with the clerk's office of the commercial court (Sec. 2 Subs. 4 CC). In principle, an SA/NV may not enter into any transaction (e.g. lease of premises or purchase of assets) until it has acquired legal personality. It is, however, possible for one or more persons to carry out a transaction on behalf of a company prior to the moment it acquires legal personality. **35**

The incorporation process takes about one to three weeks. Incorporation costs (notary fees and costs, publication costs and the 0.5 per cent registration tax on capital, excluding legal fees) for a company incorporated with a minimum capital of EUR 61,500 amount to approximately EUR 1,860. **36**

21 Many rules discussed for the SPRL/BVBA also apply to the SA/NV. These provisions will be briefly repeated in this section.

22 See Mn. 2.

23 P. Nicaise in: La société européenne: une société de type européen, JT, 2002, p. 481.

2.4 Recurrent Costs and Efforts

37 Recurrent costs and efforts relating to an SA/NV are minimal and relate only to the publication of annual accounts and their filing with the National Bank of Belgium at an annual cost of approximately EUR 400. Other costs and efforts materialise only in the event that certain corporate steps are taken which require notarisation, filing with the Crossroads Bank of Enterprises or publication.

2.5 Shares and Share Transfers

38 The shares issued by an SA/NV can be in bearer form represented by bearer share certificates (Secs. 466 and 467 CC), in registered form (Secs. 462 to 465 CC) or dematerialised shares (Secs. 468 to 475 CC). The shares can be voting as well as non-voting shares, in which case the non-voting shares cannot represent more than one-third of the capital (Sec. 480 CC). Title to bearer shares is transferred by way of handover, title to registered shares by way of endorsement and title to dematerialised shares by way of assignment.

As a general rule, shareholders may freely transfer all or part of their shares to another shareholder or a third party. Share transfers may, however, be restricted by the company's articles of association or a shareholders' agreement (Sec. 510 Subs. 1 CC).[24] These share transfer restrictions are valid, provided that they are limited in time and satisfy the corporate interest test at all times (Sec. 510 Subs. 2 CC). If share transfers have to be approved (e.g. by the board of directors) or are subject to a right of first refusal by the other shareholders, the restriction may not result in a non-transferability for more than six months as from the request for approval or the invitation to exercise the right of first refusal (Sec. 510 Subs. 3 CC).

If the seller of shares in a Belgian resident company is a Belgian individual, he will not be taxable on the capital gain realised on the sale of the shareholding, except if the sale has a speculative character (in which case the tax rate amounts to 33 per cent). If the shares are part of an important shareholding, particular rules apply.

If the seller of shares in a Belgian resident company is a Belgian company, the capital gains will not be taxable provided that the dividends distributed by the company whose shares are being sold qualify for the dividend received deduction. However, the capital gains will be taxable to the extent that they correspond to previously deducted reductions in value.

Sales of shares in Belgian resident companies are, in principle, not subject to registration duties.

2.6 Corporate Bodies

39 An SA/NV is required to hold a shareholders' meeting and to have a board of directors. The company may also have a managing director and/or general manager, a management committee and advisory committees.

2.6.1 Shareholders' Meeting

40 The annual shareholders' meeting is vested with specific powers, such as the approval of the annual accounts (Sec. 554 Subs. 1 CC), the decision to release directors and auditors from liability arising out of the performance of their duties (Sec. 554 Subs. 2 CC) and the appointment and dismissal of the directors and auditor(s) (Sec. 518 Subs. 2 and Subs. 3 CC).[25]Extraordinary shareholders' meetings decide on modifications to the company's articles of association in the presence of a notary[26] (Sec. 558 CC). Special shareholders' meetings concern a residual category of topics (e.g. replacement of directors).[27]

24 Business Law Guide to Belgium, No. 181, p. 44.
25 Van Lancker, p. 3.
26 See Mn. 11.
27 See Mn. 12.

2.6.2 Board of Directors

An SA/NV is managed by a board of directors composed of at least three persons who may, but need not, be shareholders. The minimum number of directors can be reduced to two if the company only has two shareholders (Sec. 518 CC). The directors are appointed by the shareholders' meeting and are removable at any time without cause (Sec. 518 Subs. 3 CC). 41

The board of directors has residual powers *vis-à-vis* the shareholders' meeting (Sec. 522 Subs. 1 CC) and some acts are specifically reserved for the board by the CC (Secs. 581 and 92 Subs. 1 CC).

The board of directors represents the company *vis-à-vis* third parties and in legal proceedings as plaintiff or defendant.[28] However, the articles of association may grant to one or more directors the power to represent the company alone or jointly (Sec. 522 Subs. 2 CC).

2.6.3 Managing Director and General Manager

The board of directors may grant daily management powers either to a director, the managing director (*administrateur délégué/gedelegeerd bestuurder*), the general manager (*directeur général/algemeen directeur*) or any other person (Sec. 525 CC). The person to whom the daily management is delegated represents the company within the limits of such daily management (Sec. 525 Subs. 1 CC). 42

2.6.4 Management Committee

The company's articles of association may authorise the board of directors to establish a management committee (*comité de direction/directiecomité*) enjoying legal recognition and decision-making powers (Sec. 524 *bis* CC). The scope of the powers that may be delegated to the management committee encompasses all management powers of the board of directors, except for decisions concerning the general policy of the company and all acts specifically reserved for the board by the CC. 43

2.6.5 Advisory Committee

The board of directors may also create one or more advisory committees (*comités consultatifs/adviserende comités*) (Sec. 522 CC). Only directors may be appointed as members of these committees. Advisory committees may not represent the company *vis-à-vis* third parties. 44

2.7 Duties and Liabilities of Directors

The directors are responsible for the performance of their duties in accordance with the general rules of personal contractual liability *vis-à-vis* the company and they are liable for any shortcomings in the management (Sec. 527 CC).[29] The directors are held jointly and severally liable towards the company and third parties for damages that result from non-compliance with the provisions of the CC or the articles of association (Sec. 528 Subs. 1 CC). 45

According to Sec. 530 CC, any director, former director or person who, without having been formally appointed as a director of an SA/NV, nevertheless acted in fact as a director and performs the duties of a director, may be held personally liable for all or part of the company's debts (up to the amount of the net liabilities) in the event of the company's bankruptcy when the liabilities surpass the assets, if such director has committed an act of manifest gross negligence that contributed to the company's bankruptcy. The general rules of tort liability may also apply.

In addition to the general liability of directors, the directors can be held liable for any breach of the rules relating to the protection of the company's capital listed in Sec. 610 CC.

28 Business Law Guide to Belgium, No. 203, p. 49.
29 Business Law Guide to Belgium, No. (a), p. 52.

Directors may incur criminal liability for certain offences committed while carrying out their duties (Secs. 647 to 653 CC). In some cases, directors can be held criminally liable for an offence committed by the company itself.

Under Belgian law, if, as a result of incurred losses, the net assets of an SA/NV are lower than half of the corporate capital, the directors must convene a shareholders' meeting, which must take place within two months after such loss was discovered or should have been discovered. The shareholders have to decide either to dissolve (with a special quorum and majority) the company or to continue its activities. Identical rules exist if the net assets are lower than one-quarter of the corporate capital. In such case, one-quarter of the votes of the shareholders' meeting is sufficient for a resolution to dissolve the company (Sec. 633 CC).[30]

Claims against directors in respect of activities in connection with their duties become time-barred after five years from the date such activities were performed or, if wilfully concealed, as from the date of their discovery (Sec. 198 Subs. 1 CC). The five year term applies to any kind of liability, including tort liability.

46 Directors' liability is insurable. Such insurance is almost invariably obtained by the company for the benefit of its directors and premiums are normally paid by the company. The insurance company cannot be obliged to cover damages caused deliberately. Criminal or tax penalties and fines can never be insured against.

47 Specific information and reporting duties must be complied with in the case of a conflict of interest on the part of a director and a member of the management committee[31] (Secs. 523 and 524 *bis* CC).[32]

According to the Royal Decree of 24 October 1934, a judge may prohibit a person from acting as director if such person has been convicted by a criminal court for criminal actions defined in Article 1 of the Royal Decree. When convicted for criminal actions in the context of an insolvency of a company, a person may be prohibited from carrying out any commercial activity (Art. 1 *bis*). The judge has a wide discretion but the interdiction may not be shorter than three years or longer than ten years.

2.8 Shareholders' Liability

48 As a general rule, shareholders may not be held liable for the debts incurred or transactions carried out by the company. Their maximum exposure is in principle limited to the amount of their contribution to the company's capital (Secs. 61 and 437 CC).

As for the SPRL/BVBA, the shareholders of an SA/NV may be held personally liable, namely in the event of "piercing the corporate veil" (Sec. 456 CC).[33]

2.9 Capitalisation and Financing

2.9.1 Basic Concepts

49 As for the SPRL/BVBA, the SA/NV financing regulations are based on the concept of a restricted share capital counterbalancing the notion of limited shareholder liability. The share capital of the company is therefore intended to form a capital fund which represents the minimum amount available to the company's creditors.

2.9.2 Minimum Share Capital

50 The minimum share capital of an SA/NV is EUR 61,500 (Sec. 439 CC). The capital must be entirely subscribed (Sec. 441 CC).

30 Business Law Guide to Belgium, No. 5. 309-310, p. 67.
31 A conflict of interest arises when the direct or indirect personal interest of a director conflicts with a decision to be taken by the board of directors.
32 Van Lancker, p. 30.
33 See Mn. 17.

At least one-quarter of the par or accountable value of each share must be paid up upon the issuance of the shares (either at the incorporation of the company or upon a capital increase); a contribution in kind must be fully paid up within five years of the incorporation (Sec. 448 Subs. 2 CC).

2.9.3 Maintenance of Capital and Liquidity

(i) System

The SA/NV benefits from an effective capital protection system which compensates for the absence of personal liability of shareholders. Capital is protected by allocation of net profits to a legal reserve until such reserve amounts to 10 per cent of the capital (Sec. 616 CC). **51**

Directors also have the obligation to convene a shareholders' meeting when losses cause net assets to fall below half of the registered capital in order to decide on the dissolution or continuation of the company (Sec. 633 CC). In addition, any interested party may request the dissolution of the company when the net assets have fallen below EUR 61,500 (Sec. 634 CC).

In the case of a capital decrease (not below the legal minimum amount) through repayment to shareholders or through exemption from the obligation to pay up shares, a two-month waiting period, starting from the publication of the capital decrease decision in the Annexes to the Belgian State Gazette, applies before the repayment or exemption can take place, in order to allow the creditors of the company to request security for their claims which have fallen due (Sec. 613 Subs. 1 CC).

(ii) Distributions

The annual shareholders' meeting decides on the distribution of profits. The articles of association may also stipulate certain rules as to profit distribution. **52**

There are restrictions on the payment of dividends so as to prohibit net assets from falling below the level of paid-up or, if superior, called-up capital plus the amount of reserves not available for distribution (Sec. 617 CC).

If certain conditions are fulfilled, the board of directors can distribute an interim dividend during the second half of the business year (Sec. 618 CC).

(iii) Acquisition of Own Shares and Related Financing

As for the SPRL/BVBA, there are restrictions on the acquisition (Sec. 620 CC) or the acceptance in pledge (Sec. 630 CC) by an SA/NV of its own shares, profit sharing certificates or certificates.[34] Financial assistance in view of the acquisition of the company's shares by third parties is prohibited. **53**

Subsidiaries may not hold shares (or profit sharing certificates) in a parent company which is an SA/NV, if these shares together represent more than 10 per cent of the voting rights of the parent company. Strict rules must be complied with where the parent SA/NV controls the subsidiary (Sec. 631 CC). **54**

Two independent companies, at least one of which is an SA/NV with its registered office in Belgium, may not each own shares (or profit sharing certificates or certificates) in the other company representing more than 10 per cent of its voting rights (Sec. 632 CC). **55**

(iv) Company as Lender or Guarantor

The grant of a security or guarantee (regardless of the beneficiary) by an SA/NV is regulated in the same manner as for the SPRL/BVBA.[35] **56**

34 See Mn. 24.
35 See Mn. 26.

(v) Company as Borrower

57 There are no specific restrictions applying to shareholders financing the company. With regard to the treatment of shareholder loans the same rules apply for an SA/NV as for the SPRL/BVBA.[36]

2.10 Publication and Filing Requirements

58 These requirements are to a large extent identical to those for a SPRL/BVBA.[37]

2.11 Financial Reporting

59 Annual accounts must be approved by the shareholders' meeting within six months of the closing of the financial year (Sec. 92 § Subs. 1 CC) and must be filed with the National Bank of Belgium 30 days thereafter (Sec. 98 CC).[38]

The annual accounts must be drawn up in accordance with Belgian GAAP. The drawing up of annual accounts in accordance with other accounting principles such as US GAAP or IAS/IFRS is not permitted unless an authorisation thereto has been obtained from the Ministry of Economic Affairs (Sec. 125 CC). Since 2005, listed companies must draw up their consolidated annual accounts in accordance with the IAS/IFRS principles.

The annual accounts of a company which does not qualify as a small company[39] must be audited by an auditor who is a member of the Institute of Certified Auditors (*Institut des Reviseurs d'Entreprises/Instituut der Bedrijfsrevisoren*) (Secs. 15, 141 and 142 CC).

In companies where no auditor is required to be appointed, each shareholder has an individual right to audit the corporate books and accounts.

2.12 Employee Participation in Corporate Bodies

60 Specific rules are provided for the issue of shares to employees of a company or of its subsidiaries (Sec. 609 CC). However, employees do not have the right to appoint members of an SA/NV's corporate bodies.

36 See Mn. 27.
37 See Mn. 28.
38 See Mn. 30.
39 See Mn. 20.

III. Cyprus

*by Stelios Triantafyllides (M.A., LL.M.) and Elena Papandreou (LL.B.)**

Literature: Gower's Principles of Modern Company Law; Palmer's Company Law (21st Edition – M. Schmitt/H. Thompson); Cypriot Companies Law, Chapter 113

1 The Private Limited Liability Company

The law regarding registered companies in Cyprus derives from the Cypriot Companies Law, Chapter 113, as amended, (the "Companies Law"), which is almost identical to the English Companies Act of 1948. The Companies Law broadly provides for two forms of companies: companies limited by shares and companies limited by guarantee (Sec.3 Subs.1 and 2 Companies Law). 1

In the case of a company limited by shares, each shareholder is a co-owner of the company and the extent of his rights and duties is measured according to the size of his shareholding. The liability of a shareholder *vis-à-vis* the debts of the company is limited to the unpaid amount, if any, on any shares held by him (Sec. 3 Subs. 2(a) Companies Law). 2

Companies limited by shares are sub-divided into public and private companies. In order to qualify as a private company ("*Idiotiki etaireia*" or "Private Limited Liability Company"), a company must satisfy four criteria with respect to the contents of its articles of association (Sec. 29 Companies Law): 3

a) the articles of association must restrict the right to transfer its shares;
b) the number of its members must be limited to 50;
c) the articles should prohibit an invitation to the public to subscribe for its shares or debentures; and
d) the issue of bearer shares should be prohibited.

Companies whose articles of association do not satisfy all four of the above criteria are public companies and form a residual separate category. There are approximately 160,000 private companies registered in Cyprus in contrast to less than 1,000 public companies (the latter estimated by the authors due to lack of figures). 4

Companies limited by guarantee may be registered with or without a share capital and are used invariably for the purpose of non-profit organisations. 5

1.1 Export of Company

It is not possible under the laws of the Republic of Cyprus ("Cyprus Law") to relocate a Private Limited Liability Company to a foreign country irrespective of whether or not that country is another member of the European Union ("Member State"). 6

1.2 Transformation into a Foreign Entity

Under Cyprus Law it is not possible to transform a domestic company into a foreign entity. A merger with an S.E. likewise is not possible. 7

1.3 Incorporation

A Private Limited Liability Company is set up by at least one person by subscribing and signing his name to the memorandum and articles of association (Sec. 3 Subs. 1 and Sec. 8 Companies Law). The memorandum and articles of association are delivered to the Department of the Registrar of Companies and Official Receiver (the "Registrar of Companies") and the Registrar of Companies will register the company and certify that the company is incorporated as a limited liability company. 8

* *Triantafyllides & Sons*, Nicosia.

9 The procedure to incorporate a company usually takes a week. The registration fees payable to the Registrar of Companies for the incorporation of a Private Limited Liability Company with a share capital of EUR 3,000 amount to EUR 300. If the share capital is higher, then the incorporation fees increase by approximately 0.6 per cent of the authorised share capital (Regulation for Companies (Stamp Duties and Rights) of 1992 to 2004).

1.4 Recurrent Costs and Efforts

10 Recurrent costs and efforts concerning a Private Limited Liability Company are generally as follows:
(a) preparation and filing of returns with the tax authorities;
(b) preparation of the audited financial statements and filing thereof with the tax authorities and the Registrar of Companies;
(c) filing of the annual return with the Registrar of Companies (which is an annual "summary" of the corporate picture of the company); and
(d) filing with the Registrar of Companies of any changes in the corporate structure as and when they take place, such as changes in the board of directors, capital increases and transfers of shares.

11 Other than the costs in (a) and (b) above, which depend on the size and complexity of the particular company, the annual costs for corporate housekeeping are minimal.

1.5 Shares and Share Transfers

12 The shares of a Private Limited Liability Company are transferable in the manner provided by the articles of association of the company. Typically, in order to transfer shares in a Private Limited Liability Company, the following procedure is required:
(a) an instrument of transfer is signed by the transferor and transferee. It is noted that this is a legal requirement and pre-requisite for a transfer, as provided by Sec. 73 of the Companies Law;
(b) other existing shareholders should waive any pre-emption rights they may have;
(c) the transferor returns to the company his existing share certificate for cancellation;
(d) the board of directors of the company approves the transfer;
(e) the secretary of the company enters the transferee as a shareholder in the Register of Members of the company;
(f) the company issues a share certificate in the name of the transferee;
(g) the company notifies the Registrar of Companies of the transfer; and
(h) the Registrar of Companies issues a new certificate of shareholders.

13 It is noted that the transfer is completed on the completion of item (e).

1.6 Corporate Bodies

14 Cyprus Law provides for two compulsory bodies for a Private Limited Liability Company: the board of directors and the general meeting.

1.6.1 Board of Directors

15 A Private Limited Liability Company may have one or several directors. Every company shall also have a secretary who is considered to be an officer of the company. A sole director cannot also be the secretary (Sec. 170 and Sec. 171 Subs. 1 Companies Law). It is noted that this restriction does not apply in the case of a private company with a single shareholder (Sec. 171 Subs. 1 Companies Law).

16 The directors carry out the business of the company as agents of the company. The directors are not, as such, employees of the company, neither are they servants of the company. The relationship between the company and its directors is generally regulated by the general principles of principal

and agent.[1] In addition, the directors have a fiduciary duty towards the company. Any officer (director or secretary) of the company is deemed to have apparent authority to bind the company notwithstanding any limitation of his/her authority in the articles of association of the company or otherwise, unless the specific action of the director is beyond his/her duty imposed by law (Sec. 33A Companies Law).

1.6.2 General Meetings

General meetings are intended to be the means whereby the members/shareholders exercise control over the management. The general meeting is, for example, not only responsible for the appointment and dismissal of the directors but its approval is required also for a number of business transactions.[2] 17

Resolutions of the general meeting are passed by a simple majority of the votes present and voting at a meeting, except for matters for which a special resolution is required (75 per cent of the votes present at voting) such as the passing of resolutions for the reduction of capital, amendment to the articles of association, amendment to the objects of the company, liquidation etc. (Sec. 135 Subs. 1 and 2 Companies Law). The general meeting is not entitled to give instructions to directors. 18

1.7 Duties and Liabilities of Directors

The directors are responsible for managing the day-to-day affairs of the company. In carrying out the above function, they have certain statutory and common law duties. These include the following: 19

(a) directors have an obligation to disclose to any meeting any interest they may have in a particular transaction (Sec. 191 Companies Law; Palmer p. 566);
(b) directors have a common law duty to avoid any conflict of interest;
(c) directors have a common law duty to act as fiduciaries towards the company, which requires them to act in the utmost good faith;[3]
(d) directors have a duty to manage the affairs of the company in accordance with the provisions of Cyprus Law generally and in accordance with the memorandum and articles of association; and
(e) directors are required to display in the discharge of their duties the reasonable degree of skill expected from a person of their knowledge and experience.

Failure to comply with any of these duties will lead to the relevant director being liable to the company for breach of duty. 20

The law also provides for a number of instances in which the directors have personal criminal liability. Such instances are included both in the Companies Law and in other legislation. Examples of this are as follows: 21

(a) directors are criminally liable if they make a false statement in a prospectus (Sec. 44 Companies Law);
(b) directors are criminally liable if they willfully make a false statement in any one of a number of documents which the company has a legal obligation to provide (Sec. 373 Companies Law).

Additionally, the directors of a Private Limited Liability Company cannot borrow money from the company and the company cannot guarantee or secure any loan given to its directors for any third party (Sec. 182 Subs. 1 Companies Law). It is noted that this provision used to apply only to public companies but, due to recent amendments to the law, the provision seems to apply to Private Limited Liability Companies as well, even though it is not clear that this is, in fact, the effect of the amendment. 22

If the directors declare an interim dividend and at the end of the year according to the annual accounts it is shown that, for the whole of the relevant year, there were no profits available for

1 Palmer p. 526; *Jacobus Marler estates v. Marler* (1916) 85 L.JP.C167.
2 Gower p. 553.
3 Palmer p. 526.

distribution with which to justify the relevant interim dividend, then the directors are personally liable for paying the amount of any such deficit to the company.

1.8 Shareholders' Liability

23 The liability of the shareholders of a Private Limited Liability Company is limited by the memorandum to the amount, if any, unpaid on the shares held by them respectively (Sec. 3 Subs. 2(a) Companies Law).

24 Generally, neither the legislature nor the judiciary has gone very far in depriving shareholders of the advantages of incorporation and the corporate veil has been pierced mainly: (a) if it is in the interests of the company's creditors, where the company has not complied with certain provisions of the Companies Law or where the company has traded fraudulently; (b) if, again, principally but not exclusively, in the interests of the company's creditors, where there is a group of connected companies which it is thought should be treated as one; and (c) to protect the interests of the tax authorities.[4]

1.9 Capitalisation and Financing

1.9.1 Basic Concepts

25 The memorandum of a Private Limited Liability Company must state the amount of share capital with which the company proposes to be registered and the division thereof into shares of a fixed amount (Sec. 4 Subs. 4(a) Companies Law). This is the authorised capital, which is of importance only in relation to the fees payable to the Registrar of Companies on the formation of the company. Some or all of the authorised capital will have to be subscribed, thus constituting the issued share capital.[5] The issued share capital may consist partly of paid-up capital and partly of uncalled capital.

1.9.2 Minimum Share Capital

26 There is no minimum share capital in a Private Limited Liability Company. The capital can be paid in cash or in kind.

1.9.3 Maintenance of Capital and Liquidity

(i) System

27 Cyprus has strict rules for the maintenance of capital. In this regard:

(a) The company may not reduce its share capital without following strict procedures, which include obtaining the approval of the court.
(b) The company is unable to buy back its own shares except in exceptional circumstances which are provided by Secs. 57A and 57F of the Companies Law.
(c) The company cannot provide financial assistance directly or indirectly for the acquisition of its own shares.
(d) Dividends must not be paid out of capital and must only be paid out of profits.

(ii) Distributions

28 The general rule is that dividends must not be paid out of capital and they can only be paid out of profits. A company may declare either a final dividend or an interim dividend. This is stated in most articles of association including Table A of the Companies Law.[6]

4 Gower, p. 136; *Matero Ltd v. The Republic of Cyprus.*
5 Gower pp. 217 and 218.
6 See also Palmer p. 652.

(a) Final Dividend
- (i) The final dividend can be declared with respect to any financial year after the audited financial statements for that particular year have been completed;
- (ii) the audited financial statements must show profit available for distribution for that particular period;
- (iii) the board of directors recommends to the annual general meeting the declaration of dividend. Invariably, the articles of association provide that the dividend to be distributed by the annual general meeting cannot exceed the amount recommended by the board of directors; and
- (iv) thereafter, the annual general meeting declares a dividend.

(b) Interim Dividend
- (i) At any given time, the directors have the power to declare a dividend for a year for which no audited financial statements have yet been prepared;
- (ii) they do so on the assumption that, when the audited financial statements for the particular year are prepared, they will show that the whole year had sufficient profits to justify the declaration of the said dividend;
- (iii) however, if at the end of the year and by the relevant audit it is shown that for the whole of the relevant year there were no profits available for distribution with which to justify the relevant interim dividend, then the directors are personally liable to pay the amount of any such deficit to the company; and
- (iv) a company may declare an interim dividend more than once a year.

(iii) Acquisition of Own Shares and Related Financing

The general principle is that a company cannot buy back its own shares since this would amount **29** to an unlawful reduction of capital.[7] It is also noted that the law contains provisions which enable a company to issue redeemable preference shares (Sec. 57 Companies Law). Nevertheless, the law imposes strict conditions on the funds which can be used to redeem such shares. In effect, these are profits that would otherwise have been available for distribution as dividend. Further, it is possible to redeem the premium on any such shares out of the share premium account.

It is noted that the Companies Law has specific provisions relating to the ability of a company to buy back its own shares (Secs. 57A to 57F Companies Law). Even though these sections do not specifically state that they apply only to public companies, the effect of the wording thereof clearly results in this being available only to public companies which are listed on the stock exchange.

(iv) Company as Lender or Guarantor

A company may give loans to third parties. Further, a company may provide guarantees to third **30** parties provided that there is commercial justification for it to do so and/or it obtains corporate benefit. According to case law, this is a business issue to be decided by the board of directors of the company when approving the transaction.[8]

It is not lawful for a company to give, whether directly or indirectly, by means of a loan, guarantee, the provision of security or otherwise, any financial assistance to purchase its own shares or those of its holding company and, if it does so, the transaction will be void. The only exceptions are where the ordinary business of the company is the lending of money and where a loan is made in the ordinary course of business or to enable employees to acquire shares (Sec. 53 Subs. 1 Companies Law; Gower, p. 227).

7 Sec. 53 of the Companies Law; Gower p. 225; *Trevor v. Whitworth* (1887) 12 App. Cas. 409 K.4.

8 *Rolled Steel Products (Holdings) Limited v. British Steel Corp and others* [1985] 3 All ER.

(v) Company as Borrower

31 A company may obtain loans from third parties, including its shareholders. In the event of insolvency, shareholder loans generally rank pari passu with other unsecured creditors.

1.10 Publication and Filing Requirements

32 A company must file with the Registrar of Companies full particulars of its corporate structure including:
(a) its memorandum and articles of association;
(b) its authorised and issued capital;
(c) its shareholders;
(d) its members of the board of directors and the secretary;
(e) the address of its registered office;
(f) any charges credited against any of its assets; and
(g) a copy of its audited financial statements.

33 In this regard, the company must file its annual return with the Registrar of Companies specifying the above and, further, it is under an obligation to notify the Registrar of Companies whenever there is a change to any of the above particulars during the course of the year.

34 The company file registered with the Registrar of Companies is open to the public and any interested person can review the documents in the file and request a certificate detailing any of the above particulars as well as copies of any documents submitted to the Registrar of Companies. Failure to comply with the filing obligation may result in a fine for the company for every day during which the default continues and ultimately in the deletion from the register. Penalties, however, are rarely enforced in practice.

Third parties may rely on the register content unless they know that filings were not made in time. The register cannot be accessed online.

1.11 Financial Reporting

35 A company must prepare annual audited financial statements. In this regard:
(a) the first set of audited financial statements may refer to a period which does not exceed 18 months after the incorporation of the company;
(b) thereafter, the audited financial statements must refer to the immediately preceding financial year;
(c) the audited financial statements must be prepared within 12 months of the expiration of the period to which they refer; and
(d) the financial statements must be drawn up in accordance with the International Financial Reporting Standards (IFRS) (Sec. 142 Subs. 1(a) Companies Law).

Small companies are exempt from the obligation to submit the financial statements to an audit by an auditor. According to Section 152A Subs. 2 Companies Law, the term "small company" is defined as follows: A company of which at least two of the following three criteria do not exceed, for the whole financial year, the following thresholds: (i) the total assets (without subtracting liabilities) which appear on the balance sheet CYP 2 million (approximately EUR 3.46 million); (ii) net turnover CYP 4.1 million (approximately EUR 7.1 million); (iii) number of employees, on average, 50 individuals. Provided that a company which initially satisfies the above criteria, loses the character of a small company only if it exceeds the above criteria in two whole financial years.

1.12 Employee Participation in Corporate Bodies

36 There is no requirement or restriction on the participation or representation of employees of a company in its corporate bodies.

2 The Public Limited Liability Company

Public companies in Cyprus ("*Dimosia etaireia*" or "Public Limited Liability Company") offer limited shareholder liability and are a residual separate category. Their articles of association do not satisfy all four criteria of Sec. 29 of the Companies Law (which specifies the criteria of qualifying as a Private Limited Liability Company).[9] **37**

2.1 Export of Company

As in the case of a Private Limited Liability Company, it is not possible under Cypriot Law to relocate a public company to a foreign country irrespective of whether or not it is another Member State. **38**

2.2 Transformation into a Foreign Entity

Under Cypriot Law it is not possible to transfer a domestic public company into a foreign entity. A potential merger with an S.E. is not provided for. **39**

2.3 Incorporation

A public company is set up in the same manner as a Private Limited Liability Company, with the following differences: **40**

(a) a public company is set up by at least seven persons (Sec. 3 Subs. 1 Companies Law);
(b) the name of a public company must end with the words "Public Limited" (Sec. 4 Subs. 1(a)(ii) Companies Law). The minimum authorised and issued share capital of a public company is CYP 15,000 (approximately EUR 26,000) (see Sec. 4A Subs. 1 Companies Law);
(c) the minimum authorised and issued share capital of a public company is CYP 15,000 (approximately EUR 26,000) (see Sec. 4A Subs. 1 Companies Law);
(d) a public company is unable to commence business unless it has issued a prospectus for the subscription of the share capital or, if it has done so, it delivers to the Registrar of Companies a statement in lieu of a prospectus. The Registrar of Companies thereafter certifies that the public company is entitled to commence business (Sec. 104 Subs. 1 and 2 Companies Law); and
(e) a public company cannot commence its business unless it is supplied by the Registrar of Companies with a certificate which confirms that the nominal value of the issued share capital is at least equal to CYP 15,000 (approximately EUR 26,000) (Sec. 104(3) Companies Law).

On the assumption that there will be no public offering, the procedure to register a public company takes about two weeks and the incorporation fees payable to the Registrar of Companies will be, with minimum share capital of CYP 15,000 (approximately EUR 26,000), approximately CYP 150 (EUR 260). If there is to be an offering to the public, the timing and costs may vary substantially, depending on the prospectus to be issued. **41**

2.4 Recurrent Costs and Efforts

A public company would typically face costs and efforts comparable to those of a Private Limited Liability Company. It is noted that the above statement does not address any issues of filings etc. with any stock exchange on which the shares of the public company may be listed. **42**

2.5 Shares and Share Transfers

In order to transfer shares in a public company, the following procedure is followed: **43**

(a) the transferor and transferee sign an instrument of transfer;
(b) the old share certificate is returned to the public company for cancellation;

9 See Mn. 3.

(c) the public company enters the new shareholder in the Register of Members as a member in relation to the shares which have been transferred; and
(d) the public company issues a new share certificate in the name of the transferee.
It is noted that the transfer is completed on the completion of item (d).

44 It is noted that, unlike the procedure to transfer shares in the Private Limited Liability Company, the approval of the board of directors is not required and the Registrar of Companies is not notified of the transfer of shares (which is only done at the stage of the annual return).

45 It is noted that the above does not apply to public companies the shares of which are listed with any stock exchange.

2.6 Corporate Bodies

46 Corporate bodies of a public company are the same as in a Private Limited Liability Company.[10] There are, however, additional requirements in the Companies Law on corporate governance such as:
(a) the articles of association of a public company must include the principles which define the number and the procedure for the appointment of the directors who have a duty to manage the public company and represent it to third parties (Sec. 4 Subs. 5 Companies Law); and
(b) the pre-emption rights of the shareholders for the issue of shares cannot be limited or excluded by the articles of association but only by a decision of the general meeting. The directors have an obligation to present to the general meeting a report in writing, which must state the reasons for limitation or exclusion of the pre-emption rights and the justification for the proposed issue price (Sec. 60B Subs. 5 Companies Law).

2.7 Duties and Liabilities of Directors

47 The duties and liabilities of the directors of a public company are comparable to those of the directors of a Private Limited Liability Company.[11] Furthermore, in cases where losses in previous years result in a public company losing 50 per cent of its issued capital or in cases where, in the opinion of its directors, its corporate purpose is under question, the directors have an obligation to convene an extraordinary general meeting not later than 28 days after the reduction was first known to its directors and the extraordinary general meeting needs to be held not later than 56 days after the decision to convene such a meeting in order to examine whether the company needs to be dissolved (Sec. 169F Subs. 1 Companies Law).

Omission by the directors of a public company to act as above constitutes a civil offence and they are liable to damages. This liability is personal, unlimited and joint and several (Sec. 169F Subs. (2) Companies Law).

2.8 Shareholders' Liability

48 As in the case of a Private Limited Liability Company, the liability of the shareholders of a public company is limited to the amounts, if any, unpaid on the shares respectively held by them (Sec. 3 Subs. 2(a) Companies Law).

2.9 Capitalisation and Financing

2.9.1 Basic Concepts

49 The same principles that apply to a Private Limited Liability Company apply to a public company.[12]

10 See Mn. 14 et seq.
11 See Mn. 19 et seq.
12 See Mn. 25.

2.9.2 Minimum Share Capital

The minimum share capital of a public company is CYP 15,000 (approximately EUR 26,000) (Sec. 4A Subs.1 Companies Law). No allotment shall be made of any share capital of a public company unless the amount stated in the prospectus is the minimum amount which, in the opinion of the directors, must be received by the issue of share capital that has been subscribed and the sum payable on application for the amount so stated has been paid and received by the company. The amount so stated in the prospectus shall be reckoned exclusively of any amount payable otherwise than in cash and is referred to as the "minimum subscription" (Sec. 47 Subs. 1 and 2 Companies Law). **50**

2.9.3 Maintenance of Capital and Liquidity

(i) System

The system of preservation and maintenance of the capital of a public company is, by and large, identical to the system which applies to a Private Limited Liability Company,[13] subject to the conditions which are set out here below. **51**

(ii) Distributions

Just as in the case of a Private Limited Liability Company,[14] the Companies Law imposes strict conditions for the making of any distributions by a public company. If anything, these restrictions are stricter than in a Private Limited Liability Company. **52**

A public company may reduce its share capital by following the reduction of capital procedures (Secs. 64 and 65 Companies Law).

A public company can only declare dividends to its shareholders out of its net profits according to the principles described in relation to a Private Limited Liability Company.[15]

Further, a public company cannot declare dividends to its shareholders if, at the end of the latest financial year, its net assets, as they appear in the annual accounts, or could end up as a result of such distribution, are less than the sum of the issued capital and the reserves the distribution of which is prohibited by the law or the articles of association (Sec. 169A Companies Law). The amount to be distributed to the shareholders may not exceed the amount of the results of the last audited financial year, increased by the profits that have been brought forward from the last financial year and the retention from the reserves which are available for this purpose, decreased, however, by the amount of the losses that have been brought forward from the previous financial year, as well as by the amounts which have been moved to reserves according to the law or the articles of association (Sec. 169A Subs. 2 Companies Law).

A public company may declare interim dividends if the following requirements are satisfied:

(a) Interim accounts are drafted in which it appears that the amounts available for distribution are sufficient (Sec. 169C Subs. (a) Companies Law).

(b) The amount to be distributed cannot exceed the amount of the profits of the last financial year, for which the annual accounts have been audited, increased by the profits that have been brought forward from the last financial year and the retention from the reserves which are available for this purpose, and decreased by the amount of the losses that have been brought forward from the previous financial year as well as by the amounts that have been moved to reserves according to the law or the articles of association (Sec. 169C Subs. (b) Companies Law).

13 See Mn. 27.

14 See Mn. 28 et seq.

15 See Mn. 28.

(iii) Acquisition of Own Shares and Related Financing

53 The law allows a public company to buy back part of its own shares by following strict procedures (Secs. 57A to 57F Companies Law). The relevant conditions are designed to ensure that, when any buyback takes place, there is full transparency and this is only done in cases where such buyback will not affect the solvency of the public company.

(iv) Company as Lender or Guarantor

54 The same principles that apply to a Private Limited Liability Company apply to a public company.[16]

(v) Company as Borrower

55 The same principles that apply to a Private Limited Liability Company above apply to a public company.[17]

2.10 Publication and Filing Requirements

56 The same principles that apply to a Private Limited Liability Company apply to a public company.[18]

2.11 Financial Reporting

57 The same principles that apply to a Private Limited Liability Company apply to a public company.[19]

2.12 Employee Participation in Corporate Bodies

58 There is no requirement or restriction on the employees of a company to participate or be represented in the corporate bodies.

16 See Mn. 30.
17 See Mn. 31.
18 See Mn. 32.
19 See Mn. 35.

IV. Czech Republic

*by Lukas Sevcik**

1 The Limited Liability Company ("s.r.o.")

Literature: Dědič, Jan, Obchodní zákoník: komentář (1st edition, Prague, Polygon 2005); Dvořák, Tomáš, Společnost s ručením (2nd edition, Prague, ASPI 2005) Commercial Code – Obchodní zákoník: Act No. 513/1991 Coll., as amended (Prague, Trade Links 2004)

The limited liability company (*společnost s ručením omezeným,*"s.r.o.") is the most common corporate structure used in the Czech Republic to achieve the concept of limited shareholder liability, is generally preferred by enterprises with a limited number of investors and is usually used by small to medium-sized enterprises. The statutory corporate governance framework permits a high degree of flexibility in the drafting of the memorandum of association. In 2003 approximately 208.000 limited liability companies were registered in the Czech Republic in contrast to approximately 16.000 stock corporations. 1

1.1 Export of Company

An s.r.o. may transfer its registered office (corporate seat) to a foreign country[1] irrespective of whether or not it is another EU Member State, and vice versa, where an international agreement binding the Czech Republic so provides,[2] (Sec. 26 Subs. 1 ObchZ[3]) and in cases and under conditions stipulated by EC law (Sec. 26 Subs. 4 ObchZ).[4] 2

Czech law does not prevent an s.r.o. from moving its entire business abroad and does not set any special requirements for foreign entities wishing to establish their business in the Czech Republic in the form of a subsidiary or a branch. 3

1.2 Transformation into a Foreign Entity

Czech law does not expressly provide for the transformation of a domestic company into a foreign entity. An s.r.o. cannot be merged with and into an S.E. 4

1.3 Incorporation

An s.r.o. may be founded by one shareholder (an individual or a legal entity), and it may have a maximum of 50 shareholders. The founders establish a company with the execution of a memorandum of association[5] in the form of a notarial deed (Sec. 57 ObchZ). The general meeting may also adopt articles of association that regulate the internal affairs of the s.r.o. (Sec. 110 Subs. 2 ObchZ). The company will legally exist upon its entry into the commercial register.[6] 5

An s.r.o. with a sole shareholder may not be the sole founder or the sole shareholder of another s.r.o. One individual may not be a sole shareholder of more than three s.r.o. companies. The 6

* *Linklaters*, Prague. Written with the assistance of Tomáš Doležil.

1 Czech company law is based on the incorporation theory.

2 The Czech Republic has not entered into any such agreement. Therefore, the transfer of the registered office is in fact not practicable. According to the relevant literature (e.g. Pelikánová, Commentary on the Commercial Code, I. First Part, third edition, p. 263; Doležil/Salač, Current issues regarding the right of establishment of companies, Právní Rozhledy 5/2003, p. 224 et seq.), the EC Treaty cannot be viewed as an international treaty within the meaning of Sec. 26 ObchZ.

3 Czech Commercial Code, Act no. 513/1991 Coll., as amended (*obchodní zákoník*, "ObchZ").

4 The general interpretation is that this applies only to supranational entities, such as the S.E.

5 In the case where the company is founded by a sole shareholder, the memorandum of association is replaced by the so-called founding deed.

6 Commercial registers are maintained by the regional courts (*Krajský soud* or *Městský soud*) which are competent for the registered seat of the company.

prevailing view is that this restriction applies also to foreign entities, i.e. a foreign entity with a sole shareholder may not be the sole founder or sole shareholder of an s.r.o.[7]

7 The incorporation procedure may last from two to four weeks. The notarial fees for the incorporation of an s.r.o. which has the required minimum share capital of CZK 200,000 (approximately EUR 6,770) will amount to approximately CZK 5,000 (approximately EUR 170);[8] the registration fee for registration in the commercial register amounts to CZK 5,000 (EUR 170).

1.4 Recurrent Costs and Efforts

8 Recurrent costs and efforts relating to a Czech s.r.o. are not significant and relate only to the usual corporate maintenance such as annual general meetings, the production and publication of annual accounts and their filing with the collection of documents in the commercial register.[9] No regular annual fees are to be paid.

1.5 Shares and Share Transfers

9 The share capital of an s.r.o. is divided into ownership interests (*obchodní podíl*). Each shareholder holds only one ownership interest which represents the rights and duties of the shareholder and is calculated as a ratio of a shareholder's investment contribution to the amount of the share capital. The memorandum of association may provide for ownership interests (and voting rights) that differ from the proportionally calculated share based on the shareholders' contributions.

10 The transfer of an ownership interest to another shareholder requires the approval of the general meeting, unless the need for such approval is explicitly removed in the memorandum of association (Sec. 115 Subs. 1 ObchZ). Additional restrictions may be provided for in the memorandum of association. The memorandum of association may permit the transfer of an ownership interest to a non-shareholder and may also require approval by the general meeting for such a transfer. If the company has a sole shareholder, the ownership interest is transferable without restrictions (Sec. 115 Subs. 2 ObchZ).

11 An ownership interest is transferred by way of written agreement which must contain provisions regarding the purchase price or its determination and the accession of the new shareholder to the memorandum of association and signatures thereto must be notarised (Sec. 115 Subs. 3 ObchZ). The transfer will take effect between the parties upon its execution, *vis-à-vis* the s.r.o. upon its receipt by the managing director (Sec. 115 Subs. 4 ObchZ) and *vis-à-vis* the public upon registration of the new shareholders in the commercial register, which is, however, of a declaratory nature only.

12 Ownership interests in an s.r.o. do not qualify for listing on a stock exchange.

1.6 Corporate Bodies

13 The s.r.o. has two compulsory corporate bodies: the managing directors and the general meeting. The facultative body explicitly provided for in the ObchZ is the supervisory board. Further corporate bodies, such as advisory boards or shareholder committees are optional. The responsibilities of optional bodies can be freely defined but should not interfere with the statutory responsibilities of the compulsory bodies.[10]

7 Štenglová/Plíva/Tomsa, Commercial Code, 9th edition, p. 340; Dědič, Commercial Code, Commentary, First Part (Prague, Polygon 2002), p. 960. In practice, it may be unclear which foreign companies are considered limited liability companies. The Twelfth Directive in this context specifies one member company in each individual EC Member State (see Part 1, I, Mn. 62). As regards the companies from non-EC Member States, the specified characteristics of each such company would have to be considered to see whether the company was a limited liability company.

8 This does not include VAT or any other additional copies of documents.

9 The annual accounts of medium-sized and large s.r.o.s must be audited (Sec. 20 Subs. 1(b) Accounting Act). This will result in further costs being incurred. For more detailed information, see Mn. 47.

10 The statutory responsibilities of the compulsory corporate bodies are rigid and mandatory.

1.6.1 Managing Directors

An s.r.o. may have one or several managing directors (*jednatel*) appointed by the general meeting who exclusively represent the company *vis-à-vis* third parties (Sec. 133 Subs. 1 ObchZ). They can act on behalf of the s.r.o. solely or jointly (however, a managing director may not represent the s.r.o. jointly with a proxy holder (*prokurista*)).[11] The manner of acting on behalf of the company is registered in the commercial register. **14**

Restrictions on representing the s.r.o. stipulated by the memorandum of association, articles of association and the general meeting are not effective *vis-à-vis* third parties. **15**

1.6.2 Shareholders' Meeting

The ObchZ provides for powers[12] of the general meeting which may be extended by the memorandum of association. Shareholders exercise their rights to manage and supervise the s.r.o.'s activities through its general meeting to the extent and in the manner set forth in the memorandum of association or articles of association (Sec. 122 ObchZ). Furthermore, the general meeting is entitled to give direct instructions and guidelines to the managing directors (Sec. 135 Subs. 2 in connection with Sec. 194 Subs. 4 ObchZ). However, nobody (individual shareholders, controlling entity, etc.) is entitled to give direct instructions to the management in respect of commercial management, unless a controlling agreement is concluded.[13] **16**

Resolutions of the shareholders' meeting are passed by a simple majority of the votes cast, unless the ObchZ or the memorandum of association requires a higher majority (Sec. 127 Subs. 3 ObchZ). Higher thresholds (generally involving a two-thirds majority) apply in certain cases – for example the passing of resolutions amending the memorandum of association and the articles of association, and increasing the share capital (Sec. 127 Subs. 4 ObchZ). **17**

1.6.3 Supervisory Board

If a supervisory board is established,[14] it is responsible for supervising the managing directors' compliance with their duties and has the right to inspect all company files. There must be at least three members of the supervisory board, who are to be appointed by the general meeting.[15] **18**

11 High court decision No. 7 Cmo 55/99. The company acts through the managing directors. The proxy holders act for the company.

12 The powers of the general meeting include: (i) approval of transactions made in the name of the company prior to its incorporation; (ii) approval of the company's ordinary, extraordinary and consolidated financial statements and, in the instances stipulated by law, interim financial statements, distribution of its profit and settlement of any loss; (iii) approval of the memorandum of association and its amendments; (iv) decision-making on an increase or reduction in the registered capital or admission of a specific investment contribution in kind, or approval of the setting off of a monetary receivable from the company against a company receivable in the form of payment of an investment contribution; (v) the appointment, removal and remuneration of the managing directors; (vi) the appointment, removal and remuneration of the members of the supervisory board; (vii) expulsion of a member of the company in accordance with Secs. 113 and 121 ObchZ; (viii) the appointment, removal and remuneration of a liquidator, and decision-making on whether to wind up the company with liquidation, if the articles of association so allow; (ix) decision-making on transfer or lease of an enterprise or a part thereof to, or on conclusion of such contract with, a controlled entity; (x) decision-making on a merger, transfer of business assets to a sole member, division, or conversion of legal form; (xi) approval of a controlling agreement, a contract on profit transfer and a contract with a silent partner, and amendments thereto; (xii) approval of a contract on performance of an office; and (xiii) any other matters entrusted to the general meeting by law or the memorandum of association. Unless the memorandum of association provides otherwise, the general meeting authorises and removes a proxy holder. The general meeting may reserve the right to decide on other matters falling within the powers of other company bodies.

13 Under a controlling agreement, the controlled entity agrees to be subject to unified management (including commercial management) by another entity. The controlling entity is entitled to give instructions to the controlled entity's statutory body, including those which might be disadvantageous to the controlled entity, but which are in the interests of the controlling entity or another entity within a holding group. The duty of the person of the controlled entity's statutory body to perform with due managerial care is not thereby affected.

14 This is at the sole discretion of the founders and shareholders.

15 See Mn. 67.

1.7 Duties and Liabilities of Directors

19 Managing directors must act with due managerial care (i.e. with the diligence of a prudent businessman) and their responsibility cannot be limited. In the event of a breach, the managing director must prove that he/she has acted with due managerial care. Those managing directors who caused the breach are personally jointly and severally liable to the company (Sec. 135 Subs. 2, Sec. 194 Subs. 5 and 6 ObchZ). Managing directors who are personally jointly and severally liable to the company guarantee jointly and severally obligations of the s.r.o. towards third persons (including the shareholders) if third parties cannot be satisfied by the company because the said company is insolvent or has halted its payments.[16] Claims against managing directors lapse after a period of four years. Managing directors are not liable if they have followed an instruction from the general meeting and such instruction is in line with the law. Czech law does not regulate or restrict in any manner insurance of the managing directors, and premiums for such D&O insurance may be paid by the s.r.o.[17]

20 Managing directors must fulfil certain qualification criteria, in particular, a clean criminal record[18] and no involvement in recent bankruptcy proceedings[19] (Sec. 135 Subs. 2, Sec. 194 Subs. 7 ObchZ).

21 A person cannot become a managing director of an s.r.o. if he/she has been the statutory body or a member of a statutory body over which bankruptcy has been declared or rejected due to insufficient assets within a period of one year prior to the declaration of the bankruptcy or the rejection thereof due to insufficient assets. The disqualification lasts for three years and the person can be discharged by means of: (i) the person's appointment by a two-thirds majority at the general meeting of the s.r.o.; or (ii) the person's confirmation in his office by the same majority of votes (Sec. 38 l ObchZ).

22 The commercial management of an s.r.o. is within the remit of the managing directors and, if there is more than one managing director, management decisions are taken by a majority of them, unless the memorandum of association specifies otherwise (Sec. 134 ObchZ). The managing directors have other statutory obligations, e.g. arranging for the necessary filings to be made with the commercial register and convening the annual shareholders' meeting.

1.8 Shareholders' Liability

23 Generally, a "piercing of the corporate veil" is not known under Czech law, which looks to protect the principle of limited liability. Shareholders are personally jointly and severally liable for the obligations of the company only up to the amount of unpaid capital contributions as registered in the commercial register.

24 Questions regarding the responsibilities of controlling entities are regulated by special legal provisions setting out the system of holding company law (Sec. 66 a et seq. ObchZ). In addition, any person (including a shareholder) substantially influencing the behaviour of the company is liable in the same manner as the managing directors (Sec. 66 Subs. 6 ObchZ).

16 Those managing directors who did not cause the breach are not liable to the company nor do they guarantee the obligations of the company towards third parties.

17 However, please note that the payment of premiums is a non-tax deductible expense.

18 Managing directors must not have been convicted of (i) an intentional criminal offence and sentenced to a term of imprisonment exceeding a period of one year; (ii) an intentional criminal offence, the facts of which are related to business activities; or (iii) a criminal offence caused by negligence, the facts of which are related to the scope of business activities.

19 (i) no bankruptcy may have been declared or concluded over a managing director's assets or a court settlement re-confirmed; (ii) during the past three years no proposal for the declaration of bankruptcy over a managing director's assets may have been filed or rejected due to insufficient assets; and (iii) no court or administrative body has imposed on a managing director a prohibition of activities related to the performance of trades pertaining to the company's scope of business or a similar field

1.9 Capitalisation and Financing

1.9.1 Basic Concepts

In line with the Second Directive,[20] the s.r.o. financing regulations are based on the "principle of real capital contribution and maintenance" (Sec. 58 ObchZ). 25

If the s.r.o.'s final loss represents half or more of the company's total share capital (or if the s.r.o. anticipates such a result), the managing directors must convene an extraordinary general meeting and propose to the shareholders the best solution to this situation (e.g. a capital increase, a contribution to other capital funds or winding up the company) (Sec. 128 Subs. 2 and Sec. 193 Subs. 1 ObchZ). 26

Should the s.r.o. become insolvent,[21] the managing directors are obliged to initiate insolvency proceedings. 27

1.9.2 Minimum Share Capital

The minimum share capital of an s.r.o. is CZK 200,000 (approximately EUR 6,770) (Sec. 108 Subs. 1 ObchZ). The minimum amount of a shareholder's contribution is CZK 20,000 (approximately EUR 670). The capital can be contributed in cash or in kind (Sec. 109 ObchZ).[22] 28

In the case of contributions in kind, a shareholder is obliged to pay an additional amount to the company (or to compensate it otherwise) if the contribution in kind does not reach the value declared in the expert opinion (Sec. 59 Subs. 7 ObchZ). 29

If a receivable from a third party is contributed as a contribution in kind to the share capital, the shareholder guarantees the payment of the receivable up to the amount stated in the expert opinion (Sec. 59 Subs. 6 ObchZ). 30

1.9.3 Maintenance of Capital and Liquidity

The concept of s.r.o. financing is based on European legislation. However, it has not been quite so developed by Czech case law. 31

(i) System

The "principle of real capital contribution and maintenance" applies (Secs. 58, 59 and 109 ObchZ).[23] Contributions in kind must correspond to the type of business activities carried out by the s.r.o. The share capital may be reduced only by means of a formal reduction procedure which protects the minority shareholders and the company's creditors. 32

With reference to Sec. 11 of the Second Directive,[24] Sec. 135 and Sec. 196 a Subs. 3 ObchZ regulate the transfer from shareholders to the company of those assets with a value of greater than 10 per cent of the share capital of the company.[25] The consideration for such assets must be valued 33

20 See Part 1, I, Mn. 39 et seq.

21 A company is deemed to be insolvent when: (i) it is unable to meet its obligations towards two or more creditors for more than three months after the maturity of the obligations. The company is deemed to be unable to meet its obligations when it has ceased paying its creditors; or (ii) it is overburdened with debts. The company is deemed to be overburdened with debts if it has two or more creditors and its mature obligations exceed its assets.

22 Where the capital is rendered in cash, at least 30 per cent of the share capital plus the share premium must be paid up on the date of application for registration in the commercial register, provided this is not less than CZK 100,000 (approximately EUR 3,385). The full amount is required where there is only a sole founder (Sec. 111 ObchZ). Contributions in kind must be described in the memorandum of association or in the declaration of the shareholder. Contributions in kind must be further valued by an independent expert who is appointed by the court (Sec. 59 Subs. 3 ObchZ) and fully paid by the date of application for registration of the company in the commercial register (Sec. 59 Subs. 2 ObchZ).

23 Czech case law has, however, not developed the concept of "hidden contributions".

24 See Part 1, I, Mn. 39 et seq.

25 This regulation also regulates asset transfers from the company to shareholders and asset transfers between related entities. However, it excludes transfers made in the ordinary course of business.

by an independent expert appointed by a court. If the transfer is made within three years of the company's registration, it must also be approved by the general meeting.

34 Shareholders may further contribute to other capital funds to increase the equity of an s.r.o. These contributions can only be returned to the shareholders to the extent by which their amount exceeds the company's losses (Sec. 121 ObchZ).

35 A reserve fund is obligatory. It must be gradually contributed to until it contains an amount equivalent to at least 10 per cent of the share capital, unless the memorandum of association provides for a higher amount. The reserve fund may be used only for coverage of the company's losses (Sec. 124 ObchZ).

(ii) Distributions

36 Dividends may only be paid to shareholders of the s.r.o. when the general meeting has approved the payment of dividends on the basis of the company's annual statement for the previous accounting period. The law explicitly prohibits the making of dividend prepayments before the general meeting has decided to pay dividends. The profit which can be distributed is based on profit from the current financial year plus undistributed profit from previous years minus obligatory payments to reserve funds and minus uncovered losses from previous years. A company may not distribute profit if such profit distribution might cause the equity capital to fall below the value of the share capital. (Sec. 123 Subs. 2 and Sec. 178 ObchZ).

(iii) Acquisition of Own Shares and Related Financing

37 An s.r.o. may not acquire its own ownership interests by agreement (Sec. 120 Subs. 1 ObchZ). An s.r.o. may, however, become the holder of its own ownership interest in a situation envisaged by ObchZ. In such situations, the ownership interest is to be sold to the shareholders or third parties with the approval of the general meeting. If the sale fails, either the share capital is to be reduced or the ownership interests are to be divided and distributed to the shareholders according to the ratio of their existing shareholdings (Sec. 115 Subs. 5 and 6 ObchZ). As long as the s.r.o. holds title to its ownership interests, it cannot exercise the related shareholder rights.

38 An s.r.o. may not acquire ownership interests in controlling entities by agreement or provide any other assistance in this regard (Sec. 120 Subs. 3 and Sec. 161 b, 161e and 161j ObchZ).

39 An s.r.o. may not provide financial assistance in connection with the acquisition of its own ownership interest (Sec. 120 Subs. 2 and Sec. 161 e ObchZ).

(iv) Company as Lender or Guarantor

40 An s.r.o. may give loans and credits or grant guarantees or any other type of security to third parties (including its shareholders). If these are given or granted to related persons,[26] these must be approved in advance by the general meeting and made on an arm's length basis (Sec. 135 Subs. 2 and Sec. 196 a Subs. 1 ObchZ and Sec. 23 Subs. 7 ZDP[27]). The same applies if a loan or guarantee is provided to a person who may be simultaneously represented by a related person.

41 Granting a loan or guarantee to a related person in breach of Sec. 196 a ObchZ causes the loan agreement or guarantee to become invalid.[28]

(v) Company as Borrower

42 If the s.r.o. is a borrower or recipient of a guarantee or security, the same principle applies as above.[29] However, loans provided by a controlling entity to an s.r.o. are generally allowed without

26 Managing directors, supervisory board members, proxy holders or any other persons entitled to act on behalf of the s.r.o.

27 Czech Income Taxes Act, Act No. 586/1992 Coll., as amended (*zákon o daní z příjmů*, "ZDP").

28 Supreme Court judgments No. 29 Odo 430/2002 and No. 29 Odo 2011/2000.

29 See Mn. 40.

the prior approval of the general meeting. In the event of bankruptcy the rank equal with non-shareholder loans.

Under the thin capitalisation rule, interest paid on loans from related parties is generally only tax-deductible to the extent that such loans do not exceed four times the borrowing company's equity (Sec. 25 Subs. 1(w) ZDP). **43**

1.10 Publication and Filing Requirements

An s.r.o. is registered in the commercial register.[30] In most cases the registration of new facts in the commercial register is of a declaratory nature. If a third party relies on the information entered in the commercial register, it is protected against the company in the event that the information in the commercial register is proved to be untrue.[31] **44**

The commercial register maintains a collection of documents in which a wide range of documentation and information must be filed.[32] Documents deposited there are accessible to the public and can be copied. The commercial register automatically publishes information about the deposit of documents in the commercial bulletin. Intentional failure to deposit documents constitutes a criminal offence, should such failure affect the rights of third persons. **45**

1.11 Financial Reporting

An s.r.o. must draw up its annual accounts in so timely a manner that the general meeting can resolve on them within six months of the end of the business year.[33] The annual accounts must consist of a balance sheet, a profit and loss statement and an annex[34] (Sec. 18 UZ[35]). The annual accounts must be drawn up in accordance with Czech Generally Accepted Accounting Principles ("Czech GAAP") for statutory purposes. The drawing up of annual accounts in accordance with other accounting principles (such as US GAAP or IAS/IFRS) is not permitted. Group annual accounts may, however, be drawn up in accordance with international reporting standards (Sec. 23(a) of the Act on Accounting) (although this does not release the single group companies from the obligation to draw up their annual accounts in accordance with Czech GAAP). **46**

Auditing of the financial statements is mandatory if an s.r.o. meets at least two of the following three criteria in two consecutive accounting years: (i) its balance sheet total exceeds CZK 40,000,000 (approximately EUR 1,353); (ii) its annual net turnover exceeds CZK 80,000,000 (approximately EUR 2,707); and (iii) the average number of employees in the given accounting period exceeds 50. If the financial statements must be audited, the s.r.o. must also draw up an annual report. The annual report consists of the financial statements, audit report, report on the relationship between the s.r.o. and related entities and other specific information required by law. **47**

1.12 Employee Participation in Corporate Bodies

In general, employees are not represented in the corporate bodies of an s.r.o. If, however, an s.r.o. has established a supervisory board and has more than 50 employees who are employed on more **48**

30 The commercial register is also accessible over the internet at www.justice.cz. Although the internet version of the commercial register is reliable, the information should be verified by an original extract issued by the appropriate commercial register as this is the only official source of information about a company.

31 The principle is based on the First Directive (See Part 1, I, Mn. 38).

32 The deed of incorporation, the articles of association, shareholder resolutions, including any new articles of association (every time the articles of association are amended), shareholder resolutions on the appointment or dismissal of managing directors, the annual accounts, ordinary, extraordinary and consolidated financial statements, the report on related entities, etc.

33 The business year may be the calendar year or any other 12-month period chosen.

34 The annex contains notes to the accounts relating to accounting methods used.

35 Czech Act on Accounting, Act No. 563/1991 Coll., as amended (*zákon o účetnictví*, "UZ").

than a half-time basis (based on weekly hours), one-third of the supervisory board is elected by the employees.[36]

2 The Stock Corporation ("a.s.")

Literature: Dědič, Jan, Obchodní zákoník: komentář (1st edition, Prague, Polygon 2005); Dědič, Jan; Kříž, Radim; Štenglová, Ivana, Akciové společnosti (5th edition, Prague, C.H.Beck 2003);CommercialCode –Obchodní zákoník: Act No. 513/1991 Coll., as amended (Prague, Trade Links 2004)

49 The stock corporation (*akciová společnost*, "a.s.") is the second corporate entity offering limited shareholder liability in the Czech Republic. It is designed for larger businesses and its governance structure and rules on capital protection are particularly strict.

2.1 Export of Company

50 The principle of incorporation theory, including the option to transfer the registered office, applies to an a.s. accordingly.[37]

51 The same regulation applicable to an s.r.o. in respect of the business's movement across the EU also applies to an a.s.[38]

2.2 Transformation into a Foreign Entity

52 Any such transformation would have to be carried out in the same manner as for an s.r.o.[39] However, an a.s. may merge with or into an S.E.

2.3 Incorporation

53 An a.s. may be founded by a sole founder, which can be either an individual or a legal entity. The number of shareholders is not limited. The founders establish an a.s. with the execution of the founding agreement[40] in the form of a notarial deed. The articles of association, the most important corporate document of an a.s., is attached to the founding document (Sec. 172 ObchZ). A stock corporation can be also founded by way of a public offer of shares (Sec. 164 ObchZ), which is not common practice in the Czech Republic. The company will legally exist upon its entry into the commercial register (Sec. 62 ObchZ).

54 The incorporation procedure may last from three weeks to two months.[41] The notarial fees for the incorporation of an a.s. with a minimum share capital of CZK 2,000,000 (approximately EUR 67,700) amount to approximately CZK 20,000 (approximately EUR 677).[42] In addition, the fee for registration in the commercial register will amount to CZK 5,000 (approximately EUR 170).

2.4 Recurrent Costs and Efforts

55 The annual corporate maintenance costs of an a.s. are usually higher than those of an s.r.o. The costs depend on the number of board member and shareholders and the volume of the business. An a.s. with a sole shareholder and a sole member of the board of directors would face costs and efforts comparable to those in an s.r.o.[43] In a large a.s., costs for an ordinary and extraordinary

36 The articles of association may: (i) increase the number of employee-elected supervisory board members (however, this may not exceed the number elected by the general meeting); and (ii) lower the threshold of employees for employee elections.

37 See Mn. 2.

38 See Mn. 3.

39 See Mn. 4.

40 In case of a sole shareholder the founding agreement is replaced by a founding deed.

41 See Mn. 7.

42 This does not include VAT or any other additional copies of documents.

43 See Mn. 8.

shareholders' meeting (convocation, advisers' fees, security measures), for various reports and auditing may easily reach millions of CZK. Also, the majority of corporate transactions, such as a capital increase or a merger, require more formal, costly and time-consuming procedures.

2.5 Shares and Share Transfers

The share capital of an a.s. is divided into a certain number of shares with a specified nominal value. The shares may be either registered shares (issued to a named shareholder)[44] or bearer shares. Shares may be issued as share certificates (Sec. 156 Subs. 1 ObchZ) or they may be issued in de-materialised form as uncertificated (book-entry) shares registered in the shareholder's account at the Securities Centre (*Středisko cenných papírů*) (Sec. 4 ZCP[45]). The Securities Centre, as the governmental agency that keeps records of all book-entered securities issued in the Czech Republic, will be replaced by the Central Securities Deposit (*Centrální depozitář cenných papírů*) in 2006. Certificated shares may be issued in the form of global share certificates replacing a certain number of certificated shares which would otherwise need to be issued (Sec. 5 Subs. 3 ZCP). Only bearer certificated shares can fully ensure the anonymity of the shareholders. **56**

Shares of different classes, common and preferred, may be issued if the articles of association provide for multiple classes of shares and describe the rights attached to such different classes of shares. Identical rights must be attached to all shares of a given class. The total nominal value of preferred shares may not exceed half of the registered capital. Preferred shares may have a priority right to dividends and any liquidation surplus, and may be issued without voting rights. However, if a priority dividend has not been declared by the general meeting or if the a.s. is late with the payment of the priority dividend, the non-voting preferred shares have the same voting rights as common shares until the next priority dividend is declared by the general meeting or the late priority dividend is paid. **57**

Share purchase agreements do not require written form. Bearer shares are transferred by handing over the share certificate, if not agreed otherwise, whilst registered shares are transferred by way of a handover of the endorsed shares (Sec. 156 Subs. 6 and 7 ObchZ and Secs. 17 and 18 ZCP). The endorsement must identify the purchaser and contain the date of the transfer and signature of the seller. A transfer of registered certificated shares is effective in relation to an a.s. only when the transfer is evidenced to the a.s. and recorded in the shareholders' register.[46] Book-entered shares are transferred with the registration of their transfer in the customer's account kept with the Central Securities Deposit (Sec 99 ZKT[47]). The transfer of shares does not require an entry in the commercial register. However, a sole shareholder of an a.s. must be registered in the commercial register. **58**

2.6 Corporate Bodies

The a.s. is required to have three corporate bodies: the board of directors (*představenstvo*); the supervisory board (*dozorčí rada*); and the shareholders' meeting (*valná hromada*). **59**

2.6.1 Board of Directors

An a.s. is managed by a board of directors with at least three members, unless the a.s. has a sole shareholder, in which case the number of members of the board of directors may be lower (Sec. **60**

44 A holder of registered shares has to register his (business) name, address and registered seat in the shareholder register of the company in order to be able to exercise his shareholder rights. In case of book-entered shares, the shareholders' list is replaced by the electronic evidence (Sec. 156 Subs. 2 and 3 ObchZ).

45 Czech Securities Act, Act No. 591/1992 Coll., as amended (*zákon o cennýh papírech*, "ZCP").

46 See Mn. 8 et seq.

47 Czech Act on Capital Markets, Act No. 256/2004 Coll., as amended (*zákon o podnikání na kapitalovém trhu*, "ZKP").

194 Subs. 3 ObchZ). Unless the articles of association state otherwise, each member of the board of directors may act on behalf of the a.s. independently.[48]

61 The board of directors is exclusively in charge of the management of the company and cannot be instructed by the supervisory board or the shareholders' meeting, unless a controlling agreement is concluded.[49] However, certain business transactions require the supervisory board's approval[50] or – in rare cases – the approval of the shareholders' meeting.[51]

62 The articles of association and the general meeting may restrict the authority of the board of directors to represent the a.s., but a breach of such restrictions does not influence the validity of the performed legal acts.

63 The maximum term of office for board members is five years, but this can be renewed. The body responsible for the appointment and dismissal of board members also approves management agreements concluded between the a.s. and the board members.

2.6.2 The General Meeting

64 The general meeting is the body in which the shareholders exercise their rights and decide on the most important issues of an a.s. (Sec. 184 Subs. 1 ObchZ). Pursuant to Sec. 194 Subs. 1 ObchZ, the general meeting appoints and removes the members of the board of directors (unless the articles of association stipulate that the supervisory board does so) and, with the exception of those elected by employees, the members of the supervisory board.[52] The Czech Commercial Code lists acts falling within the power of the general meeting (mainly in Sec. 187 ObchZ) and the articles of association may provide for additional powers of the general meeting.[53] Sec. 194 Subs. 4 ObchZ regulates the instructions and guidelines of the general meeting.[54]

65 Resolutions of the general meeting are passed by a simple majority of the votes cast, unless the ObchZ or the articles of association require a higher majority (Sec. 186 Subs. 1 ObchZ). Higher thresholds (generally involving a two-thirds majority or a three-quarters majority) apply in certain cases – for example, the passing of resolutions amending the articles of association, increase of the share capital, the dissolution of the company and delisting (Sec. 186 Subs. 2 to 5 ObchZ).

2.6.3 Supervisory Board

66 An a.s. must have a supervisory board, which is obliged to oversee the manner in which the board of directors exercises its powers and the way the business of the a.s. is conducted (Sec. 197 ObchZ). For this purpose, it has the right to examine all records and documents of the a.s. including the financial statements, minutes of the board of directors, etc. (Sec. 198 ObchZ). Under certain circumstances, the supervisory board has the right to convene a general meeting of shareholders

48 It is common for the articles of association to limit the power of the individual members of the board of directors and to stipulate the manner of their acting on behalf of the a.s. See Mn. 14 on acting jointly with a proxy holder.

49 Please see Mn. 16.

50 The supervisory board's approval is, for instance, required for the conclusion of a contract on the basis of which an a.s. would acquire or dispose of property whereby the value of property which it is proposed to acquire or dispose of within one accounting period would exceed one-third of the a.s.'s equity capital according to the last ordinary financial statements or consolidated financial statement, if the a.s. draws up consolidated financial statements. If an a.s. issues registered shares, the approval of the general meeting for such contract is necessary. The provision of Sec. 196 a (4) ObchZ applies accordingly.

51 An a.s. may conclude a loan or credit with a director, proxy holder or other person entitled to act on behalf of the a.s., or with persons close to them, or conclude a contract on securing the obligations (debts) of these persons, or a contract on the transfer, free of charge/for no consideration, of the company's property to any such person only with the prior approval of the general meeting and only under terms customary in business transactions.

52 In the case of an a.s. whose employees number more than 50 people who are in a working relationship and whose collective working time exceeds half the total weekly working time, one-third of the supervisory board members are elected by the employees. The articles of association may stipulate that a larger number of members of the supervisory board be elected by the employees, but this number may not exceed the number of members elected by the general meeting.

53 Powers not listed in the ObchZ or in the articles of association may not be assumed by the general meeting.

54 See Mn. 16.

(Sec. 199 ObchZ). The supervisory board designates one of its members to represent the a.s. in actions against members of the board of directors (Sec. 199 ObchZ). Supervisory board members have to act with due managerial care when exercising their powers.

A supervisory board must have at least three members, the number must be divisible by three and, if the a.s. has more than 50 employees, one-third of the supervisory board is elected by the employees.[55] 67

2.7 Duties and Liabilities of Directors

The duties and responsibilities of the members of the board of directors are comparable to those of the managing directors of an s.r.o.[56] Members of the board of directors have to act with due managerial care and their responsibility cannot be limited (Sec. 194 Subs. 5 and 6 ObchZ). Their liability is comparable with that of the managing directors of an s.r.o.[57] They must also observe confidentiality as far as the company's business matters are concerned.[58] If an act of the board of directors requires the prior approval of the general meeting or the supervisory board, breaching such restrictions does not cause the performed acts to be invalid. 68

The main duty of the members of the board of directors is that of commercial management of an a.s. Board members must ensure that all obligations stipulated by the law are fulfilled. The board of directors also has other statutory obligations, including arranging for necessary filings to be made with the commercial register, convening the annual shareholders' meeting, reporting to the supervisory board and, above all, obtaining the approval of the shareholders or the supervisory board for certain business transactions if such approval is required by law or the memorandum of association. 69

2.8 Shareholders' Liability

The shareholders of an a.s. are in principle not liable for the obligations of the company, given the principle of limited liability.[59] 70

2.9 Capitalisation and Financing

2.9.1 Basic Concepts

The capitalisation and financing of an a.s. is also based on the general concept of the "principle of real capital contribution and maintenance". The same principles as apply to the s.r.o. apply also to the a.s.[60] 71

As in the case of the s.r.o., the same principles apply in the case of a negative economic situation (Sec. 193 Subs. 1 ObchZ) or an application for insolvency of an a.s.[61] 72

2.9.2 Minimum Share Capital

The minimum share capital is CZK 2,000,000 (approximately EUR 67,600). If an a.s. is formed by way of a public offer of shares, the share capital must be at least CZK 20,000,000 (approximately EUR 676,000) (Sec. 162 Subs. 3 ObchZ). Contributions can be either monetary or in kind.[62] 73

55 See Mn. 89 for employee representation in corporate bodies.

56 See Mn. 14 et seq.

57 See Mn. 19 – 22.

58 This might complicate the due diligence process of a potential target.

59 See Mn. 23 and 24.

60 See Mn. 25.

61 See Mn. 26 and 27.

62 Where the capital is rendered in cash, at least 30 per cent of the share capital plus the share premium must be paid in on the date of application for registration in the commercial register. The full amount is required where there is only a sole founder (Sec. 111 ObchZ). Contributions in kind must be described in the memorandum of association or in the declaration of the shareholder. Contributions in kind must be further valued by an independent expert,

74 Shareholders of an a.s. are liable for the value of contributions in kind to the same extent as are the shareholders of an s.r.o.[63]

2.9.3 Maintenance of Capital and Liquidity

(i) System

75 Due to the partial anonymity of its shareholders, the a.s. provides for even stronger capital protection than is the case for the s.r.o. Contributions in kind must also correspond to the type of business activities carried out by the a.s. The share capital may be reduced only by means of a formal reduction procedure which protects the minority shareholders and the company's creditors.

76 The same principles apply to an a.s. as for an s.r.o. regarding the transfer of assets from shareholders to the company or vice versa having a value higher than 10 per cent of the share capital of the company.[64]

77 In contrast to an s.r.o., the ObchZ does not regulate contributions to the other capital funds of an a.s. However, such contributions can be made and are in principle based on an agreement between the shareholder and the company. It is advisable that contributions to the other capital funds in an a.s. be regulated in the company's articles of association.

78 A reserve fund is obligatory. Regular contributions must be paid into the fund until it contains an amount equivalent to at least 20 per cent of the share capital. The reserve fund may only be used to cover the company's losses.

(ii) Distributions

79 The ObchZ restricts distributions of profits where the company's equity would be distorted. In certain situations where a shareholder is late in the fulfilment of its obligations towards the company, the law prohibits the shareholder from receiving a dividend (Sec. 178 Subs. 1 ObchZ).

80 Further, the right to receive dividends can only be transferred separately after the decision of the general meeting on dividends has been taken. This does not apply in the case that coupons (representing the right to receive dividends) have been issued (Sec. 178 Subs. 12 ObchZ).

(iii) Acquisition of Own Shares and Related Financing

81 An a.s. may acquire its own shares only in situations explicitly envisaged by Sec. 161 a ObchZ. Shares subscribed in breach of this prohibition must be jointly and severally paid for by the shareholders who become the owners of these shares.

82 An a.s. may acquire its own shares when the acquisition is authorised by the shareholders' meeting (Sec. 161 Subs. 1 ObchZ). Such authorisation may only be given for a maximum term of 18 months for a maximum of 10 per cent of the registered share capital and the company must have enough funds for the creation of a special reserve fund.[65] Sec. 161 Subs. 2 and 3 ObchZ provide for other special situations in which the company may acquire its own shares.[66] An a.s. may, in principle, acquire share of controlling entities under similar conditions to acquisition of its own shares (Sec. 161 ObchZ).

83 Sec. 161 e ObchZ prohibits an a.s. from providing financial assistance in connection with the acquisition of its own shares, particularly in the form of a loan or the granting of security. Any such transactions are void.

appointed by the court (Sec. 59 Subs. 3 ObchZ), and fully paid by the date of application for registration of the company in the commercial register (Sec. 59 Subs. 2 ObchZ).

63 See Mn. 29 and 30.

64 See Mn. 33.

65 The special fund must be cancelled or reduced if the company disposes of its shares or interim certificates fully or partly, or uses them for reducing its registered capital. The special reserve fund may not be used in any other way.

66 If the acquisition prevents the company from suffering significant loss or if the shares are to be distributed to the company's employees.

(iv) Company as Lender or Guarantor

An a.s. may give loans and credits under the same conditions as an s.r.o. (Sec. 196 a Subs. 1 and 2 ObchZ).[67] **84**

(v) Company as Borrower

In situations in which an a.s. is a borrower or recipient of a security, the same principles and restrictions mentioned above in connection with an s.r.o. also apply to an a.s.[68] **85**

2.10 Publication and Filing Requirements

These requirements and applicable principles correspond to those of an s.r.o.[69] **86**

2.11 Financial Reporting

The accounting rules are generally identical to those of an s.r.o.[70] **87**

The rules on auditing of the financial statements are generally identical to those of an s.r.o.[71] **88**

2.12 Employee Participation in Corporate Bodies

One-third of the supervisory board must consist of employee representatives if the company has more than 50 employees who are employed on more than a half-time basis (based on weekly hours). The articles of association may only improve the position of the employee representatives.[72] **89**

67 See Mn. 41 et seq.
68 See Mn. 42.
69 See Mn. 44.
70 See Mn. 46.
71 See Mn. 47.
72 The articles of association may provide for improvements as listed in Mn. 48.

V. Denmark

*by Niels Bang Sørensen**

1 The Limited Liability Company ("ApS")

Literature: Søren Friis Hansen, Anpartsselskaber (Thomson 1998); Ida Rosenberg, ApS-loven med kommentarer (GadJura 1996)

The ApS (*Anpartsselskab,*"ApS") was intended as the most common corporate entity in Denmark to achieve limited shareholder liability for small enterprises. However, the ApS is also used by large international groups, particularly in the form of holding companies, as the ApS is eligible to elect entity classification under the US tax rules in CFR 301.7701-1ff (known as the "check-the-box" regulations). In this way, a private company may elect transparency for US tax purposes. The statutory company law requirements are not strict and permit a high degree of flexibility in the drafting of the articles of association. In October 2005 approximately 117,000 limited liability companies were registered in Denmark, in contrast to 39,000 stock corporation. 1

1.1 Export of Company

Most Danish legal scholars are of the opinion that Denmark applies the registration (incorporation) criterion when determining the nationality of a company.[1] It is accepted for an ApS to relocate its de facto corporate seat or its entire business activities to a foreign country, provided that the registration is kept in Denmark and certain basic corporate documents are available at a Danish contact address. Thus, the "Überseering" judgment[2] of the ECJ does not represent a challenge for Danish law as it prescribes for the recognition of a company validly incorporated in a Member State which moves its de facto corporate seat to another country. However, the ECJ judgment in "Centros",[3] which permitted two Danes to incorporate a UK private limited company with the sole purpose of establishing a branch in Denmark to carry out the entire business and thereby avoid Danish statutory capital requirements, has been difficult to accept for the Danish authorities. Danish law recognises such a secondary establishment; however, this was seen by the authorities as a circumvention of the Danish minimum capital requirements.[4] 2

1.2 Transformation into a Foreign Entity

Danish law contains no rules providing for transformation of an ApS into a foreign entity. The incorporation criterion allows for a move of the de facto corporate seat and business activities to a foreign country.[5] Another way to achieve this result is to contribute the assets of the ApS to a company incorporated abroad against shares. However, both methods will trigger Danish exit taxation whereby the assets are taxed as if they had been sold. An ApS cannot be merged into an S.E. 3

* *Gorrissen Federspiel Kierkegaard,* Copenhagen.

1 See Schans Christensen, Kapitalselskaber (Thomson 2004), p. 79.

2 See Part 1, I, Mn. 17 et seq.

3 See Part 1, I, Mn. 15 et seq.

4 After Centros, the Danish Parliament adopted legislation (now Sec. 11 a of Act no. 289 of 28 April 2003) introducing a requirement for a guarantee if the equity (net capital) of a limited liability company is lower than DKK 125,000, i.e. the exact size of the minimum share capital for an ApS: see Mn. 21. This must be seen as contrary to the said ECJ case law. Comparable statutory provisions with intended cross-border effect have been set aside in the ECJ judgment "InspireArt" (dated 30 September 2003, C-167/01).

5 See Mn. 2.

1.3 Incorporation

4 An ApS may be formed by one or more promoters. The promoters must sign a memorandum of association, which must contain a draft of the articles of association (Sec. 4 Subs. 1 of the Danish Limited Liability Companies Act ("ApSL")). The company will legally exist upon its registration with the Commerce and Companies Agency.

5 The length of the incorporation procedure depends on whether the filing of the incorporation documentation with the Commerce and Companies Agency is done online with immediate registration (most law firms have access to do this) or by post. The online registration takes 15 to 20 minutes whereas a filing in the traditional way normally takes two to four weeks. There are no notarial or other fees charged for the incorporation of an ApS.

1.4 Recurrent Costs and Efforts

6 The only statutory recurrent costs and efforts relate to the preparation and auditing of the annual accounts.

1.5 Shares and Share Transfers

7 It is possible to have different classes of shares with different rights attaching to them, for example, by having voting and non-voting shares, and/or shares with different dividend rights.

8 Shares in an ApS are transferred by having the new owner entered in the shareholders' register (Sec. 16 Subs. 2 ApSL). As the ApSL does not provide for share certificates, title to a share is solely evidenced by such registration. The company must be informed of any share transfer, enter the transfer in the shareholders' register and issue a confirmation (Sec. 16 Subs. 3 ApSL). In practice, the seller and the buyer must execute a written share transfer document in order to prove the share transfer *vis-à-vis* the company. Depending on the circumstances and the parties, such documents vary from a simple one page agreement to a long-form share purchase agreement. No taxes are levied on a transfer of shares.

9 An ApS is not prohibited by law from offering its shares to the public and this would not trigger a prospectus requirement. However, a public offering rarely happens as the shares of an ApS are not negotiable securities and therefore not suitable for offering to a large number of investors. An ApS cannot be listed on a Danish stock exchange.

1.6 Corporate Bodies

10 The shareholder(s) are free to choose whether one or more managers or a board of directors or both a management and a board of directors shall be in charge of the business of an ApS. In case the company has only one managerial body, such body shall perform all the managerial duties vesting in the board of directors and the managers. The ApS shall have a board of directors if it is required to have employee representation on the board of directors (Sec. 19 Subs. 1 and 2 ApSL).[6]

1.6.1 Managing Directors

11 A manager alone may bind the company with respect to affairs lying within his scope of responsibilities. The powers of the managing director(s) may be restricted either through the articles of association or by way of rules of procedure. Outside the scope of such powers, the company shall in principle be bound by legal obligations entered into by the entire board of directors or by any member of the board of directors or of the management. However, such power to bind the company may be (and in practice always is) limited by the articles of association so that the powers to bind the company may only be exercised by several members jointly[7] or by one or more specific members

6 Regarding employee representation, see Mn. 34 et seq.

7 Such a rule of signature could for example have the following wording: "The company shall be bound by the joint signature of one manager and one member of the board of directors.".

individually or jointly (Sec. 24 ApSL). Such limitations are general and apply regardless of the specific matter.[8]

If the company has both a board of directors and a management, the managing directors shall be in charge of the day-to-day business. This includes ensuring that the bookkeeping of the company is conducted in compliance with the relevant rules of law and that the asset management is carried out in a proper manner (Sec. 20 Subs. 1 ApSL). 12

1.6.2 Shareholders' Meeting

The shareholders' right to make decisions concerning the company shall be exercised at general meetings save where the shareholders agree to make decisions in a different manner.[9] The shareholders' meeting has the power to decide on all company matters. 13

All business transacted shall be determined by a simple majority of votes in the absence in the ApSL or in the articles of association of any provision containing stricter requirements (Sec. 32 ApSL).[10] Resolutions to alter the articles of association shall only be valid if at least two-thirds of the votes cast are in favour of the alteration unless the articles of association provide otherwise (Sec. 33 Subs. 1 ApSL). Furthermore, certain far-reaching resolutions altering the articles of association must be adopted by all shareholders (Sec. 34 ApSL). 14

1.6.3 Board of Directors

If the company has both a board of directors and a management, the board of directors shall be the supreme managerial body making decisions regarding transactions which are unusual or of great significance. The board of directors shall *inter alia* ensure that the bookkeeping and asset management are controlled in a manner satisfactory in consideration of the position of the company (Sec. 20 Subs. 1 ApSL). 15

1.7 Duties and Liabilities of Directors

In respect of the management of the company, the managers and directors have no specific duties other than those outlined above.[11] There are no specific duties of directors and officers relating to financing. The supreme managerial body shall regularly review the company's financing. The directors are not obliged (but are entitled) to apply for insolvency proceedings when the company is unable to pay its debts.[12] 16

Members of the board of directors and of the management who, in the performance of their duties, have caused damage to the company, shareholders, creditors of the company or any third party due to wilful misconduct or negligence shall be liable for damages.[13] The acts and omissions of each member will be assessed individually, but if several persons are found to be liable, they shall be jointly and severally liable for damages. The directors are bound by the instructions of the general meeting but cannot rely on an instruction to carry out any action without liability. Common sense and applicable law must always be applied by the directors. Legal proceedings may be instituted even if the company in general meeting has previously passed resolutions releasing the directors from liability, if information which was in all essentials correct and complete has not been given to 17

8 Provided that such matter is of a nature or size outside the scope of the ordinary powers mentioned.

9 Rules governing this may be included in the articles of association (Sec. 28 ApSL). Thus, the shareholders may adopt a scheme where for example the company has a management only and this board may take any and all decisions on the company's affairs. The shareholders can of course choose to reinstate the shareholders' meeting by amending the articles of association to this effect.

10 In the case of an equality of votes, the result shall, in the absence of any provision to the contrary in the articles of association, be determined by the drawing of lots.

11 See Mn. 12 and 15. See, however, also Mn. 32 and 33 regarding the annual report.

12 The directors will, however, be liable for damages if they expose a creditor to a credit risk which is unforeseeable to that creditor and which is so considerable that the creditor very probably will suffer a loss.

13 This follows from general principles of the Danish law of tort. Liability insurance for the members of the board of directors is permitted. The company may pay the premium to a reasonable extent.

the company in general meeting concerning the resolution or the matters on which the proceedings are based, before the resolution was passed. The general statute of limitation for claims is five years.

1.8 Shareholders' Liability

18 The shareholders are in principle not liable for the obligations of the company (Sec. 1 Subs. 2 ApSL), and no court of law has explicitly stated the principle of piercing the corporate veil.[14]

19 On the other hand, shareholders are liable to the ApS for the repayment of any illegal payments made to them in breach of the provisions of the ApSL such as, for example, illegal shareholder loans (Sec. 49 ApSL).

20 Furthermore, a shareholder shall be liable to compensate any loss inflicted upon the company, other shareholders or any third party if, by committing wilful misconduct or a grossly negligence act, he has violated the provisions of the ApSL or the articles of association of the company.[15]

1.9 Capitalisation and Financing

1.9.1 Basic Concepts

21 The amount to be paid for a share shall not be less than the nominal amount of the share (Sec. 13 Subs. 1 ApSL). The size of the share capital, which must be fully paid-up, shall be stated in the articles of association and is registered with the Companies and Commerce Agency.

1.9.2 Minimum Share Capital

22 The minimum share capital of an ApS is DKK 125,000 (approximately EUR 16,750) or the equivalent in Euro, but can be stated in the articles of association in Danish Kroner or Euro (Sec. 1 Subs. 3 ApSL). The capital can be rendered in cash or in kind. Partial contributions, for example payment of 50 per cent until registration, and the rest upon demand by the company, are not possible.

1.9.3 Maintenance of Capital and Liquidity

(i) System

23 The share capital is intended to form a capital fund which is the minimum amount available to creditors. Therefore, the preservation of the ApS's share capital is of great importance. Non-cash contributions against shares must have a value, which can be expressed as a financial equivalent. Claims on promoters or subscribers cannot be included, irrespective of whether collateral security has been provided for such claims. A valuation expert, typically a state authorised public accountant, shall prepare a valuation report on the company's acquisition of any assets. The valuation report shall be produced for the use of the company in general meeting, and the board of directors shall furnish a written statement concerning the acquisition. If the company takes over an existing business, a balance sheet must be prepared as an acquisition balance sheet for the acquired undertaking and be provided with an auditor's unqualified report (Secs. 7 and 39 ApSL).

24 No shareholder is obliged to provide further financing. If, after the drawing up of the memorandum of association and up to 24 months after the registration, the company enters into agreements relating to acquisitions from a promoter or a shareholder who is known to the company, such acquisitions shall be approved by the shareholders if the consideration corresponds to at least 10 per cent of the share capital and amounts to not less than DKK 50,000, and it is not an ordinary business transaction (Sec. 9 ApSL).

25 If the company loses 40 per cent or more of its share capital, the supreme managerial body of the company must report to the shareholders on the financial position of the company within six

14 However, the ruling of the Danish Supreme Court mentioned in Mn. 53 will also apply to ApS companies.

15 This is no longer stated in the ApSL but still applies as it follows from general principles of the Danish law of tort.

months and propose any measures to be taken, which would provide full cover of the share capital or make a proposal for the dissolution of the company (Sec. 52 ApSL).

(ii) Distributions

A reduction of the share capital, for example by repayment to the shareholders, may take place if the ApS preserves at least the minimum share capital and the creditors have been invited via an advertisement in the Official Gazette to prove their claim within three months (Secs. 46-47 ApSL). A dividend distribution may be made as an ordinary dividend at the annual general meeting in accordance with the approved annual accounts of the preceding accounting reference period, or as an extraordinary dividend decided by the board of directors according to an authorisation adopted by the general meeting and inserted in the articles of association (Secs. 44 and 44a ApSL).[16] **26**

(iii) Acquisition of Own Shares and Related Financing

An ApS is not allowed to subscribe or hold shares in itself or shares in its parent company. Any such shares should be sold as soon as possible without causing a detrimental effect to the company and not later than three years from the date of acquisition (Sec. 51 ApSL). **27**

An ApS is furthermore prohibited from granting loans to finance the acquisition of shares in itself or shares in its parent company. Nor may an ApS make assets available for, or provide assets as security in connection with, such acquisition (Sec. 49 Subs. 2 ApSL). **28**

(iv) Company as Lender or Guarantor

An ApS is not allowed to grant loans to or provide security for its shareholders or the members of its board of directors or the management of the company or of its parent company (Sec. 49 Subs. 1 ApSL). This prohibition on the granting of loans or provision of security applies equally to anyone related to any such shareholder, member of its board of directors or manager of the company by way of marriage or as a lineal ancestor or descendant, or by being particularly close to the person in any other way. However, the prohibition does not apply to loans provided to a parent company nor to security for the liabilities of a parent company (Sec. 50 Subs. 1 ApSL) if such parent company is governed by the First Directive.[17] **29**

(v) Company as Borrower

The granting of loans by shareholders to the ApS and shareholders providing security for the ApS is allowed and is not subject to any specific rules. For tax purposes, a loan must be made on normal commercial terms (arm's length). If the company's main creditor(s) so require, such a loan may be subordinated to other debts. **30**

1.10 Publication and Filing Requirements

A wide range of documentation and information must be filed with the Commerce and Companies Agency.[18] The Agency's files are open to the public and any person can review the filed **31**

16 A dividend distribution may be made from the results for the year (the profits for the year) and other reserves which are eligible for distribution after deduction of any loss carried forward from previous years. In addition, accumulated profits of the current financial year may be distributed as an extraordinary dividend.

17 See Part 1, I, Mn. 38. The latter condition does not transpire from the ApSL but is the current position of the Commerce and Companies Agency.

18 For example, the memorandum of incorporation, the articles of association, shareholder resolutions and the new articles of association following amendment, the annual accounts, resolutions on the appointment or the dismissal of board members or managing directors, and the names and addresses of managing directors and board members. The consequences for not filing within the prescribed time limits depend on the type of filing. The annual accounts shall be filed not later than five months after the end of each accounting year: see Mn. 33. In respect of the annual report fines are imposed on the members of the board of directors and ultimately the company may undergo compulsory dissolution. Amendments to the articles of association (including, for example, share capital increases and change of

documents and request a copy at the Agency's offices in Copenhagen. Online access to the basic corporate information is available.[19] A compiled summary thereof as well as a summary of historic information such as capital increases, amendments to the articles of association, the management etc. can be reviewed and printed by registered users upon payment of a minor fee. In general, the register of the Agency is up-to-date, but a third party cannot rely on its contents without making sure that newly made decisions, if any, have been filed. The files will show if a filing has been made but not yet registered.

1.11 Financial Reporting

32 The annual report must consist of a balance sheet, a profit and loss statement and notes to the accounts. For each accounting year, a management report must be prepared and for a parent company consolidated accounts must be worked out. The annual report must be drawn up in accordance with the Danish Financial Statements Act and Danish GAAP.[20]

Certain relief from financial reporting requirements is granted to small and medium-sized enterprises. In Denmark small enterprises are those not exceeding two of the following limits as at the balance sheet date in two consecutive financial years: (i) a balance sheet total of DKK 29 million (approximately EUR 3,887,400), (ii) a revenue of DKK 58 million (approximately EUR 7,774,740), and (iii) an average number of 50 full-time employees during the financial year. Medium-sized enterprises are those which are not small enterprises and which do not exceed two of the following limits as at the balance sheet date in two consecutive financial years: (i) a balance sheet total of DKK 119 million (approximately EUR 15,951,740), (ii) a revenue of DKK 238 million (approximately EUR 31,903,485), and (iii) an average number of 250 full-time employees during the financial year. Small companies are released from the requirement to draw up a cash flow statement. Furthermore, compared to large enterprises both small and medium-sized companies may draw up less detailed annual accounts and have one extra month to do so (five months instead of four months).[21]

33 The annual audited report shall be approved in general meeting (or by another body appointed so to do in the articles of association).[22] It must be filed with the Commerce and Companies Agency for publication immediately upon such approval and no later than five months after the end of the accounting year.[23]

signature rule), election of new board members or accountants have no effect *vis-á-vis* third parties until they have been registered by the Agency. The approach of the Agency towards late filings is generally relaxed, but certain late filings do have consequences. For example, a capital increase will not be valid if filed more than 12 months after it has been resolved (Sec. 36 Subs. 2 ASL), and a late filing of a merger plan means that a new merger plan must be executed by the board of directors of the merging companies (Sec. 134 d ASL).

19 For example, corporate name(s), the company's address, share capital, the name and address of the managing directors, board members and auditor firm. The Agency's web address is: www.eogs.dk.

20 With respect to the application of IAS and US GAAP, see Mn. 64. The Financial Statements Act sets up four classes of accounts (A, B, C and D) where the A class contains the most basic requirements and the D class the most demanding. Depending on its financial size, an ApS will be covered by either class B or C.

21 In October 2005 the Danish Minister of Economic and Business Affairs has put forward draft legislation proposing that –in addition to the above – very small companies shall not be required to have their annual accounts audited by an auditor if they are not exceeding two of the following limits as at the balance sheet date in two consecutive financial years: a balance sheet total of DKK 3 million (approximately EUR 402,145), a revenue of DKK 6 million (approximately EUR 804,290), and an average number of 25 full-time employees during the financial year. Such companies shall still be required to submit their annual accounts to the Commerce and Companies Agency.

22 See Mn. 13.

23 The accounting year may be the calendar year or any other 12-month period chosen.

1.12 Employee Participation in Corporate Bodies

An ApS must have a board of directors if it falls within the statutory rules about employee representation.[24] In companies which have had a total staff of on average at least 35 employees over the last three years, the employees are entitled to elect a number of members to the board of directors. The number of directors so elected may equal up to half the number of other members of the board of directors, provided that this is not less than two directors. If the number of members to be elected to the board of directors does not constitute a whole number, the number shall be rounded up (Sec. 22 Subs. 1 ApSL). **34**

The employees of a parent company and its subsidiaries registered in Denmark shall be entitled to elect, from among the employees, a number of members to the board of directors of the parent company (group representation) if the parent company and the said subsidiaries have had an average of at least 35 employees over the last three years (Sec. 22 Subs. 2 ApSL). If, furthermore, the parent company itself is subject to employee representation,[25] the employees of the parent company shall be entitled to elect two board members. The total number of members of the board of directors in the parent company elected by the employees shall correspond to half the number of members of the board of directors, provided that this is not less than three members. **35**

2 The Stock Corporation ("A/S")

Literature: Erik Werlauff, Selskabsret (5th edition, DJØF 2004); Jan Schans Christensen, Kapitalselskaber (Thomson 2004)

The stock corporation (*Aktieselskab*, "A/S") is the other important corporate entity offering limited shareholder liability in Denmark. The advantage of a stock corporation is that it has access to capital markets and therefore greater scope for raising funds to finance its business activities. However, as this could result in a large number of shareholders, its governance structure is stricter than that of the ApS. **36**

2.1 Export of Company

The Danish rules on the relocation of a domestic company to a foreign country are based on the incorporation theory and will apply to an A/S in the same manner as for an ApS.[26] **37**

2.2 Transformation into a Foreign Entity

Such transformation would have to be carried out in the same manner as for an ApS.[27] In addition, an A/S can be merged into an S.E. registered in another EU Member State.[28] **38**

2.3 Incorporation

An A/S may be formed by one or more promoters. The promoters shall sign a memorandum of association, which must contain a draft of the articles of association (Sec. 3 Subs. 1 of the Danish Stock Corporations Act ("ASL")). The company will legally exist upon its registration with the Commerce and Companies Agency. **39**

The length of the incorporation procedure and the connected costs are the same as for an ApS.[29] **40**

24 See Mn. 10. In companies which are not subject to the statutory rules, the articles of association may confer upon the employees of the company and of the group, respectively, the right to elect two or more members to the board of directors (Sec. 22 Subs. 4 ApSL).

25 See Mn. 34.

26 See Mn. 2.

27 See Mn. 3.

28 See Part 1, I, Mn. 75 and Part 2, S.E., Mn. 6 et seq. and 11 et seq.

29 See Mn. 5.

2.4 Recurrent Costs and Efforts

41 The annual efforts required to maintain an A/S can either be minimal as for an ApS,[30] or considerably more extensive if, for example, the A/S is listed on a stock exchange. If so, costs for shareholders' meetings (convening the meeting, advisers' fees, etc.), compliance with corporate governance and other stock exchange requirements may be significant.

2.5 Shares and Share Transfers

42 It is possible to have different classes of shares with different rights attaching to them, for example, shares with different dividend rights. All shares shall carry voting rights, but the voting power of certain shares may be increased, provided that such increase does not exceed ten times the voting power of any other share of the same amount (Sec. 67 ASL).

43 Shares in an A/S may be registered by name or to bearer. If a registered share has changed owner, the name of the new shareholder shall be entered in the register of shareholders if he makes a request to that effect and proves his title. The company may issue share certificates. If any shareholder so requires, or if the shares are negotiable instruments or issued to bearer, share certificates shall be issued for all of the shares (Sec. 21 ASL), unless the shares are issued through a securities centre, and/or the company's shares are quoted for sale in an authorised market place.[31] Bearer shares and negotiable shares are transferred by handing over the share certificate endorsed to the acquirer.[32] For companies which have not issued share certificates, or whose shares have not been issued through a securities centre, notification of a share changing hands must be witnessed by an entry in the register of shareholders (Sec. 25 a ASL). In practice, the seller and the buyer must execute a written share transfer document in order to prove the share transfer *vis-à-vis* the company. Depending on the circumstances and the parties, such documents vary from a simple one page agreement to a long-form share purchase agreement containing representations and warranties, etc. If share certificates have been issued, the share certificates may simply be endorsed to the acquirer. No taxes are levied on a transfer of shares.

2.6 Corporate Bodies

44 The A/S is required to have three corporate bodies: one or more managing directors, the board of directors and the shareholders' meeting.

2.6.1 Managing Directors

45 A manager may bind the company to the same extent as a manager in an ApS.[33] In the same way as for an ApS, the power to bind the company may be (and in practice always is) limited by the articles of association so that the powers to bind the company may only be exercised by several members jointly or by one or more specific members individually or jointly (Sec. 60 ASL).[34]

46 The management shall be in charge of the day-to-day business of the company and shall in that capacity follow the directions and guidelines provided by the board of directors. The day-to-day business shall not include transactions which are unusual or of great significance in consideration of the position of the company. The management may only undertake such transactions pursuant to a specific authorisation given by the board of directors, save where a resolution of the board of directors cannot be awaited without major inconvenience to the business of the company (Sec. 54 Subs. 2 ASL).

30 See Mn. 6.
31 See Sec. 7 Subs. 1 of the Act on Securities Trading.
32 If a negotiable share is registered by name it is, however, necessary for the acquirer also to have the transfer entered in the shareholders' register in order to obtain voting rights and rights to dividend.
33 See Mn. 11.
34 See further details in Mn. 11.

In the absence of any provision in the articles of association providing for a larger board, the management shall consist of one to three members appointed by the board of directors (Sec. 51 ASL). No statutory maximum term of office is applicable. 47

2.6.2 Shareholders' Meeting

The shareholders' right to make decisions concerning the company must be exercised at the general meetings (Sec. 65 Subs. 1 ASL). The shareholders' meeting is responsible for the appointment and removal of the members of the board of directors to the extent these are not appointed by the employees (Sec. 49 Subs. 2 ASL).[35] The appointment of one or more auditors and the adoption of the annual report must also take place in general meeting (Sec. 69 Subs. 2 ASL). 48

The shareholders' meeting has the power to decide on all matters of the company unless a subject is made the exclusive competence of the board of directors by the ASL. Resolutions to alter the articles of association shall be passed at general meetings by a majority of at least two-thirds of (i) the votes cast and (ii) the voting share capital represented at the meeting (Sec. 78 ASL). Further majority requirements apply to certain far-reaching resolutions altering the articles of association. 49

2.6.3 Board of Directors

An A/S shall have a board of directors of not less than three members (Sec. 49 Subs. 1 ASL). The board of directors shall ensure proper organisation of the business of the company, appoint (and dismiss) the managing director(s) and provide directions and guidelines for the management's carrying out of the day-to-day business. The board of directors shall be responsible for transactions which are unusual or of great significance to the position of the company. Furthermore, the board of directors shall consider from time to time whether the financial position of the company is sound in the context of the company's operations, and it shall ensure that the bookkeeping and asset management is controlled in a manner satisfactory to the position of the company (Sec. 54 Subs. 3 ASL). 50

2.7 Duties and Liabilities of Directors

In respect of the management of the company, the managers and directors have no specific duties other than those outlined above.[36] There are no specific duties of directors and officers relating to financing, except that the board of directors shall regularly review the company's financing. The directors are not obliged (but are entitled) to apply for insolvency proceedings when the company is unable to pay its debts.[37] 51

Members of the board of directors and of the management who, in the performance of their duties, have caused damage to the company due to wilful misconduct or negligence, are to be made liable for damages. This shall also apply where damage has been inflicted upon shareholders, creditors of the company or any third party by a violation of the provisions of the ASL or the articles of association (Sec. 140 ASL).[38] The acts and omissions of each member will be assessed individually, but if several persons are found to be liable, they shall be jointly and severally liable for damages. The directors are bound by the instructions of the general meeting but cannot rely on an instruction to carry out any action without liability. Common sense and applicable law must always be applied by the directors. Legal proceedings may be instituted even if the company in general meeting has previously passed resolutions releasing the directors from liability, if information which was in all essentials correct and complete has not been given to the company in general meeting concerning 52

35 For details on employee representation please refer to Mn. 65 et seq.

36 See Mn. 45 et seq. and 50. See also Mn. 64 regarding the annual report.

37 The directors will, however, be liable for damages if they expose a creditor to a credit risk which is unforeseeable to that creditor and which is so considerable that the creditor very probably will suffer a loss.

38 Liability insurance for the members of the board of directors is permitted and increasingly common in A/S companies. The company may pay the premium to a reasonable extent.

the resolution or the matters on which the proceedings are based, before the resolution was passed (Sec. 144 Subs. 2 ASL).[39] The general statute of limitation for claims is five years.

2.8 Shareholders' Liability

53 The shareholders are in principle not liable for the obligations of the company (Sec. 1 Subs. 2 ASL), and no court of law has explicitly stated the principle of piercing the corporate veil. In a case where (i) the assets of two sister companies could not be clearly separated, (ii) one of them contained the liabilities and went bankrupt whereas the other gained the profits of their common activities, and (iii) the companies did not appear as two separate entities *vis-à-vis* third parties, the Danish Supreme Court has stated that the tax authority as a compulsory creditor, could direct its claim in the bankruptcy estate against both companies.[40]

54 Shareholders are liable to the A/S for the repayment of any illegal payments made to them in breach of the provisions of the ASL such as, for example, illegal shareholder loans. Furthermore, a shareholder shall be liable to compensate any loss which he may have inflicted upon the company, other shareholders or any third party if by committing wilful misconduct or a grossly negligent act he has violated the provisions of the ASL or the articles of association of the company (Sec. 142 ASL).

2.9 Capitalisation and Financing

2.9.1 Basic Concepts

55 The total amount of share capital of an A/S which has been subscribed shall equal the share capital stated in the articles of association and the nominal value of the shares with the addition of any premium shall be fully paid-up (Secs. 11 and 13 ASL). The size of the share capital is registered with the Companies and Commerce Agency.

2.9.2 Minimum Share Capital

56 The minimum share capital of an A/S is DKK 500,000 (approximately EUR 67,000) or the equivalent in Euro, but can be stated in the articles of association in Danish Kroner or Euro (Sec. 1 Subs. 3 ASL). The capital can be rendered in cash or in kind. Partial contributions, for example payment of 50 per cent until registration, and the rest upon demand by the company, are not possible.

2.9.3 Maintenance of Capital and Liquidity

(i) System

57 The share capital is intended to form a capital fund which is the minimum amount available to creditors. The system ensuring the value of non-cash contributions against shares is the same as that for an ApS.[41] As the minimum share capital is more significant in an A/S, the rules on

39 If shareholders representing at least one-tenth of the share capital have opposed a resolution conferring exemption from liability or renouncing the right to institute proceedings, any shareholder may institute legal proceedings that the party or parties be ordered to pay the company damages for the loss sustained (Sec. 144 Subs. 3 ASL). If the company enters into insolvent liquidation by order of the court and the date of notice occurs within 24 months from the holding of the general meeting which granted exemption from liability or which renounced the right to institute legal proceedings, the estate in insolvent liquidation by order of the court may bring an action for damages notwithstanding such resolution by the company in general meeting (Sec. 144 Subs. 4 ASL).

40 UfR 1997.1642 H (Midtfyns Festival).

41 See Mn. 23 et seq. The relevant provisions of the ASL are Sec. 6, 6a and 6b. However, the company's acquisition of assets from a promoter or a shareholder who is known to the company, apart from acquisitions covered by the memorandum of incorporation, must be approved by the company in general meeting in any case if the acquisition takes place in the period from the date of drawing up the memorandum of association and up to 24 months after the registration of the company, and the consideration amount equals or exceeds one-tenth of the share capital (Sec. 6 c ASL).

loss of share capital are, however, less strict. Where at any time the company has lost half its share capital, the board of directors shall convene a general meeting within a maximum period of six months therefrom and make a statement at the meeting concerning the financial position of the company and, if required, propose any measures to be taken, including the dissolution of the company (Sec. 69 a ASL).

(ii) Distributions

A reduction of the share capital, for example by repayment to the shareholders, may take place if the A/S preserves at least the minimum share capital and the creditors have been invited via an advertisement in the Official Gazette to prove their claim within three months (Secs. 44, 44a and 46 ASL). The rules on dividend distribution (Secs. 109 and 109a ASL) are identical to those contained in the ApSL.[42] **58**

(iii) Acquisition of Own Shares and Related Financing

An A/S shall not acquire its own shares whether in ownership or by charge if, as a result of such acquisition, the accumulated nominal value of own shares held by the company or its subsidiaries exceeds 10 per cent of the issued share capital. Shares shall only be acquired pursuant to an authorisation valid for no more than 18 months granted to the board of directors by the company in general meeting (Sec. 48 ASL).[43] **59**

An A/S shall not subscribe its own shares (Sec. 48 h ASL). Furthermore, Sec. 115 Subs. 2 ASL prohibits an A/S from granting loans to finance the acquisition of shares in itself or shares in its parent company. Nor shall an A/S make assets available or provide assets as security in connection with such acquisition. **60**

(iv) Company as Lender or Guarantor

The restrictions regarding the provision of loans and guarantees to shareholders, etc. in an A/S (Secs. 115 and 115a ASL) are identical to those contained in the ApSL.[44] **61**

(v) Company as Borrower

The granting of loans, or the providing of security, to an A/S by shareholders is allowed and is not subject to any specific rules. For tax purposes, a loan must be made on normal commercial terms (arm's length). If the company's main creditor(s) so require, such a loan may be subordinated to other debts. **62**

2.10 Publication and Filing Requirements

These requirements correspond to the requirements of an ApS.[45] **63**

42 See Mn. 26.

43 Certain exemptions apply to the prohibition. If compelled to do so in order to avoid serious and imminent detrimental effects, a stock corporation may acquire own shares without an authorisation from the company in general meeting (Sec. 48 a ASL). Furthermore, the provisions of Sec. 48 shall not prevent a stock corporation from acquiring own shares as part of a reduction of the share capital, as part of a takeover of capital assets by way of a merger, de-merger or in any other manner, to satisfy a statutory obligation of redemption incumbent upon the company, or as part of a purchase at a compulsory sale of fully paid-up shares to satisfy an outstanding account due to the company (Sec. 48 b ASL). Specific rules govern the obligation to sell shares acquired in accordance with, or contravention of, the said provisions.

44 See Mn. 29.

45 See Mn. 31.

2.11 Financial Reporting

64 These requirements correspond to the requirements of an ApS.[46] The audited annual report shall, however, always be approved by the general meeting of shareholders. The drawing up of annual reports based on other accounting principles such as US-GAAP is not permitted. As from 1 January 2005, the application of IAS has been mandatory in consolidated accounts for A/Ss listed on a stock exchange.[47]

2.12 Employee Participation in Corporate Bodies

65 As outlined above a board of directors of at least three members is mandatory in an A/S. The board of directors shall be elected by the company in general meeting. In companies which have had a total staff of on average at least 35 employees over the last three years, the employees of the company are entitled, in addition to the members elected by the company in general meeting, to elect from among themselves a number of board members equalling up to half the number of members of the board of directors who are elected in general meeting, provided that this is not less than two members (Sec. 49 Subs. 2 ASL). If the number of employee members to be elected does not constitute a whole number, the number shall be rounded up.

66 The provisions regarding group representation in an A/S (Sec. 49 Subs. 3 ASL) are identical to those contained in the ApSL.[48]

46 See Mn. 32 et seq. The Financial Statements Act sets up four classes of accounts (A, B, C and D) where the A class contains the most basic requirements and the D class the most demanding. An A/S not listed on a stock exchange will be covered by either class B or C depending on its financial size. A listed A/S is covered by class D.

47 See Part 1, I, Mn. 54. Whether IAS shall also be mandatory for the annual report, and whether other A/S and ApS companies shall be submitted to IAS, is optional for each Member State: see Article 5 of the Regulation.

48 See Mn. 35.

VI. Estonia

*by Raino Paron (LL.M.) and Heili Haabu**

1 The Limited Liability Company ("OÜ")

Literature: M. Ots, V. Peep, T. Puri and M. Tropp, "Äriõigus. Osaühing. Aktsiaselts. Näidised ja kommentaarid" (Käsiraamatute Kirjastus, Tallinn 2005)

The most commonly used legal form for corporate entities in Estonia is the limited liability company (*osaühing*, "OÜ"). An OÜ is a company with limited liability characterised by smaller capital requirements (as compared to the other type of limited liability company under Estonian law – the stock corporation) and a simple management structure. OÜs tend to be closely-held businesses formed and managed by a relatively small group of shareholders. In October 2005 approximately 65,000 limited liability companies were registered in Estonia, in contrast to approximately 6,000 stock corporations. 1

1.1 Export of Company

While Estonian company law does not prohibit Estonian companies from carrying out business activities in a foreign jurisdiction (neither at incorporation nor at a later point in time), the relocation of the management of the company to a foreign state is not governed by Estonian law. 2

Under Estonian law, the seat of a legal person is the location of the management board and the application for entry of a company in the Commercial Register must be submitted to the registry of the city or county court of the seat of the company. Therefore, the registered office of the management board must be located in Estonia. However, Estonian law does not require management board members of a company to be Estonian residents (at least half of the management board members must be residents of the Member States of the European Economic Area or Switzerland, however). Considering the above, Estonian law does not prevent relocation of the *de facto* seat of the company to another Member State, provided that the company retains a contact address in Estonia.

1.2 Transformation into a Foreign Entity

Transformation of a domestic company into a foreign entity and merger with a foreign entity or an S.E. is not expressly regulated under Estonian corporate law. This objective may be achieved by the transfer of the enterprise to a foreign company. 3

1.3 Incorporation

An OÜ may be incorporated by one or several persons by concluding a deed of formation (in the case of a single founder) or a foundation agreement and approving the articles of association of the company (Art. 138 of the Commercial Code ("ÄS")). The foundation documents must be notarised by an Estonian notary public. A company shall exist legally as from its entry in the Commercial Register (Art. 2 ÄS). 4

The expected timeframe for the incorporation and registration of an OÜ is approximately three weeks from the filing of all documents with the Commercial Registry.[1] The stamp duty for the registration of an OÜ with the Commercial Registry is 0.2 per cent of the share capital of the company, but must not be less than EEK 3,000 (approximately EUR 190) and not more than EEK 20,000 5

* *Raidla & Partners*, Tallinn.

1 In practice, the preparation of documents, gathering of the necessary power of attorneys and excerpts from foreign registries (where the company is founded by foreign legal entities), translation thereof and finding a suitable time for the founders for the notary's appointment may take another two weeks or longer.

(approximately EUR 1,280). In addition, the founders shall pay a notary fee, the amount of which depends on the proposed share capital and whether there is one founder or several.[2]

1.4 Recurrent Costs and Efforts

6 The only annual obligation of an OÜ is the filing of the annual report with the Commercial Registry. In addition, specific corporate resolutions require notarisation and filing with the Commercial Registry. In certain cases, a notice must also be published regarding the adoption of a particular resolution. The notary fee and stamp duty related to such steps generally remain below EUR 50. There is no annual registration fee.

1.5 Shares and Share Transfers

7 The shares in an OÜ are treated as belonging to a single class. However, the company's articles of association may provide that certain rights or benefits attach to a particular individual's share. Shares in an OÜ must have a par value of EEK 100 (approximately EUR 6) or a complete multiple thereof.

Shares in an OÜ are freely transferable to other shareholders of the company. Existing shareholders also have a pre-emptive right to buy shares offered for sale to a third party. The right of pre-emption of other shareholders may be precluded by the articles of association.

As a rule, a share transfer agreement shall be notarised. The notarisation requirement does not apply, however, if shares in the company are registered with the Estonian Central Register of Securities (*Väärtpaberite Keskregister*, "ECRS") (Art. 150 ÄS).[3]

The notary fee levied on a transfer of shares depends on the transaction value.[4] The respective fee may be paid by the parties in equal proportions or in another way as agreed between the parties.

8 Since no share certificates are issued under Estonian law, title to shares (unless registered with the ECRS) can only be verified by a series of notarial transfer deeds.

1.6 Corporate Bodies

9 An OÜ is governed by a general meeting of shareholders and a management board. In addition, OÜs whose management board has fewer than three members and whose share capital exceeds EEK 400,000 (approximately EUR 25,560) must have a supervisory council. The shareholders' general meeting may also appoint a procurator (*prokurist*) for the company. If the company has a supervisory council, the procurator is appointed by the supervisory council instead.

1.6.1 Management Board

10 The management board is an executive body charged with day-to-day management duties. The management board of an OÜ may consist of one or several members elected for three years, unless the articles of association of the company provide for a shorter term. The Commercial Code does not set forth restrictions on the renewal of the term of office of board members. Members of the management board are elected by the shareholders' meeting or, if the company has a supervisory council, the supervisory council.

11 Every member of the management board may represent the company in all legal acts, unless the articles of association prescribe a joint right of representation for some or all of the members of the board. Joint representation shall apply with regard to third parties only if it is entered on the Commercial Register (Art. 181 ÄS). Other restrictions on the management board to do with representation of the company (e.g. the scope of transactions which the management board may

2 In the case of a single founder and minimum share capital, the notary fee is approximately EEK 390 (approximately EUR 25).

3 Registration of shares of an OÜ with the ECRS is optional.

4 For example, the fee for notarisation of a share sale agreement the object of which is a share in OÜ with the par value of EEK 40,000 (approximately EUR 2,560) is approximately EEK 780 (approximately EUR 50).

conclude without having to apply for the prior consent of the shareholders or the supervisory council) may be set forth in the articles of association or by a resolution of the shareholders of the supervisory council. Since such restrictions cannot be entered on the Commercial Register, the restrictions do not apply with regard to third parties.

1.6.2 Shareholders' Meeting

The general meeting of shareholders constitutes the superior corporate body of an OÜ and resolutions are adopted at regular or extraordinary shareholders' meetings. Alternatively, shareholders of an OÜ are also permitted to reach decisions via post. In addition to adopting resolutions on issues explicitly placed within the responsibilities of the shareholders by law (such as the appointment of management board members, approval of annual accounts and adoption of business plans), shareholders' meetings may also decide all other issues relating to the management of the company. In the case of deciding issues which fall within the responsibilities of the management board or supervisory council, the shareholders are liable in the same manner as members of the management board or supervisory council. **12**

Resolutions of a general meeting are adopted if over one-half of the votes cast at the general meeting are in favour of the resolution (in the case of adopting resolutions in a written procedure, over one-half of the votes represented by all shares), unless the law or the articles of association stipulate a greater majority requirement. **13**

1.6.3 Supervisory Council

The supervisory council, if appointed, engages in surveillance and longer-range management activities. Members of the supervisory council are elected by the shareholders' meeting. **14**

1.7 Duties and Liabilities of Directors

Members of a company's management board must fulfil various general duties for the company, including upholding a fiduciary duty of loyalty, acting with due diligence, performing their duties with sufficient skill and in a manner commensurate with their knowledge and abilities, and acting to maximise benefits to the company and to prevent any losses. A strict confidentiality requirement also applies where members of the management board learn of facts that the company has a legitimate interest in keeping confidential. **15**

Members of the management board who cause damage to the company by violation of their obligations will be held jointly and severally liable for compensation for the damage caused. The liability of the management board members does not depend upon their individual culpability. The limitation period for filing claims against management board members is five years under the Commercial Code (Art. 187 ÄS). **16**

The members of the management board shall not bear liability if they act pursuant to a lawful resolution of the shareholders' general meeting or any other competent body of the legal person. **17**

The Commercial Code does not provide for a possibility to delegate duties of the management board to individual board members or a committee of directors. **18**

The liability of the members of managing bodies of a company may be limited or restricted only in the internal relationship between the company and such board members. The company may waive its right to file claims against the board member either in the mandate agreement concluded with such member or by entering into a compromise agreement with the board member when a claim has already arisen. A third party creditor may, nevertheless, file a claim against the board member liable for the damage in case the assets of the company alone are not sufficient to satisfy the claims of the creditor. **19**

Estonian law does not prohibit members of managing bodies of a company from obtaining civil liability insurance or the company from paying such insurance payments. Related premiums may be paid by the company. **20**

21 A debtor in bankruptcy proceedings or any other person from whom the right to engage in economic activity has been taken away pursuant to law may not be a member of the management board. The articles of association of the company may prescribe other persons who may not be members of the management board (Art. 180 ÄS).

22 The management board members are required to immediately submit a bankruptcy petition in the case of insolvency of the company, if the insolvency is not of a temporary nature (Art. 180 ÄS). The bankruptcy petition may be filed by each member of the management board, regardless of whether such member is authorised to represent the company alone in legal acts (Art. 13 of the Bankruptcy Act, *Pankrotiseadus*, effective as of 1 January 2004 ("PankrS")). In the case of a breach of this obligation, the creditors of the company may file claims against the board members if their claims cannot be satisfied from the company's assets.

1.8 Shareholders' Liability

23 Shareholders of a company are not held personally liable for the obligations of the company. However, if a shareholder has wrongfully caused damage to a third party, to another shareholder, or to the company itself, the shareholder will be held liable for such damage. A shareholder will not be liable for any damage caused if the shareholder did not participate in the adoption of the resolution which resulted in damage or if the shareholder voted against the resolution (Art. 183 ÄS).

1.9 Capitalisation and Financing

1.9.1 Basic Concepts

24 Shareholders of an OÜ are generally liable for the company's obligations only to the extent of the amount paid for their shares. Share capital must be fully paid-up before the entry of the company on the Commercial Register and shareholders' contributions may not be refunded to the shareholders. The share capital of an OÜ is protected by imposing certain obligations on the management board as well as the general meeting of shareholders. The minimum share capital required by law must be maintained at all times.

1.9.2 Minimum Share Capital

25 The minimum share capital of an OÜ is EEK 40,000 (approximately EUR 2,560). Unless a company's articles of association prescribe otherwise, shares must be paid for in cash. However, the articles of association may provide for the option of making contributions in kind (Art. 140 ÄS).[5] Partial contributions for shares (e.g. 50 per cent at registration and 50 per cent upon demand) are not allowed.

1.9.3 Maintenance of Capital and Liquidity

26 The Commercial Code provides rules for guaranteeing that the share capital of the company is paid-up before the company exists legally as well as for ensuring that the capital is protected later, during the period that the company operates.

(i) System

27 After the execution of the foundation agreement or deed of formation, the founder(s) must open a start-up account with an Estonian bank for the purpose of paying in the share capital. Where the articles of association of the company provide for the option of making contributions in kind, such contributions must be valued pursuant to the procedure stipulated in the articles of association. If the value of a contribution in kind exceeds EEK 40,000 (approximately EUR 2,560) or if all

5 A contribution in kind is anything that can be valued in monetary terms and that is transferable to the company. A contribution in kind may also be a proprietary right, including a legal claim.

contributions in kind collectively form more than one-half of the share capital, an auditor shall audit the valuation of the contribution in kind.

A bank certificate confirming transfer of the share capital to the start-up account of the company must be enclosed with the foundation documents that are filed with the Commercial Registry. In the case of contributions in kind, documents certifying the value of the contribution in kind as well as its transfer to the company must be appended to the registration application of the company with the Commercial Register.

Contributions paid by a shareholder may not be refunded and no interest is paid on contributions. **28**

The share capital of a company is protected by imposing certain obligations on the management **29** board as well as the general meeting of shareholders. The management board must ensure that a legal reserve of at least 10 per cent of the share capital is created by way of retaining profits generated by the company. The management board is required to convene a general meeting if the net assets of the company are less than one-half of the share capital, less than EEK 40,000 (approximately EUR 2,560) or another minimum share capital provided by law. The general meeting of shareholders must then decide upon one of the following: a reduction or increase in share capital on the condition that the net assets would thereby form at least one-half of the share capital and at least EEK 40,000 (approximately EUR 25,560); the implementation of other measures as a result of which the net assets of the company would comply with the above requirements; or dissolution, merger, division or transformation of the company or the submission of a bankruptcy petition.

(ii) Distributions

Dividends may be paid annually to the shareholders from net profit or from undistributed profit **30** from previous years from which losses from previous years have been deducted, on the basis of the approved annual balance sheet. Where the net assets of the company are less than or would be less than the total of the share capital of the company, a dividend shall not be paid to the shareholders (Art. 157 ÄS). No payments are made to the shareholders from the reserve capital of the company (Art. 161 ÄS). Interim dividends are not allowed.

If a shareholder is paid a dividend which the shareholder does not have a right to receive, the shareholder shall return the payment if the shareholder knew or should have known that the payment was made to the shareholder without basis. A shareholder shall also promptly return any other payment made illegally to the shareholder upon becoming aware of the illegality of the payment (Art. 158 ÄS).

(iii) Acquisition of Own Shares and Related Financing

A company shall generally not acquire or take as security its own shares. The acquisition or **31** taking as security of its own shares by an OÜ is permitted if: (1) this occurs within one year after adoption of a shareholders' resolution which specifies the terms and conditions and term for the acquisition or taking as security of shares and the sums to be paid for the shares; and (2) the shares are paid for from assets exceeding the share capital, reserve capital and premiums (Art. 162 ÄS). There is no maximum percentage of shares which may be acquired by an OÜ.

The company's own shares shall not grant the company any rights of a shareholder and the **32** company must transfer its own shares or terminate the taking as security of its own shares within one year after the acquisition or taking as security. Where the shares acquired by the company are not transferred or the taking as security is not terminated during such term, the shares shall be cancelled and the share capital shall be reduced accordingly (Art. 163 ÄS).

An OÜ may not grant a loan to a third party or guarantee a loan taken by a third party in order to **33** acquire a share in the company.

(iv) Company as Lender or Guarantor

An OÜ may not grant a loan: (1) to one of its shareholders whose shares represent more than **34** 5 per cent of the share capital; (2) to a shareholder or member of its parent undertaking whose shares represent more than 5 per cent of the share capital of the parent undertaking; (3) to a person to acquire a share of the company; or (4) to a member of its management board or supervisory council or its procurator (Art. 159 ÄS). The guaranteeing of loans taken by such persons is also prohibited under the Commercial Code.

35 A subsidiary may, however, grant a loan to its parent undertaking or a shareholder or a member of its parent undertaking which belongs to the same group as the subsidiary as well as guarantee loans taken by such companies if this does not harm the financial status of the company or the interests of creditors (Art. 159 ÄS).

(v) Company as Borrower

36 Shareholder loans to the company are generally allowed. Considering the extensive liability of the management board members under the Commercial Code, conclusion of a loan agreement with a shareholder on other than fair market terms is likely to result in liability for the board members.

Estonian law does not provide a special regulation for shareholder loans in case of crisis of the company. They rank pari passu with non-shareholder claims.

1.10 Publication and Filing Requirements

37 Certain information regarding companies has to be published in the official publication "*Ametlikud Teadaanded*". Other information must be submitted to the Commercial Register and is made accessible via the electronic database of the register. Information published in the official publication "*Ametlikud Teadaanded*" includes the following: information regarding insolvency, reduction of share capital, liquidation proceedings, merger, division and transformation resolutions, and compulsory dissolution of the company.

The Commercial Registry is decentralised in Estonia and is maintained by four first instance courts. The Commercial Registry can also be accessed online.[6] Information that is made available via the Commercial Register consists of general data regarding the company (such as the registry code, address, share capital, fields of activity), information about members of corporate bodies and commercial pledge, articles of association, and annual reports. Third parties may rely on the information available in the Commercial Registry.

Upon failure to file information required by law or upon submission of false information to the Commercial Registry, a fine of up to EEK 24,000 (approximately EUR 1,535) may be imposed both on the company as well as each management board member of the company. In addition, a company may be dissolved by a court judgment and deleted from the Commercial Registry if certain information is not filed with the registrar, e.g. if the term of authority of the management board members has expired more than two years previously and a new management board has not been elected (information on the new members of the management board has not been filed with the Commercial Registry) or if the company has not submitted the annual report to the Commercial Registry within six months after the expiry of the term provided by law and does not submit the annual report after a caution has been issued to the company by the registrar.

1.11 Financial Reporting

38 The management board is responsible for organising the accounting of the company. After the end of the financial year, the board must prepare the annual accounts and activity report pursuant to the procedure provided for in the Accounting Act (*Raamatupidamise seadus*, effective as of 1 January 2003, "RPS"). The annual accounts consist of main statements (a balance sheet, income statement, cash flow statement and statement of changes in owner's equity) and notes on the accounts. The annual accounts must be prepared in compliance with the RPS and with internationally accepted accounting and reporting principles. In addition, the accounting policies and presentation formats used in accounting must be in accordance with at least one of the following two accounting

6 http://info.eer.ee/ari/ariweb_package.avaleht.

frameworks: (1) accounting principles generally accepted in Estonia[7] or (2) international financial reporting standards ("IFRS"). The same rules apply to group annual accounts.

The annual accounts, together with the management report and profit distribution proposal, shall be presented to the shareholders for approval. Where the company has an auditor or a supervisory council, the conclusion of the auditor and the opinion of the supervisory council shall be appended to the reports. The management board shall submit the approved annual report to the Commercial Register together with the profit distribution proposal (and the auditor's report if auditing is compulsory)[8] not later than six months after the end of the financial year.

1.12 Employee Participation in Corporate Bodies

Employees are not entitled to board representation (or representation in the supervisory council of the company) under Estonian law. 39

2 The Stock Corporation ("AS")

Literature: M. Ots, V. Peep, T. Puri and M. Tropp, "Äriõigus. Osaühing. Aktsiaselts. Näidised ja kommentaarid" (Käsiraamatute Kirjastus, Tallinn 2005)

A stock corporation (*aktsiaselts*, "AS") is another type of company with limited liability under Estonian law, characterised by greater capital requirements and more numerous classes of shares than OÜs. ASs are required to register their shares with the ECRS and to submit to independent audits. The management structure of ASs must include a supervisory council in addition to the shareholders' meeting and the management board. 40

2.1 Export of Company

As explained above, under Estonian law the seat of a legal person is the location of the management board and only companies located in Estonia can apply for registration in the Commercial Register. Therefore, it is not possible to relocate an Estonian company to another Member State under the Commercial Code currently applicable in Estonia. However, relocation of the *de facto* seat of the company is not prevented under Estonian law, provided that the company has a contact address in Estonia. 41

2.2 Transformation into a Foreign Entity

Estonian law does not provide a procedure for transformation of a domestic company into a foreign entity or merger of a domestic company with a foreign entity or S.E. The objective could be achieved by transfer of the enterprise to a foreign company. 42

2.3 Incorporation

The process of incorporation of an AS is similar to that of an OÜ. Apart from certain differences in the foundation documents resulting from a more complicated corporate structure and the requirement to register the shares with the ECRS, the same rules apply. 43

The expected timeframe for the incorporation and registration of an AS is the same as that of an OÜ – approximately three weeks from the filing of all documents with the Commercial Registry. 44

7 The accounting principles generally accepted in Estonia are based on internationally accepted accounting and reporting principles, as provided by RPS and supplemented by guidelines issued by the Estonian Accounting Standards Board

8 OÜs are required to engage an auditor if the company's share capital exceeds EEK 400,000 (approximately EUR 25,560), if the company's articles of association so provide or if auditing is required by law. Pursuant to the RPS, an annual report of the company must be audited if two of the following indicators have been exceeded as at the closing day of the respective financial year (*aruandeaasta bilansipäev*): (i) the net turnover (*netokäive*): EEK 10,000,000 (approximately EUR 639,000); (ii) balance sheet total (*bilansimaht*): EEK 5,000,000 (approximately EUR 319,500); (iii) number of employees: 10.

The stamp duty for the registration of an AS with the Commercial Registry is 0.2 per cent of the share capital of the company, but must not be less than EEK 4,000 (approximately EUR 260) and not more than EEK 40,000 (approximately EUR 2,590). In addition, the founders shall pay a notary fee, the amount of which depends on the proposed share capital and whether there is one founder or several.[9]

2.4 Recurrent Costs and Efforts

45 As in the case of OÜs, the only annual obligation of an AS is the filing of the annual report with the Commercial Register. The cost of notarisation of corporate resolutions and stamp duties related to applying for changes in the registry card of the company in the Commercial Register generally remains below EUR 50.

2.5 Shares and Share Transfers

46 The shares in an AS must have a par value of EEK 10 (approximately EUR 0.6) or a complete multiple thereof and are subject to registration with the ECRS. The shares in an AS may be divided into different classes, each of which may be granted different rights. The Commercial Code provides examples of two possible classes of shares: ordinary shares and preferred shares. Ordinary shares typically entitle the shareholder to participate in general meetings, to participate in the distribution of profits and, upon dissolution, to receive a portion of the company's remaining assets (Art. 226 ÄS). The second class of shares, preferred shares, consists of non-voting shares that grant shareholders a preferential right to receive dividends and to participate in the distribution of the company's remaining assets upon dissolution (Art. 237 ÄS).

Shares in an AS are freely transferable, but the company's articles of association may confer a right of pre-emption on other shareholders. In such cases, the transferor must notify the management board of the conclusion of the share transfer agreement and the board must inform the other shareholders who may exercise a right of pre-emption (Art. 229 ÄS).

Unlike in the case of OÜs, no notarisation requirement is applied to a sale of shares in an AS. All transactions involving shares of ASs are registered with the ECRS. Shares are deemed to be transferred as of the entry of the transfer in the share ledger kept by the ECRS. The costs relating to the transfer of shares of an AS are limited to the service fee of the bank where the securities account has been opened (generally, such fees do not exceed EEK 300 (approximately EUR 19)).

2.6 Corporate Bodies

47 The AS is required to have three corporate bodies: the management board (*juhatus*), the shareholders' meeting (*aktsionäride üldkoosolek*) and the supervisory council (*nõukogu*).

2.6.1 Management Board

48 The management board of an AS consists of one or several members elected by the supervisory council. The duties of the management board of an AS are the same as those of an OÜ: day-to-day management and representation of the company in its relations with third parties. The right of the management board members to represent the company may be restricted so that some or all of the board members may only represent the company jointly.

49 When managing a company, the management board must comply with the lawful orders of the supervisory council. Transactions which exceed the limits of day-to-day economic activities may only be concluded by the management board with the prior consent of the supervisory council.

50 The management board members are elected by the supervisory council for a term of three years, unless the articles of association provide for a shorter term. No restrictions are provided on the renewal of the term of office of management board members.

9 In the case of a single founder and minimum share capital, the notary fee is approximately EEK 840 (approximately EUR 55).

2.6.2 Shareholders' Meeting

The general meeting of shareholders is the supreme decision-making forum of ASs. Resolutions may be adopted at either regular or extraordinary general meetings. Unlike in the case of OÜs, shareholders of an AS may not adopt resolutions in a written procedure without convening a meeting. 51

The responsibilities of the shareholders' meeting of an AS to adopt resolutions is analogous to that of the shareholders' meeting of OÜs. However, the shareholders' meeting of an AS may only adopt resolutions in matters falling within the responsibilities of the management board or supervisory council of the company if so demanded by the respective management body. The shareholders are jointly liable in the same manner as members of the management board or supervisory council for damage caused by resolutions adopted under such conditions (Art. 298 ÄS). 52

2.6.3 Supervisory Council

Members of the supervisory council (a minimum of three in number) are elected by the shareholders' general meeting for the term of five years, unless the articles of association stipulate a shorter term. The supervisory council engages in surveillance and longer-range management activities. Re-election of council members is not restricted under Estonian law. 53

2.7 Duties and Liabilities of Directors

The duties and liabilities of the members of the management board are to a material extent the same as those of the management board of an OÜ.[10] 54

As is the case with OÜs, the main duties of the members of the management board of an AS include the duty to act with due diligence and in a manner loyal to the company, preventing damages and performing their obligations to the maximum benefit of the company. The same liability rules apply as to the members of the management board of an OÜ (liability does not depend upon their individual culpability). 55

Members of the supervisory council must comply with the same rules. However, the liability of the council members is limited to damage wrongfully caused by them.

2.8 Shareholders' Liability

As is the case with OÜs, the shareholders of an AS are not held personally liable for the obligations of the company. However, if a shareholder has wrongfully caused damage to a third party, to another shareholder, or to the company itself, the shareholder will be held liable for such damage. A shareholder will not be liable for any damage caused if the shareholder did not participate in the adoption of the resolution which resulted in damage or if the shareholder voted against the resolution (Art. 289 ÄS). 56

2.9 Capitalisation and Financing

2.9.1 Basic Concepts

As is the case with an OÜ, the share capital of an AS must be fully paid-up before entry of the company to the Commercial Register and shareholders' contributions may not be refunded to the shareholders. The minimum share capital required by law must be maintained at all times. 57

10 See Mn. 15 et seq.

2.9.2 Minimum Share Capital

58 The minimum share capital of an AS is EEK 400,000 (approximately EUR 25,560). The capital can be rendered in cash or in kind, if such possibility is provided in the articles of association. Partial contributions are not allowed.

2.9.3 Maintenance of Capital and Liquidity

(i) System

59 Monetary contributions must be transferred to the start-up account of the company opened with an Estonian bank. Contributions in kind are subject to appraisal pursuant to the procedure provided in the articles of association of the company as well as compulsory auditing by an independent auditor. Otherwise, the same regulations apply as to OÜs.[11]

Contributions paid by the shareholders may not be refunded, and no interest is paid on contributions. Where the net assets of the company are less than one-half of the share capital, less than EEK 400,000 (approximately EUR 25,560) or another minimum required by law, the shareholders' general meeting must decide a reduction of share capital, implementation of other measures so that the share capital of the company would comply with the above requirements, or dissolution, merger, division or transformation of the company or submission of a bankruptcy petition.

(ii) Distributions

60 As is the case with OÜs, dividends may be paid annually to the shareholders of an AS from net profit or from undistributed profit from previous years from which losses from previous years have been deducted, on the basis of the approved annual balance sheet. Interim dividends are not allowed. A shareholder shall promptly return any other payment made illegally to the shareholder.[12]

(iii) Acquisition of Own Shares and Related Financing

61 A company shall generally not acquire or take as security its own shares. The acquisition or taking as security of its own shares by an AS is permitted if: (1) this occurs within one year after adoption of a resolution of the shareholders which specifies the terms and conditions and term for the acquisition or taking as security of shares and the sums to be paid for the shares; (2) the sum of the nominal values of the shares held or taken as security by the company does not exceed one-tenth of the share capital; and (3) the shares are paid for from assets exceeding the share capital, reserve capital and premiums (Art. 283 ÄS).

The company's own shares shall not grant the company any rights of a shareholder and the company must transfer its own shares or terminate the taking as security of its own shares within one year after the acquisition or taking as security. Where the shares acquired by the company are not transferred or the taking as security is not terminated during such term, the shares shall be cancelled and the share capital shall be reduced accordingly (Art. 284 ÄS).

62 An AS may not grant a loan to a third party or guarantee a loan taken by a third party in order to acquire shares in the company.

(iv) Company as Lender or Guarantor

63 An AS may not grant a loan: (1) to a shareholder whose shares represent more than 1 per cent of the share capital; (2) to a shareholder or member of its parent undertaking whose shares represent more than 1 per cent of the share capital of the parent undertaking; (3) to a person to acquire shares of the company; or (4) to a member of its management board or supervisory council or its

11 See Mn. 27.
12 See Mn. 30.

procurator (*prokurist*). The guaranteeing of loans taken by such persons is also prohibited under the Commercial Code.

A subsidiary may, however, grant a loan to its parent undertaking or a shareholder or a member who belongs to the same group as the subsidiary as well as guarantee loans taken by such companies if this does not harm the financial status of the company or the interests of creditors (Art. 281 ÄS).

(v) Company as Borrower

Shareholder loans to ASs are generally allowed, as for OÜs.[13] **64**

2.10 Publication and Filing Requirements

These requirements correspond with the requirements in OÜs.[14] **65**

2.11 Financial Reporting

These requirements generally correspond with the requirements in OÜs,[15] except for the following. Certain ASs, namely the credit institutions, financial holding companies, mixed-activity holding companies, insurance companies and companies, the shares or other securities issued by which are quoted on a stock exchange in Estonia or a Member State, cannot choose between the accounting principles generally recognised in Estonia and IAS/IFRS and must, upon preparation of financial statements, use the accounting policies and presentation formats in accordance with IAS/IFRS. **66**

All ASs, regardless of their size, must have their annual accounts audited by an independent auditor.

2.12 Employee Participation in Corporate Bodies

Employees are not entitled to representation on the management board or supervisory council under Estonian law. **67**

13 See Mn. 36.
14 See Mn. 37.
15 See Mn. 38.

VII. Finland

*by Sakari Helminen (LL.Lic.)**

1 The Limited Liability Company ("Oy")

Literature: Timonen in: Pöyhönen (ed.), An Introduction to Finnish Law (Kauppakaari 2002), Chapter 5.2.5: Limited Company; Kyläkallio/Iirola/Kyläkallio, Osakeyhtiö (Edita 2002); Schultén af, Osakeyhtiölain kommentaari I ja II, commentary (Talentum 2002/2004)

The limited liability company (*Osakeyhtiö*, "Oy") is the most common corporate form used in Finland to achieve the concept of limited shareholder liability. The Finnish Companies Act (734/1978 as amended) (*Osakeyhtiölaki*, "OYL") applies to both limited liability companies and stock corporations (*Julkinen osakeyhtiö*, "Oyj").[1] The main difference between the Oy and Oyj is that the shares of an Oyj may be admitted to public trading. The statutory corporate governance framework is not restrictive and permits a high degree of flexibility for both the Oy and the Oyj. In September 2005 approximately 188,000 limited liability companies were registered in Finland, in contrast to only 209 stock corporations (only 138 of which were listed). 1

The OYL is currently under complete review. The final legislative bill was submitted to Parliament on 2 September 2005 and the new Act will enter into force as of 1 September 2006.[2] 2

1.1 Export of Company

The incorporation theory is applied in Finland,[3] which allows both Oys and Oyjs to move their head office and/or entire business activities from Finland to any other country without the threat that the company would deem to be dissolved or to have lost its legal personality under Finnish law. However, the only way to change the registered office (i.e. the place where the company is registered) is to first dissolve the company in Finland and thereafter incorporate it in another country.[4] This will change, if proposals for the Tenth[5] and Fourteenth Directives[6] are accepted and implemented in EU Member States, after which the future would be quite different with reference to the mobility of companies between different Member States. 3

1.2 Transformation into a Foreign Entity

The OYL does not provide any rules for the transformation of a domestic company into a foreign entity. However, a similar end result can, for example, be achieved by transferring the business of the Oy by way of an asset deal to a foreign entity.[7] 4

1.3 Incorporation

The procedure of forming an Oy is an easy one and there is no need for any notarial deed. An Oy will legally exist upon its entry into the trade register *(Kaupparekisteri)* held by the National Board of Patents and Registration (*Patentti-ja rekisterihallitus*)[8] (Sec. 2 Subs. 14 OYL). According to the 5

* *Hannes Snellman Attorneys at Law Ltd,* Turku/Helsinki.

1 See Mn. 48 et seq. You may find some basic information about Finnish enterprises, Acts, trade register and financial markets at the following websites: www.enterprisefinland.fi, www.finlex.fi (Acts), www.prh.fi (trade register) and www.hex.com (financial markets).

2 See a summary in English at www.om.fi. The central aim of the proposed reform is to enact a flexible Companies Act, which would permit shareholders and the company to organise their business activities as efficiently as possible while providing, at the same time, sufficient protection to both minority shareholders and creditors.

3 Helminen 2001 p. 28 and Savela 2003 p. 37.

4 Issues related to the S.E. are not dealt with here. See Part 1, I, Mn. 75 and Part 2, S.E., Mn. 4 et seq.

5 See Part 1, I, Mn. 55 et seq.

6 See Part 1, I, Mn. 67.

7 See Mn. 4.

8 See www.prh.fi, also in Swedish and in English.

proposed new Companies Act, articles of association can be very short,[9] because the proposed Act contains many new default provisions on matters that are to be currently mandatorily addressed in the articles of association.[10]

6 It is possible to establish and register an Oy in one day, but normally the length of the registration procedure varies from one to two weeks once the documents have been completed. The registration fee in 2005 is EUR 330.

1.4 Recurrent Costs and Efforts

7 Recurrent costs and efforts relating to an Oy are relatively minimal and are in connection mainly with the auditing and drafting of annual accounts of the company. There is no cost for the filing of annual accounts with the trade register. Neither is there any annual registration fee to be paid by the company to the trade register. The costs for auditing, bookkeeping and other external financial management vary from company to company. A rough estimation of the total annual cost of external financial management is about 0.5-1 per cent of turnover of the company, but in some fields of business the costs can be much lower than 0.5 per cent of the turnover of the company.

1.5 Shares and Share Transfers

8 All shares of an Oy entitle their holders to equal rights in the company (Sec. 3 Subs. 1 OYL). However, the articles of association may stipulate that the company shall or may have shares with different rights. Shares may, for example, differ from each other with regard to distribution of the assets of the company (including dividends) and/or the number of votes attached to them.[11] According to the proposed new Companies Act, non-voting shares would also be possible in the future.

9 Shares in an Oy can basically be freely transferred[12] by way of a commercial agreement made by and between the seller and the purchaser (Sec. 3 Subs. 2 OYL). There is no need for any notarial approvals. At the request of a shareholder, the board of directors has to issue share certificates for the shares (Sec. 3 Subs. 7 OYL). However, share certificates in an Oy are rare and shareholding in an Oy is normally proven by an extract from the company's share and shareholder registers. Share and shareholder registers, which are kept at the head office of the company, are open to public inspection and anyone has the right to obtain a copy of all or part of the share and shareholder registers (Sec. 3 Subs. 12 OYL).

10 According to the Act on Transfer Tax (931/1996 as amended) transfer tax amounting to 1.6 per cent of the transfer price is levied when shares in an Oy are transferred and either the transferor, the transferee, or both are Finnish residents, Finnish branch offices of foreign credit institutions, or Finnish branch offices of foreign investment services institutions. The transferee is liable to pay the transfer tax. When shares are transferred to a foreign transferee (as defined in the Act on Transfer Tax), the transferor is obliged to collect the transfer tax from the transferee (Sec. 16). If the transferor has not collected the tax from the foreign transferee, he may, in the final instance, be responsible to the State for payment of the tax (Sec. 23). Transfer tax must normally be paid within two months of concluding the transfer (Sec. 21.1).

11 Shares and other securities of an Oy may not be admitted to public trading, e.g. on a stock exchange or a similar market place. The concept of public trading is defined in the Securities Market Act (Sec. 1 Subs. 3) (495/1989 as amended). However, an Oy is not prohibited from issuing its

9 However, this is not very probable in practice.

10 Only the following matters have to be indicated in the articles: 1) the trade name of the company; 2) the municipality in Finland where the domicile of the company will be located; and 3) the company's field of business.

11 According to the Companies Act, however, the number of votes carried by a share may not be more than 20 times the number carried by another share (Sec. 9 Subs. 3 OYL). The proposal for the new Companies Act intends to abolish this restriction.

12 However, provisions in the articles of association of an Oy quite often restrict free transferability of the shares. See also Mn. 53 according to which an Oy may also be incorporated in the book-entry system.

shares to the public (e.g. via private placement).[13] In this case the public would have to be informed of the fact that the securities may not be admitted to public trading. Before admitting the company's shares to be listed on a stock exchange (e.g. via an IPO) the Oy must first be converted into an Oyj (Sec. 1 Subs. 2 OYL).

1.6 Corporate Bodies

An Oy's organisation and structure can be based on a two-tier or a one-tier board system. In a two-tier board system an Oy's organisation consists of a supervisory board, a board of directors and possibly a managing director. In a one-tier board system the organisation consists of a board of directors and possibly a managing director. The OYL provides for three compulsory corporate bodies: the board of directors, the general meeting of the shareholders and an auditor.[14] A company with a share capital of over EUR 80,000 must also have a managing director; otherwise a managing director is optional. A supervisory board is optional and allowed only in companies with a share capital of at least EUR 80,000. Furthermore, the articles of association may contain, for example, provisions for advisory or management boards or nomination committees. However, the duties and responsibilities of the corporate bodies defined in the OYL may not be transferred to such optional committees or boards. According to the proposed new Companies Act, all share capital requirements or restrictions with reference to the corporate bodies mentioned above are to be abolished and, henceforth, the shareholders would have more opportunities to organise their corporate governance structure as best suits them. 12

1.6.1 Managing Director

An Oy may have one managing director and one deputy managing director. In companies with a share capital of at least EUR 80,000, a managing director is mandatory (Sec. 8 Subs. 3 OYL). In practice, it is very common to have a managing director in all sizes of companies. The managing director is appointed by the board of directors or, if so stipulated in the articles of association, by the supervisory board.[15] The managing director has the right to represent the company in matters pertaining to his duties (i.e. day-to-day management) (Sec. 8 Subs. 13 OYL). Moreover, the articles of association may stipulate that the managing director has the right to sign on behalf of the company, i.e. the managing director's right to bind the company is as broad as that of the board of directors. The right to represent and sign on behalf of the company may be restricted in the articles of association by stipulating that only two or more persons together have the right to sign on behalf of the company. No other restrictions may be entered in the trade register (Sec. 8 Subs. 12 OYL). 13

The managing director is in charge of the day-to-day management of the company in accordance with the instructions and orders given by the board of directors. The managing director is also responsible for ensuring that bookkeeping complies with relevant laws and that financial matters are being handled in a reliable manner (Sec. 8 Subs. 6 OYL). 14

1.6.2 The General Meeting of Shareholders

The general meeting (i.e. shareholders' meeting) is considered to be the highest body in an Oy and it has the right to give instructions to other corporate bodies.[16] However, in practice, the general meeting quite often resolves only matters specifically assigned to it according to the OYL, such as amendment to the articles of association and issuance of new shares. 15

The shareholders may, without holding a general meeting, unanimously resolve an issue falling under the responsibility of the general meeting. The decision has to be made in writing and it must 16

13 However, please note that, *inter alia*, the Securities Market Act regulates the issuing of Oys' shares to the public in more detail.

14 In practice, auditors are authorised public accountants despite the fact that Finnish law also allows the use of unqualified auditors in many cases.

15 The nomination right of the supervisory board would be abolished by the new Companies Act.

16 Huttunen p. 30 et seq.

be dated and signed. If there is more than one shareholder, at least two of them have to sign the written decision (Sec. 9 Subs. 1 a OYL).

17 Resolutions of the general meeting are passed by a simple majority of the votes cast and, in the case of an equality of votes, the chairman has the casting vote. Higher thresholds (generally involving a 75 per cent majority of votes cast and of the shares represented at the meeting) apply in certain cases, for example, the passing of resolutions amending the articles of association (Sec. 9 Subs. 13-15 OYL).

1.6.3 Board of Directors

18 Each Oy must have a board of directors. If the number of board members is less than three, one deputy member shall be elected. If the Oy's share capital equals or exceeds EUR 80,000, at least three board members must be elected.[17] The board members are normally appointed by the general meeting. If an Oy has a supervisory board, then the supervisory board appoints the members of the board of directors unless otherwise stipulated in the articles of association (Sec. 8 Subs. 11 a OYL).[18] In addition to that the articles of association may stipulate that a minority of the board members may be appointed in another manner, e.g. by the personnel of the company (Sec. 8 Subs. 1 OYL).[19] The board of directors is responsible for the management and proper running of the operations of the company (Sec. 8 Subs. 6 OYL). The board of directors also has the statutory right to represent the company and sign its trade name (Sec. 8 Subs. 12 OYL).

1.6.4 Supervisory Board

19 The supervisory board's main function is to supervise the board of directors and the managing director (Sec. 8 Subs. 11-12 OYL). The supervisory board's position in comparison to the status of the other corporate bodies is quite minor and, as a result, very few supervisory boards are established. The supervisory board as a corporate body does not have the right to represent the company or sign on behalf of the company. The members of the supervisory board are appointed by the general meeting, unless the articles of association stipulate that a minority of the members may be appointed in another manner, e.g. by a certain shareholder.

1.7 Duties and Liabilities of Directors

20 The core of the statutory duties of the board directors and managing director are expressed in the OYL as follows: "The board of directors shall be responsible for the due organising of the administration and operations of the company" and with respect to the managing director as follows: "The managing director shall be in charge of the day-to-day management of the company in accordance with the instructions and orders given by the board of directors" (Sec. 8 Subs. 6 OYL).[20] The OYL also obliges the managing director and the board of directors to take care of several special duties including, *inter alia*, arranging for the necessary filings to be made in the trade register. The board of directors or managing director may not undertake an act or a measure which is likely to cause unfair wealth to a shareholder or to a third person at the cost of the company or another shareholder. In addition, they may not comply with a resolution made by the general meeting or another corporate body which is void due to non-compliance with the OYL or the articles of association (Sec. 8 Subs. 14 OYL). Moreover, several other Acts, especially in the areas of tax and environmental law, address the duties of directors. The directors must perform their corporate duties with proper care always taking into account the best interests of the company.

17 According to the proposed new Companies Act, the minimum size of the board of directors of any Oy would be one ordinary and one deputy board member.

18 According to the proposed new Companies Act, the supervisory board appoints the board members if so stipulated in the articles of association.

19 This means that the general meeting or the supervisory board has to appoint the majority of the board members.

20 See Mn. 14 and 19.

The members of the board of directors and of the supervisory board as well as managing director (hereinafter "directors") may be held liable not only for their acts but also for their omission. This liability is defined in the OYL as follows: "A founder, a member of the board of directors, a member of the supervisory board and the managing director is liable for the damage he has caused to the company intentionally or by negligence in his office. The same is applicable to damage caused to a shareholder or a third party by violating this Act or the articles of association of the company" (Sec. 15 Subs. 1 OYL). Liability for damage caused to the company arises from negligence, whether or not wilful. Liability for damage caused to a shareholder or a third party can only arise from a specific breach of the OYL or the articles of association. The liability of members of the board of directors and of the supervisory board is scrutinised individually. If two or more members are held liable, liability is joint and several. Mere abstaining from voting or an allocation of responsibilities is not sufficient to release a director from liability for a resolution taken. However, those matters can be taken into account when evaluating a director's negligence and in some rare circumstances these can decrease a director's liability or abolish it. Subjective criteria, e.g. special expertise or lack of expertise, may have an effect on the liability. E.g. lack of expertise may decrease a director's negligence to the appointing shareholders and special expertise may increase it with respect to shareholders and third parties. **21**

If the general meeting grants a discharge from liability to the directors, the company is not precluded from asserting a claim for damages if the general meeting arrived at its discharge decision in reliance upon incorrect or incomplete information. Nor does discharge from liability restrict a bankruptcy estate or a trustee of the company in reorganisation from suing on behalf of the company, provided that the action is brought within two years of the discharge decision. **22**

A claim in the name of the company cannot be brought (unless the action is based on a punishable act) against the directors later than three years from the end of the financial period during which the decision was made or the measure was taken (Sec. 15 Subs. 7 OYL). A claim in the name of a shareholder or a third party shall be brought against the directors, as a general rule, within 10 years of the damage.[21] **23**

The extent of liability is not limited by law.[22] Since there are no express limitations, the liability covers economic damage and loss as well as property and personal damage.[23] D&O insurance is allowed and the payment of related premiums by an Oy is permitted. **24**

A person who is legally incompetent or declared bankrupt may not act as a director. Also, a person who has been convicted by the court and thereby banned from business operations in accordance with the special provisions of the Act on Ban on Business Operation (1059/1985) cannot act as a director. The term of restriction is a minimum of three years and a maximum of seven years. **25**

The board of directors has in certain circumstances an obligation to apply for insolvency proceedings according to the OYL (Sec 13. Subs. 2 OYL).[24] **26**

1.8 Shareholders' Liability

It is questionable if the concept of piercing the corporate veil is approved in Finland.[25] According to the OYL, the shareholders cannot be held personally liable for the obligations of the company. However, in some very rare cases, it might be possible to argue in favour of piercing the corporate veil. **27**

21 Savela 1999 p. 171. According to the proposed new Companies Act, all above mentioned claims should be brought against the directors within five years.

22 According to the proposed new Companies Act, directors' liability to the company can in some circumstances be restricted if so stipulated in the articles of association.

23 However, property and personal damage are, in practice, unlikely to occur.

24 See Mn. 34.

25 Savela 1999 p. 228.

1.9 Capitalisation and Financing

1.9.1 Basic Concepts

28 The share capital, premium fund and some other funds are regarded as restricted equity, which cannot be distributed to the shareholders without a specific procedure that secures creditors' interests (Sec. 11 Subs. 6 OYL). The share capital is intended to form a capital fund which is the minimum amount available to the company's creditors.[26] The share capital can, in this way, be seen as a counterpart to the rule of limited liability of the shareholders.

29 If the proposed new Companies Act enters into force, probably the most important reform would be a changeover to a true non par value system.[27] These new rules would make it possible to issue shares below par value, i.e. the nominal value of the shares, and to enter the subscription price partly or wholly in free equity account. Therefore there would be no need for a separate premium fund, as there would be no par value and hence no premiums either. These proposed changes, which would allow more leeway in investing in the capital of a company, in no way endanger the principles and provisions concerning the equality of the shareholders or the protection of creditors.

1.9.2 Minimum Share Capital

30 The minimum share capital of an Oy is EUR 8,000 (Sec. 1 Subs. 1 OYL). The capital can be rendered in cash or in kind,[28] (Sec. 4 Subs. 6 and Sec. 2 Subs. 4 OYL). The share capital and possible premium are to be wholly in the ownership and possession of the company before an increase in the share capital and possible premium can be notified for registration (Sec. 4 Subs. 8 a and Sec. 2 Subs. 9 OYL).

1.9.3 Maintenance of Capital and Liquidity

(i) System

31 The distribution of profits and other uses of company assets are regulated in different Sections of the OYL.[29] Several methods of distribution as stipulated in the OYL are considered as comprehensive and other ways of distributing assets are considered unlawful. A shareholder will be held liable to return any assets he has obtained from an Oy contrary to the OYL unless he was justified in assuming that the distribution of the funds took place in accordance with the OYL (Sec. 12 Subs. 5 OYL). Also, the persons participating in or implementing any such decision may be liable to compensation for any deficiency existing after the above-mentioned repayment.

32 Reduction in the share capital requires, *inter alia*, the permission of the registration authority if the amount by which the share capital is reduced is used for a purpose other than covering a loss shown on an adopted balance sheet, i.e. the creditor protection rules. The same or similar system applies when other restricted funds of an Oy are distributed. Distributable assets are defined in the OYL and can be distributed without the need for any permission from creditors or authorities (Sec. 12 Subs. 2 OYL).

33 According to the proposed new Companies Act, the provisions for the distribution of assets are clarified in such a way that no distribution of assets is allowed if the distribution could result in an

26 It has been discussed whether the concept of the minimum share capital should be maintained. The creditors may be protected even if the provisions of the minimum share capital are abolished.

27 In accordance with true non par value systems, the connection between the share capital and shares is breaking. This means that shares could be issued without increasing the share capital and the share capital could be increased without issuing new shares.

28 However, the nature of a contribution in kind shall only consist of property of financial value to the company. A commitment to perform work or services cannot constitute a contribution in kind (Sec. 2 Subs. 4 and Sec. 4 Subs. 6 OYL).

29 E.g. in Sec. 6 (Lowering the share capital and redeemable shares), Sec. 7 (Own shares) and Sec. 12 (Distribution of assets) OYL.

Oy becoming insolvent.[30] Also, the provisions on the unlawful distribution of assets are proposed to be clarified by a general rule according to which a business transaction that reduces the assets of an Oy without a sound business reason is considered to be an unlawful distribution of assets.

Provisions for a compulsory liquidation procedure are a Finnish peculiarity. According to these provisions, if the equity of an Oy in the balance sheet is less than half of the share capital, the board of directors shall without delay convene the general meeting to consider placing the company in liquidation. In the first general meeting, the shareholders can make either a decision to place the company into liquidation or decide to continue the company's operations. However, if the equity is still less than half of the share capital 12 months after the first general meeting, the shareholders must at the second general meeting make a decision to place the company in liquidation (Sec. 13 Subs. 2 OYL).[31] **34**

(ii) Distributions

The general meeting decides on the distribution of dividends and other assets of the company. **35** The general meeting may not decide to distribute as a dividend an amount greater than that proposed or approved by the board of directors. However, shareholders holding a minimum of one-tenth, or smaller amount stipulated in the articles of association, of all the shares may demand that the dividend to be distributed shall equal at least half of the profits from the financial period after certain deductions (Sec. 12 Subs. 4 OYL).[32]

The distribution of dividends may not exceed the aggregate amount of the annual profits and **36** profits from previous years shown on the adopted balance sheet from which the losses and certain other non-distributable items have been deducted (Sec. 12 Subs. 2 OYL). The shares provide equal rights to the distribution of company's assets if not otherwise stipulated in the articles of association.

According to the proposed new Companies Act, the general meeting may authorise the board of **37** directors to decide on dividends. The new provisions would also allow dividends on the basis of the financial statements drawn up and adopted at any moment, which would make it possible to distribute profits arising from the current financial year.

(iii) Acquisition of Own Shares and Related Financing

An Oy may acquire its own shares and accept, but only in certain circumstances, its own shares **38** as collateral.[33] Neither an Oy nor its subsidiary enterprises may subscribe for the shares in the Oy (Sec. 7 Subs. 2 OYL). Shares acquired shall be assigned within three years[34] of the acquisition or else the share capital shall immediately be lowered by an amount equal to the aggregate nominal value of the shares acquired through invalidation of the shares (Sec. 7 Subs. 8 OYL). An Oy may not exercise shareholder rights, e.g. voting rights connected to the acquired shares. The articles of association may also stipulate that the Oy has the right or obligation to redeem its own shares by lowering its share capital (Sec. 6 Subs. 9 OYL).[35]

An Oy may not acquire all of its own shares and so at least one of the shares must be owned by **39** someone else (Sec. 7 Subs. 6 OYL).

30 This new restriction is called for, as the mere evaluation of the distributable assets in the balance sheet of an Oy is not enough to present a reliable view of its financial situation.

31 Based on the proposed new Companies Act, these provisions will be replaced with a provision according to which if the losses of an Oy are greater than its own equity then the board of directors is required to make a register notification in order to inform the public of the financial situation of the company.

32 The distribution of a dividend may, however, not exceed the amount of freely distributable assets, nor may a shareholder demand that more than 8 per cent of the equity of the company be distributed as dividend.

33 According to the proposed new Companies Act, the company can accept its own shares as collateral. However, it is clear that the value of the collateral should be quite low.

34 According to the proposed new Companies Act, there is no time limit within which the acquired shares of an Oy have to be assigned further.

35 According to the proposed new Companies Act, the articles of association may stipulate that the company has the right or obligation to acquire or redeem its own shares either by lowering its share capital or by not doing so.

40 An Oy may not grant a loan or provide collateral or any other assets for the sake of the recipient party acquiring shares in the Oy or in another company belonging to the same group ("financial assistance") (Sec. 12 Subs. 7 OYL). According to the proposed new Companies Act, the scope of application of the prohibition against financial assistance would be limited to the acquisition of the Oy's own shares and the shares of the parent company. Therefore, the financing of the acquisition of shares in a sister company would not, as a general rule, be prohibited. The correct interpretation of the provisions for financial assistance is in some circumstances demanding and thus the prohibition on financial assistance must be carefully considered when planning acquisitions that might involve financial assistance.

(iv) Company as Lender or Guarantor

41 An Oy may grant loans or provide guarantees to third parties.[36] However, according to the OYL, loans and collateral provided to a party belonging to the "inner circle" of an Oy[37] are allowed only within the limits of freely distributable assets of the Oy and against obtaining safeguarding collateral. Notwithstanding the above restrictions, monetary loans and collateral may be granted, for example, to a party belonging to the inner circle, if the debtor is a group company limited by shares (Sec. 12 Subs. 7 OYL). If the proposed new Companies Act enters into force it would abolish inner circle lending regulation. However, inner circle lending would be governed by the general principles of the OYL (for example, principles of equal treatment of shareholders and the object of the company) and thus inner circle lending would not be freely accepted in the future either. Due to tax regulations, the company should require a moderate interest to be paid for the loan granted.

(v) Company as Borrower

42 Shareholder loans and provision of collateral to an Oy are allowed. Due to tax regulations, the interest on the loan should not exceed the interest that a financing institution would require for a similar loan. According to the OYL, a shareholder is not obliged to provide additional funding for the company. However, it is possible to stipulate in the articles of association that a shareholder has an obligation to make specific payments to the company. In the event of insolvency, shareholder loans are treated similarly as any other non-shareholder to the company.

1.10 Publication and Filing Requirements

43 A wide range of documentation[38] and information must be filed with the National Board of Patents and Registration ("NBPR"), some of which will be published in the national trade register journal (*Kaupparekisterilehti*). There is no additional filing obligation in respect of foreign shareholders. The trade register is centralised, but there are several offices in different locations in Finland. The trade register is open to the public and any person can review and obtain copies of the filed documents. Some of the filed information is gathered in an extract of the trade register (*Kaupparekisteriote*) and anyone can request such official extract, which includes, for example, basic information about the company, the share capital and its reductions and increases, and the names and addresses of the board of directors, auditors and managing director. A third party can normally rely on the content of the register. There can be different consequences for not filing the necessary documents in the trade register. E.g. an amendment of the articles of association shall not enter into force before it is registered in the trade register.

44 The annual accounts of the company shall be submitted to the trade register within two months of the profit and loss account and balance sheet being adopted (Sec. 11 Subs. 14 OYL). The NBPR can

36 However, the principles of profit maximisation and the object of the company should be taken into account when giving loans or granting collateral to third parties.

37 According to the OYL, the inner circle includes, *inter alia*, a shareholder holding a minimum of 1 per cent of the shares or the votes in a company (Sec. 1 Subs. 4 OYL).

38 E.g. a deed of incorporation and the articles of association (Sec. 12 Statute of Trade Register (*Kaupparekisteriasetus*, 208/1979 as amended)). See also Mn. 7.

order the company to go into liquidation or delete it from the trade register if the above-mentioned documents have not, in spite of a request of the NBPR, been submitted to the NBPR within one year of the end of the financial period of the company (Sec. 13 Subs. 4 OYL).

The NBPR also operates electronically. Please visit the website of Electronic NBPR at www.prh.fi. **45**
Information is provided in Finnish, Swedish and English.

1.11 Financial Reporting

An Oy must draw up its annual accounts[39] within six months of the end of the financial year.[40] **46**
The Oy's annual accounts are in practice drawn up in accordance with the Finnish Accounting Act (*Kirjanpitolaki*) and Statute (*Kirjanpitoasetus*). The drawing up of both individual annual accounts and group annual accounts in accordance with international accounting principles (i.e. IAS/IFRS) is, however, also permitted for an Oy. The only requirement is that an Oy's bookkeeping, annual accounts and administration are audited in accordance with the Finnish Accounting Act (*Tilintarkastuslaki*) and approved by an Authorised Public Accountant as defined in Finnish Accounting Act.

Certain relief from financial reporting requirements is granted to small enterprises, which are those not exceeding two of the three following criteria during the financial year and the one immediately preceding it: balance sheet total of EUR 3,650,000; a turnover of EUR 7,300,000 and average number of employees 50 (Sec. 3 Subs. 9 The Finnish Accounting Act 1336/1997 as amended). Small companies are – amongst others – released from the requirement to draw up cash flow statement and a report of operation.[41]

1.12 Employee Participation in Corporate Bodies

In general, employees are not represented in the corporate bodies of an Oy. However, there is an **47**
Act on personnel representation in the administration of undertakings (725/1990 as amended)(*Laki henkilöstön edustuksesta yritysten hallinnossa*) which must be enforced in companies with 150 employees or more. The representation must be organised by agreement between the employer and employees, or, in the absence of such an agreement, in accordance with the provisions of the Act. In the latter case, the employees shall have the right in accordance with the selection of the Oy[42] to elect employees' representatives to the supervisory board, board of directors or to management groups or similar bodies that together cover the profit units of the company. The number of personnel representatives has to be between one and four, but no higher than one quarter of the number of the other members of the chosen body. The rights and obligations of the personnel representatives are outlined in detail in the above-mentioned Act.

39 The annual accounts consist of profit and loss account, balance sheet, annual report and annexes (Sec. 3 Subs. 1 Finnish Accounting Act).

40 The financial year may be the calendar year or any other 12-month period chosen. When setting up or closing down the business or changing its financial year, the financial year may be shorter or longer than 12 months but never exceeding 18 months (Sec. 1 Subs. 4 Finnish Accounting Act).

41 However, annual accounts of an Oy must then be supported by certain specific notes to annual accounts (Sec. 11 Subs. 9 OYL).

42 Consequently, it is very unusual that the personnel representatives would be, for example, board members in an Oy.

2 The Stock Corporation ("Oyj")

Literature: Please see limited liability company (Oy).

48 The stock corporation (*Julkinen osakeyhtiö*, "Oyj") is another corporate form offering limited shareholder's liability in Finland. For the differences between an Oy and an Oyj, please see Mn. 1 and 2.

2.1 Export of Company

49 As for an Oy.[43]

2.2 Transformation into a Foreign Entity

50 As for an Oy.[44]

2.3 Incorporation

51 As for an Oy.[45] An Oyj is, however, normally established by changing an Oy into an Oyj in accordance with special provisions in the OYL (Sec. 17 OYL).[46] Changing the structure of a limited liability company can be done without any tax consequences.

2.4 Recurrent Costs and Efforts

52 An unlisted Oyj typically faces costs and efforts comparable to those for an Oy.[47] However, in listed Oyjs costs for arranging shareholders' meetings, compulsory communications etc. may easily reach considerable sums of euros a year.

2.5 Shares and Share Transfers

53 The regulation concerning share certificates and transferability of shares with reference to an unlisted Oyj is the same as applies to an Oy.[48] However, if the Oyj's shares are admitted to public trading the Oyj must incorporate its shares in the book-entry system unless the Financial Supervision Authority (*Rahoitustarkastus*) grants an exemption for a special reason (Sec. 4 Subs. 25, Act on the Book-entry System (826/1991, as amended) (*Laki arvo-osuusjärjestelmästä*). The Finnish Central Securities Depository (*Suomen Arvopaperikeskus Oy*) may provide that a security of the Oy may also be incorporated in the book-entry system. The book-entry system is a paperless system where, for example, share transfers are registered electronically. This system does not use any shares or other certificates.[49] Stock Exchange regulations normally deny any restriction on free transferability of shares with respect to the shares that are admitted to public trading. Otherwise, the shares in an Oyj may differ from each other as in an Oy.[50]

43 See Mn. 3.

44 See Mn. 4. However, European Company Statute (ECS) and its related Directive concerning employee involvement within the European Company (see Part 1, I, Mn. 75 and Part 2, S..E., Mn. 12 et seq.) make it possible for public limited companies from different EU Member States to create an S.E. by means of a merger between such companies. ECS facilitates the transfer of a company's seat and makes, to some extent, cross-border transactions possible, thus it could be seen as a step forward to fulfilling the demands of the single European market. In Finland a couple of Oyjs have already been converted to an S.E.

45 See Mn. 5 and 6. The registration fee for changing the structure of a limited liability company in 2005 is EUR 330. There is no need for any notarial deed when changing the limited company form.

46 An Oyj can also be transformed into an Oy.

47 See Mn. 7.

48 See Mn. 9.

49 Please visit the website www.hex.com for more detailed information.

50 See Mn. 8.

Share transfers are generally subject to the same regulations as transfers of shares in an Oy.[51] However, transfers of shares through a stock exchange in a public sale as defined in Chapter 1, Section 2 of the Securities Market Act are free from transfer tax (Sec. 15 Subs. 5 The Act on Transfer Tax). **54**

2.6 Corporate Bodies

As for an Oy,[52] the OYL forms the basis for corporate governance while the details are left to companies and the self-regulatory bodies of businesses, i.e. corporate governance recommendations that apply to listed companies. Oyjs listed on the Helsinki Stock Exchange must comply with the new Finnish Corporate Governance Recommendation (which entered into force on 1 July 2004) ("Recommendation") or explain the reasons for deviating from the Recommendation.[53] An Oyj must give information on its compliance with the Recommendation both in its annual report and on its website. The Recommendation also includes some provisions regarding corporate bodies. These will be outlined below. **55**

2.6.1 Managing Director

As for an Oy.[54] According to the Recommendation, the managing director should not be elected as chairman of the board. The proposed new Companies Act allows the managing director to occupy both positions at the same time. **56**

2.6.2 Board of Directors

As for an Oy.[55] According to the Recommendation, the board has to comprise at least five directors and the directors shall be elected for a term of one year. There is no such restriction in the proposed new Companies Act. **57**

2.6.3 The General Meeting of Shareholders

As for an Oy.[56] **58**

2.6.4 Supervisory Board

As for an Oy.[57] The general tendency is to restrict the power of the supervisory board. In accordance with this, the Recommendation recommends that the supervisory board's powers shall be restricted to supervision of the management and issuing instructions. **59**

2.7 Duties and Liabilities of Directors

As for an Oy.[58] D&O insurance is common in listed Oyjs and the repayment of related premiums by Oyjs is permitted. **60**

2.8 Shareholders' Liability

As for an Oy.[59] **61**

51 See Mn. 9 et seq.
52 See Mn. 12 et seq.
53 You will find the new Finnish Corporate Governance Recommendation in English at www.keskuskauppakamari.fi.
54 See Mn. 13.
55 See Mn. 18.
56 See Mn. 15 et seq.
57 See Mn. 19.
58 See Mn. 20 et seq.
59 See Mn. 27.

2.9 Capitalisation and Financing

2.9.1 Basic Concepts

62 The OYL applies to both Oyjs and Oys. There are a couple of different provisions concerning these corporate forms and these differences are dealt with below.[60]

2.9.2 Minimum Share Capital

63 The minimum share capital of an Oyj is EUR 80,000 (Sec. 1 Subs. 2 OYL).[61]

2.9.3 Maintenance of Capital and Liquidity

(i) System

64 Provisions concerning capital maintenance and liquidity are in many respects the same as for an Oy.[62]

(ii) Distributions

65 As for an Oy.[63]

(iii) Acquisition of Own Shares and Related Financing

66 The basic conditions on purchase and redemption of an Oyj's own shares are the same as for an Oy.[64] Unlike an Oy, an Oyj may acquire only a limited number of its own shares. The number of shares belonging to an Oyj and its subsidiary organisations is not allowed to exceed, after the acquisition, 10 per cent of the share capital or the voting rights carried by all the shares of the Oyj (Sec. 7 Subs. 6 OYL). Shares acquired in breach of the above-mentioned restriction must be assigned immediately, but at the latest within six months[65] of the acquisition. The board of directors may be authorised by the general meeting to acquire its own shares. Such authorisation may be given for a maximum period of 12 months. Under the proposed new Companies Act, this would be for a period of up to 18 months.

67 Provisions concerning financial assistance are the same as those for an Oy.[66]

(iv) Company as Lender or Guarantor

68 As for an Oy.[67]

(v) Company as Borrower

69 As for an Oy.[68]

60 See Mn. 28 and 29.
61 See also Mn. 30.
62 See Mn. 31 et seq.
63 See Mn. 35 et seq.
64 See Mn. 38 and 39.
65 According to the proposed new Companies Act, the shares must be assigned at the latest within one year.
66 See Mn. 40.
67 See Mn. 41.
68 See Mn. 42.

2.10 Publication and Filing Requirements

These requirements according to the OYL[69] correspond in many respects with the requirements for an Oy.[70] However, unlike an Oy, an Oyj must according to the OYL, for example, notify a decision on a new issue for registration in the trade register within one month of the decision. 70

2.11 Financial Reporting

As for an Oy.[71] However, if the Oyj's shares are admitted to public trading as set forth in the Finnish Securities Market Act or traded in any other stock exchange that is regulated within another EU Member State, then an Oyj's group annual accounts must be drawn up in accordance with IAS/IFRS accounting standards. If an Oyj is not obliged to draw up group annual accounts and its shares are admitted to public trading as set out above, it must draw up its annual accounts in accordance with IAS/IFRS accounting standards. 71

Oyjs are not exempted from any financial reporting requirements, regardless of their size.

2.12 Employee Participation in Corporate Bodies

As for an Oy.[72] 72

69 However, if an Oyj's shares are admitted to public trading, then the Oyj's filing and communication obligations (due to e.g. the Finnish Security Markets Act) become more onerous.

70 See Mn. 43 et seq.

71 See Mn. 46.

72 See Mn. 47.

VIII. France

*by Alain Garnier and Virginie Buseine**

Literature: Charvériat/Couret, Sociétés Commerciales (Editions Francis Lefebvre 2005); Cozian/Viandier/Deboissy, Droit des sociétés, (18th edition, Litec 2005); International series – France (business law/taxation/social law) (4th edition, Editions Francis Lefebvre 2004)

1 Although French corporate law historically considered the two standard forms of companies having limited shareholder liability as being the SARL (*société à responsabilité limitée*) and the SA (*société anonyme*) (French equivalents of the English private limited company and public limited company), the SAS (*société par actions simplifiée*), which is a more flexible corporate vehicle, has become widely used since its creation in 1994. In January 2004 approximately 985,000 SARL's were registered in France, in contrast to approximately 128,000 SA's and 63,600 SAS's.

1 The Stock Corporation ("SA")

2 The *Société anonyme* ("SA") is a company characterised by the limited liability of its shareholders and the free transfer of shares in the company. It was conceived in the nineteenth century as a method for permitting the collection of public savings. It is today a commonly used structure.

1.1 Export of Company

3 The nationality of the company is related to the location of its registered office (Sec. L.210-3 of the Commercial Code (*Code de Commerce*, "C.Com")). Consequently, a company registered in France which relocates its registered office to another country will not be entitled, under French law, to keep its French nationality.

4 However, according to French case law, if the official registered office is not "real and serious", then the registered office could be deemed located at the place of actual management. Accordingly, if it can be proved that the place of actual management is located abroad, it could then be argued in a court that the registered office should be deemed to be in the jurisdiction of the place of actual management. Assuming that the law of the jurisdiction where the place of actual management is located would accept it, a foreign court could then, for example, in the case of insolvency proceedings, decide on the winding up of the company.

5 There is no record of a French court taking the decision to apply to a company registered in France the law of the country where the company has its effective place of business. Decisions of that nature in the future should be unlikely after the ECJ judgments Überseering and Inspire Art.[1]

6 Similarly, there does not seem to be much relevant case law from foreign courts.

1.2 Transformation into a Foreign Entity

7 French law does not prohibit the transformation of a domestic company into a foreign entity, but there is very little authority on this question, which accordingly remains unclear and also depends on the law of the host jurisdiction. Otherwise, the operation can be achieved by the transfer of the business which is run by the SA to a foreign company. It will be possible to merge an SA with an S.E.

1.3 Incorporation

8 An SA may be set up with a minimum of seven shareholders (Sec. L.225-1 C.Com). The incorporation of an SA requires the following formalities: (i) the draft articles being signed; (ii) a search for trademarks and trade names being carried out at the trade mark office (INPI); (iii) premises being

* *Linklaters*, Paris. Written with the assistance of Cyril Boussion.

1 See Part 1, I, Mn. 17 et seq.

found; (iv) the future auditors being contacted; (v) a bank account being opened; (vi) a meeting of the first board of directors to be held in order to appoint the executives; (vii) announcement in a legal journal; (viii) registration with the tax authorities; (ix) filing a request for incorporation at the *Centre de Formalités des Entreprises* (a filing office for the Companies' Registry); and (x) opening and registration of the corporate books.

9 To obtain legal existence, an SA must be registered in the Companies' Registry (*registre du commerce et des sociétés*) (Sec. L.210-6 C.Com). The registry is kept at the Commercial Court of the *département* (French administrative area) in which the company has its corporate seat. The precise length of the incorporation procedure is difficult to predict. It usually takes one or two weeks but it can be shortened to three days in case of urgency. The total cost of incorporation is approximately EUR 500.[2]

10 Before incorporation, prospective shareholders incur unlimited personal liability for acts carried out in the name of the company. Upon incorporation, acts carried out prior to incorporation which are listed in an exhibit attached to the articles are deemed to have been carried out by the company without further formalities for ratification (Sec. L.210-6 C.Com).

1.4 Recurrent Costs and Efforts

11 Once the publication of annual accounts and their filing with the Companies' Registry have been paid for, the annual costs of running an SA per se are minimal. Of course, there will be other, significant costs depending on the number of employees and shareholders in the company. For example, in a large SA, costs involved for the organisation of an ordinary general meeting (giving notice of the meeting, announcements in a legal journal, etc.) can be very significant.

1.5 Shares and Share Transfers

12 It is possible to have different classes of shares with differing rights attaching to them (e.g. voting and non-voting shares, or shares with different dividend rights).

13 Ownership of shares in an SA is evidenced by an entry made in the share accounts maintained by or on behalf of the SA.

14 Shares in an SA are in principle freely transferable but this may be controlled or restricted to a limited extent by provisions set out in the articles of association (Sec L.228-23 et seq. C.Com). Existing shareholders can benefit from a right of approval or a pre-emptive right.

15 A share transfer is evidenced by a share transfer form and by the recording of such transfer in a share transfer register. *Ad valorem* duty is payable at a rate of 1 per cent, limited to a maximum of EUR 3,049 (1.1 per cent, limited to a maximum of EUR 4,000 as from 1 January 2006) (Sec. 726 of the General Code on Taxation (*Code Général des Impôts*, "CGI")).

1.6 Corporate Bodies

16 There are two possible types of management: the standard structure, consisting of a board of directors (*Conseil d'Administration*) which elects a chairman (*Président*); or a form of management structure in which a management committee (*Directoire*) manages the SA under the control of a supervisory board (*Conseil de Surveillance*) elected by the shareholders.

1.6.1 Management of an SA with a Board of Directors

(i) Board of Directors

17 The board of directors manages the company within the limits of the company's object, and subject to the powers reserved for the general meeting of shareholders. The board of directors

2 Approximately EUR 380/430 for the mandatory announcement in a legal journal, EUR 40 for the filing at the *Centre de Formalités des Entreprises*, and EUR 60 for Companies' Registry fees.

deals with any issue relating to the day-to-day running of the company and implements any control measures which its members consider necessary (Sec. L.225-35 C.Com).

Vis-à-vis third parties, the company is bound by any action of the board, even if it does not fall within the limits of the company's object, unless it can be proved that such third party knew the acts of the board exceeded the company's object (Sec. L.225-35 C.Com). 18

The board of directors appoints a president and may also appoint a general manager[3] (Sec. L.225-47 C.Com). 19

The president: (i) chairs the board of directors; (ii) organises and conducts the work of the board of directors; and (iii) informs the general meeting of the work being carried out by the board of directors (Sec L.225-53 C.Com). The president also supervises the management bodies of the company and, in particular, ensures that the directors are in a position to carry out their activities. 20

The general manager can act in all circumstances on behalf of and in the name of the company, within the parameters of the company's objects and subject to the rights conferred by law on the general meetings of shareholders (Sec. L.225-56 C.Com). The general manager also represents the company in its dealings with third parties. 21

(ii) Shareholders' Meeting

Decisions at an ordinary general meeting ("OGM") of shareholders relate to the appointment or removal of directors, the appointment of statutory auditors, approval of accounts, approval of transfer of the registered office, decisions on whether profits will be distributed or retained, etc. (Sec. L.225-98 C.Com). 22

An extraordinary general meeting ("EGM"), formed by all current shareholders, has sole power to alter the articles of association (Sec L.225-96 C.Com). 23

1.6.2 Management of an SA with Supervisory Board and Management Committee

In this structure, a non-executive supervisory board (elected by the shareholders) controls a management committee (elected by the supervisory board) which manages the SA (Sec. L.225-68 C.Com). 24

Members of the management committee are appointed by the supervisory board which also designates from amongst them the president of the management committee (Sec. L.225-59 C.Com). 25

Members of the supervisory board are not personally liable for mismanagement of the company. The management power of the management committee is similar to that of the general manager.[4] 26

1.7 Duties and Liabilities of Directors

Directors of French companies must comply with company law and the provisions of the articles of association in addition to maintaining certain management standards. In the case of non-compliance with these provisions or failure in his duty of care towards the company, a director may be held liable. In some instances criminal liability may arise from the same circumstances. Directors are generally exposed to individual liability (but they can be held jointly and severally liable if a fault has been committed on a joint basis and if there is no possibility to determine each director's personal liability). 27

In addition to the general liability of the management, if, during an insolvency procedure, the Commercial Court establishes that there are insufficient assets, the management may be held liable for all or some of the debts of the company if a "management negligence" has been committed by the directors and is the cause of part or all of the insufficiency of assets (Sec. L.624-3 C.Com and Sec. L.651-2 as at 1 January 2006). 28

3 See Mn. 20 et seq.
4 See Mn. 21.

29 Directors are in general only liable *vis-à-vis* the company. A liability *vis-à-vis* the shareholders is unusual and even liability *vis-à-vis* third parties only occurs in very rare cases (the director's fault must not be related to his activities as director).

30 No decision by the shareholders' meeting regarding the directors' services for the past business year can release the directors from their liability (Sec. L.225-253 C.Com).

31 Claims against managers become time-barred after three years.

32 D&O insurances are allowed and common and related premiums may be paid by the company.

33 The directors must apply for insolvency proceedings if the company is unable to pay its debt as they fall due (Sec. L.621-1 C.Com and Sec. L.631-4 C.Com as at 1 January 2006). Over-indebtedness in the balance sheet does not trigger, as such, the duty to apply for insolvency proceedings.

34 The president, the general manager and, to a lesser extent, any other director may be personally liable for breach of legal or regulatory provisions applicable to the company, breach of the articles of association and breach of the duty of care. Directors may also be found personally liable for their conduct under general principles of negligence (Sec. L.225-251 C.Com).

1.8 Shareholders' Liability

35 Shareholders are only liable for losses up to the amount of their contributions (Sec. L.225-1 C.Com). However, a shareholder may support the debts of the company if this shareholder is a *de facto* or *de jure* director of the insolvent company and if such director has committed "management negligence" before the beginning of the insolvency proceeding and the management negligence is the cause of part or all of the insufficiency of assets.

1.9 Capitalisation and Financing

1.9.1 Basic Concepts

36 The share capital of the company is an instrument of financing as well as a security for creditors of the company. In the event of a reduction in the registered capital to an amount lower than the minimum share capital, any interested party may apply to the courts for the dissolution of the company. This dissolution may not be ordered if the situation has been cured by the date on which the court is due to give its judgment on the merits of the case (Sec. L.224-2 C.Com).

1.9.2 Minimum Share Capital

37 The minimum share capital of an SA is EUR 37,000 (Sec. L.224-2 C.Com) (if the company is to offer its shares to the public, then the minimum amount is increased to EUR 225,000), of which 50 per cent must be paid up upon incorporation with the balance payable within five years of registration. The capital may only be increased if the existing shares have been paid up in full.

38 Shares may be paid for in cash or by contributions in kind, but contributions in kind are subject to valuation by a specific auditor appointed by a court (Sec. L.225-8 C.Com). Shares subscribed in kind must be paid for in full at the time of their issue.

1.9.3 Maintenance of Capital and Liquidity

(i) System

39 Any agreement between the company and its chairman, one of its directors or one of its shareholders holding a percentage of voting rights greater than 10 per cent must be submitted to the board for prior approval (Sec. L.225-38 C.Com). The same applies to agreements in which one of the persons referred to in the preceding sentence is indirectly interested. Agreements which fail to gain approval will nevertheless be effective. However, the interested person as well as the chairman and other directors can bear the costs of such agreements if they are harmful to the company. An

agreement which has not been approved may also be declared null and void by the courts if such agreement has an adverse effect on the company.

If, as a result of losses duly recorded in the accounting documents, the company's equity capital falls below half of its share capital, a shareholders' meeting must be called within four months of the approval of the accounts revealing the said loss to decide whether the company should be prematurely dissolved (Sec. L.225-248 C.Com). **40**

(ii) Distributions

Once the annual accounts are approved and the existence of distributable sums is recorded, the general meeting determines the amount to be allocated to shareholders in the form of dividends (Sec. L.232-12 C.Com). **41**

If it derives from a balance sheet established during or at the end of the financial year and certified by a statutory auditor that the company has a distributable profit at the time considered, interim dividends up to such profit may be distributed before the approval of the accounts by the general meeting for the financial year concerned (Sec. L.232-12 C.Com).

Any dividend distributed in breach of the rules indicated above is a sham dividend and is subject to criminal sanctions.

It is also possible for the general meeting to allow the distribution of free reserves (Sec. L.232-11 C.Com).

A distribution may be granted in cash or in shares (Sec. L.232-18 C.Com). **42**

(iii) Acquisition of Own Shares and Related Financing

Apart from when the share capital is reduced by means of a cancellation of shares (Sec. L.225-207 C.Com) or when the company wishes to allot shares to its employees (Sec. L.225-208 C.Com), an unlisted SA is not allowed to acquire its own shares (Sec. L.225-206 C.Com). **43**

As an exception, a listed SA is authorised, albeit under strict conditions, to purchase its own shares, in particular with a view to improving the financial management of its own capital stocks. **44**

Indeed, the general meeting of a listed SA may authorise the board of directors, to buy a certain number of shares representing up to ten per cent of the company's share capital (Sec. L.225-209 C.Com.). The general meeting determines the operation's aims and terms and conditions, and its ceiling. Such authorisation must not be given for a period in excess of eighteen months.

Shares bought by the company to be used as consideration in certain transactions (mergers, split-off, contribution in kind) can not exceed five per cent of the share capital.

Pursuant to Section L.225-216 C.Com, a company shall not advance funds, grant loans or provide a pledge of security for the subscription or purchase of its own shares by a third party. Nevertheless, the provisions of this Section do not apply to ordinary transactions by credit institutions, nor to operations carried out to enable employees of the company, one of its subsidiaries or a company included in a group savings scheme to purchase shares in the company.

(iv) Company as Lender or Guarantor

Directors other than legal entities are prohibited from contracting loans from the company irrespective of their form, from arranging for the company to grant them a loan or to provide for other borrowing whatsoever, or from arranging for the company to stand as surety for them or to act as their guarantor in respect of their obligations to third parties (Sec. L.225-43 C.Com). **45**

Loans, not falling within the scope of Section L.225-216 C.Com,[5] granted by a company to its shareholder, must (i) comply with the company's corporate object (ii) be authorised under the procedure applicable to agreements between connected parties[6] and (iii) satisfy French corporate benefit concerns. Regarding corporate benefit concerns, a company, as a general rule, must receive

5 See Mn. 44.
6 See Mn. 39.

some real and adequate benefit in consideration for entering into a transaction. Furthermore, there may be criminal sanctions[7] against the director of a company who, acting in bad faith, misuse the assets or the credit of the company or the authority or voting rights he holds in the company with a view to favouring another company in which he is are directly or indirectly interested. Where the companies involved are part of the same group, a group interest can be recognised according to the *Cour de cassation* (France's highest court), thus preventing the transaction from falling within the scope of this prohibition.[8]

46 Loans and securities to third parties are not specifically restricted. A banking licence will however be required if third-party loans or guarantees are provided on a regular basis.

(v) Company as Borrower

47 Loans to an SA by its shareholders are permitted if the shareholder holds at least 5 per cent of the share capital (Sec. L.312-2 of the Monetary and Financial Code (*Code Monétaire et Financier*, "CMF")). Such loan may rank pari passu with the loans granted by non-shareholders.

1.10 Publication and Filing Requirements

48 Within a month of any increase or reduction in the share capital and conversion into a different type of legal entity, the company must provide the Companies' Registry with two copies of the minutes of the meeting approving the amendment, and two copies of the updated articles of association.[9]

49 If a formality in respect of a change has not been carried out, judges will often consider that the change is not binding upon third parties or the company. In theory, the chairman may be held liable in consequence of the breach. Thus, third parties can rely on the content of the Companies' Registry (Sec. L.123-9 and Sec. L.210-9 C.Com).

50 The following must be filed with the Clerk's office of the Commercial Court in the jurisdiction in which the company is incorporated:
- all minutes of shareholders' meetings, including those amending the articles of association;
- the annual accounts; and
- the report of the statutory auditors.

If the company does not file its annual accounts with the Clerk's office, it may be sentenced to a EUR 1,500 fine.

Furthermore, at the request of any interested party or the *procureur de la République*, the president of the Commercial Court, ruling in summary proceedings, may enjoin, subject to a penalty, the directors of any legal person to file the documents and instruments with the Companies' Registry which this legal person is required to do by the acts or regulations (Sec. L.123-5-1 C.Com).

Documents filed with the Companies' Registry are available to the public, in particular on www.infogreffe.fr.

51 The board of directors or the management committee, as the case may be, must send or make available to the shareholders documents enabling them both to take decisions based on factual knowledge and to have an informed judgment on the management and progress of the company and its business (Sec. L.225-108 C.Com).

7 SA: Sec. L. 242-6 3° C.Com, SAS: Sec. L.242-6 3° and Sec. L.244-1 C.Com. SARL: L.214-3 4° C.Com.

8 Three criteria must then be met: (i) the "assisting" company must receive some benefit (i.e., the benefit may derive from the existence of a business relationship or a financial relationship); (ii) the financial assistance provided must not exceed the "assisting" company's financial capabilities nor greatly exceed the benefit received by the latter; and (iii) the companies involved must form part of a genuine group operating under a common strategy aimed at a common objective.

9 Sec. 49, *Décret* 30 Mai 1984.

1.11 Financial Reporting

An SA must prepare its annual accounts at the end of the financial year. These annual accounts must consist of a balance sheet, profit and loss account and an appendix (Sec. L.123-12 C.Com). Annual accounts must be honest and truthful and must ensure a fair representation of the assets, financial situation and results of the undertaking (Sec. L.123-14 C.Com). They must be drawn up in accordance with French GAAP. While the use of IFRS accounting principles is not permitted (except for the consolidated accounts (Sec. L.233-24 C.Com)), French GAAP is progressively being converged with IFRS. **52**

Annual accounts of an SA always need to be audited (Sec. L.225-228 C.Com).

1.12 Employee Participation in Corporate Bodies

It is possible (but not compulsory) that a member of the board be elected by the employees (Sec. L.225-27 C.Com). Furthermore, if a company has more than 3 per cent of its share capital held by its employees, a general meeting of the shareholders must appoint at least one employee as member of the board (Sec. L.225-23 C.Com). Employee representatives, however, do not have voting rights. **53**

2 The Simplified Stock Corporation ("SAS")

The *Société par actions simplifiée* ("SAS") is a new corporate form introduced in response to the lack of flexibility in French company law which was hindering the setting up of joint ventures in France. The SAS is now widely used, not only for joint ventures or as a holding company, but also within groups of companies (in order to simplify corporate management) or even between individuals. **54**

Although the statutory provisions relating to the SA remain, to a large extent, applicable to the SAS, the relations between shareholders and the management structure of an SAS are mostly governed by the provisions included in its articles of association, which may be drafted in the most flexible way. **55**

An SAS, contrary to an SA, can not be listed or used as a vehicle to collect public savings (Sec. 227-2 C.Com).

2.1 Export of Company

An SAS is subject to the same rules as an SA.[10] **56**

2.2 Transformation into a Foreign Entity

French law does not provide for the transformation of an SAS into a foreign entity. The same principles as those applicable to an SA also apply to an SAS.[11] **57**

2.3 Incorporation

It is possible to set up an SAS with a single shareholder (Sec. L.227-1 C.Com). The SAS may be created either *ab nihilo* or by transformation of another company. **58**

The formal rules which have to be followed for the creation and registration of an SAS are the same as those applicable to an SA.[12] **59**

10 See Mn. 3 et seq.
11 See Mn. 7.
12 See Mn. 8 et seq.

2.4 Recurrent Costs and Efforts

60 Evaluation of the annual costs in an SAS is done by reference to the same principles that apply to an SA.[13] The average cost for the mandatory annual filings in an SAS with a single shareholder is EUR 40.

2.5 Shares and Share Transfers

61 Rules relating to the ownership and transfer of shares in an SAS are the same as those applicable to an SA.[14]

62 Shareholders are free to include in the articles of association certain provisions in respect of the transfer of shares. These may include, for instance: (i) the non-transferability of shares (provided that such a prohibition does not exceed 10 years); (ii) the prior approval of shareholders for any transfer of shares to third parties; (iii) a clause in respect of the change of control of any of the shareholders (a breach of such clause will entail the non-applicability of the voting rights attached to the shares or the exclusion of the shareholder); (iv) the squeeze-out of a shareholder (Sec. L.227-13 et seq. C.Com); (v) pre-emption rights; (vi) tag-along/drag-along rights.

63 If a provision is included in the articles of association, it becomes binding on third parties. Any transfer of shares in breach of the provisions will be null and void.

2.6 Corporate Bodies

64 The articles of association freely determine the form of management (Sec. L.227-5 C.Com), such as the procedure and existence of a board (which is not compulsory) or committee, the required qualification of the chairman and the appointment, removal or recommendation procedures for a manager or chairman.

2.6.1 Management of the Company

65 As regards the management, the law solely requires the SAS to have a chairman (*Président*), who may be a legal entity or an individual (Sec. L.227-6 C.Com). He must be designated in the articles of association (Sec. L.225-16 C.Com). As a control measure, shareholders have to appoint one or more auditors (Sec. 227-9 C.Com).

66 When the chairman is a legal entity, the legal representative of such entity is in charge of the management of the SAS (Sec. L.227-7 C.Com).

67 Save with respect to the chairman, the articles of association may create bodies and freely set up their names, functions and decision-making procedures.

2.6.2 Decision Making

68 Shareholders are free to determine in the articles of association the decision-making process and majority requirements (i.e. they can decide that decisions will be taken in a general meeting, or simply without holding a meeting, by obtaining the signature of all shareholders).

69 However, the law provides that the following decisions have to be taken collectively by the shareholders: approval of the annual accounts; increase, amortisation or reduction in the share capital; approval of a merger, a de-merger or a winding-up of the SAS; appointment of the statutory auditors; and allocation of the profits after approval of the annual accounts (Sec. L.227-9 C.Com).

70 The principle of proportionality of voting rights (one share, one vote) does not apply to an SAS. The voting rights of shareholders may be freely determined by the articles of association (e.g. veto rights, limitation of voting rights etc.). The only limits are that a shareholder cannot be excluded from collective decisions and cannot be deprived of his/her voting rights.

13 See Mn. 11.
14 See Mn. 12 et seq.

2.7 Duties and Liabilities of Directors

The liability of officers of an SAS is similar to that applicable to an SA (Sec. L.227-8 C.Com).[15] **71**

The chairman represents the company in dealings with third parties and is vested with full powers **72**
of management to act in all circumstances on behalf of the company within the parameters of the company's objects (Sec. L.227-6 C.Com).

In relation to third parties, the company is responsible for all acts of the chairman, even for **73**
those which do not fall within the company's objects, unless the company can prove that the third party knew the act exceeded the company's objects or unless the third party could not have been unaware of the objects, given the circumstances (Sec. L.225-35 C.Com). Publication of the articles of association is not sufficient, in itself, to constitute this proof.

Restrictions contained in the articles of association on the powers of the chairman are not binding **74**
vis-à-vis third parties.

2.8 Shareholders' Liability

The same principles as those applicable to an SA apply.[16] **75**

2.9 Capitalisation and Financing

2.9.1 Basic Concepts

The capitalisation and financing of an SAS is based on the same principles as those which apply **76**
to the SA.[17]

2.9.2 Minimum Share Capital

The minimum capital requirement is the same as that applicable to an SA. Nevertheless, an SAS **77**
is not entitled to be listed on a stock exchange or otherwise to offer its shares to the public (Sec. L.227-2 C.Com). In contrast to an SA, it is possible to set up an SAS with a variable (i.e. floating) share capital.

2.9.3 Maintenance of Capital and Liquidity

As regards the preservation and maintenance of the company's capital and liquidity, the SAS is **78**
subject to the same rules as the SA.[18] However, since an SAS cannot be listed,[19] rules regarding the acquisition of its own shares by a listed SA are not applicable to an SAS.[20]

2.10 Publication and Filing Requirements

The publicity requirements are the same as those applicable to an SA.[21] **79**

2.11 Financial Reporting

As for an SA,[22] the accounts must be drawn up in accordance with French GAAP and always **80**
need to be audited (Sec. L.227-1 C.Com).

15 See Mn. 27 et seq.
16 See Mn. 35.
17 See Mn. 36 et seq.
18 See Mn. 39 et seq.
19 See Mn. 77.
20 See Mn. 44.
21 See Mn. 48 et seq.
22 See Mn. 52.

2.12 Employee Participation in Corporate Bodies

81 Provisions applicable to an SA regarding employee participation in the board of directors or supervisory board do not apply to an SAS. Equivalent rights may be exercised by representatives of the works council *vis-à-vis* a corporate body to be defined in the articles of association of the SAS (in practice, this is often the chairman of the SAS).

3 The Limited Liability Company ("SARL")

82 The *Société à responsabilité limitée* ("SARL") is a company characterised by the limited liability of its shareholders, the restrictions on the transfer of shares in the company, the option to have a sole shareholder and almost no share capital requirement. It was conceived after the First World War, following the German model of the GmbH, with the aim of incorporating small and medium businesses. Nevertheless, this form of company can not issue negotiable securities (other than bonds) or use public funds. The SARL is today the most commonly used structure in France, but in practice only for small businesses.

3.1 Export of Company

83 An SARL is subject to the same rules as an SA.[23]

3.2 Transformation into a Foreign Entity

84 Any such transformation would have to be carried out in the same way as that for an SA. [24]

3.3 Incorporation

85 It is possible to set up an SARL even with only a single shareholder (Sec. L.223-1 C.Com). The SARL may be created either *ab nihilo* or by transformation of another company.

86 The formal rules which have to be followed for the constitution and registration of the SARL are the same as those applicable to the SA. [25]

3.4 Recurrent Costs and Efforts

87 Evaluation of the annual costs in an SARL is done by reference to the same principles that apply to an SA.[26] The average cost for the mandatory annual filings in one-shareholder SARL is EUR 40.

3.5 Shares and Share Transfers

88 In an SARL, transfers of shares to third parties are restricted by statute: any transfer to a non-shareholder must be approved by a majority of shareholders holding at least 75 per cent of the capital. Failing such approval, pre-emption rights operate in favour of the other shareholders. There are no restrictions on transfers to other shareholders, unless otherwise provided in the company's articles of association.

89 Transfers need to be evidenced by a formal written agreement. In the case of an SARL, a transfer duty of 4.8 per cent is imposed in respect of all share transfers (as from 1 January 2006, the transfer duty rate will be 5 per cent).

90 The purchaser is usually responsible for the payment of the transfer duty but purchasers and sellers remain both jointly and severally liable *vis-à-vis* the French Treasury for the payment of this duty.

23 See Mn. 3 et seq.
24 See Mn. 7.
25 See Mn. 8 et seq.
26 See Mn. 11.

3.6 Corporate Bodies

3.6.1 Management of the Company

An SARL has a simple management structure. The SARL is managed by one or more managers (*gérants*) appointed by the shareholders (Sec. L.223-18 C.Com). The manager of the company cannot be a legal entity. Each manager has unlimited power to deal with third parties in the company's name and no internal restrictions (e.g. a list of actions which the manager(s) cannot take without the members' approval or a requirement that the managers must act jointly) will bind a third party unless the company proves that the third party knew of the restriction. **91**

An SARL has to appoint one or more auditors if two of the following thresholds are overtaken: (i) a balance sheet of EUR 1,550,000, (ii) a turnover of EUR 3,100,000, and (iii) 50 employees (Sec. L.223-35 C.Com). **92**

Apart from the manager(s), the articles of association may create bodies and freely set up their names, functions and their decision-making procedures. **93**

3.6.2 Decision Making

Shareholders are free to determine in the articles of association the decision-making process and majority requirements (i.e. they can decide that decisions will be taken in a general meeting, or simply, without holding a meeting, by obtaining instead the signature of all shareholders) (Sec. L.223-26 C.Com). **94**

However, the law provides that the approval of the annual accounts has to be made collectively by the shareholders in a general meeting. Furthermore, the majority requirements for the extraordinary general meetings (including increase, amortisation or reduction in the share capital; approval of a merger, a de-merger or a winding-up of the SARL) are not freely determinable in the articles of association. **95**

3.7 Duties and Liabilities of Directors

An SARL manager is subject to the same rules as an SA director.[27] **96**

3.8 Shareholders' Liability

An SARL is subject to the same rules as an SA. **97**

3.9 Capitalisation and Financing

3.9.1 Basic Concepts

In contrast to an SA, the share capital of an SARL is now merely an instrument of financing of the company, since there is no minimum share capital requirement.[28] **98**

3.9.2 Minimum Share Capital

There is no minimum share capital requirement for an SARL. The only requirement is to indicate in the articles of association the amount of share capital (Sec. L.223-2 C.Com). **99**

Shares may be paid in cash or by contributions in kind, but contributions in kind are subject to valuation by a specific auditor appointed by a court (Sec. L.223-9 C.Com). Shares subscribed in kind must be paid in full at the time of their issue. **100**

27 See Mn. 27 et seq.
28 See Mn. 98 et seq.

3.9.3 Maintenance of Capital and Liquidity

(i) System

101 In contrast to the SA system,[29] there is no prior approval requirement for the agreement between the company and its manager or one of its shareholders, except when the agreement is entered into with a non-shareholder manager and the company and the company has no statutory auditor (Sec. L.223-19 C.Com).The annual general meeting must, however, approve the agreement between the company and its manager or one of its shareholders. Agreements which fail to gain approval will nevertheless be effective. However, the manager (and the shareholder if it is relevant) will then bear any damage (if any) suffered by the company as a result of such agreements.

102 If, as a result of losses duly recorded in the accounting documents, the company's equity capital falls below half of its share capital, a shareholders' meeting must be called within four months of the approval of the accounts revealing the said loss to decide whether the company should be prematurely dissolved (Sec. L.223-42 C.Com).

(ii) Distributions

103 An SARL is subject to the same rules as an SA.[30]

(iii) Acquisition of Own Shares and Related Financing

104 Apart from when the share capital is reduced by means of a cancellation of shares, an SARL is not allowed to acquire its own shares (Sec. L.223-34 C.Com).

(iv) Company as Lender or Guarantor

105 Managers and shareholders other than legal entities are prohibited from contracting loans from the company irrespective of their form, from arranging for the company to grant them a loan or to provide for other borrowing whatsoever, or to arrange for the company to stand as surety for them or act as their guarantor in respect of their obligations to third parties (Sec. L.223-21 C.Com).

106 For loans and securities to a third party, an SARL is subject to the same rules as an SA.[31]

(v) Company as Borrower

107 An SARL is subject to the same rules as an SA.[32]

3.10 Publication and Filing Requirements

108 The publicity requirements are the same as those applicable to an SAS.[33]

3.11 Financial Reporting

109 As for an SA, the accounts must be drawn up in accordance with French GAAP.[34] In contrast to an SA, accounts of an SARL need to be audited only if certain thresholds are met.[35]

29 See Mn. 39 et seq.
30 See Mn. 41.
31 See Mn. 46.
32 See Mn. 47.
33 See Mn. 48 et seq.
34 See Mn. 52.
35 See Mn. 92

3.12 Employee Participation in Corporate Bodies

110 Provisions applicable to an SA regarding employee participation in boards of directors or supervisory boards do not apply to an SARL.[36]

36 See Mn. 53.

IX. Germany

*by Carsten Flaßhoff (LL.M.) and Dr. Michael Krömker**

1 The Limited Liability Company ("GmbH")

Literature: Ebke/Finkin, Introduction to German Law (Kluwer 1996), Chapter 5 B III: The Limited Liability Company; Baumbach/Hueck, GmbH-Gesetz, commentary (17th edition, Beck 2000); Scholz, GmbH-Gesetz, commentary (9th edition, Otto Schmidt 2000/2002)

The GmbH (*Gesellschaft mit beschränkter Haftung,*"GmbH") is the most common corporate form used in Germany to achieve the concept of limited shareholder liability.[1] The statutory corporate governance framework is not strict and permits a high degree of flexibility in the drafting of articles of association. In contrast to the stock corporation (*Aktiengesellschaft,*"AG")[2] the shareholders have considerable capacity to influence the GmbH and can even give direct instructions to the management. 1

As a consequence of the latest ECJ rulings (cases "Überseering"[3] and "InspireArt"[4]) the GmbH as a corporate form is facing increased competition from foreign limited liability companies which were incorporated and registered under more flexible regimes in other Member States, but are solely operating in Germany. In light of this legal practitioners and law scholars are demanding the Limited Liability Companies Act ("GmbHG") to become more flexible. In 2005 the federal government proposed to satisfy these demands by lowering the minimum capital requirement from EUR 25,000 to EUR 10,000, which was rejected as insufficient in the legislative proceedings. A more fundamental reform is under discussion but no official governmental proposal has been presented yet. 2

1.1 Export of Company

While the ECJ judgments "Überseering" and "InspireArt"[5] do permit foreign entities to move their entire business and management to Germany in compliance with the principles of freedom of establishment under the EC Treaty, German law prevents a GmbH from relocating to a foreign country irrespective of whether or not it is another EU Member State. In accordance with the Real Seat Theory,[6] a decision by the shareholders to relocate either the corporate seat (registered office) or the seat of effective management of a GmbH to a foreign country would be deemed to constitute a dissolution of the company and would lead to its removal from the commercial register[7] and subsequent loss of its legal identity. 3

1.2 Transformation into a Foreign Entity

German law does not expressly provide for the transformation of a domestic company into a foreign entity. According to an ECJ judgment in the case SEVIC[8] such lack of express statutory provisions cannot serve as a basis for denying companies from another Member State to merge into a German company and have such merger registered in a German commercial register. Although the ECJ did not have to rule on the opposite case – a merger of a German entity into an entity located in another Member State and registration of such merger in such other Member State – the SEVIC 4

* *Linklaters Oppenhoff & Rädler,* Cologne.

1 In 2004 approximately 970,000 GmbHs were registered in Germany, in contrast to approximately 16,000 AGs.

2 See Mn. 44 et seq.

3 See Part 1, I, Mn. 17 et seq.

4 See Part 1, I, Mn. 19.

5 See Fn. 3 and 4.

6 See Part 1, I, Mn. 9.

7 Hueck/Fastrich in: Baumbach/Hueck, GmbH-Gesetz, Sec. 4 a Mn. 10; Emmerich in: Scholz, GmbHG, Sec. 4 a Mn. 6.

8 ECJ judgment dated 13 December 2005 (case C-411/03, SEVIC).

judgment, due to its broad wording, might be interpreted as abolishing also categorical restrictions on those out-bound cross-border mergers within the EU.

Apart from that, cross-border transformations could only be achieved indirectly by transferring the business of the GmbH to a foreign company. If done by way of an asset deal, this would result in an adverse tax effect, as hidden reserves would be realised. A tax neutral transfer could only be effected by way of a series of steps involving the transformation of the GmbH into a German limited partnership (*Kommanditgesellschaft*) with a foreign partner and the subsequent collapse of the lim-ited partnership which would result in all its assets and liabilities accruing to its only remaining foreign partner. Contrary to the stock corporation, a GmbH may not be directly converted into an S.E.[9]

1.3 Incorporation

5 A GmbH is set up by way of a notarial deed of incorporation executed by at least one incorporator (Sec. 10 GmbHG). The company will legally exist upon its entry into the commercial register held by the Local Court (*Amtsgericht*) competent for the company's corporate seat (Sec. 11 GmbHG).

6 The precise length of the incorporation procedure is difficult to predict and may vary from one to eight weeks.[10] The notarial fees for the incorporation of a GmbH with a minimum share capital of EUR 25,000 will amount to approximately EUR 500. In addition, registration in the commercial register and publication in the Federal Gazette will cost between EUR 130 and EUR 180.

1.4 Recurrent Costs and Efforts

7 Recurrent costs and efforts relating to a German GmbH are minimal and relate only to the publication of annual accounts and their filing with the commercial register[11] at an annual cost of approximately EUR 70. Other costs and efforts only materialise in the event that certain corporate steps are taken which require notarisation, filing with the commercial register or publication.

1.5 Shares and Share Transfers

8 In general, shares in a GmbH with equal nominal value convey equal rights to all of its shareholders, such as voting rights or dividend entitlements. However, the articles of association may attach different rights to certain shares or to all shares held by a particular shareholder and thereby create different classes of shares.

9 Shares in a GmbH are transferred by way of a notarial transfer deed (Sec. 15 GmbHG).[12] The transfer deed has to be notarised by a German notary public who will charge fees based on a statutory fee table which is linked to the value of the shares.[13] As German corporate law does not provide for share certificates in a GmbH, title to a share is solely evidenced by way of an uninterrupted chain of such notarial transfer deeds.[14] There is no transfer tax levied on a share transfer.[15] The articles of association may provide for a variety of transfer restrictions, e.g. pre-emption rights or the requirement of prior approval of the transfer by the managing directors or

9 See Mn. 46 and Part 2, S.E., Mn. 6 et seq. and 10 and seq.

10 To a large extent, it depends on the resources of the actual commercial register and whether or not the commercial register operates electronically. Due to these uncertainties, the acquisition of already incorporated and registered shelf-companies is common in Germany.

11 The annual accounts of middle-sized and large GmbHs (companies exceeding two of the following criteria: a balance sheet total of more than EUR 3,438,000; a turnover of more than EUR 6,875,000; more than 50 employees) must be audited (Sec. 316 Subs. 1 Sentence 1 German Commercial Code). This will result in further costs being incurred.

12 Apart from this, shares in a GmbH, like any other assets, may also be transferred by way of global succession, e.g. by way of a merger or spin-off in accordance with the German Transformation Act or by way of last will.

13 Alternatively, German courts have accepted a notarisation by certain Swiss notary publics. As their fees are substantially less than the fees of German notary publics high value share transfers are often notarised in Switzerland.

14 Or by documents proving a global succession (see Fn. 12).

15 If the company owns real property, however, the transfer of 95 or more per cent of the shares in the company will trigger real estate transfer tax (Sec. 1 Subs. 3 No. 3 and 4 Real Estate Transfer Tax Act).

the shareholders' meeting (Sec. 15 Subs. 5 GmbHG).Once a share transfer has been effected, the company must be informed of the event (Sec. 16 GmbHG). The managing directors are then required to file an amended shareholder list with the commercial register (Sec. 40 Subs. 1 Sentence 1 GmbHG).

The lack of share certificates[16] means that there is no public market for GmbH shares. Although a GmbH is not prohibited by law from issuing its shares to the public, in practice it is impossible for it to be engaged in an initial public offering of its shares. Where a GmbH intends to issue its shares to the public, it is usually first converted into an AG. **10**

1.6 Corporate Bodies

The GmbHG provides for two compulsory corporate bodies: the managing directors and the shareholders' meeting. Further corporate bodies, such as advisory boards or shareholder committees, the duties of which can be freely defined in the articles of association, are optional. In the event that the GmbH has more than 500 employees in Germany, a two tier board structure is mandatory and a supervisory board must be established. **11**

1.6.1 Managing Directors

The GmbH may have one or more managing directors, who in principle can be foreigners. The managing directors exclusively represent the company *vis-à-vis* third parties (Sec. 35 Subs. 1 GmbHG). They can be awarded joint power of representation (whereby a managing director may only represent the GmbH together with another managing director or a *Prokurist* – namely a holder of a special statutory authority to represent the company) or sole power of representation (whereby a managing director may represent the company alone). **12**

The managing directors are responsible for the management of the company. The internal powers of the managing directors may, however, be restricted either through the articles of association or by way of rules of procedure, the latter being the most flexible and common, as rules of procedure do not require a prescribed form and are not available on public record. **13**

1.6.2 Shareholders' Meeting

The shareholders' meeting has overall competence on all matters related to the company on which it wishes to decide.[17] The shareholders' meeting is amongst other things responsible for the appointment and dismissal of the managing directors[18] and the approval of the annual accounts. It may also draw up a catalogue of business transactions which require the prior approval of the shareholders' meeting. Furthermore, the shareholders' meeting is entitled to give direct instructions to the managing directors, who in turn have to comply with these instructions.[19] **14**

Resolutions of the shareholders' meeting are passed by a simple majority of the votes cast (Sec. 47 Subs. 1 GmbHG). Higher thresholds (generally involving a 75 per cent majority) apply in certain cases, for example the passing of resolutions amending the articles of association (Sec. 53 Subs. 2 GmbHG), or if agreed upon in the articles of association. **15**

16 Note that a GmbH is not prohibited from certificating its shares, though this rarely happens. The certificates, however, would not be bearer instruments but solely serve as (disprovable) pieces of evidence regarding title to the share(s). I.e. even in this case the shares would not be transferred by way of endorsement but, as outlined, by way of a notarial transfer deed.

17 Zöllner in: Baumbach/Hueck, Sec. 46 Mn. 60; K. Schmidt in: Scholz, Sec. 46 Mn. 1; Ebke/Finkin Chapter 5 B III 6 b, p. 161.

18 In GmbHs with more than 2000 employees this responsibility is by statute assigned to the supervisory board (Sec. 31 Co-Determination Act).

19 U.H. Schneider in: Scholz, Sec. 37 Mn. 5 et seq., 10 et seq.

1.6.3 Supervisory Board

16 In the event that a supervisory board is mandatory or where the shareholders have decided to set up a voluntary supervisory board with the rights and duties defined in the Stock Corporation Act ("AktG"),[20] it will be responsible for ensuring the managing directors comply with their duties and will only take management decisions which are economically feasible for the company.

1.7 Duties and Liabilities of Directors

17 The managing directors are not only responsible for managing the daily business of the GmbH but will also have certain other statutory obligations, including arranging for necessary filings to be made with the commercial register, convening the annual shareholders' meeting, reporting to the supervisory board (if one exists) and obtaining the approval of the shareholders for certain business transactions if such approval is required. The managing directors must perform their duties using the diligence of a prudent businessman and, in the event of breach, are personally liable to the company for any damages (Sec. 43 GmbHG). In addition to their general liability, the managing directors can also be held liable for any repayment of the share capital in breach of capital maintenance rules (Sec. 43 Subs. 3 GmbHG) and for any acquisition by the company of its own shares beyond the limits stipulated in Sec. 33 GmbHG.[21] In this regard they cannot claim in their defence that they had been instructed by the shareholders.[22] The liability becomes time-barred after a period of five years (Sec. 43 Subs. 4 GmbHG).

18 Where the company is unable to pay its debts or is over-indebted from a balance sheet perspective, the managing directors are obliged to apply for insolvency proceedings within three weeks of becoming aware of the situation (Sec. 64 GmbHG). A violation of this duty not only makes the managing directors personably liable but is also a criminal offence.[23]

19 In general, the managing directors are jointly and severally liable (Sec. 43 Subs. 2 GmbHG). Under certain conditions a prior allocation of duties between several managing directors may release those managing directors not responsible for the relevant duties from their liability. However, they may still be liable if they failed to supervise their co-managing directors.[24] Discharge of the managing directors in the annual meeting of shareholders releases them from all claims by the company which were apparent to the shareholders at the annual meeting.[25]

20 D&O insurance is common and the payment of related premiums by the GmbH is permitted. Liability to third parties will only exist in a number of rare cases, e.g. where a managing director fraudulently exploits the trust a third party has in him.[26]

1.8 Shareholders' Liability

21 Generally, a piercing of the corporate veil is rare under German law, which looks to protect the principle of limited liability. There are, however, certain situations which may lead to shareholder liability. These can be divided in two principal groups.

22 First, shareholders are liable to the GmbH for the repayment of any illegal payments made to them in breach of the provisions of the GmbHG relating to the protection of the company's capital and liquidity.[27]

20 This will be mandatory where co-determination is applicable; see Mn. 42. Note that where the supervisory board is not mandatory the shareholders are free in broadening or limiting its rights and duties in the articles of association.

21 See Mn. 32 for details.

22 Federal Supreme Court in: BGHZ 125, 366, 372; Zöllner in: Baumbach/Hueck, Sec. 43 Mn. 41; U.H. Schneider in: Scholz, Sec. 43 Mn. 98.

23 If convicted by a criminal court in the context of an insolvency of a company a person cannot act as a managing director for a period of five years after the judgment (Sec. 6 Subs. 2 GmbHG).

24 Zöllner in: Baumbach/Hueck, Sec. 43 Mn. 23.

25 Zöllner in: Baumbach/Hueck, Sec. 46 Mn. 26.

26 Federal Supreme Court in: BGHZ 87, 27, 126, 181; Emmerich in: Scholz, Sec. 13 Mn. 67; U.H. Schneider in: Scholz, Sec. 43 Mn. 223 et seq.; Ebke/Finkin Chapter 5 B III 7, p. 162 et seq.

27 For details, see Mn. 24 et seq.

Secondly, the shareholders can be held liable for any claims arising out of a tort committed by them in their capacity as shareholder. This will principally occur in relation to any "action endangering the existence of the company" (*existenzvernichtender Eingriff*), a concept limited to cases of fraudulent behaviour. Such a case will exist should a shareholder withdraw assets from the company which are required for the settlement of obligations of the company to third parties and such action not only puts the company in danger of becoming insolvent but also leads to the company's insolvency.[28] It is not yet ultimately clarified whether the tort triggers a liability to the company or to third-party creditors. 23

1.9 Capitalisation and Financing

1.9.1 Basic Concepts

The GmbH financing regulations are based on the concept of a restricted share capital counterbalancing the notion of limited shareholder liability. The share capital of the company is therefore intended to form a capital fund, being the minimum amount available to the company's creditors. The GmbHG applies the "principle of real capital contribution and maintenance",[29] meaning that the share capital stated in the articles of association has to be available to the company and is under no circumstances to be paid back to the shareholders. A loss of half of a company's share capital will place the managing directors under an obligation to call a shareholders' meeting (Sec. 49 Subs. 3 GmbHG); the loss of the entire share capital triggers the duty to apply for insolvency proceedings (Sec. 64 Subs. 1 Sentence 2 GmbHG). 24

1.9.2 Minimum Share Capital

The minimum share capital of a GmbH is EUR 25,000 (Sec. 5 Subs. 1 GmbHG). The capital can be rendered in cash or in kind (Sec. 5 Subs. 4 GmbHG). In principle it must be fully available to the managing directors, although the amount to be rendered before the date of application for registration in the commercial register will vary.[30] 25

1.9.3 Maintenance of Capital and Liquidity

The concept of GmbH financing is protected by a sophisticated system of provisions found in the GmbHG and rulings of the Federal Supreme Court (*Bundesgerichtshof*, "BGH"). 26

(i) System

The "principle of real capital contribution and maintenance" not only ensures the payment of cash contributions to the company, but also prevents a shareholder from circumventing the strict regulations of Sec. 5 Subs. 4 and Sec. 9 c Subs. 1 Sentence 2 GmbHG on contributions in kind[31] by contributing cash to the GmbH and selling to the GmbH the item to be actually contributed shortly afterwards. Any such hidden contribution in kind will not only make the acquisition of the 27

28 Federal Supreme Court in: BGHZ 149, 10 and 151,181; Emmerich in: Scholz, Sec. 13 Mn. 81 et seq.; Hueck/Fastrich in: Baumbach/Hueck, Sec. 5 Mn. 6.

29 U.H. Schneider in: Scholz, Sec. 19 Mn. 1 et seq.; Hueck/Fastrich in: Baumbach/Hueck, Sec. 19 Mn. 1 et seq.

30 Where the capital is rendered in cash, at least half the share capital must be paid in on the date of application for registration in the commercial register (the full amount or an equivalent security is required where there is only one incorporator) (Sec. 7 Subs. 2 Sentence 2 GmbHG). Contributions in kind have to be allowed in the articles of association and must at the very least have the intrinsic value of the share to be subscribed by the new shareholder (Sec. 8 Subs. 1 No. 5 GmbHG). Additionally, upon incorporation the shareholders have to draw up a report on the intrinsic value of the in-kind contributions (Sec. 5 Subs. 4 Sentence 2 GmbHG) which will be assessed by the commercial register. This report does not necessarily need to be audited by an independent auditor. In practice, however, the contribution report is usually audited as the contributor may want to ensure he is not liable to the company in the event the actual value of the in-kind contribution falls short of the value he has undertaken to contribute. Finally, note that contributions in kind must be rendered completely by the date of the application for registration of the company in the commercial register (Sec. 7 Subs. 3 GmbHG).

31 See Mn. 25 and Fn. 30.

"contributed" item by the GmbH invalid but will also trigger the duty on the shareholder to render the cash contribution again.[32]

28 Sec. 30 GmbHG prohibits the repayment of share capital to the shareholders (i.e. to the extent the net assets of the company do not exceed the protected share capital, any payment to a shareholder without equivalent compensation is forbidden and, if made, must be repaid). In the event the recipient of the illegal payment cannot make the repayment, the other shareholders will be liable for the amount (Sec. 31 GmbHG).

29 Pursuant to Sec. 32a/b GmbHG, external financing by shareholders will be subject to certain restrictions in the event of a so-called company "crisis", which is deemed to be the moment when a shareholder, being a prudent businessman, would have contributed new equity to the company or would have put the GmbH into liquidation or insolvency proceedings.[33]

(ii) Distributions

30 Distributions of profits to shareholders usually have to be made on the basis of a shareholders' resolution deciding on the utilisation of annual profits.[34] Such distributions must be made from annual profits or profits carried forward from previous years after deduction of losses carried forward (Sec. 29 Subs. 1 GmbHG). Although not expressly prohibited, "hidden distributions", for example by giving financial advantages to a shareholder in business transactions which are not on arm's-length terms, may be problematic in two aspects. First, they would only be allowed if all shareholders are treated equally and the registered share capital is not repaid in violation of Sec. 30 GmbHG. Second, such hidden distributions could trigger adverse tax effects.[35] Even though statutory law does not provide for a minimum dividend, the Federal Supreme Court has entitled minority shareholders to an equitable dividend.[36]

31 Advance dividends are generally allowed if – at the time of their payment – an annual result at least equalling the advance dividend is to be expected and the payment does not constitute a repayment of share capital. The advance dividend has to be adopted by the shareholders' meeting (Sec. 46 No. 1 GmbHG). Under a different concept there is also the possibility to make quasi-interim dividends. On the basis of a shareholders' resolution the capital reserve of the company can be dissolved and the reserved amount be paid out any time during the fiscal year of the company.

(iii) Acquisition of Own Shares and Related Financing

32 A GmbH may not subscribe to its own shares. Nevertheless, at a later stage it may acquire its own shares and receive its own shares as a security provided the shares are fully paid-up (Sec. 33 Subs. 1 GmbHG). However, the acquisition by the company of its own shares will require the creation of a statutory reserve for own shares in the balance sheet. This reserve must be created without reducing the restricted share capital or any capital reserve provided for in the articles of association (Sec. 33 Subs. 2 GmbHG). As long as the GmbH holds title to the repurchased shares, it cannot exercise most shareholder rights attached thereto (e.g. voting rights, right to dividends).[37]

33 There is no maximum percentage of shares which may be repurchased by the GmbH, although the GmbH may not entirely own itself. Furthermore, the company is not obliged to redeem the repurchased shares, though this will often happen where permitted in the articles of association (Sec. 34 Subs. 1 GmbHG).

34 There are no specific rules in German law governing the provision of financial assistance by a GmbH in the acquisition of its own shares by a third party. However, the general rules relating to the equal treatment of shareholders and the maintenance of share capital[38] must be observed.

32 U.H. Schneider in: Scholz, Sec. 19 Mn. 40, 42; Hueck/Fastrich in: Baumbach/Hueck, Sec. 19 Mn. 11.
33 For details see Mn. 37.
34 Sec. 42 a Subs. 2 Sentence 1, 46 No. 1 GmbHG.
35 Emmerich in: Scholz, Sec. 29 Mn. 96 et seq.
36 Federal Supreme Court in: BGHZ 23, 156 et seq.
37 Federal Supreme Court in: NJW 1995, 102 (1028); Hueck/Fastrich in: Baumbach/Hueck, Sec. 33 Mn. 18 et seq.
38 See Mn. 26 et seq.

Furthermore, the financial assistance may not take place if the company itself issues new shares (e.g. in case of a capital increase) as, in this particular case, the contribution made by the shareholder would not be deemed to be "fully available to the company".[39]

(iv) Company as Lender or Guarantor

A GmbH may give loans to, or grant guarantees for the benefit of, third parties. To the extent these are given to or granted for the benefit of shareholders, the company must ensure that the share capital remains intact (Sec. 30 GmbHG).[40] Where the share capital is not fully available anymore, loans to shareholders are only permitted under the strict condition that they are made on arm's length terms, are in the best interest of the company and are fully secured and that there is no reasonable doubt that the shareholder is able to satisfy the repayment claim.[41] **35**

Granting security to a shareholder will only be a violation of capital maintenance rules where it can be established that the secured party will claim payment under the security and the share capital would consequently be infringed.[42] **36**

(v) Company as Borrower

Shareholder loans to the company are generally allowed. However, they are restricted where there is a "crisis" in the company (Sec. 32a/b GmbHG).[43] If at such point a shareholder does not contribute equity to the company but only grants a shareholder loan or refrains from claiming back an existing loan, any such loans will be considered to rank last in any subsequent insolvency proceedings. These rules also apply to third-party loans which are secured by a shareholder (Sec. 32 a Subs. 2 GmbHG), but do not apply to loans, if the lender, in the event of a crisis in the company, acquires shares in the company in order to overcome the situation (Sec. 32 a Subs. 3 GmbHG). **37**

It should be noted in general that case law on the entire system of intra-group borrowings ((iv) and (v)), cash pools etc. is currently becoming ever stricter. Such measures thus require a careful review before being implemented. **38**

1.10 Publication and Filing Requirements

A wide range of documentation and information must be filed with the commercial register,[44] some of which will also have to be submitted for publication in the Federal Gazette. The commercial register file is open to the public and any interested person can review the filed documents and request a commercial register excerpt reflecting the principal corporate information (e.g. the share capital, the names of the managing directors and *Prokurists*, capital increases and amendments to the articles of association) as well as copies of any documents submitted. Unless a third party inspecting the commercial register has knowledge to the contrary, it can rely on the information contained therein (Sec. 15 HGB). Certain corporate changes only become effective upon registration in the commercial register. A violation of filing obligations cannot result in a deletion of the company from the commercial register but is only enforced by imposing fines. For example, not **39**

39 Federal Supreme Court in: BGHZ 80, 129 (143); Sec. 8 Subs. 2 Sentence 1 GmbHG; Hueck/Fastrich in: Baumbach/Hueck, Sec. 30 Mn. 16.

40 See Mn. 28.

41 Federal Supreme Court in: BGHZ 80, 129 (143); Sec. 8 Subs. 2 Sentence 1 GmbHG; Hueck/Fastrich in: Baumbach/Hueck, Sec. 30 Mn. 3; U.H. Schneider in: Scholz, Sec. 19 Mn. 40.

42 Hueck/Fastrich in: Baumbach/Hueck, Sec. 30 Mn. 19; Westermann in: Scholz, Sec. 30 Mn. 31 b.

43 See Mn. 29.

44 The deed of incorporation and articles of association (Sec. 8 Subs. 1 GmbHG); the shareholder resolution plus the new articles of association every time the articles of association are amended (Sec. 54 Subs. 1 Sentence 1 GmbHG); shareholder resolutions on the appointment or dismissal of managing directors (Sec. 39 Subs. 1, Sec. 46 No. 5 GmbHG); the personal data of the managing directors and the shareholders (the latter in the form of a shareholder list) upon incorporation and in the event of changes thereof (Sec. 8 Subs. 1 No. 3, Sec. 40 Subs. 1 Sentence 1 GmbHG); the annual accounts immediately after presentation to the shareholders, but no later than 12 months after the end of the business year (Sec. 325 Subs. 1 Sentence 2 HGB).

filing the annual accounts may trigger a fine of up to EUR 25,000, which, however, is only enforced upon request of any third party (Sec. 335 a Commercial Code ("HGB")).

40 Commercial registers are kept with Local Courts on a decentralised basis (an additional centralised register is under discussion). Online access is currently being introduced, but is not yet available in all Federal States.[45]

1.11 Financial Reporting

41 A GmbH must draw up its annual accounts within three months of the end of the business year.[46] The annual accounts must consist of a balance sheet, a profit and loss statement and an annex[47] (Sec. 264 HGB).[48] The annual accounts must be drawn up in accordance with German GAAP. The drawing up of annual accounts in accordance with other accounting principles, such as US GAAP or IAS/IFRS, is not permitted.[49] An exception applies to large companies,[50] which may additionally publish their annual accounts in the Federal Gazette in accordance with IAS/IFRS but are not released from the basic requirement to draw up annual accounts and submit them to the commercial register in accordance with German GAAP. Group annual accounts, however, are allowed to be solely drawn up in accordance with IAS/IFRS (though this does not release the single group companies from the obligation to draw up their annual accounts in accordance with German GAAP).[51] The annual accounts must be audited by an independent auditor/auditing firm (Sec. 316 HGB) unless the company is a small GmbH.[52]

1.12 Employee Participation in Corporate Bodies

42 In general, employees are not represented in the corporate bodies of a GmbH. Where, however, a GmbH has more than 500 employees, a supervisory board (*Aufsichtsrat*) must be created.[53] The supervisory board is, above all, responsible for controlling the management (Sec. 111 AktG). Furthermore, it has to draw up a catalogue of business transactions which require the prior approval of the supervisory board. However, supervisory board decisions can always be overruled by the shareholders' meeting.[54] The existence of a supervisory board therefore mainly ensures that employee issues are sufficiently considered by the management of the company.

45 Access and availability status can be obtained at www.handelsregister.de.

46 The business year may be the calendar year or any other 12-month period chosen.

47 The annex contains notes to the accounts relating to accounting methods used.

48 A company exceeding two of the following criteria (i) a balance sheet total of EUR 4,015,000, (ii) a turnover of EUR 8,030,000, (iii) a workforce of more than 50 employees in the annual average must additionally draw up a management report on the economic situation of the GmbH. Small GmbHs (not exceeding two of the above criteria) have an extra three months to draw up their annual accounts (Sec. 264 Subs. 1 Sentence 3 HGB). Small companies may – amongst others – furthermore draw up far less detailed annual accounts and do not need to file to the commercial register their profit and loss accounts (but the balance sheet). Medium-sized enterprises (exceeding two of the afore-mentioned thresholds but not exceeding two of the three following thresholds: (i) a balance sheet total of EUR 16,060,000, (ii) a turnover of EUR 32,120,000, (iii) a workforce of more than 250 employees in the annual average) may draw up and file to the register shorter annual accounts. Both small and medium-sized enterprises only need to publish in the Federal Gazette the fact that they have filed their annual accounts – but not the actual annual accounts (which large enterprises are required to publish).

49 Merkt in: Baumbach/Hopt, HGB, 31st ed. 2003, Intro. Sec. 238 Mn. 8 e, Sec. 238 Mn. 11, Sec. 243 Mn. 4 et seq. Note that for the purpose of internal – or group – reporting a company may of course additionally draw up its annual accounts in accordance with foreign accounting principles; however, not in lieu of the "official" annual accounts which must comply with German GAAP.

50 Large companies are those exceeding the criteria for medium-sized companies laid out in Fn. 48.

51 Merkt in: Baumbach/Hopt, HGB, 31st ed. 2003, Intro. Sec. 238 Mn. 8 e, Sec. 238 Mn. 11, Sec. 243 Mn. 4 et seq.

52 See Fn. 48.

53 The degree of employee participation depends on the number of employees. Sec. 1 Subs. 1 No. 3 of the Employee Participation Act (*Drittelbeteiligungsgesetz*) provides that in a GmbH with 500 or more but less than 2,000 employees, one-third of the supervisory board has to consist of employee representatives (so-called "small co-determination"). For a GmbH with more than 2,000 employees, Sec. 6, 7 Subs. 1 of the Co-Determination Act (*Mitbestimmungsgesetz*) provides for a supervisory board, half the members of which have to be employee representatives (so-called "large co-determination").

54 Sec. 52 Subs. 1 GmbHG, Sec. 111 Subs. 4 Sentence 3 AktG; Zöllner in: Baumbach/Hueck, Sec. 52 Mn. 64 et seq.

In companies with more than 2000 employees a so-called labour director (*Arbeitsdirektor*) with the same rights and duties as the other managing directors has to be appointed (Sec. 33 Co-Determination Act). In companies in the coal and steel industry the labour director cannot be appointed against the votes of the employee representatives on the supervisory board (Sec. 13 Subs. 1 Coal and Steel Co-Determination Act). The labour director is responsible for all management matters relating to employment and social issues. **43**

2 The Stock Corporation ("AG")

Literature: Ebke/Finkin, Introduction to German Law (Kluwer 1996), Chapter 5 B I: The Stock Company; Hüffer, Aktiengesetz, commentary (6th edition, Beck 2004); Münchener Handbuch des Gesellschaftsrechts, Vol. 4, Aktiengesellschaft (2nd edition, Beck 1999)

The stock corporation (*Aktiengesellschaft*, "AG") is the other important corporate form offering limited shareholder liability in Germany. Its advantage is its easy access to capital markets and therefore its greater scope for raising funds to finance its business activities. However, as this will usually result in a large number of shareholders, its governance structure and rules on capital protection are particularly strict. **44**

2.1 Export of Company

German restrictions on the relocation of a domestic company to a foreign country are based on the Real Seat Theory and will apply to an AG in the same manner as to a GmbH. The relocation of an AG to another EU Member State and the keeping of its identity as a German AG must therefore be considered impossible.[55] **45**

2.2 Transformation into a Foreign Entity

Any such transformation would have to be carried out in the same manner as for a GmbH.[56] The transformation into an S.E. in accordance with the respective laws, however, is possible.[57] **46**

2.3 Incorporation

An AG is set up by way of a notarial deed of incorporation executed by at least one shareholder (Sec. 23 Subs. 1 and Sec. 2 AktG). The company will legally come into existence upon its entry into the commercial register held by the Local Court competent for the company's corporate seat (Sec. 41 AktG). **47**

The precise length of the incorporation procedure is difficult to predict and may vary from two weeks to several months.[58] The notarial fees for the incorporation of an AG with a minimum share capital of EUR 50,000 amount to approximately EUR 750. In addition, the registration and publication of the event in the Federal Gazette will cost between EUR 130 and EUR 180. **48**

2.4 Recurrent Costs and Efforts

The annual efforts required to maintain an AG can be either relatively minimal or considerably high depending on whether the AG is run with a small number of employees and few shareholders or as a large enterprise having a significant number of shareholders and/or more than 500 employees.[59] A small AG would typically face costs and efforts comparable to those of a GmbH.[60] In a **49**

55 See Mn. 2.

56 See Mn. 3.

57 See Part 2, S.E., Mn. 6 et seq. and 10 and seq.

58 To a large extent, it depends on the resources of the actual commercial register and whether the commercial register operates electronically. Due to these uncertainties, the acquisition of shelf-companies, which are already incorporated and registered, is common in Germany.

59 Where there are more than 500 employees, one-third of the supervisory board must comprise employee representatives. In this case, meetings of the supervisory board become more costly.

large AG, costs for an ordinary shareholders' meeting (convocation, advisers' fees, catering for shareholders, security measures) may easily reach thousands of euros; extraordinary shareholders' meetings, which require more intensive preparation and which could become litigious, can cost more than EUR 100,000.

2.5 Shares and Share Transfers

50 Shares in an AG can either be bearer shares or registered shares.[61] The articles of association can provide for different classes of shares (Sec. 11 AktG), for example for preference shares (*Vorzugsaktien*) which have no voting rights but entitle the holder to a preference dividend. Traditionally bearer shares are transferred by handing over the share certificate whilst registered shares can either be transferred by way of handover or endorsement (Sec. 68 Subs. 1 AktG). Share certificates, however, are not mandatory. In companies with a larger number of shareholders shares are often represented by one global share certificate only which is held by a deposit institution. In this case the transfer of individual shares is effected by way of electronic bookings done between the deposit institution and the transferor's and the transferee's custodian bank.[62] There is no transfer tax levied on a share transfer.[63] Transfers of shares do not require notarial form. Transfers of registered shares are often subject to the approval of the company. This requirement has to be stipulated in the articles of association. The approval is usually given by the board of directors (Sec. 68 Subs. 2 AktG).

2.6 Corporate Bodies

51 The AG is required to have three corporate bodies: the board of directors (*Vorstand*); the supervisory board (*Aufsichtsrat*); and the shareholders' meeting (*Hauptversammlung*).

2.6.1 Board of Directors

52 The board of directors consists of one or more members and exclusively represents the company *vis-à-vis* third parties (Sec. 78 AktG). Its members can either be awarded sole or joint power of representation.[64]

53 The board of directors is exclusively in charge of the management of the company (Sec. 76 Subs. 1 AktG). In contrast to the GmbH, the board of directors is independent and not subject to binding instructions from the supervisory board or from the shareholders' meeting.[65] However, certain business transactions require the supervisory board's approval[66] or – in rare cases – the approval of the shareholders' meeting.[67]

54 The supervisory board is responsible for the appointment and dismissal of members of the board of directors (Sec. 84 Subs. 1 AktG), whose maximum term of office is five years. This term, however, can be renewed.

60 See Mn. 6.

61 A holder of registered shares has to register his name, date of birth and address in the shareholder register of the company in order to be able to exercise his shareholder rights (Sec. 67 AktG).

62 Wiesner in: Münchener Handbuch, Vol. 4, Sec. 14 Mn. 14; Hüffer, Sec. 68 Mn. 3; RGZ 77, 268, 276; RGZ 86, 154, 157.

63 If the company owns real property, however, the transfer of 95 or more per cent of the shares in the company will trigger real estate transfer tax (Sec. 1 Subs. 3 No. 3 and 4 Real Estate Transfer Tax Act).

64 For details regarding the distinction, see Mn. 12.

65 Assmann/Lange/Sethe in: Ebke/Finkin, Introduction to German Law, Chapter 5 B I 8 (c), p. 149; Hüffer, Sec. 76, Mn. 10; Wiesner in: Münchener Handbuch, Vol. 4, Sec. 19 Mn. 18.

66 See Mn. 56.

67 See Mn. 56.

2.6.2 Shareholders' Meeting

The shareholders' meeting is the representative body of the shareholders in which they can exercise their rights (Sec. 108 Subs. 1 AktG). Pursuant to Sec. 119 Subs. 1 No. 1 AktG, the shareholders' meeting is responsible for the appointment of the members of the supervisory board to the extent that no individual delegation rights are stipulated in the articles of association and that certain members are not appointed by the employees.[68] Further competencies include the formal approval of the auditors, of the members of the board of directors and the supervisory board (Sec. 119 Subs. 1 No. 3 AktG), the appointment of auditors and the utilisation of balance sheet profits (Sec. 119 Subs. 1 No. 4, No. 2 AktG). Resolutions of the shareholders' meeting are passed by a simple majority of the votes cast (Sec. 137 Subs. 1 AktG) unless the articles of association (Sec. 133 Subs. 2 AktG) or the AktG provide for higher majority requirements. **55**

The shareholders' meeting generally may not decide on management issues, given the exclusive management competence of the board of directors (Sec. 76 Subs. 1 AktG). However, there are certain measures which require the shareholders' approval. Among these are amendments to the articles of association (Sec. 119 Subs. 1 No. 5 AktG). Additionally, according to decisions by the Federal Supreme Court (e.g. in the "*Holzmüller*" case[69]), the board of directors must obtain shareholder approval if a business transaction will severely affect the financial interests of the shareholders. In a recent judgment (the "*Gelatine*" case[70]) the Federal Supreme Court clarified that the obligation to obtain shareholder approval is limited to very exceptional cases, for example when 80 per cent or more of the company's assets are transferred to a subsidiary. **56**

2.6.3 Supervisory Board

Pursuant to Sec. 95 AktG the supervisory board must have at least three members and, depending on the amount of share capital, will have a maximum number of between nine and 21 members. It is obliged to monitor whether the board of directors complies with its duties and takes management decisions which are economically feasible for the company (Sec. 111 Subs. 1 AktG), and it generally decides on the approval of the annual accounts (Sec. 172 AktG). Pursuant to Sec. 111 Subs. 4 AktG, the supervisory board must draw up a catalogue of management decisions which require the approval of the supervisory board in order to ensure effective supervision. The maximum term of office of the members of the supervisory board is five years (Sec. 102 Subs. 1 AktG); reappointment is possible. **57**

2.7 Duties and Liabilities of Directors

The duties of the members of the board of directors are comparable to those of the managing directors of a GmbH.[71] Except in certain rare instances, shareholder approval is not required for a business transaction.[72] However, the board of directors must obtain supervisory board approval for those business transactions which the supervisory board has reserved for its approval (Sec. 111 Subs. 4 AktG). **58**

Like the managing directors of a GmbH, the members of the board of directors of an AG must perform their duties using the diligence of a prudent businessman and, in the event of breach, are liable to the company (Sec. 93 AktG). Unlike in a GmbH, the discharge of the board of directors by the annual meeting of shareholders does not constitute a release from their liability. D&O insurance is common and the payment of related premiums by the AG is permitted. Liability to third parties will only arise in a number of rare cases. The same applies to the members of the supervisory board (Sec. 116. AktG). **59**

68 For details on employee representation, please refer to Mn. 42 above and Mn. 73 below.
69 Federal Supreme Court in: BGHZ 83, 122 et seq.
70 Federal Supreme Court in: ZIP 2004, 993 et seq.
71 See Mn. 17 et seq.
72 See Mn. 56.

60 In addition to the general liability of the members of the board of directors, they can also be held liable for certain breaches of provisions regarding the protection of the company's share capital (Sec. 93 Subs. 3 AktG). In this regard they can only claim that the payments made by them were based on a legal shareholders' resolution, but not that the action was approved by the supervisory board (Sec. 93 Subs. 4 Sentence 2 AktG). The liability becomes time-barred after a period of five years (Sec. 93 Subs. 6 AktG).

2.8 Shareholders' Liability

61 As is the case with a GmbH, the shareholders of an AG are in principle not liable for the obligations of the company, given the principle of limited liability. A liability to the company is only given in consequence of a breach of the provisions of the AktG relating to the protection of the company's capital and finances.[73]

62 It has not yet been decided by the Courts if direct claims of third parties against a shareholder based on the so-called tort of an "action endangering the existence of the company" (*existenzvernichtender Eingriff*)[74] are available in the context of an AG. However, it is very likely that legal practice will also apply this principle to shareholders of an AG.

2.9 Capitalisation and Financing

2.9.1 Basic Concepts

63 As is the case with a GmbH, the capitalisation and financing of an AG is based on the general concept of the "principle of real capital contribution and maintenance".[75] Accordingly, the loss of the restricted share capital will oblige the members of the board of directors to apply for insolvency proceedings (Sec. 92 Subs. 2 Sentence 2 AktG).

2.9.2 Minimum Share Capital

64 The minimum share capital of an AG is EUR 50,000 (Sec. 7 AktG). The capital can be rendered in cash or in kind (Sec. 27 Subs. 1 AktG). The part of the contributions which has to be rendered[76] immediately has to be fully available to the board of directors at the date of the application for registration of the company. The incorporation process is subject to a statutory review by the first board of directors and the first supervisory board (Sec. 33 Subs. 1 AktG). As part of the review, the level and availability of the contributions must be assessed. In addition, in certain cases a second audit by an independent auditor will be required, in particular when a member of the supervisory board or the board of directors has been involved in the incorporation or has subscribed to shares of the company or if contributions in kind are provided for (Sec. 33 Subs. 2 AktG).

2.9.3 Maintenance of Capital and Liquidity

(i) System

65 Due to the anonymity of shareholders of the AG, the law provides for an even stronger capital protection than is the case for the GmbHG. Hidden contributions in kind are likewise prohibited and make the acquisition of the "contributed" item by the AG invalid and trigger the shareholder's duty

73 For details see Mn. 63 et seq.

74 Federal Supreme Court in: BGHZ 149, 10 and 151, 181; this principle applies to a GmbH – see Mn. 20.

75 Hüffer, Sec. 1, Mn. 11, 12.

76 Where the capital is rendered in cash, at least a quarter of the share capital must be paid in on the date of application for registration in the commercial register (the full amount or a security is requested if there is only one incorporator) (Sec. 36 a AktG). Contributions in kind must be allowed in the articles of association and must at least have the intrinsic value of the shares to be subscribed by the new shareholder (Sec. 36 a Subs. 2 AktG). Contributions in kind have to be rendered completely within a period of five years of the date of application for registration of the company in the commercial register (Sec. 36 a Subs. 2 Sentence 2 AktG). Assmann/Langel/Sethe in: Ebke/Finkin, Introduction to German Law, Chapter 5 B I 3 (ii), p. 141.

to render the cash contribution again (Sec. 27 Subs. 3 AktG).[77] In addition, any agreement between the company and its incorporators, or a shareholder holding more than 10 per cent of the registered share capital of the company, concluded within two years of the registration of the company in the commercial register will require the approval of the shareholders' meeting and registration in the commercial register; otherwise any such transaction is void (Sec. 52 Subs. 1 AktG).

(ii) Distributions

Distributions to shareholders may only be made out of balance sheet profits after deduction of losses carried forward and amounts to be put into the statutory reserves (Sec. 57, 58 AktG). Hidden distributions, e.g. by way of an agreement between the company and a shareholder not meeting fair market terms, will be considered invalid and will trigger a repayment claim of the company.[78] Interim dividends are not allowed before the end of a business year. **66**

(iii) Acquisition of Own Shares and Related Financing

Except for certain limited cases, an AG is not allowed to acquire its own shares (Sec 71 Subs. 1 AktG). One of the most relevant exceptions is an authorisation by the shareholders' meeting (Sec. 71 Subs. 1 No. 8 AktG). Such authorisation may only be given for a maximum term of 18 months and may only authorise the acquisition of a maximum of 10 per cent of the registered share capital. A significant number of AGs make use of such authorisations, mostly to utilise such shares as an acquisition currency in an M&A transaction or in order to strengthen a weak stock market price of the company. In the cases where the AG is allowed to acquire its own shares it is not entitled to exercise the rights attached to these shares. **67**

In addition, Sec. 71 a AktG prohibits an AG from providing financial assistance in the acquisition of its own shares, particularly in the form of a loan or the granting of security. Any such legal transactions are void. **68**

(iv) Company as Lender or Guarantor

Loans and securities to third parties are not restricted. If granted by an AG to its shareholders, they are allowed so long as they meet market conditions; otherwise they would be considered an illegal distribution.[79] **69**

(v) Company as Borrower

Shareholder loans to an AG are generally allowed, as is the case for a GmbH. However, shareholders having a financing responsibility[80] may face the risk that in the event of a "crisis" of the company – meaning when the company can no longer obtain third-party financing on market conditions – shareholder loans cannot be paid back and will be considered to rank last in any insolvency proceedings. A financing responsibility is usually assumed if a shareholder holds more than 25 per cent of the share capital of the company.[81] The principles also apply to third-party loans secured by a shareholder. **70**

2.10 Publication and Filing Requirements

These requirements correspond with the requirements in a GmbH.[82] **71**

77 The same applies in the case of capital increases (Sec. 183 Subs. 2 AktG).

78 Hüffer, Sec. 57 Mn. 8 et seq., 23; Kantenwein in: Münchener Handbuch, Vol. 4, Sec. 49 Mn. 55 et seq.

79 Hüffer, Sec. 57 Mn. 8; Kantenwein in: Münchener Handbuch, Vol. 4, Sec. 49 Mn. 74.

80 BGHZ 90, 381, 390.

81 Hüffer, Sec. 57 Mn. 18; Wiesner in: Münchener Handbuch, Vol. 4, Sec. 16 Mn. 44; Federal Financial Court in: WM 1984, 625, 627.

82 See Mn. 39.

2.11 Financial Reporting

72 These requirements to a large extent correspond with the requirements in a GmbH.[83] As of 31 December 2005 listed AGs, however, must draw-up their group annual accounts in accordance with IAS/IFRS. US-GAAP group reporting remains permitted for an interim period ending 31 December 2007 as regards groups which are listed in the USA.

2.12 Employee Participation in Corporate Bodies

73 As outlined above, a supervisory board is mandatory in an AG. In addition, one-third of the supervisory board must consist of employee representatives if the company has more than 500 employees. Where the AG has more than 2,000 employees, half the members of the supervisory board must be employee representatives.[84] Unlike in a GmbH, the shareholders' meeting does not generally have the right to overrule supervisory board decisions.

83 See Mn. 41.

84 For details regarding employee participation in corporate bodies, see Mn. 42 et seq.

X. Greece

by Katia Papantonopoulou and Christina Zakopoulou (M.Sc.equiv.)[*]

1 The Limited Liability Company ("EPE")

Literature: Perakis, Law of the Limited Liability Company (Nomiki Vivliothiki 1994); Rokas, Trading Companies (Ant.N. Sakkoulas Publishers 1996); L. Kotsiris, Greek Company Law, (Sakkuolas 1989)

The limited liability company structure (*Eteria Periorismenis Efthinis, "EPE")* is quite common for smaller businesses and family enterprises. Although an EPE is categorised under the capital companies, it includes some personal elements such as, for instance, the possibility that the law gives to the partners the right to participate in management and represent the company. It is organised in a more flexible way than the Société Anonyme (*Anonymi Etairia*, "A.E."[1] so that the rights and duties of the partners may be regulated with considerable freedom, provided however that the transfer of the parts is strictly regulated by law. In contrast to the A.E., the EPE is not subject to state supervision and control. 1

In 2001 approximately 24,500 EPE's were registered in Greece, in contrast to approximately 30,000 A.E.'s.

1.1 Export of Company

It is partly accepted by legal theory[2] that an EPE is allowed to move its corporate seat to another country without losing its legal personality.[3] In practice, such a relocation of the corporate seat would be subject to the amendment of the articles of association of the company. The resolution regarding this must be adopted by the partners' meeting. The consent of all the partners is required. 2

Furthermore, it should be noted that, according to Greek law, an EPE is not entitled to maintain two or more registered seats. As a result, a company which moves its corporate seat to another country shall adopt the legal structure of the foreign country.

1.2 Transformation into a Foreign Entity

Greek corporate law does not explicitly provide for the transformation of a domestic company into a foreign entity. However, such a transformation can be achieved by transferring the whole business of the company to a foreign company. Furthermore, in the event that the EPE relocates its corporate seat to another country, it shall be transformed into the corresponding legal structure of the foreign country, according to the law and the rules of the foreign country. Greek corporate law does not provide for the possibility of merging an EPE with an S.E. 3

1.3 Incorporation

Apart from further formalities an EPE is established by means of a notarial deed by at least one partner (*monoprosopi eteria periorismenis efthinis*) ("one partner EPEs"). The company will exist legally upon its registration with the Registry of EPEs held by the competent Court of First Instance and the publication of its articles of association in the Official Gazette, Sec. 3 Subs. 1 Law 3190/1955 "on Companies with Limited Liability", ("L. 3190/1955"). 4

The incorporation procedure usually requires five days from the execution of the articles of association of the company. The notarial fees for the incorporation of an EPE will amount to approximately EUR 500. Registration and publication fees (Official Gazette and registration fees to 5

* *M. & P. Bernitsas Law Offices*, Athens.

1 See Mn. 30 et seq.

2 Kiantos in: Private Law of International Trade 2002, p. 171, 175, 176.

3 Under Greek private international law the corporate seat of the company is considered to be the de facto seat of the company, i.e. the seat where the management of the company actually operates and not the seat referred to in the articles of association of the company.

the Greek Chamber of Industry and Commerce) amount to approximately EUR 450. Additionally, capital concentration tax in the amount of 1 per cent of the share capital will have to be paid.[4] Should the company's capital exceed the amount of approximately EUR 29,350, a lawyer has to be present at the drafting and execution of the notarial deed and accordingly a part of his fees has to be paid to the competent Bar Association.

1.4 Recurrent Costs and Efforts

6 The annual financial statements of the company and the auditors' report (in cases where the company is obliged to appoint an auditor)[5] are subject to publication formalities at an annual cost of EUR 240. In addition, the company must pay to the Greek Chamber of Industry and Commerce annual contribution fees amounting to approximately EUR 130. The EPE is not required to pay an annual registration fee to the Registry of EPEs.

1.5 Shares and Share Transfers

7 An EPE does not issue shares. Each partner participates in the company's share capital with one or more company parts (*eterika meridia*). The minimum nominal value of each part amounts to EUR 30. Subject to probable restrictions (if any) in the articles of association, the company parts are transferable only by means of a notarial deed *inter vivos*, (Sec. 28 Subs. 1 L. 3190/1955). The transfer is subject to transfer tax. The transfer shall come into effect towards the company as of the respective registration in the partners' book, for which both the transferor and transferee are entitled to apply (Sec. 28 Subs. 3 L. 3190/1955). The transfer must also be published in the Official Gazette (Sec. 31 Subs. 2 L. 3190/1955).

8 Since an EPE does not issue shares, it cannot issue its shares to the public. In the event that the company intends to issue its shares to the public, it must be converted into an S.A.

1.6 Corporate Bodies

9 L. 3190/1955 provides that the partners' meeting is compulsory, with the administrator(s) (*diaxeiristis*) acting as legal representative(s).

1.6.1 Meeting of Partners

10 The partners' meeting is the highest corporate body in the hierarchy of an EPE and is entitled to decide on any matter related to the EPE (Sec. 14 Subs. 1 L. 3190/1955), including: amendments to the articles of association, the appointment and removal of the administrator(s) and their release from any responsibility, and the approval of the balance sheet and distribution of profit.

11 The decisions of the partners' meeting, unless otherwise provided by law or the articles of association, are taken by a majority of over half the total number of partners representing more than one half of the company's capital (Sec. 13 L. 3190/1955). Higher quorums apply, for example, for the change of the company's nationality and an increase of the obligations or responsibility of the partners or a reduction of the rights conceded by the company's articles of association (consent of all partners) and any amendment of the articles of association (majority of three-quarters of the total number of partners representing three-quarters of the total company capital (Sec. 38 Subs. 1 of L. 3190/1955)). The resolutions of the partners' meeting are binding for the administrator(s), including absent or dissenting partners.

1.6.2 Administrator(s)

12 The administration of an EPE and the representation thereof *vis-à-vis* third parties is undertaken by all partners, acting jointly, unless otherwise agreed. By virtue of the articles of association or a

4 The amounts to be paid are calculated on the company's share capital.
5 See Mn. 28.

decision of the partners' meeting, the administration and representation of the company may be entrusted to one or more partners or non-partners (administrators) for a definite or an indefinite period of time (Sec. 17 Subs. 1 L. 3190/1955). In the event that the administration has been entrusted to more than one person and it has not been agreed otherwise, the administrators shall act jointly (Sec. 17 Subs. 2 L. 3190/1955).

1.7 Duties and Liabilities of Directors

The administrator(s) represent an EPE and exercise on behalf of the EPE any act within the scope of the EPE's objects, as has been specified by the articles of association of the company, with the exception of any issues belonging to the competence of the partners' meeting by virtue of the law or the articles of association. **13**

The administrator(s) are liable towards the company, its partners and any third parties for damages resulting from any violation of L. 3190/1955, the articles of association or any negligent fault in the company's management (Sec. 26 Subs. 1 L. 3190/1955). Where the administrator(s) have acted jointly, they are jointly and severally liable (Sec. 26 Subs. 1 L. 3190/1955). Administrators that do not participate in acts of administration may not be held liable. Administrators, acting individually, are responsible for their individual acts. In certain cases a dissenting co-administrator may be held liable where the other administrators adopted an unlawful decision to the company's detriment. **14**

The meeting of partners may release the administrator(s) from any liability for compensation, or quit from its claims against the administrator(s) or decide not to initiate a company legal action against them. In this case, however, partners or third parties may individually initiate the company legal action for damages. The release of the administrator(s) from their liability by the meeting of partners likewise does not affect individual actions regulated by the general provisions of the Greek Civil Code on obligations, damages and unlawful conduct.

Claims of the company against the administrator(s) are subject to a five-year statutory limitation (Sec. 26 Subs. 2 L. 3190/1955). D&O insurances are not used in Greece.

The administrator(s) are not obliged to apply for insolvency proceedings unless the meeting of partners decides to initiate such insolvency proceedings.[6] Creditors may also file petition to the court requesting insolvency proceedings, provided that satisfactory evidence has been presented regarding cessation of the payments by the company.

1.8 Shareholders' Liability

Partners who cause the invalidity of the company are held fully liable, without any limitation *vis-à-vis* the other partners and third parties for any damages resulting from such invalidity (Sec. 7 Subs. 5 L. 3190/1955). **15**

Partners are not personally liable. Generally, piercing the corporate veil is rare under Greek law. However, in theory, it is possible where the corporate veil is used by a partner in an abusive manner and contrary to good faith and this is upheld by the court. In practice, the common cases in relation to the corporate veil being pierced are the cases where the corporate veil is used by a parent company in an abusive manner and contrary to good faith with a view to avoiding assuming liability for the actions of its subsidiaries. **16**

1.9 Capitalisation and Financing

1.9.1 Basic Concepts

Since an EPE (and not its partners) is liable for the company's liabilities, the company's share capital is the sole guarantee for the company's creditors. Therefore, the share capital stated in the articles of association: (a) must be fully paid-up at the incorporation; and (b) must be available **17**

6 See Mn. 17 for the administrator(s)' duty to call for a partners' meeting in the case of loss of half of the share capital.

to the company during its operation. It is also important to note that in the event of loss of one-half of the share capital, the administrator(s) must call a partners' meeting in order to decide on the dissolution of the company or a decrease in the company's share capital (Sec. 45 Subs. 1 L. 3190/1955).

1.9.2 Minimum Share Capital

18 The minimum share capital of an EPE is EUR 18,000 and must be fully paid-up at the time of the company's incorporation. The share capital can be rendered in cash or in kind. However, at least half of the minimum capital must be paid for in cash at the establishment of the company (Sec. 4 Subs.1 L. 3190/1955).[7]

1.9.3 Maintenance of Capital and Liquidity

19 The concept of the preservation and maintenance of the company's share capital is protected by various provisions of L. 3190/1955.

(i) System

20 The notarial deed by means of which the articles of association of an EPE are drafted must contain, *inter alia*, certification by the founders relating to the payment of the capital. In the absence of such certification, the articles of association shall not be deemed to comply with all requirements of law (Sec. 4 L. 3190/1955).

21 Pursuant to the provisions of L. 3190/1955, a departing or excluded partner may receive the value of his participation in the company's share capital under certain conditions and formalities. The departure or exclusion of a partner usually results in a reduction in the company's share capital.

(ii) Distributions

22 Unless there is a contrary provision in the articles of association of an EPE, the partners are entitled to participate in the net profits deriving from the annual balance sheet, pro rata to their participation in the company's share capital (Sec. 32 Subs. 1 L. 3190/1955). The partners' meeting decides on the distribution of net profits arising after deducting from gross profits any expense, loss, or eventual retention for the creation of ordinary and extraordinary reserve capital following the approval of the balance sheet for the preceding fiscal year.

23 Pursuant to Sec. 35 Subs. 2 L. 3190/1955, where a distribution of non-realised profits has been made, the partners who received such profits must return them.[8] The company or its creditors are entitled to raise an action against the partners who received the non-realised profits.

(iii) Acquisition of Own Parts and Related Financing

24 The company may not acquire its own parts in the share capital (Sec. 18 Subs. 4 L. 3190/1955).

(iv) Company as Lender or Guarantor

25 Greek law does not provide for restrictions in relation to the company acting as lender or guarantor to any third party, including its partners. Within this scope, the administrator(s) are entitled to

7 Payment of the capital in kind is permitted only under the following conditions: (i) the articles of association of an EPE provide for the possibility of paying the capital by contributions in kind; (ii) the contributions in kind must also reflect a financial/monetary value; (iii) the evaluation of the contributions in kind made at the time of the company's incorporation is effected subsequent to a Report of valuation, prepared by a three-member Committee of Experts, appointed by the Minister of Development.

8 Non-realised profits are considered to be: (i) the profits which do not derive from the annual balance sheet; (ii) the profits distributed in violation of the balance sheet; and (iii) the profits distributed according to an incorrect or illegal balance sheet.

conclude loans, simple or with real or other security, on movable or fixed assets of the company, under any terms and conditions.

(v) Company as Borrower

It is common in practice that the company obtains the required funds by means of borrowing from its partners. The provisions of L. 3190/1955 protect third parties' interests against the partners becoming creditors of the company. Pursuant to Sec. 32 Subs. 1 L. 3190/1955, loans by the partners to the company secured by right *in rem* on the company's assets are prohibited. The constitution of a right *in rem* in violation of the said prohibition is null and void but the loan granted by the partner to the company is still valid. In the event of the winding-up of the company upon the declaration of its bankruptcy, third parties' claims and partners' claims against the company rank equally.[9] **26**

1.10 Publication and Filing Requirements

A wide range of information about the Company needs to be filed with the Registry of EPEs[10] kept at the Court of First Instance of the district where the company's seat is located and published in the Official Gazette. The Registry of EPEs is open to the public and any interested person may review – upon application to the Secretariat of the Court of First Instance – the filed documents and may request a copy of the corporate information filed within the Registry. To the extent that the partners' meeting results in the amendment of the articles of association, such amendment must be filed within the Registry of EPEs kept at the Court of First Instance of the district where the company's seat is located and published in the Official Gazette. The filing and the publication is full proof of such information. **27**

A fine of at least EUR 59 shall be imposed on any person who intentionally violates any peremptory or prohibitory provision of administrative laws (Sec. 458 of the Greek Penal Code). The penalties shall be imposed, *inter alia*, on any administrator violating the provisions of L. 3190/1955 in relation to the registrations and publications duties.

1.11 Financial Reporting

At the end of the fiscal year, EPE's administrator(s) are obliged to prepare an inventory of all the EPE's assets and liabilities, with a detailed description of each item. An EPE's annual financial statements (i.e. the balance sheet, the profit and loss account, the distribution results table, the appendix) are prepared by the administrator(s) based on the said inventory (Sec. 22 Subs. 1 L. 3190/1955). An EPE not exceeding certain thresholds[11] is exempt from the obligatory audit of its financial statements (Sec. 23 Subs. 2 L. 3190/1955). Apart from this financial reporting requirements are equal for all companies irrespective of their size. The annual financial statements must be drawn up in accordance with the national general accounting rules. Pursuant to Sec. 134 Subs. 2 of L. 2190/1920, the drawing up of the financial statements in accordance with the EU's international accounting standards is permitted provided that the partners' meeting has approved the application of such standards (IAS/IFRS) for at least five successive fiscal years. The drawing up of the financial statements in accordance with US GAAP is not permitted. **28**

9 Rocas in: Journal of Commercial Law 1968.

10 The articles of association upon incorporation and in the event of any amendments thereof (e.g. increase or reduction in the share capital, change of the objects of the company (Sec. 8 and Sec. 38 Subs. 4 L. 3190/1955)), the company's seat, the personal data of the partners upon incorporation and, in the event of changes thereto, the corporate data of the company's administrator(s), the corporate data of the company's service agent (Sec. 8 Subs. 4 L. 3190/1955), the annual financial statements (Sec. 22 Subs. 4 L. 3190/1955).

11 According to Sec. 42 a Subs. 4 of Codified Law 2190/1920 "on Sociétés Anonymes", those EPEs may not exceed two of the following three criteria: (i) a total balance sheet of EUR 1,500,000; (ii) net turnover of EUR 3,000,000; and (iii) an average of 50 employees during the financial year.

1.12 Employee Participation in Corporate Bodies

29 In principle, employees are not represented in corporate bodies. However, pursuant to L. 1365/1983 "on the socialisation of the public corporations or the public utility corporations", employees are entitled to appoint usually two members to the boards of directors of the public utility corporations of the public sector.

2 The Stock Corporation ("A.E.")

Literature: E. Perakis, The Law of the Company Limited by Shares, (2nd edition, Nomiki Vivliothiki 2002); I. Papayiannis, The Law of the Companies Limited by Shares (Sakkoulas 1997); L. Kotsiris, Greek Company Law (Sakkoulas 1989)

30 The stock corporation or Société Anonyme (*Anonymi Etairia*, "*A.E.*") is the purest form of capital company, offering *inter alia* legal personality, limited shareholder liability and easy exit of the shareholder by means of transfer of the shares. It is the only company structure which enjoys access to the capital markets. An A.E. is subject to direct state supervision since there are various interests which need to be protected.[12]

2.1 Export of Company

31 The same principles as for an EPE apply.[13] A change of the company's nationality and relocation of its corporate seat is effected by means of a resolution of the general meeting of shareholders, adopted by a majority of two thirds of the votes represented at the general meeting (Sec. 29 Subs. 3 and Sec. 31 Subs. 2 of the Codified Law 2190/1920 "on Sociétés Anonymes", ("C.L. 2190/1920"), as currently in force).

2.2 Transformation into a Foreign Entity

32 The same principles as for an EPE apply. However, it should be accepted that an A.E. can be merged with a foreign entity by means of absorption of either the A.E. by the foreign entity or the foreign entity by the A.E.

2.3 Incorporation

33 Apart from other formalities, an A.E. is set up by means of a notarial deed containing the articles of incorporation (*katastatiko*) executed by at least two shareholders. The company acquires legal personality as of the date of its registration with the Registry of A.E.s (Sec. 7 b Subs. 10 C.L. 2190/1920). The constitutional document and the approval are published in the Official Gazette (Issue on Sociétés Anonymes and Limited Liability Companies).

34 The incorporation procedure usually requires one month from the execution of the articles of incorporation.[14] The notarial fees for the incorporation of an A.E will amount to approximately EUR 1,500. In addition, the company must pay publication fees to the Official Gazette amounting to EUR 450 and registration fees to the Greek Chamber of Industry and Commerce amounting to EUR 375. A mandatory fee must also be paid to the competent Bar Association prior to the

12 State supervision occurs not only at the time of the company's establishment but also during its function. In exercising state supervision, the state authority may refuse the approval of the decision of the company's corporate body or impose penal sanctions. State supervision is not always exercised by the competent Prefecture. According to the company's objects, supervision may be exercised by the Ministry of Development. In the case of companies listed on the Athens Stock Exchange supervision is also exercised by the Stock Exchange Committee and the Capital Market Committee.

13 See Mn. 2.

14 In the event that the share capital of an A.E. does not exceed the amount of EUR 300,000, the competent Prefecture is obliged to proceed with the approval and the registration of the articles of incorporation of the company on the same date as the filing of the constitutional document with the said Prefecture.

execution of the notarial deed. Finally, a special tax charge[15] amounting to 1 per cent of the company's share capital and a special charge[16] amounting to 1 per cent of the company's share capital must be paid.

2.4 Recurrent Costs and Efforts

C.L. 2190/1920 provides for a number of documents and particulars which need to be submitted to the competent Prefecture and published in the Official Gazette; therefore, the annual costs for maintaining an A.E. are considerably higher than those incurred by an EPE. The annual financial statements of the company along with the auditors' report are also subject to publication formalities at an annual cost of EUR 450 plus the publication fees for at least two newspapers.[17] In addition, the company shall be required to pay annual contribution fees to the Greek Chamber of Industry and Commerce amounting to approximately EUR 375. **35**

2.5 Shares and Share Transfers

Shares in an A.E. can be in the form of either registered or bearer shares. Shares are further classified into preference shares with or without voting rights[18] and redeemable shares.[19] It may also be provided in the articles of association that the transfer of registered shares is subject to an approval either of the shareholders' general meeting or the board of directors. **36**

The share certificate embodies the legal relationship between the company and the shareholder.[20] Registered shares are transferred by means of a private share sale and purchase agreement or by means of a notarial deed, executed by both the seller and the purchaser. The transfer of the shares is subject to 5 per cent transfer tax, payable by the transferor of the shares.[21] The transfer of the ownership is carried out by means of an entry in the Shareholders' Book. The seller must also endorse an annotation on the respective share certificates. Bearer shares are transferred by means of an agreement between the two parties and the simple handover of the share certificate from one party to the other (Sec. 35 Commercial Code and Sec. 1034 Greek Civil Code).

An A.E. may issue shares to the public under certain conditions provided by law. **37**

2.6 Corporate Bodies

An A.E. is required to have the following corporate bodies: the general meeting of shareholders and the board of directors.[22] **38**

15 Capital concentration tax, payable to the competent Revenue Office.

16 It is payable in favour of the Competition Committee to the National Bank of Greece.

17 The publication fees for the newspapers depend on the size of the publication (calculated at approximately EUR 8.5 per square centimetre for each publication).

18 Preference shares entitle their holders to special "privileges" not enjoyed by ordinary shareholders, such as the right of receipt of the first dividend (which amounts to at least 6 per cent of the paid-up capital) prior to the ordinary shares, and preferred payment of dividends from previous financial years during which no dividend was distributed (Sec. 3 Subs. 1 C.L. 2190/1920).

19 Shareholders whose shares are redeemable retain their rights to the repayment of their investment and participation in the distribution of the first dividend, which may be received only by shares which have not been redeemed (Sec. 15 a Subs. 4 C.L. 2190/1920).

20 The above legal relationship, however, exists even if a share certificate has not been issued. It results from the special book of registered shares kept by the company ("Shareholders' Book") where the shares are registered ones and from the receipt issued by the company after the payment of the value of the share.

21 The transfer tax is levied on capital gains obtained by both Greek and non-Greek tax residents, unless (i) a Double Taxation Avoidance Treaty is in force between Greece and the foreign state where the seller is established, (ii) the seller is not permanently established in Greece and (iii) the seller qualifies as a tax resident of the foreign state.

22 According to Greek legal theory, the auditors are the third corporate body. Due to their independence, we have refrained from outlining the auditors in more detail.

2.6.1 General Meeting of Shareholders

39 The general meeting of shareholders is the supreme corporate body and is entitled to decide on any matter related to the A.E. Its decisions are binding for absent or dissenting shareholders (Sec. 33 of C.L. 2190/1920). Amongst others the general meeting of shareholders is solely competent for deciding upon amendments to the articles of incorporation, including increases or reductions in the share capital,[23] the appointment of the members of the board of directors and auditors and the approval of the annual financial statements.

40 The general meeting has a quorum when shareholders representing at least one-fifth of the fully paid-up share capital are present (Sec. 29 Subs. 1 of C.L. 2190/1920). The resolutions of the general meeting are adopted with the absolute majority of the votes represented thereat (Sec. 31 Subs. 1 of C.L. 2190/1920). Exceptionally, for example regarding decisions concerning a change in the company's nationality or object, an increase in the shareholders' obligations, or an increase in the company's share capital which is not provided for in the articles of incorporation, a two-thirds majority shall be required, given that two-thirds of the paid-up capital is present or represented at the meeting (Sec. 29 Subs. 1, 3, 5 and Sec. 31 Subs. 2 of C.L. 2190/1920). The articles of association may provide for a higher quorum or majority.

2.6.2 Board of Directors

41 The board of directors is elected by the general meeting of shareholders and consists of at least three members. The term of their office may not exceed six years (Sec. 19 Subs. 1 of C.L. 2190/1920). The company is managed and represented by the board of directors. The members of the board of directors act collectively. However, the company's articles of association may provide that one or more members of the board of directors or other persons are entitled to represent the company in general or in certain matters, acting jointly or severally (Sec. 18 Subs. 2 of C.L. 2190/1920).

2.7 Duties and Liabilities of Directors

42 The board of directors is competent for deciding about any subject related to the company's management and the administration (management and disposal) of the company's assets (Sec. 22 Subs. 1 of C.L. 2190/1920). In general, it decides about any matter regarding the company within the objects of the company, with the exception of those for which the general meeting of shareholders has exclusive competence, according to law or the articles of association.

Each member of the board of directors (and the managing director) is liable towards the company for any fault committed by him in course of the management of the company's affairs (Sec. 22 a Subs. 1 of C.L. 2190/1920), arising from a breach of duties imposed on him by law or the company's articles of association or resolutions of the meeting of the shareholders. In view of the fact that the Board of Directors is a collective corporate body, its members are considered to be jointly liable towards the company in the event of a breach by all of them of their obligations arising from the articles of association or the law. A director shall be released from such joint liability provided he proves that he did not participate in the commission of the breach. It is not sufficient for a director to show that he did not participate in the adoption by the board of the decision in question or that he voted against such decision at the board meeting, nor that he was absent from such meeting (unless such absence is justified). Instead, the director must make every effort to cancel the execution of the said decision. The allocation of specific tasks amongst the members of the board serves as evidence that the director did not participate in the breach committed, unless the board, as a corporate body, failed to exercise the supervision required. D&O insurances are not used in Greece.

43 It has been accepted by Greek legal theory[24] and part of Greek jurisprudence that the company's creditors can raise claims against the members of the board and the managing directors only by

23 With the exception provided in Sec. 13 of C.L. 2190/1920.

24 Rocas in: Trading Companies.

means of an oblique action (*plagiastiki agogi*)[25] provided that the A.E. has not waived such claims against them in accordance with the provisions of Sec. 22 a Subs. 4 C.L. 2190/1920.[26]

Members of the board of directors are, also, liable for the debts owed by the company to the State or other public organisations. They are, also, criminally liable in the event of: (i) an evasion of the tax obligations of the company; and (ii) a breach of certain labour law provisions.

The prior instruction by the shareholders' meeting to carry out a particular action releases the managing directors from their liability for such particular action, provided that such action does not constitute a tort. Claims against the members of the board of directors and the managing directors are subject to a three-year statutory limitation, commencing as of the execution of the breach, which is extended to 10 years in the event of wilful misconduct (Sec. 22 a Subs. 5 C.L. 2190/1920).

Greek Law does not provide for a form of director's disqualification in the event of the company's **44** insolvency. Regulations regarding the initiation of insolvency proceedings and the calling of a shareholders' meeting in case of a loss of half of the share capital are comparable to those regarding the EPE.[27] The managing directors may face criminal or civil liability following the insolvency of the company.

2.8 Shareholders' Liability

As is the case with an EPE, subject to rare exceptions, the shareholders of an A.E. are not **45** personally liable.[28]

2.9 Capitalisation and Financing

2.9.1 Basic Concepts

The capitalisation and financing of an A.E. is based on the general concept of real capital con- **46** tribution and maintenance. Thus, in the event that the shareholders fail to transfer the amounts corresponding to their shares in the initial share capital to a bank account in the company's name and the board of directors does not certify the payment of the initial share capital by the shareholders within two months of the company's establishment, the decisions of the Prefecture relating to the approval of the company's establishment shall be revoked (Sec. 11 Subs. 5 and Sec. 48 Subs. 1(a) of C. L. 2190/1920). It should further be noted that, where the total equity of the company is less than one-tenth of its share capital, the decisions of the Prefecture relating to the approval of the company's establishment shall also be revoked (Sec. 48 Subs. 1(c) of C. L. 2190/1920).

2.9.2 Minimum Share Capital

The minimum share capital of an A.E. is EUR 60,000 and must be paid within two months of the **47** establishment of the A.E. (i.e. within two months of the registration of the decision approving establishment with the competent Prefecture) (Sec 8 Subs. 2 and Sec. 11 Subs. 1 of C.L. 2190/1920). The minimum capital can be formed by contributions in cash or in kind in return for shares in the company.[29]

25 Under certain conditions a creditor can enforce the rights of his debtor as against third parties in case this latter fails to do so (Sec. 72 Greek Code of Civil Procedure).

26 Although (i) it has been accepted by the prevailing legal theory and jurisprudence that the discharge of the board from liability does not necessarily constitute a waiver of the company from any claims it may have against the individual members of the board and (ii) Subs. 1 of Sec. 35 of C.L. 2190/1920 provides that the discharge of the members of the board of directors is without prejudice to any liability of the members towards the company for any fault committed during the management of the company's affairs, there have been some cases, although few, where the courts have ruled that the discharge of the members of the board from any liability (by means of a resolution of the shareholders' meeting) abolishes in essence the right of the company to claim damages, unless Sec. 22 a of the C.L. 2190/1920 applies.

27 See Mn. 14.

28 See Mn. 15 et seq.

29 The conditions are the same as in an EPE. See Mn. 18.

2.9.3 Maintenance of Capital and Liquidity

48 As is the case with an EPE, the concept of the preservation and maintenance of the company's share capital is protected by various provisions of C. L. 2190/1920.

(i) System

49 The amount of the share capital is blocked by the company in the sense that shareholders do not have the right to take it back. In particular, except for certain cases of reduction in share capital, no distribution whatsoever can be made to the shareholders, in case that, on the closing date of the last financial year, the amount of the company's equity, as shown in the balance sheet, is or will be after such a distribution less than the company's share capital increased by those reserves not distributable pursuant to the articles of incorporation (Sec. 44 a Subs. 1 of C.L. 2190/1920).

50 The stability of the share capital is also guaranteed by the provisions of Sec. 10 of C.L. 2190/1920, according to which, within two years from the commencement of the company's operations, as well as within two years from any capital increase, the acquisition of any asset by a company against a consideration exceeding one-tenth of the paid-up share capital is prohibited and null and void, if the sellers are (in simplified terms) the founders of such company, shareholders holding more than one-twentieth of the company's paid-up share capital, members of its board of directors, certain relatives thereof or their husbands and wives; and/or the seller has acquired the asset to be transferred from any of the above persons/entities within 12 months following the execution of the articles of incorporation of the relevant company or completion of the increase in share capital.[30]

(ii) Distributions

51 The net profits of the company are derived from the actual gross profit after deduction of expenses, losses, depreciation and corporate liabilities (Sec. 45 Subs. 1 of C.L. 2190/1920). The net profits are distributed as follows: (a) at least one-twentieth of the net profits must be deducted every year in order to create the ordinary reserve;[31] (b) at least 6 per cent of the paid-up share capital must be distributed to the shareholders (first dividend); (c) any remaining profits are disposed of according to the company's articles of incorporation (Sec. 45 Subs. 2 of C.L. 2190/1920). The general meeting of shareholders may decide that profits distributable to the shareholders after the payment of the first dividend are allocated for the increase in share capital through the issue of new shares granted to the shareholders without payment, in lieu of an additional dividend (Sec. 45 Subs. 3 of C.L. 2190/1920).

The payment of interim dividends is permitted under certain conditions provided for in Sec. 46 of C.L. 2190/1920. In particular, the company's accounting report must have been published at least 20 days prior to such distribution in a daily newspaper and in the Official Gazette (Issue on *Societes Anonymes* and Limited Liability Companies). Such accounting report must also be submitted to the Ministry of Development or the competent Prefecture (depending on which authority exercises the state supervision). The distribution of the interim dividends may not exceed one-half of the net profits declared in the accounting report.

52 Any amount distributed to the shareholders in violation of the provisions of Sec. 44 a, 45 and 46 of the C.L. 2190/1920 shall be returned by those who have received it, if the company proves that the said shareholders were aware or (taking into account the circumstances) ought to have been aware that such distributions were not lawful (Sec. 46 a of C.L. 2190/1920).

30 Such invalidity does not apply if the relevant acquisition has been approved by the general meeting and the Ministry of Development. The approval of the Ministry of Development is granted after the asset to be acquired has been evaluated by a special independent administrative committee.

31 Such deduction ceases to be obligatory when the ordinary reserve reaches an amount at least equal to one-third of the share capital (Sec. 44 of C.L. 1290/1920).

(iii) Acquisition of Own Shares and Related Financing

An A.E. generally is prohibited from acquiring its own shares even if the said acquisition is not effected by the company itself but by a person acting in his own name but on behalf of the company (Sec. 16 Subs. 1 of C.L. 2190/1920). However, Greek law provides for some strict exceptions to the prohibition on the company acquiring its own shares.[32] 53

Companies whose shares are listed on the Athens Stock Exchange may proceed to the acquisition of up to 10 per cent of the total of their shares through the Athens Stock Exchange, in order to support their stock exchange price when it is deemed that such price is significantly lower than the price corresponding to the market data, the financial situation and prospectus of the company. Such acquisition is subject to the prior approval of the general meeting of the shareholders for a period up to 12 months from the date of the said approval (Sec. 16 Subs. 5 et seq. C.L. 2190/1920).

The company's own shares acquired by it are taken into account for the establishment of the quorum at the general meeting of shareholders, but the right to vote attaching to these shares is suspended (Sec. 16 Subs. 4 C.L. 2190/1920).

Pursuant to Sec. 23 a Subs. 1 b of C.L. 2190/1920, loans by the company to third parties, and credits granted to them in any manner whatsoever, as well as guarantees granted to third parties with the purpose of acquiring company shares are absolutely prohibited and are null and void.

(iv) Company as Lender or Guarantor

Pursuant to Sec. 23 a Subs. 1 a of C.L. 2190/1920, loans by the company to founders, members of the board of directors, general managers or managers of the company, relatives up to the third degree by blood or by marriage included, or to the husbands or wives thereof, as well as credits granted to them by any manner or guarantees granted in their favour to third parties, are totally prohibited and are null and void. 54

(v) Company as Borrower

As is the case with an EPE, it is common practice that the company obtains the required funds by means of borrowing from its shareholders. However, it is accepted in legal theory that, in the event that the company is not reliable, the loans from shareholders to the company should be deemed not as third party funds but as company's own funds, which guarantee the payment of its liabilities towards its creditors. As a result, the claims of the shareholders in relation to the payment of their loans prior to the satisfaction of the claims of the third party creditors will be considered as abusive (Sec. 281 Greek Civil Code) and will be considered to rank last in any insolvency proceedings only if the shareholder exercises a dominant influence on the company's administration or operations, even if he holds less than the 20 per cent of the share capital or the voting rights.[33] 55

2.10 Publication and Filing Requirements

A wide range of the company's acts and particulars are submitted to the competent supervising authority[34] and published in the Official Gazette pursuant to Sec. 7 a Subs. 1 of C.L. 2190/1920.[35] 56

32 (i) acquisitions in view of a reduction of share capital, decided by the general meeting of shareholders in accordance with the company's articles of association, (ii) acquisitions as a result of a universal transfer of assets, (iii) acquisitions of fully paid shares, which derive from enforcement proceedings effected for the payment of the company's claims, (iv) acquisitions of own shares by the banking companies by order of a third party, (v) fully paid-up shares acquired free of charge, as donations, (vi) acquisitions for distribution to the company's employees or to the employees of an affiliated company.

33 Gologina-Oikonomou in: The accountability of the loans by the shareholders, EED D/2002, p. 940 et seq.

34 See Mn. 10.

35 The following acts and particulars are subject to publication: (a) the decisions of the supervising authority relating to the company's establishment as well as the approved articles of incorporation; (b) the decisions of the supervising authority relating to the approval of the amendment or codification of the company's articles of association as well as the amended articles of association; (c) the appointment or the cessation for any reason of the persons who: (i) exercise the company's management; (ii) represent the company jointly or severally; or (iii) carry out regular audits;

The filing with the Prefecture of the company's acts and particulars and the publication of the same in the Official Gazette is full evidence of such information and provides a degree of transparency in relation to the legal nature, the financial strength and the authorisations of the members of the board of directors.

The commercial registers are not organised on a central basis, since each Prefecture keeps its own Commercial Registry, which may not be accessed online.

Any director, or any member of the board of directors, representative, agent or liquidator of the company that fails to submit promptly to the competent Prefecture the documents required by law, or the articles of association, or has not provided information or has provided false information to the supervising authority in relation to the exercise of the said supervision, is punished by a penalty of not less than EUR 1,000 (Sec. 61 C. L. 2190/1920).

Any person who violates the provisions regarding the publication duties in the Official Gazette as set out by law, is punished by an imprisonment sentence of a maximum duration of three months, as well as by a penalty of not less than EUR 1,000 (Sec. 62 a C. L. 2190/1920).

57 Provided that third parties justify their legitimate interest, they may review – upon application to the Secretariat – the filed documents and may request a copy of the corporate information filed with the Registry. However, the competent supervising authority may deny such request.

2.11 Financial Reporting

58 An A.E. must draw up its annual financial statements (i.e. the balance sheet, the profit and loss account, the distribution results table, the appendix) within four months of the expiry of the corresponding fiscal year (Sec. 17 Subs. 8 Code of Books and Particulars). The company's annual financial statements must be audited by independent auditors and be approved by the annual general meeting of shareholders convened therefore within six months of the expiry of the fiscal year.[36] The listed A.E.s must also draw up three-month interim and six-month interim accounting statements. The annual financial statements must be drawn up in accordance with the national general accounting rules. Regarding the non-listing A.E and the non-affiliated companies, the drawing up of the financial statements in accordance with the EU's international accounting standards is permitted provided that the general meeting of shareholders has approved the application of such standards for at least five successive fiscal years (Sec. 134 Subs. 2 C. L. 2190/192). The drawing up of the financial statements in accordance with US GAAP is not permitted.

2.12 Employee Participation in Corporate Bodies

59 The same provisions apply as with regard to the EPE.[37]

(d) the decision regarding the revocation of the decision of the Prefecture approving the company's establishment; (e) any decision for the increase or reduction in the company's share capital; (f) the minutes of the board of directors by means of which the payment of the share capital is certified, either at the time of the company's establishment or following an increase thereof; (g) the annual financial statements along with the relevant reports of the Board of Directors and the auditors; (H) the winding-up of the company, the court decision declaring the company invalid as well as the court decisions declaring the resolutions of the general meetings as void; (i) the appointment and replacement of the liquidators, the balance sheets of the liquidators as well as the final balance sheet thereof; and (j) any other acts or particulars, the publication of which is required by other provisions.

36 The fiscal year may be the calendar year or any other 12-month period chosen.

37 See Mn. 29.

XI. Hungary

*by Dr. Csaba Berecz (LL.M.) and Dr. Eszter Fedák**

1 The Limited Liability Company ("Kft.")

Literature: Dr. Judit Gál – Dr. Ursula Vezekényi, Cégjogi tanácsadó (HVG-ORAC Lap-és Könyvkiadó Kft., Budapest 2001); Tamás Sárközy, A magyar társasági jog Európában (HVG-ORAC Lap–és Könyvkiadó Kft., Budapest 2001)

The limited liability company (*korlátolt felelősségű társaság*, "Kft."), the most common corporate form of limited liability company used in Hungary, is established with initial capital comprising predetermined primary shares (i.e. business quotas) of the members (i.e. shareholders). 1

The main legal rules regulating the establishment, registration and operation of Kft.s are set out in the Companies Act[1] ("Gt.") and the Company Registration Act[2] ("Ctv."). The rules provided under Gt. and Ctv. with regard to the Kft. are mandatory, save when Gt. explicitly allows the parties to depart from certain provisions (Sec. 9 Subs. 1 Gt.).

In June 2005 there were approximately 217,000 Kft.s registered in Hungary, in contrast to approximately 4,300 Gt.s.

1.1 Export of Company

From 1 May 2004, the relevant decisions of the ECJ are applicable in Hungary. Therefore, the export of companies into Hungary is possible under the same conditions as in the EU Member States. On the other hand, Hungarian company law is based on the real seat concept,[3] thus the relocation of Hungarian companies to a foreign country results in the loss of their status as a legal entity.[4] 2

1.2 Transformation into a Foreign Entity

The transformation provisions in Gt. prevent Hungarian companies from transforming into any other company form except for the ones provided under Gt. Therefore, the transformation of a Kft. into a foreign entity is not allowed under Hungarian law.[5] 3

1.3 Incorporation

A Kft. is set up by way of articles of association[6] executed by all founding members in the form of a notarial deed or a deed countersigned by an attorney (Sec. 10 Gt.).[7] The company will legally exist upon its entry into the company register held by the County Court/Metropolitan Court acting 4

* *Berecz & Andrékó Linklaters,* Budapest. This chapter has been written with the assistance of Dr. András Lendvai, Dr. Rita Szudoczky and Dr. Ákos Nagy.

1 Act CXLIV of 1997 on Business Associations. It is important to note that preparations for a new Companies Act are underway and the new Companies Act is expected to be announced during the second half of 2006.

2 Act CXLV of 1997 on the Register of Companies, Public Company Information and Court Registration Proceedings. It should be noted that the Company Registration Act is expected to be amended in light of the new Companies Act.

3 Interestingly, the Hungarian Private International Code (Decree 13 of 1979 on Private International Law) sets out the incorporation concept as a basic rule for the determination of the applicable law to legal entities.

4 From 8 October 2004, the rules on European companies (S.E.), namely Council Regulation 2157/2001, entered into force in Hungary. Thus, by means of the transformation of Kft.s and Rt.s into S.E.s, the relocation of Hungarian companies with limited liability will be possible in an indirect way.

5 The indirect transformation into an S.E. is possible from 8 October 2004 as set out in Fn. 4 above.

6 In the case of a Kft. owned by a sole member, the term "deed of foundation" is used for the founding document of the Kft. (Sec. 171 Subs. 2 Gt.). In the following, articles of association will also stand for deed of foundation save where required otherwise by the context.

7 The articles of association may be executed by the representative of the founders based on a power of attorney, which must be in the form of a notarial deed or private deed with full evidencing power (Sec. 10. Subs. 2 Gt.). The

as the Court of Registration (*Cégbíróság*) in the territory where the company's corporate seat is located (Sec. 16 Subs. 2 Gt.).[8]

5 The statutory deadline for the registration procedure is 30 working days[9] from the date of submission of the application[10] (Sec. 44 Subs. 3 Ctv.). The administrative fees for the registration of a Kft. are HUF 100,000 (approximately EUR 400) for stamp duty and a HUF 25,000 (approximately EUR 100) publication fee.[11]

1.4 Recurrent Costs and Efforts

6 Recurrent costs and efforts in connection with a Kft. relate to the publication of annual accounts and their filing in the commercial register;[12] other costs may be incurred in the event certain corporate steps are taken which require notarisation, filing in the commercial register or publication.[13] There is no annual registration fee for the company register, however, for the registration of a Kft. as well as any change in the company data a pre-determined fee must be paid.[14] If the amount of the registered capital exceeds HUF 50,000,000 (approximately EUR 201,000) or the number of full time employees exceeds 200 on an annual average, the election of a supervisory board, auditor and representatives of the employees for the supervisory board will be mandatory resulting in significantly higher operational costs.

1.5 Shares and Share Transfers

7 Business quotas in a Kft. are transferred by way of a business quota transfer agreement to which the provisions of civil law apply. Share certificates on business quotas are not recognised by Gt. There are statutory pre-emption rights established by Gt.[15] and the members are also entitled to set out restrictions on the transfer of business quotas in the articles of association.[16] Once a business

articles of association must be in the form of a notarial deed or countersigned by an attorney or the in-house legal counsel of the member (Sec. 10 Subs. 3 Gt.).

8 During the period between the filing of the application for registration with the Court of Registration and the registration itself, a Kft. may perform business activities in a "pre-company" form. However, no activity the pursuance of which is subject to a licence to be issued by a public authority can be pursued by a pre-company until the actual registration of the Kft. Moreover, during this period certain strategic decisions must not be made: the articles of association may not be amended, no change in the members of the Kft. can take place, the Kft. may not be transformed or terminated without legal successor and no legal action may be taken in order to exclude a member from the Kft. (Sec. 14 Subs. 1, 3 and Sec.15 Subs. 1Gt.).

9 If the Court of Registration fails to meet this deadline, the head of the Court of Registration shall arrange for the registration within eight days of the expiry of the deadline. If the head of the Court of Registration fails to comply with the above obligation, the registration shall be deemed to be made by law on the ninth day following the expiry of the 30-day deadline referred to above (Sec. 42 Subs. 2, 3 Ctv.). The deadline for registering any changes to the registered corporate data of a Kft. is 45 working days from the date of filing the relevant application and the same rules apply to this deadline as in the case of the initial registration procedure (Sec. 44 Subs. 3 Ctv.). Legal representation is mandatory in registration proceedings at the Court of Registration (Sec. 21 Subs. 2 Ctv.)

10 The deadline for registration may be extended if the Court of Registration orders the submission of supplemental documents for the registration process (Sec. 41 Ctv.).

11 Sec. 45 Subs. 1 (b) of Act XCIII of 1990 on duties and Sec. 3 Subs. 1 (b) of Decree No. 9/1998 (V.23.).

12 An amount of HUF 10,000 (approximately EUR 40) is payable for the publication of the annual report of a Kft.

13 The publication fee payable in relation to the changes to a Kft.'s registered corporate data is HUF 15,000 (approximately EUR 60). A decreased amount of publication fee is payable in the case of the submission of the application and the underlying documents by electronic way (Sec. 3 Subs. 2 and Sec. 3/A of Decree No. 9/1998 (V.23.)).

14 Stamp duty payable for the registration of any changes (save for the change to the amount of the registered capital) in the corporate records is HUF 5,000 or HUF 8,000 (approximately EUR 20 or 32) depending on the number of changes. An amount equal to 40 per cent. of the amount of stamp duty payable for the initial registration must be paid as stamp duty for the registration of any change to the amount of the registered capital (Sec. 45 Subs. 3-5 of Act XCIII of 1990 on duties).

15 The other members of the Kft., the Kft. or a person appointed by the members' meeting of the Kft., in this order, have a statutory pre-emption right over business quotas intended to be transferred by means of a contract of sale to a person who is not a member of the Kft. (Sec.134 Subs. 2 Gt.).

16 In general, business quotas may be freely transferred amongst the members of the Kft., however, the members may grant a pre-emption right to each other in the articles of association (Sec.134 Subs. 1 Gt.). Moreover, a transfer of

quota transfer has been effected, the managing director of the Kft. shall be informed of the event by way of a notification by the acquirer to which strict formality requirements[17] apply (Sec. 138 Subs. 3 Gt.). The managing director shall then file the amended members' list with the Court of Registration (Sec. 157 Subs. 3, 4 Gt.).[18] A business quota, if so provided for in the articles of association, can have different rights attached to it (Sec. 133 Subs. 1 Gt.).

As there is no share certificate issued for business quotas in a Kft., a public offering of the business quotas in a Kft. is not possible and the collection of members from the public is expressly prohibited (Sec. 122 Gt.). There is no tax levied upon the transfer of business quota, only a negligible amount of fee payable for the registration of the change of the members in the company register.[19] **8**

1.6 Corporate Bodies

Gt. provides for two compulsory corporate bodies: the managing director (*ügyvezető*) and the members' meeting (*taggyűlés*). If the registered capital exceeds HUF 50,000,000 (approximately EUR 210,000), or the Kft. has an annual average of more than 200 employees, a supervisory board must also be established (Sec 31 Subs. 2 (b), (c) Gt.).[20] **9**

1.6.1 Managing Directors

The Kft. may have one or several managing directors (Sec. 156 Subs. 1 Gt.).[21] The appointment of the managing directors is the responsibility of the members' meeting (Sec. 150 Subs. 2 (g) Gt.). The managing directors have general authorisation to represent the company *vis-à-vis* third parties (Sec. 39 Subs. 1 Gt.). They can be awarded joint power to sign on behalf of the Kft. (whereby a managing director may sign on behalf of the Kft. only together with another managing director or an authorised employee) or sole power to sign on behalf of the Kft. (whereby a managing director may sign on behalf of the company alone) (Sec. 17 Subs. 2 Ctv.). **10**

The managing director may not be given instructions by the members of the Kft. or by his employer regarding the duties pertaining to his office (Sec. 22 Subs. 2 Gt.). The members' meeting may withdraw the managerial competence of the managing director only if so allowed by the articles of association (Sec. 22 Subs. 4 Gt.). This restriction is not applicable to a one-member Kft. or to a Kft. where one of the members has a holding of greater than 75 per cent. Furthermore, in the case of a one-member Kft., the member may instruct the managing director in writing (Sec. 22 Subs. 5, 6 Gt.). **11**

business quotas to a third party may be made subject to the consent of the company and the articles of association may rule out the business quota transfer by a way other than a business quota sale and purchase agreement (Sec. 137 Gt.).

17 The notification on the acquisition of the business quotas addressed to the managing director shall be in the form of a notarial deed or private deed with full evidencing power. The acquirer shall also state in the notification that it is aware of the provisions of the articles of association of the Kft. and recognizes them as binding on itself (Sec. 138 Subs. 3 Gt.).

18 Changes to the members of a Kft. must also be registered in the Kft's company register held by the competent Court of Registration.

19 See Fn. 13.

20 A Kft. may choose an auditor to review the books of the company. The election of an auditor is mandatory if the Kft. is a one-member company or the registered capital of the Kft. exceeds HUF 50,000,000 (approximately EUR 201,000) (Sec. 41 Subs. 1, 2 Gt.).

21 Managing directors may be private individuals elected from amongst the members or third parties (Sec. 22 Subs. 3 and Sec. 156 Subs. 1 Gt.).

1.6.2 Members' Meeting

12 The supreme corporate body of the Kft. is the members' meeting which has to be convened at least once a year (Sec. 150 Subs. 1 Gt.). The most important strategic decisions fall within the exclusive powers of the members' meeting (Sec. 150 Subs. 2 Gt.).[22]

13 As a general rule, the resolutions of the members' meeting are passed by a simple majority of votes (Sec. 19 Subs. 1 Gt.), but higher thresholds (usually 75 per cent) specified by law and the articles of association apply in certain cases.[23]

1.6.3 Supervisory Board

14 The supervisory board which consists of at least three or a maximum of 15 members, is not involved in the management of the company; it has solely a controlling and monitoring role. However, the articles of association may empower the supervisory board to exercise certain managerial rights (the appointment, removal and decision on the remuneration of managing directors, the approval of transactions)[24] (Sec. 33 Subs. 1 Gt.). The appointment of the members of the supervisory board is the responsibility of the members' meeting (Sec. 150 Subs. 2 (h) Gt.).

1.7 Duties and Liabilities of Directors

15 Managing directors represent, and sign on behalf of, the Kft., *vis-à-vis* third parties, exercise the employer's rights in respect of the Kft.'s employees, convene the members' meeting, maintain the members' list of the company and report the required data and information to the Court of Registration etc. (Sec. 26 Subs. 1, Sec. 28 Subs.1, Sec. 152 Subs. 1 and Sec. 157 Subs. 1. Gt.).

16 Managing directors must fulfil their managerial duties in the best interests of the company with the increased degree of care expected of someone occupying such a position (Sec. 29 Subs. 1 Gt.).

Gt. governs general rules of liability of managing directors with regard to breaches of the provisions relating to the maintenance and preservation of registered capital. D&O insurances are not expressly regulated under Hungarian law and thus have to be considered as allowed.

17 The managing directors are liable to the company according to the rules of Hungarian civil law for the damages which they cause to the company by their culpable breach of the law, the articles of association, the resolutions made by the members' meeting of the company or their managerial duties (Sec. 29 Subs. 1 Gt.).[25]

22 In the case of a one-member Kft., no members' meeting operates. The sole member is entitled to decide on all matters falling within the scope of competence of the members' meeting by law. The sole member must inform the managing director of the Kft. in writing of all such decisions (Sec. 172 Subs. 1 Gt.).

23 E.g. amendment of the articles of association, decision on the dissolution of the Kft., etc (Secs. 159 and 168 Gt.).

24 The supervisory board shall report at the next meeting of the members' meeting on the measures it has taken within the transferred power. If, within the transferred power, the supervisory board has refused to approve a legal transaction, the executive officers of the company are entitled to convene the members' meeting. In such cases, the supreme body of the company may approve the legal transaction by a majority of three quarters or more of the votes. (Sec. 33 Subs. 2, 3 Gt.).

25 According to Sec. 339 Subs. 1, 2 of Act No. IV of 1959 on the Hungarian Civil Code ("Civil Code"), the person causing damage (i.e. the managing director) to another person (i.e. the Kft.) is liable for such damage and must indemnify the person incurring the damage. The person causing the damage can only be relieved from liability if he is able to prove that he acted in a manner that can generally be expected in the actual situation. The Civil Code also provides that the court shall, under special and equitable circumstances, be entitled to grant partial exemption from liability to a person liable for damages.

Indemnification shall be due immediately upon the occurrence of the damage.[26] According to the general rules, compensation can be claimed within five years from the date the claim becomes due.[27]

Managing directors having joint signing authority on behalf of a Kft. are jointly and severally liable for any culpable breach of the law, the articles of association, the resolutions made by the members' meeting of the company or their managerial duties (Sec. 29 Subs. 2 Gt.).[28]

Managing directors are liable *vis-à-vis* the company and the company will be held liable for losses which were caused to third parties by a managing director (Sec. 29 Gt.). The managing director is not liable to apply for insolvency proceedings; however, the managing director must convene the members' meeting when the company ceases to pay its debts (Sec. 152 Subs. 2 Gt.).

A person with a criminal conviction cannot act as a managing director, unless exempted of the detrimental effects of the conviction. Nor can a person who has been prohibited from carrying out a profession by a court order act as a managing director at a company pursuing the business activity to which the prohibition relates. Also, a person who has been an executive officer for at least one year during the two years prior to the initial date of liquidation of a company terminated during liquidation proceedings, may not be a managing director in another company for three years following the initial date of liquidation of the company, provided that he had not been elected managing director to avoid liquidation. Following the ex-officio removal of a company from the company register pursuant to the decision of the Court of Registration, a person who was a managing director of that company for one year before the removal cannot be the managing director of another company for two years (Sec. 23 Gt.).[29] In the case of one-member Kft.s, any person holding an executive position (or supervisory board membership) in the sole member of the Kft. may not be elected as a managing director (or supervisory board member) of the Kft. (Sec. 172 Subs. 3 Gt.). **18**

In the case of a one-member Kft. the member is entitled to withdraw the competence of the (non-member) managing director and give instructions to him. The withdrawal exempts the (non-member) managing director of its liability (Sec. 22 Subs. 5 Gt.). **19**

1.8 Shareholders' Liability

The liability of the members of a Kft. to the Kft. is limited only to providing the capital contributions undertaken in the articles of association. As a general rule, the members are not liable for the obligations of the Kft. (Sec. 121 Subs. 1 Gt.). Notwithstanding the foregoing however, Hungarian law provides for the piercing of the corporate veil under certain conditions and thus, members of a Kft. may bear full and unlimited liability for the obligations of the Kft. in special circumstances as set out by the relevant legal provisions. (Sec. 296 Gt.). **20**

Those special conditions and circumstances include, *inter alia*, the following: **21**

(i) if a member holds more than 50 per cent of the votes in a Kft. and, due to his influence, the company pursues a constant detrimental business policy and as a result, in the event of

26 Sec. 360 Subs. 1 of the Civil Code. The person responsible for the damages must indemnify the injured party for pecuniary and non-pecuniary damages. On the grounds of indemnification, compensation must be provided for: (i) any depreciation in value of the property of the person incurring the damage, (ii) any pecuniary advantage lost due to the damage, (iii) any non-pecuniary damage, as well as (iv) the indemnity or costs necessary for the reduction or elimination of the pecuniary and non-pecuniary losses sustained by the injured person (Sec. 355 Subs. 1 and Subs.4 of the Civil Code).

27 Sec. 324 Subs. 1 and Sec. 326 Subs. 1 of the Civil Code. However, in respect of damages caused by a criminal offence, the period of limitation for a claim shall not expire as long as the criminal offence remains punishable under the Statute of Limitations (Sec. 360 Subs. 4 of the Civil Code).

28 Joint and several liability means that the injured party can claim its entire damages from any managing director. If any of the managing directors pays the whole amount to the injured party, the damages cannot be claimed from the other managing directors by the injured person, but the managing director who paid such amount can claim the payment of a proportional share of the damages from the other managing directors.

29 Additional restrictions also apply to managing directors as set out in Gt. (e.g. restrictions on acquisition of interest in other companies, etc.)

liquidation, the Kft. is not able to fulfil its obligations towards its creditors, a creditor may claim for piercing of the corporate veil in the liquidation proceeding (Sec. 296 Subs. 1 Gt.);

(ii) if a member holds more than 75 per cent of the votes in a Kft. and, due to his influence, the Kft. pursues a constant detrimental business policy which significantly jeopardises the fulfilment of the Kft.'s obligations, a member or a creditor may claim for piercing of the corporate veil (Sec. 296 Subs. 3 Gt.);

(iii) members of a Kft. who have passed a resolution in respect of which they knew, or should have known given reasonable care, that such resolution was obviously contrary to the significant interests of the company, shall bear unlimited, joint and several liability for all resulting damages (Sec. 19 Subs. 2 Gt.);

(iv) members who have abused the limited liability provision to the detriment of the creditors may not make reference to such limited liability in the event of the termination of a Kft and shall bear full and unlimited liability for any unpaid obligations of the terminated Kft. (Sec. 56 Subs. 3 Gt.).[30]

1.9 Capitalisation and Financing

1.9.1 Basic Concepts

22 Gt. provides security for the creditors of a Kft. in the form of "minimum share capital".[31] The registered capital has to be available to the Kft. and under no circumstances can it be paid back to the members.

1.9.2 Minimum Share Capital

23 The minimum share (registered) capital of a Kft. is HUF 3,000,000 (approximately EUR 12,100) (Sec. 124 Subs. 4 Gt.). The Kft. may only be registered if all contributions in kind were made available to the company and at least one-half of each contribution in cash and in total at least HUF 1,000,000 (approximately EUR 4,030) has been paid up altogether (Sec. 126 Subs. 1 Gt.). Where all cash contributions have not been paid up until registration, the manner and time of payment of the remaining cash contribution must be provided for in the articles of association. All cash contribution must be paid up within one year following registration (Sec. 127 Gt.).[32] In the case of a one-member Kft., all contributions in kind must be provided and all cash contributions must be paid up in full prior to the submission of the application for registration (Sec. 171 Subs. 3 Gt.).

1.9.3 Maintenance of Capital and Liquidity

(i) System

24 The basic rule is that if a Kft. does not have equity which is at least equal to the minimum amount of registered capital set by Gt. for two consecutive financial years,[33] it has to transform to another form of company (Sec. 61 Subs.1, 2 Gt.). If the equity in the company decreases to one-half of the registered capital set out in the articles of association or below the minimum registered capital set out in Gt. for a Kft.,[34] the members' meeting must be convened without delay in order to provide for the necessary measures (Sec. 152 Subs. 2 Gt.).[35]

30 The liability of the member is unlimited, in particular if such member disposed of the assets of the company as if they had been his own, or if the member reduced the assets of the company for the benefit of others or himself in a way in which the member knew or should have known with due care that the company would not be able to satisfy its obligations towards third parties as a result thereof (Sec. 56 Subs. 4 Gt.).

31 The provisions of Gt. are based on the continental concept of providing security for the creditors as opposed to the common law approach where this is to be achieved by way of extensive disclosure obligations.

32 See also Mn. 25.

33 And the members of the company do not provide the required amount within three months after the acceptance of the annual report prepared for the second financial year.

34 The decrease must be evident from the balance sheet and the books of the company.

35 This is also the case where the company has stopped payments and its assets do not cover its debts.

25 The capital can be rendered in cash or in kind (Sec. 12 Subs. 1 Gt.).[36] At foundation, the cash contribution must not be less than 30 per cent. of the registered capital and HUF 1,000,000 (approximately EUR 4,030) (Sec. 124 Subs. 5 Gt.). Members who have knowingly approved the contribution in kind of any member at a value exceeding its actual value, or who otherwise acted fraudulently during the foundation bear unlimited, joint and several liability for all resulting damages (Sec. 128 Gt.).

26 The members may not reclaim from the Kft. the contributions they provided and they are entitled only to dividends in proportion to the contributions already provided (Sec. 141 Subs. 1 Gt.).

27 Save for the reduction in the registered capital and remuneration for ancillary services, no payments from the registered capital may be made to the members. Payments that have been made contrary to this prohibition must be repaid to the company (except for dividends received by the members in good faith) (Sec. 142 Subs. 1, 2).

(ii) Distributions

28 Dividends may be paid on the basis of a members' resolution.[37] No dividends may be paid to members if, as a result of such payment, the equity of the Kft. does not at least equal its registered capital (Sec. 141 Subs. 3 Gt.). Unless otherwise provided by the articles of association, dividends shall be distributed to the members in proportion to their capital contributions (Sec. 141 Subs. 2 Gt.). The members are not obliged to repay dividends received in good faith (Sec. 141 Subs. 5 Gt.).[38]

(iii) Acquisition of Own Shares and Related Financing

29 Based on a resolution of the members' meeting,[39] the Kft. may acquire a maximum of one third of its business quotas from its assets in excess of its registered capital provided that the business quota to be acquired by the Kft. has been fully paid up. The Kft. cannot exercise voting rights based on the business quota acquired. Within the period of one year following the purchase, the Kft. must dispose over the own business quota or must convey them to the members,[40] without compensation, or must withdraw such business quota[41] (Sec. 143 Subs. 1, 2 and 3 Gt.). There are no specific rules governing the provision of financial assistance by a Kft. in the acquisition of its own business quota.

30 A one-member Kft. may not acquire its own business quota (Sec. 173 Subs. 1 Gt.).

(iv) Company as Lender or Guarantor

31 A Kft. may give loans or grant guarantees to third parties. If these are given to members of the Kft., the company must ensure that no payment is made to the members from the registered capital and that the approval of this transaction falls within the exclusive authority of the members' meeting (Sec. 150 Subs. 2 (j) Gt.).

(v) Company as Borrower

32 There are no restrictions on the granting of loans by members to the Kft. but the members are not obliged to ensure sufficient funding of the company. The members' meeting may decide

36 Contributions in kind constituting a part of the registered capital may be any marketable object or intellectual work of monetary value, or any right representing monetary value. Contribution in kind can only be objects, intellectual property or rights capable of being subject to execution, which can be transferred by the company without the consent of a third party (Sec.124 Subs. 3. Gt.)

37 Prior to the approval of the annual report, interim dividends may be paid if, on the basis of the interim balance sheet, it is likely that the conditions for paying dividends at the end of the financial year will be satisfied (Sec. 141 Subs. 4 Gt.).

38 This provision does not apply to interim dividends received during the financial year (Sec. 141 Subs. 5 Gt.)

39 Passed by a majority of three-quarters or more of the votes.

40 In proportion to their capital contributions.

41 Pursuant to the rules of share capital reduction.

on additional payments to be made by the members in order to cover losses only if there is an authorisation to this effect in the articles of association (Sec. 132 Subs. 1 Gt.).[42]

In the event of liquidation shareholder loans rank pari passu with non-shareholder claims.

1.10 Publication and Filing Requirements

33 When establishing a Kft., several documents and certain information must be provided to the Court of Registration at which the statutory company register is held.[43] The company register and the documents filed with the Court of Registration are publicly available and anyone can review these or request a copy of them[44] (Sec. 3 Subs. 1-4. Ctv.).[45]

34 Third parties can rely on the content of the company register. The company may only rely on data or documents registered in the company register if that data was published in the Company Gazette, except if the company proves that the data or document have already been made known to third parties.[46] Until the contrary is proved, the good faith of the person acquiring any right for compensation by relying on the data registered in the company register or published in the Company Gazette, must be presumed. The company cannot rely on any company data against any third party acting in good faith which is notified to the Court of Registration and registered in the company register to be untrue. If the data filed with the register and published in the Company Gazette are different, any third party can rely on the data which was published in the Company Gazette unless the company proves that the correct data registered in the company register was made known to the third party (Sec. 10 Ctv.).[47]

35 If documents necessary for registration have not been filed with the Court of Registration along with the application for registration or the stamp duty was not paid or paid only in part, the application for the registration of the company can be rejected within eight days following the date of submission. Within eight days following the receipt of the order of rejection, the documents can be submitted again for registration (Sec. 26 Ctv.). Each Kft. is registered at the competent county court acting as Court of Registration in the territory where the company has its registered seat (i.e. in the case of companies with their registered seat in Budapest, by the Metropolitan Court acting as Court of Registration). The company register, including information on all companies, can also be accessed online.[48]

In the case of a foreign corporate member, its original company extract together with the official Hungarian translation thereof must also be filed along with the application for registration.

If the company fails to apply for its registration within 30 days from the date of signing the articles of association or fails to report any change in the data registered in the company register within the same deadline from the date of the change,[49] the person responsible for making the court filing (i.e. in the case of a Kft., the managing director) may be subject to a penalty amounting to between HUF 50,000 and HUF 500,000 (approximately EUR 200 to EUR 2,000) (Sec. 22 Subs. 2 Ctv.).

42 The detailed rules on additional payments can be found in Sec. 132 Subs. 1, 2, 3 and 4 Gt.

43 Following the registration of the company in the company register, the Court of Registration shall arrange for the registered corporate data of the company to be published in the Company Gazette (Sec. 7 Subs. 1 Ctv.).

44 Save for certain exceptions, e.g. no copies may be requested of the specimen signatures of the managing directors.

45 In respect of the disclosure obligations regarding the annual accounts, please see Mn. 38.

46 Until the 16th day following the publication however, any third party may prove that he did not have the possibility to inform about the data or documents (Sec. 10 Subs. 1 Ctv.).

47 Third parties can rely on documents and data in relation to which the company failed to fulfil its notification and publishing obligations, unless the document has no legal effect without its publication (Sec. 10 Subs. 4 Ctv.).

48 www.microsec.hu. However, access to this website is subject to subscription.

49 Except for a change to the amount of the registered capital, where the deadline for the submission of the application for registration is 60 days from the date of the relevant decision (Sec. 29 Subs. 4 Ctv.).

1.11 Financial Reporting

The annual report of a Kft. must be drawn up in accordance with the Accounting Act[50] ("Számv."). The annual report comprises the balance sheet, the profit and loss account and the notes on the accounts. A business report shall also be prepared concurrently with the annual report (Sec. 19 Subs. 1 Számv.). Certain relief from financial reporting requirements is granted to companies which do not exceed two out of the three following criteria during two continuous financial years: (i) a balance sheet total of HUF 500,000,000 (approximately EUR 2,010,000); (ii) an annual net turnover of HUF 1,000,000,000 (approximately EUR 4,020,000); (iii) a workforce of 50 employees per annum on average (Sec. 9 Subs. 2 Számv.). Companies meeting the above requirements are – amongst other things – released from the requirement to draw up a management report on the economic situation of the company (business report) and may draw up less detailed annual accounts (simplified annual accounts) (Secs. 96-98 Számv.). 36

The approval of the annual report falls within the exclusive authority of the members' meeting (Sec. 150 Subs. 2 (a) Gt.). If an auditor is elected, [51] he must examine the authenticity and legal compliance of the annual report. Without a statement of opinion by the auditor, the members' meeting may not decide on the annual report (Sec. 42 Subs. 1 Gt.). 37

A Kft. must deposit with the Court of Registration the annual report approved by the members' meeting and, in the case of a compulsory audit, also containing the auditor's statement of approval or the auditor's refusal to grant such approval, as well as the resolution on the appropriation of the after-tax profit within 150 days of the balance sheet date of the subject year. A parent company must deposit with the Court of Registration its consolidated annual report within 180 days of the balance sheet date of the consolidated annual report (Sec. 153 Számv.).[52] 38

A Kft. is not permitted to draw up its accounts in accordance with US GAAP or IAS/IFRS. However, from 1 January 2005, in accordance with the requirements of Regulation (EC) No. 1606/2002 on the application of international accounting standards, parent companies must prepare their consolidated annual report in accordance with the IAS/IFRS.[53] A Kft. not falling under the scope of this Regulation may prepare its group annual accounts in accordance with IAS/IFRS (Sec. 10 Subs. 2-3 Számv.). 39

1.12 Employee Participation in Corporate Bodies

Kft.s which have an annual average of more than 200 employees shall allow employees to take part in the supervisory board of the Kft.[54] In such cases, one third of the supervisory board shall comprise employees' representatives [55] (Sec. 36 Subs. 1 Gt.). 40

50 Act C of 2000 on Accounting.

51 As to the requirements set out in the Companies Act relating to the election of an auditor at Kft.s, please see Fn. 20. An audit of the annual accounts of Kft.s is also mandatory under the Számv., save for Kft.s where the election of an auditor is not required by law and the average annual net turnover does not exceed HUF 50,000,000 (approximately EUR 201,000) in the previous two financial years (Sec. 155 Subs. 2, 3, 5 Számv.).

52 Simultaneously with the deposit, the annual report approved by the members' meeting and, in the case of a compulsory audit, also containing the auditor's statement of approval or the auditor's refusal to grant such approval must also be sent to the relevant office of the Ministry of Justice for disclosure purposes (Sec. 154 Subs. 1, 7 Gt.)

53 With regard to any matter not governed under the promulgated international accounting standards, the provisions of Számv. must be applied in harmony with the promulgated international accounting standards.

54 Following a statement of opinion of the trade unions operating at the company, the employees' representatives on the supervisory board shall be nominated by the works council from among the employees. Persons nominated by the works council shall be elected as members of the supervisory board by the company's supreme body at its first meeting following such nomination, unless statutory grounds for disqualification exist in respect of the nominees. In this case, a new nomination shall be requested. On the supervisory board, employees' representatives shall have the same rights and obligations as all other members. If the opinion of the employees' representatives differs unanimously from the majority standpoint of the supervisory board, the minority standpoint of the employees' representatives shall be stated at the meeting of the company's supreme body (Sec. 37 Gt.).

55 In the event of an uneven number, such one third shall be calculated in such a way to be more favourable for the employees (Sec. 36 Subs. 1 Gt.).

2 The Stock Corporation ("Rt.")

Literature: A részvénytársaság, edited by Tamás Sárközy (HVG-ORAC Lap-és Könyvkiadó Kft., Budapest 1998); A társasági és a cégtörvény kommentárja, edited by Tamás Sárközy (HVG-ORAC Lap-és Könykiadó Kft., Budapest 2004); Business law in Hungary, edited by László Kecskés (Közgazdasági és jogi könyvkiadó, Budapest 1998)

41 A stock corporation (*részvénytársaság*, "Rt.") is a business organisation founded with a share capital (subscribed capital) consisting of shares of a pre-determined number and face value (Sec. 175 Subs. 1 Gt.). Only Rt.s may issue securities representing the shareholders' rights (Sec. 2 Subs. 4 Gt.).

The main legal rules regulating the establishment, registration and operation of Rt.s are set out in the Gt. and the Ctv. The rules provided under Gt. and Ctv. with regard to the Rt. are mandatory, save when Gt. explicitly allows the parties to depart from certain provisions (Sec. 9 Subs. 1 Gt.).

2.1 Export of Company

42 The same provisions of Hungarian law are applicable to Rt.s as to Kft.s.[56]

2.2 Transformation into a Foreign Entity

43 Any transformation may be carried out in the same manner as provided for Kft.s.[57]

2.3 Incorporation

44 An Rt. may operate as a private or public Rt.[58] The foundation of an Rt. may take place by means of private or public foundation (Sec. 177 Gt.).

45 When establishing a private Rt., the founders undertake to subscribe for all the shares of the Rt. A private Rt. is established by a deed of foundation signed by all the founding shareholders (Sec. 10 Subs. 1, 2 Gt.).[59] A public Rt. is established by way of subscription of its shares in a public foundation procedure. The statutes of a public Rt. is approved by its founding general meeting (Sec. 10 Subs. 1, 2, Sec. 212 Subs. 1 Gt.)

46 The Rt. comes into existence on the date of its registration at the Court of Registration (Sec. 16 Subs. 2 Gt.). The deadline for the registration of an Rt. in the company register corresponds to the deadline applicable in the case of a Kft.[60] HUF 600,000 (approximately EUR 2,400) is payable in the case of a public Rt. and HUF 100,000 (approximately EUR 400) in the case of a private Rt. for stamp duty, whilst a HUF 25,000 (approximately EUR 100) publication fee is payable in both cases.[61]

2.4 Recurrent Costs and Efforts

47 It is difficult to assess the costs and efforts required for the maintenance of an Rt., as these depend on the ownership structure, on whether the Rt. is public or private and on the number of employees

56 See Mn. 2.

57 See Mn. 3.

58 An Rt. shall be considered a private one if its shares are not issued publicly and an Rt. shall be considered public if (at least some of) its shares have been publicly offered (Sec. 177 Subs. 2, 3 Gt.). The shareholders' meeting of an Rt. may resolve to change the form of operation of the company in accordance with the provisions relating to the modification of the statutes/deed of foundation and with regard to the legal regulations applicable to securities (Sec. 178. Subs. 1 Gt.)

59 In the case of a private Rt., the term "deed of foundation", while in the case of a public Rt., the term "statutes" is used for founding document. The statutes/deed of foundation should be prepared by way of a notarial deed or should be countersigned by an attorney or the in-house legal counsel of the founder (similar to the case of a Kft.) (Sec. 10 Subs. 2, 3 Gt.). In the following, the term "deed of foundation" will also stand for statutes save where required otherwise by the context.

60 See Mn. 5.

61 Sec. 45 Subs. 1(a) and (b) of Act XCIII of 1990 on duties and Sec. 3 Subs. 1(b) of Decree No. 9/1998 (V.23.).

hired by the Rt. A small private Rt. would typically face costs and efforts comparable to those of Kft.s.[62] A private Rt. may save significant recurrent costs by appointing one individual as executive officer, solely to carry out the duties of the board of directors.

2.5 Shares and Share Transfers

Shares in an Rt. may be either bearer shares or registered shares.[63] Bearer shares are transferred by handing over the share certificate (or by any other way which puts the buyer in possession). Registered shares may be transferred by blank or full endorsement. If the shares are dematerialised, they shall be registered shares and the transfer of the shares will take place upon the debiting and crediting of the security accounts of the contracting parties[64] (Secs. 179-180 Gt.). In the case of a transfer of registered shares, the selling shareholder must notify the Rt's board of directors of the sale of its shares in the Rt. within eight days of the date of the transfer in order for the selling shareholder be removed from the share register of the Rt. The transfer of registered shares becomes effective and the buying shareholder may exercise its shareholder's rights vis-à-vis the Rt. only after its registration in the share register has taken place (Sec. 198 Subs. 2, 3 Gt.) **48**

It is possible to have different classes of shares with different rights attached to them, i.e. issuing shares with different voting or dividend rights attached to them (Sec. 181 Gt.). There is no tax levied upon the transfer of shares.

2.6 Corporate Bodies

An Rt. is required to have three corporate bodies: the shareholders' meeting (*közgyűlés*), the board of directors (*igazgatóság*), and the supervisory board (*felügyelő bizottság*). The details of an Rt.'s organisational structure are outlined in the founding documents and in the by-laws of the corporate bodies.[65] **49**

2.6.1 Board of Directors

The board of directors is the managing body of the Rt. and consists of between three and 11 individuals (Sec. 240 Gt.). The members of the board of directors represent the Rt. *vis-à-vis* third parties (Sec. 21 Subs. 3 and Sec. 39 Subs. 1 Gt.). The members of the board of directors can be given either sole or joint authority to sign on behalf of the Rt. The appointment of the members of the board of directors is the responsibility of the shareholders' meeting (Sec. 233 (d) Gt.), however, the deed of foundation can transfer this right to the supervisory board (Sec. 33 Gt.).[66] **50**

The independence of the members of the board of directors is similar to the provisions in relation to a Kft.[67] **51**

A private Rt. may decide that no board of directors be elected, but instead that the rights and obligations of the board of directors shall be carried out by a sole executive officer (Sec. 244 Gt.). **52**

62 See Mn. 6.

63 Within these types of shares, certain categories may exist (ordinary, preferred, employee, interest bearing and redeemable shares). Preferred shares may be further classified into different classes (preference on dividends, liquidation preference, voting rights and, in the case of private Rt.s, pre-emption rights on the stocks).

64 A private Rt. may issue registered shares only (Sec. 179 Subs. 2 Gt.). Under Sec. 408 Subs. 1 of Act CXX of 2001 on capital markets, publicly issued printed shares must have been transformed into dematerialised shares by 31 December 2004. The deed of foundation of private Rt.s may set out restrictions in respect of the transfer of the shares (Secs. 201-202 Gt.)

65 In the case of an Rt., the appointment of an auditor is mandatory (Sec. 41 Subs. 1 (a) Gt.). The rules regulating the appointment and duties of an auditor correspond to the requirements applicable to a Kft.

66 As in the case of a Kft., the transfer of certain competence of the shareholders' meeting to the supervisory board of an Rt. is allowed. See Mn. 14.

67 See Mn. 11.

2.6.2 The Shareholders' Meeting

53 The shareholders' meeting is the supreme body of the Rt., consisting of all shareholders in the company (Sec. 232 Gt.).[68]

54 The shareholders' meeting must be convened at least once a year as set out in the deed of foundation.[69] As a general rule, the shareholders' meeting passes its resolutions by a majority of votes, however, in certain matters specified by law and the deed of foundation, a majority of 75 per cent of votes is required for passing a resolution (Sec. 237 Gt.).[70]

2.6.3 Supervisory Board

55 The establishment of a supervisory board is mandatory at Rt.s and the provisions relating to the supervisory board correspond to the requirements applicable to a Kft.[71] The appointment of the members of the supervisory board is the responsibility of the shareholders' meeting (Sec. 233 (d) Gt.).

2.7 Duties and Liabilities of Directors

56 The duties of the members of the board of directors of an Rt. are similar to those of a managing director of a Kft.[72] The specific duties of a member of the board of directors arising from the position may not be the subject of an employment relationship (Sec. 240 Subs. 2 Gt.).

57 The same qualification principles and liability rules outlined in respect of the managing directors of a Kft are applicable to the members of the board of directors of an Rt.[73] However, in addition to these common rules of liability of executive officers of Kft.s and Rt.s, Gt. contains an exemption from the liability rules for the members of the board of directors of an Rt. If the damages were caused by a resolution of the board of directors, a member of the board of directors who did not take part in the decision or voted against the resolution and informed the supervisory board thereof in writing within 15 days of the decision shall not be liable (Sec. 29 Subs. 2 Gt.).

2.8 Shareholders' Liability

58 As a general rule, the obligation of the shareholders to the Rt. is limited to the provision of the face value or issue price of the shares (Sec. 175 Subs. 1 Gt.). Notwithstanding the foregoing however, the provisions of Hungarian law relating to piercing of the corporate veil as described relating to a Kft.[74] are also applicable to an Rt.

68 In the case of an Rt. owned by a sole shareholder, the rights and obligations of the shareholders' meeting are exercised by the sole shareholder (Sec. 270 Gt.).

69 In the case of a private Rt., the convening of the shareholders' meeting shall take place by means of invitations sent to the shareholders at least 15 days prior to the day of the shareholders' meeting and, in the case of a public company, by means of an announcement published according to the provisions of the statutes no later than 30 days prior to the day of the shareholders' meeting (Sec. 234 Subs. 3 Gt.).

70 At least two-thirds of the votes are required for rendering resolutions regarding, for example, the modification of the deed of foundation, the termination of the Rt., the reduction in the registered capital, or the acceptance of a public offer relating to the shares of the Rt. (Sec. 237 Gt.).

71 See Mn. 14.

72 See Mn. 15.

73 See Mn. 16 et seq.

74 See Mn. 20 et seq.

2.9 Capitalisation and Financing

2.9.1 Basic Concepts

The basic principles stated with regard to the Kft. also pertain to the Rt.,[75] with the difference that the rules relating to the maintenance and preservation of the share capital of the Rt. are more sophisticated and detailed than in the case of the Kft. **59**

2.9.2 Minimum Share Capital

The minimum share (registered) capital of the Rt. is HUF 20,000,000 (approximately EUR 80,500) (Sec. 203 Subs. 1 Gt.). **60**

An Rt. may only be registered if all contributions in kind were made available to the company[76] and at least 30 per cent of the face value or issue price of each share but at least HUF 10,000,000 (approximately EUR 40,250) contribution in cash has been paid up altogether[77] (Secs. 211, 216 Subs. 3, 219 Subs. 2 Gt.). In the case of providing contribution in kind, the auditor's evaluation of the contribution in kind must be attached to the deed of foundation (Sec. 208 Gt.).[78]

2.9.3 Maintenance of Capital and Liquidity

(i) System

If an Rt. does not have equity which is at least equal to the minimum registered capital set out in the Gt. for two consecutive financial years,[79] it has to transform to another form of company (Sec. 61 Subs. 1, 2 Gt.). **61**

The capital can be rendered in cash or in kind (Sec. 12 Subs. 1 Gt.). In the case of an Rt. there is no provision for the proportion of contribution in cash and in kind as in the case of a Kft. In the case of contributions in kind, an auditor's report must be prepared which shall describe and evaluate the contribution[80] (Sec. 208 Subs. 1 Gt.). Save for the reduction in share capital, shareholders may not be exempt from the obligation of rendering their contributions and they cannot, during the existence of the Rt., reclaim the contributions they have made (Sec. 222 Subs. 1 Gt.). **62**

The prior approval of the shareholders' meeting is required for any agreement on the transfer of property to be concluded within two years of the date of the Rt.'s registration between the Rt. and one of its founders or between the Rt. and one of its shareholders holding at least 10 per cent of the voting rights, where the value of the compensation to be provided by the Rt. equals at least one-tenth of its share capital (Sec. 211/A Subs. 1 Gt.). **63**

(ii) Distributions

The Rt. is allowed to make any disbursement[81] from its own funds to a shareholder, on the basis of its shareholding in the Rt., in the cases outlined in Gt. and only if the conditions set out in Számv. are satisfied, save for the exception of the reduction in the share capital. No disbursement can be **64**

75 See Mn. 22.

76 Save when the value of the contribution in kind is less than 25 per cent. of the amount of the registered capital. In this case, the deed of foundation may allow the provision of the contribution in kind by the end of the fifth year following the registration of the Rt. (Sec. 222 Subs. 1 Gt.)

77 The total amount of the face value or issue price of the shares must be paid within one year following the registration of the Rt. (Sec. 222 Subs. 1 Gt.)

78 The founders must attach to the deed of foundation the reasons and the facts on the basis of which they determined the value of the contribution in kind lower than it was determined in the auditor's evaluation (Sec. 209 Gt.).

79 And the shareholders of the Rt. do not provide the required amount within three months after the acceptance of the annual report prepared for the second financial year.

80 In addition, the auditor's report must include a statement of the auditor as to whether the value of such contribution – as previously determined by the founders – complies with the number and face value of the shares to be provided in exchange, as well as a description of the valuation considerations applied by the auditor. The appointed auditor of the Rt. cannot conduct a preliminary assessment of the value of contributions in kind (Sec. 208 Subs.1 Gt.).

81 Any payment made in cash or otherwise shall be regarded as a disbursement (Sec. 223 Subs. 2 Gt.).

made if the company's equity capital either is less than its registered capital or it would be reduced to less than the registered capital, were the payment made. Any payment made in breach of these provisions must be repaid to the Rt., provided that the Rt. can prove the bad faith of the shareholder (Sec. 223 Subs. 1, 3 Gt.).

65 If a shareholder receives any payment, on a basis other than its shareholding in the Rt., which would not be permitted under Sec. 223 Subs. 1 Gt. and which is otherwise incompatible with the prudent management of the Rt., the payment must be repaid to the Rt. provided that the Rt. can prove the bad faith of the shareholder (Sec. 226 Subs. 1 Gt.).

66 Shareholders are entitled to dividends in cash or in kind.[82] Shareholders shall be entitled to receive dividends only in proportion to their paid-up capital contributions (Sec. 224 Subs. 1 Gt.).[83]

67 The shareholders' meeting may make a decision[84] for the payment of interim dividends between the approval of two consecutive annual reports if the deed of foundation so provide and if conditions set out in Gt. are met (Sec. 225 Subs. 1 Gt.).

(iii) Acquisition of Own Shares and Related Financing

68 The Rt. is not entitled to subscribe for its own shares or, in the case of a private Rt., assume them (Sec. 226/A Subs. 1 Gt.).

69 The Rt. may acquire its own shares[85] if its board of directors has been appropriately authorised by the shareholders' meeting (Sec. 226/A Subs. 2 Sentence 1 Gt.). The Rt. may only acquire those shares for which a shareholder paid the face value or issue price in full and if the same shareholder provided his contribution in kind to the company in full (Sec. 226/A Subs. 3 Gt.).

70 The Rt. may not acquire its own shares if the conditions to distribute a dividend are not satisfied (Sec. 226/A Subs. 4 Gt.). The aggregate face value of all of the shares acquired or held by the Rt. during its existence may not exceed 10 per cent of its share capital at any given time (Sec. 226/A Subs. 5 Gt.). A one-member Rt. cannot acquire its own shares (Sec. 271 Gt.).

71 Where the Rt. has acquired its own shares in violation of the law, the shares involved must be alienated within one year of the date on which they were acquired. In the event of failure to comply with the legal obligation of alienation, the Rt. must take immediate action to redeem the shares involved and reduce the company's share capital (Sec. 226/D Subs. 2 Gt.).

72 Voting rights are not attached to the own shares acquired by the Rt., and such shares do not count for the purposes of a quorum or in connection with pre-emptive subscription rights. Any dividend that is payable on the Rt's own shares is taken into account in the same way as pertaining to the shareholders with respect to the dividends payable on their shares, unless otherwise prescribed in the deed of foundation (Sec. 226/E Gt.).

73 Gt. prohibits an Rt. from providing financial assistance in the acquisition of its shares. In particular, the Rt. may not provide any loan or undertake guarantee, nor can it pay any of its financial liability prematurely, if the sole purpose of such operations is to assist any third person in the acquisition of shares issued by the Rt. Any such contract is null and void (Sec. 226/H Subs. 1, 2 Gt.).[86]

82 In kind dividend may be paid only if so allowed by the deed of foundation (Sec. 224 Subs. 1 Gt.).

83 The shareholders' meeting may adopt its decision, upon the recommendation of the board of directors presented with the consent of the supervisory board, for the payment of dividends simultaneously with the approval of the annual report (Sec. 224 Subs. 3 Gt.).

84 The deed of foundation of the Rt. may grant authorisation to the board of directors to decide, subject to the prior consent of the supervisory board, on the payment of interim dividends in place of the shareholders' meeting (Sec. 225. Subs. 2 Gt.).

85 The provisions of Secs. 226/A-226/E Gt. pertaining to the acquisition of own shares of an Rt. also apply in the cases where the shares of an Rt. are acquired by a joint-stock company or a limited liability company in which the Rt. controls – directly or indirectly – over 50 per cent of the voting rights or in which the Rt. has a controlling influence (Sec. 226/F Subs. 1 Gt.).

86 The prohibition does not apply if such operations are intended to assist in the acquisition of shares, whether directly or indirectly, by the Rt's employees, including the employees of companies under the Rt's majority or overall control or by any organisation founded by the said employees for this purpose (Sec. 226/H Subs. 3 Gt.).

(iv) Company as Lender or Guarantor

Loans and securities to third parties are allowed save for the prohibition of financial assistance.[87] If granted by an Rt. to the shareholders, the general provisions on illegal distributions shall be respected.[88] 74

(v) Company as Borrower

Shareholder loans to the company are generally allowed. They rank pari passu with non-shareholder claims in the event of liquidation. 75

2.10 Publication and Filing Requirements

Generally, these requirements for an Rt. correspond with the requirements set forth for a Kft.[89] A public Rt. faces additional publication and filings requirements provided for by other provisions of Hungarian law and regulations applying to the public trading of shares.[90] 76

2.11 Financial Reporting

Generally, the requirements for an Rt. correspond with the requirements set forth for a Kft.[91] Additional financial reporting obligations applicable to public Rt.s are set out in other provisions of Hungarian law and regulations relating to the public trading of shares.[92] 77

2.12 Employee Participation in Corporate Bodies

The rules regulating employee participation in the supervisory board for an Rt. correspond with the requirements applicable to a Kft.[93] 78

87 See Mn. 73.
88 See Mn. 64 et seq.
89 See Mn. 33 et seq.
90 E.g. Act CXX of 2001 on capital markets, internal regulations of the stock exchange, etc.
91 See Mn. 36 et seq. As to the requirements set out in the Companies Act relating to the election of an auditor at Rt.s, please see Fn. 65. An audit of the annual accounts of Rt.s is also mandatory under the Számv. (Sec. 155 Subs. 2, 3, 5 Számv.).
92 See Fn. 90 above.
93 See Mn. 40.

XII. Ireland

*by Maura McLaughlin**

1 The Private Company Limited by Shares ("PCLS")

Literature: Courtney, The Law of Private Companies (2nd edition, Butterworths 2002); Keane, Company Law in the Republic of Ireland (3rd edition, Butterworths 2000); Forde, Company Law (3rd edition, Round Hall Sweet & Maxwell 1999)

The private company limited by shares ("PCLS") is overwhelmingly the most popular form of company used in Ireland to limit the liability of shareholders. As distinct from a public company limited by shares ("PLC"),[1] a PCLS restricts the rights of its members to transfer their shares, and cannot have more than 50 members or offer its shares to the public. Although the schedules to the Companies Act, 1963 ("CA, 1963") contain model articles of association for various types of companies, a high degree of customisation is possible in drafting these documents. At the end of 2004 there were approximately 138,000 private companies registered in Ireland, in contrast to approximately 1,100 public companies. 1

1.1 Export of Company

Companies may not be incorporated in Ireland unless they will carry out an activity[2] and have a registered office in Ireland (this considerably restricts the availability of shelf companies). A decision by the shareholders to discontinue all of a company's activities in Ireland or to cease to have a registered office in Ireland would render the company liable to be struck off the register of companies maintained by the Companies Registration Office ("CRO") in Dublin, notwithstanding the ECJ judgements in the cases Überseering and Inspire Art.[3] 2

1.2 Transformation into a Foreign Entity

While Irish companies may convert from one form of company to another (for example, from a PCLS to a PLC and back), Irish law does not provide for the transformation of an Irish company into a foreign entity. There is generally no barrier to the share capital, assets or business of an Irish company being acquired by a foreign entity, subject to the requirements of national or European competition rules. 3

Alternatively, pursuant to the European Company Statute, it should now be possible for Irish PLCs to merge with PLCs incorporated in other Member States to form an S.E. However, the S.E. Directive[4] and the necessary administrative changes to company incorporation procedures have yet to be implemented in Ireland.

1.3 Incorporation

A PCLS is set up by filing the memorandum and articles of association of the company and a Form A1 with the CRO, together with a fee (for ordinary incorporations[5] currently EUR 100 for paper filings and EUR 50 for electronic filings). There is no statutory minimum capital requirement for a PCLS. 4

* *Arthur Cox,* Dublin.

1 See Mn. 31 et seq.

2 "Activity" means any activity that a company may be lawfully formed to carry on and includes the holding, acquisition or disposal of property of any kind.

3 See Part 1, I, Mn. 17 et seq. and 19.

4 See Part 1, I, Mn. 76 and Part 2, S.E., Mn. 1 et seq.

5 See Mn. 5.

The Form A1 must be signed by the company's subscribers, and by its directors and secretary to evidence their consent to act as such. The Form also incorporates a statutory declaration that the requirements of the Companies Acts have been complied with, and as to the activity in which the company is being formed to engage.

5 Three incorporation schemes are available (ordinary, Fé Phrainn and CRODisk), which take between five and 15 working days approximately to incorporate a company. The faster incorporation schemes are less flexible and more expensive.

1.4 Recurrent Costs and Efforts

6 A PCLS is obliged to make annual returns to the CRO giving details of its issued and authorised share capital, shareholders, directors and secretary and attaching its statutory accounts (including directors' and auditor's reports). The fee for the return is currently EUR 40 for paper filings and EUR 20 for electronic filings.

In addition, a PCLS is required to make filings with the CRO upon the occurrence of certain other events (for example, an increase in share capital, change of directors, etc.). Fees for making these filings are currently in the range of EUR 35 to EUR 100 for paper filings and nil to EUR 50 for electronic filings.

1.5 Shares and Share Transfers

7 It is permissible to have different classes of shares in a PCLS (or in a PLC), with different rights attaching to each. The authority to issue different classes of shares must be included in the memorandum of association or the articles of association. The most common share types are ordinary shares and preference (or "preferred") shares, and it is possible to have a number or classes or ordinary and/or preference shares in a company, each with differing rights. Preference shares may have preferential rights over the ordinary shares in relation to any or all of dividends, voting rights and capital. Where a company has different classes of shares, the rights attaching to any class may not be altered without the consent of three-quarters of the shares in that class.

8 The articles of association of a PCLS will provide for the issue of share certificates and transfers of the shares in the company, and will usually give the directors absolute discretion to decline to register any transfer. In order to effect a transfer of shares in a PCLS, the transferor must execute a "proper instrument of transfer". Where fully paid-up shares are transferred, a standard pre-printed stock transfer form is invariably used. The articles of a PCLS also often provide that the instrument of transfer (usually the stock transfer form) need only be executed by the transferor, and not the transferee.

9 Under Irish law, shareholders' title to their shares is not dependent on possession of a share certificate, so the transfer of shares in a PCLS (or a PLC) may not be effected by the mere physical transfer of the share certificate. Shareholders acquire legal title to their shares upon being entered into the register of members maintained by the company. A transferee may not be registered as a shareholder until the stamp duty on the transfer has been paid to the Revenue Commissioners. Stamp duty is currently levied at the rate of 1 per cent of the consideration (or the market value, if higher) for the transfer. The transferee is responsible for paying the stamp duty.

10 Shares in a PCLS may not be offered to the public and a private company, by definition, is one that, in its articles, prohibits an invitation to the public to subscribe for any shares of the company (Sec. 33(1)(c) CA, 1963). However, prior to the implementation of Directive 2003/71/EC (the "Prospectus Directive") on 1 July 2005 the general view of legal practitioners was that it was permissible for PCLS' to make offers of shares or debentures pursuant to private placings and other restricted offerings that did not come within the statutory definition of "offer to the public" as interpreted by the Irish courts. Since the implementation of the Prospectus Directive, the opinion of practitioners has been divided as to whether this situation has altered to entirely prohibit offers of securities by PCLS'. At the time of writing, the author's view is that the position has not changed as a result of the implementation of the Prospectus Directive and that restricted offerings of securities

by PCLS' are permissible, but the intervention of the legislature, the regulatory authorities or the courts will be required to definitively settle the point.

1.6 Corporate Bodies

In a PCLS, the management of the company is shared between the members in general meeting and the board of directors. The articles of association of a PCLS govern the mechanism for the appointment of directors. When a company is incorporated the first directors are usually appointed in writing by the subscribers of the memorandum or a majority of them. Post-incorporation, the articles will usually provide for additional directors to be appointed by the existing directors; such appointments may be subject to confirmation by the members at the next annual general meeting of the company. The shareholders may remove a director by passing an ordinary resolution in general meeting (Sec. 182(1) CA, 1963). **11**

1.6.1 Board of Directors

Most Irish companies include a provision in their articles of association pursuant to which the management of the company's business is delegated to its directors, permitting the exercise by the directors of any powers of the company which are not expressly reserved to the members in general meeting. The powers of the directors may be restricted by the articles of association or their service contracts. **12**

A PCLS must have a minimum of two directors (Sec. 174 CA, 1963). At least one director must be resident in Ireland, or the company will be required to take out a bond securing payment of certain fines and penalties. The cost to a company of obtaining a bond is currently less than EUR 2,000 for a two year bond, and less than EUR 3,500 for a four year bond. **13**

1.6.2 Shareholders' Meeting

The members in general meeting may give directions to the directors that are not inconsistent with the terms of the articles of association. Furthermore, various actions by a company require prior sanction at a general meeting including changes to the memorandum and articles of association, the provision of financial assistance for the acquisition of the company's own shares, and the entry into a substantial property transaction with a director. In addition, if directors exceed their delegated authority or act in breach of their duties, a subsequent ordinary resolution of the members in general meeting may ratify their action, provided that it is within the company's capacity. **14**

Ordinary resolutions of the shareholders are passed by a simple majority of the votes cast. A 75 per cent majority is required for certain matters, including the passing of resolutions amending the articles of association, converting a PCLS to a PLC or vice versa, or approving the provision of financial assistance for the acquisition of the company's own shares. Where a company's articles permit, a written resolution signed by all of the shareholders can usually be substituted for a resolution passed at a general meeting. **15**

1.7 Duties and Liabilities of Directors

The directors have statutory obligations, including arranging for filings with the CRO and convening the shareholders' meetings. Breach of these obligations may result in fines and even imprisonment, or personal liability for debts of the company, as well as disqualification from acting as a director of any company. Under Irish company law the limitation period within which a summary prosecution against a director must be initiated is three years, unless the person against whom the proceedings are to be brought is outside Ireland at the expiry of this period (in which case, it is six months from the date on which he next enters Ireland). However, it is also possible for proceedings to be commenced at any time within three years from the date on which evidence sufficient to justify the bringing of the proceedings comes to the knowledge of the initiator of the proceedings **16** (usually a liquidator during the course of a winding-up). There is no statutory limitation period on the prosecution of indictable offences under the Companies Acts, 1963-2005.

In addition, directors owe fiduciary duties to the company: to exercise their powers in good faith and in the interests of the company as a whole; not to make undisclosed personal profits from their position; and to perform their duties with due care, skill and diligence. Directors may be liable to account to the company for any profits earned by them or indemnify the company for any losses caused by them as a result of any breach of their fiduciary duties. D&O insurance is common and the payment of related premiums by the company is permitted. Where directors realise that a company is insolvent, the Irish courts have held that they have an additional duty to wind up the company.

A director is not automatically responsible under Irish law for the actions of other directors, but where a function of the board or an individual director has been delegated, the board or the individual director (as appropriate) must ensure that their delegate is performing that function satisfactorily. If they do not, depending on the circumstances of the case, they may be held to have failed in their duty of supervision or control and be liable accordingly.

Historically, directors' duties have been considered by Irish law to be owed to the company itself, and not to shareholders, employees or creditors of the company. This has resulted in difficulties where the director who is alleged to have breached his duties also controls a majority of the company's shares, since he can then use his shareholding to block any attempt by minority shareholders to take enforcement action against him. To address this, in some circumstances the courts will permit a shareholder to bring a "derivative action" to seek a remedy, for example where the board or a director have acted illegally or there has been a fraud on the minority (for example, if corporate assets have been misappropriated). There is also a statutory remedy (Sec. 205 CA, 1963) where shareholders complain that the company's affairs are being exercised in an oppressive manner or with disregard to the interests of the members.

However, Sec. 52 Companies Act, 1990 states that the matters to which directors are to have regard in the performance of their functions shall include the interests of the company's employees in general, as well as the interests of its members. In addition, where a company is insolvent (or nearly so), the Irish courts have held that the directors owe duties to the company's creditors. The position of Irish law with respect to the tortious liability of directors to those who foreseeably rely on their actions is not clear, but it is thought that, in appropriate circumstances, the general principles of the law of negligence would apply to directors *vis-à-vis* third parties.

1.8 Shareholders' Liability

17 Save where expressly permitted by statute, the Irish courts have been reluctant to disregard the separate legal personality of a company unless incorporation is being used for an improper, illegal or fraudulent purpose.

1.9 Capitalisation and Financing

1.9.1 Basic Concepts

18 The capital maintenance rules are intended to preserve the company's capital to meet the claims of its creditors in the event of a winding-up.

1.9.2 Minimum Share Capital

19 In contrast to a PLC, the minimum issued share capital of a PCLS may be as little as EUR 0.01 for a single-member company. Shares may be paid up in cash or non-cash consideration, and need not be paid up in full upon issue. Where shares are paid up in non-cash consideration, the company must make a return to the CRO attaching the subscription contract (or giving particulars thereof), and stating the number and nominal amount of shares allotted and the extent to which they are to be treated as paid-up.

1.9.3 Maintenance of Capital and Liquidity

The capital maintenance rules are largely based on statute. Any reduction in the capital of a limited company must be sanctioned by the high court and a special resolution of the members of the company. In addition, where the net assets of a company are half or less of the amount of the company's called-up share capital, the directors are required by statute (Sec. 40(1) Companies (Amendment) Act, 1983) to convene an extraordinary general meeting of the company to consider what measures should be taken. **20**

(i) System

The preservation of the capital and liquidity of a PCLS is largely the responsibility of the directors, who must have regard to the capital maintenance rules, the test of solvency (whether the company can pay its debts as they fall due), their statutory and fiduciary duties, and any restrictions set out in the articles of association or any shareholders' agreement of the company. **21**

(ii) Distributions

Distributions may only be made out of the net accumulated realised profits of the company. The articles of association will usually provide that directors may pay interim dividends without the sanction of the members in general meeting, but final dividends must be declared by the general meeting and shall not exceed the amount recommended by the directors. Directors of companies who authorise the payment of dividends otherwise than out of distributable profits may be personally liable to repay those sums to the relevant company, whether or not they are recipients of the dividends. **22**

(iii) Acquisition of Own Shares and Related Financing

Irish company law distinguishes between off-market and market acquisitions by a company of its own shares. Since shares in a PCLS cannot be listed or traded, acquisitions by a PCLS will be off-market.[6] To make such an acquisition, a PCLS must be permitted to do so by its articles of association, the terms of the proposed contract of purchase must be approved in advance by a special resolution of the members in general meeting, and the purchase monies must be paid from profits available for distribution. The acquisition must not result in the nominal value of the issued share capital of the company which is not redeemable being less than one-tenth of the nominal value of the total issued share capital of the company. **23**

A company may not redeem any of its shares which are redeemable unless the shares are fully paid-up. If the shares redeemed are to be cancelled, the redemption monies may be paid out of profits available for distribution or the proceeds of a fresh issue of shares. Where the shares redeemed are to be retained as treasury shares or there is a premium payable upon redemption, such redemption monies must be paid out of profits available for distribution. If a PCLS wishes to re-issue treasury shares derived from a redemption or repurchase, a price within the "re-issue price range" set by members of the company must be obtained. **24**

A PCLS may not provide financial assistance for the purchase of or subscription for its own shares, subject to certain exceptions (the payment of the advisers' fees of subscribers to the company, payment of up to 10 per cent commission in connection with an allotment of shares, in connection with an employees' share scheme, etc). Private companies, but not PLCs, may validate the provision of financial assistance by using the statutory "whitewash" procedure; this involves the directors swearing a statutory declaration of solvency, and the members passing a special resolution to approve the assistance. Transactions in breach of the prohibition on financial assistance are voidable and may result in the fining or imprisonment of the company's officers. In addition, any **25**

6 See Mn. 44 for a discussion of market purchases.

director making a statutory declaration of solvency without reasonable grounds may be liable to imprisonment or a fine.

(iv) Company as Lender or Guarantor

26 A PCLS may give loans or grant guarantees to third parties. However, transactions between Irish companies and their directors or "relevant" or "connected" persons of the directors are strictly regulated. Transactions between directors or connected persons and a company involving non-cash assets of the requisite value must be approved in advance by an ordinary resolution of the company. Only in very limited circumstances will a company be permitted to provide loans, quasi-loans, credit, guarantees or security in favour of directors and relevant persons.

Transactions between a company and its shareholders which are not on arm's length terms may amount to illegal distributions if the terms of such transactions result in the company's assets being passed to shareholders at an undervalue. Breaching the restrictions on transactions between a company and its directors may result in the directors having to account to the company for any gain they made, or to indemnify the company for any losses it suffered, and in some circumstances can result in a fine or imprisonment.

(v) Company as Borrower

27 Shareholder loans to the company are generally allowed but are not required by statute. In the event of insolvency they rank pari passu with non-shareholder claims. However, in practice, shareholder often subordinate their loans on the request of financial institutions.

1.10 Publication and Filing Requirements

28 A wide range of documentation and information must be filed with the CRO (including shareholder resolutions, annual returns stating the identity of the directors and shareholders, and annual accounts), and any member of the public can review and request copies of the documents filed. Nevertheless, the shareholders of Irish companies may enter into private contractual agreements regulating their rights and obligations *inter se* which, provided they do not amount to a written resolution amending the articles of association of the relevant company, will not need to be filed with the CRO or available for public access.

Almost all of the information filed with the CRO is available for public inspection at www.cro.ie. Basic information (name, number, date of incorporation and registered office) may be checked free of charge. Company printouts or copy documents are available for a small charge (between EUR 2.50 and EUR 12).

The CRO's files are available to the public for information purposes, and should not be conclusively relied upon by third parties. For example, a director of a company is duly appointed from the time that he is appointed in accordance with the articles of association of the company, not the time that the relevant filing is made with the CRO. Therefore, a director may have authority to act on behalf of a company despite not being registered as a director of the company with the CRO.

The enforcement by the CRO of penalties for non-filing is increasingly strict. Failure to make the necessary filings will usually amount to a breach of the Companies Acts, 1963-2005. In particular, failure to file an annual return may result in a company being struck off the register and dissolved. Every company, regardless of whether it is trading or not, is required to file an annual return with the CRO and a late filing penalty of up to EUR 1,200 per return may be imposed for breach of this filing obligation.

1.11 Financial Reporting

29 Copies of the annual accounts of each PCLS (comprising a balance sheet, profit and loss account, directors' report and auditors' report) must be sent to every shareholder at least 21 days before the company's annual general meeting. The format of and disclosure of specified information in the

accounts is stipulated by statute, subject to the overriding requirement that the accounts must show a true and fair view of the state of affairs of the company. Certain relief from financial reporting requirements is granted to small and medium-sized Irish companies.

A PCLS (but not a PLC) may qualify as a "small company" if, both in the relevant financial year and the preceding financial year, it satisfies the following conditions: (a) its balance sheet total does not exceed € 1,500,000; (b) its turnover does not exceed € 1,500,000; (c) its average number of employees did not exceed 50; (d) it is not within certain specified categories of company (e.g. a charitable company, or a parent undertaking or subsidiary undertaking within the meaning of the European Communities (Companies: Group Accounts) Regulations, 1992). The directors of a "small company" may elect to dispense with the requirement to appoint an auditor or to produce audited accounts in a financial year. Members holding 10% in aggregate of the voting rights in the relevant company have the power to veto the directors' decision to avail of the small company exemption. Where a company takes advantage of the small company exemption, the company's abridged balance sheet (but not its profit and loss account or a directors' report) must be filed with the Companies Registration Office, together with a statement by the directors that the company satisfies the conditions for the exemption and acknowledging the company's obligations to keep proper books of account and prepare accounts which give a true and fair view of the state of affairs of the company.

A PCLS (but not a PLC) may qualify as a "medium-sized company" if, both in the relevant financial year and the preceding financial year, it satisfies the following conditions: (a) its balance sheet total does not exceed € 6,000,000; (b) its turnover does not exceed € 12,000,000; and (c) its average number of employees did not exceed 250. A medium-sized company may not dispense with the audit requirement altogether, but may file an abridged balance sheet and profit and loss account with the Companies Registration Office, and is exempted from the requirement to disclose particulars of turnover by way of note to its annual accounts.

Irish companies whose securities are admitted to trading on a regulated market of any EEA State[7] and who prepare consolidated accounts, must prepare those accounts for financial years commencing on or after 1st January 2005 in accordance with International Financial Reporting Standards ("IFRS"). For Irish companies with only debt securities admitted to trading, the requirement to prepare consolidated accounts in accordance with IFRS applies only to financial years starting on or after 1st January 2007.

Irish companies whose securities are not admitted to trading on a regulated market or who do not prepare consolidated accounts, whether they are a PLC or a PCLS, can choose to present their statutory financial statements in accordance with either Irish GAAP or IFRS. At the time of writing, there is no requirement for all Irish companies to switch from Irish GAAP to IFRS by a specified deadline.

1.12 Employee Participation in Corporate Bodies

In general, employees are not represented on the board of directors of a PCLS and do not have any special information or participation rights. **30**

2 The Public Company Limited by Shares ("PLC")

Literature: Courtney, The Law of Private Companies (2nd edition, Butterworths 2002) Chapter 28; Keane, Company Law in the Republic of Ireland (3rd edition, Butterworths 2000); Forde, Company Law (3rd edition, Round Hall Sweet & Maxwell 1999)

The public company limited by shares ("PLC") is the most common form of public company in Ireland, although probably less than 1 per cent of Irish companies are PLCs. The key advantages of a PLC are that it can have more than 50 members and may, in certain circumstances, offer its shares to the public. These allow PLCs to raise capital from a wider spectrum and larger number of investors than a private company. **31**

7 To have equity securities admitted to trading on a regulated market in Ireland, a company must be a PLC.

2.1 Export of Company

32 The same restrictions apply as to a PCLS.[8]

2.2 Transformation into a Foreign Entity

33 The same restrictions apply as to a PCLS.[9]

2.3 Incorporation

34 A PLC is incorporated in the same way as a PCLS, but must have a minimum of seven initial shareholders. The memorandum of association must state that the company is a PLC and include the words "public limited company" or "p.l.c." in the name of the company. In addition, the share capital of the company must be at least EUR 38,092.14, 25 per cent of which must be fully paid-up.

35 A PLC may not do business or exercise any borrowing powers until the CRO has issued a "trading certificate" to the company. In order for a trading certificate to be issued, a statutory declaration (Form 70, together with a fee of EUR 300) must be filed with the CRO confirming that the minimum capital requirements have been complied with and certain other matters. A PLC which does not obtain a trading certificate within one year of its incorporation may be struck off the register of companies.

2.4 Recurrent Costs and Efforts

36 The annual costs and efforts required to maintain a PLC vary widely. A small PLC should require costs and efforts comparable to those required for a PCLS.[10] In a PLC with a large number of shareholders, the administrative costs of complying with statutory requirements in relation to the company's shareholders may be considerable. The regulatory costs of a listed PLC are even greater, given the ever-increasing compliance and disclosure obligations of such companies.

2.5 Shares and Share Transfers

37 The shares of unlisted PLCs will normally be held in certificated form. Where shares in a PLC are "certificated" (that is, where paper share certificates have been issued to shareholders), the mechanics of share transfers do not differ significantly from those for a PCLS.

Listed PLCs will usually have provisions in their articles providing for shares in the company to be held in "uncertificated" form so that transfers can be made, and dividends paid, electronically. Regulation 5 of the Companies Act 1990 (Uncertificated Securities) Regulations 1996 disapplies any rule of law requiring the execution under hand or seal of a document in writing for the transfer of uncertificated shares in a listed PLC through a relevant system. However, most listed Irish PLCs have shares issued in both certificated and uncertificated form.

2.6 Corporate Bodies

38 The corporate structure and division of power between the shareholders and directors of a PLC is fundamentally the same as that of a PCLS.[11] However, where a PLC has a large number of shareholders who are not involved in the management of the company, the interests of the share-holders and the directors may diverge. With respect to listed PLCs, the concerns of shareholders arising from this divergence have led to a growth in corporate governance regulations. Broadly, these are intended to ensure accountability and full disclosure by the directors to shareholders. Most corporate governance regulations (for example, the Combined Code on Corporate Governance

8 See Mn. 2.
9 See Mn. 3.
10 See Mn. 6.
11 See Mn. 11 et seq.

appended to the Irish Stock Exchange's Listing Rules) are aimed primarily at listed companies, but are perceived as "best practice" for companies with substantial numbers of shareholders.

2.7 Duties and Liabilities of Directors

The duties of the directors of a PLC are fundamentally the same as those of the directors of a PCLS.[12] However, the director of a listed PLC may be subject to additional disclosure and compliance obligations imposed by the rules of the market on which the company's shares are listed or the requirements of institutional shareholders or corporate governance bodies. **39**

2.8 Shareholders' Liability

As is the case with a PCLS, the shareholders of a PLC are in principle not liable for the obligations of the company in excess of the amount paid up on their shares, but the separate legal personality of the company may be disregarded in certain circumstances.[13] **40**

2.9 Capitalisation and Financing

2.9.1 Basic Concepts

The rules on capitalisation and financing apply to a PLC in the same way as to a PCLS,[14] save for the variations described below. **41**

2.9.2 Minimum Share Capital

The share capital of a PLC must be at least EUR 38,092.14, 25 per cent of which must be fully paid-up. A PLC may not accept an undertaking to do work or perform services for the company or any other person as consideration for an issue of shares, or an undertaking to be performed more than five years after the allotment. Non-cash consideration for the allotment of shares in a PLC must be independently valued to ensure its adequacy. All shares allotted by a PLC must be paid up to at least 25 per cent of their nominal value and all of any premium payable thereon. **42**

2.9.3 Maintenance of Capital and Liquidity

(i) Distributions

The same rules apply as for a PCLS,[15] and in addition a PLC may not make a distribution if the amount of its net assets is less than the aggregate of the company's called-up share capital and its undistributable reserves, or to the extent that the distribution would reduce its net assets to less than that aggregate. **43**

(ii) Acquisition of Own Shares and Related Financing

A PLC may purchase its shares off-market[16] or, if it is listed or has dealing facilities on a stock exchange, on-market. A general authority to make market purchases must be obtained in advance from the shareholders in general meeting, which shall specify the maximum number of shares which may be acquired, the maximum and minimum prices which may be paid for such shares, and the date on which the authority will expire (which must not be more than 18 months from the date of the authority). **44**

12 See Mn. 16.
13 See Mn. 17.
14 See Mn. 18 et seq.
15 See Mn. 22.
16 See Mn. 24.

45 The prohibition on financial assistance applies equally to PLCs, but PLCs may not use the "whitewash" procedure to validate financial assistance that would otherwise be illegal.[17]

(iii) Company as Lender or Guarantor

46 The same rules apply to PLCs as to PCLSs.[18]

(iv) Company as Borrower

47 The same rules apply to PLCs as to PCLSs.[19]

2.10 Publication and Filing Requirements

48 These requirements correspond with the requirements in a PCLS.[20] In addition, a shareholder must disclose to a PLC his acquisition or disposal of any interest in shares in the company which results in his shareholding amounting to more than, or becoming less than, 5 per cent of the issued share capital of a class carrying voting rights at general meetings of the company. This is in addition to the requirements for disclosure of interests in listed shares.

2.11 Financial Reporting

49 The accounting rules applicable to a PCLS correspond with the requirements for a PLC, save that a number of the exemptions available to private companies with respect to the contents of their statutory accounts are not available to PLCs.[21]

2.12 Employee Participation in Corporate Bodies

50 In general, the employees of a PLC are in the same position as those of a PCLS.[22]

17 See Mn. 25.
18 See Mn. 26.
19 See Mn. 27.
20 See Mn. 28.
21 See Mn. 29.
22 See Mn. 30.

XIII. Italy

*by Gianluca Ghersini and Giovanna Puppo**

1 The Limited Liability Company ("S.r.l.")

Literature: MAFFEI ALBERTI A. (a cura di), Il nuovo diritto societario. Commento sistematico al d. lgs. 17 gennaio 2003 aggiornato al d. lgs. 28 dicembre 2004 n. 310. Vol. III (Cedam, Padova 2005). COTTINO G., BONFANTE G., CAGNASSO O., MONTALENTI P., Il nuovo diritto societario. Commento al d. lgs. 17 gennaio 2003 n. 6, d. lgs. 17 gennaio 2003 n. 5, d. lgs. 11 aprile 2002 n. 61. Aggiornamento al d. lgs. 310/2004, Vol. III (Zanichelli 2005). NICOLINI G., STAGNO D'ALCONTRES A. (a cura di), Società di capitali. Commentario, Vol. III. AA.VV., La riforma della società a responsabilità limitata (Ipsoa, Milano 2003)

The S.r.l. (*Società a responsabilità limitata*, "S.r.l.") represents the most common corporate pattern used in Italy by small or middle-sized commercial entities and holding companies. The statutory corporate governance framework permits a high degree of flexibility in the drafting of articles of association. In contrast to the stock corporation (*Società per Azioni*, "S.p.A."), quotaholders play a key role in the direction of the S.r.l. 1

In June 2005 there were approximately 617,000 S.r.l.s registered in Italy, in contrast to approximately 41,600 S.p.A.s (231 of which were listed at the Milan Stock Exchange).

1.1 Export of Company

Although recent case law of the ECJ[1] permits foreign entities to move their entire business and management into each Member State in compliance with the principles of freedom of establishment under Sections 43 and 48 of the EC Treaty, Italian law[2] allows the S.r.l. to relocate its registered office to a foreign country only if such transfer is carried out in compliance with the laws of all the states concerned (i.e. Italian laws and the laws of the host state).[3] However, Italian companies may transfer their de-facto seat to another Member State still maintaining their Italian registration and status as an Italian entity pursuant to Sec. 25 of Law no. 218/95. 2

1.2 Transformation into a Foreign Entity

Italian law does not expressly provide for the transformation of a domestic company into a foreign entity. This can be achieved indirectly by means of: (i) a merger of the S.r.l. with a foreign legal entity; or (ii) the transfer/contribution in kind of the S.r.l. business to a foreign company. The mergers between legal entities having their registered offices in different states are effective only if they are carried out in compliance with the laws of all the states concerned (i.e. in compliance with the laws governing all the entities involved in the merger) (Sec. 25 of Law no. 218/1995 on conflict of laws). An S.r.l. cannot be merged with an S.E. 3

1.3 Incorporation

The S.r.l. is set up by means of a contract (or unilateral deed in the case of a sole quotaholder) to be concluded before a notary public in the form of a public deed (Sec. 2463 ICC). The S.r.l. does not officially exist and cannot start its operations until the company has been registered with the 4

* *Gianni, Origoni, Grippo & Partners*, Milan.

1 See Part 1, I, Mn. 17 et seq.

2 Sec. 25 of Law no. 218/95 of 31 May 1995 on conflict of laws.

3 The decision of the quotaholders to relocate abroad the registered office of the S.r.l., involving an amendment of the articles of association, Sec. 2480 ICC, has to be drafted in the form of a public deed by an Italian notary public and does not become effective until its registration with the companies' register (Sec. 2436 ICC). Pursuant to Sec. 2473 ICC, the dissenting quotaholders are entitled to withdraw from the company.

companies' register. Any actions carried out by the company before the date of its registration imply the personal liability of those who have acted on behalf of the company (usually the directors).

5 The costs for the incorporation of an S.r.l. with statutory minimum capitalisation are approximately EUR 3,000 plus VAT for the notarial fees. Timing for incorporation may vary from one to six weeks depending on the complexity of the deal (for example, in the case of contributions in kind).

1.4 Recurrent Costs and Efforts

6 Recurrent costs and efforts relating to an S.r.l. are minimal and relate only to the filing of the annual accounts and quotaholders' list (approximately EUR 125), the stamp duty on the corporate books (approximately EUR 310) and the annual registration fee due to the companies' register (approximately EUR 370, to be increased depending on the company's turnover, plus EUR 120 for each business unit in Italian territory).[4]

1.5 Shares and Share Transfers

7 The corporate capital of the S.r.l. is divided into "quotas", which constitute the participations in the company, and cannot be represented by shares.[5] The "quotas" may be freely transferred, unless the articles of association provide for specific restrictions. The agreement between the transferor and the transferee is not subject to specific formalities (Sec. 2469 ICC). The transfer is enforceable towards the S.r.l. and third parties if: (i) the agreement results from a public deed or from a written agreement with signatures certified by a notary public; (ii) the agreement has been filed with the Companies' Register; and (iii) the new quotaholder is registered in the quotaholders' ledger of the company (Sec. 2470 ICC).

8 The lack of share certificates means that there is no public market for S.r.l. quotas. The S.r.l. is prohibited by law from issuing securities to the public or to solicit investments (Sec. 2468 ICC). Whenever an S.r.l. intends to issue securities to the public, it is usually first transformed into an S.p.A.

1.6 Corporate Bodies

9 The S.r.l. provides for one compulsory corporate body of quotaholders, which decides by way of quotaholders' meetings or written decisions. The appointment of a board of directors, the duties of which can be freely defined in the articles of association, is optional. The board of statutory auditors is required only in special cases identified by law.[6]

1.6.1 Directors

10 If nothing is provided for in the articles of association, all the quotaholders are directors of the S.r.l. Otherwise, the management of the company can be assigned only to certain quotaholders or non-quotaholders with resolutions adopted by all of the quotaholders. If so provided for in the articles of association and save for specific decisions which require a collective resolution of the directors, resolutions of the directors can be taken by means of written consultation or directors' written consent (Sec. 2475 ICC).

11 The S.r.l. may have one or several directors. The directors are appointed by the quotaholders. If several directors are appointed, they constitute the board of directors. The articles of association, however, may provide for a different decision-making model (Sec. 2475 ICC). Decisions concern-

4 In addition to the above, additional costs may be required upon the occurrence of certain corporate events (for example, extensive losses, amendments to the articles of association, etc.).

5 The existence of quotas is evidenced by an entry in the quotaholders' ledger.

6 See Mn. 15.

ing certain matters must be taken, in any case, by means of a board of directors' resolution (Sec. 2481 ICC).[7]

The directors are granted with powers to represent the S.r.l. generally *vis-à-vis* third parties (Sec. 12
2475-bis ICC). They can be awarded joint or several power of representation.[8]

1.6.2 Quotaholders' Meeting

The quotaholders' meeting has overall competence on all matters related to the company on 13
which it wishes to decide. Decisions concerning certain matters[9] must be taken, in any case, by means of a quotaholders' resolution (Sec. 2479 ICC).

Unless differently provided for in the articles of association, decisions of the quotaholders are 14
generally taken by means of quotaholders' meetings (Sec. 2479-bis ICC).[10] If so provided for in the articles of association,[11] decisions of the quotaholders can be taken by means of written consultation or quotaholders' written consent (Sec. 2479 ICC).

1.6.3 Board of Statutory Auditors

Appointment of the board of statutory auditors by the quotaholders is compulsory only in the 15
cases set forth by Sec. 2477 ICC.[12]

1.7 Duties and Liabilities of Directors

The duties of the directors of an S.r.l. depend on the effective choice that is made in the articles 16
of association with respect to the management of the company and on the allocation of functions. However, generally speaking, the duties of the directors of an S.r.l. are substantially the same as those of the directors of a S.p.A.[13]

In the S.r.l., only an interest which is in contrast with the interests of the company is regulated 17
(Sec. 2475-ter ICC). Agreements entered into in the name of the company by directors who have conflicting interests may be annulled where such conflict was known by third parties which entered into such agreements. The other directors (and the statutory auditors, if any) may challenge resolutions approved with the decisive vote of director(s) who have conflicting interests, provided that such resolutions have caused damages to the company (Sec. 2475-ter ICC).

The directors of an S.r.l. are jointly responsible towards: (i) the company for damages connected 18
to the violation of their duties; and (ii) individual quotaholders or third parties who have suffered

7 The drafting of the financial statements, the drafting of the merger plan and the spin-off plan and the decision to increase the corporate capital are reserved to the exclusive competence of the board of directors.

8 Limitations to the powers of directors resulting from the articles of association, even if published, cannot be enforced against third parties, unless evidence is given that they intentionally acted to the prejudice of the company (Sec. 2475-bis ICC).

9 (i) approval of the financial statements and relevant dividend distribution, if any; (ii) appointment of the directors, if any; (iii) appointment of the board of statutory auditors, if any; (iv) amendments to the articles of association; (v) any decision related to operations which can significantly affect the corporate purpose or which can have a significant impact on the quotaholders' rights.

10 Quotaholders' meetings are validly taken if quotaholders representing the majority of the corporate capital are in attendance and relevant resolutions are validly taken if approved by the majority of the quotaholders in attendance. Higher thresholds apply in certain cases, for example the passing of resolutions amending the articles of association (Sec. 2479 no. 4 ICC).

11 Save for specific decisions which require a formal meeting (i.e. amendments to the articles of association the approval of the annual accounts or any decision related to operations which can significantly affect the corporate purpose or which can have a significant impact on the quotaholders' rights).

12 The following cases entail mandatory appointment of statutory auditors: (i) corporate capital higher than EUR 120,000; (ii) exceeding two of the following limits for two years in a row (a) total value of assets higher than EUR 3,125,000 for two financial years in a row; b) total value of sales higher than EUR 6,250,000 for two fiscal years in a row; c) average number of employees higher than 50 for two fiscal years in a row, it being understood that, should the company fail to match such thresholds for two years in a row, appointment of the statutory auditors shall no longer be necessary; (iii) company obliged to draw up consolidated balance sheet.

13 See Mn. 62 et seq.

damage that derives "directly" from the negligent or fraudulent action of the directors (Sec. 2476 ICC). The ICC does not explicitly provide, in relation to the S.r.l., for the responsibility of the directors towards creditors (as is the case for directors of a S.p.A.).[14] The joint liability towards the company does not apply to directors who: (a) have not been negligent, and (b) if informed of the relevant action/omission, have formally raised their disagreement (Sec. 2476 ICC).

19 The approval of the financial statements by the quotaholders does not release the directors and the auditors, if appointed, from liability which arises during the management of the S.r.l. (Sec. 2476 ICC). Unless differently provided for by the articles of association, the liability action against the directors may be settled and/or waived by the company.[15] The liability action against the directors becomes time-barred after five years, starting from the date when they relinquish their office.

20 In addition to their general liability, the directors may face specific additional risks in the event of insolvency of the company and may be subject even to criminal sanctions in the event that they delay the bankruptcy process.[16]

21 Under Italian law, the directors (or the company in favour of the directors) may enter into a D&O insurance policy covering the civil liability with respect to damages caused to third parties (e.g., the company, the company's creditors, quotaholders or other third parties).

1.8 Shareholders' Liability

22 Generally, a piercing of the corporate veil is rare under Italian law, which looks to protect the principle of limited liability (*autonomia patrimoniale perfetta*) (Sec. 2462 ICC). The S.r.l., as well as the S.p.A., is a limited liability company, in which the quotaholders' liability is limited to the amount of the capital of the company subscribed by the quotaholder(s). Therefore, situations which may lead to a quotaholder liability must be deemed exceptional.[17]

23 In the case of insolvency of an S.r.l. with a sole quotaholder, limitation of liability for the company's obligations is subject to the fulfilment of both of the following requirements: (i) capital contributions fully paid-in; and (ii) publicity requirements correctly performed. Non-performance would lead to unlimited liability (Sec. 2462 ICC).

24 A specific case of direct liability of a parent company is provided for companies engaged in the so-called activities of direction and coordination (*direzione e coordinamento*), Sec. 2497 ICC.[18] The parent company[19] is held liable towards the shareholders and the creditors for the harm caused to the integrity of the company's assets if, abusing of its exercise of a dominant influence, it acted in violation of the principles of proper corporate and business management of the company subject to

14 It seems, however, that this omission does not exclude the responsibility of the directors towards creditors for violation of the obligations concerning the preservation of the "integrity of the company's assets".

15 The settlement/waiver of a liability action must be taken by the majority of the quotaholders representing at least two-thirds of the corporate capital and such resolution must not be opposed by quotaholders representing at least one-tenth of the corporate capital. It does not affect the right of the individual quotaholder and third party to be compensated.

16 In the event of losses which reduce the capital of the S.r.l. below the minimum required by law (i.e. EUR 10,000), the directors have a duty to call a quotaholders' meeting and either liquidate the company or recapitalise the same (Sec. 2482-ter ICC).

17 Typical of the S.r.l. is the liability of the quotaholders who intentionally decided or authorised the performance of acts which caused damages to: (i) the company; (ii) the other quotaholders; or (iii) a third party; in this case, the said quotaholders are subject to the same liability as the directors (Sec. 2476 ICC).

18 In the absence of any legislative indication or case law on the matter, it can be said that direction and coordination by a could be defined as the actual exercise of a dominant influence on the companies subject to it. As an example, such dominant influence could be possibly represented by a steady stream of instructions on management methods, the raising of finance, budgetary policy, the choice of contracting parties etc. In the absence of proof to the contrary, it is presumed by Italian corporate law that direction and coordination is engaged by entities which: (i) are obliged to consolidate their financial statements; (ii) control other companies according to Sec. 2359 ICC; or (iii) carry out direction and coordination activities on the basis of a contract or according to clauses of their articles of association, regardless of whether control exists in a formal sense, Sec. 2497-sexies ICC.

19 Within a corporate group, not only the company that is the ultimate shareholder of the chain of control, but also the intermediate companies in the chain, may be considered as a possible directing and coordinating entity. Investigation must be carried out on a case by case basis, depending on the effective source of the exercise of a dominant influence, if any.

it. However, the liability of the parent company is excluded when "compensatory advantages" are detected in the overall activity of the group of companies.[20] The creditors of the company subject to direction and coordination may bring action against the directing and coordinating company only if their claims have not been satisfied by the company subject to it, Sec. 2497 ICC.[21]

1.9 Capitalisation and Financing

1.9.1 Basic Concepts

The rules governing an S.r.l. with respect to contributions are significantly different from the relevant provisions set forth for a S.p.A. The S.r.l. is capitalised upon incorporation by means of capital contributions by the founding quotaholder(s) and may subsequently receive additional financing by means of a capital increase, contributions in cash, contributions of property in kind, or assignment of receivables. With exclusive reference to the S.r.l., capital contributions can be replaced by a bank guarantee or insurance policy.[22] If the articles of association so provide, the S.r.l. is entitled to receive financing from third parties by means of issuance of special securities (*titoli di debito*) (Sec. 2483 ICC).[23] **25**

1.9.2 Minimum Share Capital

The minimum corporate capital of the S.r.l. is equal to EUR 10,000 (Sec. 2463 ICC). The capital can be paid by way of cash, by contribution in kind as well as by assignment of receivables. In contrast to the S.p.A. (Sec. 2342 ICC), if the articles of association so provide, it is possible to provide any kind of asset which can be economically evaluated to the S.r.l. as capital contribution. However, if such is the case, it is provided that the work done or the supply of services is assisted by a bank guarantee or insurance coverage (Sec. 2464 ICC). When a contribution consisting of property in kind or receivables is made, an expert's report shall be attached to the articles of association (Sec. 2465 ICC).[24] In contrast to the S.p.A., the expert may be chosen directly by the quotaholders. **26**

1.9.3 Maintenance of Capital and Liquidity

(i) System

The minimum corporate capital must be entirely subscribed at the time of the incorporation. One-quarter of the corporate capital (the total amount in the case of incorporation by a sole quotaholder) must be paid-in and placed into a non-interest bearing account prior to the incorporation. This cash deposit is returned to the company after its registration with the companies' register. The company is entitled to receive from the quotaholders the uncalled portion of the subscribed capital, if any, and the directors are empowered to claim the balance from the quotaholders. No capital increase can be resolved until the subscribed capital is fully paid-in. **27**

20 Compensatory advantages may be noticed: (i) when a damage is non-existent in light of the entire result of the direction and coordination; or (ii) when a damage is entirely eliminated, also further to actions taken specifically for such purposes.

21 A company which is effectively subject to the direction and coordination of a legal entity must comply with certain mandatory disclosure obligations which are required for the purpose of allowing third parties (and possible minority shareholders) to gain prior knowledge of the company's membership to a group, Sec. 2497-bis ICC.

22 Quotaholders are entitled, at any time, to replace the guarantees above by paying in their capital contributions (Sec. 2464 ICC).

23 The said securities may be subscribed only by professional investors who, in case of subsequent circulation of the same to non-professional investors other than the company's quotaholders, are liable for the repayment of such securities by the issuing company (Sec. 2483 ICC).

24 The report shall contain a description of the property or receivables contributed, the value assigned to each item of property or receivable, the standards of evaluation applied, as well as an attestation that the value ascribed is not lower than the par value, increased by the premium, if any, of the corporate capital issued against contribution. The expert is liable for the damages caused to the company, the quotaholders or any third party.

28 Under corporate principles of Italian law, the corporate capital of the S.r.l., as well as of the S.p.A., is seen as a reference point to determine the relevance of losses incurred by such company, in particular with respect to mandatory procedures/formalities and subsequent corporate capital reduction.

29 If the corporate capital is reduced by over one-third as a consequence of losses incurred, the directors must call a quotaholders' meeting in order to take the appropriate measures.[25] If the loss incurred is not reduced (or expected to be reduced) below one-third within the following financial year, the quotaholders' meeting must reduce the corporate capital accordingly. Alternatively, the quotaholders may inject new funds through a capital contribution or waiver of receivables (Sec. 2482-bis ICC).

30 If the corporate capital, because of the losses, falls below the minimum requirement set forth by law, the directors must immediately call the quotaholders' meeting to resolve upon the reduction of the corporate capital and subsequent increase of the corporate capital for an amount not lower than the minimum, or upon the transformation of the company into another corporate form (Sec. 2483-ter ICC).

31 Capital maintenance rules also apply in the event of a voluntary reduction of the corporate capital, which takes place by means of amendment of the articles of association decided by the quotaholders (Sec. 2482 ICC).

(ii) Distributions

32 Distribution of profits to quotaholders is made on the basis of a resolution of the quotaholders deciding upon the utilisation of annual profits, resulting from the validly approved annual accounts.[26] In the event of losses, profits may not be distributed unless the capital has been restored or reduced accordingly (Sec. 2478-bis ICC).[27] Advance dividends are not allowed.

(iii) Acquisition of Own Quotas and Related Financing

33 The S.r.l. may not purchase or accept its quotas as security from the quotaholders nor can it provide loans or securities for the purchase or subscription of its quotas (Sec. 2474 ICC). However, the newly enacted Sec. 2501-bis ICC may be seen as a kind of "safe harbour": provided that the procedural requirements set forth by this section are followed, an MLBO transaction[28] is permitted and should not be viewed and re-characterised as a scheme aimed at circumventing the prohibition of financial assistance, unless it is proved that it has been intentionally conceived for this purpose.

(iv) Company as Lender or Guarantor

34 The company may act as lender to or as guarantor of the obligations of its quotaholders, associated companies and third parties provided that: (i) such activities fall within the company's corporate purposes and are justified by a corporate benefit; and (ii) the relevant decisions do not involve a conflict of interest (Sec. 2475-ter ICC).[29]

25 The board of directors must draft an interim asset statement to which the statutory auditors or the external auditor, if any, must add their comments and consequently submit them to the quotaholders' meeting.

26 The S.r.l. cannot perform "hidden distributions" of profits. However, several informal benefits may be attributed by the company to the quotaholders (for example, by way of compensation to quotaholders appointed as directors). The consequences and validity of such benefits must be verified on a case by case basis.

27 Once distributed, profits may not be claimed back by the company if the quotaholders received them in good faith based upon annual accounts regularly approved evidencing the corresponding net profits (Sec. 2478-bis ICC).

28 A "merger leveraged buyout": Namely an M&A transaction whereby the purchaser incorporates an Italian special purpose vehicle ("SPV"); (ii) the SPV is capitalised by the purchaser by means of a shareholder loan; (iii) the SPV then uses such funds to acquire a controlling interest of another company ("target") and finally (iv) the target is merged into the SPV. Such transactions were seen as a circumvention of the rules on financial assistance before the new Sec. 2501-bis ICC was introduced in January 2004.

29 The director/quotaholder cannot guarantee its personal obligations.

(v) Company as Borrower

Quotaholders' loans are allowed, but if the company faces a situation of excessive financial indebtedness with respect to its net assets or a situation in which a capital contribution would have been advisable, any financings[30] granted to the company: (i) may only be reimbursed to the quotaholder after repayment of the company's creditors; and (ii) if repaid within one year preceding the declaration of bankruptcy of the company, are to be returned to the company (Sec. 2467 ICC). In the event of bankruptcy shareholder loans are treated as subordinated claims. **35**

1.10 Publication and Filing Requirements

A wide range of documentation and information must be filed with the competent local companies' register.[31] The consequences for not filing the documents with the companies' register depend on the nature of the document at issue.[32] The companies' register is decentralised and held by the local chamber of commerce whereby the company has its registered office. Its records are open to the public and can be accessed online[33] upon payment of a fee and any interested person can review the recorded documents and request a chamber of commerce survey detailing the main corporate information as well as copies of major documents filed.[34] **36**

1.11 Financial Reporting

The S.r.l. must draw up its annual accounts within 120 days of the end of the business year.[35] The board of directors has exclusive competence for the drawing up of the financial statements, while the quotaholders' meeting has the exclusive competence for its approval.[36] The annual accounts must be drawn up in accordance with provisions of law and Italian GAAP. The drawing up of annual accounts in accordance with other accounting principles such as US GAAP or IAS/IFRS is not permitted for the S.r.l. **37**

Certain relief from financial reporting requirements is granted to small enterprises. In Italy small enterprises are those not exceeding two of the three following criteria: (i) a balance sheet total of EUR 3,125,000, (ii) a turnover of EUR 6,250,000, (iii) a workforce of 50 employees in the annual average, for two years in a row. Small companies may draw up the annual accounts in an abridged form (*bilancio in forma abbreviata*) (Sec. 2435-bis ICC). If the small enterprise is an S.r.l., it is released from the requirement to appoint a board of statutory auditors and does not need to have its annual accounts audited by an independent auditor, unless obliged to draw up consolidated balance sheet.

The accounting review of the annual accounts of the S.r.l. is carried out directly by the quotaholders, if the board of statutory auditors is not appointed (Sec. 2476 ICC). S.r.l.s having: (i) a

30 If the conditions set forth by Sec. 2467 are met, the S.r.l. treats any shareholders' financing, regardless of its form, as if it were contribution to equity.

31 For example, the following documents must be filed with the companies' register: (i) the articles of association and any amendment thereof; (ii) the appointment/dismissal/resignation of directors and statutory auditors, if any; (iii) the fact that the company is held or ceases to be held by a sole quotaholder; (iv) the annual accounts; and (v) the quotaholders' list.

32 For example, failure to comply with publicity requirements in case of the appointment of a director may entail the unenforceability towards third parties of such appointment; failure to comply with publicity requirements in the case of the S.r.l. with a sole quotaholder entails the exclusion of limited liability for the obligations which arise during the period of non-performance of the said fulfilments.

33 www.cerved.it.

34 As regards additional filing obligations for foreign entities and individuals, prior to incorporation each quotaholder, as well as each director, must obtain a taxpayer number (*codice fiscale*) in Italy. Where a quotaholder is a legal entity, a taxpayer number must also be applied for its legal representative.

35 If so provided for in the articles of association, the deadline may be extended by up to 180 days.

36 The annual accounts consist of: (i) a balance sheet (*stato patrimoniale*); (ii) a profit and loss account (*conto economico*); and (iii) a note to the financial statements (*nota integrativa*) and must be completed with the report on the management (*relazione sulla gestione*), and an auditors' report (*relazione dei sindaci*), if appointed (Sec. 2423 ICC). If the conditions set forth under Sec. 2435-bis ICC are met, it is possible to draw up the annual accounts in an abridged form (*bilancio in forma abbreviata*).

corporate capital higher than EUR 120,000; (ii) exceeding two of the following limits for two years in a row (a) a total value of assets higher than EUR 3,125,000 for two financial years in a row; (b) a total value of sales higher than EUR 6,250,000 for two fiscal years in a row; (c) an average number of employees higher than 50 for two fiscal years in a row, must appoint a board of the statutory auditors, which shall carry out the accounting review of the annual accounts (Sec. 2477 ICC).

The annual accounts of S.r.l.s require auditing by external independent auditors if the quotaholders decide in that way (Sec. 2477 ICC) unless the company is obliged to draw up a consolidated balance sheet. If such is the case, S.r.l.s, like S.p.A.s, regardless of their size, must have their annual accounts and consolidated balance sheet audited by either an individual auditor (*revisore contabile*) or by an auditing firm (*società di revisione*) duly enrolled in the relevant register held at the Italian Ministry of Justice (Sec. 2409-bis ICC).

1.12 Employee Participation in Corporate Bodies

38 Employees are not entitled to appoint members of, or be represented in, the corporate bodies of the S.r.l.

2 The Stock Corporation ("S.p.A.")

Literature: RAGUSA MAGGIORE G., Trattato delle società. Le società di capitali. La società per azioni. Formazione della società per azioni. Nuovo diritto societario (Cedam, Padova 2003). CAVALLO BORGIA R., Delle società per azioni. Vol. IV (Zanichelli/Soc. Ed. del Foro Italiano, Bologna/Roma 2005). MAFFEI ALBERTI A. (a cura di), Il nuovo diritto societario. Commento sistematico al d. lgs. 17 gennaio 2003 aggiornato al d. lgs. 28 dicembre 2004 n. 310. Vol. I e II (Cedam, Padova 2005). COTTINO G., BONFANTE G., CAGNASSO O., MONTALENTI P., Il nuovo diritto societario. Commento al d. lgs. 17 gennaio 2003 n. 6, d. lgs. 17 gennaio 2003 n. 5, d. lgs. 11 aprile 2002 n. 61. Aggiornamento al d. lgs. 310/2004, Vol. I e II (Zanichelli 2005)

39 The stock corporation (*Società per Azioni*, "S.p.A.") is the other important corporate entity offering limited shareholder liability in Italy. Its advantage is that it has easy access to capital markets and therefore greater scope for raising funds to finance its business activities. However, as this will usually result in a large number of shareholders, its governance structure and rules on capital protection are particularly strict.

2.1 Export of Company

40 The importing and exporting of stock companies is regulated by substantially the same rules applicable to the S.r.l.[37]

2.2 Transformation into a Foreign Entity

41 The transformation of a domestic stock company into a foreign entity is regulated by substantially the same rules applicable to the S.r.l.[38] However, an S.p.A. can be merged with and into an S.E.

2.3 Incorporation

42 The procedure for incorporation of the S.p.A. is similar to the one provided for the S.r.l. [39]

43 The costs for the incorporation of the S.p.A. are EUR 5,000 plus VAT for the notarial fees.[40]

37 See Mn. 2.

38 See Mn. 3.

39 See Mn. 4.

40 The amount of the above notarial fees is based on the assumption that the company is incorporated with the minimum capitalisation required by Italian law.

2.4 Recurrent Costs and Efforts

The annual efforts required to maintain an S.p.A. can be either relatively minimal or considerably high depending on whether the S.p.A. is run with few shareholders or as a large enterprise having a significant number of shareholders. Costs may raise significantly if the S.p.A. is listed on the stock exchange. 44

2.5 Shares and Share Transfers

The stock capital of the S.p.A. is represented by shares. Shares are indivisible (Sec. 2347 ICC) and – in general – must all be of equal value and grant their holders the same rights (Sec. 2348 ICC). It is possible to issue shares without nominal value (Sec. 2346 ICC). Given that the total value of the shares has to be equal to the stock capital value, it is possible to grant to the shareholders a number of shares having a total nominal value different from the relevant capital contribution (Sec. 2346 ICC). 45

It is possible to issue virtually any categories of shares granting various rights, with reference both to dividend distribution and right to vote, if so provided for in the articles of association. All shares of the same category are required to confer the same rights (Sec. 2348 ICC). The aggregate value of the shares endowed with special voting rights may not exceed 50 per cent of the corporate capital of the company, while shares with multiple voting rights are not permitted (Sec. 2351 ICC).[41] 46

In contrast to the S.r.l., the issuance of shares against work done or supply of services in favour of the company is not permitted. However, these types of assets can be compensated with special financial instruments (*strumenti finanziari*), which can be issued provided that they do not grant the right to vote in the shareholders' meeting (Sec. 2346 ICC). 47

Transfer of nominative shares (being the usual type of shares) is implemented by way of endorsement of the share certificate authenticated by a notary public (Sec. 2355 ICC).[42] The articles of association may impose various limitations on the circulation of the shares. They can also be locked-up for a period not exceeding five years (Sec. 2355-bis ICC). 48

2.6 Corporate Bodies

With reference to corporate governance, three alternative systems are permitted for the S.p.A.: (i) traditional; (ii) dualistic (two-tier board); (iii) monistic (one-tier board). The choice between the three systems has to be taken carefully, since it deeply affects the role and function of the shareholders' meeting. If nothing is provided for in the articles of association, the traditional system applies (Sec. 2380 ICC). 49

In the traditional structure, the shareholders' meeting is in charge of the appointment of two separate bodies: the board of directors and the board of the statutory auditors. 50

In the Dualistic pattern – clearly inspired by the German experience – a supervisory board (*Consiglio di Sorveglianza*) appoints, controls and has the power to call off, the managing board (*Consiglio di Gestione*) (Sec. 2409-novies ICC). The shareholders' meeting appoints the supervisory board (Sec. 2409-duodecies ICC), which is in charge of approving the financial statements (Sec. 2409-terdecies ICC). 51

41 The following categories of shares are officially recognised or accepted: (i) deferred shares (*azioni postergate*) (Sec. 2348 ICC); (ii) tracking shares with monetary rights related to the economic results of certain business sectors of the company (*azioni correlate*) (Sec. 2350 ICC); (iii) redeemable shares (*azioni riscattabili*); (iv) shares preferred in the distribution of profits and in the capital repayment in the case of a winding-up (*azioni privilegiate*); (v) shares devoid of voting rights, with voting rights limited to certain matters and conditional on the occurrence of certain events (Sec. 2351 ICC).

42 The individual/entity resulting as endorsee on the share certificate by way of a continuous series of endorsements is entitled to exercise corporate rights and to request the registration of transfer in the shareholders' ledger of the company. In the case of saving shares (*azioni di risparmio*) (i.e. shares devoid of voting rights, but granted with increased economic privileges, which may be issued only by companies listed on the Italian Stock Exchange), the transfer is executed by way of delivery of the to-bearer share certificates (*certificati al portatore*).

52 The Monistic system, borrowed from Common Law, represents a simplified corporate structure. The management of the company is assigned to the board of directors by the shareholders' meeting (Sec. 2409-sexiesdecies ICC). An audit committee (*Comitato per il Controllo sulla Gestione*) has to be appointed from among the directors by the board of directors (Sec 2409-octiesdecies ICC).[43] The audit committee is in charge of overseeing the adequacy of the company organisation, administration, accounting and control systems (Sec. 2409-octiesdecies ICC) but not of the financial auditing of the annual accounts.

2.6.1 Board of Directors

53 Under the traditional model, which is currently still the most common in Italy,[44] the board of directors consists of one or several members and is granted with a general power to represent the company *vis-à-vis* third parties (Sec. 2384 ICC). Its members can either be awarded sole or joint power of representation.

54 Under the traditional model, as a result of their appointment, the directors of an S.p.A. are entrusted with the general and exclusive duty to manage the company (Sec. 2380-bis ICC). Enforceability towards third parties of limitations to powers of directors are regulated by substantially the same rules applicable to the S.r.l.

55 The directors' maximum term of office is three years and they are eligible for re-election, unless the articles of association provide otherwise (Sec. 2383 ICC).

2.6.2 The Shareholders' Meeting

56 The shareholders' meeting is the representative body of the shareholders in which they can exercise their rights. The shareholders' meeting may be ordinary[45] or extraordinary (Sec. 2363 ICC).[46]

57 The shareholders' meeting generally may not decide on management issues given the exclusive management competence of the board of directors (Sec. 2380-bis ICC).[47]

2.6.3 Board of Statutory Auditors

58 In contrast to the S.r.l., the appointment of the board of statutory auditors (*Collegio Sindacale*) is mandatory for the S.p.A. The statutory auditors control the legality and adequacy of a company's organisational structure and its functioning (Sec. 2403 ICC).

59 The financial audit of an S.p.A. shall be carried out by either an individual auditor or by an auditing firm (*revisore contabile*), both of which shall be duly enrolled in the relevant register held at the Italian Ministry of Justice (Sec. 2409-bis ICC).

43 In the traditional system, at least half of the members of the board of directors must meet the independence requirements for eligibility as members of the board of statutory auditors (Sec. 2409-septiesdecies ICC).

44 And which, unless the articles of association provide otherwise, applies to all S.p.A.s by operation of law (Sec. 2380 ICC).

45 The ordinary shareholders' meeting: (i) approves the annual accounts; (ii) appoints and revokes the directors, the statutory auditors and the external auditor, if any; (iii) decides the level of compensation for directors and auditors; (iv) considers liability actions against directors and auditors; (v) considers the subject matters attributed to its jurisdiction by law and the authorisations required by the articles of association for the performance of certain acts by the directors (the above without prejudice to the liability of the directors for actions performed) (Sec. 2364 ICC).

46 The extraordinary shareholders' meeting resolves upon any matter involving an amendment of the articles of association and the appointment, revocation or replacement of the liquidators (Sec. 2365 ICC). Certain matters involving amendment of the articles of association (such as the merger resolution, the opening or closing of secondary offices, the reduction/increase of the corporate capital) can be delegated to the board of directors, if the articles of association so provide (Sec. 2365 ICC).

47 The only management issue reserved to the exclusive competence of the shareholders' meeting is the decision to acquire an interest in an unlimited liability entity (*società di persone*) (Sec. 2361 ICC).

2.7 Duties and Liabilities of Directors

The directors of the S.p.A. have a general duty to carry out the management of the company with the care that is required in relation to the office and their specific skills (Sec. 2392 ICC). **60**

In case a director has an interest[48] in a certain matter to be resolved upon by the board of directors: (i) he shall inform the other directors and the statutory auditors; and (ii) the resolution approving the matter shall sufficiently illustrate the reasons and the interest the company has in taking that action/decision (Sec. 2391 ICC). **61**

Normally, an S.p.A. is managed by a board of directors and by managing directors, who have been delegated some powers by the board.[49] With respect to delegated matters, the managing (i.e. executive) directors have a duty to (a) take care that the organisation of the company is adequate for its size and activities, (b) act within the limits of the conferred powers and (c) report to the board at least once per semester. The non-executive members of the board have a supervisory duty towards the actions taken by the managing directors (Sec. 2381 ICC). **62**

The directors may be jointly liable towards: (i) the company for damages resulting from the violation of their duties[50] (Sec. 2392 ICC); and/or (ii) the creditors of the company, for the violation of the duty to preserve the "integrity of the company's assets" (Sec. 2394 ICC); and/or (iii) individual shareholders or third parties, for damages deriving "directly" from their negligent or fraudulent actions (Sec. 2395 ICC).[51] **63**

Breach of the provisions relating to financial assistance and purchase of own shares (Sec. 2357 ICC) entails exposure to liability action for the directors of the company pursuant to Sec. 2393 ICC and may trigger criminal sanctions pursuant to Sec. 2628 ICC. **64**

The joint liability towards the company does not apply to the directors who have formally dissented from the decision of the board causing the prejudice. In the event of conflict of interest, the director in breach is responsible for the damages deriving from his action or omission to act (Sec. 2391 ICC).[52] In the case of appointment of managing directors, the non-executive members of the board remain nevertheless liable if they (a) breached their duty to collect information from the latter, or (b) being aware that a detrimental action was being carried out, did not impede or limit the consequences thereof (Sec. 2392 ICC). **65**

Statute of limitations for liability actions, D&O insurance, directors' disqualifications and liability in case of insolvency are regulated by substantially the same rules applicable to the S.r.l.[53] **66**

2.8 Shareholders' Liability

Shareholder liability and piercing the corporate veil are regulated by substantially the same rules applicable to the S.r.l.[54] **67**

48 Not necessarily in conflict with the interest of the company.

49 The board, in any case, has the power to give guidelines to the managing directors and/or to revoke the delegation and/or take back the power to decide on a specific matter that was previously delegated.

50 The liability action must be taken (and the settlement/waiver thereof is possible if not objected) by a minority of shareholders representing at least one-fifth of the corporate capital (one-twentieth for companies listed on the stock exchange) (Sec. 2393-bis ICC).

51 In this case liability action is in tort, and it becomes time-barred after five years, starting from the date of the wrongdoing by the director(s).

52 Acting for a personal interest in conflict with the interest of the company might also generate criminal liabilities (Sec. 2634 ICC).

53 See Mn. 21 et seq.

54 See Mn. 22 et seq.

2.9 Capitalisation and Financing

2.9.1 Basic Concepts

68 The rules governing the S.p.A. with respect to capitalisation and financing are to some extent different from the rules applicable to the S.r.l. There is a public market for shares, and the S.p.A. may issue a wide range of marketable financial instruments and bonds.[55]

2.9.2 Minimum Share Capital

69 The minimum share capital of the S.p.A. is EUR 120,000 (Sec. 2327 ICC). The capital can be rendered in cash or in kind as well as by means of assignment of receivables. When a contribution consisting of property in kind or receivables is made, a court-appointed expert's report is required (Sec. 2343 ICC). The contents of the expert's report and liability are regulated by substantially the same rules applicable to the S.r.l. Sole shareholding is regulated by substantially the same rules applicable to the S.r.l. (Sec. 2325 ICC and Sec. 2362 ICC).

2.9.3 Maintenance of Capital and Liquidity

(i) System

70 Capital maintenance rules are substantially the same as the rules applicable to the S.r.l.[56] Of interest in the case of the S.p.A. is the possibility of creating assets destined for specific operations (*patrimoni destinati ad uno specifico affare*) whereby the company allocates certain assets to specific operations. The assets so divided cannot be seized by the general creditors of the company (Sec. 2447-quinquies ICC).[57]

(ii) Distributions

71 Distributions to shareholders are regulated by substantially the same rules applicable to the S.r.l.[58] Advance dividends are only allowed on the basis of annual accounts certified by independent auditors.

(iii) Acquisition of Own Shares and Related Financing

72 The S.p.A. cannot (directly or indirectly) purchase its own shares, unless the said shares are fully paid-in and the purchase is made by using the profits available for distribution and/or the available reserves, resulting from the last approved financial statements (Sec. 2357 ICC). The S.p.A. cannot purchase more than 10 per cent of its shares.[59] The shares purchased in violation must be sold within one year. Failing such sale, the shares must be cancelled promptly and the capital of the company must be reduced accordingly.

55 Such instruments do not attribute the status of shareholder, except for bonds convertible into shares (*obbligazioni convertibili*), but may grant specific corporate prerogatives such as right to profits and/or to appointment of corporate bodies (Sec. 2351 ICC).

56 See Mn. 27 et seq.

57 Such a result may be obtained through the use of two different legal mechanisms: (i) the constitution of a separate set of assets to be exclusively destined to certain operations (*patrimonio destinato*) (Sec. 2447-bis ICC); or (ii) the entering into a financing agreement to be reimbursed exclusively by the profits of a certain operation (*finanziamento destinato*) (Sec. 2447-decies ICC). The separate set of assets may not be created: (i) for an aggregate value exceeding the 10 per cent of the net assets of the company; and (ii) for the exercise of activities reserved by law to qualified operators, subject to the regulatory regime.

58 See Mn. 32.

59 Additional requirements (e.g., authorisation of the shareholders' meeting, par value of the shares, etc.) must be met by the company in order to purchase its own shares.

The S.p.A. cannot finance the acquisition of its own shares and cannot issue guarantees for the purchase of, or subscription to, such shares (Sec. 2358 ICC). The S.p.A. cannot accept its own shares as a security (not even through a fiduciary company or an interposed person).[60] 73

(iv) Company as Lender or Guarantor

Loans and securities to third parties are regulated by substantially the same rules applicable to the S.r.l.[61] 74

(v) Company as Borrower

The S.p.A. may acquire funds by means of the issuance of bonds (*obbligazioni*), which can be convertible or not convertible into equity (Sec. 2410 ICC), and by means of shareholders' loans.[62] The restriction on the reimbursement of shareholder loans in the case of insolvency provided for the S.r.l.[63] does not apply to the S.p.A. unless the shareholder granting the loan abuses his direction and coordination powers to the detriment of the company. In the event of bankruptcy shareholder loans are treated as subordinated claims. 75

2.10 Publication and Filing Requirements

Publication/filing requirements are regulated by substantially the same rules applicable to the S.r.l.[64] 76

2.11 Financial Reporting

The drawing up of the annual accounts of the S.p.A. is regulated by substantially the same rules applicable to the S.r.l.[65] The S.p.A. listed on the stock exchange, banks and insurance companies, even if not listed, are obliged to adopt IAS/IFRS starting from the consolidated financial statements approved after 1 January 2005 and annual accounts approved after 1 January 2006. 77

S.p.A.s listed in the stock exchange must have their annual accounts and consolidated balance sheets audited by an independent auditing firm (*società di revisione*) duly enrolled in the relevant register held by the CONSOB (Italian Stock Exchange Authority) (Sec. 155 of Legislative Decree no. 58/1998 ("TUF")).

Private S.p.A.s whose shares are extensively owned by the public (*società che fanno ricorso al mercato del capitale di rischio*) (Section 2325-bis ICC) must have their annual accounts and consolidated balance sheet audited by an independent auditing firm (*società di revisione*) duly enrolled in the relevant register held at the Italian Ministry of Justice, under the supervision of CONSOB (Italian Stock Exchange Regulatory Authority) (Sec. 2409-bis ICC).

Private S.p.A.s obliged to draw up a consolidated balance sheet, must have their annual accounts and consolidated balance sheet audited by either an individual auditor (*revisore contabile*) or by an auditing firm (*società di revisione*) duly enrolled in the relevant register held at the Italian Ministry of Justice (Sec. 2409-bis ICC).

Private S.p.A.s not obliged to draw up a consolidated balance sheet may have their annual accounts audited by either an external auditor (individual auditor or auditing firm duly enrolled in the relevant register held at the Italian Ministry of Justice) or by the board of statutory auditors, if the articles of associations so provide (Sec. 2409-bis ICC).

60 The only exceptions to these provisions are provided for the case that a company intends to facilitate the acquisition of shares by its employees (as well as by the employees of companies belonging to the same group).

61 See Mn. 34.

62 Whether certain restrictions apply to the reimbursement of shareholders' loans if the company, which receives the shareholders' loans, is an S.r.l. (Sec. 2467 ICC), such rules on thin cap do not apply to the S.p.A., unless a case of "direction and coordination" (see Mn. 1, 8 above) occurs.

63 See Mn. 35.

64 See Mn. 36.

65 See Mn. 37.

2.12 Employee Participation in Corporate Bodies

78 Employee participation/representation in corporate bodies is regulated by the same rules applicable to the S.r.l.[66]

66 See Mn. 38.

XIV. Latvia

*by Peteris Dalderis and Lauris Zubulis**

1 The Limited Liability Company ("SIA")

Literature: Strupišs, Komerclikuma komentāri, commentary Part I A (A. Strupiša juridiskais birojs 2003); Strupišs, Komerclikuma komentāri, commentary Part III (A. Strupiša juridiskais birojs 2003)

A limited liability company (*sabiedrība ar ierobežotu atbildību*, "SIA") is one of the three corporate forms (besides the stock company and additional liability company) allowed by Latvian company law. The SIA is the most common company form used in Latvia. In contrast to other corporations, the governance framework of an SIA is not thoroughly prescribed by law. The shareholders enjoy a considerable degree of freedom in forming the structure and decision-making schemes of an SIA. 1

According to the statistics published by the holder of the electronic database of the Latvian Commercial Register, SIA "Lursoft", the total number of limited liability companies incorporated in Latvia was approximately 78,000 in October 2005, in contrast to approximately 1,270 stock corporations.[1]

1.1 Export of Company

The export of companies is not expressly regulated by Latvian law. Legal practice, however, indicates that it is not possible to move an SIA's corporate seat to another country (even a Member State of the EU) and the Latvian Commercial Register will not register an SIA with a corporate seat abroad. On the other hand, the business activities of a Latvian SIA can be partly or fully carried out in another country without losing the company's legal identity under Latvian law. The company will nevertheless still be required to file tax reports etc. under Latvian law. 2

1.2 Transformation into a Foreign Entity

Again, this issue is not expressly regulated by Latvian law. However, legal practice shows that transformation of a Latvian company into a foreign entity without a previous winding-up is not possible. The relevant provisions of the Commercial Law (Komerclikums, "KCL") provide only for transfer of the corporate property. Recently, a new law on European Stock Corporations ("EKL") has entered into force. The EKL mainly regulates the incorporation and employee involvement in an S.E. However, an SIA may not be the forming entity of an S.E. 3

1.3 Incorporation

An SIA can be established by one or more persons by registering it in the Commercial Register (Sec. 140 KCL). For registration, certain documents such as the articles of association and foundation agreement have to be submitted. Some of the documents (the application to the Commercial Register and the certificate of authenticity of the signatures of members of the board) need a certification by a notary. An SIA legally exists from the moment of its entry into the Commercial Register (Sec. 1 Subs. 1 KCL). 4

All registrations in the Commercial Register have to be made within three working days of submitting the application. The total costs of registration amount to approximately LVL 139 (approximately EUR 210), including the LVL 100 (approximately EUR 150) fee for registration, the LVL 24 (approximately EUR 40) fee for publication in the Official Gazette *Latvijas Vēstnesis* and the 5

* *Glimstedt and Partners,* Riga.

1 See Mn. 36 et seq.

LVL 15 (approximately EUR 20) fees of the public notary. The fees of a notary do not depend on the size of the share capital.

1.4 Recurrent Costs and Efforts

6 An SIA faces only few annual formalities, i.e. submitting the annual report and monthly tax reports to the authorities. Where an SIA is a small business and does not exceed two of the following economic figures: (1) the total sum of the balance is below LVL 100,000 (approximately EUR 150,000); (2) the net turnover is below LVL 200,000 (approximately EUR 300,000); or (3) the number of employees is below 25, the annual report may be certified by any person the shareholders have elected. If the company exceeds any two of the above-mentioned criteria, the affirmation of a sworn auditor is required, whose service will cost at least LVL 500 (approximately EUR 750). A member of the board must be re-elected every three years; failing this, a new member must be elected to the board. Annual general meetings ("AGMs") are required by law at least once a year. The law does not prescribe any specific expensive actions to be taken in connection with the AGM and therefore the convening of an AGM cannot be regarded as a considerable cost. Moreover, the law provides for the possibility of passing AGM resolutions without holding a physical meeting.

1.5 Shares and Share Transfers

7 All shares in an SIA entitle their holders to the same rights; no classes of shares are allowed. The KCL does not provide for share certificates for an SIA. The management board is obliged by law to create a shareholders' register and to update it (Sec. 187 KCL). Shareholders may freely transfer their fully paid-up shares. However, the KCL entitles the other shareholders to the right of pre-emption in the case of sale of the shares. Other types of share transfer (e.g. transferring as a gift) are allowed only upon other shareholders' approval.

8 The law does not prescribe any specific form of share transfer instrument and therefore the transfer may be executed by a private deed. However, a share transfer is legally effected only upon entering it into the shareholders' register (Sec. 136, Subs. 2 KCL). The KCL further obliges the management board of an SIA to submit the updated shareholders' register to the Commercial Register after each share transfer (Sec. 187, Subs. 6 KCL). No transfer taxes or registration fees are levied on the transfers of shares. Although an SIA is not prohibited from issuing its shares to the public, the practical realisation of the public offering is implicated by the lack of a market for the SIA shares and by the shareholders' right of pre-emption.

1.6 Corporate Bodies

9 According to Latvian law, an SIA shall have two mandatory bodies: (1) the shareholders' meeting (*dalībnieku sapulce*); and (2) the management board (*valde*). The shareholders may establish a supervisory board and other bodies not required by law (Sec. 209 KCL). The powers and responsibilities of such bodies (except the supervisory board) can be freely defined in the articles of association.

1.6.1 Management Board

10 The management board may consist of one or several members (Sec. 221 Subs. 2 KCL). Members of the management board are appointed by resolution of the shareholders (Sec. 224 Subs. 1 KCL). The management board may make any decisions concerning the company that do not fall within the exclusive authority of the shareholders' meeting. If there are several members of the management board, they manage the company together (Sec. 222 KCL).

11 According to Latvian law, members of the management board have joint power of representation (Sec. 223 Subs. 1 KCL). However, shareholders can decide to grant sole power of representation to the members of the management board. All other kinds of limitations on the power of representation of members of the management board will not be binding on third parties. A provision in the articles of association according to which members of the management board are allowed to represent the

company only together with specific unregistered proxy holders (*prokurists*) will be void (Sec. 223 Subs. 3 KCL).

1.6.2 Shareholders' Meeting

The shareholders' meeting has exclusive authority in the most important matters concerning the company: amendments to the articles of association; changes in the share capital; the appointment of members of the management board, supervisory board and auditors; the approval of the annual report; the utilisation of profits; bringing an action against a shareholder or a member of the supervisory or management board; and the reorganisation or termination of the SIA (Sec. 210 Subs. 1 KCL). The scope of this authority can be extended by the articles of association. In addition, the shareholders' meeting may make decisions that are usually made by the management board. Shareholders who voted for such a decision are jointly liable for damages to the company caused by their decision (Sec. 210 Subs. 2 KCL). **12**

The shareholders' meeting is able to make binding decisions when the shareholders present represent more than half of the paid-up share capital. The shareholders' meeting passes resolutions by a simple majority of the votes cast (Sec. 212 Subs. 1 KCL). Higher thresholds apply only in certain cases, for example, amending the articles of association and reorganisation of the SIA (Sec. 218 KCL). **13**

1.6.3 Supervisory Board

The supervisory board of an SIA has the same powers and responsibilities as the supervisory board of a stock company (Sec. 220 Subs. 2 KCL).[2] It is responsible for protecting the interests of the shareholders from illegal or economically unreasonable decisions of the management board. **14**

1.7 Duties and Liabilities of Directors

The management board has to manage the daily business of the SIA and fulfil other obligations prescribed by law, the articles of association or resolutions of the shareholders' meeting. The management board must perform its duties using the diligence of a prudent manager (Sec. 169 KCL). The members of the management board are jointly liable *vis-à-vis* the company. However, a member of the management board may be excluded from the joint liability if it is proven that he has performed his duties using the diligence of a prudent manager. Liability of the members of the management board *vis-à-vis* third parties exists only in the quite rare cases of committing a tort. Generally all claims against the management board become time-barred after 10 years. D&O liability insurance is permitted in Latvia and the related premiums may be paid by the company. **15**

The management board does not bear liability *vis-à-vis* the company if the particular action that resulted in damages for the company was taken in good faith in accordance with the shareholders' instructions. Further, the shareholders may expressly release the management board from liability for particular past actions. However, the shareholders' resolution on a general release of the management board from their liability (for example, in connection with approval of the annual report) will not be valid. **16**

The management board is obliged to apply for insolvency proceedings if any one of the following conditions exists: (1) the company is not able to pay its debts within three weeks of the debts becoming due and no settlement is reached with the creditors; and (2) the liabilities of the company exceed its assets. Failure to comply with this requirement may lead to a criminal conviction of the members of management board.[3] **17**

Members of the management board may be convicted for specific criminal offences, e.g. malicious insolvency, or held liable for specific administrative offences, e.g. engaging in business activities without registration of the company in the Commercial Register. If a member of the **18**

2 See Mn. 46.
3 See Mn. 18.

management board is convicted for criminal offences the court may, apart from a prison sentence and fines, prohibit him from engaging in any business activities for up to five years. Administrative offences of a member of the management board usually lead to fines.

1.8 Shareholders' Liability

19 Piercing the corporate veil is allowed only in rare cases explicitly given in law. The principle of the shareholders' limited liability is not respected in cases when interests of the company's creditors need to be protected. Creditors can raise two kinds of claims against the shareholders of an insolvent company. First, they can demand to payment of the fully-non-paid shares (Sec. 66 Law on the Insolvency of Companies ("LUUM")). Second, they can ask the court to recognise the contracts concluded in the five years before the company became insolvent as void (Sec. 69 LUUM). As a consequence of a successful action, creditors can demand the return of property or money to the SIA.

Furthermore, the shareholders who have received a sum of money from the company without legal grounds are obliged to pay it back and to recover the damages in cases where they had knowledge of the illegality of the payment (Sec. 162 KCL).

1.9 Capitalisation and Financing

1.9.1 Basic Concepts

20 The basic principle of the capitalisation and financing of an SIA is that the liability of the company is limited to property belonging to it. The minimum property guaranteed to creditors is the share capital. The share capital must always be available to the company. According to Sec. 219 KCL, the management board has to convene the shareholders' meeting and submit a report about the situation and possible solutions if losses exceed half the share capital or there is a danger of the company's insolvency. Possible solutions can be the winding-up of the company, initiating the insolvency procedure, issuing a guarantee to the creditors of the SIA etc. Shareholders have no obligation to support the company in a financial crisis.

1.9.2 Minimum Share Capital

21 The minimum share capital of an SIA is LVL 2,000 (approximately EUR 3,000) (Sec. 185 KCL). The contributions can be rendered in cash or in kind (Sec. 151 KCL). If the non-cash investments constitute more than half of the share capital or their combined value is more than EUR 6,000 their value has to be estimated by certified experts. At least half of the share capital of an SIA must be rendered before the date of the application for registration of the company in the Commercial Register. Another 50 per cent can be paid within one year of the date of registration (Sec. 146 KCL).

1.9.3 Maintenance of Capital and Liquidity

(i) System

22 Contributions made by shareholders to the share capital are the property of the company (Sec. 151 Subs. 2 KCL) and may not be repaid to the shareholders.

23 According to the KCL, shareholders may have joint liability in the case where another shareholder did not pay up his share in the term stipulated in the foundation agreement and they knew or should have known of his inability to perform such duty (Sec. 166 Subs. 3 KCL). Also, shareholders who have approved the evaluation of contributions in kind have a joint obligation to compensate for the difference between the asserted and real value (Sec. 154 Subs. 6 KCL).

24 Sec. 139 Subs. 1 KCL permits a shareholder to receive payments from the company in the form of the price for the sale of goods subject to the shareholders' approval of this transaction. The law provides this limitation only in the first two years after the establishment of the SIA if the price exceeds 5 per cent of the share capital.

(ii) Distributions

Distributions of profits to shareholders must be made on the basis of a shareholders' resolution deciding on the utilisation of annual profit. Dividends are paid only for fully paid-up shares according to the face value of all shares and only in the form of cash. Sec. 161 Subs. 4 KCL prohibits payment of dividends if the total of the company's equity does not exceed the paid-up share capital. Dividends paid illegally must be returned to the SIA by the shareholder regardless of whether or not he knew about the illegality of the payment (Sec. 162 KCL). Dividends may be calculated and paid only once a year (Sec. 161 Subs. 5 KCL). **25**

All payments that a shareholder receives from the company, with the exception of dividends and some other specified payments (Sec. 182 Subs. 1 KCL) are considered to be illegal and have to be paid back to the SIA (Sec. 182 Subs. 2 KCL). In addition, the use of the SIA's property free of charge, the sale to the company of goods for a higher price than their market value and receiving services from the SIA for a lower price than their market value are illegal and result in the same obligation as an illegal payment. **26**

(iii) Acquisition of Own Shares and Related Financing

The KCL prohibits an SIA from acquiring its own shares with the exception of certain cases listed in Sec. 192 Subs. 1 KCL. In the majority of these cases, the company receives its own shares on the basis of the law itself (no contract is required) without any obligation for payment. The law does not set any limits as to the number of own shares that an SIA may acquire. Creation of a reserve for the company's own shares is not required. An SIA has to sell its shares within one year, or the share capital will be reduced by the face value of the company's own shares. An SIA does not receive any of the shareholders' rights and its shares are not taken into account when the representation of the shares is to be determined for voting or other rights. **27**

There is no prohibition by law of financial assistance by an SIA in the acquisition of its own shares by a third party. Such financial assistance can be illegal if it discriminates against some of the shareholders. According to Sec. 198 KCL, the procedure of paying up new shares and consequently granting a loan from the company as the means of payment shall be determined by resolution of the shareholders' meeting. **28**

(iv) Company as Lender or Guarantor

An SIA has the right to give loans and guarantees to third parties and to the shareholders without any limitation. However, these contracts can be declared void during the insolvency procedure if is established that the company has deliberately caused damages to its creditors by such contracts, and the contracting party has been aware thereof. If the contracting party in such contract is a shareholder, the law presumes his knowledge of the creditors' damages (Sec. 69 Subs. 1 and 2 LUUM). **29**

(v) Company as Borrower

The shareholders of an SIA are free to finance the company by way of issuing loans to it. There is no obligation imposed on them to ensure sufficient funding of the SIA. According to Sec. 107 Subs. 4 LUUM, the shareholders who have issued loans to the company are in the same group of creditors in the insolvency procedure as any other creditors. **30**

1.10 Publication and Filing Requirements

The KCL defines a set of information that companies are obliged to register and update with the Commercial Register. The registered information is made available to the public in the Commercial Register and any third party can rely on it. The Commercial Register is available electronically on the internet (www.lursoft.lv), but the electronic database is managed by a private company and, **31** legally, it may not be regarded as binding. It is, however, general market practice that companies rely on the information contained in the electronic database.

32 The following information concerning an SIA has to be made public in the Commercial Register: the name of the company, including the indication of the type of company (SIA); personal information about the members of the management board, the specific unlimited proxy holders (*prokurists*) and the auditor; its share capital; its legal address and its term if the SIA was created for a certain period of time only (Sec. 8 Subs. 3 KCL). Other data, such as the identity of shareholders, may be obtained from the Commercial Register as it is contained in the submitted documents. The annual report of the SIA has to be filed each year in the Commercial Register. Any interested person has the right to review the register or to make copies. Finally, all companies are obliged to submit tax reports to the tax authority on a monthly, quarterly or annual basis.

33 Failure of the management board to file the requested documents in the Commercial Register may lead to administrative fines in an amount up to EUR 300. The Commercial Register generally enforces the fines on a strict basis. Failure of the management board to submit tax reports to the tax authority may in accordance with Sec. 35 of the Law on Taxes and Duties ("LNN") lead to forced winding-up of the company. However, this ultimate sanction is hardly ever applied.

1.11 Financial Reporting

34 The annual report of an SIA consists of two parts: the financial review (balance, profit and loss statement) and the report of the management board about the company's development over the last 12 months. The beginning and the end of the financial year can be determined in the articles of association by the shareholders.

Certain relief from the financial reporting requirements is granted to smaller companies although the term "small and medium-sized companies" is not used in the Latvian legislation. Where a company does not exceed any two of the following criteria it may use a simplified form of balance sheet: (i) the total sum of the balance is below EUR 1,500,000 (= LVL 1,000,000); (ii) the net turnover is below EUR 3,400,000 (= LVL 2,400,000); or (iii) the number of employees is below 250 (Sec. 24 LUGP). Further, these companies are released from the obligation to publish their annual reports in the Official Gazette *Latvijas Vēstnesis*(Sec. 66, Subs. 4 LUGP). On the other hand, companies exceeding the above-mentioned criteria are granted seven months period of time for preparing the annual report and submitting it to the authorities while the other companies have only four months (Sec. 66, Subs. 1 LUGP).

Some further simplification of the balance sheet is permitted in respect to the companies not exceeding any two of the following criteria: (i) the total sum of the balance is below EUR 150,000 (= LVL 100,000); (ii) the net turnover is below EUR 300,000 (= LVL 200,000); or (iii) the number of employees is below 25 (Sec 54. LUGP). Additionally, these companies are released from the obligation to draw up a management report on the company's economic situation and do not need to have their annual reports audited by sworn auditors (Sec. 62 and Sec. 66, Subs. 2 LUGP).

Bookkeeping of companies (regardless of whether an individual one or a group) is permitted only in accordance with the standards indicated in the Law on Annual Accounts of Companies Sec. 5 Subs. 1 ("LUGP"). Publicly traded companies (which are usually only ASs)[4] are an exception being obliged to apply the IAS standards to their bookkeeping. Finally, the application of the IAS bookkeeping standards only is allowed in respect to group annual reports. All companies, however, are allowed additionally to draw up their annual reports according to the IAS and make them public.

1.12 Employee Participation in Corporate Bodies

35 There is no mandatory representation of employees in the corporate bodies of an SIA.

4 See Mn. 8; for details on the AS see Mn. 36 et seq.

2 The Stock Corporation ("AS")

Literature: Strupišs, Komerclikuma komentāri, commentary Part I A (A. Strupiša juridiskais birojs 2003); Strupišs, Komerclikuma komentāri, commentary Part III (A. Strupiša juridiskais birojs 2003)

The stock corporation (*akciju sabiedrība*, "AS") is the other most significant type of company with limited shareholder liability. Although its governance structure and rules on capital are considerably stricter that those of an SIA, the attraction of an AS is based on its easier access to the capital markets. **36**

2.1 Export of Company

The possibilities and restrictions regarding the export of an AS are the same as for an SIA.[5] **37**

2.2 Transformation into a Foreign Entity

Generally, the transformation of an AS into a foreign company is not possible under Latvian law. The only exception is the foundation of an S.E. An S.E. may be formed by merger of a Latvian AS with another entity or by transformation of a Latvian AS into an S.E. **38**

2.3 Incorporation

The procedure and preconditions for incorporation are the same as in the case of an SIA.[6] The only difference in the costs by comparison with an SIA is the amount of the registration fee, which is LVL 250 (approximately EUR 375). **39**

2.4 Recurrent Costs and Efforts

The annual costs and efforts required to maintain an AS may be substantially higher than for an SIA, as an AS, in difference from an SIA, shall always establish and maintain a supervisory board consisting of at least three members. Further, as the law only permits physical AGMsin an AS, the costs for convening these meetings may be greater than in an SIA. **40**

2.5 Shares and Share Transfers

The shares of an AS may be bearer or registered, certificated or dematerialised. Further, there can be different classes of shares in an AS depending on the rights attached thereto, for example dividend rights and voting rights. The shares may be transferred by handing over the share certificate (in case of certificated registered shares), by endorsement (in the case of certificated bearer shares) or by transfer to the acquirer's account (in the case of dematerialised shares). For recording of the owners of the registered shares and the transactions therewith the company shall create and update a shareholders' register. The shareholders of an AS can transfer their shares without any restrictions or previous permissions from the company's board unless otherwise prescribed by the company's articles of association (Sec. 238 KCL). The transfer of shares does not need to be registered in the Commercial Register. No transfer taxes are levied on transfers of shares. **41**

2.6 Corporate Bodies

An AS is required to have three corporate bodies: the management board (*valde*), the supervisory board (*padome*) and the shareholders' meeting (*akcionāru sapulce*). **42**

5 See Mn. 2.
6 See Mn. 4 and 5.

2.6.1 Management Board

43 The management board may consist of one or several members, however if the company's shares are in public circulation, the management board shall consist of at least three members (Sec. 304 KCL). The maximum term of office is three years but this may be renewed. Members of the management board are appointed and dismissed by the supervisory board.

44 The management board may make any decisions concerning the company's operation that do not fall within the exclusive authority of the shareholders' meeting and the supervisory board. In certain cases, the supervisory board's approval will be necessary. The members of the board have joint power of representation but sole representation can be awarded (Sec. 303 Subs. 1 KCL).

2.6.2 Shareholders' Meeting

45 The shareholders' right to decide on matters regarding the AS is restricted to the authority of the shareholders' meeting as defined in the KCL. The shareholders' meeting is entitled to pass resolutions regarding the annual report, the utilisation of profits, the appointment of members of the supervisory board and auditors, the amount of their salary, changes to the share capital, amendments to the articles of association, the issuing of shares and the reorganisation or termination of the AS (Sec. 268 Subs. 1 KCL). The shareholders' meeting can make decisions irrespective of the number of shareholders present unless the articles of association provide for a certain quorum. A decision is binding if a majority of the shareholders present voted for it. In certain cases, for example changes of the share capital, a two-thirds majority of votes is necessary (Sec. 284 Subs. 2 KCL).

2.6.3 Supervisory Board

46 The supervisory board must consist of at least three members (if the shares are in public circulation, the minimum number of members is five) but not more than 20 (Sec. 295 KCL). The maximum term of office of the members is three years (Sec. 296 Subs. 1 KCL). Reappointment is possible. The main tasks of the supervisory board are to appoint the members of the management board and to monitor whether the decisions of the management board are lawful and economically feasible.

2.7 Duties and Liability of Directors

47 Members of the management board of an AS have similar duties to those of an SIA.[7] The articles of association can provide that for important matters the management board must obtain the supervisory board's approval. However, such approval may not always release the members of the management board from their liability *vis-à-vis* the company (Sec. 169 Subs. 4 KCL).

2.8 Shareholders' Liability

48 The shareholders of an AS are liable only in the exceptional cases.[8]

2.9 Capitalisation and Financing

2.9.1 Basic Concepts

49 As in the case of an SIA, the basic principle of the capitalisation and financing of an AS is that the liability of the company is limited to property belonging to it. The minimum property guaranteed to the creditors is the share capital. The share capital must always be available to the company.

7 See Mn. 15 et seq

8 See Mn. 19.

2.9.2 Minimum Share Capital

The minimum share capital of an AS is LVL 25,000 (approximately EUR 37,425) (Sec. 225 Subs. 1 KCL). 25 per cent of the share capital (but not less than the minimum share capital) shall be paid in cash at the date of the application for registration (Sec. 146 Subs. 4 KCL). The remaining part of the capital must be rendered in cash or in kind within one year of signing the foundation agreement. The contributions in kind must be evaluated by independent experts. The experts' report is published in the Official Gazette. **50**

2.9.3 Maintenance of Capital and Liquidity

(i) System

KCL provides for the same capital protection for an AS as for an SIA.[9] The most important exceptions are the following. Where losses exceed half of the share capital or there is a danger of insolvency, the duly conducted shareholders' meeting must make a decision concerning the improvement of the company's financial condition (Sec. 271 KCL). Any agreement between the company and a member of the management board requires the approval of the supervisory board (Sec. 292 Subs. 1 KCL). **51**

(ii) Distributions

The same legal requirements apply to the distribution of profits to shareholders in an AS as in an SIA,[10] with the exception being the procedure of decision-making about the utilisation of profits. The dividends are paid according to a resolution of the shareholders' meeting which has been informed of the management board's proposal and the supervisory board's report (Sec. 268 Subs. 1 KCL). Dividends may be calculated and paid only once a year (Sec. 161 Subs. 5 KCL). **52**

(iii) Acquisition of Own Shares and Related Financing

With the exception of certain cases (generally the same as in an SIA[11]), an AS is not allowed to acquire its own shares (Sec. 240 Subs. 1 KCL). The mere authorisation of the acquisition by the shareholders' meeting is not sufficient if the preconditions of the above-mentioned provision are not fulfilled. The equity of an AS after acquisition of its own shares must be greater than the share capital (Sec. 240 Subs. 6 KCL). Sec. 241 KCL prohibits an AS from providing any direct or indirect financial assistance in the acquisition of its own shares. **53**

(iv) Company as Lender or Guarantor

Loans and securities to third parties are restricted in the same way as in the case of an SIA.[12] In addition, the approval of the supervisory board may be necessary if the loan granted by the company does not fall within the scope of the usual business of the AS and the articles of association of the company provide that the management board needs the approval of the supervisory board in important matters (Sec. 294 Subs. 1 KCL). **54**

(v) Company as Borrower

Shareholders' loans and the granting of a security to an AS are allowed as in the case of an SIA.[13] **55**

9 See Mn. 22 et seq.
10 See Mn. 25 and 26.
11 See Mn. 27.
12 See Mn. 29.
13 See Mn. 30.

2.10 Publication and Filing Requirements

56 These requirements correspond with the requirements for an SIA.[14]

2.11 Financial Reporting

57 These requirements correspond with the requirements for an SIA.[15]

2.12 Employee Participation in Corporate Bodies

58 The participation and representation of employees in an AS are the same as in an SIA.[16]

14 See Mn. 31 et seq.
15 See Mn. 34.
16 See Mn. 35.

XV. Lithuania

by Elijus Burgis (LL.M.) and Akvilė Bosaitė[*]

1. The Limited Liability Company ("UAB")

Literature: Mikelėnas/Bartkus/Mizaras/Keserauskas, Commentary on the Second Book ("Persons") of the Civil Code of the Republic of Lithuania (Justitia 2002)

A limited liability company (*Uždaroji akcinė bendrovė*, "UAB") is the most common corporate form for making investments in Lithuania. In contrast to a stock corporation (*Akcinė bendrovė*, "AB"),[1] the minimum share capital in a UAB is particularly small, a UAB is relieved of any fairly expensive disclosure of information and the transfer of shares in a UAB is quite limited. These factors combine to enable founders of a UAB to organise a group of shareholders from well-known and reliable entrepreneurs. 1

In August 2005 there were approximately 51,000 UABs registered in Lithuania, in contrast to approximately 780 ABs.

1.1 Export of Company

The issue of the possibility of moving the centre of administration of a company incorporated under the law of Lithuania to another state without moving its registered office is not considered by applicable legislative acts. Under Lithuanian legislation the legal capacity of a company is directly linked with the registration of a company. Hence, incorporation theory is applicable in Lithuania rather than real seat theory.[2] 2

A company must have its registered office situated in the Republic of Lithuania (Sec. 2 Subs. 7 Law on Companies (*Akcinių bendrovių įstatymas*,"ABĮ"). The Civil Code (*Civilinis kodeksas*, "CK") defines the registered office as the place where the permanent managing body of a legal person is seated. Where the registered office differs from the actual place of the seat of the company's managing bodies, third parties have a right to treat the registered office of a legal person as the place where the permanent managing body is seated (Sec. 2.49 CK). However, the above legal provisions do not deal with the issue of whether the real seat of management can be transferred to a foreign country without transferring the registered office. If the company does not perform any activities in Lithuania and does not have its managing bodies seated in Lithuania, but has its registered office in Lithuania, it is still treated as a legal person of the Republic of Lithuania. In such a case it should be regarded as retaining legal capacity and being subject to the corporate laws of the Republic of Lithuania. In practice, however, it could hardly be possible to have a centre of administration in a country other than Lithuania because of administrative requirements that each legal person incorporated and having its registered office in Lithuania is required to perform.[3] 3

As a result of the above, it is most likely that the corporate laws of the Republic of Lithuania do not allow the "export" of companies because of the direct link between the centre of administration and the registered office which has to be situated in the Republic of Lithuania. 4

1.2 Transformation into a Foreign Entity

Based on the incorporation theory, Lithuanian law does not provide for the transformation of a domestic company into a foreign entity. Hence, the transfer of a UAB's business or assets to a foreign company will not be considered as the transformation of a UAB into a foreign entity. Moreover, if the sale of a UAB's shares to a foreign company is effected, then a UAB will be 5

* *Bernotas & Dominas Glimstedt,* Vilnius.

1 See Mn. 51 et seq.

2 Mikelėnas/Bartkus/Mizaras/Keserauskas, p. 126.

3 See Mn. 8 and 48.

deemed to be a Lithuanian company with a foreign capital participation that in principal has no impact on the legal identity of the UAB.

1.3 Incorporation

6 A UAB is set up by an incorporation agreement (or in case of one founder, by an incorporation statement) executed by all founders or their duly authorised persons. A UAB is subject to registration with the Register of Legal Entities (Sec. 11 ABĮ). Prior to registration, the founders must obtain a certification from a notary public that the documents of incorporation are in conformity with applicable laws as well as a verification of the data to be included in the Register of Legal Entities (pre-registration procedure).[4]

7 The length of the incorporation procedure may vary from one to three weeks.[5] The notarial and registration fees for the incorporation of a UAB, irrespective of the share capital, will amount to approximately LTL 500 (approximately EUR 150).

1.4 Recurrent Costs and Efforts

8 The greatest recurrent costs and efforts for a UAB pertain to the drawing preparing and filing of annual financial statements,[6] the costs of which depend on the size of the company. Further, although relatively small, other costs relate to the calling of the annual shareholders' meetings and the maintenance of at least one corporate body, i.e. the managing director ("managing director"). Other costs and efforts only materialise in the event that certain corporate steps are taken which require notarisation, filing or publication. Notably, no annual registration fee is payable to the Register of Legal Entities.

1.5 Shares and Share Transfers

9 Shares in a UAB may be either material (material shares or share certificates) or non-material (book-entry) (Sec. 40 ABĮ). Shares may be of several classes, namely ordinary shares,[7] preference shares[8] and employee shares[9] (Secs. 42 and 43 ABĮ). All shares of the same class carry equal proprietary and non-proprietary rights. However, rights attached to the shares of different classes may vary (e.g. such differences may relate to voting rights, rights to receive dividends, etc.).

10 Unless the articles of association explicitly provide otherwise, the sale[10] of the shares in a UAB is subject to stringent procedural requirements. A shareholder intending to sell any part of its shares held in the company is required to notify the managing director thereof and specify the number of shares intended for sale and the sale price. A pre-emptive right in respect of the acquisition of all shares offered for sale for the indicated sale price is vested in any current shareholder of a UAB

4 In Lithuania trade names do not require separate registration and are protected from the date of submission of an application to register a company with the aforementioned Register of Legal Entities.

5 The length of the incorporation procedure may also be subject to the additional incorporation steps which may be taken upon a request from the founders (e.g. temporary reservation of the company name with the Register of Legal Entities).

6 The financial statements of a UAB must be audited if the UAB meets at least two of the following criteria: (a) its annual net revenue exceeds approximately EUR 2.9 million; (b) the value of assets shown in the balance sheet exceeds approximately EUR 1.45 million; and (c) the average annual number of employees exceeds 50. This will result in further costs being incurred.

7 They carry all proprietary and non-proprietary rights of a shareholder.

8 These shares may constitute up to one-third of the share capital only. A holder of a preference share takes priority over other shareholders in receiving dividends. However, a holder of a preference share is not awarded the right to vote, unless the articles of association stipulate otherwise.

9 These are issued for the subscription of employees of the company only (with the exception of employees serving as the managing director, board members and members of the supervisory council of the company). An employee may transfer his employee shares to other employees of the company only. Such restriction period may not exceed three years.

10 No restrictions are applied when a UAB's shares are transferred in another manner (other than by sale) (Sec. 47 ABĮ).

(Sec. 47 ABĮ). However, in the case of a share transfer, the number of shareholders in a UAB may not exceed 250.

Title to material shares is transferred by making a relevant entry on a material share (a share certificate), i.e. an endorsement. The transfer of non-material shares is effected by executing a written share transfer agreement. The transfer of title to non-material shares is recorded by entries in the personal securities accounts of a transferor and a transferee (Sec. 46 ABĮ), which are as a general rule held and managed by the managing director of the company. Therefore, title to the shares is evidenced by a material share or a share certificate (combined with an uninterrupted chain of endorsements) or the appropriate entries in the shareholders' securities accounts (as the case may be). **11**

No special tax levies are imposed in the case of share transfer and general taxation rules are applied. Therefore a transferor is obliged to pay income tax of 15 per cent on the surplus (in the case of an individual) or tax of 19 per cent (combined of the profit tax and social tax) on the surplus (in the case of a corporate entity), although exemptions are allowed. **12**

The law prohibits public trading of shares in a UAB (Sec. 2 Subs. 4 ABĮ). Hence, the shares and debentures of a UAB may not be listed on the Stock Exchange (i.e. the Vilnius Stock Exchange, which is the only stock exchange in Lithuania). **13**

1.6 Corporate Bodies

Pursuant to the ABĮ, every UAB must have at least two bodies, namely the managing director (*vadovas*) and the shareholders' meeting (*visuotinis akcininkų susirinkimas*). Further corporate and supervisory bodies of the company (i.e. the board (*valdyba*) and/or the supervisory council (*stebėtojų taryba*)), the duties of which are laid down in principle in the ABĮ, are optional. **14**

1.6.1 Managing Director

The managing director, being a natural person, is the compulsory single-person corporate body of a UAB. He enjoys the exclusive right of representing the company *vis-à-vis* third parties (Sec. 37 ABĮ). However, upon a decision of the shareholders, the managing director may be awarded joint power of representation[11] (whereby the managing director may only represent the company together with a board member. **15**

The managing director is appointed and dismissed from office by the board, or by the supervisory council if the board is not formed or by the shareholders' meeting if the supervisory council is not formed either (Sec. 37 ABĮ). Some ambiguity is introduced by the legal status of the managing director. On the one hand, the managing director is an employee of the company employed under a labour contract and enjoying certain protections under labour law. On the other hand, he is the corporate body of the company, the legal status of which is governed by civil law.[12] **16**

The managing director is responsible for the day-to-day management of the company. He is legally independent and may not be instructed by shareholders with respect to management issues falling within the powers of corporate bodies of the company (i.e. the managing director and the board). If a board exists, then certain transactions may be entered into by the managing director based only on a decision of the board (Sec. 37 ABĮ).[13] The powers of the managing director may be restricted by the articles of association, however, only to the extent permitted by law. Notwithstanding the above, no restriction of the managing director's powers may be employed by the company in trying to escape liability through invocation of the *ultra vires* doctrine (Sec. 2.83 CK).[14] **17**

11 The joint power of representation has to be established in the articles of association and notified to the Register of Legal Entities (Sec. 2.83 Subs. 2 CK).

12 The Ruling of the Supreme Court of Lithuania (*Lietuvos Aukščiausiasis Teismas*) in the civil case No. 3K-3-1203/2001 *AB "Laivitė" v. G. Radzevičius* dated 28 November 2001.

13 See Mn. 16.

14 Only breach of the joint power of representation may induce implementation of the *ultra vires* doctrine.

1.6.2 Shareholders' Meeting

18 The powers of the shareholders' meeting are statutorily established and include the right of decision on issues vital to the company. Generally, the shareholders' meeting makes decisions on the appointment and dismissal of supervisory or corporate bodies, amendments to the articles of association, restructuring, reorganisation or transformation of the company or on other issues which are not routine. This results in an absolute prohibition on the assignment of powers of the shareholders' meeting to other bodies of the company (Sec. 19 Subs. 5 ABĮ).

19 Notably, the shareholders' meeting may not decide on management issues falling within the powers of other bodies of the company nor on those issues which by their essence are the functions of the corporate bodies (Sec. 20 Subs. 2 ABĮ). Still, the shareholders are free to draft the articles of association to the extent permitted by law and to lay down that certain decisions on business transactions adopted by the board (or by the managing director if no board exists) will require the approval of the shareholders' meeting (Sec. 34 Subs. 5 ABĮ). However, the prior instructions or approval of the shareholders to carry out a particular action does not release the managing director or board members from their liability for such action.

1.6.3 Board

20 The board is an optional collegial corporate body of the company. The board must have at least three members, who may be elected for a period not exceeding four years; reappointment is also possible (Sec. 33 ABĮ). The board is elected by the supervisory council (if one exists) or by the shareholders' meeting.

21 In the event that the shareholders opt to form a board, the latter will be responsible for the appointment and removal of the managing director, calling the shareholders' meeting, drawing up the operating policy of the company, etc. The board will adopt only those corporate decisions which are economically feasible for the company[15] (Sec. 34 ABĮ). If no board exists, its powers are legally assigned to the managing director of the company.

1.6.4 Supervisory Council

22 The supervisory council is a collegial supervisory body appointed by the shareholders' meeting responsible for the effective monitoring of the functions performed by the company's corporate bodies (Sec. 32 ABĮ). The supervisory council is an optional body of a UAB and is not used very often.

23 Pursuant to Sec. 31 ABĮ, the supervisory council must have at least three members and not more than 15 members, whose term of office may not exceed four years; re-election is also possible. In pursuance of achieving a genuine division of powers in the company, the ABĮ stipulates that powers of the supervisory council may not be assigned to other bodies of the company.

1.7 Duties and Liabilities of Directors

24 The members of any body of the company must perform their duties using the diligence of a prudent businessman and be loyal to the company. In addition to his general duties, the managing director is responsible for the proper fulfilment of the requirements for the acquisition by the company of its own shares (Sec. 54 ABĮ), as well as being obliged to apply for insolvency proceedings if (i) the company is insolvent and will not be able to settle with its creditors and the creditors have not applied for insolvency proceedings; or (ii) the company has publicly announced or otherwise informed a creditor that the company is not able to settle with it.

15 E.g. (i) decisions to transfer, invest or lease long-term assets of the company the book value of which exceeds 1/20 of the company's share capital; (ii) decisions to issue guarantees or sureties which create liability in respect of the company over 1/20 of the company's share capital; and (iii) decisions for the company to become a founder or a member/shareholder of other legal entities, etc.

As a general rule, the managing director and board members are liable *vis-à-vis* the shareholders and the company only (i.e. it is the company and not the managing director which is responsible *vis-à-vis* the third party creditors[16]). Consequently, board members who made decisions detrimental to the interests of the company are exposed to joint and several liability. The managing director as a single-person corporate body faces individual liability for any management decision (save for those decisions attributed to the competence of the board, if a board exists). The managing director is not released from his liability even in the case of an allocation of responsibilities between his co-managing directors. The general approval of the managing director's services for the past business year in the annual shareholders' meeting is not common and therefore does not release the managing director from his liability. In the event of a material breach, the managing director may face not only civil but also administrative or criminal punishment. For some particular administrative or criminal actions a court even may deprive a person of the right to act as a managing director for a time period fixed by the court on a case-by-case basis. 25

Different limitation periods are applied with respect to decisions made and transactions entered into by the corporate bodies of the company. Thus, claims against the decisions of the managing director or the board of the company become time-barred after 30 days from the day when the claimant found out or should have found out about the contested decision. For claims against transactions entered into by the corporate bodies, general rules are applied, i.e. such claims are time-barred after 10 years from the day when the claimant found out or should have found out about the contested transaction.[17] 26

If a member of any corporate body acts *ultra vires* and the company performs a transaction improperly, then the member acting *ultra vires* has several liability towards third parties (Sec. 2.83 Subs. 3 CK). The risks of the members of corporate bodies are increased due to the fact that, although allowed, D&O insurance, the insurance-related premiums of which may be paid by the company, is very uncommon in Lithuania. 27

1.8 Shareholders' Liability

Although rare, there are certain situations which may lead to a shareholder's liability. These can be divided into two principal groups. 28

First, the company is entitled to recover dividends paid out to a shareholder provided that shareholder knew or should have known that dividends were allocated and/or paid in breach of the provisions of applicable laws (Sec. 60 ABĮ). 29

Secondly, a shareholder can be held liable to third parties for any claims arising out of its fraudulent acts due to which the company is not able to fully perform its commitments to the creditors (Sec. 2.50 Subs. 3 CK). However, the liability of a shareholder will be several only. The very fact of the fraudulent acts will be adjudicated as a shareholder's fault, and no limited liability could therefore be invoked. For example, a shareholder will be held responsible if that shareholder causes a UAB to transfer assets to a newly incorporated entity of such shareholder, resulting in the insolvency of the UAB.[18] 30

1.9 Capitalisation and Financing

1.9.1 Basic Concepts

The separation of the company's assets from the shareholders' assets is the underlying concept of the company's financing regulations. Thus, the shareholders do not enjoy an ownership right to any portion of the company's assets save for the right to receive a part of the company's profit 31

16 With the exception of cases referred to in Mn. 27.

17 The Ruling of the Supreme Court of Lithuania in civil case No. 3K-3-230/2005 *UAB Coris Vilnius" v. S. M. Masedunskas* dated 4 April 2005.

18 The Ruling of the Supreme Court of Lithuania in civil case No. 3K-3-124/2004 *UAB "Göllner spedition" v. S. Beinorius and A. Beinorienė* dated 18 February 2004.

(dividend) and a part of the residual assets of the company in liquidation, and no other forms of repayment of share capital may be used.[19]

32 As a rule, the share capital is intended to satisfy the interests of the creditors, employees and other *bona fide* third parties (i.e. the "external" financial indicator). Therefore, it is the equity capital[20] which is the "internal" key financial indicator of the company. In the case where the equity capital falls below one half of the share capital of the company, the management and the shareholders will be called to implement measures counterbalancing the equity capital and the share capital (Sec. 38 Subs. 3 ABĮ).

1.9.2 Minimum Share Capital

33 The minimum share capital of a UAB is approximately LTL 10,000 (approximately EUR 2,900) (Sec. 2 Subs. 4 ABĮ). The initial contributions for the subscribed shares comprising not less than one-quarter of the nominal value of such shares must be paid up by a shareholder in cash. The aggregate amount of the initial contributions in cash must be equal to the statutorily established minimum amount of the share capital (Sec. 8 ABĮ). The initial contributions for the shares must be fully paid up before the application to a public notary.[21] The remaining part of the contribution for the subscribed shares must be paid within 12 months of the execution of the incorporation agreement/incorporation statement (Sec. 8 Subs. 2 ABĮ).

1.9.3 Maintenance of Capital and Liquidity

34 The underlying principal of preservation of the company's capital lies in the requirements for the shareholders to contribute the minimum share capital of the company in cash and preserve equity capital equal to not less than half of the share capital.

(i) System

35 Pursuant to Sec. 45 ABĮ, payments for shares by the shareholders may be made in cash[22] and/or in kind.[23] Assets withdrawn from public circulation as well as works and services may not be used as contributions in kind. The underlying idea is therefore that the company must have a real financial benefit from any contribution in kind. Where the above requirements are breached, the company shall be deemed to acquire the improperly paid-up shares itself or the increase in the share capital may result in the invalidation thereof.

36 In contrast to the restrictions on shareholders receiving repayment of the share capital,[24] to a large extent there are no prohibitions on shareholders financing the company. The shareholders are entitled to make new contributions by subscribing newly issued shares, granting loans,[25] and financing the company in the form of shareholders' contributions for the purpose of covering losses of the company (Sec. 49 ABĮ).[26] However, in the latter case, the shareholders will not be entitled to receive any shares or other benefit from the company (i.e. so-called "unremunerated" financing).

19 Railaitė in: Manager's World, p. 45.

20 The equity capital consists of the registered share capital, the share premium account, the revaluation reserve, the legal reserve (i.e. mandatory reserve), the reserve for own shares, other reserves and the inappropriate result (profit/loss), (Sec. 38 Subs. 1 ABĮ).

21 See Mn. 6.

22 See Mn. 33.

23 Contributions in kind have to be evaluated by an independent asset appraiser prior to the contributing thereof (Sec. 8 Subs. 8 ABĮ). Contributions in kind may only be paid if a decision of the shareholders' meeting is issued to that effect. The said decision must specify the item contributed as a contribution in kind, the person contributing in kind and the value of that item (Sec. 45 ABĮ).

24 See Mn. 31.

25 See Mn. 43.

26 I.e. to restore the equity capital of the company to an amount equal to half of the share capital.

(ii) Distributions

The distribution of profits (i.e. dividends) to the shareholders may only be made on the basis of a decision of the shareholders' meeting regarding the approval of the annual financial statement and the utilisation of annual profits, i.e. no interim dividends are possible. If, upon the approval of the annual financial statement, the shareholders' meeting issues no decision on the distribution of profits then the profit will be considered as inappropriate profit which will be moved to the results of the company in the following financial year.[27] **37**

Announcement of dividends is prohibited if thereafter the equity capital of the company would become lower than the protected capital of the company,[28] or the company is insolvent or would become insolvent after the payment of dividends, or the results of the financial year available for appropriation are negative (Sec. 60 ABĮ). **38**

(iii) Acquisition of Own Shares and Related Financing

Pursuant to Sec. 54 ABĮ, a UAB may purchase[29] its own shares provided the shares are fully paid up.[30] The purchase of shares must be based on the decision of the shareholders' meeting. Prior to the acquisition of shares, a reserve for own shares must be formed. Such reserve must amount to not less than the aggregate amount of the issuance price of the shares intended for acquisition by the company. However, having purchased its own shares, the company may not enjoy any proprietary or non-proprietary rights attached to such shares. Notably, the acceptance of its own shares by the company as a security for the discharge of any obligation will also be considered as the acquisition of the company's own shares (Sec. 54 Subs. 8 ABĮ). **39**

The company is restricted from acquiring its own shares if: (i) this would result in the equity capital being less than the aggregate amount of the share capital, legal reserve and reserve for own shares; or (ii) the aggregate par values of own shares being acquired by the company together with the par values of other own shares already held by the company would exceed one-tenth of the share capital. **40**

The following specific rules govern the provision of financial assistance by a UAB in the acquisition of its own shares by a third party: (i) if the shares of the company are acquired by its subsidiary, the shares are treated as having been acquired by the parent company; (ii) where the shares of the company are subscribed for or acquired by a person acting on his own behalf but for the benefit of the company and using its funds, the shares are treated as having been subscribed for or acquired by the company. **41**

(iv) Company as Lender or Guarantor

A UAB enjoys rights of granting loans and issuing guarantees or sureties to third parties and its shareholders provided the company meets certain legal requirements.[31] However, enjoyment of these rights must be profitable to the company. **42**

27 Railaitė in: Manager's World, p. 45.

28 The protected capital consists of the aggregate amount of the share capital, the legal reserve, the revaluation reserve and the reserve for own shares.

29 The company is solely entitled to purchase its own shares from other shareholders of the company. Thus, pursuant to Sec. 44 Subs. 6 ABĮ, the subscription for its own shares by the company is prohibited.

30 The above requirement has one exception pursuant to which the company shall be deemed to acquire own shares which were not fully paid up by a subscriber. However, in such a case the company must transfer the said shares to other persons or reduce its share capital by cancelling those shares thereafter (Sec. 45 Subs. 12 ABĮ).

31 These requirements are as follows: (i) a company's income from the said activities may not comprise the significant part of its aggregate income (Sec. 2 Subs. 42 Law on Financial Institutions (*Finansų įstaigų įstatymas*, "FĮĮ")); (ii) a company's funds lent to third parties may not exceed the amount of its equity capital; and (iii) a company may not make advance payments, give loans or offer security for the discharge of its obligations to third parties if such actions are aimed at enabling other persons to acquire shares in that company (Sec. 44 Subs. 9 ABĮ).

(v) Company as Borrower

43 There are no general legal restrictions regarding providing the company with a loan, surety or guarantee. However, in pursuance of preserving the capital of the company, the aggregate amount of the funds borrowed by a company from non-professional lenders[32] may not exceed its equity capital.[33]

44 The shareholders are not legally committed to ensuring the sufficient funding of the company. Shareholders' loans to the company are in principal allowed, although certain restrictions are applied. Hence, when the company borrows from its shareholders: (i) it may not pledge or mortgage its assets to those shareholders; and (ii) the interest rate may not be higher than the average interest rate offered by commercial banks in the lender's domicile (Sec. 15 Subs. 1 ABĮ). No specific rules regarding the ranking of shareholders' loans in insolvency proceedings are applied, i.e. they have neither preference over nor inferiority to other loans.

45 In addition, the company may issue debentures (Sec. 55 ABĮ). However, it is still a novelty for a UAB to do so.

1.10 Publication and Filing Requirements

46 Information on every UAB incorporated in Lithuania is kept with the Register of Legal Entities. The Register of Legal Entities is the centralised official state register open to the public, and may be accessed online.[34] Any person can, for a fixed fee, obtain copies of documents filed by any UAB and request excerpts detailing the principal corporate information of the company in question.

47 A *bona fide* third party may rely on the content of the Register of Legal Entities. Therefore, a transaction entered by a person which in the Register of Legal Entities is indicated as having signatory power on behalf of the company would be binding on the company.

48 The law provides for an exhaustive list of information and documentation which must be filed by a UAB with the Register of Legal Entities.[35] In certain cases, information relating to a UAB must be announced publicly.[36] As a general rule it is the managing director who is responsible for filing or announcing the information. Thus, in the case where the managing director fails to file the information with the Register of Legal Entities when due, he may be subject to a fine ranging from approximately EUR 29 up to approximately EUR 1450. In certain cases (e.g. not filing the annual accounts for more than two years or not renewing the information about the company for more than five years) a UAB may ultimately be liquidated at the instigation of the manager of the Register of Legal Entities. Although, due to their novelty, neither of the above sanctions yet have been imposed, it is more a question of time than probability.

1.11 Financial Reporting

49 The financial statements of a UAB must be drawn up and approved by the shareholders' meeting within four months of the end of the business year.[37] Additionally, the board or the managing director (if no board exists) must draw up an annual report on the activities of the company (Sec. 36 ABĮ).

32 Only the Bank of Lithuania, financial institutions, insurance companies and other persons capable of evaluating the risks associated with lending are considered as professional lenders (Sec. 2 Subs. 29 FĮĮ).

33 Sec. 3 Subs. 4 FĮĮ.

34 www.kada.lt.

35 *Inter alia*, a registration certificate of a parent company (where a founder is a foreign legal person); an incorporation agreement/an incorporation statement (Sec. 7 Subs. 6 ABĮ); the articles of association, and any shareholders' decisions regarding amendments to the articles of association (Sec. 4 ABĮ); decisions on the appointment and dismissal of members of corporate or supervisory bodies; explicit data about the sole shareholder and the members of other bodies of the company, including a *prokurist*; information about any licence held by the company (Sec. 2.66 CK); annual accounts; an annual report on the activities of the company (Sec. 36 ABĮ); etc.

36 The scope of information which must be publicly announced is limited to certain fundamental cases, for example, change of the company name.

37 For the requirements for having the annual financial accounts audited, see Mn. 8.

Certain relief from financial reporting requirements is granted to small enterprises. Small enterprises (irrespective whether it is a UAB or an AB) are those not exceeding two of the three following criteria for the two consecutive years: assets shown in the balance sheet of approximately EUR 1,448,100, annual net revenue of approximately EUR 2,027,400, a workforce of 10 employees in the annual average. Small companies may draw up and file to the Register of Legal Entities shorter and less detailed annual financial accounts, i.e. shorter balance sheet and profit (loss) statement and no cash flow account. In addition, UABs (but not ABs) enjoy release from auditing requirements, provided they meet certain criteria.[38]

The financial statements must be drawn up in accordance with the Law on Financial Statements (*Įmonių finansinės atskaitomybės įstatymas*, "ĮFAĮ") and Lithuanian Accounting Standards ("LAS"),[39] i.e. business accounting standards approved by the Accounting Institute of the Republic of Lithuania. A UAB is not committed to drawing up its financial statements in accordance with International Accounting Standards ("IAS") although they are permitted and may be used in parallel with LAS.

1.12 Employee Participation in Corporate Bodies

Employees are not represented in the corporate or supervisory bodies of a UAB. **50**

2 The Stock Corporation ("AB")

Literature: Mikelėnas/Bartkus/Mizaras/Keserauskas, Commentary on the Second Book ("Persons") of the Civil Code of the Republic of Lithuania (Justitia 2002)

In Lithuania, the other corporate entity offering limited shareholder liability is the stock corpo- **51**
ration (*Akcinė bendrovė*, "AB"). In comparison with a UAB, the advantage of an AB is that its shares may be listed on the Stock Exchange, which facilitates the raising of new capital in the market: the company's financing becomes more flexible at optimal costs. However, shareholders are particularly remote from the day-to-day business of the company, and this may give rise to conflicts of interest relating to corporate governance.

2.1 Export of Company

As for a UAB, the incorporation theory is the decisive factor regarding the possibility of export- **52**
ing an AB abroad.[40]

2.2 Transformation into a Foreign Entity

Rules on transformation of an AB into a foreign company are the same as for a UAB.[41] However, **53**
in contrast to a UAB, an AB may be merged with an S.E.

2.3 Incorporation

Principally, the incorporation of an AB has the same procedure as for a UAB,[42] but with some **54**
additional steps. Namely, prior to payment of the initial contributions for the shares, the founders must open a general securities account with the Central Securities Depository (*Centrinis depozitoriumas*) (Sec. 46 Subs. 3 Law on Securities Market (*Vertybinių popierių rinkos įstatymas*, "VPRĮ"). After the payment of all the initial contributions for the shares, the founders of the AB must draw up the statutory report and approve the same at the incorporation meeting.

38 For details see Mn. 8.
39 Sec. 15 ĮFAĮ.
40 See Mn. 2 et seq.
41 See Mn. 5.
42 See Mn. 6 et seq.

55 The length of the incorporation procedure may vary from one to eight weeks.[43] The notarial and registration fees for the incorporation of an AB, irrespective of the share capital, will amount to approximately LTL 500 (approximately EUR 150).

2.4 Recurrent Costs and Efforts

56 The annual costs and efforts required to maintain an AB are significantly higher in comparison to those of a UAB. Every AB must audit its financial statements, the costs of which depend on the size of the company and may in certain cases reach up to EUR 20,000. Further costs relate to the calling of annual shareholders' meetings and the maintaining of at least one corporate body (the managing director). Moreover, burdensome expenses pertain to the disclosure and filing of information,[44] etc.

2.5 Shares and Share Transfers

57 Only non-material (book-entry) shares may be issued by an AB. Shares of an AB may be of several classes, namely ordinary shares, preference shares and employee shares,[45] (Secs. 42 and 43 ABĮ). All shares of the same class carry equal proprietary and non-proprietary rights. As for a UAB, rights attached to the shares of different classes may vary. The transfer of shares is effected by executing a written share transfer agreement, except for cases where shares are transferred on the Stock Exchange. An entry in the shareholders' securities accounts is direct proof of the right of ownership to the securities specified thereby. Shareholders' securities accounts may be managed by professional account managers only (Sec. 46 VPRĮ).

58 The shares in an AB may be offered for sale and traded in publicly on the Stock Exchange. Currently, there are two trading lists on the Stock Exchange: (a) the official trading list; and (b) the current trading list. Shares not registered in the above trading lists are considered as unlisted securities.

59 Unlisted shares may not be offered for sale using the services of professional account managers. As a general rule, transactions for the sale and purchase of shares admitted to the official or current list may be executed on the Stock Exchange.

2.6 Corporate Bodies

60 As in the case of a UAB, an AB must have at least two bodies, namely the managing director and the shareholders' meeting. The setting up of collegiate bodies for supervision and management facilitates a more efficient and transparent management process. Therefore, a board and supervisory council are preferred[46] although not compulsory.

2.6.1 Managing Director

61 The rules on the appointment and scope of powers of the managing director are to a large extent the same as in the case of a UAB.[47]

2.6.2 Shareholders' Meeting

62 The shareholders do not participate in the direct management of the company. Generally, they only contribute their property to the share capital of the company and appoint persons to be in charge of the supervision or management of the company (as the case may be).

43 The length of the incorporation procedure may also be subject to additional incorporation steps which may be taken (e.g. temporary reservation of the company name with the Register of Legal Entities, or drafting of a prospectus).

44 See Mn. 75.

45 See Mn. 9.

46 Principle II of the recommended Corporate Governance Code for Companies Listed on the Vilnius Stock Exchange of Lithuania, approved by the Management Board of the Vilnius Stock Exchange of Lithuania.

47 For details see Mn. 15 et seq.

The powers of the shareholders' meeting are statutorily established and are no different from those of a UAB.[48] As in the case of a UAB, the powers of the shareholders' meeting are exclusive and may not be assigned to any other bodies of the company (Sec. 19 Subs. 5 ABĮ). 63

2.6.3 Board

The board is a collegial management body, which is responsible for the strategic management of the company and which performs other key functions of corporate governance. In principal, the formation and powers of the board of an AB are no different from those of a UAB.[49] However, the board has some additional duties relating to the public trading of an AB's shares. Therefore, the board must publicly publish its opinion concerning every tender offer to acquire the shares of an AB (Sec. 18 VPRĮ). 64

2.6.4 Supervisory Council

The supervisory council is a collegial supervisory body responsible for the effective monitoring of the functions performed by the company's corporate bodies. The formation and functions of the supervisory council are the same as in the case of a UAB.[50] 65

2.7 Duties and Liabilities of Directors

The duties and liabilities of the members of the management and supervisory bodies of an AB are to a large extent the same as in the case of a UAB,[51] save for the additional duties of the managing director regarding the disclosure of information relating to an AB.[52] 66

2.8 Shareholders' Liability

As with the shareholders of a UAB, the shareholders of an AB bear liability for the company's obligations only for the amount they pay for the shares, although certain exceptions exist.[53] 67

2.9 Capitalisation and Financing

2.9.1 Basic Concepts

The recognition of a company's exclusive right to own its assets through the right of ownership is the underlying concept of company financing regulations. Notably, as in the case of a UAB, equity capital is the main indicator in respect of the day-to-day financials of an AB.[54] 68

2.9.2 Minimum Share Capital

The minimum share capital of an AB is approximately LTL 150,000 (approximately EUR 44,000) (Sec. 2 Subs. 3 ABĮ). As is the case with a UAB, the minimum share capital has to be rendered in cash and any capital above the said minimum threshold can be rendered in cash or in kind.[55] The initial contributions for the shares must be fully paid up before the application to a public notary. 69

48 See Mn. 18 et seq.
49 See Mn. 20 et seq.
50 See Mn. 22 et seq.
51 See Mn. 24 et seq.
52 See Mn. 75.
53 For details see Mn. 28 et seq.
54 See Mn. 31 et seq.
55 See Mn. 33.

2.9.3 Maintenance of Capital and Liquidity

(i) System

70 The rules on the preservation and maintenance of the capital of an AB are to a large extent the same as in the case of a UAB.[56] However, as the shares of an AB may be traded publicly, it is easier to convert the shares into cash and therefore to benefit from the greater liquidity of the shares.

(ii) Distributions

71 Distribution of profits to the shareholders may only be made on the basis of a decision of the shareholders' meeting regarding the approval of the annual financial statement and the utilisation of annual profits, i.e. no interim dividends are allowed. The rules pertaining to the disbursement of dividends are the same as for a UAB.[57]

(iii) Acquisition of Own Shares and Related Financing

72 The legal requirements and procedure pertaining to the purchase of its own shares by an AB are analogous to those of a UAB[58] save for the requirement laid down in Sec. 54 Subs. 1 ABĮ pursuant to which, prior to the acquisition of its own shares, an AB must submit a voluntary tender offer.[59]

(iv) Company as Lender or Guarantor

73 As is the case with a UAB, loans and securities to third parties are allowed if certain requirements are met.[60]

(v) Company as Borrower

74 As is the case with a UAB, a loan or granting of any security by a third person or a shareholder to an AB is generally allowed.[61] However, in contrast to a UAB, the issuance of debentures is quite common in an AB, especially taking into account: (i) the possibility of publicly trading in an AB's debentures (Sec. 55 ABĮ); and (ii) the fact that there are no obligations regarding the securitisation or the redemption thereof.

2.10 Publication and Filing Requirements

75 Data about every AB is kept with the same Register of Legal Entities as in the case of UABs. The publicity and filing requirements and the consequences for breach thereof for an AB are generally the same as for a UAB,[62] with the additional obligation for an AB to disclose information on every material event of the company[63] (Sec. 2 Subs. 9 VPRĮ). Moreover, an AB, whose securities are admitted to the official or current trading list must disclose a pro forma balance sheet and a profit (loss) account, a semi-annual report, an annual prospectus-report, etc.

56 See Mn. 34 et seq.
57 See Mn. 37 et seq.
58 See Mn. 39 et seq.
59 A tender offer means the procedure of announcing a company's (person's) intention to acquire part or all of the securities of a company (Sec. 17 VPRĮ).
60 For detailed legal and procedural requirements see Mn. 42.
61 See Mn. 43 et seq.
62 For details see Mn. 46 et seq.
63 A material event is an event related to the company's activity which might have a significant influence on the market price of the company's securities, e.g. most of the decisions of the shareholders' meeting, the supervisory council and the board of the company; change of the company's name or address; a judicial decision on the company's rehabilitation; a decision to restrict the company's activity, or suspend or revoke authorisation to engage in its main activity; preliminary results (net profit/loss) of the company's activity over the accounting period (quarter, year), etc.

2.11 Financial Reporting

An AB's financial statements must be drawn up in accordance with the ĮFAĮ and LAS. Those ABs whose securities have been publicly traded are obliged to draw up their accounts in accordance with IAS (Sec. 15 Subs. 5 FAĮ). **76**

2.12 Employee Participation in Corporate Bodies

These requirements correspond with the requirements for a UAB.[64] **77**

64 See Mn. 50.

XVI. Luxembourg

*by Jean-Michel Schmit (LL.M.) and Nicolas Gauzès**

1 The Limited Liability Company ("S.à r.l.")

Literature: Metzler, Le Régime Juridique et Fiscal des Sociétés à Responsabilité Limitée dans le Grand-Duché de Luxembourg (Sirey, Bruylant and Buck, 1933)

The limited liability company (*Société à responsabilité limitée*, "S.à r.l.") is a corporate form used in Luxembourg for companies which do not need to solicit funds from the public or to obtain listing of their shares on the stock exchange (Sec. 179 et seq. of the law of 10 August 1915 relating to commercial companies as amended (the "LLC")). An S.à r.l. comprises a limited number of shareholders (one to 40 shareholders) (Sec. 181 LLC) who can transfer their shares only to third parties that are not shareholders, if such transfer is approved by the shareholders' meeting voting with a special majority of the holders of three-quarters of the share capital (Sec. 189 LLC). 1

1.1 Export of Company

According to Luxembourg law, the domicile of a commercial company is located at the place of its principal establishment, which is deemed to be located at the company's registered office (Sec. 2 LLC). A decision to move the place of the principal establishment of an S.à r.l. to a foreign country results in the company ceasing to be subject to Luxembourg law. However, subject to the law of the foreign country into which the place of the company's principal establishment is moved, the transfer of the place of the principal establishment of an S.à r.l. into a foreign country will not be considered as a dissolution of the S.à r.l. and the company will continue to exist in the foreign country without losing its legal identity.[1] 2

1.2 Transformation into a Foreign Entity

The shareholders of an S.à r.l. may by unanimous vote resolve to change the company's nationality and hence transform the S.à r.l. into a foreign entity (Sec. 199 LLC). From a Luxembourg company law point of view, such a resolution will not be considered a dissolution of the company and the company will continue to exist without losing its legal identity.[2] 3

1.3 Incorporation

The S.à r.l. is set up by way of a notarial deed of incorporation (Sec. 4 LLC) and legally exists immediately upon execution of the said notarial deed by the founding shareholders and the notary. An S.à r.l. shall at all times have a minimum of one and a maximum of 40 shareholders (Sec. 181 LLC), which may be corporate entities and/or individuals. 4

The precise length of the incorporation procedure may vary, but is achievable within one week.[3] The notarial fees for the incorporation of an S.à r.l. are proportionate to the amount of the subscribed capital.[4] As a general rule, a capital duty of 1 per cent of the subscribed capital is also due. In addition, there will be registration costs with the Luxembourg Trade and Companies Register 5

* *Linklaters Loesch*, Luxembourg. The authors wish to thank Jean-Paul Spang, *Linklaters Loesch*, for his most helpful suggestions and observations.

1 The recent ECJ rulings in the cases Überseering and InspireArt (see Part 1, I, Mn. 17 et seq. and 19) should not have any consequence for this.

2 Amendments to the LLC dealing with the European Stock Corporation (S.E.) which will result from the implementation of a recent draft bill (no. 5352) which has not yet been adopted in Parliament, will not apply to S.à r.l. and will thus have no effect on the transformation of a domestic S.à r.l. into a foreign entity.

3 Given the limited costs and time required to incorporate a new company in Luxembourg, it is unusual to use an existing shelf-company.

4 For an S.à r.l. with the minimum share capital of EUR 12,400, the notary fees will amount to approximately EUR 500 + 12 per cent VAT.

(*Registre du Commerce et des Sociétés*)[5] and costs of publication in the Luxembourg Official Gazette (*Mémorial C*) proportionate to the length of the text of the notarial deed of incorporation.[6]

1.4 Recurrent Costs and Efforts

6 Recurrent costs and efforts relating to an S.à r.l. are not substantial. Often the company is registered with a domiciliary agent, who will also provide ancillary services, such as the preparation, publication and filing of the annual accounts with the Luxembourg Trade and Companies Register.[7] The fees of the domiciliary agents vary from one domiciliary agent to another and depend on the services provided.[8] Other costs only materialise in the event certain corporate steps are taken which require notarisation, filing with the Luxembourg Trade and Companies Register or publication. There is no annual registration fee due to the Luxembourg Trade and Companies Register.

1.5 Shares and Share Transfers

7 The share capital of an S.à r.l. is divided into shares which must have an equal par value of at least EUR 25,[9] or the equivalent amount in any foreign currency. All shares must be fully paid up and in registered form.

An S.à r.l. can issue different classes of shares with different financial rights attaching to them. Each of the shares, regardless of any class of shares, must however at all times give right to one vote.

8 The shares may not be issued to the public and are not freely transferable to non-shareholders. The law imposes certain minimum restrictions, which may be strengthened by the articles of incorporation. The transfer of shares to a non-shareholder is subject to the approval of the shareholders representing at least three quarters of all the shares (Sec. 189 LLC). Share transfers must be documented in writing in a notarial deed or in an agreement under private seal. *Vis-à-vis* the company and third parties, the transfer is effective when it has been accepted by, or notified to, the company (Sec. 190 LLC). A share transfer must also be filed with the Luxembourg Trade and Companies Register and published in the Luxembourg Official Gazette. No transfer taxes are levied in Luxembourg on a transfer of shares.

1.6 Corporate Bodies

1.6.1 Managers

9 An S.à r.l. is managed by one or several managers (*gérants*), which may be shareholders or not and which may be corporate entities or individuals (Sec. 191 LLC).[10] The managers are appointed by the shareholders for a limited or an unlimited period of time. The appointments must be filed with the Luxembourg Trade and Companies Register and be published in the Luxembourg Official Gazette. Unless the articles provide for the contrary, the managers are only removable for valid reasons.

10 Every manager has the power to perform any acts necessary or useful for the accomplishment of the object and purpose of the company. These powers cover all acts that are not expressly reserved by law to the decision of the shareholders. The managers represent the company *vis-à-vis* third

5 EUR 145.

6 For an average length bilingual text (e.g. English/French), the publication costs will be around EUR 500 to EUR 750.

7 The annual accounts of middle-sized and large S.à r.l. (companies exceeding two of the following criteria: a balance sheet total of more than EUR 3,125,000; a turnover of more than EUR 6,250,000; more than 50 employees) must be audited (Sec. 256). This will result in further costs being incurred.

8 For domiciliation services only, the annual cost may be estimated at a minimum of EUR 2,000 to EUR 3,000.

9 Following conversion to euro the exact amount is EUR 24.79 (Sec. 182 LLC).

10 There are no manager's qualification requirements under the law. Accordingly, anybody can in principle be appointed as managers of a Luxembourg S.à r.l. Disqualification rules, however, apply in cases of insolvent liquidation. Sec. 444-1 of the Commercial Code.

parties. They can be awarded joint or individual power of representation (Sec. 191bis LLC). The articles of incorporation may further restrict the powers of the managers, but such restrictions are not binding on third parties, even if the restrictions have been published.

1.6.2 Shareholders' Meeting

The powers of the shareholders' meeting are those which the company law and the articles entrust to it, namely, without limitation, the election and removal of the managers and of the statutory auditors, the approval of the annual accounts and the allocation of any available profits and any amendments to the company's articles, including the increase or reduction in the company's share capital, the transfer of the company's registered office (except within the same municipality) and the company's dissolution and liquidation. **11**

In principle, resolutions by the shareholders are adopted at general meetings. They may, however, also be adopted in writing, if there are not more than 25 shareholders (Sec. 193 LLC). As a general rule, decisions are validly adopted by the favourable vote of shareholders representing more than one half of the corporate capital. Special requirements as to quorum and majority are, however, applicable to the amendment of the articles of incorporation and to the approval of a transfer of shares to a third party.[11] **12**

1.6.3 Auditors

The auditing of the business of the S.à r.l. by one or more statutory auditors is only required where the S.à r.l. has more than 25 shareholders. The auditor(s) are designated in the articles of incorporation and/or (re-)appointed by the shareholders' meeting (Sec. 200 LLC). **13**

In certain circumstances,[12] the auditing must be entrusted to an independent auditor duly licensed in Luxembourg (*réviseur d'entreprises*). In such circumstances, the law does not require the appointment of a statutory auditor in addition to the independent auditor. **14**

1.7 Duties and Liabilities of Managers

The managers are not only responsible for managing the daily business of the S.à r.l., but also have certain other statutory obligations, including, for example, arranging for necessary filings to be made with the Luxembourg Trade and Companies Register, convening the annual shareholders' meeting and reporting to the auditor. **15**

Should the company become insolvent, the managers of the company must, according to law (Sec. 440 of the Commercial Code), voluntarily file for bankruptcy within one month.

Managers are liable (i) severally but not jointly towards the company for any misconduct in the management of the company's affairs, but which do not constitute a violation of legal or statutory provisions; and (ii) jointly and severally towards the company, the shareholders and third parties for acts which constitute a violation of legal or statutory provisions (Sec. 192 and 59 LLC). The managers can be discharged from such liability in the case of a violation to which they were not a party, provided no misconduct is attributable to them and they have reported such violation to the first general meeting after they had acquired knowledge thereof. Any claims against the managers, for actions taken by them in that capacity, become time-barred after five years as from the time of such actions, or if they were fraudulently concealed, from the discovery thereof. **16**

Once a year, after adoption of the company's balance sheet, the general meeting shall vote specifically as to whether discharge is given to the managers. Such discharge is valid and the managers' liability can no longer be sought by the company, provided the balance sheet on the

11 Transfers of shares must be approved by shareholders representing at least three-quarters of all the shares and amendment of the articles of association must be approved by a majority of the shareholders representing at least three-quarters of all the shares. Change of the company's nationality and increase of the obligation of the shareholders require unanimity.

12 Companies exceeding two of the following criteria: a balance sheet total of more than EUR 3,125,000; a turnover of more than EUR 6,250,000; more than 50 employees.

basis of which the discharge is given contains no omission or false information concealing the true situation of the company. Such a discharge has no impact on the possible liability of the managers towards third parties.

A managers' insurance may be subscribed and the payment of the related premiums by the company is permitted.

In addition to the general liability of the managers, Luxembourg law provides for specific criminal offences, notably where a manager of an S.à r.l. issues shares or bonds to the public, distributes dividends in the absence of available funds, acquires own shares with funds of the company that are not available, provides financial assistance for the subscription of shares or abuses the company's assets.

17 Where serious faults have been committed by the manager(s) and have contributed to the company's bankruptcy, Luxembourg courts may extend the corporate bankruptcy to the said manager(s) (Sec. 495-1 of the Commercial Code). The law also provides for criminal offences relating to the wrongful management of the company (Sec. 162 et seq. LLC).

1.8 Shareholders' Liability

18 The liability of the shareholders of an S.à r.l. is limited to the shareholders' initial and subsequent contributions to the company's capital. However, where a shareholder is held by a Luxembourg court to have *de facto* acted as manager of the company and has committed serious faults which have contributed to the company's bankruptcy, the courts may extend the corporate bankruptcy to such shareholder (Sec. 495-1 of the Commercial Code).

1.9 Capitalisation and Financing

1.9.1 Basic Concepts

19 The share capital of an S.à r.l. is intended to form a capital fund which is the minimum amount available to the company's creditors.

1.9.2 Minimum Share Capital

20 The minimum share capital of an S.à r.l. is EUR 12,400[13] or the equivalent amount in any foreign currency. It must be fully subscribed and paid up immediately upon incorporation either in cash or in kind.

21 In the case of an issue of new shares, the existing shareholders have no preferential subscription rights.

1.9.3 Maintenance of Capital and Liquidity

(i) System

22 Any contributions to the capital of an S.à r.l. must immediately be paid up by the shareholders and may be paid in cash or in kind. To avoid "hidden" contributions in kind any transaction of the company with a shareholder exceeding 10 per cent of the share capital within a period of 24 months after incorporation requires the approval of the shareholders' meeting.

23 The shareholders may decide to reduce the share capital provided the capital remains above the required minimum.

24 Nothing prevents the shareholders from financing the S.à r.l. by other means including shareholders' loans. Thin capitalisation rules, however, prohibit an excessive financing by means of debt rather than equity from a tax point of view.

13 Following conversion to euro the exact amount is EUR 12,394.68 (Sec. 182 LLC).

(ii) Distributions

Distributions of profits to shareholders usually have to be made on the basis of a shareholders' resolution deciding on the utilisation of the available annual profits. Such distributions can only be legally made from available annual profits or profits carried forward from previous years after deduction of losses carried forward. Prior to the utilisation of the annual profits to distribute a dividend to the shareholders, 5 per cent of the said annual profits must, however, be allocated to a legal reserve until such reserve amounts to 10 per cent of the subscribed capital of the company (Sec. 197 LLC). **25**

The law does not expressly provide for nor expressly prohibit the payment of interim dividends upon the decision of the managers. In the absence of legal certainty, the question of whether to pay out interim dividends shall be assessed carefully on a case by case basis. **26**

There is no express reference to the concept of hidden distributions under Luxembourg company law, but certain transactions may be considered as hidden distributions from a tax perspective and have negative tax consequences. **27**

(iii) Acquisition of Own Shares and Related Financing

In the absence of any legal provision or express prohibition in relation to the purchase and redemption of own shares by an S.à r.l., the question of whether an S.à r.l. may acquire or redeem its own shares shall be assessed carefully on a case by case basis. **28**

An S.à r.l. may not provide any financial assistance to a third party to acquire the shares issued by the S.à r.l.[14] **29**

(iv) Company as Lender or Guarantor

An S.à r.l. may give loans or grant guarantees to the undertakings forming part of the group of the company, including to its shareholder(s) or exceptionally to third parties, provided the said activity falls within the company's object, the company derives a benefit therefrom and the loans are made on arm's length terms. **30**

(v) Company as Borrower

Shareholders' loans to an S.à r.l. are generally allowed. In the event of insolvency they rank pari passu with non-shareholder loans. **31**

An S.à r.l. may borrow funds from third parties. It may issue debentures and other similar debt instruments, but only on a purely private basis (Sec. 188 LLC). **32**

1.10 Publication and Filing Requirements

A wide range of documentation and information must be filed with the Luxembourg Trade and Companies Register, some of which, including the identity of the shareholders, must also be published in the Luxembourg Official Gazette. **33**

Documents and extracts of documents will only be valid *vis-à-vis* third parties from the day of their publication in the Luxembourg Official Gazette unless the company concerned proves that the relevant third parties had prior knowledge thereof.

Non-compliance with the publication requirements under the law (for example, with respect to the annual accounts) can, as the case may be, be considered as a serious contravention of the law and lead to the compulsory dissolution and liquidation of the company concerned by order of the Luxembourg District Court (*Tribunal d'Arrondissement*).

The Luxembourg Trade and Companies Register is open to the public and any person can review the filed documents and request an excerpt from the Luxembourg Trade and Companies Register

14 By application of the principle set by Sec. 49-6 concerning S.A. and in combination with the penalties set by Sec. 168, which also apply to managers of an S.à r.l.

detailing the main corporate information of an S.à r.l., as well as copies of any documents that the company has filed with the Luxembourg Trade and Companies Register.

Third parties can rely on the information available at the Luxembourg Trade and Companies Register, unless the company concerned can bring evidence that the relevant third party had knowledge of other information. The publications in the Luxembourg Official Gazette are available online.[15]

1.11 Financial Reporting

34 An S.à r.l. must draw up its annual accounts comprising the balance sheet, the profit and loss account and the notes to the accounts within six months of the financial year end (Sec. 197 and Sec. 163 LLC). The annual accounts must be prepared in accordance with Luxembourg GAAP. The drawing of annual accounts in accordance with other accounting principles such as US GAAP or IAS/IFRS is generally not yet permitted.[16]

Certain relief from financial reporting requirements is granted to small companies. In Luxembourg small companies are those not exceeding two of the three following criteria: (i) a balance sheet total of EUR 3,125,000, (ii) a turnover of EUR 6,250,000, (iii) a workforce of 50 employees in the annual average. Small companies may draw up less detailed annual accounts, do not need to draw up a management report on the economic situation of the company and do not need to have their annual accounts audited by a licensed independent auditor (*réviseur d'entreprises*).

1.12 Employee Participation in Corporate Bodies

35 Luxembourg company law does not currently provide for the participation or the representation of the employees in corporate bodies.

2 The Stock Corporation ("S.A.")

Literature: Corbisier, Droit des Sociétés, Tableau Comparatif des Droits Luxembourgeois, Belge et Français et Textes Légaux Luxembourgeois (Bruylant, 2000)

36 The stock corporation (*Société anonyme*, "S.A.") is another important corporate entity offering limited shareholder liability. An S.A. must have a minimum of two shareholders, without, however, any maximum number of shareholders. As opposed to an S.à r.l., the transfer of shares in an S.A. is free, unless the transferability has been restricted by agreement or in the articles of association. An S.A. may solicit funds from the public and obtain listing of its shares on a stock exchange. Compared to the S.à r.l., it thus has better access to capital markets and therefore greater scope for raising funds to finance its business activities. The shareholding in an S.A. (except for the founding shareholders) may be kept anonymous.

2.1 Export of Company

37 The general provisions of Luxembourg law regarding the domicile of a commercial company apply to an S.A. in the same manner and under the same conditions as for an S.à r.l. and the possibilities and restrictions regarding the exporting of an S.A. are thus identical to those of an S.à r.l.[17]

15 http://www.legilux.public.lu.

16 The law provides that the Ministry of Justice can grant certain exemptions to the Luxembourg GAAP requirements. This provision aims at allowing the Ministry of Justice to permit certain companies to draw their annual accounts up in accordance with IAS/IFRS.

17 See Mn. 2.

2.2 Transformation into a Foreign Entity

A transformation of a Luxembourg S.A. into a foreign entity is carried out in the same manner as for an S.à r.l.[18] 38

2.3 Incorporation

The incorporation process of an S.A. is substantially identical to the incorporation process of an S.à r.l., except that an S.A. must have two founding shareholders (Sec. 26 LLC).[19] 39

The length and the costs relating to the incorporation procedure of an S.A. are identical to those incurred by an S.à r.l. (except that the minimum notarial fees and the minimum capital duty to be paid will be somewhat higher, as they are proportionate to the share capital, and as the minimum share capital of an S.A. is somewhat higher than the minimum share capital of an S.à r.l.).[20] 40

2.4 Recurrent Costs and Efforts

Recurrent costs and efforts relating to an S.A. are not substantial and are identical to those incurred by an S.à r.l.[21] 41

2.5 Shares and Share Transfers

The share capital of an S.A. is divided into shares which must have an equal par value of at least EUR 1.24, or the equivalent amount in any other currency (with or without indication of such value) (Sec. 37 LLC). 25 per cent of the par value of the shares must be paid up immediately upon subscription. Shares can either be in registered form or bearer shares. Holders of bearer shares can always request the conversion of their shares into registered shares, and vice versa, unless the articles specifically prohibit the conversion from registered shares into bearer shares. Shares not fully paid up must remain in registered form until payment in full has been made. 42

An S.A. can issue different classes of shares with different financial rights attaching to them. An S.A. can also issue non-voting shares within the limits provided for by law.

The shares may be issued to the public and are freely transferable unless the law, the articles or an agreement among shareholders restrict the transferability. Bearer shares are transferred by delivery and registered shares by agreement between the transferor and the transferee. *Vis-à-vis* the company and *vis-à-vis* third parties, the transfer of registered shares is effective upon registration in the company's shareholders' register. No transfer taxes are levied in Luxembourg on a transfer of shares. 43

2.6 Corporate Bodies

2.6.1 Board of Directors[22]

An S.A. is managed by a board of directors which comprises at least three directors who are appointed by the shareholders for a period not exceeding six years.[23] The directors can be corporate entities or individuals. They are re-eligible for election and may be removed at any time with or without cause by a simple majority vote of the shareholders' meeting (Sec. 51 LLC). The 44

18 See Mn. 3. A unanimous vote is required in accordance with Sec. 67-1 LLC.

19 Once the LLC has been amended in accordance with a recent draft bill (no. 5352), which has not yet been adopted in Parliament, dealing with the European Stock Corporation (S.E.), it will be possible to set up an S.A. with one shareholder only.

20 For an S.A with the minimum share capital of EUR 31,000, the notary fees will amount to approximately EUR 1,000 + 12 per cent VAT.

21 See Mn. 6.

22 The draft bill no. 5352 (see Fn. 19) offers a choice between the existing one-tier system with a board of directors and a new two-tier system with a supervisory board (*conseil de surveillance*) and a management board (*directoire*).

23 Under draft bill no. 5352, an S.A. which has one sole shareholder may have a board of directors comprising one director only.

appointments must be filed with the Luxembourg Trade and Companies Register and be published in the Luxembourg Official Gazette.

45 The board of directors has the power to perform any acts necessary or useful for the accomplishment of the object and purpose of the company.[24] These powers cover all acts that are not expressly reserved by law to the decision of the shareholders. The board of directors represents the company *vis-à-vis* third parties (Sec. 53 LLC). Directors can be awarded joint or individual power of representation. The articles of incorporation may further restrict the powers of the board of directors, but such restrictions are not binding on third parties, even if they have been published.

2.6.2 Day-to-day Management

46 The day-to-day management and the representation within such day-to-day management of an S.A. may be delegated by the board of directors to one or several directors, managers or other agents, which may be shareholders or not, acting individually or jointly. The delegation in favour of a member of the board of directors must be previously authorised by the general meeting of shareholders (Sec. 60 LLC).

2.6.3 Shareholders' Meeting

47 The powers of the general meeting are those which company law and the articles entrust to it, namely, without limitation, the election and the removal of the directors and of the statutory auditors, the approval of the annual accounts and the allocation of any available profits, any amendments to the articles of the S.A., including an increase or reduction in the company's share capital, the transfer of the company's registered office (except within the same municipality) and the company's dissolution and liquidation.

48 A general meeting must be held at least once a year at the date, hour and place specified in the articles. Any other general meeting may be convened by the board of directors or by the statutory auditor. It must be convened upon the request of shareholders representing 20 per cent of all the shares issued (Sec. 70 LLC).

49 The procedure to be followed during a shareholders' meeting may be laid down in the articles. The range of provisions that the articles may contain on that point is extremely wide. In principle, resolutions of the general meeting of shareholders are adopted by simple majority of the votes cast, but special requirements as to quorum and majority are applicable to the amendment of the articles of incorporation.[25]

2.6.4 Auditors

50 The auditing of the business of an S.A. is carried out by one or more statutory auditors, who may be shareholders or not. The statutory auditors are appointed by the general meeting of shareholders for a period which may not exceed six years (Sec. 61 LLC).

51 In certain circumstances,[26] the auditing must be entrusted to an independent auditor duly licensed in Luxembourg. In such circumstances, the law does not require the appointment of a statutory auditor in addition to the independent auditor.

2.7 Duties and Liabilities of Directors

52 The board of directors is not only responsible for managing the daily business of the S.A., but also has certain other statutory obligations, including, for example, arranging for necessary filings to

24 Any director having a personal interest in a transaction conflicting with that of the company may not take part in the deliberation of the board of directors.

25 Amendment to the articles of association must be approved by shareholders representing at least two-thirds of all the shares. Change of the company's nationality and increase of the obligations of the shareholders require unanimity.

26 Companies exceeding two of the following criteria: a balance sheet total of more than EUR 3,125,000; a turnover of more than EUR 6,250,000; more than 50 employees.

be made with the Luxembourg Trade and Companies Register, convening the annual shareholders' meeting and reporting to the auditor (Sec. 53 LLC).

The directors must submit to the general meeting of shareholders the question of whether to dissolve the company if one-half or three-quarters of the company's corporate capital is lost. If they fail to do so, the directors may personally be declared jointly and severally liable *vis-à-vis* the company for any increase in the loss incurred (Sec. 100 LLC).

Should the company become insolvent, the board of directors must, according to law (Sec. 440 of the Commercial Code), file for bankruptcy within one month.

In principle, the directors do not contract any personal liability deriving from the liabilities of **53** the company (Sec. 58 LLC). Directors are however liable (i) severally but not jointly towards the company for any misconduct in the management of the company's affairs, but which does not constitute a violation of legal or statutory provisions; and (ii) jointly and severally towards the company, the shareholders and third parties for acts which constitute a violation of legal or statutory provisions (Sec. 192 and 59 LLC). The directors can be discharged from such liability in the case of a violation to which they were not a party, provided no misconduct is attributable to them and they have reported such violation to the first general meeting after they had acquired knowledge thereof. Any claims against the directors, for actions taken by them in that capacity, become time-barred after five years as from the time of such actions, or if they were fraudulently concealed, from the discovery thereof.

Once a year, after adoption of the company's balance sheet, the general meeting shall vote specifically as to whether discharge is given to the directors. Such discharge is valid and the directors' liability can no longer be sought by the company, provided the balance sheet on the basis of which the discharge is given contains no omission or false information concealing the true situation of the company. Such a discharge has no impact on the possible liability of the directors towards third parties.

A directors' insurance may be subscribed and the payment of the related premiums by the company is permitted.

In addition to the general liability of the directors, Luxembourg law provides for specific criminal offences, notably where a director of an S.A. issues shares or bonds to the public, distributes dividends in the absence of available funds, acquires own shares with funds of the company that are not available, provides financial assistance for the subscription of shares or abuses the company's assets.

Where serious faults have been committed by one or several directors and have contributed to **54** the company's bankruptcy, Luxembourg courts may extend the corporate bankruptcy to the said director(s) (Sec. 495-1 of the Commercial Code) and disqualification rules may apply (Sec. 444-1 of the Commercial Code). The law also provides for criminal offences relating to the wrongful management of the company (Sec. 162 et seq LLC).

2.8 Shareholders' Liability

The liability of the shareholders of an S.A. is limited to the shareholders' initial and subsequent **55** contributions to the company's capital. However, where a shareholder is held by a Luxembourg court to have *de facto* acted as manager of the company and has committed serious faults which have contributed to the company's bankruptcy, the courts may extend the corporate bankruptcy to such shareholder (Sec. 495-1 of the Commercial Code).

2.9 Capitalisation and Financing

2.9.1 Basic Concepts

The share capital of an S.A. is intended to form a capital fund which is the minimum amount **56** available to the company's creditors.

2.9.2 Minimum Share Capital

57 The minimum share capital of an S.A. is EUR 31,000[27] or the equivalent amount in any foreign currency. It must be fully subscribed and at least one-quarter of each share must be paid up in cash or in kind. If a share premium is payable, it must be paid in full.

58 Besides the subscribed capital, there may be an authorised capital, i.e. the authority granted to the board of directors to from time to time increase the subscribed capital and issue additional shares within the authorised limit (Sec. 32 LLC). The authorisation granted to the board of directors to increase the share capital may not be granted for a period exceeding five years.

59 Where new shares are issued for cash, the existing shareholders have a statutory preferential right to subscribe for these shares. However, the shareholders' meeting, voting with the quorum and majority rules applicable to amendments to the articles, may resolve to limit or waive that preferential right (Sec. 32-3 LLC). The statutory preferential subscription right of existing shareholders does not exist where new shares are issued against payment in kind.

2.9.3 Maintenance of Capital and Liquidity

(i) System

60 Upon subscription of new shares, the shareholders must immediately pay in at least 25 per cent of the par value of the new shares subscribed for and 100 per cent of any share premium paid on the said shares. Contributions may be paid in cash or in kind. In case of a contribution in kind, the value of the said contribution must be appraised by an independent auditor duly licensed in Luxembourg (*réviseur d'entreprises*) (Sec. 32-1 Subs. 5 LLC).

61 The shareholders may decide to reduce the share capital provided the capital remains above the required minimum. Specific provisions are applicable where the share capital is reduced by reimbursement of part of the capital to the shareholders.

62 Nothing prevents the shareholders from financing an S.A. by other means including shareholders' loans. Thin capitalisation rules, however, prohibit an excessive financing by means of debt rather than equity from a tax perspective.

63 In the event of a loss of half or three-quarters of the corporate capital, the directors must convene the general meeting of shareholders to resolve on the possible dissolution of the company (Sec. 100 LLC).

(ii) Distributions

64 Distributions of profits to shareholders usually have to be made on the basis of a shareholders' resolution deciding on the utilisation of the available annual profits. Such distributions can only be legally made from available annual profits or profits carried forward from previous years after deduction of losses carried forward. Prior to the utilisation of the annual profits to distribute a dividend to the shareholders, 5 per cent of the said annual profits must, however, be allocated to a legal reserve until such reserve amounts to 10 per cent of the subscribed capital of the company (Sec. 72 LLC).

65 In the second half of the financial year, the board of directors, if so authorised by the articles of incorporation, may pay out an advance payment on dividends from the profit of the current financial year; in so doing the board of directors has to comply with the requirements laid down in law (Sec. 72-2 LLC).

66 There is no express reference to the concept of hidden distributions under Luxembourg company law, but certain transactions may be considered as hidden distributions from a tax perspective and have negative tax consequences.

27 Following conversion to euro the exact amount is EUR 3,986.69 (Sec. 26).

(iii) Acquisition of Own Shares and Related Financing

An S.A. may acquire a maximum of 10 per cent of its own fully paid-up shares subject to the prior authorisation to do so by the general meeting, which shall also determine the terms and conditions of the proposed acquisition. The acquisition may not have as a consequence that the net asset value of the company falls below the company's share capital and any undistributable reserves (Sec. 49-2 LLC). Among the rights attaching to the shares, the voting rights of its own shares held by the S.A. are suspended and if the said shares are included among the assets shown in the balance sheet, a non-distributable reserve of the same amount shall be created among the liabilities (Sec. 49-5 LLC). **67**

An S.A. may also issue redeemable shares, which will be redeemable subject to the terms and conditions laid down in the articles and in law (Sec. 49-8 LLC). **68**

An S.A. may not provide any financial assistance to third parties to acquire the shares issued by the S.A. (Sec. 49-6 LLC). **69**

(iv) Company as Lender or Guarantor

An S.A. may give loans or grant guarantees to third parties, including to the shareholder(s) of the company, provided the said activity falls within the company's object, the company derives a benefit therefrom and the loans are made on arm's length terms. **70**

(v) Company as Borrower

Shareholders' loans to an S.A. are generally allowed. In the event of insolvency they rank pari passu with non-shareholder loans. **71**

An S.A. may borrow funds from third parties. It may issue debentures or similar debt instruments in private and in public. **72**

2.10 Publication and Filing Requirements

A wide range of documentation and information must be filed with the Luxembourg Trade and Companies Register, some of which must also be published in the Luxembourg Official Gazette. **73**

Documents and extracts of documents will only be valid *vis-à-vis* third parties from the day of their publication in the Luxembourg Official Gazette unless the company concerned proves that the relevant third parties had prior knowledge thereof.

Non-compliance with the publication requirements under the law (for example, with respect to the annual accounts) can, as the case may be, be considered as a serious contravention of the law and lead to the compulsory dissolution and liquidation of the company concerned by order of the Luxembourg District Court (*Tribunal d'Arrondissement*).

The Luxembourg Trade and Companies Register is open to the public and any person can review the filed documents and request an excerpt from the Luxembourg Trade and Companies Register detailing the main corporate information of an S.A., as well as copies of any documents that the company has filed with the Luxembourg Trade and Companies Register.

Third parties can rely on the information available at the Luxembourg Trade and Companies Register, unless the company concerned can bring evidence that the relevant third party had knowledge of other information. The publications in the Luxembourg Official Gazette are available online.[28]

2.11 Financial Reporting

The accounting rules applicable to an S.A. correspond to those applicable to an S.à r.l.[29] **74**

28 http://www.legilux.public.lu.
29 See Mn. 34.

2.12 Employee Participation in Corporate Bodies

75 Luxembourg company law does not generally provide for the participation or the representation of employees in corporate bodies. The only S.A.s for which an employee participation at board level is required are those which have at least 1,000 employees working in Luxembourg, or in which the Luxembourg State holds a participation of at least 25 per cent, or which have been granted a government concession, in which case the board of directors must comprise nine directors at least one-third of whom represent the employees (Secs. 22 and 24 of the law of 6 May 1974 on worker's councils and on the representation of employees in S.A.s.).

XVII. Malta

*by Andrew Muscat**

1. The Limited Liability Company ("Ltd")

Literature: B.M. Hannigan, Farrar's Company Law (London: Butterworths 2003); L.C.B Gower, Gower's Principles of Modern Company Law (7th edition, London: Sweet & Maxwell 2003); Oscar Grech, Notes on the Companies Act

The private limited liability company ("Ltd")[1] is the most common corporate form used in Malta in order to achieve the concept of shareholder limited liability. It differs from the public company ("plc") mainly in that it cannot freely offer its shares to the public and in that the number of shareholders is limited to 50. 1

There are at present approximately 22,000 to 23,000 limited liability companies registered in Malta, in contrast to only 55 public companies.

1.1 Export of Company

The Companies Act 1995 ("CA") does not prohibit a company registered in Malta from moving its central place of business to another jurisdiction. Indeed, the real seat theory is not followed in Malta and in terms of Maltese law an Ltd would retain its identity as a Maltese Ltd even if it moves its central place of business to another jurisdiction. 2

1.2 Transformation into a Foreign Entity

This is regulated by the Continuation of Companies Regulations 2002.[2] An Ltd registered in Malta may be continued abroad and be transformed into a foreign entity if the law of an approved country or jurisdiction so allows and the consent of the register in Malta is obtained. Furthermore, the Ltd must apply to the proper authority of the selected country or jurisdiction. A request to the Registrar for his consent must be accompanied by a declaration signed by at least two directors of the Ltd. When the instrument of continuation is issued by the relevant authority of the foreign country, the company shall be deemed to have ceased to be a company incorporated in Malta and the Registrar will strike off the name of the company from the register.[3] 3

Maltese law does not provide for the possibility of an Ltd merging with an S.E.

1.3 Incorporation

An Ltd is only validly constituted if a memorandum of association is entered into and subscribed by at least two persons (Sec. 68 CA) but, in the case of a private exempt company, an Ltd may be also registered with one single member provided certain conditions are fulfilled. Together with the memorandum, one may also register articles of association, prescribing regulations for the company. 4

The memorandum and articles are delivered for registration to the Registrar who will issue a certificate of registration if he is satisfied that the provisions of the CA have been complied with. Provided all the documents required and delivered for registration are correct, the incorporation procedure is completed within a day or two. On registration, the company shall come into existence 5

* *Mamo TCV Advocates,* Valetta.

1 A private company may be designated by any name, but such name shall end with the words "private limited company" or "limited" or its abbreviation "ltd". Where a private company is an investment company with variable share capital, the name of the company will have to be followed by the words "investment company with variable share capital" or by "SICAV" followed by the words "private limited company", "limited" or its abbreviation (Sec. 70 of the Companies Act 1995 ("CA").

2 Regulations 11 to 17 of the Continuation of Companies Regulations issued under the CA.

3 This will evidence that the local Ltd has been transformed into a foreign entity.

and shall be authorised to commence business (Sec. 77 CA). Under the Companies Act (Fees) Regulations,[4] registration costs depend on the amount of authorised share capital.[5] The process of incorporation is completed within a few days.

1.4 Recurrent Costs and Efforts

6 The recurrent costs of an Ltd required by law are usually minimal. They refer to the preparation of audited financial statements and their filing with the Registrar. Annual fees must also be paid upon the delivery of the annual return. Other acts or documents which may be required from time to time and which are subject to registration and publication may also be subject to costs.

1.5 Shares and Share Transfers

7 It is possible for an Ltd to have different classes of shares, with each class having different rights attaching to such shares.

Shares in an Ltd may be transferred by means of a private writing or any other form which the directors may approve (Sec. 118 CA). For a company to register a transfer of shares, a proper instrument of transfer or an authentic copy thereof has to be delivered to the company. Within two months of such registration, the company should issue new certificates in respect of shares that have been transferred (Sec. 120 CA). Within 14 days after the date on which a transfer of any such shares is registered with the company,[6] the company must deliver to the Registrar for registration a notice of the transfer. Default in complying with this requirement does not lead to the nullity of the transfer, but every officer of the company who is in default is liable to a penalty. The articles of association generally impose restrictions on the transfer of shares (such as pre-emption rights or a discretion on the part of directors to decline to register any transfer of shares).

A share transfer gives rise to the obligation on the part of the transferee to pay duty under the Duty on Documents and Transfers Act (Chapter 364 of the Laws of Malta). Moreover, if such transfer constitutes a capital gain, the transferor must pay income tax on such gain (Income Tax Act – Chapter 123 of the Laws of Malta).

8 An Ltd is prohibited from offering to the public, whether for cash or otherwise, shares or debentures of the company. An Ltd is also restricted from allotting or agreeing to allot shares in or debentures of the company with a view to offering all or any of those shares or debentures to the public (Sec. 209 CA).

1.6 Corporate Bodies

9 An Ltd has two bodies: a board of directors and a general meeting. The Ltd must also have a company secretary.

1.6.1 The Board of Directors

10 An Ltd is required to have at least one director. However, the representation of the company does not necessarily vest in the directors, but may be exercised by such other person or persons as may be provided in the memorandum.[7]

11 Directors must act within the powers given by law or by the memorandum and articles of association. As regards third parties, anything done by the directors which exceeds the limits of their

4 Issued under the CA.

5 Schedule to Regulation 2, Companies Act (Fees) Regulations. Registration of an increase in authorised share capital, annual return and other documents are also subject to fees.

6 Or, in the case of a *causa mortis* transmission, within one month from the date on which any such shares transmitted *causa mortis* have been registered in the name of the person entitled to be registered as the holder thereof.

7 In the event that such representation ceases to be vested in any person or persons, a new appointment will have to be made by an ordinary resolution at a general meeting.

authority or powers shall be binding on the company, unless that act exceeds the powers granted to the directors by virtue of the CA.

1.6.2 The Shareholders' Meeting

The general meeting of the shareholders is the representative body of the shareholders, by means of which they can exercise their rights. An Ltd must hold an annual general meeting in addition to any other meetings in that year, known as extraordinary general meetings.[8] The general meeting has the power, *inter alia*, to appoint and remove directors and to approve the audited financial statements. 12

Ordinary resolutions are passed by members having the right to attend and vote holding in the aggregate shares entitling the holders thereof to more than 50 per cent of the voting rights attached to shares represented and entitled to vote at the meeting, or such higher percentage as the memorandum or articles may prescribe. On the other hand, where extraordinary resolutions are required to be taken by an Ltd, notice specifying the intention to propose the text of the resolution as an extraordinary resolution and the principal purpose thereof must be duly given. Moreover, such resolution must be passed by a number of members having the right to attend and vote at any such meeting holding in the aggregate not less than 51 per cent in nominal value of the shares conferring that right, or such other higher percentage as the memorandum or articles may prescribe (Sec. 135 CA). 13

1.6.3 The Company Secretary

An Ltd must have a secretary who will be responsible for the keeping of various minute books, registers and other records.[9] Moreover, the secretary of an Ltd is to ensure that proper notices of all meetings are given and that all returns and other documents of the company are prepared and delivered in accordance with the requirements of the CA. The directors of an Ltd have the power to appoint and remove the company secretary. A sole director cannot also act as the company secretary, unless the company is a private exempt company. 14

1.7 Duties and Liabilities of Directors

The directors are bound to act honestly and in good faith in the best interests of the company. They are obliged to promote the well-being of the company and are responsible for the general governance of the company, proper administration and management and the general supervision of its affairs (Sec. 136A CA). Other duties may be assigned by the memorandum or articles. 15

The directors must perform their duties with the degree of care, diligence and skill which would be exercised by a reasonably diligent person.[10] The directors shall be jointly and severally liable in damages to the company for any breach of duty, provided that where a particular duty has been

8 The annual general meeting shall be specified as such in the notices calling it. Not more than 15 months shall elapse between the date of one annual general meeting and the next (Sec. 128 CA).

9 These are:
- The minute book of general meetings of the company;
- The minute book of the meetings of the board of directors;
- The register of members; and
- Such other registers and records as the company secretary may be required to keep by the board of directors.

10 The directors are prohibited from:
- Making personal gain from confidential company information;
- Using any property, information, or opportunity of the company for their own or anyone else's benefit except with the consent of the company in general meeting or except as permitted by the company's memorandum or articles of association;
- Making secret or personal profits from their position without the consent of the company;
- Obtaining benefit in any other way in connection with the exercise of their powers except with the consent of the company in general meeting or except as permitted by the company's memorandum or articles of association;
- Exercising the powers they have for the purposes for which the powers were conferred and shall not misuse any such powers.

entrusted to one or more of the directors, only such director or directors shall be liable in damages (Sec. 147(1) CA). Where the directors incur personal liability towards the company for any breach of duty, the CA specifies that this liability is in respect of damages. This means that liability in these cases is one of tort, barred by the period of limitation of two years.

Besides the general liability of the directors described above, the directors may also incur liability for breaches of provisions relating to the safeguarding of share capital.[11] If the company subscribes for its own shares in the case of an increase in the issued share capital, the members and directors shall be jointly and severally liable to pay for these shares unless they can prove that the breach occurred through no fault of their own (Sec. 105 CA). Moreover, in the case of a winding-up, they can also be held liable if they make payments out of capital in respect of a redemption or purchase of the company's own shares.[12]

Under the provisions of the CA (Sec. 218(1) CA), if the company is unable to pay its debts, the directors may apply to the court for the dissolution and winding up of the company. Although there is no obligation on the directors to make this application, they may be held liable towards the creditors for wrongful trading if a company has been dissolved and is insolvent and it appears that they knew or ought to have known, prior to the dissolution of the company, that there was no reasonable prospect that the company would avoid being dissolved due to its insolvency and the directors failed to take every step they ought to have taken with a view to minimising the potential loss to the company's creditors (Sec. 315 and 316 CA). Liability for fraudulent or wrongful trading is ordered by the court.

Where directors perform acts which exceed the powers granted to them by virtue of the CA, such acts are not binding on the company. In such case, it may be possible for third party creditors to make a claim directly against the directors.

The CA does not specify whether shareholders may instruct directors to carry out a particular action. However, such instruction is not generally possible, unless specific power is given to the general meeting in the memorandum or articles of association. In such case, the directors would probably be released from liability to the company for the particular action. When the shareholders approve the financial statements of the previous financial year in the annual general meeting, such approval is not to be inferred as releasing the directors from liability for acts done over the past business year. In Malta, D&O insurance is allowed and the related premiums may also be paid by the company.

A person shall not be qualified for appointment or to hold office as director of a company if: (i) he is interdicted or incapacitated or is an undischarged bankrupt; (ii) he has been convicted of any of the crimes affecting public trust or of theft or of fraud or of knowingly receiving property obtained by theft or fraud; (iii) he is a minor who has not been emancipated; or (iv) he is subject to a disqualification order for breaches of the CA (Sec. 142 CA).

1.8 Shareholders' Liability

16 As a general rule, the members' liability is limited to the amount, if any, unpaid on the shares respectively held by each of them. Members are not generally liable for the obligations of an Ltd.

17 When a distribution or payment is made by an Ltd to a shareholder in contravention of the CA and the shareholder has reasonable grounds to believe that the distribution was so made, he will be obliged to repay it back to the company.

11 For example, they may be liable to a penalty if they do not call a general meeting under Sec. 104 CA described in Mn. 56 below, or if they are guilty of wrongful trading prior to dissolution under Sec. 316 CA.

12 Indeed, if the company's assets and the amounts paid by way of contribution are not sufficient for the payment of its debts and liabilities and the dissolution occurs within 12 months of the date of such payment, the directors who authorised such redemption or purchase are liable to contribute to make good the insufficiency. Moreover, the directors may be jointly and severally liable with the person from whom the shares were redeemed or purchased to contribute to make up for that part of the capital used to purchase or redeem the company's own shares (Sec. 217 CA).

18 The lifting of the corporate veil in Malta may occur both on a statutory as well as a judicial basis. The statutory cases[13] of the lifting of the corporate veil are listed in the CA. As regards the judicial lifting of the corporate veil, the Maltese Courts[14] tend to follow English cases and it is accepted that the separate juridical personality of the company may be put aside where the paramount interest of justice so requires or if the inroad is required to prevent fraud from being committed.[15]

1.9 Capitalisation and Financing

1.9.1 Basic Concepts

19 The Ltd is formed by means of a capital divided into shares held by its members. The principle of capital maintenance considers the company's share capital as a capital fund available to the company's creditors. This principle seeks to ensure that the share capital is not returned to the shareholders unless certain stringent conditions are met (Secs. 83, 104 to 116 CA). The loss of the issued share capital and the inability of the Ltd to pay its debts may result in the winding-up of the company.

1.9.2 Minimum Share Capital

20 The minimum share capital of an Ltd must be not less than Lm 500 (approximately EUR 1,200).[16] Where the authorised share capital is equal to the minimum, it must be wholly subscribed and where it exceeds such minimum, at least that minimum must be subscribed. Not less than 20 per cent of the nominal value of each share taken up shall be paid up on the signing of the memorandum (Sec. 72(3) CA).

The consideration for the acquisition of shares in a company may only consist of assets capable of economic assessment. Future personal services and in general any undertakings to perform work or supply services may not be given by way of consideration. Where, on original subscription or otherwise, shares are issued for a consideration other than in cash, the full consideration must be transferred to the company within five years from the date the company is authorised to commence business or from the date of the decision to issue the shares, as the case may be. Moreover, a report on any consideration other than in cash must be drawn up before the company is registered or before the shares are issued, as the case may be, by one or more experts who are independent of the company and approved by the Registrar. The report must be delivered to the Registrar for registration before the company is registered or before the shares are issued, as the case may be, and in default, the Registrar shall refuse to register the company or the return of the allotments of the shares so issued. In the latter case, the issue is also considered to be null and void (Sec. 73 CA).

1.9.3 Maintenance of Capital and Liquidity

21 The CA contains detailed provisions regulating the maintenance of the company's share capital, including rules regulating the reduction of share capital, the duty of directors where the company is

13 Sec. 214(3) CA – If a company ends up without at least two members and remains so for a period of more than six months, the sole remaining member, after the six months, will become solely and personally liable for debts contracted after the six months have elapsed. He will be jointly and severally liable with the company.
Sec. 315 CA – Persons who were knowingly parties to the carrying on of the business during winding–up with the intent to defraud creditors of the company may be held personally responsible without any limitation of liability for all or any of the debts of the company.
Section 316 – Under this Section, liability refers only to directors and applies only if they knew or ought to have known prior to the dissolution of the company that there was no reasonable prospect that the company would avoid being dissolved due to its insolvency. This is known as wrongful trading and only applies if the company is in liquidation.

14 *Dr. Jose' Herrera v Tancred Tabone et. – Court of Appeal, 22 January 1992, Edward and Giovanna Leone Enriquez v Dr. Anthony Farrugia pro et nomine, 1995.*

15 The most common instances of judicial lifting of the corporate veil take place in cases of fraud or improper conduct.

16 Approximately EUR 1,200.

unable to pay its debts, the prohibition of financial assistance,[17] the redemption of preference shares and the conditions for the acquisition by a company of its own shares (Secs. 83, 104 – 116 CA).

(i) System

22 Shareholders are liable for the capital they have subscribed for. This means that they must pay up any issued share capital not yet paid-up whenever there are calls for payment in accordance with the articles of association. If the shareholder fails to pay any call or instalment of a call on the day appointed for payment thereof, any share in the company may, as long as provision to that effect is contained in the memorandum or articles of association and provided certain procedures usually contemplated in the articles of association are followed, be forfeited in favour of the company or the shareholder may surrender any or all of his shares in favour of the company (Sec. 112 CA).

23 A company may not subscribe for its own shares, whether on original subscription or on any subsequent subscription. If the company subscribes for its own shares on original subscription, the subscribers to the memorandum shall be jointly and severally liable to pay for these shares. If the company subscribes for its own shares in the case of an increase in the issued share capital, the members and directors shall be jointly and severally liable to pay for these shares unless they can prove that the breach occurred through no fault of their own (Sec. 105 CA). An Ltd, subject to certain strict conditions, may acquire is own shares (Sec. 106 CA).

24 For the protection of creditors, any reduction of the issued share capital shall not take effect until three months from the date of the publication of the statement relating to the resolution for such reduction. If a creditor whose debt existed prior to such publication objects by writ of summons filed within these three months, the court will uphold the objection or allow the reduction on sufficient security being given.[18]

(ii) Distributions

25 Distributions of profits to shareholders can only be made out of profits available for that purpose.[19] These distributions cannot consist of an acquisition or redemption of the company's own shares or a reduction in issued share capital. When a distribution is made by an Ltd to a shareholder in contravention of the CA and the shareholder has reasonable grounds to believe that the distribution was so made, he will be liable to repay it back to the company (Sec. 204 CA).

A company's profits available for distribution are its accumulated, realised profits, so far as not previously utilised by distribution or capitalisation, less its accumulated, realised losses, so far as not previously written off in a reduction or reorganisation of issued share capital duly made (Sec. 192 CA). If these conditions are satisfied, the company is not obliged to await the end of the accounting period to pay out dividends, but it may pay out "interim" or "advance" dividends, provided "initial" or "interim" accounts are prepared (Sec. 197 CA).

(iii) Acquisition of Own Shares and Related Financing

26 An Ltd may acquire any of its own shares otherwise than by subscription, provided that provision is made by the memorandum or articles of the Ltd. Furthermore, authorisation is required by an extraordinary resolution, which resolution shall determine the terms and conditions of such acquisition. A number of other strict conditions are also imposed by the CA (Secs. 106 to 110 CA).

17 For the purpose of an acquisition or subscription made or to be made by any person of or for any shares in the company or its parent company.

18 Moreover, the total or partial waving of any unpaid part of issued share capital and the release of the shareholders from their obligation to pay up that unpaid part shall be considered as a reduction in share capital (Sec. 83 CA).

19 These are the Ltd's accumulated, realised profits as long as they were not previously utilised by distribution or capitalisation, less its accumulated, realised losses as long as they were not previously written off in a reduction or reorganisation of issued share capital (Sec. 192 CA).

The acceptance of the company's own shares by way of pledge or other form of security shall be treated as an acquisition by the company of such shares and thus subject to the same restrictions as specified above (Sec. 111 CA). 27

Ordinary shares cannot be redeemed. Preference shares may be redeemed, but only if duly authorised by the memorandum and articles. Such preference shares may only be redeemed out of the profits of the company or out of the proceeds of a fresh issue of shares. 28

Sec. 110 Subs. 1 (b) of the Companies Act (Chapter 386 of the Laws of Malta) provides that it shall not be lawful for an undertaking: to give, whether directly or indirectly, and whether by means of a loan, guarantee, the provision of security or otherwise, any financial assistance for the purpose of an acquisition or subscription made or to be made by any person of or for any shares in the company or its parent company. This provision does not apply to transactions effected with a view to the acquisition of shares by or for the company's employees or the employees of a group company; or to the provision of financial assistance by an investment company with fixed share capital for the purpose of or in connection with the acquisition of its fully paid up shares by another undertaking. These exceptions however do not apply if such transactions or financial assistance have the effect of reducing the net assets of the company below the amount of issued share capital plus those reserves which may not be distributed under the provisions of the Companies Act or the company's articles.

(iv) Company as Lender or Guarantor

The CA does not prohibit an Ltd from making loans or from guaranteeing the obligations of third parties. The CA provides that, unless otherwise provided in its memorandum or articles, a company shall have the power to guarantee the obligations of any third party and, for such purpose, to hypothecate or charge its undertakings, property and uncalled capital (Sec. 136 CA). The CA, however, prohibits loans or guarantees in favour of directors (unless the company is a private exempt company) (Secs. 144 and 211 CA). 29

Loans or guarantees in favour of shareholders are also allowed provided they are justifiable and meet market conditions. 30

(v) Company as Borrower

The company, unless otherwise provided in its memorandum or articles, shall have the power to borrow money and, for such purpose, to hypothecate or charge its undertakings, property and uncalled capital and to issue debentures (Sec. 136 CA).[20] Moreover, the CA does not prohibit shareholders from making loans to an Ltd or from guaranteeing loans made to an Ltd. There are no statutory provisions considering shareholders' loans as last ranking in insolvency proceedings. Nor is the shareholder obliged to ensure sufficient funding for the company. The company may also be a recipient of a security. 31

1.10 Publication and Filing Requirements

An Ltd must register a wide range of documentation and information with the registrar of companies, some of which must also be submitted for publication in the Government Gazette and some of which must also be published in one or more local newspapers. The registry of companies is open to the public and any interested person may view registered documents[21] and also obtain copies thereof. The register is also available online.[22] 32

Default in filing the documents which must be registered under the CA has different consequences depending on the nature of the document. Indeed, failure to register some documents, for example those relating to a change in directors or a share transfer, may result in fines being

20 In an Ltd these cannot be issued to the public but only to shareholders (Sec. 209(2)(a) CA).

21 These include the memorandum and articles of association as well as any amendments, the share capital or any increases in such capital, and the names of the directors.

22 www.mfsa.com.mt.

imposed on the officers of the company who are in default. Failure to register other documents may also result in the nullity of the transaction to be effected by such registration. An alteration to the memorandum and articles of association, for example, is not effective until it is registered. These consequences are enforced. Since the registration of documents is an obligation imposed by law on the company, third parties may rely on the contents of the register.

If a company fails to deliver the annual accounts to the Registrar, or the accounts delivered to the Registrar do not comply with the provisions of the CA, every officer of the company who is in default will be liable to a penalty, and, for every day during which the default continues, to a further penalty (Sec. 183(10) CA). The failure to file annual accounts may be one of the circumstances which is taken into account by the Registrar in determining whether to declare a company to be "defunct". This involves a procedure whereby the company is struck off the register of companies without being wound up.

1.11 Financial Reporting

33 The company must prepare accounts and any other financial statements which may be required according to generally accepted accounting principles and practice in adherence to International Accounting Standards as may be issued from time to time by the International Accounting Standards Board.[23] For each accounting period, the directors and the company's auditors must also prepare a report. The annual accounts, directors' report and auditors' report must be laid before the general meeting for its approval. These documents must also be delivered to the Registrar for registration.[24]

The CA grants certain exemptions to "small companies" and certain classes of Ltds. Under Sec. 185 CA "small companies" are defined as companies which on their balance sheet dates do not exceed the limits of two of the three following criteria: (i) balance sheet total: Lm 1,100,000 (approximately EUR 2,560,000) (ii), turnover: Lm 2,200,000 (approximately EUR 5,120,000), (iii) average number of employees during the accounting period: 50. These "small companies", whether Ltds or plcs, may draw up abridged balance sheets and abridged layouts of profit and loss account and abridged notes to the accounts. Moreover, those Ltds which on their balance sheet dates do not exceed the limits of two of the three following criteria: (i) balance sheet total: Lm 20,000 (approximately EUR 46,700), (ii) turnover: Lm 40,000 (approximately EUR 93,400), (iii) average number of employees during the acounting period: 2; may also draw up the above-mentioned accounts in an abridged form. These private companies are furthermore also exempt from the strict requirements of Chapter IX of Part V of the Companies Act which provides complex procedures for the appointment, resignation, removal and appointment of auditors, including the requirement to be audited by an independent auditor. They are also exempt from the obligation of drawing up an auditors' report to the company members on all annual accounts of the company.

1.12 Employee Participation in Corporate Bodies

34 The CA does not require employee participation or representation. Nonetheless, this does not in any way hinder employees from joining a trade union. Furthermore, employees can be shareholders of an Ltd.

23 The individual accounts comprise the balance sheet, the profit and loss account and the notes to the accounts. A company's annual accounts must also be approved by the board of directors.

24 An Ltd. is required to keep proper accounting records with respect to most of its activities:
(a) all sums of money received and expended by the company and the matters in respect of which the receipt and expenditure takes place;
(b) the assets and liabilities of the company;
(c) if the company's business involves dealing in goods:
  (i) statements of stocks held by the company at the end of each accounting period of the company;
  (ii) all statements of stocktakings; and
  (iii) except in the case of goods sold by way of ordinary retail trade, statements of all goods sold and purchased, showing the goods and the buyers and sellers in sufficient detail to enable all these to be identified.

2. The Stock Corporation (Public Limited Company "Plc")

Literature: B.M. Hannigan, Farrar's Company Law (London: Butterworths 2003); L.C.B Gower, Gower's Principles of Modern Company Law (7th edition, London: Sweet & Maxwell 2003); Oscar Grech, Notes on the Companies Act

The stock corporation is known in Malta as the public limited company ("plc"). It also offers limited shareholder liability. Generally, the plc may freely offer its shares to the public. The limited liability of shareholders facilitates the raising of capital from the public. This will often result in a large number of shareholders and consequently the rules on its governance and capital protection are quite strict. A plc's shares may also be listed on the Malta Stock Exchange. In such case, the plc will also be regulated by various stock exchange regulations. **35**

2.1 Export of Company

The CA does not prohibit a plc from moving its central place of business to another jurisdiction. The real seat theory is not followed in Malta and in terms of Maltese law the plc would retain its identity as a Maltese company even if it moves its central place of business to another jurisdiction. **36**

2.2 Transformation into a Foreign Entity

These requirements correspond to the requirements in an Ltd.[25] **37**

However, plcs quoted on a recognised stock exchange have the additional requirement of providing the Registrar with evidence of the consent of the said exchange and of the listing authority in Malta to the company continuing in another jurisdiction.[26]

Maltese law does not provide for the possibility of a plc merging with an S.E.

2.3 Incorporation

The plc is only validly constituted if a memorandum of association is entered into and subscribed by at least two persons (Sec. 68 CA). Together with the memorandum, articles of association may also be registered. **38**

The memorandum and articles are delivered for registration to the Registrar who will only register them if he is satisfied that the provisions of the CA have been complied with. On registration, the company shall come into existence and shall be authorised to commence business (Sec. 77 CA). Under the Companies Act (Fees) Regulations,[27] registration costs depend on the amount of authorised share capital.[28] The process of incorporation is completed within a few days. **39**

2.4 Recurrent Costs and Efforts

The recurrent costs of a plc required by law are minimal. They refer to the preparation of audited financial statements and their filing with the Registrar. Annual fees must also be paid upon the delivery of the annual return.[29] Other acts or documents which may be required from time to time and which are subject to registration and publication may also be subject to costs. Costs would also be involved in relation to the holding of ordinary and extraordinary general meetings. Plcs which have their shares quoted on the stock exchange also incur additional costs. **40**

25 See Mn. 3.

26 Regulation 13(d) – Continuation of Companies Regulations – issued under the CA.

27 Issued under the CA.

28 The minimum registration fee payable by a plc is Lm 255 (assuming the minimum authorised share capital is equal to that prescribed by law (Lm 20,000)). If the authorised share capital exceeds Lm 20,000, additional fees are payable. The total fees payable cannot exceed Lm 750 (Schedule to Regulation 2, Companies Act (Fees) Regulations).

29 Schedule to Regulation 2, Companies Act (Fees) Regulations.

2.5 Shares and Share Transfers

41 As for an Ltd, a plc may also have ordinary and preference shares.[30] The CA provides that ordinary shares are not redeemable, and every company must at all times have ordinary shares.[31] A plc may also issue debentures.[32]

Shares in a plc may be transferred by means of a private writing or any other form which the directors may approve (Sec. 118 CA). For a company to register a transfer of shares, a proper instrument of transfer or an authentic copy thereof has to be delivered to the company. Within two months of such registration, the company should issue new certificates in respect of shares that have been transferred (Sec. 120 CA). The articles of association do not usually impose restrictions on the transfer of shares. The registration requirements and tax implications applicable to the Ltd also apply to the plc.[33] Shares which are listed on the Malta Stock Exchange are transferred in accordance with applicable stock exchange rules.

2.6 Corporate Bodies

42 The plc has two bodies: a board of directors and a general meeting. The plc must also have a company secretary.

2.6.1 Board of Directors

43 Every plc shall have at least two directors. Directors must act within the powers given by law or by the memorandum and articles of association. All acts of the directors bind the company, unless they exceed the powers granted to the board by virtue of the CA (Sec. 137(1) CA). The memorandum or articles may vest representation in persons other than the directors.

44 The directors are responsible for the general governance of the company, its proper administration and management and the general supervision of its affairs (Sec. 136A CA). Although the directors are independent, they must act within the powers given by law or by the memorandum and articles of association. Moreover, certain business transactions require the approval of the general meeting.[34]

45 Unless otherwise provided in the memorandum or articles, directors other than the first directors shall be appointed by ordinary resolution of the company at the general meeting (Sec. 139(4) CA). A company may remove a director before the expiration of his period of office by a resolution taken at a general meeting (Sec. 140(1) CA).

2.6.2 The Shareholders' Meeting

46 The general meeting of the shareholders is the representative body of the shareholders, by means of which they can exercise their rights. Every company must hold an annual general meeting each year. It may also hold any other meetings in that year, known as extraordinary general meetings (Sec. 128 CA). The general meeting has the power, *inter alia*, to appoint and remove directors and to approve the audited financial statements.

30 Ordinary shares or equities carry residual rights of participation in the income and capital of the company, but have no right to a fixed dividend. Preference shares generally carry fixed dividends and may be redeemable. The ordinary shareholders may receive the remainder of the distributable surplus after the preferential rights of the preference shareholders have been satisfied.

31 Where the share capital is divided into different classes of shares, the memorandum of every company must state the rights attaching to the shares of each class (Sec. 72(5) CA).

32 These are documents evidencing an indebtedness which is normally, but not necessarily, secured by a charge over property.

33 See Mn. 7.

34 For example, an increase in issued share capital (Sec. 85 CA).

The general meeting cannot decide on management issues as these fall within the powers of the board of directors. However, there are many measures which require the shareholders' approval.[35] 47

2.6.3 Company Secretary

Every plc, like an Ltd, must have a company secretary. The company secretary cannot be the sole director of the company and may be removed by the directors. 48

2.7 Duties and Liabilities of Directors

These requirements correspond to the requirements in an Ltd.[36] In the case of a plc, however, directors also incur liability and may be obliged to compensate the company and the allottee if they permit or authorise the allotment of any share capital of a plc without receiving the minimum subscription (Sec. 97 CA). 49

2.8 Shareholders' Liability

Shareholder liability corresponds to that mentioned under the Ltd.[37] 50

The lifting of the corporate veil also applies to plcs and its requirements correspond to those mentioned under the Ltd.[38] 51

2.9 Capitalisation and Financing

2.9.1 Basic Concepts

These requirements correspond to the requirements in an Ltd.[39] 52

2.9.2 Minimum Share Capital

A plc cannot have an authorised share capital of less than Lm 20,000 (approximately EUR 46,700), and this must be subscribed by at least two persons. Where the authorised share capital is equal to the above minimum, it must be fully subscribed in the memorandum. Where it exceeds such minimum, at least that minimum shall be subscribed. Moreover, not less than 25 per cent of the nominal value of each share taken up shall be paid up on the signing of the memorandum (Sec. 72(3) CA). It is not lawful for a plc to issue any form of application for its shares or debentures unless the company is registered. Furthermore, the form must be issued with a prospectus which complies with the requirements of the CA. 53

As regards contributions in kind, the same rules relating to an Ltd are applicable.[40]

2.9.3 Maintenance of Capital and Liquidity

(i) System

The CA contains various provisions for the preservation of the company's capital (Secs. 83, 104 to 116 CA). Where the net assets of a plc are one-half or less of its called-up issued share capital, the directors shall, not later than 30 days from the earliest day on which that fact is known to any director of the company, convene a general meeting for the purpose of determining what steps should be taken to deal with the situation, including a consideration of whether to dissolve the company (Sec. 104 CA). A company may not subscribe for its own shares, whether on original 54

35 Examples include alterations and additions to the memorandum and articles of association, the amalgamation or division of the company, as well as winding-up.

36 See Mn. 15.

37 See Mn. 16.

38 See Mn. 18.

39 See Mn. 19.

40 See Mn. 20.

subscription or on any subsequent subscription (Sec. 105 CA). A plc, subject to certain strict conditions, may acquire is own shares.[41]

(ii) Distributions

55 A company cannot make any distributions except out of profits available for this purpose. Moreover, a plc may only make a distribution at a given time if the amount of its net assets is not less than the aggregate of its called-up issued share capital and undistributable reserves, and if the distribution does not reduce the amount of those assets to less than that aggregate (Sec. 193 CA). Also, where a distribution is made by a company to a member in contravention of the CA (Sec. 192 to 208 CA) and that member knows or has reasonable grounds to believe that it is so made, he shall be liable to repay it to the company (Sec. 204 CA).

If the above conditions are satisfied, a plc is not obliged to await the end of the accounting period to pay out dividends, but it may pay out "interim" or "advance" dividends, provided "initial" or "interim" accounts are prepared (Sec. 197 CA). The CA provides special requirements in respect of the interim and initial accounts to be prepared for a proposed distribution by a plc. For example, interim accounts must be properly prepared and the balance sheet and profit and loss account must give a true and fair view of the state of the company's affairs as at the balance sheet date or the period in respect of which the accounts were prepared, respectively. A copy of the interim accounts must also have been delivered to the Registrar for registration. On the other hand, initial accounts have the additional requirement of necessitating a report by the company's auditors stating whether, in their opinion, the accounts have been properly prepared.

(iii) Acquisition of Own Shares and Related Financing

56 A company may acquire its own shares otherwise than by subscription only if provision is made in the memorandum or articles and authorisation is given by extraordinary resolution (Sec. 106 CA). The CA also imposes other strict conditions for such acquisition (Secs. 106 to 110 CA). These conditions and the relative exceptions are basically in line with those listed in the Second Directive[42]

Only preference shares may be redeemed. Where a company is duly authorised by the memorandum or articles to issue preference shares which are redeemable, such shares may only be redeemed out of the profits of the company or out of the proceeds of a fresh issue of shares (Sec. 115 CA).

57 The acceptance of the company's own shares by way of pledge or other form of security shall be treated as an acquisition by the company of such shares and thus subject to the same restrictions as specified above (Sec. 111 CA).

The rules governing financial assistance for Ltds equally apply to plcs.[43]

(iv) Company as Lender or Guarantor

58 These requirements correspond to the requirements in an Ltd.[44]

(v) Company as Borrower

59 These requirements correspond to the requirements in an Ltd.[45]

41 See Mn. 56 et seq.
42 See Part 1, I, Mn. 39 et seq.
43 See Mn. 28.
44 See Mn. 29.
45 See Mn. 31.

2.10 Publication and Filing Requirements

These requirements correspond to the requirements in an Ltd.[46] However, a plc whose shares are listed on the Malta Stock Exchange has to comply with certain stock exchange regulations. **60**

2.11 Financial Reporting

These requirements correspond to the requirements in an Ltd.[47] **61**

2.12 Employee Participation in Corporate Bodies

These requirements correspond to the requirements in an Ltd.[48] **62**

46 See Mn. 32.
47 See Mn. 33.
48 See Mn. 34.

XVIII. The Netherlands

*by Pieter Riemer and Henk Arnold Sijnja**

Literature: P. van Schilfgaarde, Van de BV en de NV (Revised by Jaap Winter) (Deventer: Kluwer 2003); J.M.M. Maeijer, Mr. C. Asser's handleiding tot de beoefening van het Nederlands burgerlijk recht. 3. Vertegenwoordiging en rechtspersoon. Deel III. De naamloze en de besloten vennootschap (Deventer: W.E.J. Tjeenk-Willink 2000) ("Asser/Maeijer 1994 (2-III)"); Steven R. Schuit, Corporate law & practice of The Netherlands (Updated by Barbara Bier) (Deventer: Kluwer 2002).

The B.V. (*besloten vennootschap*) and the N.V. (*naamloze vennootschap*) are the corporate forms used in the Netherlands to carry out commercial business activities. Both the B.V. and N.V. are entities based on the contributed capital of their participants (i.e. founders and/or shareholders) and whose capital is divided into shares. The B.V. and N.V. are solely liable for the obligations entered into in their own name.[1] Shareholders are only liable to the amount of the nominal share capital contributed by them on the issued share capital (Secs. 2: 192 and 81 Dutch Civil Code (*Burgerlijk Wetboek*, "DCC")). Within the confines of statutory law, both the B.V. and N.V. can be organised to the business needs of the entrepreneur. The legal regime for both the B.V. and N.V. is equivalent. 1

In October 2005 approximately 633,000 B.V.s were registered in the Netherlands, in contrast to approximately 4,400 N.V.s.

1 The Limited Liability Company ("B.V.")

There is wide flexibility as to the B.V.'s organisation, so that it can be used for very many different business purposes. In practice, the B.V. is very often used to carry out business activities, including for family-owned businesses, joint ventures, management and holding purposes, investment purposes and as a sub-holding company within a group. The B.V., in combination with the friendly Dutch tax climate, offers an interesting corporate business form for international business purposes. 2

Recently, the Dutch government has begun actions aimed at making the B.V. more attractive. These actions may result in a simplification of the rules governing the B.V. and flexibility of the rules. At this stage improvements include less mandatory law, cancellation of unnecessary restrictive rules, more freedom for shareholders to organise the company to suit their needs and intentions, a decrease in the administrative burden and an adaptation to actual national and international practice. 3

1.1 Export of Company

While the latest judgments of the ECJ (cases "Überseering"[2] and "InspireArt"[3]) do permit foreign entities to move their entire business and management to the Netherlands in compliance with the principles of freedom of establishment under the EC Treaty, Netherlands law prescribes that the statutory seat of a company must be in the Netherlands in order for it to be recognised as a Dutch company.[4] The B.V. may have its headquarters and carry out its activities outside the Netherlands. 4

1.2 Transformation into a Foreign Entity

A Dutch company cannot transfer its statutory seat to a jurisdiction other than the Netherlands and cannot otherwise convert itself into a non-Dutch corporate legal form. In exceptional circumstances, such as in cases of war and revolution, a Dutch company may transfer its corporate seat to other parts of the Kingdom of the Netherlands (the Netherlands Antilles) or other jurisdictions.[5] 5

* *Linklaters*, Amsterdam.

1 Statutory law provides for some exceptions to this general rule for the protection of a B.V.'s creditors, in particular in relation to the preservation of the company's equity.

2 See Part 1, I, Mn. 17 et seq.

3 See Part 1, I, Mn. 19.

4 The "incorporation theory" (Sec. 1: 10, 2: 177 Subs. 3, 2: 66 Subs. 3 DCC).

5 Statute Law on the voluntary transfer of corporate seat (*Rijkswet vrijwillige zetelverplaatsing van rechtspersonen*) and the Act on the voluntary transfer of corporate seat to third countries (*Wet vrijwilllige zetelverplaatsing derde landen*).

6 In order for a B.V.'s business activities to continue to be carried out by a foreign legal corporate form, the B.V. must transfer its business through an asset sale to the relevant foreign entity or be dissolved and wound-up such that its business will by means of a liquidation distribution transfer to the foreign shareholder (if any). A foreign entity which carries out business activities in the Netherlands will be considered to have a branch office of that foreign entity.

1.3 Incorporation

7 A B.V. is set up by way of a notarial deed of incorporation executed before a Dutch civil law notary. The B.V. must be incorporated by at least one incorporator. Individuals and legal entities, including foreign individuals and entities, can be an incorporator. All shares can be held by one individual or entity. The Ministry of Justice must issue a certificate of no objection before the notarial deed can be executed. Before issuing the certificate, the Ministry will verify whether there is a risk of abuse of the corporate form.[6]

8 The company will legally exist upon execution of the notarial deed of incorporation. The incorporation must be registered with the Commercial Register of the Chamber of Commerce in the same district as the statutory seat of the company. Until registration with the Commercial Register, the managing directors of the company are jointly and severally liable for the company's legal acts.

9 Assuming that the shares of the company will be paid in cash, a B.V. can normally be incorporated within a week once an application for the declaration of no objection has been filed with the Ministry of Justice. The notarial fees for the incorporation of a B.V. with a minimum EUR 18,000 share capital will amount to approximately EUR 2,500 exclusive of office expenses and VAT. In addition, the fees payable to the Ministry of Justice in connection with the certificate of no objection and a trade name search by the Chamber of Commerce amount to EUR 90,76 and EUR 83 (maximum) respectively. The advertisement costs of publication of certain changes to the company data in the Dutch State Gazette are EUR 12,84 excluding VAT as a minimum.

1.4 Recurrent Costs and Efforts

10 The fees payable to the Chamber of Commerce in connection with the registration of the company with the Commercial Register depend on certain criteria set by the Chamber of Commerce, including the funding of the company. The annual registration fee varies between EUR 140 and EUR 880. Recurrent costs and efforts relating to the publication of annual accounts and their filing with the Commercial Register amount to approximately EUR 25 on average for advertisement in the Dutch State Gazette. Other costs and efforts only materialise in the event that certain corporate steps are taken which require notarisation, filing with the Commercial Register or publication in the Dutch State Gazette or nationally distributed newspapers.

1.5 Shares and Share Transfers

11 A B.V. can only issue registered shares. It cannot issue certificates for those registered shares.

12 A distinction can be made into types of shares and classes of shares. Types of shares are ordinary shares,[7] preference shares,[8] cumulative preference shares[9] and priority shares.[10]

6 The certificate can be refused only on certain limited grounds, all related to the (bad) credentials of those who will determine the company's policy, the risk of unlawful use of the company or the possibility that creditors will be prejudiced.

7 Shares in respect of which no particular arrangements apply. These are the most common form of shares.

8 Shares which give the holders thereof a preference over ordinary shareholders in dividend payments. It is possible that these shares also have preference over ordinary shares in the proceeds upon liquidation of the company.

9 Shares which entitle the holder thereof to the payment of any dividends which have not been paid over previous years (e.g. because there were not sufficient profits to meet the dividend rights attached to the shares), with preference over the dividend rights attached to ordinary shares.

10 Shares which give special voting rights to the holder thereof. It is possible that certain resolutions of the shareholders' meeting are subject to the approval of the holders of priority shares or binding nomination rights of priority shareholders.

Also a distinction in classes of shares (of the same type) can be made. Very often classes are created to categorise (groups of) shareholders. Classes of shares are often used by joint ventures or highly leveraged buy-outs. The different classes of shares can be identified by using letters, i.e. "A" shares and "B" shares, etc. By creating different classes of shares, the rights attached to[11] these shares can be varied, by including provisions to that effect in the company's articles. **13**

Registered shares are transferred by way of a deed executed before a Dutch civil notary. The transfer must be acknowledged by the B.V., without which the new shareholders cannot exercise their shareholder rights. Usually, the B.V. is a party to the deed of transfer for acknowledgement of the transfer. Otherwise, the notarial deed must be served to the company by a Dutch court bailiff. **14**

In principle, no taxes are due in connection with the transfer of shares. **15**

Pursuant to mandatory provisions the transfer of registered shares in a B.V. must be restricted. For this purpose, the articles must include a transfer restriction clause. Such transfer restriction clause can take the form of either: (i) the transfer of shares to the prospective buyer is subject to the approval of a corporate body as designated in the articles (e.g. the management board, supervisory board, if any, or the shareholders' meeting); or (ii) the shareholder must offer the shares to all shareholders first. A combination of the two transfer restriction provisions is also possible. **16**

It is possible to work out transfer restriction provisions in a shareholders' agreement in addition to the provisions in the articles of association.[12]

1.6 Corporate Bodies

Unless the large company regime (*structuurregime*) applies,[13] the law prescribes that a B.V. shall have at least two corporate bodies: the management board and the shareholders' meeting.[14] Further corporate bodies, such as a supervisory board or committees, the duties of which can be freely defined in the articles of association, regulations of the management board and/or supervisory board, are optional.[15] **17**

1.6.1 Large Company Regime

In the event that the "large company regime" applies to the company, a two tier board structure is mandatory and a supervisory board must be established.[16] **18**

The special powers of the supervisory board vary, according to whether the company concerned is partially exempted from the large company rules or not. The supervisory board of a non-exempt large company has the following special powers:

(i) the power to elect, suspend and remove the managing directors;
(ii) the power to approve or reject certain specified resolutions of the management board; and
(iii) the power to make nominations to the shareholders' meeting for its own vacancies.

11 For example, the different classes of shares entitle the holders thereof to make binding nominations for the appointment of managing directors, so as to ensure that each category of shareholders is represented on the company's management board.

12 B.C.M. Waaijer, Aandeelhoudersovereenkomsten (Deventer: Kluwer).

13 See Mn.18 et seq.

14 Companies that do not meet the criteria of a large company may voluntarily apply the large company regime (Sec. 2: 267, 157 DCC). An important reason for (listed) companies to voluntarily adopt the large company regime was that shareholders' influence on the company's governance was restricted under the old large company regime. The Act pertaining to changes to the large company regime, which came into force on 1 October 2004, gave shareholders greater influence on the company's governance once more.

15 Except that the powers and responsibilities attributed to corporate bodies other than the management board, supervisory board and shareholders' meeting cannot be the same as those of these three bodies.

16 Companies that meet the following criteria must have a supervisory board subject to the large company regime: the company's issued capital plus reserves equal at least EUR 16,000,000; it or its "dependent company" has established a Works Council, as required by law; and the company, together with its dependent companies, normally employs 100 or more persons in the Netherlands (Sec. 2: 263 Subs. 2, 153 Subs. 2 DCC).

The special powers of the supervisory board of a partially exempt large company are limited to those set forth under (ii) and (iii) above. In this situation, the power to appoint managing directors remains with the shareholders. Foreign-based groups of companies or internationally active groups of companies with a Dutch holding company are often subject to the partially exempt large company rules.

The articles may subject additional resolutions of the management board to the approval of the supervisory board.[17] If the management board enters into a transaction in violation of these additional provisions in its articles of association, the company remains bound. The violation may, however, form the grounds for removal of a managing director or for other legal action.

1.6.2 Management Board

19 The management board is the executive body of the B.V. Both natural persons as well as legal entities may serve as a managing director. Managing directors may be Dutch or foreign, and do not have to be resident in the Netherlands. The management board is responsible for the day-to-day management of the company. The management board represents the company and can for and on behalf of the company enter into and execute agreements. The members of the management board (often referred to as managing directors) have collective powers and responsibilities.

20 The management board is not subordinate to any other corporate body of the company.[18] The articles may, however, subject management board resolutions to the prior approval of other corporate bodies such as the supervisory board, if any, or shareholders' meeting. The articles may stipulate that the management board shall observe any directives of another corporate body, such as the supervisory board, if any, or shareholders' meeting, regarding the general course of affairs with respect to certain matters described in the articles (Sec. 2: 239 Subs. 4, 129 Subs. 4 DCC).

1.6.3. Supervisory Board

21 Unlike the management board, the supervisory board must consist of natural persons only (Sec. 2: 250, 140 DCC). Supervisory directors may be Dutch or foreign, and they need not be resident in the Netherlands. There are no requirements as to the number of supervisory directors, unless it concerns a large company, in which case there shall be at least three supervisory directors.

22 The supervisory board shall supervise the policy of the management board and the general course of the company's affairs. In addition, the supervisory board shall advise the management board (Sec. 2: 250, 140 DCC). The supervisory directors have collective powers and responsibilities. The supervisory board is not subordinate to any other corporate body and must act in the interests of the company. The management board is required to provide the supervisory board with all information necessary for the proper performance of its duties.

23 The articles may stipulate that the management board shall observe any directives of the supervisory board regarding the general course of affairs with respect to certain matters described in the articles (Sec. 2: 239 Subs. 4, 129 Subs. 4 DCC).

24 The supervisory board may be attributed with additional powers in the articles. However, such powers may not be of such nature that they fall under the competence of the management board or shareholders' meeting.

1.6.4 Shareholders' Meeting

25 In its decision dated 21 January 1955, the Supreme Court held that the shareholders' meeting is not the highest corporate body of a company in the Netherlands to which other corporate bodies would be subordinated.[19]

17 Asser-Maeijer III, No. 381.

18 Supreme Court 21 January 1955, NJ 1959, 43 (Forumbank).

19 Supreme Court 21 January 1955, NJ 1959, 43 (Forumbank).

The shareholders' meeting has the power to resolve on the material matters relating to the company's structure and organisation and its business. Its powers include the appointment, suspension and removal of managing directors and supervisory directors, amendment of the articles of association, increase of its share capital, adoption of the annual accounts and dissolution and liquidation of the company. Important decisions relating to the B.V.'s business, i.e. material acquisitions or divestments, are also considered to be subject to the shareholders' meeting's approval.[20] If the B.V. is subject to the "full" large company regime, the supervisory board appoints, suspends and removes the managing directors. 26

Shareholders' meetings must be held in the Netherlands, provided that meetings may be held in other countries if the entire issued share capital is present or represented. 27

Resolutions are adopted by a simple majority of the votes cast unless the articles require otherwise (Sec. 2: 230, 120 DCC). Each shareholder has at least one vote. Shareholders have as many voting rights as their proportionate part in the nominal value of the entire issued capital of the company.[21] Dutch corporate law does not have the concept of non-voting shares. 28

1.7 Duties and Liabilities of Directors

Managing directors and supervisory directors must properly perform their duties (Sec. 2: 9 DCC). In addition, the B.V. and those who pursuant to the law and its articles are connected with its organisation must observe reasonableness and fairness towards each other (Sec. 2: 8 DCC). Managing directors and supervisory directors may be held personally liable to the B.V. in the case of breach of the aforementioned rules. A managing director or supervisory director has not properly performed his duties if he has been "seriously negligent".[22] 29

In principle, managing directors and supervisory directors are jointly and severally liable, unless a managing director or supervisory director can prove that the failure concerned is not attributable to him. An allocation of the duties of managing directors and supervisory directors may help in providing evidence. D&O liability insurance is widely available in the Netherlands. The company may take out D&O insurance at its own cost. The legal effectiveness of indemnification of managing directors and supervisory directors by the company is uncertain. 30

The managing directors and supervisory directors can be discharged from the performance of their duties by the shareholders meeting. Discharge is often given on the occasion of the discussion of and adoption of the annual accounts.[23] Discharge only has legal effect in respect of those matters which were known to the shareholders' meeting at the time discharge was given (either through the annual accounts or otherwise). 31

Managing directors and supervisory directors may be liable to third parties (including individual shareholders) pursuant to specific laws, such as in connection with misleading financial statements, bankruptcy, non-payment of taxes and social premiums, and on the basis of tort. 32

1.8 Shareholders' Liability

The main rule under Dutch law is that the company is exclusively liable for its own obligations. An analysis of court cases shows that the Dutch Supreme Court has accepted that a shareholder may be liable to an injured party on the basis of tort.[24] Although these cases concerned primary obligations of the company, the Supreme Court held that the shareholder was personally at fault towards the injured party as well. The fact that a shareholder fully controlled the company, that 33

20 Asser-Maeijer III, No. 258.

21 In general, shareholders may enter into agreements regulating their voting behaviour or relating to other rights they may have as a shareholder. Such agreements are binding and enforceable (Supreme Court 30 June 1944, NJ 1944/45, 465 and 13 November 1959, NJ 1960, 472).

22 Supreme Court 10 January 1997, NJ 1997, 360 (Van de Ven).

23 It is not possible, however, to stipulate that the adoption of the annual accounts shall automatically imply the discharge of the managing directors and supervisory directors (Sec. 2: 210 Subs. 3, 101 Subs. 3 DCC).

24 Supreme Court 16 June 1995, NJ 1996, 214 (Bato's Erf); 25 September 1981, NJ 1982, 443 (Osby) and 8 November 1992, 174 (Nimox/Auditrade). See also Asser-Maeijer III, No. 623.

its management was also management of the company and that it determined to a large extent the company's policy, is not in itself enough to construe liability. It may, however, result in a reversal of the burden of proof that the shareholder committed tort. Circumstances where a shareholder might be liable are: giving the impression of creditworthiness of the company; unauthorised withdrawal of assets, e.g. creating a preferential position of the shareholder as creditor above other creditors of the company; and making capital distributions to the shareholder.

1.9 Capitalisation and Financing

1.9.1 Basic Concepts

34 Dutch corporate law relating to the preservation of a company's capital is strongly based on European directives. There is a wide variety of statutory laws aimed at preserving a company's capital and protecting creditors against infringement of their claims. In addition, case law provides protection to creditors against fraudulent actions by a company and/or its corporate bodies, most notably the management board, on the basis of tort.

1.9.2 Minimum Share Capital

35 In connection with the share capital of a Dutch company, three concepts are used. First, there is the authorised capital, which is amount of share capital mentioned in the articles and up to which shares can be issued. The authorised capital is divided into shares with a certain nominal value. Second, the shares that have actually been issued, multiplied by the nominal value of these shares, constitute the company's issued capital. The issued capital must be at least one-fifth of the company's authorised capital. Finally, that part of the issued capital that has been paid for by the shareholders is the paid-up capital. The B.V. must have a minimum issued capital of EUR 18,000. If a B.V.'s equity, being the aggregate of its issued and called-up capital and the reserves that must be maintained pursuant to statute or its articles, is less than the applicable minimum capital, then it must create a reserve for the balance.

36 It can be stipulated that up to 75 per cent of the nominal value only has to be paid-up when called for by the B.V. (Sec. 2: 191, 80 DCC). It follows that the paid-up capital shall always be at least 25 per cent of the issued capital. These relative percentages are subject to the minimum capital requirements, which amounts should always have been paid-up.

A subscriber for shares must pay these up at the issue of the shares. Shares can be paid up in cash and in kind. It can be agreed that a shareholder pays up 25 per cent of the nominal value of the shares, and the remainder when called for by the B.V.[25]

37 There are also provisions aimed at preventing transactions which are not contributions on shares but have the same effect, such as a transfer of assets for consideration to the B.V. by a founder or shareholder during a certain period after the company's incorporation whereby shares were subscribed for in cash up to the mandatory minimum capital (*Nachgrunding*). Such transactions may erode the company's equity and hence they are subject to special regulations.

1.9.3 Maintenance of Capital and Liquidity

(i) System

38 Reference is made to Section 1.9.1 above.[26]

25 The contribution in kind on shares is subject to strict provisions aimed at ensuring that the company acquires "real" value at its possession. Essentially, these provisions include a valuation of the assets (and liabilities, if any) to be contributed by an independent accountant.

26 See Mn. 34.

(ii) Distributions

The possibility of distributing profits is determined on the basis of the B.V.'s annual accounts. Profits can only be distributed following the adoption by the shareholders' meeting of the annual accounts which show that the distribution is permitted. Save as otherwise provided for in the articles, each shareholder is entitled to the profit proportionate to the paid-up nominal value of his shares. Although deviating arrangements with respect to the dividend rights can be made, the bottom line is that no shareholder can be excluded from sharing in the company's profits. Profits can be distributed in cash or in kind. Provided the articles so permit, it is also possible for the company to pay interim dividends which are made during a financial year. **39**

Distributions, whether from profits or reserves, and irrespective of whether they concern dividends paid following adoption of the annual accounts or interim dividends, can only be made up to an amount that exceeds the paid-up and called up capital plus any reserve required pursuant to statutory law or the articles. **40**

(iii) Acquisition of Own Shares and Related Financing

A company may repurchase shares in its own capital in accordance with specific provisions in the law. A company may only acquire fully paid-up shares in its capital. A B.V. may only acquire that number of shares of which the aggregate nominal amount does not exceed 50 per cent of the company's issued capital. A B.V. may acquire shares in its own capital for no consideration, or for consideration, in which latter case the following additional requirements must be met. First, the company's equity after deduction of the purchase price for the shares may not fall below the sum of the company's issued and called-up capital, plus the statutory reserves and reserves that must be maintained pursuant to its articles. It follows that the purchase price must be paid from the company's freely distributable reserves. Second, the articles must permit the repurchase and the shareholders' meeting must have authorised the management board to repurchase the shares. **41**

Statutory law does not allow B.V.s and N.V.s to give financial assistance to third parties aiming to subscribe or acquire in its capital. These rules also prohibit a company from establishing security rights, guaranteeing the share price or otherwise guaranteeing or binding itself jointly and severally or otherwise with or for third parties for the above measures. As an exception to the above rule, a B.V. may grant loans for the sole purpose of acquiring shares in its capital up to the amount of its freely distributable reserves provided its articles so allow. These rules also apply to subsidiaries. **42**

The exact scope of the financial assistance rules is unclear and, potentially, a wide variety of (leveraged) M&A transactions may be covered. Case law over the past few years, however, indicates that the Dutch courts apply a restrictive interpretation of the financial assistance rules.[27] In practice, alternative financing structures are developed that deal with the financial assistance rules. As there is no conclusive case law, any structure should be carefully reviewed on its financial assistance merits.

(iv) Company as Lender or Guarantor

In principle, a B.V. may give loans, grant guarantees or provide security to third parties. On the basis of the ultra vires doctrine guidance can be found as to whether a B.V. can grant loans or provide security for the benefit of third parties, including group companies. The bottom line is that the lending or providing of security may be subject to nullification by the company if such act could not possibly be in the company's corporate interests. Indications that a transaction may be challenged on the basis of ultra vires are that the company concerned does not benefit from such transaction, that there is a disproportionate imbalance between the risks assumed by the company compared to the benefits received by it or that the company's existence would be jeopardised by the relevant transaction. It is generally recognised that within a group of companies, subsidiaries may, **43**

27 Court of Breda 3 November 1992, NJ 1993, 427 (King Air) and Supreme Court 7 May 2004, RvdW 2004, 68 (Muller q.q./Rabobank Katwijk a/d Rijn).

within the confines of their corporate interests, provide security, or otherwise provide guarantees, for the debts of other group companies, including the parent company, or provide financing to other group companies.

(v) Company as Borrower

44 Shareholder loans to the company are allowed and in principle rank equal with third-party loans in case of any insolvency of the company. The tax treatment of shareholder loans should be reviewed.

1.10 Publication and Filing Requirements

45 A wide range of documentation and information must be filed with the Commercial Register. The Commercial Register file is open to the public and any interested person can review the filed documents and request a Commercial Register excerpt detailing the principal corporate information (e.g. the share capital, the names of the managing directors, supervisory directors and legal representatives, capital increases and amendments to the articles of association) as well as copies of any documents submitted. If the B.V. has only one shareholder, details of such shareholder must be entered in the registration of the B.V. with the Commercial Register as well. Company details can be obtained through the Commercial Register's website www.kvk.nl.[28]

1.11 Financial Reporting

46 Dutch statutory law prescribes that the management board of a company must within five months of the expiration of each financial year (i) draw up the annual accounts and annual report of the company and (ii) file them at its registered offices for inspection by the shareholders. The shareholders' meeting may decide to extend this term by a maximum period of six months on the ground of exceptional circumstances.

Certain relief from financial reporting requirements is granted to small and medium-sized companies.[29] If a company (including its subsidiaries) does not exceed two of the following three criteria for two successive years it is considered a small company under Dutch law: (i) an asset total of EUR 3,650,000, (ii) a net turnover of EUR 7,300,000, (iii) an annual average of less than 50 employees. Small companies only need to file a condensed balance sheet with the commercial register of the Chamber of Commerce. Their annual accounts do not have to be audited by an independent auditor. Regarding their profit and loss accounts they have the advantage of some minor other exemptions, among which the possibility to not disclose the net turnover.

If a company (including its subsidiaries) does not exceed two of the following three criteria for two successive years it is considered a medium sized company under Dutch law: (i) an asset total of EUR 14,600,000, (ii) a net turnover of EUR 29,200,000, (iii) an annual average of less than 250 employees. Medium sized companies enjoy some minor exemptions with regard to their annual accounts. They do not have to deduct the net turnover from the gross company result and do not have to split up the accounts according to departmental/geographical origin. They can suffice with filing a condensed balance sheet with the commercial register of the Chamber of Commerce.

47 The annual accounts must be prepared in accordance with Dutch GAAP and must provide such information as will enable the reader to form a sound opinion of the assets and liabilities and profits and losses of the company. Depending on the size of the company and nature of its business

28 There is also an English version of the website available: www.kvk.nl/home/homeUK.asp. Please note not all information has been made available in the English version. An English manual for the Commercial Register's website can be found at www.kvk.nl/sectie/sectie.asp?sectieID=102. It is also possible to request an electronic excerpt from companies registered with the Commercial Register via this same website for EUR 2.50. Authenticated electronic copies of excerpts cost EUR 7.50. A copy of a company's articles of association can be requested via the website but cannot be received electronically. The Commercial Register provides a copy of a company's articles of association for EUR 11.

29 Banking and insurance companies and investment companies with a permit cannot be exempt from the general rules regarding the preparation and filing of the annual accounts.

activities, the contents of the annual accounts may vary. The management board must file the annual accounts within eight days of their adoption by the shareholders' meeting with the Commercial Register. In the event that the annual accounts are not adopted within two months of the period permitted by law, i.e. within 13 months of the end of the financial year, the management board should file the drawn up annual accounts forthwith with the Commercial Register. The annual accounts must be accompanied by the auditor's opinion and the report of the management board for the relevant financial year.

Provided certain conditions are met, a Dutch company which is a group company may be exempted from the aforesaid preparation and/or publication requirements.[30] **48**

Any interested party has the right to institute legal proceedings in court against a company in order to enforce compliance with the aforementioned publication requirements. **49**

1.12 Employee Participation in Corporate Bodies

Supervisory directors of the supervisory board of a large B.V. are appointed by the shareholders' meeting from a nomination by the supervisory board. The shareholders' meeting and the works councils have a right of recommendation for such nominations to be made. In addition, the works council has an enhanced recommendation right, which means that the supervisory board shall nominate persons recommended by the works council for one-third of the members of the supervisory board, unless the supervisory board objects to a nomination on the ground that there is an expectation that the person concerned is not capable or the supervisory board would be improperly composed following appointment of such person. In that case the works council and supervisory board must consult and try to agree on another person, failing which the Enterprise Chamber of the Amsterdam Court of Appeal (*Ondernemingskamer van het Gerechtshof te Amsterdam*) will decide. **50**

2 The Stock Corporation ("N.V.")

As outlined above, the regime of the N.V. is to a large extent identical to the regime of the B.V. **51**

On 9 December 2003 a new Dutch Corporate Governance Code was adopted. This Code became effective for companies (i.e. N.V.s) with a listing as from the financial year starting on or after 1 January 2004. The Code contains the principles and concrete provisions which, amongst others, the management board, supervisory board and shareholders of a company should observe in relation to each of the other persons involved in a company. The provisions of the Code reflect national and international best practice and may be regarded as an expression of general principles of good corporate governance. Although the Code is applicable to listed companies, the principles may accordingly be applied by private companies.

2.1 Export of Company

See Section 1.1.[31] **52**

2.2 Transformation into a Foreign Entity

See Section 1.2.[32] An N.V., however, may be merged with an S.E. subject to the applicable rules. **53**

30 Such may be the case if the financial data of the company have been included in the consolidated accounts of a direct or indirect parent company, provided these accounts are prepared and published pursuant to and in accordance with EU accounting directives (for details see Part 1, I, Mn. 48 et seq.). An important condition is that the consolidating parent company files a statement of joint and several liability with the Commercial Register of the statutory seat of the company, for the obligations arising out of transactions of the corporation.

31 See Mn. 4.

32 See Mn.5 et seq.

2.3 Incorporation

54 See Section 1.3,[33] except that the mandatory minimum issued share capital of an N.V. amounts to EUR 45,000.

2.4 Recurrent Costs and Efforts

55 See Section 1.4.[34]

2.5 Shares and Share Transfers

56 An N.V. may issue registered shares and bearer shares. For the bearer shares, certificates must be issued. If the N.V has registered shares, it may issue certificates.

57 The N.V. has the same types and classes of shares as the B.V.[35] Bearer shares are transferred by delivery of the share certificates or, as is the case with N.V.s listed on Euronext Amsterdam, if the shares have been deposited with Necigef, through a system of book entries. The Dutch Securities Giro Transfer Act (*Wet giraal effectenverkeer*, the "WGE") provides for a book-entry system for the delivery of securities, including shares. *Nederlands Centraal Instituut voor Giraal Effectenverkeer B.V.* ("Euroclear Netherlands") in Amsterdam acts as central securities depositary under the Act. Transfers take place by way of book-entry by making an entry in the records of Euroclear Netherlands and/or the member organisations concerned.

58 Registered shares are transferred by way of a deed executed before a Dutch civil law notary, similar to the B.V. With respect to the registered shares, the new shareholder can only exercise his shareholder rights after acknowledgement of the transfer by the N.V.[36]

59 The articles may only restrict the transfer of registered shares. The law allows N.V.s much more flexibility as to how a transfer of registered shares shall be restricted, albeit that a transfer restriction arrangement may not make a transfer impossible or very onerous. Bearer shares are freely transferable.

2.6 Corporate Bodies

60 See Section 1.6.[37]

2.6.1 Large Company Regime

61 See Section 1.6.1.[38]

2.6.2 Management Board

62 See Section 1.6.2.[39]

2.6.3 Supervisory Board

63 See Section 1.6.3.[40]

33 See Mn. 7 et seq.
34 See Mn. 10.
35 See Mn. 12.
36 See Mn. 16.
37 See Mn. 17.
38 See Mn. 18.
39 See Mn. 19 et seq.
40 See Mn. 21 et seq.

2.6.4 The Shareholders' Meeting

See Section 1.6.4.[41] The approval of the shareholders' meeting is required for management board resolutions involving a significant change in the company's identity or character or of that of its enterprise, including, in any event, in respect of: (i) a transfer of the company's enterprise or substantially all of its enterprise to a third party; (ii) the entering into or termination of an enduring co-operation of the company or any subsidiary which has a significant impact on the company; and (iii) the acquisition or divestment of participations with a value of at least one-third of the company's assets according to its (consolidated) balance sheet with explanatory notes in the company's last adopted annual accounts (Sec. 2: 107a DCC). 64

2.7 Duties and Liabilities of Directors

See Section 1.7.[42] 65

2.8 Shareholders' Liability

See Section 1.8.[43] 66

2.9 Capitalisation and Financing

2.9.1 Basic Concepts

See Section 1.9.1.[44] 67

2.9.2 Minimum Share Capital

See Section 1.9.2,[45] except that the N.V. must have a minimum issued capital of EUR 45,000. The N.V. must always have a paid-up capital at least equal to its minimum capital. If its issued capital, or called up part thereof, is less than the minimum capital then, at the request of the public prosecutor, the N.V. shall be dissolved. Unlike the B.V., the N.V. does not need to maintain a reserve for the shortfall. 68

Bearer shares must be paid-up in full. As regards registered shares, it can be stipulated that up to 75 per cent of the nominal value only has to be paid-up when called for by the company. It follows that the paid-up capital shall always be at least 25 per cent of the issued capital. These relative percentages are subject to the minimum capital requirements, which amounts should always have been paid-up. 69

2.9.3 Maintenance of Capital and Liquidity

(i) System

See Section 1.9.1.[46] The management board of an N.V. must convene a shareholders' meeting within three months after the management board became aware that the company's equity was equal to or fell below 50 per cent of the company's paid and called-up capital, to discuss possible measures (Sec. 2: 108a DCC). 70

41 See Mn. 25 et seq.
42 See Mn. 29 et seq.
43 See Mn. 33.
44 See Mn. 34.
45 See Mn. 35.
46 See Mn. 38.

(ii) Distributions

71 See Section 1.9.3.[47]

(iii) Acquisition of Own Shares and Related Financing

72 See Section 1.9.3,[48] provided, however, that an N.V. may only acquire that number of shares of which the aggregate nominal amount does not exceed 10 per cent of the N.V.'s issued capital.

The authorisation by the shareholders' meeting is not required if it concerns shares in an N.V. which are being purchased under an employee share participation arrangement and provided the shares are included in the price list of a stock exchange. Subject to all requirements being met, it may be possible to structure a repurchase of shares in a tax friendly manner.

73 With regard to financial assistance rules, see Section 1.9.3,[49] except that an N.V. may not grant loans for this purpose. These rules also apply to subsidiaries. The financial assistance rules do not apply to shares of an N.V. which are purchased under an employee share participation arrangement.

(iv) Company as Lender or Guarantor

74 See Section 1.9.3.[50]

(v) Company as Borrower

75 See Section 1.9.3.[51]

2.10 Publication and Filing Requirements

76 See Section 1.10.[52]

2.11 Financial Reporting

77 See Section 1.11,[53] except that listed N.V.s must prepare their annual accounts as of the financial year starting on or after 1 January 2005 in accordance with IAS/IFRS.

2.12 Employee Participation in Corporate Bodies

78 See Section 1.12.[54]

47 See Mn. 39 et seq.
48 See Mn. 41.
49 See Mn. 42.
50 See Mn. 43.
51 See Mn. 44.
52 See Mn. 45.
53 See Mn. 46 et seq.
54 See Mn. 50.

XIX. Poland

*by Dr. Cezary Wiśniewski and Michał Mieciński**

1 The Limited Liability Company ("sp. z o.o.")

Literature: Sołtysiński/Szajkowski/Szumański/Szwaja, Kodeks Spółek Handlowych, commentary (2nd edition, C.H. Beck 2002); Kidyba, Kodeks Spółek Handlowych, commentary (2nd edition, Zakamycze 2004); Litwińska, Kodeks Spółek Handlowych, commentary (1st edition, C.H. Beck 2002)

The limited liability company (*spółka z ograniczoną odpowiedzialnością*, "sp. z o.o.") is the 1
most common form of capital company used by small and medium-sized entities, which allows shareholders to exclude their personal liability for the company's liabilities. The main reasons for its popularity are the fact that there are fewer formalities in running the company, lower share capital requirements,[1] as well as a rather limited number of compulsory legal regulations, all of which make the sp. z o.o. a much more flexible form of corporate entity than its alternative under Polish law, the joint stock company (*spółka akcyjna*, "S.A.").

Today there are approximately 109,700 sp. z o.o. registered in Poland, in contrast to approximately 6,000 S.A.

1.1 Export of Company

Notwithstanding the principle of freedom of establishment under the EC Treaty, reaffirmed by the 2
latest rulings of the ECJ,[2] Polish law prohibits an sp. z o.o. from moving its corporate seat abroad. The decision to relocate the registered seat of an sp. z o.o. abroad (irrespective of whether or not it is to another EU Member State) would result in the dissolution of the company (Sec. 270 KSH[3]). There are no express legal provisions which would prohibit a de facto relocation of the management and operations of an sp. z o.o. abroad.

1.2 Transformation into a Foreign Entity

Currently, there are no legal provisions expressly providing for the transformation of an sp. 3
z o.o. into a foreign entity. This can be achieved only indirectly either by establishing an S.E. or by transferring the assets of an sp. z o.o. to a foreign entity.[4] In the latter case, no formal transformation will, however, occur, as both the sp. z o.o. and the foreign entity will retain their own legal personalities.

1.3 Incorporation

An sp. z o.o. may be incorporated by one or more persons. However, it cannot be formed solely 4
by another sp. z o.o. having itself a single shareholder (Sec. 151 KSH).[5]

Creation of an sp. z o.o. is subject to the following requirements being met:

* *Linklaters*, Warsaw.

1 The minimum admissible initial share capital of an sp. z o.o. is PLN 50,000 (approximately EUR 12,700).

2 See Part 1, I, Mn. 17 et seq. and 19.

3 Act on Commercial Partnerships and Companies Code (*ustawa – kodeks spółek handlowych*) of 15 September 2000 (Journal of Laws No. 94, item 1037, as subsequently amended) ("KSH").

4 In addition, the Tenth Directive will facilitate cross-border mergers of commercial companies between different Member States of the European Union. For details see Part 1, I, Mn. 56 et seq.

5 This restriction also applies to the formation of a single-shareholder sp. z o.o. by a foreign single-shareholder limited liability company, e.g. a German GmbH or a Dutch B.V. (ruling of the Polish Supreme Court (*Sąd Najwyższy*) of 28 April 1997, II CKN 133/97, OSNC 1997/10/154). It only applies to the establishment of a single-shareholder sp. z o.o. by another single-shareholder limited liability company. Following registration of the sp. z o.o., it is possible for all shares to be held by one shareholder, irrespective of whether or not it is a single-shareholder limited liability company.

(i) adoption of its articles of association in the form of a notarial deed;
(ii) shareholder contributions to cover the entire issued share capital of the company;
(iii) appointment of corporate bodies (management board and, if required by law or the company's articles of association, supervisory board or audit committee); and
(iv) registration in the register of entrepreneurs.

An sp. z o.o. acquires legal personality at the moment of its registration. However, an sp. z o.o. in organisation (*spółka z ograniczoną odpowiedzialnością w organizacji*) is created at the moment of the shareholders adopting the articles of association.[6]

The costs of incorporation of an sp. z o.o. include a notary fee and tax on civil legal actions (both depending on the amount of the initial share capital),[7] a court registration fee in the amount of PLN 1,000 (approximately EUR 254) and a fee for the compulsory announcement of the company's registration in the official gazette *Monitor Sądowy i Gospodarczy* amounting to PLN 500 (approximately EUR 127).

5 Whilst the time required to register an sp. z o.o. may vary from court to court, generally it takes between one and six weeks from the date of submission of the complete set of documents to register an sp. z o.o in the register of entrepreneurs.

1.4 Recurrent Costs and Efforts

6 Recurrent costs and efforts are rather low in the case of an sp. z o.o. They include, in particular, drawing up annual financial reports and filing them with the registration court, an auditors' report (if and when required by law[8]), filing income tax and VAT returns (generally once a month) and the cost of holding annual shareholders' meetings. However, certain corporate events must be documented and notarised, with their particulars being filed with the registration court or announced,[9] in which case the recurrent costs and efforts for the company may be higher.

1.5 Shares and Share Transfers

7 The minimum par value of one share is PLN 50 (approximately EUR 13). The articles of association determine whether a shareholder may hold only one or more shares. If a shareholder is permitted to hold more than one share in the company, all shares must be equal (i.e. they must have the same par value) and indivisible. The law does not allow the issue of share certificates in respect of shares in a Polish sp. z o.o. There is no public trading in shares in a Polish sp. z o.o. The lack of share certificates makes it impossible for an sp. z o.o. to be engaged in any initial public offerings. Thus, an sp. z o.o. intending to offer its shares to the public must be first transformed into an S.A.

A legal action for the transfer of shares in an sp. z o.o. must be made in writing and the signatures must be certified by a notary in order to be valid. The company must be notified in writing of the transfer of shares. The transfer is effective against the company from the moment of such notification (Sec. 187 Subs. 1 KSH). The management board of an sp. z o.o. must keep a share

6 An sp. z o.o. in organisation may acquire rights (including ownership of real estate and other rights *in rem*) and be subject to obligations, sue and be sued. Upon registration it acquires legal personality and thus becomes a registered sp. z o.o. At the same time, all rights and obligations of the sp. z o.o. in organisation are assumed by the registered sp. z o.o. The company itself and any persons who acted on its behalf are liable for any obligations incurred by the sp. z o.o. in organisation. The above personal liability ceases to exist upon approval of any actions taken on behalf of the sp. z o.o. in organisation by the shareholders' meeting (Sec. 161 Subs. 3 KSH). Furthermore, shareholders of the sp. z o.o. in organisation are jointly and severally liable for its obligations up to the value of their unpaid contributions to the company's share capital.

7 In the case of an sp. z o.o. with the minimum admissible share capital of PLN 50,000 (approximately EUR 12,700), the notary fee should not exceed PLN 1,000 (approximately EUR 254) and the tax on civil actions would amount to PLN 250 (approximately EUR 63).

8 See Mn. 35.

9 This may be required in particular in relation to events as a result of which the data disclosed in the register of entrepreneurs kept for the company changes, e.g. amendments to the company's articles of association, changes in the composition of the management board, changes in shareholdings, etc.

register[10] evidencing, *inter alia*, all current shareholdings and, following any change of these, it must file an amended shareholders' list with the registration court.

A disposal of shares (including any encumbrance *in rem* on the title to such shares) prior to registration of the company (or the registration of an increase in share capital) is null and void (Sec. 16 KSH).

The articles of association of an sp. z o.o. may provide for certain restrictions on the transfer of shares, such as the existence of pre-emption rights, a requirement for prior consent to the transfer by the company or the shareholders' meeting, etc. (Sec. 180 KSH). However, such restrictions may not result in excluding the right of a shareholder to dispose of its shares.

1.6 Corporate Bodies

An sp. z o.o. requires two compulsory corporate bodies: the management board (*zarząd*) and the shareholders' meeting (*zgromadzenie wspólników*). A supervisory body, i.e. a supervisory board (*rada nadzorcza*) or an audit committee (*komisja rewizyjna*),[11] is obligatory only when the company's share capital exceeds PLN 500,000 and there are more than 25 shareholders in the company (Sec. 213 KSH). If the above thresholds are not met, a supervisory board and/or an audit committee are only optional. 8

1.6.1 Management Board

The management board has the power both to represent the sp. z o.o. against third parties and to manage its affairs (Sec. 201 Subs. 1 KSH). 9

The management board consists of one or more members which are appointed and dismissed by a resolution of the shareholders, unless the articles of association provide otherwise (Sec. 201 Subs. 2 and 4 KSH).

Only natural persons with full legal capacity may become members of the management board. However, persons convicted by a criminal court for certain criminal actions are disqualified from taking the function of member of the management board.[12]

Only the members of the management board are authorised to represent the sp. z o.o. *vis-à-vis* third parties and this power cannot be restricted with legal effect towards third parties (Sec. 204 KSH). If the management board consists of more than one member, the members of the management board may be authorised to act individually or jointly.[13]

The management board is generally the only body authorised to manage the internal affairs of the sp. z o.o. The shareholders are not entitled to manage the company's affairs. However, through shareholders' resolutions, which are binding on the management board, the shareholders may require the management board to take actions in accordance with their wishes. Furthermore, certain actions by the management board require the shareholders' approval.[14] The list of such actions may be extended by the company's articles of association.[15] 10

10 The share register includes in particular information about shareholders (names, addresses), their title to shares, the number and par value of shares held by each shareholder and any encumbrances on such shares by way of a pledge and/or usufruct rights.

11 In practice, audit committees are very rare.

12 Most importantly criminal actions to the detriment of the company, against the economy and commercial relationships.

13 Unless the articles of association provide otherwise, the law stipulates that the sp. z o.o. must be jointly represented by two members of the management board or one member of the management board and a holder of a commercial power of attorney (*prokurent*) acting together.

14 Pursuant to Secs. 228 and 299 KSH, the following actions require a shareholders' resolution:
- (i) claims for loss or damage caused upon formation of the company, or by its management or supervision at the time of such formation;
- (ii) a disposal or tenancy of the business undertaking of the company or an organised part of it, as well as the creation of limited rights *in rem* over them;
- (iii) an acquisition or a disposal of real estate or part of such real estate by the company, unless the articles of association provide otherwise;

1.6.2 Shareholders' Meeting

11 The shareholders' meeting is the highest resolution-adopting body of the company, yet it lacks the authority to carry out the company's day-to-day management. The shareholders' meeting may pass resolutions in relation to all matters in respect of which the law and/or articles of association require a decision of the shareholders. A shareholders' resolution may also be passed in relation to any matter if the shareholders wish to express their opinion.

12 As a rule, shareholders' resolutions are passed at shareholders' meetings. However, they may also be passed without holding a shareholders' meeting if all shareholders consent in writing to the proposed decision or to a written vote.[16]

There are two types of shareholders' meetings: ordinary shareholders' meetings and extraordinary shareholders' meetings. Ordinary shareholders' meetings must be convened annually within six months of the end of the financial year. Extraordinary shareholders' meetings are held whenever they are required by law or the company's articles of association, or the corporate bodies or persons authorised to convene shareholders' meetings consider this desirable.

Holding a shareholders' meeting outside Poland is not permitted.

Generally, shareholders' resolutions are adopted by an absolute majority of the votes cast, unless the articles of association or the law provides for other special majorities in respect of specific types of decisions.[17]

1.6.3 Supervisory Board

13 In the case of an sp. z o.o., every shareholder is empowered to control the activities of the company (Sec. 212 KSH). However, this right can be limited or waived if a supervisory body (a supervisory board and/or an audit committee) is appointed in the company.

If appointed, a supervisory board has the power to exercise permanent supervision over all areas of the company's activities. The supervisory board is, however, not authorised to give binding instructions to the management board (Sec. 219 Subs. 2 KSH).

A supervisory board must consist of at least three members, which are appointed and dismissed by a shareholders' resolution. The articles of association may, however, provide for a different manner of appointment and/or dismissal of members of the supervisory board.

(iv) an acquisition of real estate or part of real estate or fixed assets for a price higher than one-quarter of the company's share capital but not less than PLN 50,000, if made before the second anniversary of the company's registration, unless such acquisition was envisaged by the articles of association.

Any of the above actions taken by the management board on behalf of the company in the absence of a shareholders' resolution (which may be passed either prior to or up to two months after such action) are null and void (Sec. 17 Subs. 1 KSH).

In addition, a shareholders' resolution is required pursuant to Sec. 230 KSH, if the company is to dispose of a right or assume an obligation the value of which exceeds double the amount of the company's share capital. In this case, very occasionally lack of a resolution does not cause invalidity), but imposes personal liability on the members of the management board to the company for any loss or damage caused.

15 If shareholders' consent for actions of the management board is only required pursuant to the articles of association and not by law, actions taken in the absence of such consent are valid and binding upon the company; however, the management board members who acted without shareholders' consent are personally liable to the company for any loss or damage caused by their actions (Sec. 17 Subs. 3 KSH).

16 No resolution may be passed by way of a written vote if relating to matters expressly reserved for decision in ordinary shareholders' meetings (such as consideration and approval of the management board's report on the operations of the company and the financial report for the financial year, division of profits or financing of losses and giving approval for the performance of duties by the members of the company's corporate bodies) or by way of a secret vote (e.g. for the appointment or dismissal of members of the company's corporate bodies).

17 A majority of two-thirds of the votes cast is required for example for resolutions amending the articles of association, reduction of share capital or dissolution of the company. A resolution concerning a substantial change in the scope of the company's activities requires a majority of three-quarters of the votes cast. A resolution on the merger of an sp. z o.o. with another capitalised company requires a majority of three-quarters of the votes cast, representing at least half of the company's entire share capital.

Members of the supervisory board are appointed for one year, unless the articles of association provide for a different term of office. Each member of the supervisory board may exercise the above right of supervision alone, unless the articles of association provide otherwise.

1.6.4 Audit Committee

An audit committee is an alternate supervisory body in an sp. z o.o. Unlike those of the supervisory board, its powers are very limited.[18] However, if no supervisory board is appointed and the audit committee is the only supervisory body of the sp. z o.o., its powers may be extended in the articles of association. Audit committees are very rare in practice. 14

1.7 Duties and Liabilities of Directors

The management board, apart from managing the day-to-day business of the company, is also responsible for carrying out certain other statutory obligations. These include, in particular, the power to convene and prepare shareholders' meetings, file applications with the registration court, ensure the publication of information regarding the company as required by law and provide information about the company's affairs to the shareholders. 15

In performing their duties, the members of the management board must exercise such diligence as is required by the professional nature of their activities. Members of the management board are personally liable to the company for any loss or damage caused by acts or omissions in breach of the law or the articles of association, unless such acts or omissions are not due to a member's personal default. If loss or damage is caused by more than one member of the management board, such members are jointly and severally liable to the company.[19] A member of the management board would not be released from the discussed liability by claiming he was acting pursuant to instructions from the shareholders (or the supervisory board). In turn, the release from liability would generally apply if the member of the management board is formally discharged from his duties by the annual ordinary shareholders' meeting closing every financial year.[20] Even a prior instruction by the shareholders to carry out a particular action which would result in an act or omission in breach of the law or the articles of association would not release the management board member from his liability.

For the sake of protection of members of the management board, the latter may be insured by means of D&O insurance, premiums for which can be paid by themselves or by the company.

Apart from the general liability of members of the management board, Polish law also provides for the specific liability of such members in relation to financing. Members of the management board may be held personally liable for any repayment of the share capital in breach of Sec. 189 KSH.[21] 16

Members of the management board of an sp. z o.o. may be held personally liable for the company's obligations towards its creditors. If a creditor's enforcement against the company proves to be ineffective, members of the management board are jointly and severally liable for the company's obligations towards such creditor. A management board member may be released from the above

18 The competence of an audit committee is limited to evaluation of the management board's reports on the operations of the company, the annual financial reports or any proposals of the management board concerning the division of profits or financing losses, as well as submission to the shareholders' meeting of an annual report on the results of such evaluation.

19 Personal liability of members of the management board is time-barred after three years from the date on which the company learns of the loss or damage and who is liable for it. In any event, such liability is time-barred after 10 years from the date of the event which caused the loss or damage to the company.
If the company does not bring an action for damage caused to it within one year of the date on which the act causing the loss or damage is discovered, each shareholder may file a writ in an action for damage caused to the company. In such a case (or if the company is declared bankrupt), the management board members may not claim that their actions were approved by a resolution of the ordinary shareholders' meeting or that the company released them from liability.

20 The release from liability does not apply in the events described in Fn. 26.

21 See Mn. 23.

liability if he can provide evidence that: (i) an application for the opening of insolvency proceedings in respect of the company was applied for on time; (ii) failure to submit such an application was not through any fault on his part; or (iii) in spite of the fact that the insolvency of the company was not applied for, the creditor suffered no damage.[22]

Furthermore, if members of the management board have, wilfully or negligently, stated untrue data in the representations made to the court regarding the shareholders' contributions to the share capital, they are jointly and severally liable together with the company towards its creditors for a period of three years from the date of the registration of the company (or of the share capital increase) (Sec. 291 KSH).

1.8 Shareholders' Liability

17 Shareholders of an sp. z o.o. are not liable for the company's obligations towards the company's creditors, unless there is a contractual obligation on shareholders (such as a guarantee in favour of a third party for the company performing its contractual obligations) or a shareholder, acting in his capacity as such, commits a tort against a third party. Neither Polish law nor Polish jurisprudence has so far recognised the concept of piercing the corporate veil.[23]

1.9 Capitalisation and Financing

1.9.1 Basic Concepts

18 The system of financing an sp. z o.o. is based on the concept of preservation of share capital. The share capital of an sp. z o.o. forms a capital fund which should be preserved at all times during the company's existence. Polish law applies the "principle of real capital contribution and maintenance" which means that share capital in the amount stated in the articles of association and registered in the register of entrepreneurs must be made available to the company and is under no circumstances to be paid back to the shareholders other than by applying the formal procedure for reduction in the company's share capital. In addition, shareholders may not receive any payments from the company which are required in order for the company to maintain its share capital, irrespective of the legal ground for such payment.

1.9.2 Minimum Share Capital

19 The minimum admissible share capital for an sp. z o.o is PLN 50,000 (approximately EUR 12,700). The share capital can be contributed in cash and/or in kind.[24] Such share capital must always be paid in full before registration of the sp. z o.o. can proceed.

1.9.3 Maintenance of Capital and Liquidity

(i) System

20 The "principle of real capital contribution and maintenance" is protected by a number of legal provisions. The system not only ensures that contributions to the company's share capital (both in kind and in cash) are made in full before the company is registered, but also prevents contributions in kind from being overvalued. Although the shareholder's own evaluation of contributions in kind is not verified by the court or by an independent auditor in the process of registration of the

22 Similar events trigger a personal liability for the members of the management board in respect of any tax arrears of the sp. z o.o. as stipulated in Sec. 116 of the Polish Tax Ordinance of 29 August 1997 (Journal of Laws No. 137, item 926, as subsequently amended).

23 For shareholders' liability for obligations of the sp. z o.o. in organisation, see Fn. 6. For a discussion of the thin capitalisation rules, see Mn. 24.

24 Polish law and Polish jurisprudence have recognised the concept of the so-called "capability of being subject to contribution in-kind", delivering certain guidelines as to whether certain items may be contributed in kind. Pursuant to these guidelines, most importantly, non-transferable rights, or performance of work, or delivery of services may not be contributed to an sp. z o.o.

company, shareholders who overvalue their contributions in kind and members of the management board who are aware of this fact are jointly and severally liable to the company to the extent of any difference between the value stated by the shareholder and the fair market value of the contribution in kind on the date of notarisation of the company's articles of association (Sec. 175 KSH).

Furthermore, the system prevents "hidden contributions in kind" by requiring shareholders' resolution approval for the acquisition of real estate or fixed assets by the company for a price higher than one-quarter of its share capital but not lower than PLN 50,000 (approximately EUR 12,700), if such acquisition occurs prior to the second anniversary of the company's registration and it was not provided for in the company's articles of association (Sec. 229 KSH). 21

Sec. 189 KSH not only prohibits the return of capital contributions to shareholders during the existence of an sp. z o.o. other than through a share capital reduction, but also prohibits the making of any payments by the company to a shareholder which are required for the purpose of maintaining full coverage of the company's share capital. 22

If the company's losses at any time exceed the sum of any supplementary and reserve capital and half of the company's share capital, the management board must convene an extraordinary shareholders' meeting, at which a resolution on the further existence of the company must be passed (Sec. 233 KSH). 23

If a shareholder receives an illegal payment from the company, he must repay the same to the company. Members of the management board who are responsible for an illegal payment to a shareholder are jointly and severally liable, together with the recipient of such repayment. If neither the recipient of an amount required for the full coverage of the company's share capital nor the member(s) of the management board responsible for such payment are able to repay such sums, the other shareholders are held personally liable for repayment of the shortfall. 24

An sp. z o.o. may also be financed by the shareholders by means other than equity.[25] External financing of an sp. z o.o. by shareholders through shareholder loans is, however, subject to certain restrictions. If the company is declared bankrupt within two years of the execution date of such loan agreement, the shareholder loan may be reclassified by operation of law as that shareholder's contribution to the company's share capital (Sec. 14 Subs. 3 KSH). As a result, the shareholder who granted the sp. z o.o. a loan will not be able to claim its repayment within the scope of the bankruptcy proceedings.[26] 25

(ii) Distributions

A shareholder is entitled to participate in the company's annual profits as reflected in the company's annual financial report and allocated for distribution amongst the shareholders under a resolution of the shareholders' meeting (Sec. 191 Subs. 1 KSH). The sp. z o.o.'s articles of association may also authorise its management board to pay to the shareholders limited advance dividend payments if the company's approved financial results for the previous year show profits. 26

25 Apart from share capital, equity financing in an sp. z o.o. includes additional payments (*dopłaty*). These may be provided for in the articles of association, which may oblige the shareholders to make payments to the company in addition to their initial contributions to the company's share capital. Additional payments are to be made by each shareholder in proportion to its shareholding. They do not result in an increase in share capital, do not require registration and do not involve the issue of new shares in exchange. Additional payments are classified as equity and are designated to a special capital reserve. They may be returned to the shareholders if not required in order to finance losses disclosed in the company's financial report. Additional payments do not need to be interest bearing and they are generally not treated as taxable income of the company.

26 In addition, Polish tax law applies certain thin capitalisation rules (Sec. 16.1 Subs. 60 and 61 of the Act on Commercial Income Tax of 15 February 1992, Journal of Laws No. 54/2000, item 654, as subsequently amended). Shareholder loans to the company are permitted; however, interest on loans granted by shareholders holding at least 25 per cent of the shares in the company (and/or by certain related parties) may be, in part, non tax-deductible. If the loan is granted by such shareholder or a related party of that shareholder and the debt figure exceeds three times the amount of the share capital of the borrowing sp. z o.o., the interest accrued upon the excess will not be treated as tax deductible for the borrower. Additionally, where the company's share capital has been increased by the conversion of loans granted by such shareholders and/or their related parties into equity, the amount of the share capital thus created may not count towards the company's thin capitalisation basis.

(iii) Acquisition of Own Shares and Related Financing

27 As a rule, an sp. z o.o. may not acquire its own shares or accept a pledge over its own shares (Sec. 200 Subs. 1 KSH).[27] There are a number of exceptions to this prohibition, which include, amongst others, the purchase of the company's own shares from a shareholder for the purpose of their subsequent redemption, and the purchase of the limited number of the company's own shares as part of merger or de-merger proceedings.

28 There is no maximum percentage of shares which may be repurchased by an sp. z o.o. However, except for any rights necessary for the maintenance of the repurchased shares, an sp. z o.o. may not enjoy any other shareholders' rights.

29 Unlike in the case of a Polish joint stock company,[28] there are no specific rules or restrictions governing the provision of financial assistance by an sp. z o.o. in the acquisition of its shares by a third party.[29]

(iv) Company as Lender or Guarantor

30 An sp. z o.o. may extend loans and grant guarantees to third parties. In the case of loans or guarantees granted to its own shareholders, the company must ensure that Sec. 189 KSH is not breached.[30]

31 Entering into a loan, credit, suretyship (guarantee) or other similar agreement with, or in favour of, a member of the management board, supervisory board, audit committee, a holder of a commercial power of attorney or a liquidator of the company, requires shareholders' approval (Sec. 15 Subs. 1 KSH).

(v) Company as Borrower

32 An sp. z o.o. may be granted loans by, and give security for third party loans from, its own shareholders. However, if the company is declared bankrupt within two years of the date on which the relevant loan agreement is concluded, the thin capitalisation regulations will apply.[31]

1.10 Publication and Filing Requirements

33 A substantial number of documents and information must be filed with the register of entrepreneurs, which is maintained by district courts located throughout Poland. Some of these, such as details of any changes to information disclosed in the register of entrepreneurs, must in addition be submitted for publication in the official gazette *Monitor Sądowy i Gospodarczy*.

34 Access to the register of entrepreneurs' files is open to the public. Any interested person may inspect the filed documents and request copies of them, as well as current and historical excerpts from the register evidencing the most important corporate details of an sp. z o.o. The information in the register of entrepreneurs is centralised, though it may not be accessed online.

Third parties may rely on the contents of the register unless they act in bad faith, i.e. unless they are aware or should be aware of the incorrectness of an entry in the register.

The non-filing of documents with the registration court is subject to fines of up to PLN 20,000 (approximately EUR 5,000) though, in practice, such fines would be imposed in vary rare cases.

27 This prohibition also applies to the acquisition of shares in the sp. z o.o. by any of its dependent companies (Sec. 200 Subs. 1 KSH). A breach of this prohibition in cases other than those allowed by law constitutes a criminal offence by the management board members or liquidators of the company who allowed such purchase, which is subject to a fine, restriction on liberty or imprisonment for up to six months (Sec. 588 KSH).

28 See Mn. 62.

29 However, the general rules relating to the maintenance of share capital and equal treatment of shareholders must be observed.

30 See Mn. 17, 21 and 23.

31 See Mn. 25.

1.11 Financial Reporting

The annual financial report of an sp. z o.o. (including, *inter alia*, its balance sheet and profit and loss account) must be drawn up within three months of the end of the financial year[32] and must be approved by the shareholders' meeting within six months of the end of the financial year. The annual accounts must be drawn up in accordance with the provisions of the PAA. In matters not regulated by the PAA, Polish GAAP may be applied. If the appropriate Polish GAAP is also silent in this respect, IAS may be applied accordingly. 35

As a rule, financial reporting, publication and auditing requirements are equal for all companies irrespective of their size. No relief is granted to small- and medium sized enterprises. Auditing, however, is only required where an sp. z o.o. exceeds certain thresholds: The annual reports of an sp. z o.o. which meet the requirements laid down by law[33] must be audited and published in the official gazette *Monitor Polski B*.

1.12 Employee Participation in Corporate Bodies

As a rule, employees are not represented in the corporate bodies of an sp. z o.o.[34] 36

2 The Stock Corporation ("S.A.")

Literature: Sołtysiński/Szajkowski/Szumański/Szwaja, Kodeks Spółek Handlowych, commentary (3rd ed., C.H. Beck 2003); Pyzioł/Szumański/Weiss, Prawo spółek (Branta 2002)

A stock corporation (*spółka akcyjna*,"S.A.") is the second type of capital company recognised by Polish law. Generally, although not necessarily, an S.A. is designed for a large number of shareholders and larger operations. Joint stock companies may be listed on the stock exchange, which gives them greater access to funds to finance their activities. Certain entities, such as banks, insurance companies or investment funds, can be set up only in the form of a joint stock company. The setting up and running of an S.A. is characterised by a greater number of formalities in comparison with that of an sp. z o.o. 37

2.1 Export of Company

The rules preventing the relocation of an sp. z o.o.[35] outside Poland can be applied *mutatis mutandis* to the transfer of an S.A.'s seat. 38

2.2 Transformation into a Foreign Entity

The transformation of an S.A. into a foreign entity may be carried out only indirectly by applying the same procedures as in the case of an sp. z o.o.[36] 39

32 A financial year is a calendar year or any other period of 12 full consecutive calendar months, as may be chosen by the company (Sec. 3 Subs. 9 Polish Act on Accounting of 29 September 1994, Journal of Laws No. 76/2002, item 694, as subsequently amended ("PAA")).

33 The requirement for the annual report to be audited and published only arises if the sp. z o.o. fulfilled at least two out of the following three conditions in the financial year immediately preceding the financial year for which the annual report is being drawn up: (i) the company had on average at least 50 employees in full time employment; (ii) the sum of the company's balance sheet assets was equal to the PLN equivalent of at least EUR 2,500,000; and (iii) the company's net income from the sale of goods and services and financial operations was equal to the PLN equivalent of at least EUR 5,000,000.

34 There are certain marginal exceptions to this rule. For example, in an sp. z o.o. which was formed from a commercialised state owned enterprise (*przedsiębiorstwo państwowe*), employees may be granted participation in the supervisory board; however, the appointment of a supervisory board is not obligatory (Sec. 11 of the Act on Commercialisation and Privatisation of State Owned Enterprises (Journal of Laws No. 171/2002, item 1397, as subsequently amended)).

35 See Mn. 2.

36 See Mn. 3.

2.3 Incorporation

40 The requirements for the formation of a joint stock company are:
(i) the signing of the S.A.'s articles of association (*statut*) by its founders[37] in the form of a notarial deed;
(ii) shareholder subscription for all shares in the S.A.;
(iii) shareholder contributions to the S.A.'s share capital;[38]
(iv) appointment of the company's management board and supervisory board; and
(v) registration in the register of entrepreneurs.[39]

An S.A. may be founded by one or more persons. However, it may not be formed exclusively by a single-shareholder sp. z o.o.[40]

At the moment of its registration, an S.A. becomes a legal person. However, once the S.A.'s articles of association are executed and all shares are subscribed for, a joint stock company in organisation is set up (Sec. 310 KSH).[41]

41 The fees payable in relation to the incorporation and registration of an S.A. are similar to those in the case of formation of an sp. z o.o.[42]

Whilst the time taken to register an S.A. varies from court to court, in general it could take from one to six weeks to register the S.A. in the register of entrepreneurs.

2.4 Recurrent Costs and Efforts

42 Annual recurrent costs and efforts for an S.A. depend on the size of the company. They can be similar to, or at least not substantially higher than, those incurred by an sp. z o.o.[43] if the number of shareholders in the S.A. is relatively small. However, if the S.A. is listed or has a significant number of shareholders, the costs for corporate housekeeping may be higher.[44] Running an S.A. is more formal than its counterpart, the sp. z o.o. It requires that minutes from all shareholders'

37 The signatories of the S.A.'s articles of association are the founders of the company. The founders do not necessarily have to be the only shareholders. Shares may also be subscribed for by other third parties who did not sign the company's articles of association but have signed a declaration in the form of a notarial deed that they wish to become shareholders of the company and they consent to its formation and the contents of its articles of association.

38 Polish law recognises two ways of obtaining share capital by an S.A.: by offering its shares to a close circle of private investors or by way of an initial public offering (the latter is regulated by the Act on Public Trading of Securities (*ustawa – prawo o publicznym obrocie papierami wartościowymi*) of 21 August 1997 (Journal of Laws No. 118, item 754, as subsequently amended)). In practice, no initial public offering is made at the stage of the company's formation.
Sec. 309 Subs. 3 KSH provides that any shares subscribed for by contributions in kind must be paid up in full by not later than the first anniversary of the company's registration. Shares subscribed for in cash must be paid for up to a minimum of one-quarter of their par value before the company's registration. If the shares are subscribed for in exchange for contributions in kind, in whole or in part, the share capital must be paid up prior to the company's registration to the extent of at least one-quarter of its nominal value. The remainder of such contributions must be paid up in accordance with the company's articles of association or a resolution of the general shareholders' meeting. Shareholders may authorise the management board to determine the term within which the remaining part of such shareholder contributions are to be paid up (Sec. 330 KSH).

39 An application for the registration of an S.A. must be filed within six months of the date of drawing up of the company's articles of association (Sec. 325 KSH).

40 This limitation applies to single-shareholder sp. z o.o.s only. A single-shareholder S.A. may be the sole founder of an S.A. As is the case for an sp. z o.o., after the company is registered, a single-shareholder sp. z o.o. may be the sole shareholder of an S.A. See Mn. 4.

41 For a discussion of the "company in organisation" concept see Mn. 4.

42 See Mn. 4. The fees will be proportionally higher than in a sp. z o.o. due to the higher minimum admissible share capital in the S.A. In the case of an S.A. with the minimum admissible share capital of PLN 500,000 (approximately EUR 127,000) the notary fee should not exceed PLN 3,210 and the tax on civil actions would amount to PLN 2,500 (approximately EUR 640).

43 See Mn. 6.

44 The recurrent costs and efforts that a listed company has to bear may be significant due to the scope of information that the company is legally required to make publicly available and submit for announcement.

meetings be notarised; shareholders' meetings must generally be convened by an announcement in the official gazette *Monitor Sądowy i Gospodarczy*[45] (which is an additional cost factor).

2.5 Shares and Share Transfers

An S.A. may issue either bearer shares or registered shares.[46] At the request of a shareholder, registered shares may be changed to bearer shares and vice versa.[47] The minimum par value of one share is PLN 0.01 (approximately EUR 0.0025). **43**

As a rule, shares in an S.A. are transferable (Sec. 337 KSH). **44**

The company's articles of association may impose certain restrictions on the transfer of shares, such as the existence of pre-emption rights, a requirement for prior consent to the transfer by the company or the shareholders' meeting, etc. Such restrictions may only apply to registered shares[48] and must not result in excluding the right of a shareholder to dispose of his shares.

Further, shareholder agreements may provide for limitations on the disposal of shares (Sec. 338 KSH).[49]

There are also certain legal restrictions on the transfer of shares. For example, shares subscribed for contributions in kind must not be transferred or pledged until the annual financial report for the financial year in which they were paid up is approved by the general shareholders' meeting (Sec. 336 KSH).

The transfer of registered shares requires that a written declaration be provided by the selling shareholder to the effect that he thereby transfers the shares either in the share certificate itself or in a separate document (e.g. in the sale agreement) and the transfer of possession of the share (Sec. 339 KSH). The transfer of a bearer share requires delivery of the share certificate.[50] **45**

The shares of listed companies have no material form (they are recorded on the shareholder's securities account). Therefore, the transfer of such shares is also in a dematerialised form and occurs by way of the appropriate record being made in the shareholder's securities account.

Generally, the transfer of shares is subject to the tax on civil law transactions in the amount of 1 per cent of the market value of the transferred shares. **46**

2.6 Corporate Bodies

There are three compulsory corporate bodies in an S.A.: the management board (*zarząd*); the supervisory board (*rada nadzorcza*); and the general shareholders' meeting (*walne zgromadzenie*). **47**

45 However, if all the shares are registered shares, a general shareholders' meeting may be convened by written notice sent to all registered shareholders by registered mail or courier at least two weeks prior to the date of the general meeting. Subject to shareholders' consent, a notice may be sent to such consenting shareholders by electronic mail (Sec. 402 KSH).

46 Apart from bearer and registered shares, the law provides for other (sub)types of shares, such as silent shares (*akcje nieme*), which are shares that are privileged in respect of dividend payment but do not carry a right to vote at shareholders' meetings (Sec. 353 KSH). Furthermore, the law provides for securities other than shares that may, or in certain circumstances must, be issued by the S.A., e.g. registered temporary certificates (*imienne świadectwa tymczasowe*), which are issued instead of bearer shares that are not paid up in full (Sec. 335 KSH); registered founder certificates (*imienne świadectwa założycielskie*), which may be issued for the benefit of the company's founders as remuneration for their services upon formation of the company (Sec. 355 KSH); or utility certificates (*świadectwa użytkowe*), which may be issued in exchange for shares that have been redeemed (Sec. 361 KSH).

47 Unless the law or the company's articles of association provide otherwise (Sec. 334 KSH).

48 Restrictions in the S.A.'s articles of association regarding the transfer of shares may not apply to bearer shares or to shares in listed companies.

49 Contractual limitations on share transfers (which may apply to both registered and bearer shares) are permitted for a specified period of time not exceeding five years from the date of execution of the shareholder agreement. Furthermore, agreements creating pre-emption rights or other priority rights are permitted, provided that such rights are established for a term not exceeding 10 years from the date of the shareholder agreement (Sec. 338 KSH).

50 Sec. 921 of the Polish Civil Code (*kodeks cywilny*) (Journal of Laws No. 16/1964, item 93, as subsequently amended).

2.6.1 Management Board

48 The management board of an S.A. may consist of one or more members and it enjoys sole power to represent the company *vis-à-vis* third parties. This authority cannot be restricted towards third parties. The members of the management board may be awarded either individual or joint powers of representation.[51]

49 The management board is responsible for most of the day-to-day management decisions of the company. Nevertheless, for certain essential transactions to be entered into by the management board on behalf of the company, the consent of the general shareholders' meeting must be obtained, otherwise such actions are null and void.[52] Furthermore, the company's articles of association may provide for instances in which the actions of the management board require the approval of the supervisory board.[53] However, neither the general shareholders' meeting nor the supervisory board is permitted to give binding instructions to the management board regarding the management of the company's affairs (Sec. 375 KSH).

50 The members of the management board are appointed and dismissed by the supervisory board, unless the company's articles of association provide otherwise (Sec. 368 Subs. 4 KSH). Nevertheless, the general shareholders' meeting is at all times entitled to dismiss or suspend members of the management board. The maximum term of office of management board members cannot exceed five years, but a reappointment is permitted (Sec. 369 KSH).

Only natural persons with full legal capacity may become members of the management board. However, persons convicted by a criminal court for certain criminal actions are disqualified from taking the function of member of the management board.[54]

2.6.2 The General Shareholders' Meeting

51 The general shareholders' meeting is the representative body of the shareholders in which they can exercise their rights as shareholders. They may adopt resolutions on the most significant matters concerning the running of the company.

Ordinary general meetings must be convened once a year within six months of the end of the financial year. The procedure for convening such meetings is formalised and generally requires publishing of an announcement in the official gazette *Monitor Sądowy i Gospodarczy*.[55] All minutes

51 See Mn. 9.

52 Pursuant to Secs. 393 and 394 KSH, the following actions of the management board require a resolution of the shareholders' meeting:
- (i) claims for loss or damage caused upon formation of the company, or by its management or supervision at the time of such formation;
- (ii) a disposal or tenancy of the business undertaking or an organised part of it, as well as the creation of limited rights *in rem* over them;
- (iii) an acquisition or a disposal of real estate or part of such real estate, unless the company's articles of association provide otherwise;
- (iv) the issue of convertible bonds, bonds carrying priority rights or subscription warrants;
- (v) a purchase of the company's own shares in the cases stipulated in the KSH;
- (vi) conclusion of an agreement in relation to management of the company or the transfer of profits; and
- (vii) an acquisition of any assets from a founder, shareholder, parent or subsidiary company for a price higher than one-tenth of the S.A.'s paid-up share capital, if made before the second anniversary of the company's registration.

Any of the above actions taken by the management board on behalf of the company in the absence of a resolution of the shareholders' meeting (which may be passed either prior to or up to two months after such action) are null and void (Sec. 17 Subs. 1 KSH).

53 Sec. 384 KSH. If supervisory board consent for actions of the management board is only required pursuant to the S.A.'s articles of association and not by law, management board actions taken in the absence of such consent are valid and binding upon the company; however, the management board members who acted without valid consent are personally liable to the company for any loss or damage caused by their actions (Sec. 17 Subs. 3 KSH).

54 Most importantly criminal actions to the detriment of the company, against the economy and commercial relationships.

55 See Mn. 42.

of general shareholders' meetings must be made in the form of a notarial deed in order to be valid (Sec. 421 Subs. 1 KSH).

2.6.3 Supervisory Board

The supervisory board is a compulsory supervisory body in an S.A. and is generally appointed by the general shareholders' meeting, unless the company's statute provides otherwise (Sec. 385 Subs. 1 KSH).[56] It must consist of at least three (in the case of listed companies at least five) members, who are appointed for a term of office which cannot exceed five years.[57] 52

Supervisory board members exercise their powers collectively; however, they may be authorised by the supervisory board to perform certain supervisory functions individually. Only supervisory board members elected by group voting may perform their supervisory functions individually (Sec. 390 KSH). 53

The supervisory board has the responsibility and powers for overall supervision of all of the company's activities (Sec. 382 Subs. 1 KSH), as well as a right to suspend members of the management board for important reasons and delegate to members of the supervisory board the temporary performance of management functions[58] (Sec. 383 KSH).

Furthermore, the supervisory board may be granted a statutory right to approve certain of the actions of the management board.[59] However, the supervisory board is prohibited by law from giving binding instructions to the management board regarding the management of the company's affairs (Sec. 375 KSH).

2.7 Duties and Liabilities of Directors

The duties of the management board in an S.A. correspond to those of the management board in an sp. z o.o.[60] 54

The liability of the management board of an S.A. is similar to that of members of the management board of an sp. z o.o. (Secs. 479 to 490 KSH).[61]

Apart from the imposition of a general liability on management board members, such members are additionally responsible for any breaches of the provisions regarding protection of the company's share capital, as well as for any benefits received by shareholders from the company in breach of the law or the company's articles of association (Sec. 350 Subs.1 KSH). 55

Unlike in the case of an sp. z o.o., [62] members of an S.A.'s management board may not be held personally liable for the company's liabilities towards third parties in the event that a creditor's enforcement against the company proves to be ineffective.

56 In order to protect minority rights, Polish corporate law provides for the appointment of the supervisory board by groups of shareholders (Sec. 385 Subs. 3 et seq. KSH). If shareholders representing at least one-fifth of the company's share capital request election of the supervisory board members by voting in separate groups, such voting must take place at the next general shareholders' meeting, irrespective of the fact that the company's articles of association may provide for a different procedure of appointment. Shareholders having the requisite number of shares, calculated by dividing the total number of shares owned by those shareholders represented at the meeting by the total number of supervisory board positions, may create a group, which will be entitled to elect one member of the supervisory board. Such group does not participate in the election of the remaining members of the supervisory board.

57 Reappointment is permitted (Sec. 386 Subs. 2 and Sec. 369 Subs. 1 KSH).

58 For a period not exceeding three months where a management board member was dismissed, has resigned or is for other reasons not able to perform his duties.

59 See Mn. 49.

60 See Mn. 15.

61 See also Mn. 15.

62 See Mn. 16. However, members of the management board are personally liable for any tax arrears of the S.A. as stipulated in Sec. 116 of the Polish Tax Ordinance of 29 August 1997 (Journal of Laws No. 137, item 926, as subsequently amended).

2.8 Shareholders' Liability

56 As it is the case with an sp. z o.o., shareholders of an S.A. are generally not personally liable for the obligations of the company. Neither Polish law nor Polish jurisprudence has recognised the concept of piercing the corporate veil so far.[63]

2.9 Capitalisation and Financing

2.9.1 Basic Concepts

57 As in an sp. z o.o., capitalisation and financing of an S.A. is based on the "principle of real capital contribution and maintenance".[64]

2.9.2 Minimum Share Capital

58 The minimum admissible share capital of an S.A. is PLN 500,000 (approximately EUR 127,000) (Sec. 308 KSH). Share capital can be contributed in cash and/or in kind.[65] Contributions in kind must be made within one year as of the S.A.'s registration. Contributions in cash must be made for at least one-quarter of the par value of the shares so paid for prior to registration. If the shares are covered solely by means of contributions in kind or by means of mixture of contributions in kind and contributions in cash, such shares must be paid for in the amount of at least one-quarter of their par value prior to registration.

In addition to share capital, an S.A. is required to carry compulsory supplementary capital for the purpose of financing losses. Such supplementary capital is retained from the company's profits. An annual amount equal to at least 8 per cent of the S.A.'s profits for any given financial year must be allocated to supplementary capital until such time as the company's supplementary capital reaches one-third of the company's share capital (Sec. 396 KSH).

2.9.3 Maintenance of Capital and Liquidity

(i) System

59 The system provides for the preservation of capital to an even greater extent than is the case for an sp. z o.o.[66] Hidden contributions in kind are likewise forbidden and the law provides various mechanisms for protection against them,[67] as well as against the overvaluation of contributions in kind.[68]

63 See Mn. 17.

64 See Mn. 18.

65 See Mn. 19.

66 See Mn. 20 et seq.

67 Pursuant to Sec. 394 KSH, an acquisition by the company of any assets from a founder, shareholder, parent or subsidiary company for a price higher than one-tenth of the S.A.'s paid-up share capital requires for its validity a resolution of the general shareholders' meeting, if made before the second anniversary of the company's registration.

68 Pursuant to Sec. 311 KSH, a report of the founders must be prepared if contributions in kind are made or the company acquires assets or pays remuneration for services provided in connection with its formation, before the company's registration. The report must be audited for its accuracy and reliability by a qualified auditor appointed by the registration court (Sec. 312 KSH). The same procedure applies if, before the second anniversary of its registration, the company intends to acquire assets from any of its founders, shareholders, parent or subsidiary companies, for a price higher than one-tenth of the company's paid-up share capital (Sec. 394 Subs. 3 KSH). In addition, shares subscribed for by contributions in kind must not be transferred or pledged until the annual financial report for the financial year in which they were paid up is approved by the general shareholders' meeting. Such shares must be retained by the company as security for any claims for damages for non-performance or improper performance of the shareholders' obligation to make contributions in kind (Sec. 336 KSH).

(ii) Distributions

The right to share in the company's profits is the main financial entitlement of shareholders in an S.A. Distributions can be made, provided the company has profits as stated in the company's audited financial report and the general shareholders' meeting resolves for the company to make a dividend distribution to the shareholders (Sec. 347 KSH). The S.A.'s statute may also authorise its management board to pay to shareholders limited advance dividend payments if the company's approved financial results for the previous year show profits. Consent of the supervisory board is required for the payment of advance dividends (Sec. 349 KSH). **60**

Shareholders who receive payments from the company in breach of the law or the company's articles of association must repay them, save for any profits received by a shareholder acting in good faith. The recipient of illegal payments, as well as members of the management board and/or the supervisory board who are responsible for such payments, are jointly and severally liable to make repayment (Sec. 350 KSH).

(iii) Acquisition of Own Shares and Related Financing

Subject to the exceptions in Sec. 362 KSH,[69] an S.A. is prohibited from acquiring or subscribing for its own shares. The company cannot exercise any of the shareholders' rights attaching to any repurchased shares, except for the right to dispose of them or to take any action necessary for the maintenance of rights deriving from such repurchased shares (Sec. 364 KSH). **61**

The provision of financial assistance by an S.A. is forbidden. The company cannot extend loans, grant security, pay dividend advances or provide any other direct or indirect financing to its shareholders or third parties for the acquisition of, or subscription for, its shares (Sec. 345 Subs. 1 KSH).[70] **62**

(iv) Company as Lender or Guarantor

An S.A. may extend loans and guarantees to third parties, including to its shareholders. Any such transactions with the company's shareholders must be made on arm's length terms, otherwise they would breach Sec. 350 KSH. **63**

Special restrictions apply if a loan, credit, suretyship (guarantee) or other similar agreement with, or in favour of, a member of the management board, supervisory board, a holder of a commercial power of attorney or a liquidator of the company is to be entered into.[71]

(v) Company as Borrower

As in the case of an sp. z o.o., shareholders may extend shareholder loans to an S.A. However, the thin capitalisation rules will likewise apply.[72] **64**

2.10 Publication and Filing Requirements

Publicity and filing requirements are similar to those applicable to an sp. z o.o.[73] **65**

69 E.g. an acquisition of shares effected in order to avert the threat of major damage to the company, or an acquisition of shares with the intention of offering them for acquisition to the company's employees, etc.

70 This prohibition does not apply to financing provided by financial institutions in the ordinary course of their business, as well as to financing provided by the company to its employees or those of an affiliated company in order to facilitate the acquisition of, or subscription for, shares issued to them by the company, provided that a special capital reserve is created from funds which in accordance with law would normally have been available for distributions amongst shareholders (Sec. 345 Subs. 2 KSH).

71 Entering into such agreements by the company requires a resolution of the general shareholders' meeting (Sec. 15 Subs. 1 KSH).

72 See Mn. 24 and 32.

73 See Mn. 33 and 34.

2.11 Financial Reporting

66 These rules are comparable with those applicable to an sp. z o.o.[74] However, the financial statements of an S.A. must always be audited and published in the official gazette *Monitor Polski B.* (Sec. 64 Subs. 1.3 PPA).

2.12 Employee Participation in Corporate Bodies

67 The rules regarding employee participation and representation in the corporate bodies of an S.A. correspond to those applicable in the case of an sp. z o.o.[75]

74 See Mn. 35.
75 See Mn. 36.

XX. Portugal

by Jorge M Bleck and Sofia Egídio[*]

1 The Limited Liability Company ("Lda")

Literature: Ventura, Sociedades Por Quotas, 3 Vols. (Almedina 1987, 1989, 1991); Abreu, Curso de Direito Comercial, Vol. II: Das Sociedades (Almedina 2002); Furtado, Curso de Direito das Sociedades (5th edition, Almedina 2004); Cordeiro, Manual de Direito das Sociedades, Vol. I (Almedina 2004)

The limited liability company (*Sociedade por Quotas*, "Lda") is traditionally the most common corporate form used in Portugal for small and medium-sized companies. The shareholders' liability is limited to the contributions established in the articles of association as share capital. The main differences as compared to the stock corporation (*Sociedade Anónima*, "SA")[1] are: (i) the joint and several liability of the shareholders for the contribution of the entire share capital; and (ii) the possibility for the shareholders to give direct instructions to the managing directors. In 2004 there were approximately 471,600 Lda.s registered in Portugal, in contrast to approximately 24,200 S.A.s (84 of which were listed). 1

The regulation concerning corporate governance is not strict and permits a high degree of flexibility in the drafting of articles of association. Despite this flexibility, the transfer of shares is subject to notarial deed and public registration with the commercial register making it easier to identify the holders of the Lda. 2

1.1 Export of Company

A company incorporated and registered in Portugal is allowed to move its business activity to another country without losing its legal identity and its registration, provided it is accepted by the law of the foreign country (Art. 3, Nr. 5 of the Portuguese Companies Code (*Código das Sociedades Comerciais*, "CC")).[2] The decision to relocate the business activity of an Lda must be passed by a 75 per cent majority of the votes corresponding to the share capital (Art. 3, Nr. 6) whereby opposing shareholders may ask for an exclusion from the company if they so wish.[3] 3

1.2 Transformation into a Foreign Entity

Portuguese law does not expressly provide for the transformation of a domestic company into a foreign entity. This would be an indirect result of transferring the business activity or corporate seat to a foreign country the laws of which do not allow the maintaining of its Portuguese legal identity. An Lda cannot be merged with an S.E. 4

1.3 Incorporation

An Lda is normally set up by way of a notarial deed of incorporation, executed by at least two incorporators[4] (Art. 7, Nrs. 1 and 2). Prior to the execution of the notarial deed of incorporation the corporate name of the Lda must be obtained. The company will legally exist upon its entry into the 5

* *Linklaters*, Lisbon. Written with the assistance of Patrícia Afonso Fonseca and Carla Gonçalves Borges.

1 See Mn. 44 et seq.

2 Hereinafter, all the provisions in the text that do not refer to any law shall refer to the CC.

3 Portuguese law does not expressly provide for the transfer of the corporate seat. Arguably, the legal framework described above shall be applied to both situations, including the voting majority to pass that decision, given the fact that moving the corporate seat will change the personal law of the company and affect third parties' and minority shareholders' interests. Lima Pinheiro, *Direito Internacional Privado*, Vol. II (2nd edition, Almedina 2002), p. 118 et seq.

4 It is possible to incorporate an Lda with a sole shareholder subject to the specific regime of "*Sociedades Unipessoais por Quotas*". Notarisation of the act of incorporation might not be necessary depending on the nature of the contributions of the sole shareholder.

commercial register (Art. 5). The company must publish its articles of association in the Official Gazette (*Diário da República*). However, according to the Decree-Law 111/2005 of 8 July, it is possible to incorporate a new Lda. in a short time[5] with some commercial register offices, provided that the corporate name is one of those previously approved by the authorities and that the articles of association to be selected are from those available from the authorities, which are very standard.

6 The length of the incorporation procedure may vary from eight to 10 weeks. The notarial and registry fees amount to approximately EUR 250 and the cost of the publication of the articles of association in the Official Gazette will vary (EUR 72 per page). Stamp tax is currently levied at 0.4 per cent of the value of the share capital and shall be borne by the incorporated company.

1.4 Recurrent Costs and Efforts

7 Recurrent costs and efforts relating to an Lda are very small and relate only to the publication of annual accounts and their filing with the commercial register.[6] The cost of filing is currently EUR 52.74 plus the publication fees of EUR 72 per page in the Official Gazette. Other costs and efforts will only be incurred in the event certain corporate steps are taken which require notarisation, filing with the commercial register or publication (for example, an increase of share capital).

1.5 Shares and Share Transfers

8 Shares in an Lda are denominated in "quotas" which can be transferred by way of a notarial transfer deed (Art. 228, Nr. 1). Unless otherwise provided for in the articles of association, the approval of the company itself is necessary, the exception being those transfers made between a shareholder and family members (Art. 228, Nr. 2 and Art. 229, Nr. 2).[7] The quota transfer will be effective in relation to the company when it approves the transfer or the company is informed of the same if such approval is not necessary (Art. 229, Nr. 3). The transfer of quotas may trigger the payment of several taxes: (i) corporate income tax, to be paid by the entity transferring the shares; (ii) real estate transfer tax, to be paid by the acquiring entity (if the company has real estate properties and at least 75 per cent of the share capital is being transferred); and (iii) stamp duty to be paid by the acquiring entity, the amount of which is not significant.

9 The CC prohibits the issue of quota certificates (Art. 219, Nr. 7). Therefore, title to a quota is solely evidenced by entry in the public commercial register. The prohibition of quota certificates implies that there is no public market for quotas. Although an Lda is not expressly prohibited by law from issuing its quotas to the public, it is in practice impossible for it to be engaged in an initial public offering of its quotas.

1.6 Corporate Bodies

10 The CC provides for two compulsory corporate bodies, the managing directors and the shareholders' meeting, and one that is optional: the audit board or a sole auditor.[8]

5 Assuming that all the required documents are delivered, the company is incorporated on the same day and the commercial registry certificate of the registry of the articles of association and the tax and social security numbers are delivered. After January 2006 it will be possible to obtain the corporate name prior to the incorporation. However, there is no possibility of presenting amended articles of association to the authorities. Any amendment shall be made subsequently.

6 The annual accounts of an Lda which does not have an audit board must be audited by an official chartered accountant, if for two consecutive years two of the following three limits are exceeded: a balance sheet total of EUR 1,500,000; a turnover of EUR 3,000,000; 50 employees. This will result in further costs being incurred.

7 If the articles of association prohibit the transfer of shares, the shareholders have the right to exit the company after 10 years (Art. 229, Nr. 1).

8 See Mn. 15.

1.6.1 Managing Directors

An Lda may have one or several managing directors, who do not necessarily have to be shareholders of the company, and who exclusively represent the company *vis-à-vis* third parties (Art. 252, Nr. 1). If more than one managing director is appointed, the majority will represent the company *vis-à-vis* third parties[9] unless the articles of association provide otherwise (Art. 261, Nr. 2). **11**

The managing directors are responsible for the management of the company. Notwithstanding this, they are bound by the instructions of the shareholders (Art. 259). **12**

1.6.2 Shareholders' Meeting

The shareholders' meeting has overall authority on almost all matters relating to the company. It has exclusive authority regarding various issues such as the removal of managing directors and audit board members, changes to the articles of association, confiscation of shares and the approval of quota transfers (Art. 246, Nr. 1). If the articles of association do not provide otherwise, the shareholders' meeting may also decide upon certain business transactions (for example, the disposal of a business, the acquisition and disposal of subsidiaries). Furthermore, it is entitled to give direct instructions to the managing directors. **13**

Resolutions of the shareholders' meeting are passed by a simple majority of the votes cast (Art. 248, Nr. 1 and Art. 386, Nr. 1). Exceptions are made for the passing of certain resolutions, including those amending the articles of association, which require a three-quarters majority of the total share capital (Art. 265, Nr. 1). **14**

1.6.3 Audit Board

The articles of association may provide for an audit board,[10] which must then comply with the rules established for this body as existing in the SA[11] (Art. 262, Nr. 1). It is responsible for supervising the company's management and accounts, as well as for ensuring compliance with the law and the articles of association (Art. 420, Nr. 1). **15**

1.7 Duties and Liabilities of Directors

Besides being responsible for managing the day-to-day business of an Lda, the managing directors also have certain statutory obligations, such as convening the annual shareholders' meeting, reporting to the audit board (if any) or obtaining the approval of the shareholders for certain business transactions when this is required. The managing directors must perform their duties using the diligence of a prudent businessman taking into account the interests of the company, the shareholders and the employees (Art. 64). A director is required to have full legal capacity and not have been convicted of guilty insolvency within an insolvency proceeding (Art. 189 of the Insolvency Code). **16**

The managing directors have a joint liability (Art. 73) and it is not possible to establish limits for that liability (for example, based on the allocation of the responsibilities of each director). In the event of guilty breach, they are personally liable to the company (Art. 72) and to the company's creditors (Art. 78). If any one of the directors is not guilty of a breach, he has the right to recover from the other directors any damages for which he has been considered liable. Even so, the managing directors are not liable to the company should the breach result from a shareholders' resolution (Art. 72, Nr. 4) or if their management is approved by a shareholders' resolution (which has to be approved with less than 10 per cent voting against the resolution) and the shareholders are aware of any breach before such approval. Furthermore, the managing directors are liable in general terms for damages directly caused to the shareholders and to third parties (Art. 79). Finally, in certain **17**

9 However, delegation by the managing directors to one sole managing director is allowed for certain acts or classes of acts.

10 Instead of an audit board, it is possible to provide for a sole auditor, who must be a chartered registered accountant (*revisor oficial de contas*).

11 See Mn. 59.

circumstances, the managing directors[12] are liable for the tax debts of the company.[13] The general statute of limitations for claims against directors is five years (Art. 174).

18 In addition to the general liability of the managing directors, they can also be held liable for any illegal payment made in breach of the provisions of Arts. 31 to 33, for any acquisition by the company of own shares in breach of Art. 220, and for breach of Art. 35.[14] These breaches are punishable through the payment of fines and in some cases by imprisonment, respectively (Arts. 514, 510 and 523).[15]

1.8 Shareholders' Liability

19 The principle of limited liability[16] has exceptions. There are certain situations imposed by law which may lead to a shareholder liability, besides those established in the articles of association.[17] The exceptions imposed by law can be divided into three groups.

20 First, when a shareholders' majority passes a resolution with the view to obtaining special advantages or benefits for either themselves or third parties and thereby cause harm to the company or to the minority shareholders, those shareholders will be jointly liable for damages caused (Art. 58, Nr. 3).

21 Secondly, the shareholders who have the right to elect or dismiss a managing director or a member of the audit board will be, in certain circumstances, jointly responsible with him towards the company and the other shareholders, to the extent they were negligent in their choice (*culpa in eligendo*) of that managing director or audit board member (Art. 83).

22 Finally, in the case of the bankruptcy of a company reduced to one shareholder, such shareholder will be responsible for the company's obligations incurred after the concentration of the quotas, where it can be proven that the provisions of the CC relating to the protection of the company's share capital and liquidity were breached in that period (Art. 84).

1.9 Capitalisation and Financing

1.9.1 Basic Concepts

23 The overall principle underlying the capitalisation and financing of an Lda is the "principle of preserving the capital intact",[18] which aims to prevent capital contributions reverting to the shareholders before third party creditors are satisfied. The share capital stated in the articles of association serves as a reference to the company's potential creditors of the minimum monetary protection available to them.

1.9.2 Minimum Share Capital

24 The minimum share capital of an Lda is EUR 5,000 (Art. 201). The share capital can be rendered in cash or in kind (Art. 25, Nr. 1). Where the capital is rendered in cash, at least half of the share capital must be paid in on the date of the notarial deed of incorporation. Deferred contributions are only allowed in the event that on the incorporation date the minimum amount of share capital

12 As well as the members of the audit board (if any).

13 In the event that the company's assets to be seized are insufficient, i.e. the managing directors have a subsidiary liability (Arts. 22 to 24 of the General Tax Law (*Lei Geral Tributária*)).

14 See Mn. 28.

15 Criminal liability is time barred after two years from the date of the breach (Art. 118, Nr. 1(d) of the Penal Code (*Código Penal, PC*)), and civil liability is time barred after five years (Art. 174).

16 See Mn. 1.

17 For instance, the articles of association may provide for a direct liability of the shareholders to the company's creditors (Art. 198) or for ancillary capital contributions (Art. 209) or supplementary contributions (Art. 210).

18 Furtado, *Curso de Direito das Sociedades* (5th edition, Almedina 2004), p. 311 et seq.; A. Almeida, *Sociedades Comerciais* (2nd edition, Coimbra Editora 1999), p. 171 et seq.

required is reached (Art. 202, Nr. 2).[19] Contributions in kind need to be valued by an independent chartered accountant who will issue an evaluation report for the purpose of the incorporation of the company (Art. 28, Nr. 1).

1.9.3 Maintenance of Capital and Liquidity

(i) System

Portuguese corporate law establishes a complex system to ensure the preservation and maintenance of the company's capital and liquidity. On the one hand, the CC applies a system of capital maintenance (registered share capital may not be paid back[20]) whilst on the other, creditors are protected: (i) through the personal liability of the managing directors *vis-à-vis* third parties should they act in breach of their duties; and (ii) pursuant to insolvency law. **25**

The "principle of preserving the capital intact" ensures the payment by shareholders of capital contributions to the company and establishes that actions of the managing directors or resolutions of the shareholders' meeting releasing any shareholder from the obligation to pay up his contribution are void (Art. 27, Nr. 1). As regards contributions in kind, the CC provides for a mandatory valuation to ensure there is a real value attributable to such contributions.[21] **26**

Certain rules are established for distributions to shareholders (Arts. 31 to 33). No distributions of any nature are allowed if: **27**

(a) the company's net situation is lower than the aggregate amount of share capital plus legal reserves, or becomes lower as a consequence of the distribution; or
(b) in the period of time between the shareholders' resolution and its execution by the directors, changes in the company's assets result in the situation detailed in (a) above; or
(c) the shareholders' resolution allowing for the distribution to the shareholders was based on incorrect accounts; or
(d) the annual profits must be used to cover accumulated deficits or to constitute legal reserves incurred in previous years.

Any amount paid to a shareholder that infringes one of the abovementioned situations must be repaid to the company upon its request or upon the company's creditors' request on its behalf (Art. 34, Nrs. 1 and 3). However, regarding points (a) and (d), shareholders will only have to repay the amount if the company or the company's creditors prove that the shareholders were aware or should have been aware of the irregularity of the payment. On the other hand, the directors that effect any illegal payment are liable for damages caused.[22] **28**

Other transactions between the company and its shareholders such as rendering of services or delivery of goods do not qualify as repayment of share capital. **29**

Under Portuguese corporate law there are no limits relating to the level of a company's indebtedness or to the granting of security. However, pursuant to Art. 35, if the accounts of the previous financial year reveal that the company's equity is lower than half of the company's share capital, the managing directors are required to expressly mention this fact in the annual management report and to propose some actions to the shareholders so that the company's equity covers a minimum of two thirds of the company's share capital.[23] **30**

19 Those deferred contributions must be paid within the next five years after incorporation, and are due according to the articles of association. In any case further to a five-year period, the payment of the deferred contributions can be claimed at any time (Art. 203., Nr. 1).

20 Except in certain cases of cancellation of shares with a reduction in share capital authorised by a court (Art. 95).

21 See Mn. 22.

22 See Mn. 37.

23 Such as dissolution of the company, reduction of the share capital or a realisation of supplementary contributions.

(ii) Distributions

31 Distributions of profits to shareholders are subject to a shareholders' resolution deciding on the utilisation of annual profits (Art. 31, Nr. 1). At least 50 per cent of the annual profits[24] shall be distributed, every fiscal year, unless the articles of association or a resolution approved by three quarters of the votes representing the whole share capital provide otherwise (Art. 217). It is mandatory to resolve on this matter in the shareholders' general meeting. Other distributions (such as profits carried forward from previous years, voluntary reserves, or other assets) to shareholders must also be approved by a shareholders' resolution but will be subject to a number of additional restrictions (Arts. 32 and 33):

(a) the net situation of the company must not be less than the amount of the share capital plus reserves that may not be distributed or become less than that amount as a result of the distribution;
(b) hidden reserves cannot be distributed.[25]

Advance dividends might be made if foreseen in the articles of association and if certain requirements are fulfilled (Arts. 297).

(iii) Acquisition of Own Shares and Related Financing

32 An Lda may acquire its own shares provided they are fully paid up (Art. 220, Nr. 1). However, own shares may only be acquired for nil consideration or for value if under an executive proceeding against the shareholder and where, for that purpose, the company has free reserves in an amount not less than double the value to be paid for the shares (Art. 220, Nr. 2).

33 The acquisition of own shares must be approved by a shareholders' resolution (Art. 246, Nr. 1(b)).

34 The legal framework on financial assistance regarding the SA is applicable to an Lda as well (Arts. 220 and 510).[26]

35 Any acquisition of own shares which does not comply with the abovementioned provisions is void (Art. 220, Nr. 3).

(iv) Company as Lender or Guarantor

36 Companies are legally entitled to provide guarantees in relation to the obligations of companies which they either control or with which they are in a group relationship, i.e. to parent or subsidiary companies[27] (upstream and downstream guarantees) (Art. 6, Nr. 3).[28]

37 Besides the abovementioned case, companies are legally entitled to provide guarantees in relation to the obligations of other entities only where there is a justified commercial benefit or interest (Art. 6, Nr. 3). If a corporate benefit cannot be demonstrated or satisfied and the company provides a guarantee, the managing directors may incur the risk of being personally liable for any damages caused to the company.

38 The company is allowed, even if it is not expressly provided by law, to act as lender. Loans to shareholders are allowed but they cannot be a way of making (hidden) distributions.

(v) Company as Borrower

39 There are no explicit restrictions to external financing by shareholders, but shareholder loans will be considered subordinated debt, and in the event of bankruptcy or a dissolution of the company due to any other cause, these loans may only be reimbursed after all debts to third parties have

24 After deduction of the losses carried forward from previous years or the amounts necessary to reintegrate mandatory reserves.

25 Should the shareholders receive any amount in breach of these mandatory provisions, see Mn. 27.

26 See Mn. 70 et seq.

27 Subsidiaries are those companies in which the company that provides guarantees: (i) has more than 50 per cent of the issued share capital; or (ii) has more than 50 per cent of the voting rights; or (iii) is able to designate the majority of members of the board of directors or audit board.

28 This legal regime is applicable to the provision of guarantees by Portuguese companies regardless of the nationality of the parent or subsidiary company that benefits from the guarantee.

been settled (Art. 245, Nr. 3(a) and Art. 48 of the Insolvency Code (*Código da Insolvência e da Recuperação de Empresas*, "IC")).[29] It should be noted that, whenever the indebtedness of a company towards its foreign shareholders is more than double the amount of equity of such shareholders in the company, interest paid in relation to the excess is not tax deductible (thin capitalisation of 2:1).

The shareholders are not required to ensure sufficient funding of the company unless the articles of association establish an obligation to make supplementary contributions or ancillary contributions[30] (Arts. 209 to 213). **40**

1.10 Publication and Filing Requirements

A large number of various documents and information must be filed with the commercial register,[31] some of which must also be submitted for publication in the Official Gazette. There are mandatory filings such as changes to the articles of association and appointment of corporate bodies. The accounts must also be filed and can be requested by anyone but are not published. The commercial register file is open to the public and any person can review the filed documents and request an excerpt from the commercial register detailing the main corporate information[32] as well as copies of any documents submitted. The certificates issued by the commercial register are official and make evidence of the registered facts. The non-filing of facts that must be filed triggers several consequences such as it not being possible to make evidence of those facts, the same not producing effects before third parties and the payment of a fine for the delay in filing the facts with the commercial register. **41**

1.11 Financial Reporting

An Lda must draw up its annual accounts within three months of the end of the business year, or within five months of the same date in the case of companies which must draw up consolidated accounts or apply the method of capital equivalence, i.e. accounts which reflect on other group companies' accounts (Art. 65, Nr. 5). The drawing up of the accounts of an Lda must be in accordance with Portuguese GAAP, which in some matters comply with the IAS, but not in others. The company's accounts only need to be audited (and filed to the commercial registry) should the company meet two of the three following criteria for two consecutive years: (i) balance total sheet of EUR 1,500,000; (ii) total net sales and other revenues of EUR 3,000,000 and (iii) an average of 50 employees during the fiscal year. For those Lda. not having an audit board,[33] the annual accounts must be approved in a shareholders general meeting. **42**

1.12 Employee Participation in Corporate Bodies

Normally, employees will not be represented in the corporate bodies of an Lda. With regard to wholly state-owned companies, the works council has the right to appoint employees' representatives as directors in a number established by the articles of association of the company. These employees will have the same rights as the other directors. **43**

29 According to Art. 48 IC, the shareholders' loans are the last ones to be reimbursed amongst other subordinated credits (e.g. director's loans, other loans from companies of the group or related persons (Art. 49, Nr. 2 IC)).

30 In these cases, the articles of association must establish limits to such contributions.

31 Art. 3 of the Commercial Registry Code (*Código do Registo Comercial,* "CRC"). The commercial register is (i) centralised in respect to the corporate name of the company and (ii) de-centralised in respect to the remaining aspects requiring registration. The registers cannot by accessed online.

32 For example, the share capital, the names of the managing directors, the identity of the shareholders, capital increases and amendments to the articles of association, etc.

33 See Mn. 15.

2 The Stock Corporation ("SA")

Literature: Ventura, Novos Estudos Sobre Sociedades Anónimas e Sociedades em Nome Colectivo (Almedina 1994); Abreu, Manual de Direito Comercial, Vol. II: Das Sociedades (Almedina 2002); Furtado, Curso de Direito das Sociedades (5th edition, Almedina 2004); Cordeiro, Manual de Direito das Sociedades, Vol. I (Almedina 2004)

44 The stock corporation (*Sociedade Anónima*, "SA")[34] is the most common investment vehicle used in Portugal for commercial transactions. The shareholders' liability is limited to the contribution of each shareholder, which is the percentage that he holds in the share capital. In contrast to the Lda, the shareholders can only resolve on matters referred to them by the board of directors or which are specifically entrusted to them by law or by the articles of association. Transfers of shares do not need to be notarised and its shares may be listed on a stock exchange.

2.1 Export of Company

45 Restrictions on the relocation of a domestic company to a foreign country will apply to an SA in the same manner as for an Lda.[35]

2.2 Transformation into a Foreign Entity

46 Any such transformation would have to be carried out in the same manner as for an Lda.[36] However, it is possible for an SA to merge with a European Company by means of an incorporation or by the incorporation of a new company.

2.3 Incorporation

47 An SA is set up by way of a notarial deed of incorporation executed by at least five incorporators (Art. 273, Nr. 1). There are, however, three exceptions: (i) where the State, directly or indirectly, has control over the majority of the share capital, the deed of incorporation may be executed by two incorporators (Art. 273, Nr. 2); (ii) where the share capital is initially wholly-owned by a company (Art. 488, Nr. 1); and (iii) the incorporation of an SA in a short time as described for the Lda.[37]

48 The incorporation procedure and costs associated with it correspond to those of an Lda,[38] but there is an additional obligation to communicate the incorporation to the Portuguese Securities Market Commission (*Comissão de Mercado de Valores Mobiliários*, "CMVM") (Art. 110, Nr. 2 and Art. 114 of the Portuguese Securities Code (*Código dos Valores Mobiliários*, "SC") and Arts. 2 and 5 of CMVM Regulation 10/2000).[39]

2.4 Recurrent Costs and Efforts

49 A small SA will normally face costs and efforts comparable to those of an Lda,[40] but in an SA the additional cost of a mandatory registered chartered accountant will always have to be considered. Furthermore, in a large SA or a listed one, the publicity and information duties (for example, calling a shareholders' meeting; the annual accounts) also increase the level of costs.

34 If it is a listed SA, the denomination will end with the expression "*Sociedade Aberta*".
35 See Mn. 3.
36 See Mn. 4.
37 See Mn. 5.
38 See Mn. 5 (in part) and 6.
39 In the case of an incorporation by a public subscription of shares, the promoters of the incorporation shall subscribe and fully pay up such number of shares as have a nominal value which corresponds, at least, to the minimum share capital; those shares are not alienable for two years from the definitive register (Art. 279, Nr. 2).
40 See Mn. 7.

2.5 Shares and Share Transfers

Shares may take the form of nominative shares, i.e. registered shares or bearer shares and may be represented by certificates or dematerialised (represented in book entry form and registered with a depository bank). The CC foresees the possibility of having different classes of shares with differing rights attaching to them if the articles of association provide so, notably preference shares without voting rights and redeemable preference shares. **50**

Dematerialised shares are transferred by registering them in the transferee's share account (Arts. 61(a), 62, 63, Nr. 1(a) and 80 SC and Art. 21 of the CMVM Regulation 14/2000).[41] **51**

Certificated shares may be transferred in a number of ways depending on the form of the shares, but commonly are transferred by delivery of the certificate to the depositary, the bank or the new holder, supported by a declaration of transfer in favour of the transferee written on the certificate and the subsequent registration of the shares by the depositary in the transferee's share account (Arts. 99, Nr. 2(b), 102 and 105 SC and Ministerial Order (*Portaria*) 290/2000).[42] The transfer of shares may trigger the payment of corporate income tax, to be paid by the entity transferring the shares, and stamp duty to be paid by the acquiring entity, the amount of which is not significant. **52**

2.6 Corporate Bodies

The law establishes two possible governance structures for the management of an SA, a one-tier structure, with a board of directors (or a sole director where the share capital does not exceed EUR 200,000) (Arts. 390 to 412), and a two-tier structure, comprising a supervisory board and a board of directors (Arts. 424 to 445). In both structures, there are also the shareholders' meeting and an audit board or a single auditor who must be a registered chartered accountant. **53**

2.6.1 One-Tier Structure

The board of directors consists of an odd number of directors (Art. 390, Nrs. 1 and 2), who may be appointed at the point of incorporation or by way of a shareholders' resolution for a maximum period of four years (Art. 391, Nrs. 1 and 3) and who can be re-elected. **54**

The board of directors is entrusted with the management of the company. The management of the company can be delegated to an executive committee also consisting of an odd number of directors or of one or more directors, if otherwise provided for by the articles of association (Art. 407, Nrs. 1 and 3). **55**

2.6.2 Two-Tier Structure

In this structure the members of the board of directors can alternatively be appointed by the supervisory board (Art. 425, Nr. 1). The board of directors have reporting obligations *vis-à-vis* the board (Art. 432), and in certain circumstances must obtain its prior consent for the performance of some acts (Arts. 431, Nr. 1 and Art. 442, nr 1). **56**

The supervisory board consists of an odd number of members, greater than the number of directors but less than 15 (Art. 434, Nr. 1), who must be shareholders but who cannot be directors of the company or other group companies (Art. 437, Nr. 1). Its members are appointed for a maximum **57**

41 Nominative, registered shares which are neither incorporated in a centralised system nor registered with a financial intermediary are transferred by registering them in the transferee's account with the issuer, i.e. the company, or with the financial intermediary acting for the issuer (Art. 64, Nrs. 1 and 2 and 80 SC and Art. 21 Regulation 14/2000).

42 The (i) listed bearer or nominative/registered shares; (ii) bearer shares represented by a single certificate; and (iii) bearer shares incorporated in a centralised system or deposited in a financial intermediary by initiative of the issuer are transferred by registering them in the transferee's account (Arts. 99, Nr. 2(a)(b), 80 and 105 SC and Art. 21 Regulation 14/2000), or, regarding (iii), by delivery of the certificate to the depositary if it is different from the one of the issuer (Arts. 105, 80 and 101, Nrs. 1 and 2 SC and Art. 21 Regulation 14/2000). Bearer shares not incorporated in a centralised system nor registered with a financial intermediary are transferred through the delivery of the certificates to the transferee or to a depositary appointed by him (Art. 101 SC).

period of four years (Art. 425 Nrs. 1 and 2) and can be re-elected. The supervisory board does not have management powers.

2.6.3 Shareholders' Meeting

58 The shareholders' meeting is composed of the shareholders who are entitled to at least one vote (Art. 379, Nr. 1).[43] The shareholders' meeting has a residual capacity on matters related to the company, since, besides having powers to decide on matters that are specifically entrusted to it by law or by the articles of association, it has powers to decide on matters that are not entrusted to any other corporate body (Art. 373, Nr. 2). As to matters related to the management of the company, the shareholders' meeting can only resolve on matters referred to it by the board of directors (Art. 373, Nr. 3).

2.6.4 Registered Chartered Accountant or Audit Board

59 The financial auditing of the company is entrusted to an auditing board[44] or to a sole auditor, who must be a chartered registered accountant (Art. 413, Nr. 1). The appointment of the audit board or the sole auditor and any substitute can be done at incorporation, or by way of a shareholders' resolution and cannot exceed four years (Art. 415, Nr. 1).

2.7 Duties and Liabilities of Directors

60 The duties of the directors are comparable to those of the managing directors of an Lda.[45] The directors must comply with the resolutions of the shareholders and the audit board, either when such bodies have exclusive capacity or the shareholders are requested by the board of directors to resolve on certain management matters (Art. 405, Nr. 1).

61 All board members must provide a guarantee for any possible liability that might arise from the performance of their duties in an amount not less than EUR 5,000. However, this guarantee can be replaced by an insurance taken out for the benefit of the company (Art. 396, Nrs. 1 and 2).[46] The company is not allowed to bear the insurance premiums if the insured amount is not less than EUR 5,000. Should the amount be higher, the company may bear the insurance premiums on a *pro rata* basis.

62 The members of the board of directors of an SA must perform their duties in the same manner as the managing directors of an Lda are required to do and have the same liability.[47]

2.8 Shareholders' Liability

63 The exceptions to the principle of limited shareholder liability in an SA correspond to those referred to with regard to an Lda,[48] taking into account that shareholders' liability is limited to the shares subscribed by the shareholders.

64 However, in the case of a sole shareholder, the parent company liability legal framework will apply. This legal framework establishes that the parent company becomes liable for the obligations of a wholly-owned company, regardless of their nature, once a period of 30 days commencing the date on which the relevant controlled company should have settled such obligations has elapsed (Art. 501). Furthermore, the parent company is liable, after termination of the group's relationship or if the company is declared bankrupt, for the wholly-owned company's annual losses to the extent

43 The articles of association may establish that above a certain limit the votes issued by a sole shareholder, in its name or in representation of another shareholder, shall not be counted. (Art. 384, Nr. 1(b)).

44 One of the members of the audit board must be a registered chartered accountant.

45 See Mn. 16 et seq., regarding management matters.

46 With the exception of public companies, the shareholders may waive the obligation of the directors to provide this guarantee in the shareholders' meeting resolution that appoints the director or in the articles of association, if they provide for the appointment of that director (Art. 396, Nr. 3).

47 See Mn. 16.

48 See Mn. 17 et seq., with exception of the regime under Art. 198.

these have not been reserved (Art. 502, Nr). 1. The rationale for this legal framework is the right of the parent company to give bidding instructions to the controlled company.

2.9 Capitalisation and Financing

2.9.1 Basic Concepts

As is the case with an Lda, the capitalisation and financing of an SA is based on the "principle of preserving the capital intact".[49] Hence, the same rules apply to the SA. 65

2.9.2 Minimum Share Capital

The minimum share capital of an SA is EUR 50,000 (Art. 276, Nr. 3). At least 30 per cent of the contributions in cash must be paid-up at the date of incorporation (Art. 277, Nr. 2). The deferred contributions must be paid-up within five years of incorporation (Art. 285, Nr. 1). Regarding contributions in kind, the legal framework corresponds to the one applied to an Lda.[50] 66

2.9.3 Maintenance of Capital and Liquidity

(i) System

The complex system established by Portuguese corporate law to ensure the preservation and maintenance of a company's capital and liquidity applies in the same terms to both an Lda and an SA.[51] However, in the case of an SA, the legal framework is stricter in relation to the acquisition of assets from shareholders.[52] 67

(ii) Distributions

The legal framework on distributions for an SA corresponds with the legal framework for an Lda.[53] However, in the case of an SA, unless the articles of association or a shareholders' resolution provide otherwise, half the annual profits[54] must be distributed to the shareholders (Art. 294, Nr. 1). Advanced dividends might be paid during the fiscal year if the articles of association provide so and it involves half of the annual profits to be distributed.[55] 68

(iii) Acquisition of Own Shares and Related Financing

The direct or indirect acquisition by an SA of its own shares is subject to a number of restrictions under Portuguese law. In general terms, a company can only acquire its own shares if the articles of association allow it and, save for some limited cases, if some requirements are complied with, such as a shareholders' resolution and where the acquisition is limited to 10 per cent of the share capital. 69

Portuguese law expressly prohibits financial assistance. A company cannot grant loans, provide funds or guarantees in order to enable a third entity to subscribe or acquire shares representing the company's issued share capital (Art. 322). This legal framework is extended to the subscription or acquisition of shares of the parent company. 70

All transactions that violate the prohibition of financial assistance are considered null and void. 71

49 See Mn. 23.

50 See Mn. 22.

51 See Mn. 23 et seq.

52 The acquisitions to be made by the company from its shareholders are, in general, subject to a prior resolution of the shareholders' meeting and a prior evaluation of the assets to be acquired, made by a chartered accountant (unless the acquisition is detailed in the objective of the company) (Art. 29).

53 See Mn. 31.

54 After deduction of the losses carried forward from previous years or the necessary amounts to reintegrate mandatory reserves.

55 The board of directors is entitled to resolve the anticipated distribution of profits based on a specific audited balance sheet prepared for such purpose (Art. 297).

72 The only two exceptions to the prohibition of financial assistance are: (i) the granting of credit by credit and financial institutions for the acquisition of own shares within the scope of its business; and (ii) transactions relating to the acquisition of shares in the company by its employees (Art. 322, Nr. 2).[56]

(iv) Company as Lender or Guarantor

73 The legal framework on this matter corresponds to the legal framework of an Lda,[57] but it should be stressed that an SA cannot grant loans, credit or securities to directors either of the company or of a company belonging to the same group (Art. 397, Nrs. 1 and 3).

(v) Company as Borrower

74 The legal framework applicable to an Lda on this matter shall be applicable by analogy to an SA (Art. 2).[58]

2.10 Publication and Filing Requirements

75 These requirements correspond with the requirements for an Lda,[59] but, in the case of a listed company, pursuant to Arts. 5 and 245 SC, the annual accounts, a management report and the audit report must be published in the Portuguese Securities Market Commission information disclosure system, any electronic means that is made available by the operator of the market or a regulated market bulletin or in a daily newspaper of national circulation.

2.11 Financial Reporting

76 These requirements correspond with the requirements for an Lda,[60] although there is an exception regarding listed companies. Note furthermore that S.A.s need to be audited even if they are small or medium-sized enterprises. The IAS Regulation[61] has determined that listed companies must prepare their consolidated accounts from 2005 onwards in accordance with the IAS/IFRS and each EU Member State has to decide if the same principles will or will not be extended to non-listed companies and to individual accounts of the listed companies. Portugal has not yet taken a decision on this subject.

2.12 Employee Participation in Corporate Bodies

77 The legal framework of these duties corresponds to the legal framework for an Lda.[62]

56 Provided in both cases that the liquid assets of the company are not reduced to below the limit of the issued share capital, plus the reserves of the company that cannot be distributable by law or pursuant to the articles of association of the company.

57 See Mn. 36 et seq.

58 See Mn. 39 et seq.

59 See Mn. 41.

60 See Mn. 42.

61 See Part 1, I, Mn 55.

62 See Mn. 43.

XXI. Slovakia

*by Daniel Torsher and Miroslav Trencan**

1 The Limited Liability Company ("s.r.o.")

Literature: Ovečková, Commercial Code, commentary (Iura Edition 2005); Suchoža, Commercial Code and related texts, commentary (Eurounion 2003)

The limited liability company (*spoločnost' s ručením obmedzeným*, "s.r.o.") is the most common corporate form used in Slovakia. It is a capital corporate entity, the assets of which are separate from those of its members. Members of an s.r.o. are liable to third parties only to the extent of their unpaid contributions registered with the commercial register (*obchodný register*). The main features distinguishing an s.r.o. from a stock corporation (*akciová spoločnost'*, "a.s.")[1] and other corporate entities in Slovakia include the extent of the liability of members for the obligations of the entity, the structure of their corporate bodies and different minimum capitalisation requirements. 1

In December 2004 there were approximately 90,000 s.r.o. registered in Slovakia, in contrast to approximately 6,800 a.s.

1.1 Export of Company

Under Sec. 26 Subs. 1 of the Commercial Code ("CC"), an s.r.o. with its registered seat in Slovakia may transfer its registered office abroad provided that such transfer is allowed under EU law or an international treaty binding on Slovakia. Since these two conditions are not currently met, the transfer of the registered seat of a Slovak s.r.o. abroad without loss of its legal identity is currently not possible. A Slovak s.r.o. can transfer its *de facto* seat abroad (subject to the laws of the host country) and keep its registered seat in Slovakia. 2

1.2 Transformation into a Foreign Entity

Slovak law does not provide for the transformation of a Slovak s.r.o. into a foreign entity. It enables domestic companies to change their corporate form, e.g. from an s.r.o. to an a.s. and vice versa. 3

1.3 Incorporation

An s.r.o. is founded by the execution of a memorandum of association or a foundation deed, if there is a single founder (Sec. 57 Subs. 3 CC). A notary must verify the signatures of the founders. A natural person who is a single member of an s.r.o. may be a sole member in no more than two other limited liability companies. An s.r.o. cannot be founded by a company which itself has a single member. 4

The legal existence of the company starts on the date of its entry into the commercial register by the registry court (*registrový súd*). An application for registration should be filed with the commercial register within 90 days of foundation. Before such application can be filed, at least 30 per cent of the monetary contributions to the registered capital must be paid up. If an s.r.o. has a single founder, the registered capital must have been fully paid up. 5

Once a complete application for registration is filed, the commercial register should register a new company within five business days. The cost of incorporation for an s.r.o. is approximately EUR 450 (excluding legal fees and capital contribution). 6

* *Linklaters,* Bratislava. Written with the assistance of Martin Bak.

1 See Mn. 39 et seq.

1.4 Recurrent Costs and Efforts

7 There are no major recurrent costs that an s.r.o. would incur in the course of its normal operations other than costs related to annual reporting and filing duties, such as the duty to file annual financial statements in the public collection of documents held with the commercial register (*zbierka listín*), or costs incurred in the regular course of its business, such as the obligation to notify the commercial register of changes to its corporate data. There is no annual maintenance fee.

1.5 Shares and Share Transfers

8 The ownership interest in an s.r.o. represents both the rights and obligations of a member as well as the participation corresponding to such ownership interest (Sec. 114 Subs. 1 CC). Slovak law does not provide for ownership interest certificates, and none are issued by an s.r.o. Since the memorandum of association must contain details regarding members of an s.r.o., and each amended memorandum of association must be deposited in the collection of documents with the commercial register, transfers of ownership interests can be tracked by reviewing the collection of documents.

9 A member may transfer an ownership interest to another member pursuant to an ownership interest transfer agreement, which must be in writing and which must contain notarised signatures of the members. Unless the memorandum of association provides otherwise, the transfer of an ownership interest from one member to another must be approved by the general meeting in advance. The memorandum of association permitting, a member may also transfer his ownership interest to a third party. In such case, a prior approval of the general meeting may be required by the memorandum of association.

1.6 Corporate Bodies

10 An s.r.o. has two compulsory bodies: the general meeting (*valné zhromaždenie*) and the executives (*konatelia*). A supervisory board (*dozorná rada*) is established only if the memorandum of association so provides.

1.6.1 General Meeting

11 The general meeting is the supreme body of an s.r.o. (Sec. 125 Subs. 1 CC). Among other things, it decides on the appointment, removal and remuneration of the executives and members of the supervisory board. It may not delegate its own powers to other corporate bodies; however, it may reserve unto itself the right to decide upon matters that otherwise fall within the authority of the other corporate bodies. The memorandum of association or the articles of association may increase the scope of matters falling within the authority of the general meeting.

12 Resolutions of the general meeting are passed by a simple majority of votes of the members present (Sec. 127 Subs. 3 CC). Unless the memorandum of association provides otherwise, a quorum of members with at least 50 per cent of all voting rights is required for the general meeting to proceed and its members are entitled to one vote for each SKK 1,000 (approximately EUR 25) of registered capital. In certain cases, two-thirds of the votes of all members are required to pass a resolution. The general meeting must be held at least once per year.

1.6.2 Executives

13 An s.r.o. may have one or more executives. If there are more executives, each one of them is entitled to act individually on behalf of the company unless the memorandum of association provides otherwise. Executives are appointed by the general meeting from among the members or other natural persons. No restrictions on the duration of the mandate or the age of an executive apply. The authority of executives may only be limited by the memorandum of association or the general meeting, although any such restriction will not be valid *vis-à-vis* third parties.

1.6.3 Supervisory Board

The supervisory board is responsible for overseeing the activities of the executives and reports to the general meeting at least once a year, or at different intervals as set out in the memorandum of association. It may require executives to submit all information and explanations on all matters of an s.r.o. and may look into all company documents; however, it does not have the authority to instruct the executives on any matter. If the interests of the company so require, the supervisory board shall convene a general meeting (Sec. 140 Subs. 2 CC). In the event a supervisory board is established, it must have at least three members who are elected by the general meeting, with the limitation that an executive may not be a member of the supervisory board. **14**

1.7 Duties and Liabilities of Directors

Executives must act with proper care and diligence and in the interests of the company and of all its members and not to their own advantage or the benefit of only certain members, or third persons (Sec. 135 a Subs. 1 CC). Executives who have breached their obligations in the course of performance of their function (i.e. not all executives) are jointly and severally liable for damages incurred by the s.r.o. as a result of their breach. An executive is not liable for damages if he can prove that during the performance of his functions he has acted with due care and in good faith that such action was in the interests of the company. Also, an executive will not be liable for damages caused to the company through actions undertaken pursuant to the terms of a resolution of the general meeting, provided, however, that liability will not be excluded where such resolution was contrary to law, the memorandum of association or the articles of association (Sec. 135 a Subs. 3 CC). **15**

As a general rule, a person cannot act as an executive of an s.r.o. if he has been convicted of certain types of criminal offences and his record has not yet been expunged. **16**

Executives are liable towards the company. Agreements between executives and an s.r.o. limiting or excluding the liability of executives are prohibited. The memorandum of association and the articles of association may not provide for such limitation or exclusion (Sec. 135 a Subs. 4 CC). Slovak law does not recognise the concept of release of executives from their liability upon approval of their services by the annual general meeting. Even if such release is granted it would be likely to be unenforceable. An s.r.o. may only waive an existing right to claim damages or agree to settle a claim for damages against an executive after three years from their occurrence, subject to approval by the general meeting and subject to there being no objections against such action by a member or members with contributions representing at least 10 per cent of the company's basic capital. Claims by the company against executives become time-barred after four years from the date when the company became aware of the damage and of the responsible executive, and at the latest after 10 years from the date when the damage occurred. D&O insurance is not prohibited. **17**

A settlement agreement between an s.r.o. and one or more of its executives will not be enforceable *vis-à-vis* a creditor of the company in circumstances where the creditor cannot recover his claim from the company (Sec. 135 a Subs. 4 and 5 CC). If a creditor cannot satisfy his claim against an s.r.o. from the company's assets, he can lodge a claim for compensation of damages caused to the company by its executives, doing so in his own name and on his own account. **18**

Executives of an s.r.o. are obliged to apply for insolvency proceedings if (i) the company has two or more creditors and is not able to fulfil its obligations within 30 days after they become due, or (ii) the company has two or more creditors and is over-indebted (although the law does not define the term "over-indebted", according to some court precedents this is deemed the case if the company's debts (regardless of their maturity or term) exceed its assets, i.e. if the company has negative equity). **19**

1.8 Members' Liability

20 An s.r.o. is liable for any breach of its obligations with its entire property, not just with its basic capital. Members are liable only to the extent of their unpaid contribution to the basic capital as evidenced in the commercial register.

21 Any abuse by a member of his member rights, especially an abuse by the majority of minority voting rights, is prohibited, as is any action that is disadvantageous to any of the members of an s.r.o and that constitutes misuse (Sec. 56 a CC). These provisions are new to the CC and are as yet untested in practice. There is no doctrine, specific legislative provisions or case law in Slovakia whereby limited liability protection of members can be reduced by piercing or lifting the corporate veil.

1.9 Capitalisation and Financing

1.9.1 Basic Concepts

22 The basic capital contributed by members to the company serves as the company's assets and source of its financing. If a member has not paid his contribution fully, he is obliged by the CC to do so within five years of the date of establishment of the s.r.o. or, in case of a new member, from the day when he became a member. The non-payment of unpaid contributions within an additional time limit may lead to an exclusion from membership (Sec. 113 Subs. 4 CC).

1.9.2 Minimum Share Capital

23 The minimum basic capital of an s.r.o. is SKK 200,000 (approximately EUR 5,000). The capital can be rendered in cash or in kind (Sec. 58 Subs. 1 CC). The minimum contribution of each member is SKK 30,000 (approximately EUR 750). If a member contributes to the minimum basic capital in kind, the memorandum of association must specify the nature of such contribution and must express the amount which the contribution in kind provides towards the total contribution of the member. A contribution in kind must be valued by expert appraisal.

1.9.3 Maintenance of Capital and Liquidity

(i) System

24 The capital of an s.r.o. is comprised of its basic capital and other capital sources, such as the reserve fund (Sec. 59 Subs. 3 CC) or other funds created from the company's profit as well as undistributed profits. Capital contributions may not be repaid in whole or in part. Payments to members as a result of a reduction in the company's basic capital are not considered repayment of capital.

Assets to be transferred from shareholders to the company with a value of greater than 10 per cent of the share capital must be valued by an independent expert appointed by a court. If the transfer is made within three years of the company's registration, it must also be approved by the general meeting.

25 The memorandum of association may stipulate that the general meeting can require members to make a payment in cash to cover the losses suffered by the s.r.o. up to 50 per cent of the registered capital and *pro rata* to each member's contribution (Sec. 121 Subs. 1 CC). An s.r.o. may receive capital from third parties, as well as from its own members (e.g. on the basis of a loan agreement between the member as lender and the company as borrower). The legal regime applicable to financing by members and external financing is the same.

(ii) Distributions

26 Distribution of profits to members is made on the basis of a resolution of the general meeting on the utilisation of profits. An s.r.o. may distribute net profit from which contributions to the reserve

fund, other funds and unpaid losses from previous years are deducted, and to which are added undistributed profits from previous years and funds created from profit which are not required by law (Sec. 179 Subs. 3 CC). Profits may not be distributed if, after a distribution, the equity of the s.r.o. would fall below the aggregate of its basic capital and funds that may not be distributed to members (e.g. the reserve fund).

Members are entitled to share profits *pro rata* to their paid contributions, unless the memorandum of association provides otherwise. An s.r.o. is prohibited from paying interest on contributions made to the company or advances on profit shares (Sec. 123 Subs. 2 CC). If any profits are paid to the members in violation of the provisions of the CC, members are obliged to return these to the company. Liability for the return of illegally paid profits is joint and several and rests with the executives who have authorised such payments (Sec. 123 Subs. 4 CC). **27**

(iii) Acquisition of Own Ownership Interests and Related Financing

Generally, the acquisition by an s.r.o. of its own ownership interests is prohibited (Sec. 120 Subs. 1 CC). In certain situations, however, the company may acquire its own ownership interest by operation of law, e.g. if a member is expelled, his ownership interest is then automatically transferred to the s.r.o., which is obliged to transfer the relevant ownership interest to another member or to a third party within six months, failing which the basic capital must be reduced. **28**

During the time a company holds its own ownership interests, it may not exercise the related rights of a member. There is no limit on the maximum percentage of ownership interests that may be acquired by the company. The provisions in the previous paragraph on the company's obligation either to transfer its own ownership interest or to correspondingly decrease its capital apply in this case also. **29**

There are no specific Slovak law rules prohibiting the provision of financial assistance by an s.r.o. in the acquisition of its ownership interests by a third party. **30**

(iv) Company as Lender or Guarantor

An s.r.o. may give loans or grant guarantees to third parties. **31**

(v) Company as Borrower

Loans to an s.r.o. by its members are allowed without restriction. In the case of insolvency, loans by the members (unless agreed in the form of subordinated debt) rank equally with ordinary claims. **32**

1.10 Publication and Filing Requirements

A wide range of documentation and information must be filed with the collection of documents held by the commercial register (Sec. 27 CC).[2] Generally, an s.r.o. must register with the commercial register all changes in its corporate matters (e.g. change in members), and must submit to the collection of documents all changes in its corporate documentation (e.g. changes to the articles of association or memorandum of association). There is no annual obligation to file changes with the commercial register or documents with the collection of documents, with the exception of annual financial statements. **33**

Information contained in the commercial register is effective against third parties from the date of publication. Third parties can rely on the content of the register. The commercial register is available online.[3] **34**

2 Act No. 530/2003 Coll. on the Commercial Register. Information entered into the commercial register regarding an s.r.o. includes: business name; registered seat; identification number; scope of business activity; identification data on the executive(s); identification data on general proxies; identification data on members of the supervisory board (if any); identification data on the members; and registered capital.

3 www.orsr.sk.

35 A company may be sanctioned if it fails to register changes in the commercial register or submit the necessary documents to the collection of documents. By way of example, if a company fails to submit its individual financial statements to the commercial register for two consecutive years a court has the duty under the CC to order the winding-up of the company (this provision is relatively new and its application has thus not yet been verified by the court) (Sec. 68 Subs. 6 CC).

1.11 Financial Reporting

36 An s.r.o must keep accounts using the double-entry bookkeeping system. Slovak accounting rules are generally being harmonised with international standards, in particular IFRS.

37 An s.r.o. must deposit its annual and extraordinary financial statements in the collection of documents after approval by the general meeting. Financial statements must be drawn up within six months of the end of the business year (Sec. 40 Subs. 1 Sentence 3 CC) which generally runs from 1 January to 31 December. An s.r.o. may opt for a different financial year, being any 12-month period. An s.r.o.'s financial statements must be audited if the s.r.o. meets any two of the following three conditions: (a) its total assets exceed SKK 20 million (approximately EUR 500,000); (b) its turnover (excluding VAT) exceeds SKK 40 million (approximately EUR 1 million); or (c) it has more than 20 employees. Companies exceeding these thresholds must also prepare an annual report consisting of their financial accounts and an auditor's report and publish their balance sheet and profit and loss accounts in the Commercial Bulletin within 30 days from the approval of their financial accounts. Companies which do not exceed at least two of the three above mentioned criteria are exempted from these requirements."

1.12 Employee Participation in Corporate Bodies

38 Employees are not required to be represented in the compulsory corporate bodies. The CC does not regulate representation of employees in the supervisory board.

2 The Stock Corporation ("a.s.")

Literature: Ovečková, Commercial Code, commentary (Iura Edition 2005); Suchoža, Commercial Code and related texts, commentary (Eurounion 2003)

39 The stock corporation (*akciová spoločnost', akc. spol.*, "a.s.") is the second important form of corporate entity in Slovakia. An a.s. is liable for its obligations with all its property and its shareholders are not liable for its obligations. An a.s. can more easily accumulate capital through the issuance of shares, and the shares are generally transferable in an expedient and simple manner.

2.1 Export of Company

40 The possibilities and restrictions regarding the export of an a.s. are the same as in the case of an s.r.o.[4]

2.2 Transformation into a Foreign Entity

41 Slovak law does not provide for the direct transformation of a Slovak a.s. into a foreign stock corporation. Under European Council Regulation No. 2157/2001 on the Statute for an S.E., implemented in Slovakia by the European Company Act,[5] it is possible to merge stock corporations from two different Member States into an S.E. Once formed, an S.E. transfers its registered seat from Slovakia to another Member State and vice versa.

4 See Mn. 2.

5 Act No. 562/2004 Coll. in force from 1 November 2004.

2.3 Incorporation

Like an s.r.o., an a.s. is incorporated upon its entry into the commercial register. An a.s. is established by means of a memorandum of association (in the case of multiple founders) or a foundation deed (in the case of a single founder), either of which must be executed in the form of a notarial deed. A draft text of the company's articles of association must be included in the memorandum of association or the foundation deed (Sec. 162 Subs. 2 Sentence 4 CC). An application for registration must be filed by the board of directors and signed by all its members. **42**

The registry court is obliged to register an a.s. within five business days. An a.s. may be established by a single founder only if the founder is a legal person, otherwise at least two founders are required. The minimum costs for establishing and incorporating an a.s. are approximately EUR 800 (excluding legal fees and the registered capital). **43**

2.4 Recurrent Costs and Efforts

The annual costs of corporate maintenance for an a.s. vary considerably, depending on the size of the enterprise. A small a.s. would typically face annual costs of a few hundred Euro. The costs for a large a.s. could be significantly higher, depending on the volume of its business activity and the extent of its corporate changes during a year. **44**

2.5 Shares and Share Transfers

Shares in an a.s. can be either registered shares or bearer shares (Sec. 156 Subs. 1 CC). A registered share may be issued as a share certificate or as a book-entered share. A bearer share may be issued only as a book-entered share. Transfers of registered shares in the form of share certificates take place by way of endorsement and delivery of the same certificate (Sec. 156 Subs. 4 Sentence 1 CC). In addition, transfers of registered shares in the form of share certificates are only effective *vis-à-vis* the company upon the entry of the transfer in the shareholders' book; the entry is effected by the board of directors upon the request of the shareholder (who must evidence such a transfer). Transfers of book-entered shares, both registered and bearer shares, take place through the central depository of shares or its members (mostly banks and financial institutions) upon registration of such transfer on the basis of corresponding and matching applications of the parties to the transfer. **45**

The company can also issue preference shares (Sec. 159 Subs. 1 CC). Preference shares are shares with preference rights on dividends. The articles of association of an a.s. may also provide for issuance of non-voting preference shares. Holders of preference shares have all other rights attached to shareholding. The aggregate nominal value of preference shares issued cannot exceed 50 per cent of the registered capital. **46**

2.6 Corporate Bodies

An a.s. has three mandatory corporate bodies: the general meeting (*valné zhromaždenie*), the board of directors (*predstavenstvo*) and the supervisory board (*dozorná rada*). **47**

2.6.1 General Meeting

The general meeting is the supreme corporate body of an a.s. It decides, *inter alia*, on amendments to the articles of association, increase or reduction of the basic capital, and the appointment of members of the board of directors and members of the supervisory board. It usually decides by a simple majority of the shareholders present. In certain cases, approval of two-thirds of the shareholders present is required (Sec. 187 Subs. 2 CC). **48**

Generally, the powers of the general meeting may be limited only in so far as the CC allows. Certain of its functions may be vested in the supervisory board should the articles of association so allow, e.g. election of members of the board of directors or approval of allocation of bonuses to **49** members of the corporate bodies. The general meeting or the articles of association may delegate the power to decide on an increase of the basic capital to the board of directors. Extending the authority of the general meeting is possible but must be explicitly provided for by the articles of association.

2.6.2 Board of Directors

50 The board of directors decides on all company matters unless these are vested in one of the other two corporate bodies by the CC or the company's articles of association (Sec. 191 Subs. 1 CC). Members of the board of directors are appointed and discharged by the general meeting for the term set by the articles of association, which may not be longer than five years (Sec. 194 Subs. 1 CC). The articles of association, resolutions of the general meeting or resolutions of the supervisory board may limit the rights of the board of directors to act on behalf of the company. Such limitations, however, are not effective *vis-à-vis* third parties.

51 Unless the articles of association provide otherwise, each director has the power of representation to act alone on behalf of an a.s. The articles of association may establish that only certain members are allowed to bind the company or that two or more directors have joint power of representation. Specification of the exact extent of powers and decision-making of the board of directors is an obligatory element of the articles of association (Sec. 173 Subs. 1(f) CC).

2.6.3 Supervisory Board

52 The supervisory board oversees the activities of the board of directors and the conduct of the day-to-day business of an a.s. It also reviews the annual, extraordinary and consolidated statutory accounts, as well as proposals for the settlement of losses or the distribution of profits, and submits its comments to the general meeting. Prior approval of the supervisory board is required for an extension of a loan, transfer or making available of the company's property for use, or securing an obligation of a member of the board of directors, other persons entitled to act on behalf of the company, their relatives or entities on behalf of which such persons are entitled to act, by the company. The articles of association may make the contract on the discharge of the position of member of the board of directors of an a.s. subject to approval by the supervisory board.

53 The supervisory board has a minimum of three members. If the company has more than 50 employees, two-thirds of the members of the supervisory board are elected by the general meeting and one-third by the employees.[6] Otherwise, all are elected by the general meeting. Its members can only be natural persons and are elected for a maximum term of five years (Sec. 200 Subs. 2 CC). A member of the supervisory board may not at the same time be a member of the board of directors, a general proxy of the company, or be otherwise registered in the commercial register as a person authorised to act on behalf of the company.

2.7 Duties and Liabilities of Directors

54 The duties of the members of the board of directors are comparable to those of the executives of an s.r.o. Liability of directors is joint and several, and applies to those directors who have acted in breach of their duties. D&O insurance coverage is not prohibited.

55 The list of serious breaches of obligations is more extensive than for executives of an s.r.o. It includes providing benefits to shareholders in breach of the CC,[7] obtaining property or providing benefits in breach of the principles established in the CC, and subscribing, acquiring or accepting as a collateral the company's own shares or shares of another company in breach of the CC, as well as issuance of shares in conflict with the CC (Sec. 194 Subs. 6 CC). Conditions for disqualification of members of the board of directors are the same as in case of an s.r.o.[8]

6 See Mn. 71.
7 See Mn. 59.
8 See Mn. 16.

Members of the board of directors are not relieved of their liability to the company if their conduct has been approved by the supervisory board (Sec. 194 Subs. 7 Sentence 3 CC). Members are not liable for damages to the company from conduct by which they have carried out resolutions of the general meeting; however, they are liable for such conduct if the resolution is in breach of law or the articles of association. As in the case of an s.r.o, generally, the concept of release of members of the board of directors from their liability upon approval of their services by the annual general meeting is not recognised and even if such release were granted it would be likely to be unenforceable. An a.s. may only waive an existing right to claim damages or agree to settle a claim for damages against a member after three years from their occurrence, subject to approval by the general meeting and subject to there being no objections against such action by shareholders whose nominal shareholdings represent at least 5 per cent of the company's basic capital. **56**

A creditor of an a.s. may lodge a claim of the company for settlement of damages against members of the board of directors if he cannot satisfy his claim from the company's property. The obligation of members of the board of directors to apply for insolvency proceedings corresponds to the obligation of executives in an s.r.o.[9] **57**

2.8 Shareholders' Liability

Under Slovak law, the shareholders of an a.s. have no liability for the company's obligations (Sec. 154 Subs. 1 Sentence 3 CC). There is no doctrine, specific legislative provisions or case law in Slovakia whereby limited liability protection of members can be reduced by piercing or lifting the corporate veil. **58**

A shareholder is required not to exercise his rights to the disadvantage of other shareholders. If he has received a share of profit of an a.s. in good faith, he is not obliged to return it. Any other benefit received by a shareholder that was given to the shareholder in breach of law or the articles of association must be returned to the company and the board of directors is obliged to claim and recover any such illegally granted benefit (Sec. 179 Subs. 9 CC). Should the board of directors fail to do so, other shareholders may claim these benefits on behalf of the company (Sec. 182 Subs. 2 CC). **59**

2.9 Capitalisation and Financing

2.9.1 Basic Concepts

The capitalisation and financing of an a.s. is based on the concept of real capital contribution and maintenance. Capital at the disposal of an a.s. can effectively be increased by issuing new shares. A resolution to increase the basic share capital of an a.s. must generally be approved at the general meeting of the company by two-thirds of the shareholders present and such decision must be recorded by way of a notarial deed. **60**

2.9.2 Minimum Share Capital

The minimum share capital of an a.s. is SKK 1,000,000 (approximately EUR 25,000). The capital can be rendered in cash or in kind (Sec. 58 Subs. 1 CC). The articles of association must specify the nominal value of all classes of shares to be issued and the aggregate of the nominal values of such shares must correspond to the amount of the registered capital (Sec. 157 Subs. 1 CC). The first general meeting (i.e. the general meeting that takes the decision on establishment of an a.s.) can only take place if the aggregate nominal value of the subscribed shares is equal to the proposed registered capital and if at least 30 per cent of the nominal value of the pledged contributions in cash have been paid up (Sec. 169 Subs. 1 CC). **61**

9 See Mn. 19.

2.9.3 Maintenance of Capital and Liquidity

(i) System

62 The principle of real capital contribution and maintenance applies particularly strictly with regard to preservation and maintenance of the capital of an a.s. An a.s. may not subscribe to its own shares and the possibilities for gaining ownership of its own shares are limited. Likewise, an a.s. may not return contributions to its shareholders, pay out interest from shareholder contributions or advance dividends, or pay profit contributions at the cost of the basic registered capital or the reserve fund.

63 As with the s.r.o., if an a.s. receives property from its founders or shareholders or their related persons for consideration exceeding 10 per cent of the value of the registered capital of the company, the value of the property must be confirmed by an expert appraisal. Any agreement for such acquisition of property must be approved by the general meeting if it is concluded within two years of the establishment of the company (Sec. 59 a Subs. 1 and 2 CC).

(ii) Distributions

64 Each shareholder is entitled to a share of the company's profits (a dividend) based on the approval of the general meeting. The right to receive a dividend is a basic right of a shareholder. The rules on distribution of profits are the same as in the case of an s.r.o.[10] When the general meeting decides upon payment of dividends, a shareholder becomes a creditor of the company to the extent of the amount of the dividend. An a.s. is prohibited from paying advances on dividends.

(iii) Acquisition of Own Shares and Related Financing

65 An a.s. may obtain its own shares only under limited conditions as set out in Sec. 161a-161f CC. An a.s. may not obtain its own shares by means of subscribing them for itself. Generally, an a.s. may become a shareholder of its own shares if the general meeting has authorised such a transaction, if the nominal value of all shares that the a.s. will have in its possession does not exceed 10 per cent of its registered capital, if such action does not result in a reduction in the company's equity to below the aggregate value of its registered capital and the mandatory equity funds (such as the reserve fund), and if the rate of issue of the subscribed shares was paid in full (Sec. 161 a Subs. 2 CC).

66 Sec. 161 b Subs. 2 CC lists exceptional cases in which a company may purchase its own shares without having to satisfy the general rule (see previous paragraph). Shares that have been transferred in breach of the law must be transferred back within one year or the registered capital of the company must be decreased accordingly. Otherwise, the court may order the winding-up and liquidation of the a.s.

(iv) Company as Lender or Guarantor

67 Loans and guarantees to third parties are not restricted. Financial assistance (i.e. advances, payments, loans, credits or securities) to third parties in relation to the acquisition of shares of an a.s. by such third persons are prohibited (Sec. 161 e CC). This prohibition does not apply to transactions by banks and other financial institutions in their normal course of business and to actions taken in connection with the acquisition of shares by the company's employees provided that this does not result in a reduction of the company's equity to below the aggregate value of the registered capital and the reserve fund.

(v) Company as Borrower

68 Shareholder loans to an a.s. are allowed. In the event of insolvency shareholder loans rank equally with ordinary claims, unless agreed in the form of subordinated debt.

10 See Mn. 26 et seq.

2.10 Publication and Filing Requirements

These requirements correspond to the requirements in an s.r.o.[11] 69

2.11 Financial Reporting

Generally, accounting rules for an a.s. correspond to those for an s.r.o.[12] Ordinary individual and extraordinary individual financial statements of an a.s. must always be audited. Audited financial statements must be deposited in the collection of documents held by the commercial register (Sec. 40 Subs. 2 CC). 70

2.12 Employee Participation in Corporate Bodies

Employees do not participate in the general meeting or the board of directors, but must be represented in the supervisory board if the a.s. has 50 or more employees at the time of election of members of the supervisory board (Sec. 200 Subs. 1 CC). Employees have the right to elect one-third of the members by law but the articles of association may increase the proportion of their representation up to 50 per cent. 71

11 See Mn. 33 et seq.
12 See Mn. 36 et seq.

XXII. Slovenia

*by Jani Soršak and Dr. Florian Kirchhof**

1 The Limited Liability Company ("d.o.o.")

Literature: Bohinc/Bratina/Knez et al., ZGD with commentary, Vols. 1 and 2 (2nd edition, Gospodarski vestnik 2002; "ZGD Commentary"); Slovenian Companies Act (Zakon o gospodarskih družbah, "ZGD") and Court Register Act (Zakon o sodnem registru, "ZSR"), Financial Operations of Companies Act (Zakon o finančnem poslovanju podjetij, "ZFPPod"), Book Entry Securities Act (Zakon o nematerialziranih vednostnih papirjih, "ZNVP") and Securities Market Act (Zakon o trgu vrednostnih papirjev, "ZTVP")

The legal form of the d.o.o. (*družba z omejeno odgovornostjo*, "d.o.o.") as a commercial company is most often used by smaller and medium enterprises in which shareholders play a more significant role. In the era of Slovenia's economic transition to a market economy and especially due to the changes in legislation allowing a relatively simple incorporation of companies, the number of d.o.o.'s significantly increased in the 1990s. However, as many of these companies were only established "on paper" and performed no real business activities, subsequent provisions in *ZFPPod* were adopted, allowing the automatic termination of such inactive companies. In 2003 there were approximately 30,600 limited liability companies registered in Slovenia, in contrast to approximately 1,100 stock corporations. 1

1.1 Export of Company

The company may not relocate its registered office abroad, including another EU Member State, without losing the legal identity of a Slovenian company. Should the company want to cancel its Slovenian legal identity and move its registered office abroad, the company would be deregistered in Slovenia, but not liquidated. However, Slovenian private international law provides that in the event the company relocates its headquarters ("factual seat") into another state while remaining registered in Slovenia, it shall be deemed that it has the host state's legal identity, provided the host state considers the company to have the host's state legal identity. It shall be noted that there is no case law where a court would apply this provision of private international law. 2

1.2 Transformation into a Foreign Entity

Slovenian company law does not expressly provide for the transformation of a domestic company into a foreign entity. In practice, this can be achieved indirectly by transferring the d.o.o. business to a foreign company. It is also possible to merge a Slovenian company into a company of another EU Member State. Slovenian law does not yet regulate the S.E. Implementation of the S.E. along with a number of other amendments to the Companies Act is expected by the end of 2005. A draft has not been disclosed yet, therefore we cannot opine on whether the S.E. Directive will indeed be implemented in full. 3

1.3 Incorporation

The d.o.o. is founded by adoption of the articles of association, which must be concluded in the form of the notary deed. The requirement for a notary deed is waived in the event of a single founder. 4

Prior to the court registration it is necessary to: (1) sign the articles of association drafted in the form of a notary deed, (2) open a bank account with a bank, to which the share capital will be credited, and (3) sign the accompanying documents required by the registry court.

* *Schönherr Rechtsanwälte*, Ljubljana.

The designated director shall file the registration request with the registry court (*Okrožno sodišče*) which has jurisdiction at the seat of the new company.[1]

The time needed for incorporation will usually take between 4 and 8 weeks. The court fee for incorporation of a d.o.o. is SIT 28,500 (approximately EUR 120) if there is only one shareholder, SIT 47,500 (approximately EUR 200) for 2 to 10 shareholders and SIT 66,500 (approximately EUR 280) for more than 10 shareholders. In addition to court fees there will be notary fees for Articles of Association and other required notarizations (e.g. notarized signatures for company representatives), and translation costs for any documents that are not produced in Slovenian. The notary fees for Articles of Association depend on the amount of share capital and start at approx. EUR 205 for a d.o.o. and at approx. EUR 285 for a d.d.

1.4 Recurrent Costs and Efforts

5 Recurrent costs and efforts relating to a d.o.o. are minimal and relate only to the filing of annual accounts with the competent tax authority.

1.5 Shares and Share Transfers

6 The participation interest in a limited liability company is a "quota", rather than a share. The quota represents the quota holder's participation in the company and may neither be issued as a share nor embodied in a certificate. "Shares" in a d.o.o. are therefore not deemed to be securities and *ZGD* uses the words "share interest" instead. Share interests in a d.o.o. may be transferred by an agreement in the form of a notarial deed.[2]

Shareholders have one vote for every complete SIT 14,000 (approximately EUR 65) of the share capital. The articles of association may determine that some shareholders have more votes for every complete SIT 14,000 of the founding share capital, or that the voting right of some partners is limited. Share transfers are exempt from VAT but the transfer may result in a capital gain tax obligation in some cases.

1.6 Corporate Bodies

7 The *ZGD* requires a d.o.o to have two mandatory corporate bodies, namely the managing director(s) and the shareholders' meeting. A supervisory board is optional, whilst further corporate bodies, such as advisory boards or shareholder committees, may be created but will have no legally recognised importance outside of the d.o.o's internal structure.

1 The following documents shall be enclosed with the registration filing: (1) the articles of association, (2) a list of the shareholders and the share interests they have assumed, (3) a report on contributions in kind if there is contribution in kind, (4) a report by a licensed auditor on the value of contributions in kind if the respective contribution's value exceeds a certain value (please see the following paragraph), (5) confirmation of the bank that the share capital has been deposited, together with a declaration that the money is at free disposal to the company, (6) a resolution appointing the director, (7) the certified signature of the director and other individuals entitled to represent the company, (8) a notarised photocopy of the director's passport if the director is not a Slovenian citizen, (9) a statement by the director that he or she has not been convicted for commercial crimes and that he or she is not liable to pay damages to a bankrupt company's creditors under Article 19 of the *ZFPPod,* (10) when shareholders participate in another Slovenian company they have to give a declaration that this company does not have any unsettled due obligations; this declaration has to be confirmed by the Tax Authority, (11) confirmation of the paid court fee, (12) where the founder is a foreign company, a translation of the respective court register excerpt. When the initial share capital is rendered with the contribution in kind, the following documents have to be enclosed: (1) a report on the contribution in kind, (2) a report from the authorised auditor on the appraisal of the value of the contribution in kind (when the value of contribution in kind exceeds SIT 14,000,000 (approximately EUR 60,000)).

2 The lack of share certificates means that there is no public market for d.o.o. share interests. In practice, a d.o.o. cannot engage in an initial public offering of its shares. The standard practice is that if a d.o.o. intends to issue its shares to the public, it is usually first converted into a d.d.

1.6.1 Managing Directors

The d.o.o. may have one or more managing directors. The managing directors represent the company exclusively *vis-à-vis* third parties (Sec. 32 Subs. 1 *ZGD*). While several directors may be awarded joint power of representation (whereby a managing director may only represent the d.o.o. together with another managing director or a *Prokurist*) or sole power of representation (whereby a managing director may represent the company solely), any limitations on the directors regarding the representation *vis-à-vis* third parties set out in the articles of association, except for the joint representation requirement, will have no effect towards third parties. 8

1.6.2 The Shareholders' Meeting

The shareholders' meeting has, *inter alia*, the following competences (Sec 439 *ZGD*): 9
(i) to adopt an annual balance sheet for founding shares,
(ii) to return subsequent payments (payment in addition to the payment of the subscribed share interests),
(iii) to divide and terminate share interests,
(iv) to appoint and recall the managing directors,
(v) to measure, inspect, and control work of directors.

Resolutions of the shareholders' meeting are adopted if voted for by a majority of the votes cast unless otherwise determined by law or the articles of association (Sec. 442 Subs. 2 *ZGD*).[3] 10

1.6.3 Supervisory Board

The most important responsibility of a supervisory board, if established, is the appointment and control of the managing directors. 11

1.7 Duties and Liabilities of Directors

The primary responsibility of the directors is the management of the daily business of the d.o.o. and to represent the d.o.o. *vis-à-vis* third parties (Sec. 449, Subs. 1 *ZGD*). The directors must perform financially sound and diligent management of the company. When performing their duties they must act using the diligence of a prudent businessman. Managing directors are obliged to file for insolvency proceedings if the company is (i) unable to pay its debts or (ii) is over-indebted within two months. Failure of the managing director(s) to do so resulting in bankruptcy, and indulgent performance of the supervisory board members and the shareholders contributing to the incapacity of the company to settle its debts, may result in their personal joint and several liability towards the creditors. Liability is limited to between SIT 5 and 15 million (EUR 20,800 to 62,500) depending on the size of the company. The limitation of liability does not apply for gross negligence or willful acts. Claims become time-barred after five years. For the relationship of a director to a d.o.o., in respect of claims originating from a director's contract with the company, rules of obligation law apply (Sec. 449 Subs. 3 *ZGD*). If the director is employed by the company, labour law should be considered as well. 12

3 In addition, a quorum is required at the shareholders' meetings. A quorum is set at the majority of the votes (50 per cent plus one vote of all the possible votes). Shareholders have one vote for every complete SIT 14,000 (approximately EUR 65) of the share capital. The articles of association may determine that some shareholders have more votes for every complete SIT 14,000 of the founding share capital, or that the voting right of some partners is limited. Higher thresholds (generally involving a 75 per cent majority) apply in certain cases, for example, the passing of resolutions amending the articles of association (Sec. 450 Subs. 1 *ZGD*). If a change in the articles of association results in the expansion of shareholders' liabilities towards the company, such a decision must be adopted by all the shareholders, except in the case of an increase of the registered capital.

1.8 Shareholders' Liability

13 As a rule, to which there should be as few exceptions as possible, Slovenian law protects the principle of the corporate veil or the principle of limited liability of the shareholders of a d.o.o. There are, however, certain situations which may lead to a shareholder liability. These are primarily due to fraudulent or negligent actions or omissions on the part of the shareholders.

14 Shareholders may be liable for the company's obligations (according to Sec. 6 Subs. 1 *ZGD*) in the following cases: (1) if they have misused the legal personality of the company to achieve a goal prohibited to them as individuals, or (2) if they have misused the company to indemnify their creditors, or (3) if, in breach of law, they have managed the assets of a legal person as their own assets, or (4) if, to their own advantage or the advantage of another party, they have impaired the property of the company and in so doing knew, or should have known, that the company would not be able to settle its obligations to third parties. Anyone who, prior to entry into the register, acts in the name and on behalf of the company is also liable for obligations arising therefrom.

15 In addition, shareholders are liable to the d.o.o. for the repayment of any illegal payments made to them in breach of the provisions to protect the share capital. If the d.o.o. is automatically struck out of the court register due to non-performance (so called "sleeping companies") some of the shareholders will remain liable for the d.o.o.'s liabilities for a year after the d.o.o. has been struck out of the court register.

1.9 Capitalisation and Financing

1.9.1 Basic Concepts

16 *ZFPPod* requires that all commercial companies, at all times, possess adequate capital with respect to the volume and type of operations undertaken in carrying out their activities and with respect to the risks to which they will be exposed in doing so ("capital adequacy"). All companies are legally required, in order to hedge themselves against liquidity risks, to formulate and carry out a policy of regular liquidity management. The capital from *ZFPPod* is not to be confused with the share capital of the d.o.o. and is not really intended to be adequate for the kind of business the d.o.o. intends to perform.[4] The bridge between the requirement that the company has adequate capital to finance its business and the share capital of the d.o.o. is, however, provided in *ZFPPod*, which provides an assumption that capital inadequacy of a company has occurred if its loss for the current year and the losses brought forward amount to one-half of the d.o.o.'s share capital. The share capital stated in the articles of association has to be available to the company and may be paid back to the shareholders only in the event of the voluntary liquidation of the company after all the debts of the company are paid.

1.9.2 Minimum Share Capital

17 The minimum share capital of the d.o.o. must equal at least SIT 2,100,000 (approximately EUR 8,850). The share capital may be contributed in kind or in cash. Prior to registration in the court register, all in kind contributions must be made in full, and no less than SIT 1.1 million in cash contribution (approximately EUR 4,620) (Sec. 410 Subs. 5 *ZGD*). Each shareholder must pay at least one-quarter of his or her share contribution. The share capital may not be rendered in kind only; at least one-third of the share capital shall be rendered in cash (Sec. 410 Subs. 3 *ZGD*), however this request is waived when the contribution in cash equals no less than SIT 1.4 million (approximately EUR 6,000) while the contribution in kind exceeds SIT 10 million (approximately EUR 42,000) (Sec. 410 Subs. 11 *ZGD*).

4 *ZGD* Commentary, Vol. 2, p. 348.

1.9.3 Maintenance of Capital and Liquidity

The concept of d.o.o. capital maintenance rules is determined not only by *ZGD*, but also by *ZFFPod*. The jurisprudence on the subject is still evolving. 18

(i) System

Assets of the d.o.o., i.e. their value, required to maintain the share capital may not be paid to the shareholders. 19

Sec. 430 Subs. 1 *ZGD* explicitly prohibits the repayment of share capital to the shareholders.[6] In the event the recipient of an illegal payment cannot make the repayment, the other shareholders will be liable for the amount to the creditors of the d.o.o. (Sec. 431 Subs. 3 *ZGD*). 20

Pursuant to Sec. 433 *ZGD*, in the event shareholders grant loans to the d.o.o. in lieu of share capital injection, as would be appropriate for a diligent shareholder, these loans are treated as the company's share capital in an eventual bankruptcy procedure. 21

(ii) Distributions

Distributions of profits to shareholders usually have to be made on the basis of a shareholders' resolution deciding on the utilisation of annual profits (Sec. 429 *ZGD*). Distribution of profits is made in proportion to the amount of share interest of each shareholder unless otherwise determined by the articles of association. Shareholders may decide to pay advance dividends which may have to be wholly or partially reimbursed if profits are not sufficient. 22

(iii) Acquisition of Own Shares and Related Financing

A d.o.o. may acquire its own share interests and receive own shares as a security, provided the share interests are fully paid-up (Sec. 435 Subs. 1 *ZGD*). The acquisition by the company of its own share interests will require the creation of a statutory reserve for own shares in the balance sheet (Sec. 435 Subs. 2 *ZGD*). As long as the d.o.o. holds the title to the redeemed share interests it cannot exercise any shareholder rights (e.g., voting rights, right to dividends). The d.o.o. may not acquire all of its share interests (Sec. 435 Subs. 3 *ZGD*). 23

Slovenian law generally allows financial assistance for the d.o.o., except if such financial assistance would constitute a prohibited repayment of share capital.

(iv) Company as Lender or Guarantor

A d.o.o. may give loans or grant guarantees to third parties. Loans to shareholders are permitted provided they are made on arm's-length terms and the interests of the other creditors of the d.o.o. are not damaged. 24

Granting security to a shareholder is allowed in principle provided it is made on arm's-length terms. 25

(v) Company as Borrower

Shareholder loans to the company are generally allowed, though they might be equitably subordinated to other claims in bankruptcy.[5] 26

1.10 Publication and Filing Requirements

A wide range of documentation and information must be filed with the court register, some of which will also have to be submitted for publication in the Official Gazette.[6] 27

5 See Mn. 21.

6 Registration of the company and commenced proceeding for termination of the company. Other filings with the court register are: transfer of share interests, decrease/increase of the share capital, amendments to the articles of

The court register file is open to the public and any interested person can review the filed documents and request a commercial register excerpt detailing the principal corporate information (e.g., the share capital, the names of the managing directors and *Prokurists*, capital increases and amendments to the articles of association) as well as copies of any documents submitted. A court register is a public register and any third party may, in good faith, rely on the contents of the register. The court register is organised as a centralised database and it is accessible online on the State portal of the Republic of Slovenia.[7] No annual registration fee is payable.

28 A company is not required to file annual accounts in the court register, though under the *ZFPPod* the company may be struck from the register for failing to submit annual accounts to the competent tax authority for two subsequent years or more.

1.11 Financial Reporting

29 The annual accounts must be drawn up in accordance with Slovenian accounting standards. Following the entry of Slovenia into the EU (1 May 2004), IAS standards may be directly applicable to some Slovenian companies, since according to the EU regulation the listed companies are obliged to prepare their financial statements in compliance with IAS adopted in the EU starting in 2005. This, however, is not applicable to a d.o.o., which may not be listed. *ZGD* requires that the Slovenian accounting standards are in accordance with the Fourth and Seventh Directives.[8]

Certain relief from financial reporting requirements is granted to small and medium-sized enterprises. In Slovenia small enterprises are those that do not exceed at least two of the three thresholds: (i) a balance sheet total of EUR 2,083,333, (ii) a turnover of EUR 4,166,667, (iii) a workforce of 50 employees in the annual average. Medium sized enterprises are those that exceed two of the afore-mentioned criteria but do not exceed two of the three following criteria: (i) a balance sheet total of EUR 8,333,333, (ii) a turnover of EUR 16,666,667, (iii) a workforce of more than 250 employees in the annual average. Banks, insurance companies and companies that are required to prepare consolidated annual accounts are deemed large companies.

Small companies, unless listed, are released from the requirement to have their annual accounts audited by an external auditor. The same unlisted small companies must submit for publication their annual accounts to the Slovenian Agency for Public Legal Records and Related Services within 3 months after the end of the financial year, while medium and large companies must do so within 8 months after the end of the financial year. Medium companies are required to produce a complete balance sheet, but may merge categories into general categories in the published balance sheet, while small companies may prepare and publish the balance sheet with general categories alone. Small and medium companies may merge certain categories in their profit-and-loss statements and are not required to disclose or explain certain accounting categories.

1.12 Employee Participation in Corporate Bodies

30 A company with more than 500 employees shall have a so-called "labour" director as the member of the board of directors, if requested by the works council.

The labour director represents the interests of the employees with special focus on employment and social questions. The labour director has the same rights as other directors.

If the d.o.o. has a supervisory board, the employees are also represented on the supervisory board (at least one-third of supervisory board members), regardless of the size of the company.

association, appointment of directors, *prokurists*, and supervisory board members (if the d.o.o. has a supervisory board).

7 http://e-uprava.gov.si/e-uprava/ Access is subject to prior registration.

8 See Part 1, I, Mn. 66 et seq.

2 The Stock Corporation (delniška družba, "d.d.")

Literature: Bohinc/Bratina/Knez et al., ZGD with commentary, Vols. 1 and 2 (2nd edition, Gospodarski vestnik 2002; "ZGD Commentary"); Slovenian Companies Act (Zakon o gospodarskih družbah, "ZGD") and Court Register Act (Zakon o sodnem registru, "ZSR"), Financial Operations of Companies Act (Zakon o finančnem poslovanju podjetij, "ZFPPod"), Book Entry Securities Act (Zakon o nematerialziranih vednostnih papirjih, "ZNVP") and Securities Market Act (Zakon o trgu vrednostnih papirjev, "ZTVP"); Michael Knaus, Commercial Company Law, Chapter 9 (1st edition, Uradni list Republike Slovenije 2002)

Stock corporations (*delniška družba,*"d.d.") exist in a smaller number in Slovenia (in comparison 31 to Limited Liability Companies) with the majority being incorporated as such due to national privatisation models. The d.d. form is mostly used by big and medium-size companies (on the basis of the share capital) and holding companies.

2.1 Export of Company

Slovenian restrictions on the relocation of a domestic company to a foreign country are based on 32 the real seat theory. Please see above.[9]

2.2 Transformation into a Foreign Entity

Please see above.[10] 33

2.3 Incorporation

A d.d. is set up by way of a notarial deed of incorporation executed by one or more shareholders 34 (Sec. 170 and Sec. 184 Subs 1. *ZGD*). In accordance with Sec. 3 Subs. 1, all companies acquire the character of a legal person by being entered in the court register held by the District Court located at the company's corporate seat. A d.d. may be founded by the procedure of simultaneous founding, (Sec. 189-204a *ZGD*) or by the procedure of successive founding (public subscription) (Sec. 205-218 *ZGD*).[11] In a simultaneous founding, the shareholders purchase all shares, while in a successive founding the shares are offered publicly.

It takes significantly longer to incorporate a d.d., because the formal requirements for a d.d. are much stricter than for a d.o.o. The court fee for incorporation of a d.d. is SIT 104,500 SIT (approximately EUR 435) for up to 50 shareholders, SIT 199,500 (approximately EUR 830) for 51 to 100 shareholders and SIT 294,500 (approximately EUR 1230) for more than 100 shareholders. In addition to court fees there will be notary fees for Articles of Association and other required notarizations (e.g. notarized signatures for company representatives), and translation costs for any documents that are not produced in Slovenian. The notary fees for Articles of Association depend on the amount of share capital and start at approx. EUR 205 for a d.o.o. and at approx. EUR 285 for a d.d.

The precise length of the incorporation procedure is difficult to predict and may vary from a few 35 weeks to several months.[12]

9 See Mn. 2.

10 See Mn. 3.

11 Stock corporations in Slovenia are far more often founded simultaneously than successively. The procedure of successive founding is much more complicated and time-consuming than simultaneous founding and is therefore rarely used.

12 The length of the incorporation process depends on the time required by (i) shareholders to adopt and sign the articles of association and to takeover the shares (simultaneous incorporation) or, on the other hand, the term for the subscription and payment of shares (successive incorporation: this will not exceed three months commencing from the day of the beginning of the subscription) and (ii) the competent companies court registry to proceed with the formal registration. The notarial fees for the incorporation of a d.d. with a minimum share capital of SIT 6,000,000 (approximately EUR 25,000) amount to approximately EUR 600. The registration fee for the incorporation of a d.d.

2.4 Recurrent Costs and Efforts

36 The annual efforts required to maintain a d.d. can be either relatively minimal or considerably high depending on whether the d.d. is run with a small number of employees and few shareholders or as a large company.[13] The large and medium-sized d.d., as well as small-sized d.d., whose shares are traded publicly, must audit their annual reports, which may represent a significant cost. There is no annual registration fee to the commercial register.

2.5 Shares and Share Transfers

37 Sec. 178 *ZGD* provides that a corporation is authorised to issue different classes of stock (e.g., common stock or preferred stock). Shares in a d.d. may either be bearer shares or registered shares. Bearer shares are transferred by handing over the share certificate whilst registered shares can be transferred by way of endorsement (Sec. 233 *ZGD*). The transfer of registered shares issued in non-material form is subject to the Book Entry Securities Act – ZNVP (*Zakon o nematerializiranih vrednostnih papirjih)*. The rights which arise for these stocks are gained by the registration of acquisition of these stocks by the possessor, in the central registry of immaterialised stocks. The transfer instrument for the transfer of title from the previous possessor of the security to its new possessor is a transfer order in paper form while the transfer is executed and registered electronically. According to Sec. 27 Subs. 4 Value Added Tax Act ("ZDDV"), transfer of securities is exempted from VAT; however, a capital gains tax may be incurred in some cases, if profit is made. Otherwise, no transfer tax is levied on the transfer of shares itself. If a registered share is transferred to another person, the transfer shall be reported to the company and evidenced. The company shall record the transfer in the share book.

2.6 Corporate Bodies

38 Every d.d. must have two corporate bodies: a board of directors (*uprava družbe*) and the shareholders' meeting (*skupščina*). The articles of association (*statut družbe*) determine whether the company will also have a supervisory board (*nadzorni svet*). In the following cases, the company is bound to have a supervisory board: (i) if its capital stock amounts to SIT 410,000,000 (approximately EUR 1,700,000), or (ii) if the average annual number of employees exceeds 500, or (iii) if the company was established successively, or (iv) if the company's shares are listed on the stock exchange, or (v) if the number of holders of registered shares is above 100 (Sec. 261 *ZGD*).

2.6.1 Board of Directors

39 The board of directors consists of one or more members and represents the company *vis-à-vis* third parties (Sec. 246 and Sec. 248 *ZGD*). If there are several members in the board of directors, they represent the company jointly, unless otherwise determined by the articles of association. The articles of association or the supervisory board, if so determined by the articles of association, may determine that board of directors' members are authorised to represent the company solely or jointly, or some of them jointly together with a *Prokurist* (Sec. 248 Subs. 2 and 4 *ZGD*). According to Sec. 250 Subs. 1 *ZGD*, the board of directors and its president are appointed by the supervisory board for a term not exceeding five years, but further consecutive re-appointments are allowed.

40 The board of directors is exclusively in charge of the management of the company (Sec. 246 Subs. 1 *ZGD*). The board of directors is independent and must neither be instructed by the supervi-

depends on the number of founders; where there are less than 50 founders, the fee will amount to approximately EUR 450.

13 A large company shall be understood to mean a company which exceeds at least two of the following criteria: (i) average number of employees not exceeding 250, (ii) annual income below SIT 4,000,000,000 (EUR 16.7 million) and (iii) average level of assets at the beginning and end of the business year not exceeding SIT 550,000,000. Banks, insurance companies and associated companies which are, under Article 53 *ZGD*, obliged to prepare consolidated annual statements are regarded as large companies.

sory board nor by the shareholders' meeting.[14] However, certain business transactions require the supervisory board's approval (Sec. 274 *ZGD*)[15] or – in rare cases – the approval of the shareholders' meeting. In the latter event, managing directors are released from liability for such an action, but a mere supervisory board approval does not release managing directors from liability for incurred damages.

The supervisory board has sole authority for the appointment and dismissal of the members and the president of the board of directors (Sec. 250 Subs. 1 *ZGD*).[16] **41**

2.6.2 The Shareholders' Meeting

The shareholders' meeting is the representative body of the shareholders in which they can exercise their rights (Sec. 281 *ZGD*). Pursuant to Sec. 282 Subs. 1 no. 3 *ZGD*, the shareholders' meeting is responsible for the appointment of the members of the supervisory board to the extent these are not appointed by the employees.[17] Further competencies include making decisions about (i) distribution of profits as proposed by the board of directors and on the basis of the opinion supplied by the supervisory board, (ii) the annual report as proposed by the board of directors and on the basis of the opinion supplied by the supervisory board, (iii) changes to the articles of association, (iv) increase and decrease of capital, (v) termination of the company and status changes (merger, affiliation), (vi) appointment of the auditor and (vii) other matters defined by the articles of association and the law (Sec. 282 Subs. 1 *ZGD*). **42**

The shareholders' meeting generally may not decide on management issues given the exclusive management competence of the board of directors (Sec. 282 Subs. 2 *ZGD*). **43**

2.6.3 Supervisory Board

Pursuant to Sec. 262 *ZGD*, the supervisory board must consist of at least three members, appointed by the shareholders' meeting. The supervisory board is obliged to monitor whether the board of directors complies with its duties and takes management decisions which are economically feasible for the company. **44**

2.7 Duties and Liabilities of Directors

The board of directors represents and acts as the agent for the company. In relation to the shareholders' meeting its responsibilities are: (i) to prepare, upon request by the shareholders' meeting, measures within the authority of the shareholders' meeting, (ii) to prepare contracts and other enactments when the validity thereof is subject to approval by the shareholders' meeting and (iii) to execute the decisions adopted by the shareholders' meeting (Sec. 249 *ZGD*). It should also give reports to the supervisory board (Sec. 256 *ZGD*). A person cannot act as a director for a period of five years after conviction for specified criminal offences (e.g., business crime, criminal offence against labour relations and social security); moreover, not within two years of completion of the sentence (Sec. 246 Subs. 4 *ZGD*). The foregoing provision is also employed for the qualifications of a managing director of a d.o.o. **45**

Like the managing directors of a d.o.o., the members of the board of directors of a d.d. must perform their duties using the diligence of a prudent businessman and, in the event of breach, are jointly and severally liable to the company for damage sustained as a result of breach of their duties to the company, unless they prove they acted with due care and integrity in performing their duties **46**

14 *ZGD* even forbids the shareholders' meeting from deciding issues concerning the management of business, except in two situations (i) if this is requested by the board of directors or (ii) if the company has no supervisory board and such matters would normally fall under the authority of the supervisory board. This does not, however, include the decisions adopted by the shareholders' meeting which are binding for the board of directors.

15 These transactions are defined by the supervisory board or by the articles of association.

16 If for any reason one or more members of the board of directors have not been appointed, they shall be appointed by court upon petition by interested parties.

17 For details on employee representation, please refer to marginal notes 30, 58.

(Sec. 258 Subs. 1, 2 and 3 *ZGD*). The same applies to the members of the supervisory board (Sec. 280 *ZGD*). A company cannot renounce its claim for damages sustained or settle its claim until three years has passed from inception of the claim. A company's claim against the members of the board can also be invoked by the company's creditors; however, only in the event that the company is not able to repay their debts (Sec. 258 Subs. 5 *ZGD*). Pursuant to Sec. 280 Subs. 2 *ZGD*, shareholders can also claim damages without prejudice to the claim of the company itself (e.g., minority shareholders' claims).

In addition to the general liability of the members of the board of directors, they can also be held liable for certain breaches of provisions relating to the protection of the company's share capital (Sec. 258 Subs. 3 *ZGD*). Members of the board of directors and the supervisory board are not required to reimburse the company and the shareholders for losses if their actions were based on a lawful resolution passed by the shareholders' meeting (Sec. 258. Subs. 4 *ZGD*).

Shareholders at an annual general meeting who resolve on a discharge of acts of the board of directors and supervisory board, by doing so authorise and approve the performance of the board of directors and supervisory board for the financial year. However, according to the *ZGD*, the discharge has no legal effect in the sense that it constitutes a waiver of claims by the company against the members of the board of directors or supervisory board (Sec 282(a) Subs. 1 and 2 *ZGD*).

Managing directors are obliged to file for insolvency proceedings if the company is (i) unable to pay its debts or (ii) is over-indebted within two months. Failure of the managing directors to do so resulting in bankruptcy (Secs. 12 and 13 *ZFPPod*), and indulgent performance of the supervisory board members and the shareholders contributing to incapacity of the company to settle its debts may result in their personal joint and several liability towards the creditors. Liability is limited to between SIT 5 and 15 million (EUR 20,800 to 62,500), depending on the size of the company. The limitation of liability does not apply for gross negligence or willful acts. Claims become time-barred after five years.

According to law and practice, a company may purchase insurance on behalf of its board of directors and supervisory board to cover any D&O liability incurred.

2.8 Shareholders' Liability

47 In general, shareholders are not liable for the obligations of the company. Shareholders may be liable for the company's obligations through the piercing of the corporate veil, which can be enforced in the same cases as already stated concerning a d.o.o. – please see above.[18]

2.9 Capitalisation and Financing

2.9.1 Basic Concepts

48 The capitalisation and financing of a d.d. is based on the general concept of the "principle of real capital contribution and maintenance". Accordingly, the loss of the restricted share capital will oblige the members of the board of directors to apply for insolvency proceedings (Sec. 371 Subs. 1 Pt. 8 *ZGD*).

2.9.2 Minimum Share Capital

49 The minimum share capital of a d.d. is SIT 6,000,000 (EUR 25,000) (Sec. 172 *ZGD*). The capital can be contributed in cash or in kind (Sec. 191 Subs. 2 *ZGD*); at least one-third of the share capital shall be rendered by contribution in cash.

At least 25 per cent of the nominal value of each monetary share shall be paid-up prior to the registration of the company. Issued shares shall not be sold for less than their par value. The incorporation process is subject to a statutory review by the new board of directors and the new supervisory board (Sec. 194 Subs. 1 *ZGD*). As part of the review, the level and availability of the

18 See Mn. 13 et seq.

contributions must be assessed. In addition, in certain cases an additional audit by an independent auditor, appointed by the court, will be required.

2.9.3 Maintenance of Capital and Liquidity

(i) System

ZGD includes provisions about capital protection. For shareholders with more than 25 per cent of the voting shares in the company, it appears that when the shareholders grant loans to the company in lieu of share capital injection, these loans are treated as the company's share capital in an eventual bankruptcy procedure. **50**

(ii) Distributions

Distributions to shareholders may only be made out of balance sheet profits (Sec. 228 Subs. 1 *ZGD*). Hidden distributions are not allowed. Advance dividends are permitted, if so provided by the articles of association and with approval of the supervisory board. They are limited to one-half of predicted profits and one-half of the profits from the preceding year, whichever is smaller. **51**

(iii) Acquisition of Own Shares and Related Financing

Except for certain limited cases, a d.d. is not allowed to acquire its own shares (Sec 240. Subs. 1 *ZGD*). One of the most relevant exceptions is when the acquisition is authorised by the shareholders' meeting (Sec. 240 Subs. 1 No.8 *ZGD*).[19] Such authorisation may only be given for a maximum term of 18 months and may only authorise the acquisition of a maximum 10 per cent of the registered share capital. **52**

Financial assistance in acquiring shares in a d.d. has to be regarded in light of the provisions on loan/guarantee for a person wishing to acquire shares in the d.d.. The company law (ZGD) treats shares (art. 244.) obtained in the name of a third person, but for the account of the company, as treasury shares (no voting rights, resale obligation) unless these are obtained under same restrictions applying for "true" treasury shares (e.g. if acquisition is necessary to prevent grave harm, universal legal succession, acquisition without compensation, acquisition to provide severance to employees, GA resolution). In practice it is very difficult to discern when the "financial assistance" would constitute a prohibited purchase of own shares and when not. In addition, should a loan be given to a shareholder to obtain the shares this could constitute repayment of the capital (unless given under fair market conditions).

(iv) Company as Lender or Guarantor

There is no direct restriction or consequence for the company granting any kind of guarantee for the obligations of its shareholders, associated companies or any third party. Protection of the creditors, if necessary, may be sought through means mentioned in previous points. **53**

However, there are some restrictions regarding loans to members of the supervisory board or the board of directors.

19 Other exceptions, when a company is allowed to acquire it's own shares, are: (i) if the acquisition is necessary for the company to prevent imminent serious damage, (ii) if the shares are to be offered for purchase to the company employees or a company associated with it, (iii) if the acquisition is necessary to give shareholders compensation according to the provisions of the present law, (iv) if the acquisition is free of charge, (v) if it wants to acquire shares at the purchasing commission, (vi) if the acquisition is based on universal legal inheritance and (vii) if the acquisition is based on an assembly decision to withdraw shares in line with the provisions on the decrease in the capital stock.

(v) Company as Borrower

54 Shareholder loans to a d.d. are generally allowed, but please see marginal note 50. The principles also apply to third-party loans secured by a shareholder (Sec. 433 Subs. 2 *ZGD*).

2.10 Publication and Filing Requirements

55 A wide range of documentation and information must be filed with the court register,[20] some of which will also have to be submitted for publication in the Federal Gazette. Financial penalties are imposed on the company, director and/or *prokurist* (person in charge) as sanction for companies failing to meet the statutory requirements of filing and publishing.

All additional filing obligations for non-residents provided in financial legislation have been repealed. Except for industry restrictions, such as exploitation of natural resources or gaming, there are no additional obligations in respect of foreign investors (shareholders) whatsoever.

56 A court register is a public register and any third party can in good faith rely on the contents of the register. A court register is organised as a centralised database and it is accessible online on the State portal of the Republic of Slovenia.[21] No annual registration fee is payable.

57 A company is not required to file annual accounts in the court register, though under the *ZFPPod* the company may be struck from the register for failing to submit annual accounts to AJPES for two subsequent years or more.

2.11 Financial Reporting

58 These requirements correspond with the requirements in a d.o.o.[22]

2.12 Employee Participation in Corporate Bodies

59 These requirements correspond with the requirements in a d.o.o.[23]

20 Annual business reports of companies, shares of which were publicly offered, either on primary or secondary markets, i.e. traded on the organised market, shall be published in a national daily. The notification by the company to its shareholders for a shareholders' meeting and the respective agenda shall be published in the national Official Gazette. The notification by the company to its shareholders to pay the remaining outstanding share capital shall also be published in the national Official Gazette. Business reports, consolidated when applicable, shall be filed with the Agency for Public Evidence ("AJPES"). The agency shall make a respective part/form of the business reports publicly available. The companies, shares of which were publicly offered, either on primary or secondary markets, i.e. traded on the organised market, shall file annual business reports with the Agency for Security Markets. Companies, shares of which are quoted, shall file the reports semi-annually. The companies should also inform the agency on a regular basis of any business event that might considerably influence the price of their shares.

21 http://e-uprava.gov.si/e-uprava/.

22 See Mn. 29.

23 See Mn. 30.

XXIII. Spain

*by Prof. Álvaro Sáinz and César Ramírez (LL.M.)**

1. The Limited Liability Company ("SL")

Literature: Ignacio Arroyo/José Miguel Embid, Comments on the Limited Liabilities Companies Act (Tecnos 1997); Manuel Broseta, Manual de Derecho Mercantil (Tecnos 2002)

The two most common forms of company in Spain are the *Sociedad Anónima* ("SA") and the *Sociedad de Responsabilidad Limitada* ("SL"). Both the SA and the SL are limited liability companies incorporated with a share capital contributed by the shareholders.[1] The shareholders have limited liability for the company's debts up to the amounts contributed as equity. 1

The Spanish legislator intended the SL to serve as the vehicle of choice for closed enterprises with a limited number of shareholders, leaving SAs for larger organisations and for publicly listed companies.

Perhaps the most frequently cited benefit of an SL is that members do not have to undergo the time-consuming and costly process of obtaining an independent expert's report for the valuation of non-cash capital contributions.[2]

Another key difference between SAs and SLs, this time related to the governance of the company, is that SAs give minority shareholders the right to be represented on the board of directors of the company in proportion to their interest in the share capital thereof. This right does not exist in the case of SLs.[3]

1.1 Export of Company

Under Spanish law, the registered office and, specifically, the location: (i) where the company has its headquarters; or (ii) where its main business activities are carried out, must be located in Spain. Thus a company whose headquarters or main business activities are outside Spain may not be considered by the Spanish authorities as a Spanish company subject to Spanish corporate legislation, even though it may have become registered in Spain.[4] 2

In this regard, the relocation of the registered office to another EU Member State is only permitted if Spain and the relevant receiving EU Member State are parties to an international treaty in force that allows such a transfer, with the company maintaining its legal identity. Should this be the case, the relevant company would no longer be a Spanish company subject to the Spanish Companies Act.[5]

* Álvaro Sáinz is a partner at *Linklaters*, Madrid. César Ramírez is a former managing associate at this firm.

1 Although "shares", "shareholders" and "shareholders' meeting" should strictly only apply to SAs, and "participations", "quotas", "members" and "members' meeting" should be used when referring to SLs, we have used "shares" and "shareholders" to refer to both types of companies.

2 Such reports are always required for SA companies. By doing away with this requirement, the law considerably reduces the time needed for completing common transactions such as contributing shares to a holding company. Nevertheless, this freedom comes with some risk: unless an independent expert's report is obtained, shareholders (and sometimes directors) are made jointly and severally liable to the company and third parties for the accuracy of the valuation given to non-cash capital contributions.

3 To add some perspective, note that SLs are far more popular than SAs among investors in Spain: as per the statistics issued by the Spanish Central Commercial Registry, an aggregate of 128,717 SLs were incorporated in 2004, while only 2,224 SAs (not all of which are listed) were incorporated in the same period.

4 The rulings by the European Court of Justice in "Überseering" and "InspireArt" (See Part 1, I, Mn. 17 et seq. and 19) have not so far moved the Spanish legislator to amend this principle.

5 While the above principle remains true for Spanish SLs (and SAs), recent legislation (entered into force on 16 November 2005) authorises relocation of SEs registered in Spain to another EU member State. This right to relocate is not however unrestricted, and the Spanish authorities are entitled to oppose the relocation for reasons of public general interest. Shareholders of an SE registered in Spain who opposed relocation are entitled to separate from the company by having the value of their shares reimbursed.

Finally, upon a discrepancy between (a) the address of the registered office and (b) the location in (i) or (ii) above, third parties will be allowed to consider the company as domiciled in either (a) or (b), at their convenience.

1.2 Transformation into a Foreign Entity

3 Under Spanish law, a domestic company cannot be transformed into a foreign entity. Determination of the company's nationality and, therefore, of the applicable law, is made under Spanish law according to the location of the company's registered office. The transformation into a foreign entity could only be achieved by transferring the SL's business to a foreign company. If done by way of an asset deal, there will be an adverse tax effect, as hidden reserves will be realised. In any event, such transfer may be effected under a neutral tax regime avoiding the realisation of hidden reserves and the accrual of other possible applicable taxes.

Spanish law has recently introduced the possibility of merging a domestic company with an S.E.[6]

1.3 Incorporation

4 The steps required to incorporate an SL in Spain are as follows:

(i) Reservation of the relevant company name.
The corporate name of the company to be incorporated must be reserved in advance.[7]

(ii) Obtaining a tax identification number.

(iii) Opening a bank account to deposit the share capital.

(iv) Execution of the public deed of incorporation.

(v) Stamp duty – this is levied at a rate of 1 per cent of the nominal value of the subscribed share capital and issuance premium, which has to be paid after execution of the public deed of incorporation and before filing with the Commercial Registry.

(vi) Filing of the deed of incorporation at the relevant Commercial Registry.[8]

5 Preparation of all necessary documents of incorporation, submission of petitions and similar legal arrangements should take around 15 days.

Once the deed of incorporation is filed with the relevant Commercial Registry, final registration of the company should be achieved within 30 days.[9]

6 Costs of incorporation depend on the amount of share capital and premium to be contributed. The main costs involve notarial fees, registration fees and stamp duty. By way of example, the notarial fees for the incorporation of an SL with the minimum share capital of EUR 3,006 may amount to EUR 300, registration fees to EUR 100 and stamp duty to EUR 30.06.

1.4 Recurrent Costs and Efforts

7 Apart from the above, Spanish companies must fulfil annual requirements, incurring additional annual ongoing costs.

6 See Spanish Act 19/2005 (implementing European Regulation 2157/2001, dated 8 October 2001, of the Council of Ministers), entered into force on 16 November 2005. The Act authorises the incorporation of SEs (including through a merger) registered in Spain, and also allows a Spanish company to be transformed into an SE. As in the case of relocation, shareholders of a domestic company who opposed the merger into an SE domiciled in another EU State are entitled to separate from the company.

7 One of the future partners (or a representative) must contact the Central Commercial Registry (*Registro Mercantil Central*) requesting use of the relevant corporate name. If the name is available, it will be reserved for a period of 15 months. The Registry will then issue a Certificate of Availability (*Certificación Negativa del Nombre*) as evidence that the name has been reserved. This certificate is valid for two months and may be renewed until the 15-month term of validity mentioned above has elapsed.

8 This is the last step needed to accomplish the incorporation process of an SL company in Spain. Note that, although the company comes into existence once the relevant deed of incorporation is executed, legal personality is not acquired until registration of the company in the relevant Commercial Registry.

9 Please note that, for foreign directors, the Spanish tax authorities require that each individual/company obtain an "NIE" (*Foreign Identification Number*). This process, consequently, may delay the registration of the company with the Commercial Registry. The same obligation applies to any foreign founder of a company.

The main annual obligations for a Spanish company are: (i) payment of corporation tax, basically dependent on the company's turnover; and (ii) approval and filing of its annual accounts at the Commercial Registry.

The shareholders' meeting to approve the annual accounts, unless "universal",[10] shall be called by notice published in the Official Gazette of the Commercial Registry and in one of the major daily newspapers circulated in the relevant province, which would cost around EUR 2,000. As a (cheaper) alternative, the by-laws may establish a different procedure such as the notice being sent to the partners' addresses registered with the relevant partners' book.[11]

The fees for filing the annual accounts at the Commercial Registry amount to around EUR 50-60.

Other agreements are more occasional and depend on the governance of the company. The costs for executing resolutions in a public deed and registering them differ on a case by-case basis and cannot be calculated beforehand.

No annual registration fee is payable to the Commercial Registry.

1.5 Quotas and Quota Transfers

SLs are not entitled to issue share certificates. The share capital is divided into quotas which are **8**
not considered as securities: as a result, an SL may not be listed on an exchange.

There are no bearer quotas in an SL: the quotas are registered to each shareholder (quotaholder) on the partners' book, kept by the relevant management body of the SL. The partners of the company do not have any special liability or obligation, their liability being limited to the capital contributed by each partner.

It is possible to have different classes of shares (quotas) with different dividend rights attaching to them, or shares that entitle the shareholder to more than one vote per share (*participaciones de voto plural o múltiple*). Non-voting shares can also be issued, provided that the aggregate par value does not exceed half of the share capital of the SL.

The transfer of an SL's quotas must be carried out by means of the relevant deed of purchase be- **9**
ing executed before a notary public (*documento público*).[12] The acquisition must also be registered in the partners' registry book for the company to acknowledge the transfer and for the acquirer to be recognised as a shareholder. For these purposes, the directors or the company secretary must be notified of the transfer so that the partners' registry book can be updated. Finally, all provisions of the law and the bylaws must be observed.

As a general rule no transfer taxes are levied on the transfer of an SL's quotas.

1.6 Corporate Bodies

The two corporate bodies are: (i) the partners' meeting; and (ii) the managing body. **10**

The general partners' meeting decides on all issues relating to the organisation and structure of the company.

The managing body can adopt the following structures: **11**

(i) a sole directorship;
(ii) two or more directors acting together;

10 According to Spanish law, a general meeting shall be deemed to have been duly called, without the relevant notices having been sent out, if the entire share capital of the company is present or duly represented and all the shareholders unanimously agree to hold a general meeting and its agenda. Such a meeting is known as a "universal" meeting (*Junta Universal*).

11 This alternative is not available to SAs.

12 Unless otherwise provided in the bylaws of the company, transfer of quotas is free when made in favour of: (i) any other quota holder; (ii) a spouse, antecedent or descendant; and (iii) companies belonging to the same group. If there are no provisions in the bylaws on the matter, the transfer will be subject to statute, meaning that the intention to sell must be announced to the managing body of the company, which in turn must announce such intention to sell to the other partners, who may opt to purchase such share; if no shareholder makes use of such pre-emptive right, the company may purchase the share itself and, if so desired, carry out a reduction of share capital; only after such procedure has been completed is the sale to a third party permissible, although the sale may also proceed if the selling shareholder does not obtain a reply to his/her offer after three months have elapsed.

(iii) two or more directors acting severally; and
(iv) a board of directors (this is a joint managing body with a minimum of three and a maximum of 12 members). Note that, among the members of the board, the directors can delegate all the representative powers of the board in favour of one or more managing directors or in favour of an executive committee.[13]

All forms of managing body can be provided for in the company's bylaws. By doing so, the partners' meeting is able to opt for any form, and change from one form to another from time to time, by passing the relevant shareholders' resolution, without the need to amend the bylaws.

1.7 Duties and Liabilities of Directors

12 In general, the managing body represents the company and has to administer and manage it with due diligence and act always for the benefit of the company. Apart from the representative powers, there are certain obligations established in Spanish legislation that directors must comply with, which mainly concern: (i) the preparation of the annual accounts of the company; (ii) the calling of the general meeting of the company; and (iii) a duty to apply for insolvency proceedings, generally whenever the shareholders have failed to do so.

13 Pursuant to Spanish company law, directors are jointly and severally liable towards the company, its partners and creditors for any damages caused as a result of actions performed or resolutions passed in breach of law or the company's bylaws, or without the due diligence required or without being in the best interests of the company.

Spanish law also recognises the right of partners and third parties in general to make claims against directors or board members for any damages suffered directly as a consequence of their conduct. Third-party claims will, in this case, need to comply with the requirements of the Spanish Civil Code on non-contractual responsibility or tort.

The responsibility of board members towards the company, partners, creditors and third parties in general will not be excluded even if the relevant board resolution or action taken contrary to the articles or in breach of the duty of care had been previously approved or subsequently ratified by a partners' resolution. On the other hand, the directors who voted against the damaging resolution would be released of any liability.

Note that the approval of the annual accounts does not discharge or release the directors from liability.

The general statute of limitations for claims against a director is four years. Spanish courts have ruled that this period runs from the date the director ceased to be a director.

D&O insurance is allowed and is common in Spanish companies. When appropriate, related premiums are paid by the company.

Finally:

(i) directors have specific obligations in connection with the acquisition by the SL of its own shares and/or financial assistance. If the SL infringes any of the obligations related to the purchase of its own shares and/or financial assistance, directors, managers and officers of the SL shall be deemed liable for such infringement, and specific sanctions and penalties shall be imposed. These sanctions expire after a period of three years; and
(ii) directors have a duty of loyalty towards the company, meaning that: (i) they are not allowed to use the name of the company to make any personal deal; (ii) they are not allowed to make any investment or deal that they have come to know about through their office as director; (iii) they must notify the board of directors of any situation leading to a conflict of interest between them and the company that will be, in any case, included in the "Corporate Governance Annual Report"; and (iv) they must report their stake in any company with a similar corporate purpose in order for this to be included in the report.

In addition to the above, certain actions carried out by the directors could lead to criminal liability.

13 In any event, note that the following may not be delegated under any circumstances: (i) the laying of accounts and balance sheets before a general meeting; and (ii) the powers granted to the board by the general meeting, unless the board is expressly authorised to do so.

1.8 Shareholders' Liability

The general principle governing corporate liability is that each company, as an independent entity, is solely responsible for its liabilities unless otherwise provided by Spanish regulations. 14

Nevertheless, the legal personality of a company may be disregarded and its shareholders or any other relevant obligor (i.e. a sister company) may be held jointly liable for the company's debts by application of the "piercing of the corporate veil" principle.

In the absence of a legal framework governing this principle, the Spanish courts have established a doctrine on the circumstances required for its application, which are as follows:

(i) the legal personality of a company is used fraudulently mainly to avoid the liability of a person which, otherwise, would be liable in accordance with article 1911 of the Civil Code; and

(ii) as a result of the above, damage is caused to a third party (i.e. the company's creditors, its employees or minority shareholders).

Given the subjective nature of requirement (i) above, the courts have often considered that certain factual circumstances may be an indication that an intention to avoid the application of article 1911 of the Civil Code exists, in particular in the case of:

(a) thin capitalisation of a company;

(b) *confusion of corporate identity:* this situation takes place if there is no clear separation between the company and its shareholder or any other relevant obligor in the ordinary course of their business; and

(c) *groups of companies:* even if a company appears to be an independent entity *vis-à-vis* third parties, it may be deemed that it is not so where it is part of a group of companies and is subject to direct and effective control from its parent company.

The "piercing of the corporate veil" principle would not be applied automatically should one or more of the above circumstances be met. On the contrary, in order to pierce the veil, the court would consider very carefully the specific merits of each case, in particular whether a violation of article 1911 of the Civil Code, as described above, has been committed, damage has been caused to a third party and such damage cannot be remedied by any other means.

1.9 Capitalisation and Financing

1.9.1 Basic Concepts

Under Spanish law, minimum capital requirements apply for SLs. This assures a minimum funding to commence and conduct business and, accordingly, strengthen the protection of creditors. 15

Rules on minimum share capital are then complemented by additional rules on maintenance of the share capital throughout the life of the company.

1.9.2 Minimum Share Capital

The minimum fully subscribed and paid-up capital is EUR 3,006. The minimum capital has to be paid in full prior to or on the date of incorporation (i.e. execution of the deed of incorporation before the notary public). It can be made either in cash or in kind. 16

1.9.3 Maintenance of Capital and Liquidity

(i) System

The minimum share capital rule is protected as of the time of incorporation: the notary will not allow the incorporation of an SL with a share capital below EUR 3,006. Additionally, an undercapitalised SL will be refused registration at the Commercial Registry. 17

Additional rules, embedding this principle, apply throughout the life of the company. Some of these rules, mostly inspired by the Second Directive,[14] have been implemented in Spanish corporate law as follows:

- the subscribed capital must be formed of assets capable of economic assessment: undertakings to perform work or supply services may not form part of these assets;
- shares must not be issued at a price lower than their nominal value;
- shareholders may not be released from their obligation to pay up their contributions; and
- a loss of half of the subscribed share capital obliges the management to call a general meeting of shareholders which must decide the measures to be taken.

(ii) Distributions

18 The distribution of dividends to partners may only be paid out of the profits for the financial year or freely available voluntary reserves, if the net book value is not and will not become, as a result of the distribution, lower than the share capital.

In any event, where losses are brought over from previous years causing the value of the net assets of the company to be lower than the share capital, profits shall be used to offset these losses.

A minimum legal reserve must be set aside and be maintained throughout the life of the company. This is set at 20 per cent of the subscribed share capital figure. For these purposes, and while the general meeting of the company shall decide freely upon the allocation of the year's profits in accordance with the approved balance sheet, at least 10 per cent of the year's profits must be set aside to build up this reserve until it reaches the 20 per cent threshold.

Advance dividends (*dividendos a cuenta*) are allowed. While only the partners may agree to distribute dividends based on an approved set of annual accounts, a resolution to advance dividends may be passed both by the partners or by the directors of the company.

(iii) Acquisition of Own Quotas and Related Financing

19 An SL may not subscribe either its own quotas, or shares or quotas issued by its parent company.

An SL may only acquire its own quotas, or shares or quotas of its parent company: (i) where such quotas/shares form part of assets acquired as a whole in a universal transfer,[15] are freely acquired or are acquired as a consequence of a court order in settlement of a claim by the company against the holder of such quotas/shares; (ii) where the quotas/shares are acquired in execution of a resolution reducing the share capital of the company; (iii) when the quotas/shares are acquired as a result of legal or administrative execution proceedings; or (iv) when the acquisition is authorised by the general partners' meeting, is made out of profits or reserves and is carried out for the purposes of, *inter alia*, acquiring the quotas of a partner who is being separated from the company.

Quotas acquired by the company by virtue of the above shall be disposed of within three years of their acquisition; and shares or quotas of a parent company shall be transferred within one year.

In the meantime, (a) rights attached to quotas held by the company are suspended for those periods and (b) a reserve of the amount of such shares must be created on the equity and liabilities side of the balance sheet, such a reserve not being available for distribution while the quotas are not disposed of or cancelled.

For regulations on financial assistance please refer to Mn. 20.

(iv) Company as Lender or Guarantor

Under Spanish law there are two main restrictions to be taken into account when deciding on granting any guarantee. These are as follows:

14 See Part 1, I, Mn. 39 et seq.

15 A type of transfer whereby the acquirer subrogates the transferor in all rights and obligations related to each asset acquired, for instance by way of a will.

(a) Financial Assistance

An SL is neither entitled to advance funds, grant loans or give guarantees, nor facilitate any form of financial assistance for the acquisition of its quotas or the quotas issued by any company belonging to the same group.[16] 20

(b) Corporate Benefit

Under Spanish law no specific restrictions or corporate benefit procedures need to be complied with. Any transaction needs to be considered on a case-by-case basis and is subject to: (i) the directors' general duty of diligence towards their company; and (ii) the obligation to comply with any applicable regulation (e.g. financial assistance issues as explained above). 21

In this regard, as directors are required to act with a duty of care and in the best interests of the company, the granting of any guarantees either in favour of the company's partners, or in favour of third parties, must be made for the benefit of the company.

(v) Company as Borrower

There is no particular rule preventing shareholders from financing their company either through the contribution of new equity or the provision of a shareholder loan. 22

Generally, a loan repayment to a shareholder will be considered as a usual third-party claim. As such, in an insolvency scenario such a repayment will be satisfied as a usual third-party claim, i.e. before contributions of the shareholders are repaid.

1.10 Publication and Filing Requirements

Once the company has been registered with the relevant Commercial Registry, Spanish legislation requires the filing and registration of a wide range of documentation and information, related to the day-to-day management of the company and any transaction affecting the company's share capital or structure. Likewise, annual accounts must be deposited annually with the relevant Commercial Registry. 23

Apart from the need to file any resolution of the company affecting its bylaws with the Commercial Registry, it is also necessary to register any foreign investment made in the company (i.e. subscription or acquisition of quotas by a foreign entity) with the Directorate of Foreign Investments. Additionally, any loans received by a Spanish company from a foreign entity, or any loans granted by a Spanish company to a foreign entity shall be declared to the Bank of Spain (*Banco de España*). Likewise, depending on the corporate purpose of the company and its activities within regulated sectors (i.e. telecommunications, insurance, etc.), other notifications may be necessary to other administrative bodies.

The relevant period to make the notifications or filings above varies, but is usually from ten to 30 days from the date the relevant corporate resolution was passed. Note also the need to publicise certain corporate resolutions, such as a reduction of capital, in newspapers.

Failure to make the relevant filings and/or publications may lead to fines being imposed, ultimately leading to the company being struck from the Commercial Registry if it persistently fails to file annual accounts (*cierre registral*). 24

In certain circumstances, however, the relevant corporate action will not be deemed to have any effect unless filed with the Commercial Registry. This is particularly so in the case of incorporation of a company (SL or SA): an unregistered company will be denied legal status. Another example is the case of new shares issued by a company: the new shares cannot be transferred unless and until the corporate resolution authorising their issuance is registered with the Commercial Registry.

16 Please note that, in contrast to SAs, financial assistance restrictions are more extensive as they not only include the acquisition of an SL's own quotas but also the quotas issued by any other company belonging to the same group (i.e. not only the parent company but also any sister companies).

Finally, *bona fide* third parties may rely on the content of the Commercial Registry. As an example, a third party contracting with a company through the company's managing director – registered as such with the Commercial Registry – will usually be protected, even in a case where the registered managing director's authority has been revoked but not yet cancelled in the Commercial Registry. This will be so except in a case where the third party actually knew about the revocation of the director's authority. The Commercial Registry can be accessed online under www.registradores.org.

1.11 Financial Reporting

25 Within a maximum of three months from the end of the financial year, the directors of the company shall prepare the draft financial statements (made up by a balance sheet, a profit and loss account, and an annual report), the management report and the proposed distribution of income or loss. Thereafter, the directors will submit these documents to the shareholders (together with the auditor's report – see below) for approval within the first six months of the end of the financial year.

The financial statements and the management report must then be audited.

Note that certain relief from financial reporting requirements is granted to small and medium-sized enterprises. In particular:

(a) Companies (whether an SL or an SA) which, during the two years preceding the end of the financial year, met at least two of the three following criteria, are entitled to present an abridged (as opposed to a full) balance sheet. These criteria are as follows:
- the total value of the items in the assets does not exceed EUR 2,374,000;
- the net annual turnover is less than EUR 4,747,996; and
- the average number of workers employed during the financial year is not greater than 50.

(b) Companies (whether an SL or an SA) which, during the two years preceding the end of the financial year, met at least two of the three following criteria, are entitled to present an abridged (as opposed to a full) profit and loss account. These criteria are as follows:
- the total value of the items in the assets does not exceed EUR 9,495,992;
- the net annual turnover is less than EUR 18,991,983; and
- the average number of workers employed during the financial year is not greater than 50.

(c) Companies (whether an SA or an SL) entitled to present an abridged balance sheet:
- are also entitled to file a far less detailed (abridged) annual report;
- need not produce any management report at all; and
- need not audit their accounts.

The drawing up of the accounts of an individual company and group annual accounts in accordance with US GAAP is not permitted under any circumstance.

Unlike the case for the consolidated accounts of listed SAs,[17] it currently remains optional for SLs to draft their consolidated accounts in accordance with IAS standards.

On the other hand, individual accounts of an SL may not currently be drafted in accordance with IAS standards.

1.12 Employee Participation in Corporate Bodies

26 Under Spanish law, employees do not have the right to appoint members of the corporate bodies of the company, although they are entitled to establish a works council.

17 See Mn. 50.

2 The Stock Corporation ("SA")

Literature: Ignacio Arroyo/José Miguel Embid, Comments on the Public Companies Act (Tecnos 2001); Manuel Broseta, Manual de Derecho Mercantil (Tecnos 2002)

The main characteristic of an SA is that its share capital is divided into shares, which are securities. In principle, such shares can be transferred without restrictions and can be traded on a public stock exchange. SA companies can issue bond instruments and may hold their own shares, subject to certain restrictions. 27

2.1 Export of Company

According to Spanish law, the same restrictions that apply to an SL also apply to an SA.[18] 28

2.2 Transformation into a Foreign Entity

Any such transformation must be carried out in the same manner as for an SL.[19] 29

2.3 Incorporation

The incorporation of an SA is carried out in accordance with the same procedures as for an SL.[20] 30

There is an alternative procedure for incorporating an SA, namely "successive formation". Essentially, this procedure involves the promoters offering the general public the possibility to subscribe shares upon the incorporation of the new entity. This system is rarely used in practice and much less so in the case of foreign investors. 31

Costs of incorporation depend on the amount of share capital and premium to be contributed. The main costs involve notarial fees, registration fees and stamp duty. By way of example, notarial fees for the incorporation of an SA with the minimum share capital of EUR 60,101.21 may amount to EUR 475, while registration fees will amount to EUR 150, and stamp duty to EUR 601.01. 32

2.4 Recurrent Costs and Efforts

The same recurrent costs and efforts that apply to an SL also apply to an SA.[21] 33

2.5 Shares and Share Transfers

The procedure of issuing shares in an SA differs depending on whether the company is listed or not. If not listed, the shares are issued on execution of the incorporation deed or by means of capital increases. If listed, issuance has to comply with certain specific regulations and is overseen by administrative authorities (including the Spanish Stock Exchange Commission, *Comisión Nacional del Mercado de Valores*). 34

Note that shares in an SA may be registered shares or (unlike an SL) bearer shares. While usually shareholders can decide whether the shares of their company will be registered or bearer shares, in some circumstances shares must necessarily be registered. This is the case, for instance, when the relevant shares are subject to pre-emptive rights, or when the shares have not been fully paid-up.

Shares in an SA need not be certificated. However, a registered shareholder is entitled to ask for their shares to be certificated by the company secretary at any time.

Transfer of shares in an SA can take place by simply physical delivery of the certificates (bearer shares) or by endorsement (bearer or registered shares). As a matter of practice, however, transfer involves a deed of transfer executed either as a private document or, more commonly, as a deed before a notary public. 35

18 See Mn. 2.
19 See Mn. 3.
20 See Mn. 4 et seq.
21 See Mn. 7.

A share transfer is, in general, free. However, the bylaws of the company may set out restrictions on the transfer of shares, such as rights of first refusal or pre-emptive rights in favour of the remaining shareholders and/or the company itself, which must be observed in any proposed transfer of shares.[22]

The same provisions concerning registration of the transfer or registered shares in the partners' book that apply to an SL also apply to an SA.[23]

Likewise, administrative authorisations may be requested if companies belonging to certain sectors of industry are to be transferred (e.g. telecommunications or insurance companies).

An SA can issue different classes of shares, with different rights in case of liquidation or winding-up of the company (in particular, economic rights), or different rights to dividends. An SA can also issue non-voting shares. Holders of non-voting shares enjoy additional rights to those held by ordinary shareholders, including a right to be paid dividends before any distributions are made to ordinary shareholders, but following the latest legislative changes there is no right to a minimum dividend (formerly set as 5 per cent of the share capital paid-up for each non-voting share). However, in certain circumstances failure by the SA to distribute the minimum dividend set out in the bylaws may result in the non-voting shares becoming ordinary shares, and as such entitled to vote.

2.6 Corporate Bodies

36 The two corporate bodies in an SA are: (i) the shareholders' meeting; and (ii) the managing body; both have the same duties as the corporate bodies in an SL.[24]

37 The managing body can adopt the following structures:

(i) a sole director;
(ii) two or more directors acting together;
(iii) two directors acting severally; and
(iv) a board of directors (this is a joint managing body with a minimum of three members). Note that among the members of the board, the directors can delegate all the representative powers of the board in favour of one or more managing directors or in favour of an executive committee.[25]

An SA's bylaws must necessarily refer to one of the four structures above; accordingly, and unlike the situation in the case of an SL, any change in the management form will therefore entail an amendment to the company's bylaws.

2.7 Duties and Liabilities of Directors

38 Directors of an SA have the same duties and liabilities as the directors of an SL.[26]

22 The first step is to verify the seller's title over the shares (this is usually done by reviewing the shareholders' registry book, previous share purchase agreements, the deed of incorporation, any deeds of increase or reduction in share capital, etc.).
Once the title of ownership has been verified, the shares will be transferred in accordance with their representation: (i) bearer shares must be transferred by public deed; (ii) registered shares represented by share certificates can be endorsed, such endorsement to be carried out under the terms of the relevant share purchase agreement. In Spain, the purchase of shares is usually done before a notary and formalised by public deed. If shares are not represented by means of certificates, they must be transferred by public deed.
If the shares are listed, transfer in the market is carried out by IBERCLEAR (the Spanish clearing and settlement system).
It is also necessary to register the acquisition of registered shares in the shareholders' registry book for the company to acknowledge the transfer and the purchaser to be recognised as a shareholder. Finally, the company's bylaws must be checked to ensure that all necessary transfer requirements have been complied with.

23 See Mn. 8.

24 See Mn. 10.

25 In any event, note that the following may not be delegated under any circumstances: (i) submission of the accounts and balance sheets to a general meeting; and (ii) the powers granted to the board by the general meeting, unless the board is expressly authorised to do so.

26 See Mn. 12 et seq.

2.8 Shareholders' Liability

The same restrictions and provisions that apply to an SL apply to an SA.[27] 39

2.9 Capitalisation and Financing

2.9.1 Basic Concepts

Under Spanish law, the requirements on minimum share capital apply to both SAs and SLs. 40

2.9.2 Minimum Share Capital

The minimum share capital that must be fully subscribed is EUR 60,101.21. However, it is 41
possible to pay only 25 per cent of the said amount on the date of incorporation, the remaining 75 per cent being paid as the bylaws may direct or, if delegated to the administrators, as established by these latter.[28]

2.9.3 Maintenance of Capital and Liquidity

(i) System

The minimum capital must be paid prior to or on the date of incorporation (i.e. execution of the 42
deed of incorporation before the notary public). It can be made both in cash and in kind. However, please note that if it is decided that the contribution be made in kind, it is compulsory to include a report in the public deed of incorporation drafted by an expert appointed by the Commercial Registry accrediting the value given by the relevant shareholder to such contribution.

The minimum share capital is strongly protected, as it ultimately represents a security for third-party creditors.[29]

A minimum legal reserve must be set aside and be maintained throughout the life of the company. The same provisions on minimum legal reserve that apply to an SL also apply to an SA.[30]

Finally, the shareholders are bound to pass a resolution whereby the registered capital of the company is decreased if, as a consequence of losses, the net worth of the company falls below two-thirds of the registered share capital and a corporate year has elapsed without the net worth having been restored.

If, on the other hand, the net worth of the company falls below half of the registered share capital, then the shareholders are bound to pass a resolution winding-up the company, or else increasing or decreasing the share capital as appropriate.

(ii) Distributions

The distribution of dividends to shareholders may only be paid out of the profit for the financial 43
year or free voluntary reserves, if the book value of net assets is not and will not become, as a result of such distribution, less than the share capital.[31]

Advance dividends (*dividendos a cuenta*) are allowed. While only the shareholders may agree to distribute dividends based on an approved set of annual accounts, a resolution to advance dividends may be passed both by the shareholders or by the directors of the company.

27 See Mn. 14.

28 Please note that Spanish legislation provides that a company must adopt the form of an SA and have a specific share capital when it performs certain commercial activities, e.g. banks, insurance companies, real estate investment funds, private TV companies, private equity companies, listed companies, securities agencies and securities companies.

29 Note the rule whereby acquisitions for value exceeding 10 per cent of the company's share capital figure made by the SA within the first two years from the date of its incorporation need prior approval by the general shareholders' meeting.

30 See Mn. 17.

31 See Mn. 18.

(iii) Acquisition of Own Shares and Related Financing

44 An SA is not permitted to subscribe its own shares, or shares issued by its parent company. An SA may only acquire its own shares, or shares of its parent company, in the following circumstances: (i) when the acquisition has been authorised by the general shareholders' meeting; (ii) the nominal value of the shares acquired, added to the shares already held by the company and its subsidiaries, does not exceed 10 per cent[32] of the share capital; (iii) the acquisition enables the acquiring company to create the required legal reserve, without reducing the capital of the reserves; and (iv) the shares are fully paid-up.

Notwithstanding the foregoing, an SA may freely acquire its own shares or shares/quotas of its parent company: (i) when the shares/quotas are acquired in execution of a resolution reducing the share capital of the company; (ii) when such shares/quotas form part of assets acquired as a whole in a universal transfer;[33] (iii) when the shares/quotas are freely acquired; and (iv) when the shares/quotas are acquired as a consequence of a court order in settlement of a claim by the company against the holder of such shares/quotas.

Shares/quotas acquired by the company by virtue of the above must be disposed of within three years of their acquisition.

For regulations on financial assistance please refer to Mn. 45.

(iv) Company as Lender or Guarantor

Apart from having to act within the scope of the corporate purpose, there are two principal restrictions to be taken into account when deciding on whether to provide security:

(a) Financial Assistance

45 An SA is not entitled to advance funds, grant loans, give guarantees or facilitate any form of financial assistance for the acquisition of its shares or of shares of its controlling company by a third party. This restriction is also extended to the scenario where the transaction affecting the shares of the relevant parent company is carried out by a foreign company (i.e. a company not incorporated in Spain acquires the shares of a company whose subsidiary provides the financial assistance).

The restriction does not apply to transactions relating to the acquisition of shares by the company's employees or employees of an associated company. Nor does it apply to transactions by banks and other financial institutions acting within their ordinary course of business.

(b) Corporate Benefit

46 Under Spanish law, no specific restrictions or corporate benefit procedures need to be complied with. However, all transactions need to be considered on a case-by-case basis, and are subject to: (i) the directors' general duty of diligence towards their company; and (ii) the requirement to comply with any applicable regulation (e.g. financial assistance issues as explained in Mn. 45 above).[34]

(v) Company as Borrower

47 The same provisions that apply to an SL also apply to an SA.[35]

32 5 per cent for listed companies.

33 A type of transfer whereby the acquirer subrogates the transferor in all rights and obligations related to each asset acquired, for instance by way of a will.

34 In this regard, as directors are required to act with a duty of care and in the best interests of the company, the granting of any guarantees, either in favour of the company's shareholders, or in favour of third parties, must be made for the benefit of the company.

35 See Mn. 22.

2.10 Publication and Filing Requirements

Apart from the general publication and filing requirements that apply to Spanish companies,[36] listed SAs must comply with the additional reporting obligations set out by the Spanish Stock Exchange Commission. **48**

2.11 Financial Reporting

Apart from the general accounting rules that apply to Spanish companies,[37] in relation to the group annual accounts, the option of using IAS standards depends on whether or not the SA is listed. As of 1 January 2005, it is compulsory for listed companies to draw up their consolidated accounts in accordance with IAS standards. **49**

Additionally, the drafting of individual accounts of banks and financial entities in accordance with IAS standards is currently allowed.

2.12 Employee Participation in Corporate Bodies

Under Spanish law, the same provisions that apply to an SA also apply to an SL with regard to employee participation in corporate bodies.[38] **50**

36 See Mn. 24.
37 See Mn. 25.
38 See Mn. 26.

XXIV. Sweden

by Svante Johansson[*]

Literature: Moberg in: Michael Bogdan, Swedish Law in the New Millennium (1st edition, Norstedts Juridik AB 2000); Andersson/Johansson/Skog, Aktiebolagslagen, En kommentar. Del I och II (Norstedts Juridik 2004); Johansson, Nials svensk associationsrätt (8th edition., Norstedts Juridik 2004)

1 The Limited Liability Company ("privat AB")

Swedish companies with limited liability (*aktiebolag*, "AB") are divided into private ABs (*privat aktiebolag*) and public ABs (*publikt aktiebolag*), both regulated by the Swedish Companies Act (*aktiebolagslagen*, "ABL"). Public ABs must have "publikt" or the abbreviation "publ" in their company names or attach the abbreviation "publ" to the company name (Ch. 28 Sec. 1 ABL). The main difference between the two types of ABs is that only public ABs are allowed to turn to the public in seeking to raise capital (Ch. 1 Sec. 7 and 8 ABL). The private AB is the most common type of AB in Sweden. There are approximately 300,000 private ABs registered in Sweden, in contrast to approximately 1,000 public Abs (of which approximately 500 are listed). 1

The statutory corporate governance framework is not strict and permits, for example, great flexibility in the drafting of the articles of association. 2

1.1 Export of Company

Swedish company law does not restrict the relocation abroad of private ABs' entire businesses and management. It also does not have any restrictions on accepting foreign legal entities moving to Sweden, since Sweden fully adheres to the incorporation principle.[1] 3

1.2 Transformation into a Foreign Entity

Swedish law does not provide for the changing of a domestic company into a foreign entity, except in relation to the rules regarding the European Company or S.E. It is not possible to merge a Swedish AB with a foreign company under Swedish law (with the exception of the S.E.). Any other transformation can only be achieved indirectly by transferring the private AB's business to a foreign company. If done by way of an asset deal, there may be an adverse tax effect as hidden reserves will be realised. 4

1.3 Incorporation

Private ABs are set up by way of a charter of incorporation, containing information on the shares, the articles of association and the minutes of the first general meeting of shareholders, which must be executed by at least one incorporator (Ch. 2 ABL). The company must be registered in the centralised commercial register held by the Swedish Companies Registration Office (*Bolagsverket*). 5

The acquisition of shelf companies which are already incorporated and registered is common, as the incorporation procedure usually takes five to six weeks. The registration fees amount to SEK 2,000 (approximately EUR 220) and acquisition of a shelf company amounts to approximately SEK 10,000 (approximately EUR 1,100). 6

1.4 Recurrent Costs and Efforts

Recurrent costs for private ABs relate to the publication and auditing of annual accounts. Filing them with the Swedish Companies Registration Office is, however, free of charge. Other costs and 7

* *Linklaters,* Stockholm. Written with the assistance of Björn Kristiansson.

1 See Part 1, I, Mn. 7 et seq.

fees only occur as a result of certain company actions which require the publication and filing of documents with the Swedish Companies Registration Office. The cost for filing, for example, a new issue of shares with the Swedish Companies Registration Office amounts to SEK 800 (approximately EUR 90).

1.5 Shares and Share Transfers

8 All shares in an AB have equal rights, unless the articles of association state otherwise. All shares must have voting rights attached to them, the maximum permitted difference in voting rights between different classes of shares being ten to one (Ch. 4 Sec. 5 ABL). Older companies may have shares with greater difference in voting rights. There are no restrictions regarding differences in rights to dividends etc.

9 Share certificates can be issued, but are not mandatory for ABs. Shares can either be issued in paper form, in which case they must be bearer shares, or through the paperless central securities depository system, kept by VPC AB ("VPC").[2] The share register is kept by the company unless the shares are dematerialised, in which case it is kept by VPC. To be able to enjoy all shareholder rights, a shareholder must be registered in the share register (Ch. 4 Sec. 37 ABL). To legally effect the transfer of title to paper shares, physical handover of the share certificates is required. Physical handover is replaced with registration in relation to paperless shares.

10 Private ABs may not have their shares, debentures or warrants listed on an exchange or an authorised marketplace. A private AB or a shareholder of the company may not direct an issue of these instruments to the public.

11 Pre-emptive rights can be provided for in the articles of association, as well as purchase option clauses and consent clauses (Ch. 4 Sec. 27 ABL).

1.6 Corporate Bodies

12 The ABL provides for the presence of four compulsory "bodies" in an AB. These are: (a) the general meeting of shareholders ("GM"); (b) the board of directors; (c) the managing director; and (d) the auditors. In the case of private ABs, a managing director is not mandatory (Ch. 8 Sec. 27 ABL). The company's highest decision-making body is the GM. The GM has to decide on certain matters, such as new issues of shares, changes to the articles of association, etc., and can decide on all matters that do not, by law or by virtue of the company's articles of association, expressly fall under the exclusive competence of another body of the company. The GM elects the company's board of directors, which in its turn appoints the company's managing director.

13 Under the Private Sector Employees (Board Representation) Act (*lag (1987:1245) om styrelserepresentation för de privatanställda*), employees appointed by the trade unions have the right to be represented on the board of ABs of a certain size. In companies with 25 employees or above, the local trade unions have the right to appoint two representatives to the board, along with two alternates. In companies with activities in several branches and at least 1,000 employees, the unions have the right to appoint three representatives and three alternates. However, the number of employee representatives may never exceed the number of other directors.

1.6.1 The Board of Directors

14 The board of directors in a private AB may consist of only one or two directors, provided that at least one alternate director is appointed (Ch. 8 Sec. 1 ABL). A person under age, with a custodian pursuant to the Parental Code, in bankruptcy or declared incapable of engaging in trade may not be a director (Ch. 8 Sec. 11 ABL). The board members are elected by the GM unless the articles of association state otherwise, but the articles cannot give the board or individual board members the right to elect any directors (Ch. 8 Sec. 8 ABL). At least half of the board must be EU residents,

2 The articles of association must include a record clause (*avstämningsförbehåll*) to be able to use the registration system (Ch. 4 Sec. 39 ABL). VPC is still the only central securities depository in Sweden.

unless an exception is granted by the Swedish Companies Registration Office (Ch. 8 Sec. 9 ABL). If neither the board of directors nor the managing director have their domicile in Sweden, the company is required to appoint a person who is domiciled in Sweden and who can accept service of documents on behalf of the company (Ch. 8 Sec. 40 ABL).

During the term of its appointment, the board of directors has full responsibility for the management and organisation of the company (Ch. 8 Sec. 4 ABL). The board's extensive decision-making ability is limited by the exclusive powers of the GM regarding, *inter alia*, the appointment of board members and auditors, the approval of the accounts, the increase or reduction of share capital and changes to the articles of association. The board is also obliged to comply with any special directions given by the GM, as long as they do not conflict with the law or articles of association. **15**

The board of directors has a duty, on an annual basis, to adopt written procedures governing its work (*arbetsordning*) (Ch. 8 Sec. 6 ABL), unless the board is composed of only one board member and one alternate. The procedures must cover the division of responsibilities among the board members, the duties of the alternates and how often board meetings should be held. **16**

The board represents the company and signs documents on behalf of the company. Furthermore, the board may authorise one or more directors, the managing director or someone else to sign on behalf of the company, if such authorisation or proxy is not prohibited by the articles of association (Ch. 8 Sec. 37 ABL). The board is entitled to revoke such authorisation. **17**

In the GM's appointment of board members, the person who receives the most votes is deemed to have been elected, unless otherwise prescribed in the articles of association (Ch. 7 Sec. 41 ABL). Dismissal of a board member requires a simple majority of the votes cast at the GM. **18**

Boards consisting of more than one board member must appoint one member to be chairman of the board (Ch. 8 Sec. 17 ABL). However, the chairman may be elected directly by the GM or by another procedure, as laid down in the articles of association. The chairman will lead the board in its work and monitor that the board fulfils its duties. **19**

The quorum requirement for board decisions is that more than half of the board members must be present, unless a higher number is prescribed in the articles of association (Ch. 8 Sec. 21 ABL). Board decisions require a simple majority among the members present, but the number of directors voting in favour must exceed one-third of the total number of board members, unless otherwise prescribed in the articles of association. In the event of deadlock, the chairman has the casting vote (Ch. 8 Sec. 22 ABL). **20**

1.6.2 General Meeting of Shareholders ("GM")

The GM is the ultimate decision-making body of an AB. An annual GM ("AGM") must be held annually or more frequently if so required by the articles of association (Ch. 7 Sec. 10 and 12 ABL). An extraordinary GM can be convened by the board of directors and must be convened if so required by the company's auditor or shareholders owning not less than one-tenth of the shares (Ch. 7 Sec. 13 ABL). As previously mentioned, the GM has exclusive authority in certain matters, for example the appointment and dismissal of board members, the adoption of the income statement and the balance sheet, the increase or reduction of share capital and amendments to the articles of association. The GM can give direct instructions to the board and the managing director, who in turn must comply with these instructions (provided they do not contravene the law or the articles of association). The GM cannot represent the company. **21**

Resolutions by the GM are passed by a simple majority of the votes cast (Ch. 7 Sec. 41 ABL). In certain cases, for example when amending the articles of association, a qualified majority is required. The majority requirement in relation to elections has been stated above. Capital increases normally require a simple majority, unless the issue of the new shares, convertibles or warrants is directed to a certain person for cash consideration (a two-thirds, and in some cases a nine-tenths, majority is then required). **22**

A GM must be held either where the seat of the board is located or in another location in Sweden provided for in the articles of association (Ch. 7 Sec. 15 ABL). **23**

1.6.3 Managing Director

24 A managing director is appointed by the board of directors, which can revoke any such appointment at any time. It is not obligatory for private ABs to have a managing director (Ch. 8 Sec. 27 ABL). In the event of a managing director being appointed, the managing director is responsible for the daily business of the company, the book-keeping and the management of assets as directed by the board (Ch. 8 Sec. 29 ABL). The managing director must be an EU resident, unless an exception is granted by the Swedish Companies Registration Office (Ch. 8 Sec. 30 ABL).

25 The managing director is entitled to represent the company and sign on behalf of the company in the daily course of business. If a board decision on a certain matter cannot be awaited, the managing director is entitled to make and execute such a decision, provided that he informs the board immediately (Ch. 8 Sec. 29 ABL).

1.7 Duties and Liabilities of Directors

26 The board of directors and the managing director, as well as the GM, may not take decisions or enter into transactions which are likely to benefit a shareholder or third party to the detriment of another shareholder or the company (Ch. 8 Sec. 41 and Ch. 7 Sec. 47 ABL).

27 According to the disqualification rules, a board member or the managing director may not take part in matters regarding agreements or court proceedings between: (a) the director and the company; (b) the company and third parties, where the director has a material interest in the matter in conflict with the company's interests; and (c) the company and a legal entity which the director may represent (Ch. 8 Sec. 23 and 34 ABL).

28 Each director of the board and the managing director must perform his or her duties with the due care and attention of a prudent businessman. The board members and the managing director are personally liable to the company for all loss caused by the management of the company, provided that the loss is as a result of negligent or intentional acts by the directors. The directors are also liable for loss suffered by the shareholders or third parties as a result of contravening, through negligence or intent, the ABL, the Annual Reports Act (*årsredovisningslagen (1995:1554)*,"ÅRL") or the articles of association. The directors' liability is personal to each director. If two or more directors cause the company damage they are jointly and severally liable. This is the case regardless of the extent to which each individual contributed to the damage (the degree of negligence may, however, be of importance regarding the liability between the directors and any action they may take against each other). A division of work may be of importance if a claim against the board arises. A director who is allocated responsibility for a certain area will most likely bear a larger liability for that area than the rest of the directors. However, the board can never divest their fundamental duties as board members, which means that the rest of the directors are not free from liability just because a board duty which was delegated to a certain director was not correctly managed. Any defect in the supervising duty may result in the whole board becoming liable due to the negligence of an individual director.

29 Unless the proceedings in respect of damages are based on criminal acts (Ch. 29 Sec. 13 ABL) the right to bring proceedings in respect of damages is limited to five years from the end of the financial year during which the liable act (or omission) occurred. The AGM shall adopt a resolution regarding discharge from liability of board members and the managing director (Ch. 7 Sec. 11 ABL). Discharge is granted individually, and means that the director is not liable towards the company in relation to actions of which the GM has been informed, i.e. actions that are covered by the annual report.

30 A director is liable for any damage which he causes third parties (shareholders, creditors, employees and others) through a breach of the ABL, applicable annual reports legislation or the Articles of Association (Ch. 29 Sec. 1 ABL). A breach of the ABL may include breaches of either explicit or implicit provisions, for example a breach of the general clause. A broader interpretation is that provisions which are referred to in the ABL are also included within this rule.

There are no special rules on D&O insurance for board directors, which means that it is allowed. However, the Swedish tax authorities have questioned whether the premium for such insurance should be taxed as income for the individual director. 31

1.8 Shareholders' Liability

The main principle under the ABL is the protection of limited liability. As a result, the issue of piercing the corporate veil has only come before the courts on a few occasions. 32

A shareholder is only liable for damage caused to the company, the shareholders or third parties as a result of contravening, through negligence or intent, the ABL, the ÅRL or the articles of association (Ch. 29 Sec. 3 ABL). Shareholders can also be liable for declaring an unlawful dividend and must repay it if it is proven that they realised, or should have realised, that the payment was not in accordance with Ch. 17 Sec. 6 ABL. 33

1.9 Capitalisation and Financing

1.9.1 Basic Concepts

The financing rules for an AB are based on the concept of a restricted share capital which constitutes a minimum amount available to the company's creditors. 34

1.9.2 Minimum Share Capital

The minimum share capital of a private AB must amount to SEK 100,000 (approximately EUR 11,000) (Ch. 1 Sec. 5 ABL) and can be paid up in cash or in kind, but contributions in kind have to be of value to the company (Ch. 2 Sec. 6 ABL). The share capital must be fully paid up on registration. Bank statements showing cash contributions or auditors' statements for contributions in kind are therefore necessary (Ch. 2 Sec. 23 ABL). The amount of the share capital must be stated in the articles of association. A company can in its articles of association prescribe a minimum and a maximum share capital where the maximum capital can be four times the minimum capital, enabling it in this way to change the share capital without amending the articles of association. 35

Loss of half of the registered share capital triggers an obligation for the board of directors to issue a notice to the GM which shall consider whether the company shall go into liquidation, unless the share capital is restored within a certain time frame (Ch. 25 Sec. 13 ABL). In the event of the insolvency of the company, loans by shareholders are not considered to be part of the share capital. Shareholders may, however, give conditional capital contributions, whereby the contribution can be repaid to the shareholder from future distributable funds. 36

1.9.3 Maintenance of Capital and Liquidity

The concept of financing ABs is regulated by the ABL as well as by case law. 37

(i) System

To protect the company's capital there are rules regarding capital contributions from shareholders when the AB is incorporated and for subsequent issues of shares or instruments that can be converted into shares or give the right to subscribe for new shares. As mentioned above, the consideration to the company for shares can be made in cash or in kind. It is up to the company to decide which form the consideration should take. If consideration in kind is allowed, the market value of the property must be used and the property has to be of benefit to the company. An obligation to work or perform services for the company is not allowed as consideration in kind (Ch. 2 Sec. 6 ABL). 38

(ii) Distributions

39 Payments from a company to a shareholder can, under the ABL, only be made in accordance with provisions relating to profit distribution, acquisition of its own shares, reduction in share capital, reserve fund or premium fund, and distribution at liquidation (Ch. 17 Sec. 2 ABL). The rules not only cover distribution of profit but also the sale of company assets below cost price, loans to shareholders, liens or sureties on a shareholder's debt to third parties and group contributions. A loan to a shareholder is considered a dividend if the shareholder's financial position indicates that, at the time of the borrowing transaction, repayment cannot be counted upon.

40 Payment made in contravention of the ABL must be returned by the recipient. If the recipient acted in good faith or is insolvent, the responsibility to cover the deficit rests with the board members, the managing director, the accountants, the shareholders and the liquidator (Ch. 17 Sec. 6 ABL). The general rule is that a payment which infringes the ABL is legally invalid.

41 The amount to be distributed is not, in the main, allowed to exceed the company's non-restricted equity (Ch. 17 Sec. 3 ABL). The proposal to pay dividends must be presented by the board and be decided upon by the GM. The GM can only resolve to distribute a dividend proposed or approved by the board (Ch. 18 Sec. 11 ABL). Notwithstanding this, however, shareholders representing 10 per cent or more of the share capital can request a dividend distribution of, after certain deductions, 50 per cent of the net profit for the year.

42 The ABL does not deal with "hidden dividends", but this issue has come before the courts. It was found that a hidden dividend not exceeding the amount allowed to be distributed and not violating shareholders' rights of equal treatment is permitted. If the dividend exceeds the amount allowed to be distributed, it is considered illegal.

43 A company can declare dividends at extraordinary GMs, based on a balance sheet adopted at an earlier GM, adjusted for previously declared and distributed dividends. Such dividends can be declared up until the next AGM wherein the new annual accounts are adopted. Interim dividends, i.e. advance dividends, are not allowed.

(iii) Acquisition of Own Shares and Related Financing

44 Only public ABs with listed shares are allowed to purchase or sell their own shares (Ch. 19 Sec. 13 ABL), even though there are rules for a limited number of special situations when all ABs may purchase their own shares (Ch. 19 Sec. 5 ABL).

45 Redemption of shares requires a GM resolution. A GM resolution to reduce share capital, combined with repayment of it to the shareholders, usually requires court permission in order to protect the creditors of the company (Ch. 20 ABL). The share capital of private ABs can never be reduced to lower than SEK 100,000 (approximately EUR 11,000) (Ch. 1 Sec. 5 ABL).

For rules on financial assistance please refer to Mn. 49.

(iv) Company as Lender or Guarantor

46 A company may make loans and offer credit, provided that such measures are part of the day-to-day business of the company, for example, trade credits in connection with the sale of goods. Loans and guarantees that cannot be regarded as a part of the company's business are regarded as dividend distributions, if the borrower's financial situation makes it impossible to repay the loan, and may therefore require GM approval.

47 Loans given outside the company's business to shareholders (and certain other persons closely connected with the company such as board members and the managing director of the company and of group companies) are prohibited in accordance with the general loan prohibition (Ch. 21 Secs. 1 and 2 ABL).

48 The general loan prohibition has four exemptions: the prohibition is not applicable when the debtor: (a) is a municipality county council; (b) is a legal person within the same group as the lending company (*Koncernundantaget*); (c) operates a business and the loan is given solely for business reasons; or (d) is a shareholder who owns less than 1 per cent of the shares and has no

decisive influence over the company. Further, the tax authority may grant an exemption from the general loan prohibition.

The special loan prohibition is applicable to everyone and provides that the company may not grant a cash loan for the purpose of financing the acquisition of its shares or shares in a subsidiary to the debtor, or to any natural or legal person closely related to him (Ch. 21 Sec. 3 and 6 ABL). The special loan prohibition is subject to one specified exemption, involving loans to employees under certain circumstances. **49**

The loan prohibition is correspondingly applicable to the furnishing of a security or guarantee. The tax authority may grant exemptions from the loan prohibition. **50**

Granting a prohibited loan does not, as a general rule, invalidate the transaction, but the person who, wilfully or with gross negligence, enters into such a transaction will be criminally liable (Ch. 30 Sec. 1 ABL). **51**

(v) Company as Borrower

Sweden does not have any specific rules on shareholder loans given to the company and shareholder security granted in favour of the company in case of a financial crises of the company. **52**

1.10 Publication and Filing Requirements

The charter of incorporation, the articles of association, GM and board resolutions, board membership details etc. must in general be filed with the Swedish Companies Registration Office, which publishes that a change in the register has been made in the Swedish National Gazette (*Post och Inrikes Tidningar*). The commercial register is open to the public and any interested person can review the filed documents and request commercial register excerpts detailing the principle corporate information of a company, for example share capital, names of the board members and articles of association, as well as copies of submitted documents. The register can be accessed online.[3] If a board director or a managing director has been registered, a third party can rely on the content of the register. Only if the third party knows that such a registration is wrongful he cannot rely on it (Ch. 27 Sec. 5 ABL). **53**

GM resolutions that require registration are null and void if not registered. Failure to make filings may incur a fine. A company that has not filed its annual accounts within 11 months from the end of its financial year,[4] is put into involuntary liquidation by the Swedish Companies Registration Office (Ch. 25 Sec. 11 ABL). **54**

1.11 Financial Reporting

An annual report must be prepared each business year according to the ÅRL and be passed by the AGM (Ch. 7 Sec. 10 ABL).[5] The report must contain a profit and loss statement, a balance sheet and a directors' report (*förvaltningsberättelse*). The annual report has to be signed by members of the board and the managing director, if one has been appointed. In the event of the annual report not being filed with the Swedish Companies Registration Office within 11 months of the end of the business year, the Swedish Companies Registration Office shall order the company into liquidation.[6] Financial reporting, publication and auditing requirements are equal for all companies irrespective of their size. No relief is granted to small- and medium sized enterprises. **55**

The annual accounts must be drawn up in accordance with Swedish GAAP (see Ch. 8 Sec. 1 of the Accounting Act (*bokföringslagen (1999:1078)*)). **56**

3 www.bolagsverket.se/in_english/index.html
4 In practice, due to other rules, this period will usually be between 12 and 13 months from the end of the financial year.
5 The business year may be the calendar year or any other 12 month period.
6 See Mn. 54.

1.12 Employee Participation in Corporate Bodies

57 As mentioned above,[7] local labour unions are entitled to appoint two representatives to the board of directors and two alternates if the company employs 25 or more persons. If the company has at least 1,000 employees, the labour union has the right to appoint three representatives and three alternates. The union and shareholder representatives are generally bound by the same duties as a member of the board of directors.

58 The Swedish Act on Co-Determination (*lag (1976:580) om medbestämmande i arbetslivet*) gives labour unions a right to information and to be involved in negotiations in all aspects of the company's business affecting the labour union or its members. The company, however, has the final decision on this matter.

2 The Stock Corporation ("publ AB")

59 Public ABs (*publikt aktiebolag*) are the other type of AB. The main advantage of public ABs over private ones is the ability to turn to the public in seeking to raise capital. However, this may result in a large number of shareholders and therefore a less flexible company. Due to the fact that both types of ABs are governed by the same law, the ABL, almost all rules are in general the same for both private and public ABs as they are, for example, regarding governance structure and capital protection.

2.1 Export of Company

60 Public ABs are treated in the same way as private ones where there are no restrictions on the relocation of such companies.

2.2 Transformation into a Foreign Entity

61 Please see the corresponding section for private ABs.[8]

2.3 Incorporation

62 Public ABs are generally incorporated in the same way as private ABs. The main difference is in the minimum share capital. For public ABs, the minimum share capital must be SEK 500,000 (approximately EUR 55,000).

2.4 Recurrent Costs and Efforts

63 Costs recur on the same basis as for private ABs.[9] However, it can generally be said that these can be higher in public ABs, especially if the company's shares are listed.

2.5 Shares and Share Transfers

64 Shares are issued and transferred in the same way as for private ABs.[10] Listed shares must, however, be registered in the central securities depository system, in which case no share certificates may be issued.

65 Pre-emptive rights (but not purchase option clauses or consent clauses) can be provided for in the articles of association but are not allowed in connection with listed shares.

7 See Mn. 13.
8 See Mn. 4.
9 See Mn. 7.
10 See Mn. 8 et seq.

2.6 Corporate Bodies

Public ABs must have, as mentioned earlier, four corporate bodies, with the appointment by the board of a managing director being obligatory (Ch. 8 Sec. 27 ABL). Furthermore, there must be at least three board members in public ABs. The managing director of a public AB is not allowed to take the position of chairman of the board of directors (Ch. 8 Sec. 49 ABL). **66**

For the roles and responsibilities of the various corporate bodies, please see the corresponding section for private ABs.[11] **67**

2.7 Duties and Liabilities of Directors

Please see the corresponding section for private ABs.[12] **68**

2.8 Shareholders' Liability

Please see the corresponding section for private ABs.[13] **69**

2.9 Capitalisation and Financing

2.9.1 Basic Concept

Please see the corresponding section for private ABs.[14] **70**

2.9.2 Minimum Share Capital

The same rules apply as for private ABs,[15] except that the minimum capital requirement for public ABs is SEK 500,000 (approximately EUR 55,000). **71**

2.9.3 Maintenance of Capital and Liquidity

The concept of financing is the same as applies to private ABs. **72**

(i) System

The same set of rules apply as for private ABs.[16] One difference is that any major agreement between the company and its incorporators or a shareholder holding more than 10 per cent of the registered share capital of the company within two years of registration of the company requires shareholder approval and registration in the commercial register (Ch. 2 Sec. 29 ABL). **73**

(ii) Distributions

Please see the corresponding section for private ABs.[17] **74**

(iii) Acquisition of Own Shares and Related Financing

Public ABs with listed shares may purchase and sell their own shares (Ch. 19 Sec. 13 ABL). Own shares may only be repurchased on a stock exchange or authorised marketplace or through a public offer made to all shareholders on a pro rata basis, as the company may only hold a maximum of 10 per cent of its own shares (Ch. 19 Sec. 15 ABL). Negotiated purchases with individual shareholders **75**

11 See Mn. 12 et seq.
12 See Mn. 26 et seq.
13 See Mn. 32 et seq.
14 See Mn. 34.
15 See Mn. 35 et seq.
16 See Mn. 38.
17 See Mn. 39 et seq.

are not allowed. The sale of own shares can be made on the exchange or authorised marketplace, or in accordance with the provisions relating to new issues of shares. Redemption of listed ABs' own shares is possible under the general share redemption rules that are generally applicable to ABs.

76 Acquisitions and sales of own shares require GM approval with a two-thirds majority and are only valid until the next AGM.

77 If a company acquires shares in contravention of the ABL, the acquisition is still valid, but the shares must be sold within three years of the acquisition.

(iv) Company as Lender or Guarantor

78 Please see the corresponding section for private ABs.[18]

(v) Company as Borrower

79 Please see the corresponding section for private ABs.[19]

2.10 Publication and Filing Requirements

80 Please see the corresponding section for private ABs.[20]

2.11 Financial Reporting

81 Please see the corresponding section for private ABs.[21]

2.12 Employee Participation in Corporate Bodies

82 Please see the corresponding section for private ABs.[22]

18 See Mn. 46 et seq.
19 See Mn. 52.
20 See Mn. 53.
21 See Mn. 55.
22 See Mn. 57 et seq.

XXV. United Kingdom

*by Steven Turnbull and James Coleman**

Literature: Gore-Browne on Companies (44th Edition, Jordan Publishing Limited, loose-leaf presentation); Gower/Davis: The Principles of Modern Company Law (7th Edition, Sweet & Maxwell 2003); Pennington's Company Law (8th Edition, Butterworths 2001)

1 The Private Company Limited by Shares ("Limited" or "Private Company")

The private company limited by shares ("private company"[1]) is the most common corporate form used in England and Wales. It is generally considered to offer a very flexible structure for the conduct of business despite not being able to offer its shares or debentures to the public (Sec. 81 CA). The principal statutory provisions relating to private companies are set out in the Companies Act 1985 ("Companies Act" or "CA") and the Companies Act 1989. In October 2005 there were approximately 2.1 million private companies registered in England and Wales in contrast to approximately 12,500 public companies. **1**

1.1 Export of Company

Whilst the registered seat of a private company must be located within England and Wales, there is nothing to prevent the central management and control of the company's affairs being effected in a foreign jurisdiction. **2**

1.2 Transformation into a Foreign Entity

There are no express provisions for the transformation of a private company into a foreign entity. In practice, this can only be achieved by transferring the business of the company to a foreign company.[2] **3**

1.3 Incorporation

A private company is quick, cheap and simple to establish. There are no minimum capital requirements, the costs of incorporation can be as little as GBP 20 (approximately EUR 30) and the registration process takes approximately five working days. Same-day registration can be requested at a cost of GBP 50 (approximately EUR 75); alternatively, it is possible to purchase a shelf company. **4**

A private company may be formed by one or more natural or legal persons. The principal corporate document required is a memorandum of association detailing, *inter alia*, the name of the company,[3] its registered office address[4] and its objects and share capital. The company's share **5**

* *Linklaters*, London.

1 For the purposes of the Companies Act 1985, a private company is defined as a company which is not a public company (Sec. 1 Subs. 3 CA). For public companies, see also Mn. 41 et seq. of this chapter. This chapter does not deal with the law applicable to unlimited companies or private companies limited by guarantee.

2 Unlike in relation to public companies, there are no provisions in Council Regulation (FL) No 2157/2001 which allow for the "merger" of private companies to form an S.E.

3 There are restrictions on the choice of name; see Business Names Act 1985 and Company and Business Names Regulations 1981 (as amended). Guidance is provided by the Publication GBF2 issued by Companies House.

4 The registered office must be located within either England or Wales.

capital does not need to be denominated in sterling and may comprise mixed currencies.[5] If articles of association[6] are not drawn up, standard articles as set out in statute will apply by default.[7]

6 To incorporate a private company, the company's memorandum and articles (if any) must be delivered to the Registrar of Companies (Companies House[8]), together with details of the director(s) and company secretary appointed (Sec. 10 Subs. 2 CA)[9] and a prescribed form statutory declaration for the incorporation process (Sec. 12 Subs. 3 CA).[10] The certificate of incorporation produced on registration constitutes conclusive evidence that the incorporation requirements have been met and the company is incorporated.[11]

1.4 Recurrent Costs and Efforts

7 Recurrent costs and efforts are minimal. In general, it is necessary to maintain a registered office in England or Wales, hold an annual general meeting ("AGM") once a year (Sec. 366 CA),[12] make certain filings with Companies House,[13] file accounts produced under UK GAAP[14] and pay an annual registration fee of GBP 30 (GBP 15 if submitted electronically) (EUR 45 and EUR 23 respectively). Costs and efforts can be reduced by all the members adopting an "elective" regime to dispense with certain statutory requirements or by all the members passing written resolutions to avoid the formalities involved in calling a meeting (Sec. 379A CA).[15]

Basic company secretarial services and maintaining a registered office by a third party provider would cost from GBP 300 (approximately EUR 450) per annum, depending on the provider and type of services required.

1.5 Shares and Share Transfers

8 Private companies have the ability to issue voting and non-voting shares in fully or partly-paid form and there is a large degree of freedom to define entitlements to income and capital and preferential ranking. Shares are generally issued in registered form, although it is possible to issue share warrants to bearer if authorised by the articles.

9 Shares in registered form are usually transferred by stock transfer form. The transferor executes the stock transfer form and delivers it with the accompanying share certificate to the transferee, who will arrange for the stock transfer form to be stamped. Stamp duty is levied at a rate of 0.5 per cent of the consideration payable by the transferee (unless the transfer is adjudicated stamp duty exempt). The transferee then submits the stock transfer form and share certificate to the company for registration. The transferee only becomes a member of the company when its name is entered in the register of members (Sec. 22 Subs. 2. CA). The articles of private companies often contain provisions to enable the directors to reject registration.[16]

5 Re Scandinavian Bank Group plc [1988] Ch 87.
6 Whereas the memorandum sets out the company's constitution, the articles govern the internal affairs of the company. See Fn. 3.
7 Table A articles as in force at the date of the company's registration (Sec. 8 Subs. 2 CA). See Companies Tables (A to F) Regulations 1985, SI 1985/805 (as amended) ("Table A").
8 Companies House, Crown Way, Maindy, Cardiff CF14 3UZ. Companies House has an electronic filing and authentication service for new incorporations.
9 Statement is made using the standard Form 10.
10 Form 12.
11 Hammond v Prentice Bros Ltd. [1920] 1 Ch 201.
12 The Government proposes to simplify decision-making for private companies by making it easier for votes to be taken by written resolution and by making AGMs "opt-in" rather than "opt-out" (Draft Company Law Reform Bill).
13 See Mn. 37.
14 Alternatively, a private company can elect to prepare individual and consolidated accounts in accordance with IFRS for financial years commencing on or after 1 January 2005. See Mn. 39.
15 For example, private companies can elect to dispense with holding AGMs, laying accounts before AGMs and annually reappointing auditors.
16 For an example see art. 24 of Table A.

1.6 Corporate Bodies

The private company has a single tier board of directors.[17] Generally, all powers of management are in the hands of the board of directors, subject to the articles and to any matters reserved to the members in general meeting. 10

1.6.1 Board of Directors

A private company must have at least one director.[18] There are no age restrictions.[19] A person may not be a director if an undischarged bankrupt or disqualified by a court from holding a directorship.[20] The articles govern the appointment of directors. Usually the board has the right to appoint directors to fill vacancies and to appoint additional persons, subject to the approval of members at the next annual general meeting. 11

The board has actual authority to represent the company as determined by the articles. Actions carried out by the board, or by persons authorised on its behalf, which exceed its authority or the company's capacity will, however, bind the company.[21] Third parties acting in good faith[22] are not only protected in this respect, but may also rely on acts of individual directors where the directors had actual or ostensible authority.[23] 12

1.6.2 General Meeting

The general meeting exercises its control over the company by a majority of members at general meeting and decides on those matters for which it is given responsibility in the articles or by the Companies Act.[24] 13

In general, a member or members holding 5 per cent or more of the issued share capital have the right to have an item placed on the agenda for an annual general meeting (Sec. 376 CA) whilst those holding more than 10 per cent have the right to call a general meeting (Sec. 368 CA). 14

1.6.3 Company Secretary

Every private company must appoint a company secretary, who will normally undertake corporate housekeeping duties, including maintaining the statutory books and registers and ensuring that statutory forms are filed with Companies House (Sec. 283 CA).[25] The secretary of a private com- 15

17 Large private companies and public companies may have non-executive directors in addition to executive directors within the one-tiered board structure.

18 A director may be either a natural or, if permitted in the articles, a legal person. However, the draft Company Law Reform Bill requires at least one director to be a natural person.

19 Unless the company is a subsidiary of a public company. See Mn. 50. The draft Company Law Reform Bill proposes to introduce a minimum age requirement of 16.

20 If, despite being an undischarged bankrupt or disqualified, a director is directly or indirectly involved in the management of a company, he will generally be liable together with the company for the debts and liabilities of the company.

21 A transaction will not be held void just because a company lacks capacity to enter into it (Sec. 35 Subs. 1 CA). The authority of the board is deemed to be free of any limitation under the company's constitution (Sec. 35A Subs. 1 CA).

22 A person is presumed to have acted in good faith unless the contrary is proved (Sec. 35A Subs. 2(c) CA). Note also Sec. 35A Subs. 2(b) and Sec. 35B CA.

23 Note the rule in Royal British Bank v Turquand [1856] 6 E&B 327, EXCH CH; Freeman & Lockyer v Buckhurst Park Properties [1964] 2 QB 480.

24 The powers reserved to members by the Companies Act include the power to change the memorandum and articles of association, the company name and share capital and various powers in relation to the issue of shares. The powers reserved by the articles may include powers in relation to the appointment of directors and declaration of dividends. Table A art. 70 makes the directors' management of the company subject to any directions given by special resolution (requiring a majority of not less than 75 per cent of members who vote) but this is rarely used. It may be easier for members to remove a director which requires a simple majority of those voting and compliance with CA formalities.

25 See Mn. 37 for details.

pany is not required to have any formal qualifications and the position is often filled by a director[26] or an employee of the company.

1.7 Duties and Liabilities of Directors

16 Each director of a private company owes certain fiduciary duties to the company[27] as well as a general duty of care.[28] The duties are owed individually but all directors who participate in a breach of duty will be jointly and severally liable. The duties are generally owed to the company, that is, to the members (both present and future) as a whole and not individual members or other companies in the same corporate group. The directors must, however, also have regard to the interests of employees (Sec. 309 CA)[29] and, when the company is about to go into liquidation or is otherwise facing insolvency, the company's creditors.[30] Breach of a fiduciary duty may result in the results of the exercise of power being either void or voidable[31] and the director concerned may be held directly liable to account for profits obtained.

17 Furthermore, directors may be held liable for failure to comply with certain Companies Act provisions, including filing obligations and the duty to maintain certain records.[32] In certain circumstances, a director may also be disqualified by a court from acting in the future as a director.[33] Where a relevant application is made, the court has an obligation to review the director's conduct in respect of a company which has either gone into insolvent liquidation or administration or where an administrative receiver has been appointed and to make a disqualification order where the director's conduct makes him unfit to be concerned in the management of a company (Sec. 6 Company Directors Disqualification Act 1986). Where a private company is, or may be, in financial difficulties, a director will have further obligations imposed under UK insolvency legislation and, if convicted of either wrongful trading (Sec. 214 Insolvency Act 1986)[34] or fraudulent trading (Sec. 213 Insolvency Act 1986),[35] may be held personally liable for certain debts and liabilities of the company.

18 A company may not generally exempt its directors from liability to the company for any negligence, default, breach of duty or breach of trust, although it may insure its directors against actions

26 A sole director cannot also be a company secretary.

27 Fiduciary duties include the duty to act bona fide and in the best interests of the company (Re Smith & Fawcett Limited [1942] CH 304), not to act for a collateral purpose (Hogg v Cramphorn Limited [1967] CH 254, Howard Smith v Ampol Petroleum [1974] AC 821), to avoid a conflict of interest and duty (Industrial Development Consultants v Cooley [1972] 2 All ER 162), to disclose personal interests (Aberdeen Railway Company v Blaikie [1854] 1 Mac 461), and not to make a secret profit (Regal (Hastings) Limited v Gulliver [1942] 1 All ER 378; [1967] 2 AC 134n, HL). There are also statutory obligations in Part X CA. For example, note the obligation to disclose to the board interests in contracts (Sec. 317 CA) and restrictions on substantial property transactions involving directors (Sec. 320 CA).

28 The standard of skill required used to be subjective, determined by reference to the director in question (Re City Equitable Fire Insurance Co Limited [1925] Ch 407). However, recently there has been a move to a more objective test – see e.g. Re Barings Plc (No 5) [1999] BCLC 433. The draft Company Law Reform Bill (March 2005) will introduce a statutory statement of directors' duties that preserves the objective/subjective test.

29 This duty is only enforceable by the company itself in the same way as any other fiduciary duty and is not directly enforceable by the employees.

30 Walker v Wimborne [1976] 50 ALJR 446. Note also liability for wrongful and fraudulent trading; see Mn. 17.

31 With regards to agreements concluded with third parties, much will depend on the knowledge of the third parties of the breach of duty (note Sec. 35 and Sec. 35A CA) and their ability to rely on the ostensible authority of the director. See Mn. 12.

32 The CA generally provides for the payment of fines (sometimes increasing on a daily basis) and/or imprisonment.

33 Company Directors Disqualification Act 1986 ("CDDA"). The grounds for disqualification are conviction of an offence, persistent default, fraud, unfitness, persistent failure to file annual accounts and wrongful and fraudulent trading.

34 A director will come within the scope of wrongful trading, and may be liable to make a contribution, where he knew or ought to have concluded that there was no reasonable prospect of the company avoiding insolvent liquidation. There will be a defence to the charge of wrongful trading where the director can demonstrate that he has taken every step to minimise the potential loss to the company's creditors as he ought to have taken (Sec. 241 Subs. 3 Insolvency Act 1986).

35 Established if, in the course of a winding-up of a company, it appears that any business of the company has been carried on with the intent to defraud creditors of the company or for any fraudulent purpose. Fraudulent trading is both a criminal and civil offence.

by the company or third parties (Sec. 309A CA). The law has recently been changed to allow a company to indemnify its directors against actions brought by third parties and to pay directors' legal costs as they are incurred, subject to disclosure requirements.[36] The time limits for bringing a claim in tort (e.g. where directors have been negligent) or for breach of contract (e.g. a contract of service) are in most cases six years from the date of the breach. In certain cases of fraudulent breaches of fiduciary duties (please refer to Fn. 28) the limitation period runs from the date the fraud is discovered.

1.8 Shareholders' Liability

English courts construe the principle of limited liability strictly and a shareholder will not generally be liable for company debts and liabilities beyond the amount payable on shares he holds in the company. The courts have, however, pierced the corporate veil where it was necessary to prevent the limited liability form from being used either for fraudulent purposes or to evade a contractual or other legal obligation. 19

1.9 Capitalisation and Financing

1.9.1 Basic Concepts

The concept of a minimum capital constituting a minimum capital fund being available to creditors is not applied under English law as far as the private company is concerned. The shareholders are instead free to decide on the measures for financing the company whilst creditor protection is mainly ensured pursuant to the fiduciary duties of directors, insolvency regulations and the principles of wrongful and fraudulent trading.[37] Where a company has a paid-up share capital, however, certain capital maintenance rules do apply.[38] 20

1.9.2 Minimum Share Capital

There are no minimum capital requirements under English company law for a private company. 21

1.9.3 Maintenance of Capital and Liquidity

(i) System

There is no single capital maintenance regime as exists in many civil law jurisdictions but there are a number of statutory provisions (Part V CA) and common law rules in relation to capital maintenance, including those summarised below. 22

Allotment of Shares. Whereas a private company may issue shares without any particular fraction of the nominal amount being paid up, shares may not be issued at a discount to their nominal value (Sec. 100 CA). With certain exceptions, where shares are issued at a premium, the aggregate value of the premium must be transferred to the company's share premium account (Sec. 130 CA) details of which must appear in the balance sheet. Any payment for shares may be made in cash or in kind. 23

(ii) Distributions

Distributions to members are governed by both statutory and common law rules. Under the statutory rules, a private company may make a distribution[39] only out of profits available for that 24

36 The Companies (Audit, Investigations and Community Enterprise) Act 2004 inserted new Secs. 309A – C and a new Sec. 337A into the CA to allow this with effect from April 2005.

37 See Mn. 16 et seq.

38 See Mn. 22 et seq.

39 "Distribution" is defined in Sec. 263 Subs. 2 CA as "every description of distribution of a company's assets to its members, whether in cash or otherwise". Expressly excepted from this definition are bonus issues, the redemption or purchase by a company of its own shares, a reduction in capital and the distribution of assets on a winding-up.

purpose, namely the company's accumulated, realised profits (so far as not previously distributed or capitalised) less its accumulated, realised losses (so far as not previously written off in a reduction or reorganisation of capital). Realised profits and realised losses are those which fall to be treated as such by generally accepted accounting principles (Sec. 262 Subs. 3 CA as applied by Sec 742 Subs. 2 CA).[40] They are determined by reference to the company's individual accounts, normally the last audited annual accounts that have been laid before the members (Sec. 270 Subs. 3 CA).

25 A shareholder who knows or has reasonable grounds for believing that a distribution or part of it has been made in contravention of statutory provisions is liable to repay it and the directors who have authorised such a distribution are likely to be personally liable. A member who is not liable under this provision may nevertheless be liable as a constructive trustee (Sec. 263 Subs. 1 CA).

26 The statutory rules are without prejudice to common law (or the articles). The main common law rule is that a private company cannot make a distribution out of capital. A distribution will be deemed to be out of capital if, following the distribution, the distributing company does not have net assets with a market value at least equal to its capital (including undistributable reserves). If there is an unlawful distribution, it is void *ab initio* and third parties receiving assets with knowledge (actual or constructive) may be held liable as constructive trustees.

27 The company's articles govern who has the power to declare and pay distributions. Most articles provide that a final dividend[41] is to be declared by the company by way of a shareholders' resolution passed in general meeting, whereas the directors have power to pay interim dividends.

(iii) Acquisition of Own Shares and Related Financing

28 The Companies Act provides a number of exceptions to the general rule that a private company cannot acquire its own shares (Sec. 143 Subs. 1 CA).[42] For example, if authorised by its articles, a private company may:

29 - issue shares which can be redeemed at the option of the company or the shareholder (Sec. 159 Subs. 1 CA) provided that, at the time of issuing the redeemable shares, some shares are in issue that are not redeemable (Sec. 159 Subs. 2 CA). Also, the redeemable shares must be fully paid and the terms of redemption must provide for payment on redemption (Sec. 159 Subs. 3 CA). Redeemable shares may be redeemed out of distributable profits, the proceeds of a fresh issue of shares made for the purposes of the redemption (Sec. 160 Subs. 1(a) CA), or out of capital if the strict provisions of the Companies Act are followed (Sec. 171 CA).[43]Shares redeemed are cancelled on redemption;

30 - purchase its own shares (Sec. 162 Subs. 1 CA) provided that the shares are fully paid, the relevant shareholder approval is obtained, payment is made in full on completion of purchase (Sec. 162 Subs. 2 CA) and some shares remain in issue that are not redeemable or treasury shares (Sec. 162 Subs. 3 CA).[44] The amount payable on purchase must be satisfied out of distributable profits or a fresh issue of shares made for the purpose or out of capital if the strict provisions of the Companies Act are followed. The shares must be cancelled on purchase;[45]

31 - reduce its share capital. Capital reductions must be authorised in a company's articles of association, a special resolution will then have to be passed by the shareholders (Sec. 135 Subs. 1 CA) and the reduction must be confirmed by a court (Sec. 136 CA). The court will consider whether the interests of creditors and shareholders have been adequately protected (Sec. 137 Subs. 1 CA). Once the court has confirmed the reduction, it must be registered with the Registrar of Companies before it becomes effective (Sec. 138 CA).

40 The Institute of Chartered Accountants in England and Wales has published guidance on this area (see its Technical Releases 07/03, 50/04, 64/04 and (in draft) 21/05.)

41 A dividend declared once the results of the year as a whole are known.

42 If breached, the company is liable to a fine and the officers responsible liable to a fine and imprisonment.

43 Only private companies may redeem or purchase shares out of capital.

44 Treasury shares are unlikely to be relevant for private companies.

45 Listed shares can be purchased and held in treasury rather than cancelled (Sec. 162A CA) but this is unlikely to be relevant to private companies given the general restriction on offering shares or debentures to the public (Sec. 81 CA).

A company (or any of its subsidiaries) is prohibited from providing financial assistance directly or indirectly for the purpose of the acquisition of shares in the company or to reduce or discharge a liability incurred for the purpose of the acquisition (Sec. 151 CA).[46] Financial assistance is broadly defined and includes assistance in the form of a gift, guarantee, indemnity, loan or other assistance which will reduce the net assets of the company to a material extent (Sec. 152 CA). There are certain exceptions, including the redemption and purchase of shares made in accordance with the Companies Act and distributions of company assets by way of a dividend (Sec. 153 CA). **32**

A private company may, however, give financial assistance if it complies with the "whitewash" procedure in the Companies Act and there is no reduction in its net assets. The whitewash involves, *inter alia*, a special resolution of the members[47] and a statutory declaration of the directors that the company can pay its debts as and when they fall due (Sec. 155 et seq. CA), supported by an auditor's report. **33**

(iv) Company as Lender or Guarantor

A private company may give loans and grant guarantees subject to compliance with the rules on corporate capacity and authorisation and corporate benefit.[48] If the loan or guarantee is being provided in the context of an acquisition or group reorganisation or restructuring, the financial assistance prohibition may apply.[49] **34**

Subject to the above, there are no restrictions on loans to shareholders although there are certain restrictions on loans to directors or on entering into guarantees or on providing security for loans made to directors (Sec. 330 Subs. 2 CA). **35**

(v) Company as Borrower

A private company is entitled to borrow monies and charge assets in order to secure its borrowings subject to compliance with the rules on corporate capacity and authorisation and corporate benefit. Shareholder loans to the company are allowed, though in practice are normally subordinated to other borrowings at the request of lending banks or other third party creditors. **36**

1.10 Publication and Filing Requirements

Companies House maintains a central register of all filings submitted to it.[50] **37**

There are a number of books and registers[51] which a private company must maintain at its registered office and make public on request. The company is also required to file once a year an Annual Return[52] confirming details of the registered office address and the identity of the directors, secretary and shareholders. In addition, filings must be made from time to time of, *inter alia*, certain resolutions, increases in or reduction of share capital, directors' powers to allot shares and the annual accounts. Filing obligations, particularly those relating to accounts and Annual Returns, are taken seriously and failure to comply can result in a fine being levied, and, in the case of persistent violations of this duty, the company can ultimately be struck from the register and its directors disqualified (Sec. 3 CDDA).[53] **38**

46 The UK Government proposes to repeal the restrictions on financial assistance by private companies (Draft Company Law Reform Bill).

47 Requires a majority of not less than 75 per cent of the votes cast in person or by proxy.

48 The corporate benefit requirement is particularly relevant for upstream guarantees and is usually satisfied by a unanimous shareholder resolution authorising or subsequently ratifying the giving of the guarantee.

49 See Mn. 32.

50 The register is open to inspection by members of the public. Some basic information is accessible online at www.companieshouse.gov.uk (Monday to Saturday 7.00 a.m. to midnight).

51 Registers of members, charges, directors, directors' interests, debenture holders, minute books and directors' service agreements. Much of the information contained in these registers is also publicly available at Companies House and the company must make filings in respect of changes to them.

52 This is done using the standard Form 363 available from Companies House.

53 See Mn. 17.

1.11 Financial Reporting

39 Directors of a private company are required to prepare annual accounts (comprising a balance sheet and profit and loss account) for each financial year (Sec. 226 CA). The directors of a parent company must also prepare consolidated group accounts for each financial year (Sec. 227 CA). Such accounts must comply with the detailed requirements of the Companies Act and give a true and fair view. In effect, this means that the accounts must be prepared in accordance with UK GAAP. They must also be audited. The annual accounts, together with a directors' report and auditor's report, must be laid before the company in general meeting and filed with the Registrar of Companies within the statutory time limits.

Less onerous accounting requirements apply to small and medium-sized companies. In the UK, small companies are those which meet at least two of the following criteria: a balance sheet total of GBP 2.8 million (approximately EUR 4.2 million) or less, an annual turnover of GBP 5.6 million (approximately EUR 8.4 million) or less and an average annual number of employees of 50 or less. Medium-sized companies are those which meet at least two of the following criteria: a balance sheet total of GBP 11.4 million (approximately EUR 17.1 million) or less, an annual turnover of GBP 22.8 million (approximately EUR 34.2 million) or less and an average number of employees of 250 or less.[54] Such small and medium-sized companies may file abbreviated accounts (Sec. 246 and 246A CA). Small companies may also be exempt from the requirement for the accounts to be audited (Sec. 249A CA).[55]. Private companies can also dispense with the requirement to lay accounts before a general meeting (Sec. 379A CA). Private companies prepare their individual and consolidated accounts in accordance with International Financial Reporting Standards (IFRS) for financial years commencing on or after 1 January 2005 (Sec. 226 and Sec. 227 CA).

1.12 Employee Participation in Corporate Bodies

40 There are no co-determination obligations on a private company as such.

2 The Public Company Limited by Shares ("Public Company")

41 The public company limited by shares ("public company") (Sec. 1 Subs. 3 CA provides a statutory definition) is a corporate form which not only offers the benefits of limited liability but, because it is not prohibited from offering its shares or debentures to the public,[56] also offers greater access to capital markets and therefore greater scope for raising funds to finance its business activities.[57] As for private companies, the principal statutory provisions relating to public companies are set out in the Companies Act 1985 and Companies Act 1989.

2.1 Export of Company

42 Please refer to Mn. 2.

54 Notwithstanding that the requirements may be met, the exemptions and exceptions will not apply to public companies, those companies which have permission under Part 4 of the Financial Services and Markets Act 2000 to carry on one or more regulated activities and those companies which carry on insurance market activities (Sec. 247A(1B) CA).

55 To qualify, the small company must not only qualify as a small company under Sec. 246 CA but its annual turnover must not exceed GBP 5.6 million (approximately EUR 8.4 million) and its balance sheet total for that year must not be more than GBP 2.8 million (approximately EUR 4.2 million).

56 Contrast the position of the private company. See Mn. 1.

57 This section does not consider the law relating to and the regulation of listed public limited companies.

2.2 Transformation into a Foreign Entity

Two or more public companies may merge to form an S.E. provided at least two of them are governed by the law of different EU member states (Article 2(1) of Council Regulation (EC) No. 2157/2001).[58] Apart from this, a true merger with a foreign entity is not possible. 43

2.3 Incorporation

A public company is quick and, aside from the obligation to comply with the minimum capital requirements,[59] cheap to establish. The costs and timing of the registration process and the documents required match those for a private company.[60] 44

A public company must, however, have a minimum number of two members (Sec. 1 Subs. 1 CA) and the memorandum must additionally state that the company is a public limited company. Furthermore, before a public company can carry on business or exercise any borrowing powers, it must obtain a trading certificate confirming satisfaction of the statutory capital requirements (Sec. 117 Subs. 1 CA).[61] 45

A public company can be created by re-registering a private company as a public limited company (Secs. 43 to 47 CA). 46

2.4 Recurrent Costs and Efforts

Recurrent costs and efforts will be greater than those for a private company because of a larger number of obligations and restrictions applicable to public companies under UK company law. For example, members of a public company may not agree an "elective" regime to dispense with certain Companies Act requirements.[62] However, recurrent costs and efforts for a small public company may continue to be insignificant. 47

2.5 Shares and Share Transfers

Please refer to Mn. 8 and 9. Shares in listed companies within CREST (the computerised system of paperless shares and transfers) can be transferred without the need for a paper stock transfer form or share certificate. Stamp Duty Reserve Tax is payable by the transferee at a rate of 0.5 per cent of the consideration. Shares in listed companies must be fully transferable.[63] 48

2.6 Corporate Bodies

As is the case for a private company, a public company has a single tier board of directors.[64] 49

2.6.1 Board of Directors

A public company must have at least two directors (Sec. 282 Subs. 1 CA).[65] Directors must not be appointed by a single resolution unless approved by all the members (Sec. 292 CA). A director of a public company (or a subsidiary of a public company) may not be appointed if over 70 years of age and must vacate his office at the end of the annual general meeting commencing next after 50

58 It is contemplated that the procedure would be based on that set out in Sec. 427A CA but this has not been tested.

59 See Mn. 56 et seq.

60 See Mn. 4 et seq.

61 Issued by the registrar of companies following submission of a prescribed form application and a specific statutory declaration (Sec. 117 Subs. 2 CA). Details of the content of the statutory declaration are set out in Sec. 177 Subs. 3 CA. Failure to obtain a trading certificate before carrying on business or exercising borrowing powers may result in criminal sanctions being imposed on the company and any officer in default (Sec. 117 Subs. 7 CA).

62 See Fn. 15.

63 Unlike in private companies – see Mn. 9.

64 Public companies, especially listed companies, may have executive and non-executive directors within the single board structure.

65 See also Fn. 18 regarding the appointment of corporate directors.

he obtains that age unless provided otherwise in the articles or the appointment is approved by the company in general meeting (Sec. 293 CA).[66] The power of the board and individual directors to bind the company is the same as for private limited companies.[67]

51 The Combined Code of Corporate Governance applies to listed companies and contains provisions on the composition, role and procedures of the board. Its provisions are not mandatory but companies are required to disclose in their annual report and accounts if they do not comply with the Combined Code and give reasons for non-compliance.

2.6.2 General Meeting

52 Please refer to Mn. 13 et seq..

2.6.3 Company Secretary

53 Every public company must appoint a company secretary (Sec. 283 CA), who must have previous experience or certain qualifications (Sec. 286 CA).[68]

2.7 Duties and Liabilities of Directors

54 Please refer to Mn. 16 et seq.

2.8 Shareholders' Liability

55 Please refer to Mn. 19. In addition, if a public company carries on business without having at least two members and does so for more than six months, the remaining member is generally liable jointly and severally with the company for the payment of the company's debts contracted during the period (Sec. 24 Subs. 1 CA).[69]

2.9 Capitalisation and Financing

2.9.1 Basic Concepts

56 In line with the requirements of the Second Directive[70] the public company must have a minimum share capital, the protection of which is ensured by stricter rules than in a private company. Common law rules as to creditor protection, however, remain applicable at the same time.

2.9.2 Minimum Share Capital

57 A public company must be incorporated with a minimum share capital of GBP 50,000 (approximately EUR 75,000) paid up at least as to one-quarter of that amount (Sec. 118 CA).[71]

66 The draft Company Law Reform Bill proposes to remove the restriction on those over 70 being directors of public companies.

67 See Mn. 12.

68 Qualifications include being a barrister, solicitor or being a member of an accountant or chartered secretary professional body.

69 This situation can be avoided in group situations by shares being partly held through a nominee.

70 See Part 1, I, Mn. 39 et seq.

71 A minimum of GBP 12,500 (approximately EUR 18,750) is therefore required when wishing to establish and carry on business using a public company. This minimum amount must be denominated in sterling. Subsequent amounts may be denominated in other currencies.

2.9.3 Maintenance of Capital and Liquidity

(i) System

As is the case for a private company, there is no single capital maintenance regime which applies to a public company. Additional statutory provisions apply to public companies reflecting the Second Directive,[72] including the provisions summarised below. 58

Allotment of Shares. A public company may not allot a share except as paid up at least as to one-quarter of its nominal value and the whole of any premium on it (Sec. 101 Subs. 1 CA). In general, if a public company allots shares otherwise than in cash, the consideration for the allotment must be independently valued by an expert (Sec. 103 Subs. 1 CA).[73] Non-cash consideration given in exchange for shares in a public company may not consist of an undertaking to do work or provide services (Sec. 99 Subs. 2 CA) or an undertaking to be performed more than five years after the date of allotment (Sec. 102 CA). 59

Serious Loss of Capital. Where the net assets of a public company are less than half its called-up share capital, the directors must convene a members' meeting to consider what steps need to be taken to deal with the situation (Sec. 142 CA). 60

(ii) Distributions

In addition to the statutory restrictions applicable to private companies,[74] a public company may only make a distribution to the extent that its net assets exceed its share capital and undistributable reserves (Sec. 264 Subs. 1 CA). 61

(iii) Acquisition of Own Shares and Related Financing

As a general rule, a public company cannot acquire its own shares (Sec. 143 Subs. 1 CA),[75] although nominees may be used subject to certain restrictions (Secs. 145 and 146 CA). Also, a public company may redeem, purchase or reduce its share capital except that: 62

- public companies are not permitted to redeem or purchase shares out of capital;[76] 63
- a public company may purchase its shares and hold them in treasury as an exception to the usual requirement for their immediate cancellation (Sec. 162A CA). The shares being purchased must be qualifying shares (Sec. 162 Subs. 4 CA)[77] and must be purchased out of distributable profits (Sec. 162A Subs. 1 CA). The aggregate nominal value of treasury shares must not at any time exceed 10 per cent of the nominal value of the issued share capital of the company (Sec. 162B Subs. 1 CA); 64
- it is implied (although not expressly stated in the Companies Act) that a public company may not reduce its share capital below the statutory minimum[78] by a purchase or redemption of shares. In relation to a reduction of capital which has the effect of bringing a public company's capital below the statutory minimum, the Companies Act expressly provides that the court order confirming the reduction of a public company's capital will not be registered unless the court otherwise directs or the company is first re-registered as a private company (Sec. 139 Subs. 2 CA). 65

72 See Part 1, I, Mn. 39 et seq.

73 The valuation provisions are set out in Sec. 108 CA. Exceptions include takeovers by exchange of shares (Sec. 103 Subs. 3 CA) and allotments of shares in connection with a proposed merger of the allotting company with another company (Sec. 103 Subs. 5 CA).

74 See Mn.24 et seq.

75 See also Fn. 39.

76 See Mn. 28.

77 Qualifying shares are those which are either officially listed on the London Stock Exchange or another EEA exchange, or which are traded on a regulated market in an EEA state.

78 See Mn. 57.

66 The whitewash procedure that allows a private company to provide financial assistance does not apply to public companies. Also, certain exceptions[79] to the prohibition on financial assistance are only permitted for public companies if the net assets are not reduced or the assistance is provided out of distributable profits (Sec. 154 CA).

(iv) Company as Lender or Guarantor:

67 Please refer to Mn. 34. Directors of public companies are more restricted in their financial dealings with the company and need to disclose more information about such arrangements in the accounts (Sec. 330 CA).

(v) Company as Borrower

68 Please refer to Mn. 36.

2.10 Publication and Filing Requirements

69 The publication and filing requirements of a public company generally match those applicable for a private company.[80] Please refer to Mn. 37 et seq. for details. A public company must, however, in addition to a register of members also maintain a register of substantial shareholdings (Sec. 211 CA).[81] A public company whose shares are listed will also have to comply with the disclosure requirements of the Listing, Disclosure and Prospectus Rules.

2.11 Financial Reporting

70 UK public companies whose securities are listed on an EU regulated market are required to produce their consolidated accounts in accordance with IFRS (dealing with the form and content of accounts) for financial years commencing on or after 1 January 2005.[82] UK public companies whose securities are UK, EU or Nasdaq/NYSE listed (but not AIM listed) must also produce a directors' remuneration report and, for financial years commencing on or after 1 April 2005, an operating and financial review (Sec. 234B CA (directors' remuneration report) and Sec. 234 AA CA (operating and financial review)). Otherwise, the accounting rules and obligations generally match those applicable for a private company.[83]

2.12 Employee Participation in Corporate Bodies

71 There are no co-determination obligations on a public company as such.

79 The exceptions are set out in Sec. 153 Subs. 4 CA and cover lending in the ordinary course of business, financial assistance for the purposes of or in connection with employee share schemes and the making of loans to persons other than to directors.

80 See Mn. 37.

81 Members have a statutory obligation to disclose the existence of substantial shareholdings (Sec. 198 CA to Sec. 219 CA. "Substantial" are, depending on the circumstances, either 3 per cent or 10 per cent shareholdings) so that this list can be maintained, and the company has the right to make inquiries of members (Sec. 212 CA).

82 EC Regulation No. 1606/2002. UK companies may also prepare their individual accounts in accordance with IFRS (Sec. 226 CA 1985 as amended by The Companies Act 1985 (International Accounting Standards and Other Accounting Amendments) Regulations 2004).

83 Although the less onerous accounting requirements applicable to small and medium-sized companies and the audit exemption for small companies do not apply to public companies. See Mn. 39. Also, shorter statutory periods apply to public companies for laying the accounts and directors' and auditor's reports before the company in general meeting.

XXVI. Excursus: Societas Europaea ("S.E.")

by Hanns-William Mülsch and Dr. Sven Piegsa (LL.M)

Literature: Manz/Mayer/Schröder, Europäische Aktiengesellschaft S.E., commentary (1st edition, Nomos 2005); Teichmann, The European Company – A Challenge to Academics, Legislatures and Practitioners, German Law Journal (2003) Vol. 4 No. 4 pp. 309-331; Werlauff, The S.E. Company – A New Common European Company from 8 October 2004, European Business Law Review (2003), 14 pp. 85-103.

1 General

The introduction of the European Company – S.E. has been one of the most ambitious and protracted projects in European company law. First drafts originate from as early as the 1970s.[1] Finally, in 2001 the Council of the European Union adopted the Regulation on the Statute for a European Company ("S.E. Regulation"),[2] having direct effect in Member States since 8 October 2004,[3] and the Directive supplementing the Statute for a European Company with regard to the involvement of employees ("S.E. Directive"),[4] which had to be transformed into national law no later than said date.[5] 1

The main features of this new kind of company, designed as a European stock corporation, are the European legal capacity, the limited liability of the shareholders, and the possibility of transferring the seat to another Member State without losing legal personality. However, the ways of establishing an S.E. are limited, as there have to be relations with more than one Member State. 2

Turning from the initial concept of creating a standardised European Company, the S.E. Regulation provides for a complex system of rules applicable to the S.E. (Art. 9 S.E. Regulation). Not all features of the S.E. are explicitly and uniformly prescribed by the S.E. Regulation.[6] An S.E. is authorised to regulate matters in its statutes[7] while other matters are expressly left for regulation by the Member States;[8] detailed or less detailed guidelines regarding the regulation are given depending on the relevant matter. If the S.E. Regulation remains silent on an issue, the relevant rule has to be sought, firstly, in provisions of laws adopted by Member States in implementation of the EC Regulation and the EC Directive, secondly, in provisions of Member States' laws which would apply to stock corporations formed in accordance with that Member State, and, thirdly, in provisions of the S.E.'s statutes which, in this respect, have to comply with the national law on stock corporations of the Member State in which the S.E.'s registered office is located. As a result, in different Member States there will be different kinds of S.E.s. 3

1 On the history of the S.E. see V. Edwards, The European Company – Essential Tool or Eviscerated Dream, Common Market Law Review (2003), Vol. 40 pp. 443 – 450.

2 Council Regulation (EC) No 2157/2001/EC of 8 October 2001, OJ L 294, 10 November 2001, p. 1. The European legislation is available online at: http://europa.eu.int/eur-lex/en/index.html

3 However, national laws implementing the S.E. Regulation into national company law are necessary, as, last but not least, the S.E. Regulation grants Member States various options. To this date, such laws have been adopted by most of the Member States.

4 Council Directive 2001/86/EC of 8 October 2001, OJ L 294, 10 November 2001, p. 22.

5 As per decision of the European Economic Area Joint Committee No 93/2002 of 25 June 2002 (OJ L 266, 3 October 2002, p. 69) the S.E. Regulation is also applicable within the countries of the European Economic Area, which are Iceland, Liechtenstein and Norway.

6 A uniform regulation can e.g. be found as regards the minimum share capital of EUR 120,000 provided for in Art. 4 para. 2 S.E. Regulation.

7 E.g. the choice between a two-tier or a one-tier board model (Art. 38 S.E. Regulation).

8 E.g. the law on minority shareholder and creditor protection in case of a transfer of seat (Art. 8 para. 5 and 7 S.E. Regulation).

2 Details

2.1 Export of Company

4 The registered office of an S.E. may be transferred to any other Member State without the S.E. losing its legal personality (Art. 8 Subs. 1 S.E. Regulation). In order to avoid liquidation of the S.E., pursuant to Art. 64 S.E. Regulation, the relocation of the registered office must always be accompanied by the transfer of the head office, as both registered and head offices have to be located within the same Member State (Art. 7 S.E. Regulation).[9] Upon transfer, the S.E. will become subject to the law on stock corporations of the Member State to which the registered office has been transferred, to the extent that this law is applicable to S.E.s which have their registered offices in that Member State.[10]

5 The transfer must follow the specific procedure stipulated in Art. 8 para. 2 S.E. Regulation: The management or administrative organ of the S.E. must draw up and publish a transfer proposal covering the main aspects of the transfer[11] and a report on the legal and economic aspects of the transfer, including its implications for shareholders, creditors and employees. The transfer proposal has to be approved by the shareholders' meeting with a majority of no less than two-thirds of the votes cast, whereby this decision may be taken as early as two months after the publication of the proposal. The Member State in which the registered office is located prior to the transfer may adopt provisions which protect minority shareholders who oppose the transfer. Finally, the S.E. has to ensure vis-à-vis the competent authority of the Member State which it is leaving that the national legal requirements on creditor protection have been fulfilled.

2.2 Transformation into a Foreign Entity

6 A direct way of transforming an S.E. into a foreign entity, i.e. an entity which is solely governed by the company law of another Member State, will be available under the national laws of the Member State in which the registered office of the S.E. is located as soon as the Tenth Directive on Cross-border Mergers has been transformed into national law.[12]

7 An indirect way of transforming an S.E. into a foreign entity is made possible by Art. 66 S.E. Regulation. This provision allows for the conversion of an S.E. into a national stock corporation governed by the company law of the Member State in which the registered office of the S.E. is located, provided that the S.E. has been in existence for at least two years. Thus, in order to transform an S.E. into a foreign entity, the registered seat of the S.E. has to first be relocated to the favoured Member State and, subsequently, the S.E. has to be transformed into a national stock corporation of that Member State.

8 As regards the applicability of the company law of another Member State, the S.E. may be partly transformed into a "foreign entity" merely by transferring its registered seat to another Member State[13] as the S.E. is governed to a great extent by the company law of the Member State in which its registered office is located.[14]

9 It has been argued that after the ECJ ruling in the case "*Überseering*" (see Part 1, I, Mn. 17 et seq.) this provision violates the principle of freedom of establishment (Art. 43, 48 EC) and is therefore not applicable, see Teichmann, German Law Review (2003) Vol. 4 No. 4 p. 315. Following this argumentation an S.E. would be able to relocate its factual seat to another Member State without relocating its registered seat at the same time.

10 See Mn. 3. However, in order to protect creditors, the change of the applicable national law will have no effect on any cause of action arising prior to the transfer of the seat, for in respect of those causes of action the S.E. is considered as having its registered office at the previous location (Art. 8 Subs. 16 S.E. Regulation).

11 Those are: new location of the registered office, the new statutes of the S.E., the transfer timetable, any implications the transfer may have on employees' involvement, and any rights provided for the protection of shareholders and/or creditors.

12 See Part 1, I, Mn. 56 et seq.

13 See Mn. 4 et seq.

14 On the importance of the Member States' law on stock corporations of see Mn. 3.

Currently, there is no legal way to transform the S.E. into an entity governed by the company law of a non EU and non EEA country.[15] 9

2.3 Incorporation

The ways of establishing an S.E. are limited (Art. 2 and 3 S.E. Regulation). Typically, the formation of an S.E. requires at least two already existing entities[16] and relations to more than one Member State. Furthermore, all of the companies participating in the formation of an S.E. must have their registered and head offices within the European Community or the European Economic Area.[17] 10

Altogether there are five ways to establish an S.E.. It may be done by way of 11

- a merger of stock corporations which are governed by the laws of different Member States (Art. 2 para. 1 and Art. 17 – 31 S.E. Regulation), 12
- a formation of a holding S.E. which holds shares in at least two companies,[18] provided that no less than two of these companies are governed by the laws of a different Member States or that no less than two of these companies have for at least two years had a subsidiary[19] governed by the law of another Member State or a branch located in another Member State (Art. 2 para. 2 and Art. 32 – 34 S.E. Regulation),[20] 13
- a formation of a subsidiary ("joint venture S.E.") through two or more companies of any kind, again provided that at least two of these companies are governed by the laws of different Member States or that at least two of these companies have for at least two years had a subsidiary[21] governed by the law of another Member State or a branch located in another Member State (Art. 2 para. 3 and Art. 35, 36 S.E. Regulation), 14
- a transformation of a stock corporation if for at least two years it has had a subsidiary governed by the law of another Member State (Art. 2 para. 5 and Art. 37 S.E. Regulation), 15
- a formation as a subsidiary of a parent S.E. (Art. 3 para. 2 S.E. Regulation). 16

The time it takes and the costs incurred in establishing an S.E. vary widely depending on the chosen way of formation, the length of the process and the respective requirements of the applicable Member States' company laws. 17

2.4 Recurrent Costs and Efforts

The recurrent costs and efforts depend very much on the law of the Member State in which the S.E. is registered and should be similar to those of a stock corporation in the respective Member State. However, a shareholders' meeting has to be held at least once a year (Art. 54 para. 1 S.E. Regulation). 18

2.5 Shares and Share Transfers

The S.E. Regulation neither provides for rules on possible classes and division of shares in an S.E.[22] nor for rules on the transfer of these shares. Therefore, these issues are governed by the national law on stock corporations of the Member State in which the S.E. has its registered office. 19

15 On the applicability of the S.E. Regulation within the countries of the European Economic Area see Fn. 5.

16 One or both of the entities can be already existing S.E.s as, in respect of formation of a new S.E., an already existing S.E. is regarded as stock corporation governed by the law of the Member State in which its registered office is located (Art. 3 para. 1 S.E. Regulation).

17 On the applicability of the S.E. Regulation within the countries of the European Economic Area see Fn. 5.

18 Stock corporations and/or limited-liability companies and/or S.E.s. The shares held by the holding S.E. must confer more than 50 % of the permanent voting rights in each of the participating companies (Art. 32 para. 2 S.E. Regulation).

19 May be any kind of company, e.g. Ltd., Plc., Partnership.

20 On formation of a holding S.E. see Oplustil, Selected Problems concerning formation of a holding S.E. (societas europaea), German Law Journal (2003), Vol. 4 No. 2 pp. 107 – 126.

21 May be any kind of company, e.g. Ltd., Plc., Partnership.

22 Art. 60 S.E. Regulation indicates that there can be different classes of shares.

2.6 Corporate Bodies

20 The S.E. Regulation provides for a corporate governance system comprised of two to three corporate bodies: the shareholders' meeting and, depending on the form adopted in the articles of association, either a two-tier management system consisting of a supervisory board and a management board or a one-tier management system with an administrative board (Art. 38 S.E. Regulation).[23] The S.E.'s statutes may permit another legal entity to be a member of one of its boards, provided that the law applicable to stock corporations in the Member State in which the S.E. has its registered office does not stipulate otherwise (Art. 47 para. 1 S.E. Regulation). Furthermore, national law may permit minority shareholders or other persons or authorities to appoint some board members (Art. 47 para. 4 S.E. Regulation).

2.6.1 Shareholders' Meeting(Art. 52 – 60 S.E. Regulation)

21 The function of the shareholders' meeting is to take basic decisions such as those concerning the appointment of the members of the supervisory board in a two-tier system or the administrative board in a one-tier system, the amendment of statutes, the transfer of the registered office,[24] the formation of a new S.E. by way of a merger with another company[25] or through establishing a holding S.E. which holds shares in the company,[26] and the transformation of the company into a national stock corporation.[27] Furthermore, the S.E.'s shareholders' meeting decides on matters for which responsibility is given to the shareholders' meeting of a stock corporation governed by the law on stock corporations of the Member State in which the S.E.'s registered office is located, or by the statutes of the S.E. in accordance with that national law.

2.6.2 Two-tier System (Art. 39 – 42, 46 – 51 S.E. Regulation)

22 As already indicated by their names, the management board is solely responsible for managing the S.E., whereas the supervisory board is responsible for controlling the management board. In order to fulfil this task, the management board is required to report to the supervisory board at least every three months and to promptly convey information of any kind which the supervisory board requests (Art. 41 S.E. Regulation). Moreover, the statutes shall list certain categories of transactions which need the approval of the supervisory board. If provided for by the law of the Member State in which the S.E. is registered, the supervisory board in addition may decide on those categories of transactions (Art. 48 S.E. Regulation).

23 The supervisory board appoints the members of the management board, whereas the members of the supervisory board are appointed by the shareholders' meeting save for employees' representatives appointed by employees in connection with a system of co-determination according to the S.E. Directive.[28] No person may be a member of both boards at the same time.

2.6.3 One-tier System (Art. 43 – 51 S.E. Regulation)

24 Should the S.E. opt for a one-tier system, the company is managed by the administrative board. However, if provided for by the Member State in which the S.E. is located, the S.E. shall have one or more managing directors who are responsible for the day-to-day management under the same conditions that apply to stock corporations whose registered office is in that Member State.

23 On the differences between a two-tier board model and a one-tier board model see P. Davis, Board Structure in the UK and Germany: Convergence or Continuing Divergence?, International and Comparative Corporate Law Journal (2001), Vol. 2 Issue 4 p. 435 et seq.

24 See Mn. 5.

25 See Mn. 12.

26 See Mn. 13.

27 See Mn. 7.

28 On employees' participation in an S.E. see Mn. 31 et seq.. If half of the members are appointed by employees, only a member appointed by the shareholders' meeting may be elected chairman of the supervisory board; in that case the chairman will have a casting vote in the event of a tie (Art. 42 S.E. Regulation).

The members of the administrative board are appointed by the shareholders' meeting. The administrative board has to have at least three members if the S.E. is co-determined according to the S.E. Directive.[29] 25

2.7 Duties and Liabilities of Directors

As regards the liability of board members concerning loss or damage sustained by the S.E. following any breach on their part of the legal, statutory or other obligations inherent in their duties, the respective provisions on stock corporations of the Member State in which the S.E.'s registered office is situated apply (Art. 51 S.E. Regulation). 26

2.8 Shareholders' Liability

The shareholders' liability is restricted to the amount to which the shareholders have subscribed (Art. 1 para. 2 S.E. Regulation). In practice, a shareholder may be held liable only if and to the extent that he has not fully paid the share capital in the first place, or if he was illegally repaid after that. However, the law of the Member State in which the S.E. is registered may provide for a piercing of the corporate veil.[30] 27

2.9 Capitalisation and Financing

The S.E. Regulation only provides for a minimum registered share capital of an S.E. in the amount of EUR 120,000 (Art. 4 para. 2 S.E. Regulation). All other issues regarding the capital of an S.E., its maintenance and changes thereto, its shares, bonds and similar securities are regulated by the law on stock corporations of the Member State in which the S.E.'s registered office is located. 28

2.10 Publication and Filing Requirements

The registration of an S.E.[31] and publication of documents and particulars concerning an S.E.[32] are, in general, governed by the law of the Member State in which the S.E. establishes or has its registered office (Art. 13 S.E. Regulation).[33] In addition, notice of an S.E.'s registration and the deletion of such a registration has to be published in the Official Journal of the European Communities (Art. 14 S.E. Regulation). 29

2.11 Financial Reporting

As regards the preparation of an S.E.'s annual and, where appropriate, consolidated accounts including the accompanying annual report and the auditing and publication of these accounts, the respective national rules for stock corporations of the Member State in which the S.E.'s registered office is located are applicable (Art. 61, 62 S.E. Regulation).[34] 30

29 On employees' participation in an S.E. see Mn. 31 et seq. If half of the members are appointed by employees, only a member appointed by the shareholders' meeting may be elected chairman of the administrative board; in that case the chairman will have a casting vote in the event of a tie (Art. 45 S.E. Regulation).

30 Hirte, Die Europäische Aktiengesellschaft, Neue Zeitschrift für Gesellschaftsrecht 2002, p. 9.

31 I.e. registration in the course of establishment (Art. 12 S.E. Regulation) and in the course of a transfer of seat (Art. 8 para. 10 S.E. Regulation).

32 E.g. proposal on the transfer of seat (Art. 8 para. 2 S.E. Regulation), amendment of articles of association (Art. 59 para. 3 S.E. Regulation), the invitation and termination of winding up, liquidation, insolvency or cessation of payment procedures and any decision to continue operating (Art. 65 S.E. Regulation).

33 The national laws on publication of companies' documents have been harmonised by the First Directive, see Part 1, I, Mn. 38.

34 The different laws of the Member States regarding annual accounts have widely been harmonised; for details see Part 1, I, Mn. 47 et seq.

2.12 Employee Participation in Corporate Bodies

31 The employee involvement in the corporate bodies of an S.E. is regulated by the national law of the Member State in which the registered office of the S.E. is to be located, whereas the various national laws have to follow the provisions of the S.E. Directive. The S.E. Directive, and thus each national law, is based upon the principles of negotiation and the protection of the status quo ante. The S.E. can only be registered if the issue of employee participation is resolved (Art. 12 para. 2 S.E. Regulation).

32 Within the process of establishing an S.E., negotiations concerning employees' involvement in the S.E. have to be carried out and may end up with an agreement. However, employees' representatives may decide that negotiations should not commence at all or should be terminated. Ultimately, the negotiations may fail.

2.12.1 Negotiations: Rules on Procedure and Agreement

33 Negotiations concerning the employees' involvement in the S.E. have to be carried out between the representatives of the management or administrative boards of the companies participating in the formation of the S.E. on the one side and a special negotiating body of employees' representatives representing proportionally all employees employed by the participating companies on the other side. These negotiations shall commence as soon as possible following publication of the draft terms of formation and the establishment of the negotiating body. In general, the negotiating period is six months.[35]

34 Any agreement which reduces existing participation rights requires the approval of two-thirds of the members of the special negotiating body if, in case of an S.E. to be established by way of a merger, participation covers at least 25 % of the overall employees employed by the participating companies, or if, in case of an S.E. to be established through creating a holding company or forming a subsidiary, participation covers at least 50 % of the overall number of employees of the participating companies.[36]

2.12.2 Breakdown in Negotiations

35 The special negotiating body may decide by a two-thirds majority of its members not to commence negotiations or to terminate negotiations already commenced.[37] As a consequence, there will be no employee participation on the board level of the S.E., and only the rules on information and consultation of employees in force in the Member States where the S.E. has employees will apply.

2.12.3 Failure of Negotiations

36 Should negotiations fail, i.e. no agreement be reached within the negotiating period, the standard rules on employee involvement provided for by the Member State in which the registered office of the S.E. is to be located will apply. Such standard rules must satisfy certain provisions laid down in the Annex of the S.E. Directive. The standard rules only apply if, in case of an S.E. being established by way of a merger, employee participation applied in one or more of the participating companies covers at least 25 per cent of the overall employees employed by the participating companies, or if, in case of an S.E. being established through creating a holding company or forming a subsidiary, employee participation covers at least 50 per cent of the overall number of employees of the participating companies.

35 The negotiating parties may decide, through joint agreement, to extend this period for up to one year.

36 In case of a formation of an S.E. by way of transformation of an existing stock corporation, the applicable national law may condition the conversion to a favourable vote of a qualified majority or unanimity on the board of the stock corporation within which employee participation is organised (Art. 37 para. 8 S.E. Regulation), thus granting employees' representatives a "veto right" if the draft terms of conversion provide for a reduction of employees' participation within the future S.E.

37 These decisions cannot be taken by the special negotiating body in case of an S.E. established by way of transformation if there is participation in the stock corporation to be transformed.

The mandatory standard rules laid down in the S.E. Directive provide for, *inter alia*, employee participation on the S.E.'s board level, i.e. on the supervisory board, if the company has opted for a two-tier system, or on the administrative board, if the company has chosen a one-tier system. The number of employees' representatives on the supervisory or administrative board has to be equal to the highest proportion of employees' representatives on any board level in force in the participating companies concerned before registration of the S.E.. In case of a formation of an S.E. by way of transformation of an existing stock corporation, all aspects of employee participation shall continue to apply to the S.E. **37**

The possible effect of the standard rules may be illustrated by the following example: An English plc with a total of 8000 employees but with no employee participation on its board of directors, and a German AG with a total of 3000 employees and a quota of employees' representative on its supervisory board of 50 per cent merge to form a London based S.E. If the negotiations on employee involvement fail (as no agreement can be reached), the standard rules on employee participation apply, since the employee participation applied in the German AG before the merger covered 27 per cent of the overall employees employed by the participating companies, and therefore the abovementioned threshold of 25 per cent is exceeded. In this case, the standard would provide for a quota of 50 per cent of employees' representatives on the S.E.'s board, as this was the highest proportion of employees' representatives on any board in force before the registration of the S.E. **38**

A Member State may stipulate that the standard rules on employee participation are not to apply in case of a formation of an S.E. by way of a merger (Art. 7 para. 3 S.E. Directive). However, in case of such an opting-out of that Member State, the S.E. can only be registered if the negotiating parties have come to an agreement on the issue of employee representation, or if none of the participating companies were governed by participation rules prior to the registration of the S.E. (Art 12 para. 2 S.E. Regulation). **39**

Index*

* Reference is made to marginal numbers. Please also refer to page XXIII.